DECONSTRUCTING *DR. STRANGELOVE*

DECONSTRUCTING
DR. STRANGELOVE

The Secret History of Nuclear War Films

SEAN M. MALONEY

Potomac Books

AN IMPRINT OF THE UNIVERSITY OF NEBRASKA PRESS

© 2020 by Sean M. Maloney

All rights reserved. Potomac Books is an imprint of the
University of Nebraska Press.

⊚

Library of Congress Cataloging-in-Publication Data
Names: Maloney, Sean M., 1967– author.
Title: Deconstructing Dr. Strangelove: the secret history of
nuclear war films / Sean M. Maloney.
Description: Lincoln: Potomac Books, an imprint of the
University of Nebraska Press, [2020] | Includes bibliographical
references and index.
Identifiers: LCCN 2019037861
ISBN 9781640121928 (hardback)
ISBN 9781640123496 (epub)
ISBN 9781640123502 (mobi)
ISBN 9781640123519 (pdf)
Subjects: LCSH: Nuclear warfare in motion pictures. | Cold
War in motion pictures. | War films—History and criticism.
Classification: LCC PN1995.9.W3 M35 2020 | DDC
791.4/658—dc23
LC record available at https://lccn.loc.gov/2019037861

Set in Arno Pro by Laura Buis.

For Dad,
who showed me the way.

"A wild goose never raised a tame gosling."—Irish proverb

CONTENTS

ILLUSTRATIONS

TABLES

ACKNOWLEDGMENTS

This is always a fun section in any book. Recounting the large number of people who assisted or observed with either curiosity or bemusement also brings to mind all of the adventures undertaken in the pursuit of this project. And there were many during the research and writing phases of *Deconstructing* Dr. Strangelove. This book involved a combination of archival research and field research, the fieldwork usually undertaken while traveling by motorcycle. My wife, Larissa, accompanied me on several of those trips, to Ashland, Nebraska; Rome, New York; Battle Creek, Michigan; and innumerable remote locations of abandoned nuclear weapons infrastructure. Always ready for an adventure under all types of climatic conditions, there she was, smiling and curious as to where we were off to next and where it fit into the puzzle. I would also like to recognize my good friends Matt Larson, Rob Silliman, Dave McDermott, Glen Barney, and their families for all of the support and assistance they provided not only during the course of this project but also back to the 1980s when we started exploring abandoned missile sites together while we were still in high school.

The original structure of the book evolved after conversations with Stephen Wrinn, who said, approximately, "Why do just *Strangelove*? Why not do the other movies too?" You can blame Steve for this crucial expansion, as the original concept would have, in retrospect, been far too narrow and less interesting. Similarly I have to profusely thank Tom Swanson for his willingness to see the project in its breadth, depth, and scope and not cut it to pieces to satisfy some fear-filled, self-limiting commercial and/or ideological procrustean bed. The publishing industry desperately needs more Tom Swansons. Fritz Heinzen, my indefatigable agent, fixer, facilitator, and close friend, was essential in getting the manuscript to print. I would particularly like to thank Mike Whitby at the Directorate of History for giving the manuscript a thorough and critical eye. The staff of the University of Nebraska Press/Potomac Books was superlative as usual.

The next group I would like to direct my thanks to contains all of the former Strategic Air Command (SAC) personnel who shared anecdotes and insights and who strongly encouraged me to balance the slanted perspective on nuclear weapons with the facts and the context of the activities they were engaged in during the Cold War. Among them I would like to thank Earl "Mac" McGill for, in addition to other things relating to B-52 operations, teaching me offset bombing. Jim Boensch instructed me on the proper care, feeding, and launch of a Minuteman II. Bill Ossenfort and Ray Hildebrant enhanced my knowledge of B-52 and KC-135 alert operations; Arnie Johnson dramatically improved my understanding of Operation Chrome Dome. This book would be deficient if Larry Eastland, John Reynolds, and Darrell Schmidt did not assist me with understanding B-58 operations. Jim Gilman explained how to repair B-47s under alert conditions. Philip Moore explained the dark arts of the long lost Blue Scout system. Finally, Maj. Gen. Bill Doyle ensured the accuracy of my understanding of the role of the airborne emergency action officer on Looking Glass aircraft. I would particularly like to thank all of the retired SAC personnel who contribute to Fans of the Strategic Air Command Facebook page and to the admins Timothy Mills, David Fransen, Jeff Jackson, Tim Mello, and Tom Renk.

The staffs of the archives I buried myself in and the museums I had access to and the FOIA entities at certain government agencies are due the bulk of my thanks. Let's start with the archives. Thanks particularly to the staff of the Air Force Historical Research Agency, especially Cathy Cox, Marcie Green, and Geoff Henson. In addition to Agency staff, other U.S. Air Force FOIA personnel crucial to this book are Theresa Corbin, Renee Kaffenbarger, Tech. Sgt. Meegan C. Haynes, Janet F. Beasley, Candice Velazquez, Crystal Delk, and Staff Sgt. LaTeasha Mayo. In this regard I would also like to thank Maj. Gen. Richard M. Clark, 8th Air Force commander, for personally signing off on the declassification of SAC records that significantly predate his and my existence on this Earth.

This book benefited from substantial field research. I can't thank the friendly, knowledgeable, and dedicated staff of the Strategic Air Command Museum enough, especially Brian York, the curator, and particularly Joe Vrana, Mark "Hambone" Hamilton, Dan Kirwan, Allen Jones, and Christina Jones from the restoration staff. The support I received from them was superlative, and the museum is truly a monument to SAC and its personnel.

The existence of the Minuteman Missile National Historic Site in South Dakota was crucial to this book, so I would like to particularly thank Superintendent Eric Leonard and all of his staff for their time and hospitality. Eric's tutorial on the politics of the MMNHS itself deserves to be converted into a dissertation, and the U.S. Parks Service should use the Leonard-led MMNHS as a model for other Cold War heritage sites.

Equally I'd like to thank Dan Kueker at the South Dakota Air and Space Museum at Ellsworth AFB for his assistance, particularly with the Minuteman II Missile Procedures Trainer, our discussion on Victor Alert, and his insights into preserving Cold War history. Another crucial entity in my journeys was the National Museum of Nuclear Science and History in Albuquerque. I want to thank the curator, David Hoover, for taking the time to walk me though his unique and fascinating collection of nuclear weapons and delivery systems.

I would like to thank the staff of the Department of Energy Nevada National Security Site for the mind-blowing tour of their vast enterprise. Thanks also to the North American Aerospace Defense Command (NORAD) for an equally eye-opening tour of the Cheyenne Mountain Facility.

The Library of Congress Manuscript Division is populated with knowledgeable, calm, cool, and collected professionals, who in their quiet and unruffled way instantly corrected errors on my part when I requested the wrong group of boxes. The staff of the small but powerful Syracuse University Special Collections archives, particularly Jacklyn Hoyt and Nichole Westerdahl, is equally efficient. Responding to someone who dropped into the University of Iowa on a Harley breathlessly requesting access to the Collins Radio Company papers was handled with alacrity by the archive staff there.

I am not sure exactly who to thank at the CIA for their impressively rapid responses to my FOIA requests. The front man for the Information and Privacy Coordinator appears to be "Michael Lavergne," obviously a pseudonym, yet I got everything I asked for in a timely fashion. Another intelligence organization could learn from them and stop pretending that material produced half a century ago actually has national security implications this far into the twenty-first century. A special word of thanks also to Michael Holm, whose detailed compilations of the Soviet Cold War air order of battle were invaluable.

There are just too many people to thank at all of the museums I visited. To the knowledgeable docents, the enthusiastic tour guides, and everybody else I encountered who are determined to preserve the history of the Cold War: thanks for your hospitality and assistance. These include the Air Mobility Command Museum, Dover, Delaware; Battleship Cove at Fall River, Massachusetts; the Greenbrier bunker in West Virginia; the Grissom Air Museum in Peru, Indiana; the Loring Military Heritage Center in Limestone, Maine; the March Field Air Museum, Riverside, California; the NASA Wallops Island Flight Facility Visitor Center, Virginia; the National Atomic Testing Museum, Las Vegas; the National Museum of the U.S. Air Force, Dayton, Ohio; Patriot's Point Museum in Charleston, South Carolina; the Pima Air and Space Museum, Arizona; the Ronald Reagan Minuteman Missile Site, Cooperstown, North Dakota; the Ronald Reagan Presidential Library and Center for Public Affairs, Simi Valley, California; the St. Mary's Submarine Museum, South Carolina; the Titan Missile Museum, Sahuarita, Arizona; the Valiant Air Command, Titusville, Florida; and, last but not least, Wings Over the Rockies Air and Space Museum at Denver, Colorado. Plus a special thanks to Harrison Ford.

Thanks also to Mike Tsukamato at the Air Force Association for his astonishingly rapid response on photographs and to Diane Rowan for facilitating that connection. Thanks also to Martin Healy and Peter London at HarperCollins and Cris Piquinela at Curtis Licensing for assisting me with permissions. And finally, thanks to Cassandra Barbour at Entertainment Clearances Inc. for providing me with guidelines for use of material owned by Sony Pictures.

DECONSTRUCTING *DR. STRANGELOVE*

Introduction

When I was growing up in the 1970s, my parents and I discussed dental hygiene over the supper table one night. This led to my mom revealing that I did not have cavities because, when I was conceived and born, our water was fluoridated. I had no idea this was a bad thing until my dad joked that it was a Commie plot. This was, incidentally, the morning after we watched the Soviet Union's nuclear-powered Kosmos 954 satellite break up in the sky on reentry over northern Canada. My dad described the hysteria surrounding fluoridation in the 1950s and told me it was a plot device in a movie that involved nuclear warfare.

In those days video cassette recorders (predecessor to DVD players, that is, a device that used video tape as opposed to digital media) were not household staples. If you wanted to see an older movie, you had to wait until it was on television, and even then it was cut to pieces with ridiculous commercials, like the ones advertising Mr. Clean right in the middle of the castle firefight in *Where Eagles Dare.*

We were lucky, however, because we had the Plaza Theatre in Calgary. The Plaza was a run-down 1940s movie house lovingly operated by film students from the University of Calgary. Every Friday and Saturday night they played an actual celluloid film. Kubrick. Lean. Hitchcock. *The Rocky Horror Picture Show.* Patrons were encouraged to dress up for the occasion (not just for *Rocky Horror*, incidentally), so, for example, when *Lawrence of Arabia* played, moviegoers wore Arab headdresses and salaamed each other. This became a problem when *Jesus Christ Superstar* played on Easter, as the crosses sometimes wouldn't fit through the door.

I got to see *Dr. Strangelove* on the big screen in all of its glory, as Kubrick intended it. Suffice it to say, I was hooked on nukes. Twenty-five years later, after watching *Fail-Safe, On the Beach, The Bedford Incident, By Dawn's Early Light,* and practically every postapocalyptic film to boot, I published my PhD dissertation, "Learning to Love the Bomb: Canada's Cold War Strategy and Nuclear Weapons, 1951–1970."

The 1964 comedy film *Dr. Strangelove; or: How I Learned to Stop Worrying and Love the Bomb* has achieved cult and now iconic status in popular culture. It is also the flagship of a entire genre of Cold War nuclear crisis films, many of which are employed in academic venues to depict the prime absurdity of the Cold War: nuclear deterrence and its possible failure. The films of the Cold War nuclear crisis genre are regularly used by educators to illustrate nuclear warfare theories of the time. The reality is, however, that the further we get away from those dangerous years, the more art takes over from life, history, and reality. The Cold War deterrent system employed millions of people and was responsible for the incredible technological world that we now enjoy. It was responsible for putting a man on the moon and returning him safely to Earth. It was responsible for the internet, the microwave, the personal computer. The Cold War defined two generations. Is it appropriate that the most visible representative of it in popular culture mocks the sincere efforts taken to protect our way of life? Or that other films treat it with the deadly seriousness of a heart attack?

Of course it is. That's the greatness of freedom of speech and expression, paradoxically guaranteed in part by the nuclear deterrent system itself. There were layers of abstraction and absurdity in places like the RAND Corporation and in other "think tanks." However, those who also served should get their due. And *Dr. Strangelove* does not give it to them. *Dr. Strangelove, Fail-Safe, The Bedford Incident,* and others are about the internal and external failures of the deterrent system. That system did not fail in real life. Why is that? How is that? Can we use *Dr. Strangelove* and related films as vehicles to help us understand the answers to those questions? Having seen the movie, even understanding that it was fiction, I always wanted to know what was really going on in that secretive world. That was impossible in the 1970s. Thirty years after the end of the Cold War, we have much better insight.

Cold War nuclear crisis films like *Dr. Strangelove, Fail-Safe,* and *The Day After* are, in many ways, very different from your average Saturday afternoon disaster flick. The idea that life on Earth can be eradicated by mechanical and chemical devices of our own manufacture is terrifying. During the course of the nuclear age, indeed from the start of it, voices on the spectrum from the merely skeptical to the vocally hysterical have been raised decrying this state of affairs. At its heart, the argument appears to be one of humanity versus inhumanity, life versus mass death. Good versus evil.

Then there was the political angle to go along with the emotional. During the twentieth century both the skeptical and the hysterical voices were generally subsumed by the ideological context of the Cold War. The co-optation of the antinuclear movement by our opponents in the Soviet Union and their allies led to simplistic guilt by association in some quarters in the West, who decided that if you were antinuclear, you served Moscow's interests, either overtly or covertly. Similarly the Soviets' deliberate instigation and activation of antinuclear themes in the media, academia, and politics made it increasingly difficult to maintain skepticism without being associated with Soviet objectives.

The collapse of the liberal consensus in the United States and its subsequent youth revolution in the 1960s merged anti–Vietnam War politics with anti-American military politics. If you were against Vietnam, you were against The Bomb, and vice versa. The United States was the Evil Empire of the 1960s. Anything associated with that empire was therefore bad. And that included nuclear weapons.

It was simply impossible to examine nuclear issues during the second half of the Cold War without being drawn into one camp or the other, especially in the polarized political landscape of the United States, where academic study of the issues was seriously divided. Every element was seen through ideological lenses. Historian Gar Alperovitz, for example, argued that the U.S. decision to use atomic weapons against Japan was really intended to intimidate the Soviet Union. If this is true, then the United States, not the Soviet Union, is responsible for initiating the Cold War. Not so, said another historian, John Lewis Gaddis: the Soviets were conducting espionage and stealing nuclear secrets during the war; therefore they were an enemy before Truman's decision to bomb Hiroshima and Nagasaki in 1945. And so on and so forth. Yea, unto the twenty-first century.

The literature on U.S. foreign policy in the 1980s and 1990s seemed fixated on using the Vietnam lens to view all topics. Bruce Cumings wrote two books in an attempt to prove that Korea was Vietnam before Vietnam was Vietnam. Others insisted that it wasn't a question of "CIA bad, KGB good." It was just "CIA bad, CIA worse." Other than John Barron and his best seller *KGB: The Secret Work of Soviet Secret Agents*, few talked about the KGB or the GRU, the Soviets' foreign intelligence services. That mentality was essentially transferred to examinations of nuclear weapons. The only material in the public domain focused on the American nuclear program, which produced an exceptionalist distortion: if one knew about American nuclear accidents, for example, and nothing about Soviet nuclear accidents, it appeared the United States was engaged in reckless endangerment of the planet. Silence from the other side of the Iron Curtain as this was useful to the Soviets in the pursuit of their objectives.

This state of affairs started to change in the 1990s with a temporary opening in various Soviet and ex–Warsaw Pact archives. That window of opportunity was exploited as much as possible until the Putin regime closed it around 2000. Declassification efforts in the United States have seriously questioned the prevailing academic notions of the Cold War so prevalent in the 1980s. The Rosenbergs *were* guilty, and there *were* numerous other "atomic spies." The design for The Bomb *was* stolen. The Communist International really *was* a global Communist conspiracy. The Weather Underground really *were* Communists trying to overthrow the United States. Stalin, the writer Martin Amis finally admitted, *was* a really, really bad guy.

In the twenty-first century it is evident that much of the scholarship dealing with the Cold War and nuclear issues from the 1980s and even into the 1990s is obsolete. This is no calumny on those who were intensely interested in studying such affairs at the time. They simply didn't have access to the information that we do now. In many cases these scholars were operating in the Cold War ideological context, which may have placed limits on the types of questions they were asking and thus the information they were looking for.

Interested parties continue to write about Cold War nuclear issues today; this is a good thing. However, in many cases the discussion is dominated by an air of sensationalism coupled with document hunting in order to reinforce existing prejudices. Some of those prejudices are holdovers from the 1960s, 1970s, and 1980s.

Take the case of John F. Kennedy requesting a study and then a plan to destroy the Soviet Union's strategic nuclear capability in 1961. In the Cold War ideological context, the information would have been framed and labeled as a "first-strike plan," that is, a morally wrong and perfidious plan. To those conversant with the Cold War ideological debate over first strike and second strike, this is a staggering revelation. The Soviet propaganda machine frequently accused the United States of planning a first strike, which the Soviets used to justify certain of their own aggressive behaviors. To those not familiar with that debate, the new documentation released from the archive just becomes a conversation between Kennedy and his staff and advisors about possible extreme options during the 1961 Berlin crisis. Since it didn't happen, what's the big deal?

This brings us to the great Cold War nuclear crisis films. They were a staple of the Cold War popular cultural milieu from the 1950s to the 1980s. Their primary purpose was to entertain an audience and make money. Their secondary function was to be skeptical about what seemed at the time to be an insane state of affairs. The methodology used was sensationalistic: to shock, to excite, and to provoke. And what was more shocking, exciting and provocative during the Cold War than the possibility of an end to life on Earth? And an end to *your* life too?

Today there is increased interest in nuclear weapons, particularly accidents. In the past decade more information on American and British nuclear accidents during the Cold War has become available. This has triggered document hunting by media personalities, their researchers, and bloggers. Some are interested in the technical aspects, for instance, how a Mark 39 nuclear bomb's safety systems worked. The Japanese refer to such people as *otaku*. The British use the term "anorak." In North America they are "geeks." Though the technical data they uncover are fantastic, many writers uncritically repeat information verbatim, without regard to policy context or personality, thus reinforcing obsolete, inaccurate, or even ideological points on topics that scholars have labored to clarify. Some writers retain an ideological agenda from the Cold War and endeavor to prove they were right back then. Some employ history and historical documents selectively to bolster an argument related to a current disarmament or environmental agenda.

The freedom to pursue these interests in the context of a free society is one reason the Cold War was fought. That said, sensationalism vis-à-vis nuclear accidents, rogue generals, and "how close we came" does not help us answer the most important question of all: Why didn't a nuclear war happen?

With supposedly rogue generals and imperfect safety systems, what exactly prevented the mass detonation of nuclear weapons between 1946 and 1991? Leaning on luck, as some do, is an intellectually lazy way out. But some combination of factors contributed to the nonuse of nuclear weapons. Sensationalism may distract and obscure an examination of these reasons.

What if nuclear deterrence policies actually deterred, and could be proven to have deterred? Then those who argued thirty and forty years ago (or today) that it really didn't or couldn't or shouldn't would be honor-bound to engage in vigorous ideological debate. But that goal is not the same as the search for historical reality. Which leads us to several important questions: What were the components of the deterrent system, and how did they actually work? And what was the role of professionalism in getting them to work?

This is where the *otaku*, the anoraks, and the geeks can significantly contribute to the larger debate. Unlike other types of history, technical data are absolutely critical to understanding nuclear history. Because the arcane language employed by the nuclear high priests was used to keep out the unworthy and the unbelievers, cracking

6

that code, understanding that language has utility in understanding why nuclear war didn't happen.

The nuclear crisis films were arguably part of why a war didn't happen. They showed viewers what could happen and what the results might look like. For example, despite attempts by some historians to downplay the effects of the film *On the Beach* and suggest the antinuclear movement had more influence, it is clear that the film played a positive role in stimulating discussion, debate, and even activism. And it is evident from newly released material that Ronald Reagan was tremendously and personally affected by the 1983 TV movie *The Day After* and that this influenced policy in a positive fashion.

However, the films mislead us when they examine how the nuclear deterrent mechanism worked. They exaggerate in some cases (*Dr. Strangelove, On the Beach*), and they sensationalize in others (*Fail-Safe*). They rely on excessive emotionalism (*Threads, The Day After*). The villains are invariably rogue American military personnel employing secret and thus antidemocratic technology. Never identified as culpable are the global political situations or the interested parties that maintain an oppressive occupational military system far in excess of defensive requirements, which forced the creation of the nuclear mechanism in the first place.

There were reasons for U.S. nuclearization, and given what we now know (or have reconfirmed) about the Communist system under Stalin, Khrushchev, and Mao, they were legitimate reasons. America's crimes, if one wishes to call them that, were miniscule compared to what went on Mao's China. Variants of the Soviet AK-47 assault rifle distributed by the Soviet Union and China have killed far more human beings on this planet than American nuclear weapons ever did.

The Cold War nuclear crisis films are thus a two-edged sword. They raised awareness of some of the larger issues surrounding the nuclear age, but they also distorted the reality of how the mechanisms actually worked and even called into question whether they could work. The films argue that the human factor will eventually cause failure; they don't show that mechanisms were put in place to prevent failure, thus presenting an unbalanced view.

Deconstructing Dr. Strangelove examines how well the Cold War crisis films stack up against historical reality, or at least as much of that reality as we can reconstruct with confidence. First, I examine the source material on which the films are based. Who wrote these books, and why? What changes were made when were they transformed into film? What were the repercussions of this process on the message? Second, I address the fact that the mental stability of senior military personnel is seriously questioned in almost all of the films and is indeed central to the drama generated by the film scenarios. It was inevitable that comparisons would be made to real people and that the fictional portrayals would influence how we think of key military leaders from the period. To what extent are those perceptions distorted? Perhaps there was more going on behind the scenes than was commonly understood. Third, the "war room," an arena where nuclear crises are played out, is a central element in all of the films. I describe what they looked like in the 1950s and 1960s. And as we will see there were in fact many war rooms. Fourth, the Strategic Air Command bomber force, like the war room, is central to almost all of the nuclear crisis films. I explain how it really worked. Could it have been released without presidential authorization? How was it supposed to be used? I have included four vignettes to illustrate how the bombers portrayed in the films would have been employed at the time using real weapons and actual targets. Fifth, I tackle the little-known and misunderstood subject of the ballistic missile force and the apparently malevolent computers they were hooked up to. The intercontinental ballistic missiles (ICBMs) were vulnerable to hijacking and launch by either humans or other computers, or both. Sixth, I discuss the nuclear submarine movies, which depicted cramped claustrophobic cylinders loaded with world-ending weapons controlled by stressed-out crews. Why did those submariners never lose their cool and launch, especially while being hunted by nuclear-armed adversaries?

Deconstructing Dr. Strangelove will take us on a journey into the past and show us what the tools of deterrence were, how they actually worked, and why. In doing so this work will provide crucial context to that highly specialized genre, the nuclear war film.

ONE

Book! Movie!

The Literary Genesis of the Cold War Nuclear Crisis Film

There is a unique genre that deals specifically with Cold War–era nuclear crises. This genre started with a "boom!" in the mid-1950s, peaked by 1965, then echoed in the early 1980s before fading away with the end of the Cold War in 1991. During the course of its run the genre contained best-selling books, some of them selling millions of copies, and numerous critically acclaimed films that are still viewed today and are even used as teaching tools or as texts reflecting the Cold War. The novels influenced the movies, and both continue to have a substantial impact on contemporary social discourse and popular culture.

But what exactly was a "nuclear crisis"? The unique historical structure of the Cold War included three constituent elements. The first was a precariously balanced world order divided between Communist totalitarian states, led by the Soviet Union and China, and the free market democracies, led by the United States. The second was the fact that these systems competed with each other for influence in the uncommitted parts of the world. This competition took myriad forms, including propaganda, covert and clandestine activities, diplomacy, development aid, space and sea exploration, and the global presence of armed forces operating in close proximity to each other in contested areas. The third element was the presence and deployment of extremely destructive weapons that relied on a scarce, unique, and secretive form of detonation. A crisis existed when all of these elements collided at discrete points in time and the possibility of nuclear weapons use became elevated as a result.

In the eighteenth and nineteenth centuries European nations competed for space in the multilateral global order, and when that competition got too intense, local or regional conflicts took place. These were usually settled using diplomacy. If diplomacy failed, nations would go to war with each other, and when one side was spent or decided that it was no longer capable of carrying on, diplomacy kicked in again and peace was declared. I know of only one film about a nineteenth-century global crisis: *55 Days at Peking* (1963), which depicts an American-led multinational mission to rescue diplomatic workers besieged by Chinese revolutionaries.

Why are there no other films dealing with nineteenth-century crises? Simply put, because such crises moved slowly and were not very dramatic. There was no sense of urgency in the nineteenth century on par with that of the late twentieth. If one were produced, such a film would consist of the participants moving back and forth between sumptuous hotels in plush carriages with lots of smoke-filled backroom deals being made over port and prostitutes. There would be footage of a lot of paper inked up with quill pens, balled up, and the text rewritten on a daily basis, to be balled up again until everybody agreed to the wording and implications. This could take days or months. It could take weeks to communicate with far-flung forces in, say, Africa or India. Movies are made about the fictional Richard Sharpe and the 94th Rifles in Spain, not about Metternich. We have to admit that, except for the average soldier in the field, the stakes were comparatively low in the nineteenth century.

Now consider a series of extremely large explosions that spread death-dealing material around the planet. Consider it happening in hours. Minutes even. Now that is dramatic. Sensational. Visceral. Urgent. Superpowers rubbing up against each other in the far-flung reaches of the Cold War are not Sharpe and the 94th Rifles sortieing out from Portugal to contribute to Napoleon's "Spanish ulcer." If he had had them, Old Boney would have used nuclear weapons to cauterize the wound. When twentieth-century superpowers collided, at whatever level, the possibility of *escalation* existed. This word was virtually unknown outside of the boardrooms of the Otis Elevator

Company prior to the 1950s. Escalation became *the* underpinning concept of the Cold War system, driving all of those fears home with an atomic-powered nail gun. We have a crisis if these forces come into contact because it could lead to nuclear weapons use and thus the End of Civilization As We Know It.

But do all of the texts we are about to discuss fit into this schema? Is it simply the possibility of an escalatory process and the presence of nuclear weapons that define the genre? Certainly there were science fiction novels, including H. G. Wells's *The World Set Free* (1914), that suggested there would be nuclear weapons in the future, and that they would be destructive. Literature dealing with "superweapons" was published throughout the twentieth century, as described in some detail by both P. D. Smith in *Doomsday Men: The Real Dr. Strangelove and the Dream of the Superweapon* (2007) and David Seed in *Under the Shadow: The Atomic Bomb and Cold War Narratives* (2013).[1] Yet most of this writing predates the Cold War and none was turned into a film or other cultural property that had lasting impact. They were speculative in nature, in some cases decades ahead of actual events, but were not really a reflection of their time.

Indeed practically the day after Hiroshima a flood of literature burst into the magazine stands and bookstores of the West. This literature took many forms: science fiction; scientific and technical nonfiction; strategic, ethical, and philosophical analyses; and more. Almost none of it was commercial enough to be converted to film. And why should it have been? To some people the bombs used against Japan were just bigger bombs. There was nothing special about "special weapons" yet.[2] There was no production line. By 1947 there was only a handful of custom-built atomic weapons, and the parameters of the Cold War would not be firmly established in the public mind until later in the 1940s.

It was only during the Korean War and the concurrent detonation of the first experimental, megaton-yield, thermonuclear weapon that the public connected an overseas crisis and the possibility of extreme levels of destruction, extending to the elimination of civilization. Apocalyptic and postapocalyptic fiction in existence at the time looked to biological or germ warfare as a world-ender: an example is George R. Stewart's *Earth Abides* (1949).

With the detonation of the Ivy Mike, Joe-4, and Castle Bravo thermonuclear devices between 1952 and 1954, a whole new level of destruction was introduced into the discourse. Ivy Mike erased an entire Pacific island, leaving a water-filled crater nearly a mile across. Footage from the Castle Bravo test showed palm trees burning from the initial pulse of heat from the detonation before they were blown to pieces and scattered by the shock wave. It did not take a great deal of imagination for the audience watching newsreels before the cartoons on a Saturday afternoon in their small-town theater to mentally replace those palm trees with human beings.

Nevil Shute Norway's *On the Beach* (1957) is considered by many to be the seminal mainstream novel dealing with the aftereffects of nuclear war. Written by a veteran best-selling author for wide distribution, *On the Beach* hit the stores and newsstands in the summer of 1957, selling over one hundred thousand copies in six weeks. It was also serialized in forty newspapers, guaranteeing widespread distribution. Eventually four million copies were in print, including mass-market paperback editions. The emotional aspects of Shute's characterizations in the novel drove home the point of nuclear weapons effects far more effectively than numbers and theories bandied about by the scientists on the talk shows and in newsmagazines. Some credit the book with invigorating the ban-the-bomb movement in the late 1950s. And as *The Day After* film personally affected President Reagan, so did *On the Beach* affect President Kennedy.[3]

Using nuclear weapons in a world where both sides possessed them could lead to a runaway situation in which larger and larger weapons were used. That, in the jargon of the day, was "escalation."[4] Escalation was bad. Escalation was frightening. But escalation contained an inherent element of suspense. Escalation could, therefore, be made exciting. And profitable. Escalation had a plot line similar to a romance novel or movie: Would he or wouldn't he fully commit? It was only a matter of time before writers started to look at escalation and its effects for dramatic purposes. And that drama translated into film rather directly and easily.

But what if there were no superheroic brave men around to save us? What if there were only flawed generals, politicians, diplomats, and bureaucrats? And what if complex circumstances related to policy, strategy, and technology already put in motion years previously produced an inexorable momentum that generated a crisis situation that led to thermonuclear destruction? Peter George dreaded that possibility. Ultimately that fear psychologically debilitated and eventually killed him. But not until he had produced two short but powerful works that extended that fear to an audience already primed for more by *On the Beach*.

Significantly, George caught the attention of the Best and the Brightest in the American think-tanks: Thomas Schelling at Harvard sent thirty-one copies of *Two Hours to Doom* (published as *Red Alert* in the United States), the basis for *Dr. Strangelove*, to his colleagues after he read it during a long airplane flight.[5] George also attracted the attention of a certain hot young filmmaker looking for something dramatic to focus on for his next Big Project.

Welshman Peter Bryan George served in the Royal Air Force during and after World War II. Attaining the rank of squadron leader in the 1950s, George was a best-selling novelist writing mysteries and spy thrillers under the pen names Byan Peters and Peter Bryant.[6] It is unclear what, exactly, he did in the RAF in the 1950s. Several websites state, without any hard data, that he worked in the intelligence community. Indeed a careful reading of *Red Alert* would suggest that he did. As with Rascovich and Trew, whom we will soon examine, it is highly probable that George accessed his social network in the RAF to collect information for use in the book. If George was an RAF intelligence officer at this time, it is also highly likely that he would have been privy to sensitive collection activities of the day. These included Project Robin, which involved extremely risky RAF radar mapping penetration and signal intelligence flights undertaken in RB-45C and Canberra jet bombers deep inside the Soviet Union in 1952–55. Such operations involved spoofing and outrunning the Soviet air defense system.[7] If George knew about these operations, he would have found them dangerous and provocative, likely contributing to his high anxiety.

George told Schelling how he decided to write *Red Alert*: "He was sitting with two others at a table in the officers' club of an American B-47 base in England in 1957 or 1958 when a bomber took off. . . . The vibration caused a coffee cup near the table edge to crash to the floor. Somebody said: 'That's the way World War III will start.' George responded by phoning his publisher, saying that for an advance he'd take three weeks leave and write the book."[8]

For the most part those seeking insight into the making of *Dr. Strangelove* glance at *Red Alert* in a cursory manner, note the readily apparent similarities and differences between the book and the film, and then move on to their primary areas of interest. This does not do justice to George and *Red Alert*. *Red Alert* is a highly sophisticated work; it is not merely a basis for *Dr. Strangelove*, and the differences between the two are important ones that highlight what Kubrick later did to distort George's original messages. Kubrick thought that *Red Alert* was too sophisticated and too technical to bring to the silver screen.

As cultural consumers we are or should be already familiar with the basic plot of *Dr. Strangelove*: a mentally unbalanced U.S. Air Force general deceives his staff and misuses a contingency plan that permits him to unilaterally respond to a Soviet attack. There is, in fact, no Soviet attack. He presents the U.S. leadership with a choice: follow up with the whole force and "win," or take their chances. He then prevents the recall of the aircraft by defending the base to the death. During the course of the crisis it is learned that the Soviets have a secret "Doomsday Device" that will destroy the world if they are attacked. Despite all efforts at diplomacy and to recall the aircraft, one B-52 succeeds against all odds because the highly trained and professional crew uses their initiative, and the world ends.

Red Alert describes a generalized Cold War environment consisting of several discrete aspects that directly influence the decision of a U.S. Air Force general to launch the thirty-two B-52K bombers of the 843rd Bomb Wing that is on airborne alert near the Soviet Union. These are not explored in the film and remain the crucial contrast between George's book and Kubrick's movie. They are the perception of failure of American Cold War policy generally; the inability of the contemporary nuclear strategy to support that policy effectively; the availability and specific configuration of the technologies surrounding the delivery of nuclear weapons; the ability to launch the forces; and the policy decisions made after the inappropriate decision to launch, which then feeds back into the crisis process, thus exacerbating it. There really was no way this could have translated to film in any coherent manner, yet *Red Alert* was influential in both popular and specialist venues.

The most important character in *Red Alert* is Brigadier General Quinten, the commander of Sonora Air Force Base in Texas, home of the 843rd Bomb Wing. George uses Quinten's conversations with his executive officer, Maj. Paul Howard, as his delivery system on matters of policy and strategy. Quinten represents those who in the 1950s believed that the Truman-era containment and Eisenhower-era massive retaliation policies were failing and dangerously so; in the novel containment consists of: "Economic aid to under-developed countries. Military aid to Europe. [American] Military strength . . . sufficient to deter any large scale aggression." Quinten asserts that the United States has spent billions in aid: "Russian watched us doing it and smiled. In a lot of countries we managed effectively to destroy colonialism. But we didn't supply a political dynamic sufficiently strong to hold off the Communists as well as replace the colonial systems we helped to end. . . . Big business . . . doesn't mean a thing to the peasants of a backward country," whereas superficial Communism does, a thin edge of the wedge which is then exploited by the force of Communist bayonets. The West was tired of war, and the Russians "figured correctly that . . . we wouldn't fight a major war over the Balkans, or the Baltic States, or even China. Those countries went under." As for massive retaliation, "While we were thinking in terms of A-bombs, Russia thought in terms of bayonets."[9]

On the technological front, the Soviets exploited Nazi scientists to work on ballistic missiles as well as exploiting the atomic bomb spy rings to develop the technological capability to "leap frog" over the Americans: "When the first two Russian satellites went into orbit the writing was on the wall." As a result, Quinten explains, "the destructive potential of weapons has increased, so the margin of retaliatory time has decreased." SAC is now vulnerable once the Soviet ICBMs come fully on line: "Three months . . . is the short period still to run before NORAD can effectively track their missiles coming in and give us time to fire off ours and get SAC off the ground."[10] George has Quinten make the classic case for preventive war, which will likely be fought before 1960, when the window of opportunity closes.

George uses briefings in the novel to explain the Soviet force structure and war planning based on it. Class 1 targets within 1,500 miles of the Soviet Union will be taken out by supersonic fighter-bombers and intermediate-range ballistic missiles. These include the SAC bomber bases in Western Europe, the aircraft carriers of the Sixth Fleet in the Mediterranean, and forces in all European and Middle Eastern NATO countries. London, Paris, and Rome will be destroyed. The Soviets have had the capability of doing this for some time, but as George's characters explain, "this was meaningless unless Class 2 targets" were destroyed. These were the SAC bases in North America and Okinawa, plus Washington, New York, and Chicago. To carry out attacks against Class 2 targets the Soviets would employ missile-launching submarines, two special regiments of Mya-4 Bison bombers, and thirty-six ICBMs; there are no American ICBMs operational yet. The ICBMs are the critical element as the submarines and bombers cannot reach all SAC bases.[11] That was a relatively accurate reflection of the state of affairs by 1960–61.

The near-operational capacity of the latest Soviet ICBM site has triggered Quentin into action. George notes in *Red Alert* that there was in 1958 a single operational Soviet ICBM site with three more about to come on line, plus the existence of two regiments of Bison bombers. This was in fact accurate information on contemporary Soviet capabilities.[12] The level of detail in *Red Alert* makes it likely that George had access to British intelligence data.

Quinten questions the efficacy of the existing civil-military relationship in the nuclear age, but this is efficacy based more on time or the lack of it during a crisis rather than any other reason. In a statement that is watered down and parodied by Gen. Jack D. Ripper, his alter ego in *Dr. Strangelove*, Quinten tells Howard, "[Clemenceau] said war was too important a matter to be left to generals. At the moment he said it, he was probably right. But now it's swung the other way. When a war can be won and lost in an hour after its starts, than war is too important to be left to politicians. The Russians know it. And they also know we don't work things that way."[13]

But that is not all. Unlike his alter ego, Quinten's motives are complex and less rooted in Freudian psychology. There is the past: "We've come a long way since Pearl Harbor. That taught us a lesson we've never forgotten."[14] This statement accurately reflects the results of studies made by theorist Albert Wohlstetter on SAC vulnerability that were conducted by the RAND Corporation throughout the 1950s.[15] Quinten believes there is a window of opportunity that will close shortly on the ICBM issue. He is also terminally ill, so there will be no personal or career consequences. But George takes pains to explain that Quinten is also motivated by his observation of the brutal rape culture of Soviet occupation forces in Austria when he was an observer there in 1945, and by the Soviet tanks crushing of Hungarian civilians in 1956. Soviet hydrogen bomb tests and satellite launches are not disconnected from these events. But the crème de la crème of atrocities, Quinten explains, is his knowledge that "troops taken prisoner in Korea [were] forced to stand naked on the ice of a frozen river while water was poured over their feet until they were part of the ice. . . . Some of them didn't give in. They lost their feet. Sometimes they lost their minds, sometimes their lives. My nephew was one of the lucky ones. He just lost his life."[16]

Brigadier General Quinten is by no means the moral equivalent of General Ripper in *Dr. Strangelove*. And one wonders how much of Quinten's experiences mirror George's. Quinten makes a choice, but that choice is driven by a plethora of factors in a complex context, not because Commie fluoridation has made it so he can't get it up any more with the babes. Of note, George is the only author in this study that does not let the Soviet Union and its leadership off the hook completely. This is a major point of divergence with the Kubrickian worldview in *Dr. Strangelove*, where anybody who is anti-

Communist is a deluded McCarthyite and therefore highly dangerous, especially if he has access to nuclear weapons. One could argue that *Red Alert* could be subtitled "The Tragedy of General Quinten."

As for the tools of destruction, George was exceptionally concerned that bombers equipped with nuclear weapons would be kept aloft at all hours of the day by aerial refueling to reduce their vulnerability to destruction on the ground by missile. This concept, airborne alert, was experimental, even radical in 1958. It plays a key role in *Red Alert* in that it permits readied aircraft to be employed within minutes of receiving their action messages by Quinten. Two characters in *Red Alert* even reference a 1958 U.S. Air Force press release on the matter and the public furor it caused at the time.[17]

On 7 April 1958 senior United Press journalist Frank Bartholomew posted a dispatch from the SAC underground command post at Offutt Air Force Base. This article was published in practically every American newspaper the next day; in the *New York Times*, reporters elaborated on it with their own information. Extensive foreign coverage followed. In his dispatch Bartholomew claimed that SAC's B-36, B-47, and B-52 bombers were in "continuous flight" on the perimeter of the Soviet Union and loaded with thermonuclear weapons, that they were kept in place via aerial refueling by KC-97 and KC-135 tankers and could be sent to strike targets in the USSR only on presidential order. The idea of a "fail-safe" point was also mentioned, with Bartholomew walking through a scenario where a plane did not get the message to return. There was also a plethora of quotes from the commander in chief of Strategic Air Command (CINCSAC), Gen. Thomas Power, and details of forward basing in Spain, the Marianas, and Britain. Though we know today that this eventually became SAC standing operating procedure, it was the first time Americans had had access to this level of detail. Within a week the Soviet Union vigorously protested this "provocation" in the United Nations and every other world venue.[18] Thus when Ambassador DeSadeski in *Dr. Strangelove* exclaims in the war room that his source was the *New York Times*, this can be taken as historically accurate.

It is evident that this was carefully planned messaging by Power, but to what extent it had the concurrence of the Eisenhower White

House is unclear. Power published the best-selling *Design for Survival* after he retired in 1964. He noted in the introduction that the first version, written in 1958, was banned by Secretary of Defense Neil McElroy. Power said that he had similar conversations with media and political figures at the time on matters discussed in the manuscript and that he was motivated by the desire to have an educated public involved in democratic processes related to defence.[19]

It is interesting that the members of the Operations Coordinating Board, the Eisenhower administration's high-level psychological operations group, agreed that "sensational newspaper publicity can make the conduct of foreign affairs more difficult. Specific[ally] reports concerning SAC procedures on which the recent Soviet complaints about irresponsible flights with nuclear weapons were undoubtedly based."[20] The Board did not blame Power; they blamed the media. They even considered, again presaging the DeSadeski scene, inviting the USSR's Premier Nikita Khrushchev to SAC headquarters so he could see for himself how the system worked, but "this proposal was not pursued further."[21]

The technological aspects of *Red Alert* explore what George believed to be serious flaws in the command-and-control process for SAC's Airborne Alert Force. It is in this area that George had many pieces of the puzzle but not the whole picture. He depicts in some detail several key processes: the fictional B-52K itself, the bomb arming process, how he believed thermonuclear weapons functioned, and the communications systems in the aircraft. Most important, however, is George's depiction of bomb design because of the role this plays in the climax of the novel. And this is what he got wrong.

The B-52K *Alabama Angel* is on its final run to its target, the ICBM complex. The crew has progressed through a complex weapons-release process that includes the in-flight insertion of the firing mechanism, something that was done on early nuclear weapons but generally not after 1958. George's thermonuclear weapon has a gun assembly primary (similar to the Little Boy bomb) but with plutonium spheres. This primary detonates along with a tritium core, which then detonates deuterium and produces a 15-megaton yield blast, remarkably close to the actual yield of the Castle Bravo shot in 1954.[22] In

1958 George conflated the failed Thin Man atomic bomb design from 1945 with some of the basic essential elements of the alternative conceptual multistage thermonuclear bomb designs of the day.

As the B-52K bomber prepares to drop, it gets hit and crashes before the arming safety process is completed. The bomb breaks up, with the secondary stage falling off and the primary detonating with a 200-kiloton yield. This yield is remarkably close to the George test shot, which was one of the first thermonuclear process experiments in the Greenhouse tests of 1951. In *Red Alert* the primary detonates on impact because it is a gun assembly device. This gives the Soviet leaders the excuse they need to stick it to the Americans, who have agreed to exchange Atlantic City for Kotlass, the city nearest to the ICBM base.

In actuality the safety mechanisms of the day were such that this could not have happened. Similarly the idea that nuclear release authority could be predelegated via something like *Dr. Strangelove's* Plan R to a wing commander that had forces on airborne alert and that no authentication system was necessary beyond the wing commander and his deployed forces does not stand up to historical reality, as we will see later. However, George could not have known that when he wrote *Red Alert*. That particular flaw gets transferred into *Dr. Strangelove* and transmitted to a broader audience.

There are many elements in *Red Alert* that do find their way unscathed into *Dr. Strangelove*. These include the Doomsday Machine, though in the book it is triggered by people, not "automatically by a computer." There is a CRM-114 communications device on board the mythical B-52K to screen incoming transmissions; it fails in both book and film. The Airborne Alert Force "X Point" (along a line from the Arctic to the Persian Gulf, where the B-52Ks turn around) was in reality called the Positive Control Point.

Other elements are not translated into the film: the concept of proportional exchange, one city for another to prevent greater war, makes it into *Fail-Safe* and, in another form, into *The Bedford Incident*, but not the film *Dr. Strangelove*. There is no Dr. Strangelove character in *Red Alert*. An important theme in *Red Alert* is that there is an inexorable, uncontrollable process in play of which a nuclear crisis is only one part, and there is no way of stopping this inevitable race to the abyss. That is what George feared the most, not rogue U.S. Air Force generals. The United States was being forced into a corner by circumstances, and the results were not going to be pretty.

George's final work, *Commander-1* (1965), makes *On the Beach* look like an exercise in ecstatic joyfulness. A U.S. Navy research submarine conducting long-term human relationship experiments in the Arctic, a sort of sexual version of the 1960 voyage of the USS *Triton*, survives and redeploys to a special survival base island, but its captain evolves into a fascist dictator and forces the survivors to take special thought control narcotics.[23] Dissenters are executed by machine gun, and a special Strangelove-esque genetic breeding program is implemented. Technically *Commander-1* belongs in the realm of postapocalyptic fiction, though it depicts a detailed third-party initiation scenario by which the war starts.

The depressive tone of *Commander-1* clearly reflected George's deepening personal turmoil over the future of the World As We Know It. He committed suicide in 1966, using the same method that one of the characters in *Commander-1* does when he can't handle the stress of "survival" any longer.[24]

Competitive Escalation: *Dr. Strangelove* and *Fail-Safe*

It took a bright young director to fully realize Peter George's fear factor on the silver screen. Getting there, however, was far more involved and convoluted that merely producing a screenplay based on *Two Hours to Doom / Red Alert*. There was a whole Kubrickian process that George's book had to pass through before Dr. Strangelove rolled out in his wheelchair and started gesticulating. That process involved the work of others. And even a pair of competitors.

In December 1959 a short story called "Abraham '59: A Nuclear Fantasy" appeared in *Dissent* magazine. "F. B. Aiken" was the pen name for an up-and-coming academic, Harvey Wheeler. Wheeler, who served in the U.S. Army, was left with a "presentiment of nuclear catastrophe" after the atomic bombing of Japan; this propelled him to study political science, which led to numerous books on American politics in the 1950s. "Abraham '59" started out as

"Abraham '56." Wheeler asked the question: What if SAC bombed the Soviet Union by accident? How could a full-scale nuclear war be prevented? He had already posed the question to colleagues, who had no solution. "Abraham" was one approach: if SAC hit a city, then the president had to somehow contact the Soviet premier and offer up an American city for destruction in exchange and stop any further escalation. Proportionality was the solution. Wheeler shopped the idea around. At a party attended by psychologist B. F. Skinner, military historian Walter Millis, and political scientist Eugene Burdick, all agreed that the "Abraham" scenario was possible and that it had to be published. There were no takers on the literary scene, but with some persistence the *Dissent* article eventually emerged.[25]

In 2000 Wheeler alleged that George had been a fiction editor at more than one of the U.S. magazines to which he'd sent "Abraham '58," implying that George plagiarized him. At this point in history there is no conclusive evidence that this occurred, and there appears to be nobody from that period still alive who can contradict Wheeler's assertion.[26] The premise of the two works is similar, and the concept of proportionality as a solution exists in both, but George's depiction has significant technical and strategic dimensions that Wheeler, who did not have anywhere near the same level of access, does not have. And unlike Wheeler, George was driven by a variety of concerns, not a singular one.

When "Abraham '59" appeared, it was at the end of a long year that saw several seminal works on nuclear affairs. Bernard Brodie from RAND published *Strategy in the Missile Age*. Albert Wohlstetter, also from RAND, published "The Delicate Balance of Terror" in *Foreign Affairs*, whose editors then turned down Thomas Schelling's "Surprise Attack and Disarmament," which riffed off of Wohlstetter. "Surprise Attack" found a home in the *Bulletin of the Atomic Scientists*. These were three high-profile pieces, all of them reinforcing the same message in different ways: the United States and its bomber force was vulnerable to ballistic missiles; there was an increased need to respond quickly to threats or attacks; and the country was vulnerable to catastrophic miscalculation because of both.[27]

The national prominence and commercial success of nuclear fear likely led Wheeler to connect with Eugene Burdick, who in 1958 had just published, with William Lederer, the notorious best seller *The Ugly American*, which drove the Eisenhower administration crazy with its depiction of the failing development competition with Communism in the decolonizing Third World. Burdick was a former naval officer, war hero, and development specialist who had degrees in psychology and philosophy.[28] Ed Kuhn, an editor at McGraw-Hill, was on the lookout for controversy and met with Burdick and Wheeler sometime in 1960 or 1961 to craft what would become *Fail-Safe*. According to Wheeler, Kuhn asked, "You fellas ever heard of a British novel with a similar plot?" Both replied in the negative. "No matter . . . I've seen it. Not very good. Back to work."[29] It was only years later, apparently, that Wheeler realized he was referring to George's *Red Alert*.

But there is more to this story. In December 1961 Burdick sent to Harris-Kubrick Pictures a "partially completed novel and outline of a novel tentatively entitled *Fail-Safe* . . . for [their] consideration in connection with the potential purchase" of film rights. According to the film historian Peter Kramer, "Kubrick was not interested in the offer, but immediately recognized the similarities between *Fail-Safe* and *Red Alert*, and hence the danger that someone else might pick up the film rights for *Fail-Safe* and produce a rival picture. In preparation of a possible plagiarism suit, Kubrick sent Burdick and his co-author Harvey Wheeler, via registered mail, a copy of *Red Alert*, 'to which we own the exclusive world-wide motion picture and allied rights.' . . . This established the fact that the two authors had indeed been familiar with *Red Alert*."[30]

Despite this, the product of Wheeler, Burdick, and Kuhn's deliberations became the *Saturday Evening Post* excerpt article on 13 October 1962, and then the runaway best-selling novel *Fail-Safe*, published in December 1962. In effect, *Fail-Safe* is an elaborate version of "Abraham '59" with as much technical detail as the three could glean from various U.S. Air Force magazines and the *New York Times*. Apparently none of the American reviewers noted its similarity to *Red Alert*; this can probably be chalked up to a not-invented-here attitude prevalent in American culture and epitomized by Kuhn's remarks to the authors.

Concurrent with the *Fail-Safe* process was Kubrick's interest in George's work. Kubrick was an omnivore, gobbling up everything on the subject of nuclear war after reading Schelling's "Delicate Balance of Terror." (Writer Terry Southern once counted sixty-three volumes on Kubrick's bookshelf dealing with nuclear affairs.) When he asked Alastair Buchan, the head of the recently established International Institute for Strategic Studies, for something to read, Buchan recommended *Two Hours to Doom* (*Red Alert* in the United States). An alternative or possibly concurrent version of this anecdote claims that Kubrick read a Schelling article in *The Observer* and another, "Men, Meteors, and War," in the September 1960 issue of the *Bulletin of the Atomic Scientists* that praised *Red Alert* effusively. Both events took place either in 1960 or 1961 and thus prior to Burdick's sending the incomplete "Fail-Safe" material to Kubrick.[31]

Then the soon to be former RANDist Herman Kahn weighed in. Kubrick read Kahn's *On Thermonuclear War*, which appeared in 1960 and achieved notoriety in days, if not hours, after its release. The auteur and the provocateur started to correspond in January 1961, and in time there were face-to-face discussions about The Unthinkable. Kahn's influence on the shift from *Red Alert* to *Dr. Strangelove* was profound.

Unlike the other commentators on nuclear war, including Schelling, who published *The Strategy of Conflict* in the same year, Kahn's tone and approach shocked, intrigued, and outraged the reading public all at once. Schelling provided an eyes-glazed-over Organization Man math text, while Kahn produced the academic equivalent of an EC Comics horror story, complete with the academic equivalent of violence, gore, and embedded morality tales. Indeed the quote most often associated with *On Thermonuclear War* was from James Newman's *Scientific American* review describing the 668-page book as "a moral tract on mass murder: how to plan it, how to commit it, how to get away with it, how to justify it."[32]

In many ways *On Thermonuclear War* is almost as much source material for *Dr. Strangelove* as *Red Alert* and thus is worth going into here. The basic argument is that the United States won't reach the year 2000—or 1965—unless it gets serious about nuclear war. To explain this, Kahn introduced the American people to the holy jargon employed by the priest-like strategists of the secretive RAND: Finite Deterrence, Counterforce as Insurance, Pre-attack Mobilization Base, Credible First Strike Capability. He challenged his readers with the concept of World Wars I through VIII and boldly asked, "Will the survivors envy the dead?"[33]

Kahn slammed Nevil Shute's *On the Beach* as "badly researched" and taken too seriously. Thermonuclear war would be extremely damaging, but there would be survivors. Therefore it was incumbent on leadership to accept the fact that national objectives would still have meaning after a catastrophic attack. Kahn tore apart "finite deterrence" and similar ideas that would later be dubbed mutual assured destruction. *On Thermonuclear War* was an assault on the abject refusal of some commentators and policymakers to seriously examine and prepare for a postattack state.

Sharon Ghamari-Tabrizi asserts that Kahn was employing the "theatre of the absurd" in *On Thermonuclear War* to get his points across, in the same way *Mad Magazine* and EC Comics engaged in social commentary using "sick" humor, a new comedy type that emerged in the United States during the 1950s.[34] For example, a whole section of the book deals with genetic mutations and appears to calculate the relative numbers of genetically disordered children in the United States, Europe, and the USSR before and after a nuclear war, prefiguring *Dr. Strangelove*'s commentary on survivors "breeding more prodigiously" after emerging from the mineshafts. Kahn even asked, "Is it just as bad to kill a man 10,000 years from now as to kill one today?" and pointed out, "Only survivors can have children."[35]

Buried amid the copious amounts of verbal debris is Kahn's argument for a robust deterrent and a creative and effective civil defense program to prevent all of this in the first place. An adjunct to that discussion emerges as the Doomsday Machine and its even more frightening relations, the Doomsday-in-a-Hurry Machine and the Homicidal Pact Machine, and with them the progenitor of the Strangelovian discussion of the "Doomsday gap."[36] This discussion clearly influenced the 1966 Dennis Feltham Jones novel *Colossus* and its derivative 1970 film, *Colossus: The Forbin Project*. However, despite Kahn's protests to Kubrick, the idea was originally mooted by physicist Leo Szilard a decade earlier,[37] and both Shute and George employed Szilard's "cobalt bombs" as plot devices in 1957 and 1958.[38]

Also of key importance in any discussion of Kahn, Wheeler, George, and Kubrick is Kahn's discussion of accidental war in *On Thermonuclear War*. Distinguishing between "accidental accidents" and "nonaccidental accidents" (pace Donald Rumsfeld and "known unknowns and "unknown unknowns"), Kahn, in some detail, references the international furor generated in April 1958 by Frank H. Bartholomew's United Press report on a possible scenario for accidental war, the story whose description of bombers in "continuous flight" had directly influenced George and *Red Alert*.[39] We are caught in a literary confluence: Wheeler claims he wrote "Abraham" in 1956, yet airborne alert did not yet exist. When "Abraham" was published in late 1959, airborne alert was a reality, the spat over the Bartholomew piece had played out, and *Red Alert* had been in print for a year. Suffice it to say the discussion of accidental war and SAC in 1958 influenced the work of Wheeler, Burdick, George, and Kahn to varying degrees. To extrapolate further, if Bartholomew's access was thanks to Gen. Thomas Power's attempt to influence the Soviets and the American public, CINCSAC himself ultimately and inadvertently played a role in the creation of *Dr. Strangelove* and *Fail-Safe*.

In any event, Kahn met with Kubrick while he and George were working on the screenplay originally titled "The Delicate Balance of Terror." This meeting resulted in the shift from the serious tone in *Red Alert* to the theater of the absurd, or, as Ghamari-Tabrizi calls it, the grotesque, that is more evident in the later version of the screenplay called "Dr. Strangelove." Kahn and Kubrick agreed that the only way to approach the subject was through comedy.[40] Around this time Kubrick also held a brainstorming session that included George and RANDists William Kaufman, Morton Halperin, and Thomas Schelling. Schelling later recalled, "We had a hell of a time getting that damn war started. . . . We finally decided that it couldn't happen unless there was somebody crazy in the Air Force. That's when Kubrick and Peter George decided they would have to do it as what they called a 'nightmare comedy.'"[41]

But that was not all. During preproduction Peter Sellers, who was going to play Maj. "King" Kong in addition to other roles, was concerned that he couldn't effectively manage a Texas accent and American colloquialisms. Kubrick reached out to Terry Southern, who flew to England and quickly read *Red Alert*. Southern, who among other things was an authentic combat veteran, altered some of the dialogue. This forced a partial screenplay rewrite by George, Kubrick, and Southern.[42] The result was the "Dr. Strangelove" screenplay and book, which differed from *Red Alert*, the "Delicate Balance of Terror" working script, and even in some minor respects the final film, *Dr. Strangelove*.

The "Dr. Strangelove" book jettisons all of George's discussion of preventive war and instead depicts alien archaeologists researching their metabook, *The Dead Worlds of Antiquity*, and finding documents hidden in the Great Northern Desert of planet Earth. The terminology differs slightly: "X point" is the term used instead of George's "fail-safe points," George's ULTECH is "Plan R," and George's CWIE is the CRM-114 discriminator. George's *Alabama Angel* becomes *The Leper Colony*, obviously spoofing the award-winning 1949 film *Twelve O'Clock High*, in which bomb group leader Gregory Peck orders his worst crews and worst leaders to fly together in a B-17 renamed *Leper Colony* in order to shape them up. The idea that something similar could happen in a squadron equipped with thermonuclear weapons is hilarious and probably was instigated by Kubrick.

The plot of the "Dr. Strangelove" book is essentially the same as the movie's; both feature Maj. "King" Kong, Gen. Buck Turgidson, Gen. Jack D. Ripper, and crew yippee-ki-yaying to Armageddon. Ripper commits suicide in his Burpelson AFB Führerbunker after his "children" surrender. Strangelove doesn't gesticulate yet. Kahn is all over the book and thus the movie. (Ghamari-Tabrizi has found seven direct Kahn quotes in the book.)[43]

Director Sidney Lumet, on the other hand, was attracted to *Fail-Safe*, believing a "kind of anti-war piece had a tremendous value [and he] felt it really could make money because it was an enormous bestseller," not to mention the fact that he could make it on the cheap.[44] This put Lumet on a collision course with Kubrick, which resulted in a legal dispute during the productions of both films in 1963: did Wheeler and Burdick plagiarize George, or did George and Kubrick plagiarize Wheeler and Burdick? Did Kubrick read *Fail-Safe* when came out in 1962 while he was working up *Dr. Strangelove*?

Fail-Safe the book, when boiled down to its essence, is a series of essays interspersed with character studies that examine the issues of accidental war and the fallibility of men and machines while one such crisis is in play. "Abraham '59" is tacked on to the end.

Set in 1967, the novel, in ways similar to *Red Alert*, flips between the SAC war room, the Pentagon war room, the White House bomb shelter, and later the cockpit of a Vindicator bomber. The authors, Burdick and Wheeler, use the SAC war room as a theater to establish how "the system" works. The players are General Bogan (CINC-SAC), his duty officer, a scientist, and a congressman. There is a Big Board, with identical counterparts in Colorado Springs and the Pentagon displaying the current threat condition and unit locations (in some ways technically correct for the 1970s). There is a discussion about Soviet missile submarines and how vulnerable the United States is to them because of the three-mile limit, the distance from a nation's coast where its territory ends and international waters begin, but Bogan explains that a "pattern of sonar buoys has been laid across the Pacific" and they can pick up sound and process it at the Kaneohe Bay facility in Hawaii. This is a reference to the real and highly classified underwater sound surveillance system employed by the United States and Canada at the time.[45]

When a UFO appears in the system, the reader is permitted to see how the system responds. Burdick and Wheeler take us through colored alert conditions and explain that there are six bomber groups on patrol kept aloft by aerial refueling. Once the alert system goes into effect, these aircraft move toward their "fail-safe points." When they arrive they require a presidential order to proceed. The president is "accompanied by a Warrant Officer who has the codes," a reference to the real "football" briefcase.

The congressman asks, "What if somebody up there or down here cracks?" and after an elaborate discussion is told there is a "psychological screening program" in place for everybody from general to private. Burdick and Wheeler have Colonel Cascio explain that "there are a number of people who believe that the Air Force has a high incidence of madmen among its crews. . . . A few years back there was a lot of upset about whether or not an individual madman, ranging from a general down to the pilot of a plane, could start a war. With this procedure we may still have the madmen around but there is nothing they can do to start a war."[46]

As the planes head for their fail-safe points, fighters reach higher states of readiness, ICBMs make preparations for launch, and bomber squadrons arm and fuel up. Bogan tells the congressman, "All out safety is an expensive thing." The Royal Canadian Air Force intercepts the UFO, an off-course airliner. Bogan explains, "What we would do is make sure that the single plane does not have a runaway pilot who wanted to commit Hari-Kiri against New York or Montreal"—somewhat ironic in the post-9/11 world.

Meanwhile, as everything returns to normal, "a small condenser blew" in the presidential command net room that houses the "fail-safe activating mechanism." The six Vindicator bombers holding at their fail-safe point (the book's description suggests that these are based on B-58 Hustler bombers) suddenly get a message on their fail-safe box, which is described as a "six-wheel-code machine." The crew check their single-sideband radios and get a "loud, pulsed drone," which suggests they are being jammed by Soviet electronic warfare systems. A check of the alternate security channel presents the same fail-safe code: CAP 811. Two of the crew verify their orders: the group will drop twelve 20-megation bombs from 60,000 feet in a pattern over Moscow, detonating them at 5,000 feet.[47]

Meanwhile, on the Washington cocktail circuit, RAND-like defense scientist Walter Grotoschele faces off with antagonists who want to debate thermonuclear war. This debate serves to explain to the reader the contending theories and policies that the United States was struggling with at the time. Grotoschele, a blend of Henry Kissinger and Herman Kahn, argues, "Every war, including thermonuclear war, must have a victor and a vanquished." While the liberal newspaper-man Foster baits him with "Get with it.... Probability and the cobalt bomb made you old fashioned ten years ago," Grotoschele responds, Kahn-like, "It is a question of who's culture survives."

Betty, the wife of SAC general Black, intervenes. "It's a Greek tragedy," she declares and promises to euthanize her children with morphine "when" it happens. Grotoschele fights back: "I'm trying to *save* your two boys, not narcotize their deaths." General Black sides with his wife and, *On the Beach*–like, suggests everybody get out their morphine.[48] Grotoschele, who gives lectures in how many decades after a nuclear war it will take to achieve medieval stan-dards of living, believes in counterforce and civil defense; Foster is into countervalue, or "finite deterrence"; and the Blacks are into despair. In an interesting historical parallel, there were apparently an abnormal number of suicides among the wives of officers attending the National War College in the late 1950s that one faculty member attributed to the depressing nature of course discussions related to the probability of nuclear war.[49]

Fail-Safe delves into technical details obviously extrapolated from open sources. As the crisis builds there is discussion of the Gold telephone system that linked a "handful of policymakers with the White House." (In reality the Gold system was the Joint Chiefs of Staff Alerting Network, the final conference call before War Emer-gency was declared.) There is an elaborate discussion of Lowry AFB in Colorado and its eighteen underground silos housing Titan mis-siles (accurate), how they are fueled up to launch (partially accu-rate), the psychology of their crews (strange and inaccurate), and that the missiles also have fail-safe points that require an order to continue or they are destroyed in flight (inaccurate). Burdick and Wheeler make sure we know all about the "miniature emergency Omaha" aircraft (code-named Looking Glass in real life) and the four KC-135 command-and-control planes scattered throughout the country to support the president and SAC, even though they play no role in events.[50]

As the clock ticks down and time runs out, the president gets a lot of advice. Some of it is contradictory and not useful: Grotoschele gets into the possibility that the Soviets might use the excuse of the accident to launch a strike while the rest of SAC is stood down. He advocates, Ripper-like, following up Group 6 with everything they have and using the accident as an opportunity. He thinks the Soviets will calculate their chances and surrender. Nobody buys into this argument. Eventually the decision is made to use the "hot line," which involves interpreters and translation (as opposed to the real Teletype system). Khrushchev is by some miracle still in charge at the other end after the Cuban debacle. And he's reasonable. The decision is made to assist the Soviets in breaching the electronic defense systems of the planes and destroying them, just like in *Red Alert*.

The Soviet premier and the U.S. president agree that if Moscow is attacked, the United States will bomb New York as a proportional compensatory measure. The American ambassador in Moscow and the Soviet ambassador at the UN in New York join the conference call so that their deaths will signal that both cities are destroyed. Vindicator 5 and Vindicator 6 are about to make it through the Soviet air defenses when the Soviets blunder and throw everything at Vindicator 6, the unarmed electronic warfare aircraft. Unlike the *Alabama Angel* in *Red Alert*, Vindicator 5 gets through. The phone screeches as the American ambassador melts. General Black, orbiting New York in his Vindicator, drops thermonuclear weapons on the city and commits suicide. The Soviet UN ambassador's phone screeches. The world is saved.

That is, until Kubrick and George sue Burdick and Wheeler. Then *Dr. Strangelove* emerges first onto the silver screen and the world ends to Strangelove exclaiming he can walk, the music of Vera Lynn, and the visuals of thermonuclear tests at Eniwetok and Bikini. Six months later, in 1964, *Fail-Safe* was released to positive reviews but low box-office returns. Black comedy, it seems, was like using sugar to help the medicine go down. *Fail-Safe* was just too calculated, too serious, too *mechanical*. *Strangelove* was humanistic by comparison. *Strangelove*'s Ripper hit every male theatergoer where it might legitimately hurt, while *Fail-Safe*'s Grotoschele and his nuclear death fetishist female companion were probably just a little too weird to handle.

In an internal memo, Carl Kaysen, Kennedy's deputy national security advisor, wrote, "Americans are entitled to the assurance that the events in the novel *Fail Safe*—or even its stepfather, *Red Alert*—do not correspond at all to the realities of our system of safeguards."[51] The air force's evaluation of *Fail-Safe* was dismissive: "There has been no evidence to indicate that the novel has had any effect other than to re-enforce the convictions of those who already believe that Military Forces, per se, are evil. . . . [A] statement pointing out the tremendous number of factual errors . . . would serve only to lend credence to the 'message' of the authors that war by accident (with U.S. Forces at fault) is inevitable."[52]

Mark Rascovich: Running Silent and Deep

Mark R. Rascovich is the most mysterious of the writers who explored Cold War nuclear crises. He wrote two books relevant to our discussion: the novel *The Bedford Incident* (1963), on which the 1965 movie is based, and *Bucher: My Story* (1970). *Bucher* is not a novel: it is the harrowing account of Lloyd M. Bucher, commanding officer of the intelligence-gathering ship USS *Pueblo*, which was seized by North Korea in 1968. Bucher and his crew were incarcerated under abominable circumstances for over a year, and the incident nearly led to war with North Korea. In neither book is there biographical data about the author. Even Rascovich's obituary is opaque, to say the least. It mentions both books, notes that he liked deep-sea fishing, and announces that he died in West Palm Beach on 13 December 1976. Nothing else, not even a picture in his hometown paper.[53]

The only other personal information is a disclaimer at the start of *The Bedford Incident*: "Some of the anti-submarine warfare techniques and equipment described in this work have been deliberately obscured. This has been done because the author has had access to certain confidential naval information imparted to him in his capacity of marine researcher and has no wish to betray such trust or embarrass his associates. This in no way impairs the validity of the story, which in essence and in spirit remains a potentially true one for as long as we live under the present circumstances."[54]

32

Rascovich was involved in oceanographic research based in Florida. In 1960 he became a research fellow with the American Museum of Natural History, where he worked on the electronic tagging of tuna. This led to a consultative role with the Inter-American Tropical Tuna Commission. He was also president of the Sailfish Club of Florida, a conservationist and sport fishing organization.[55] That research, in some capacity, appears to have overlapped with the extensive anti-submarine warfare program undertaken by the U.S. Navy in the 1950s and 1960s.

The connection to Bucher is interesting. Clearly Bucher trusted Rascovich to write what is an intensely emotional account of the *Pueblo* affair. A former enlisted sailor during World War II, Bucher served as a submarine officer from 1954 to 1964. He was not part of the Rickover nuclear "club" and as a result spent most of his time on diesel-powered submarines, including time as the executive officer aboard the uss *Ronquil*, the submarine used to depict the uss *Tigerfish* in the film version of *Ice Station Zebra*. He also served aboard the uss *Besugo*, a World War II submarine converted to an auxiliary research submarine (AGSS-321), which itself, in another strange coincidence, served as a fictional submarine in the 1957 film *Hellcats of the Navy* starring Ronald Reagan.[56] It is likely that Rascovich and Bucher worked together in some research capacity.

Many have compared *The Bedford Incident*, published in 1963, to *Moby-Dick*, and indeed Rascovich quotes Melville and otherwise makes the comparison himself throughout the work. However, to suggest that it is merely a Cold War updating of an earlier Grand Obsession is far too simplistic. *The Bedford Incident* is a microhistorical study of the Cold War itself, and it is glaringly evident that Rascovich was alarmed by an event or events that he had either heard about socially or been briefed on. The level of technical detail in the book suggests knowledge beyond exceptionally sound research. In my view, *The Bedford Incident* is the best literary depiction of the Cold War to come out of that period and deserves to be remembered as such.

Ben Munceford, journalist extraordinaire, arrives on the antisubmarine destroyer DL-113, the uss *Bedford*, while she is patrolling the

Greenland-Iceland–United Kingdom Gap, that piece of ocean that Soviet submarines have to transit if they are to interfere with or target NATO shipping, bases, and cities. Munceford's interactions with the primary characters, particularly the captain, Erik Finlander, and the West German observer and former U-Boat ace Cmdre. Wolfgang Schrepke, permit Rascovich to expound in detail on the nature of the Cold War and the dangerous and unseen aspects of it at sea.

Once on board Munceford is briefed by Commander Allison, the executive officer: "We are an active part of NATO's defenses and operate our ship virtually under wartime conditions." Munceford is "getting the impression that they are far more active than has been let on back home." He asks Allison, "You mean you fight yourselves a sort of private Cold War out here?" Allison does not answer. Finlander elaborates: "We are hunters—stalking kind of hunters—who track by ear a foe who is also intently listening to us." The captain admits that it is a "nebulous cold war without decisively obtainable tactical objectives."[57]

Munceford presses for a clearer explanation of what is really going on. Rascovich has Finlander describe this in a briefing: "Contrary to certain scuttlebutt we aren't here to spy on each other's missile ranges or atomic tests. That kind of work can be done cheaper and easier by one man in a U-2. . . . It is DEW [Distant Early Warning] Line and NORAD emissions. Soviet submarines are recording and checking out to help them penetrate our defenses when the time comes. I also suspect scouting and ranging of submarine missile firing positions. These are objectives worth tremendous risks. They are worth killing over."[58]

Munceford asks if anybody gets hurt, and Finlander responds, "Fear hurts. Unrelenting tension becomes a physical pain. Uncertainty and frustration can turn into a crippling agony. . . . This is . . . the hard core war part of the Cold War. Here we clash in the privacy of the black, empty ocean with no audience but our own conscience; both parties want to keep it that way because the stakes are such that no compromise is possible. If you doubt me, then ask yourself what the United States has left if its DEW-line and NORAD systems are cracked."[59]

Finlander's logic is a legitimate reflection of the times. If the DEW Line radar stations were "spoofed" or jammed by the Soviets in wartime because they knew what frequencies they worked on, it would seriously increase the probability of a successful nuclear bomber attack against the United States and Canada. Similarly, if the Soviets could acquire optimal firing positions for missile-launching submarines in areas difficult for NATO to respond to, it would seriously contribute to the overall strategic problem.

"We're not here to make faces at Commies over a wall," Finlander explains. "We're not in a base area indoctrinating simple-minded natives into the complex savagery of modern guerilla tactics; we're not sitting in an air conditioned blockhouse in Florida trying to shoot a bigger hole in the moon. Here we *hunt* Russians. Here we have our enemy and more than accepting his challenge, go after him without any inhibitions of containment policies or technical inferiorities."[60] For Capt. Erik Finlander, "there is nothing more demoralizing that to have the secrecy stripped from one's secret mission."

In an equally important insight into Finlander and his obsession, Rascovich explains that Finlander had been part of the 1940–41 U.S. Navy "neutrality patrols" but does not elaborate. This was a Cold War–like situation between a neutral United States and belligerent Nazi Germany that at the time resulted in unacknowledged clashes between U.S. destroyers and Nazi U-Boats, including the sinking of the USS *Reuben James*.[61] With the nuclear stakes at an all-time high, Finlander's obsession with stalking Soviet submarines is completely understandable and possibly even legitimate. This is a significant point of departure from the 1965 film version of *The Bedford Incident*.

In terms of technical detail, Rascovich clearly was familiar with aspects of contemporary anti-submarine warfare. The Soviet sub the *Bedford* is after is based on an advanced German World War II design, the Walther boat propelled by hydrogen peroxide. It is equipped with a hooded periscope to reduce reflection, has a white-painted fin or sail for Arctic operations, and uses burst radio transmissions to pass information. The *Bedford* is a "destroyer leader," a specialized anti-sub vessel equipped with the nuclear-capable Anti-Submarine Rocket (ASROC) system, a Terrier anti-aircraft missile system that can "track a RB-47 on patrol out of Thule" (a reference to actual classified "ferret" intelligence-gathering flights), a high-frequency direction-finding system connected to a multiplex emissions sensor, and a variety of active and passive sonar systems. Rascovich, surprisingly for 1963, explains the importance of what was then a highly classified oceanographic discovery that dramatically affected anti-submarine warfare: the existence of the deep sound channel. This anomaly allows sonar acquisition of targets hundreds and even thousands of miles away. In particular Rascovich notes the fact that the presence of whales interferes with sonar and targeting systems.[62]

The tactics employed by both adversaries during this cat-and-mouse game are similarly detailed and based on reality. The Soviet submarine skillfully uses the environment to conceal its activities and movements from the *Bedford*, including the use of the wreck of the World War II battlecruiser HMS *Hood* to interfere with the *Bedford*'s magnetometer detection system. The *Bedford* employs selective radar, sonar, and radio emissions in combination with icebergs and floes to screen her approach to the submarine and to a Soviet "research" ship that covertly supports the submarine deployments.[63]

The policy situation puts very real pressure on Captain Finlander. The Soviet submarine is not even one of the new Soviet nuclear-propelled submarines. If the *Bedford* cannot prevail in a cat-and-mouse game against an older submarine of lesser capability, what does that mean for the future of anti-submarine warfare and the vulnerability of North America to missile-launching submarines?[64] This reflects the actual policy and technological debate of the day: the only way to ensure a kill against a nuclear-propelled submarine at the time was thought to be a missile, or a nuclear depth charge delivered by aircraft, either land-based, from an aircraft carrier, or a helicopter based on a ship.

And the *Bedford* is not exactly invulnerable. Commander Porter, the new ship's doctor, is a reservist World War II veteran unacquainted with the new U.S. Navy. Ensign Ralston explains the futility of litter-bearing exercises: "There won't be any more old-fashioned battle casualties. If the *Bedford* was to take a hit, it would most likely be from a missile or torpedo containing at least half a ton of amatol, if not actually a nuclear warhead. . . . [It is a matter of] total oblivion or total survival."[65]

The *Bedford*'s pursuit and tracking of the Soviet submarine, dubbed "Moby Dick" by the crew, is described in suspenseful and intricate detail, similar to Alistair MacLean's depiction of submarine operations in *Ice Station Zebra*. It is clear in retrospect that Tom Clancy owed a serious debt to Mark Rascovich. Once Moby Dick is located inside Danish territorial waters, Finlander orders the ASROC missile system put on standby and targeting data from the sonars fed to the system. He then reports to his higher headquarters. Their response: Don't do anything, as there is a crisis over Berlin that is currently escalating around the city and elsewhere. Finlander rants, "Nice neutral little Sweden with her toy navy has the guts to depth charge Commie pigboats [submarines] they catch violating her shores," while the United States is sitting on its hands.

The sonar pings and the ASROC computer chatters. A series of messages arrive indicating the Berlin crisis is deteriorating and the situation is "shifting in favor of the transgressor." The *Bedford* is cleared to go ahead and interdict the submarine. Another message countermands this and tells Finlander to wait. The *Bedford* is now *part of* the escalatory process of this new crisis, and this development is recognized by higher authorities. Then Finlander is instructed to go ahead and act promptly to interdict, that is, force the sub to surface and escort it out of NATO national territory. Finlander has permission to undertake this task as part of the larger diplomatic maneuvering dynamic.[66] The movie completely departs from the book on this point, as we will see in chapter 9.

Finlander tells Munceford that his purpose is to "so exhaust [the enemy] and shatter his morale that he will be unable to accomplish the purpose of his trespass." Finlander and Commodore Schrepke, the former U-Boat man, debate this course of action. Finlander's response to Schrepke: "So I've brainwashed my crew and turned them into a bunch of schizos." Schrepke: "You have run the most appalling risks for very dubious objectives."[67] The weapons officer vomits from the tension and is replaced by a less-experienced man. In the ensuing confusion he misunderstands Finlander, who is arguing with Schrepke on the bridge, and fires an ASROC missile against Moby Dick. The Soviet submarine is subsequently destroyed by the underwater nuclear blast, and the jellied remains of her crew float to the surface amid the debris.

Schrepke tells a shocked Finlander, "What would happen if it becomes general knowledge that we sank a Soviet submarine on the high seas after deliberately tracking her for 48 hours?" Finlander replies, "All hell will break loose." Schrepke, "A nuclear hell, Erik?" Finlander's final monologue is a Rascovichian essay on the Cold War:

> The cold war! How can governments expect their military to guide their actions by such a blatantly sordid euphemism? Is there really such a thing possible as a half-war? Can one half-fight with these deadly weapons? Did those Russian submariners half-threaten us? Are they now only half-dead down there? Should I have only half-feared them when the crews of so many American ships and planes are totally dead as a result of Russian actions? Does it not all naturally culminate in the totality of death and destruction? . . . Look and see what this cold war really is. The same as any war. Death.[68]

This critical monologue makes reference to the little-known and, at the time, mostly secret fact that by 1963 Soviet forces had shot down over thirteen American reconnaissance aircraft, killing their crews, in most cases over international waters.[69] Once again this critical context is missing from the film version of *The Bedford Incident*.

Commodore Schrepke surreptitiously manipulates the ASROC fire control system to make it live, connects a power cable to the launcher that is left disconnected as part of the arming process, and, anticipating Slim Pickens's Maj. "King" Kong by nearly a year, climbs astride an ASROC missile and detonates the warhead, thus sinking the *Bedford* and ensuring that stability is put back into the Cold War system. This is a tactical version of the proportional trade-off scenario depicted in George's *Red Alert*, F. B. Aiken's "Abraham '59: A Nuclear Fantasy," *Fail-Safe*, and the film version of *Ice Station Zebra*.

Of all of the novels examined for this study, *The Bedford Incident* is the best literary exposition of the fundamental nature of the Cold War itself. The similarities with *Red Alert* and *Fail-Safe* are evident, but neither of those works was able to delve into the depths, as it were, of what the Cold War was really about as well as Rascovich did.

Antony Trew: Loose Canon

A submarine crew experiencing mental or ideological issues and exploiting the isolation of the vessel from land-based command and control to launch nuclear weapons is familiar to contemporary audiences who have experienced the claustrophobically intense film *Crimson Tide* (1995), starring Gene Hackman and Denzel Washington. Before that, Tom Clancy penned the best-selling *The Hunt for Red October* in 1984 (the subsequent film coming out in 1990 with Sean Connery in the lead). Prior to that, Thomas N. Scortia and Frank M. Robinson wrote *The Gold Crew* in 1980, which was later turned into a TV movie, *The Fifth Missile* (1986), wherein the requisite rogue U.S. Navy nuclear submarine is commanded by Robert Conrad, who was familiar to audiences from his commanding the ragtag heroic Black Sheep Squadron in a TV series.

Yet more than fifty years ago, in January 1963, an unknown South African writer published a first novel in which the captain of a nuclear ballistic missile submarine has a mental breakdown and initiates the launch processes that will strike the Soviet Union with Polaris missiles. That book, *Two Hours to Darkness*, sold nearly three and a half million copies, easily giving it international best-seller status.[70]

Antony Trew, who passed away in 1996, was apparently "wryly aware of his diminished status at Collins [publishing house] now that his book sales were in decline as fashions in thriller changed."[71] As a younger man, however, he led a remarkable life. Trew was a part-time naval officer in the South African forces in the 1920s who worked as an organizer of the South African equivalent of the American Automobile Association. When World War II started, he rejoined the naval services and deployed to the Mediterranean theater of operations. There Trew led grueling and dangerous resupply convoys into the beleaguered port enclave of Tobruk, in Libya. He then served on HMS *Versatile*, a World War I–era destroyer handling escort duty in the North Sea. (Later it was an escort for the Normandy operations.) In 1944 Trew took command of HMS *Walker*, another heavily modified World War I–era destroyer, and escorted numerous Arctic convoys, running the German gauntlet to the Soviet Union.[72]

After the war Trew returned to running the Transvaal Automobile Association and then took up novel writing. In all he wrote ten novels from 1963 to 1996. In addition to *Two Hours to Darkness*, three are Cold War novels involving either submarines or nautical espionage efforts. Stunningly, one of them, *The Zhukov Briefing* (1975), has a Soviet nuclear ballistic missile submarine running aground off Norway, which attracts competing espionage and recovery efforts. That scenario anticipated the actual 1981 grounding in Swedish waters of the nuclear weapon–equipped Soviet S-363 attack submarine in the "Whiskey-on-the-rocks" incident, when the crew was ordered to destroy the nuclear torpedoes and the sub if there were attempts to board her.[73]

Set in 1964, *Two Hours to Darkness* takes us aboard the fictional ballistic missile submarine HMS *Retaliate*, one of six Polaris missile–carrying submarines turned over to the Royal Navy by the U.S. Navy after a nuclear sharing agreement is concluded between the United Kingdom and the United States. Three of these submarines, each carrying sixteen missiles, are on station in the Baltic and North Sea: *Retaliate, Deterrent,* and *Massive.* They regularly surface to establish their location relative to their targets using long-range navigation and the high-frequency direction-finding network, and to maintain communications with a pair of transmitters: one NATO, one Royal Navy. Their targets are military targets, primarily Soviet naval bases and industry. The weapons are released by a combination of NATO, U.S. Navy, and Royal Navy actions.[74]

This description makes *Two Hours to Darkness* all the more remarkable for a novel set in 1964 and published the previous year. In 1959–60 there was substantial British debate over the acquisition of future nuclear systems. The choice was between an American-designed bomber-launched missile (Skybolt) that would be used to upgrade some of the existing "V-force" bombers (Vulcan and Victor); a land-based intermediate-range ballistic missile, Blue Streak; or a submarine-based missile like Polaris, which came in last priority. The decision was made to acquire Skybolt in 1960, but the Kennedy administration cancelled the project in 1962 and in November that year offered up Polaris instead. The Polaris sales agreement was signed in April 1963, just when *Two Hours to Darkness* was published.

The Royal Navy had four *Resolution*-class submarines constructed to each carry sixteen Polaris missiles. The first of these vessels was operationally deployed in 1967.[75]

Trew later explained his motivation for writing *Two Hours to Darkness*: "We manufacture 'super' weapons with 'super' powers of destruction, but there are no 'super' men to whom we can entrust them. They are in the hands of ordinary men, whether at the political or the operational level—men who are subject to the same emotional upsets as ordinary men anywhere."[76]

Indeed. And Captain Shadde, HMS *Retaliate's* commanding officer, becomes Trew's vehicle to explore this vital issue. The dark, low-lying, cylindrical *Retaliate*, which has "something sinister about her . . . an aura of death, perhaps," is in the Baltic conducting a "routine showing the flag visit." A pair of accidents involving the submarine while in Stockholm leads Shadde to suspect sabotage, and an investigation ensues: he pooh-poohs any other reason and sarcastically labels any officer who disagrees as part of the "It-can't-happen-here brigade." He baits one officer, asserting, "What's the good of a bloody great monster like this if it's never used?," which leads to a debate over the efficacy of deterrence.[77]

Shadde's behavior deteriorates. He rants about being English, not Scottish, Irish, or Welsh, and that the British position in the world has diminished to the point where aggressive Soviet behavior is nearly unchecked. The *Retaliate's* crew includes a U.S. Navy officer, Lieutenant Commander Gallagher, who is in charge of the Polaris missile launch system. Shadde lashes out at Gallagher, declaring that putting an American in such a position is "a dirty political trick thought up by politicians."[78]

As the book unfolds, Shadde is sarcastic, paranoid, a stern taskmaster in a clichéd Royal Navy sense, and a depressive. His marriage failing and the possibility of a charge for impaired driving, a "Dear John" letter exacerbates his situation. Psychiatry, he tells the ships doc, is "mumbo-jumbo" and a "threat and affront to naval discipline." That failing discipline means that "probably half the crew are ban-the-bomb rabble."[79]

As we learn, a deeper aggravating factor for Shadde is what we would today call an operational stress injury or posttraumatic stress disorder resulting from his wartime service. Here Trew skillfully plays off of the existing popular 1950s *Caine Mutiny* zeitgeist (best-selling book by Herman Wouk published in 1952, award-winning film in 1954). In *The Caine Mutiny* the ship's apparently eccentric, tentative, and potentially cowardly commander, Philip Francis Queeg, is revealed in the end to be suffering from years of service in the North Atlantic and the internal mutinous dynamics of his less-experienced officers shown to be out of order. Trew asks the reader to consider what happens if we have a Queeg-like character that has PTSD and may in fact be malevolent and who is in charge of sixteen megaton-yield nuclear weapons with a tentative command-and-control system.

Two characters have a dialogue asserting that the possibility of "unauthorized firings" is media-driven political drivel: "You'd need too many different people in too many different places."[80] Here Trew embarks on a multipage explanation of what he believes the authorization and firing process is or will be. He envisions that the Polaris missile–carrying submarines manned by the British are tasked, targeted, and released by NATO's supreme allied commander Atlantic, the Royal Navy's fleet officer submarines, and then *Retaliate* and her crew. An American Chiefs of Staff representative is part of the process in the two headquarters, with a U.S. Navy officer on board to authenticate and handle the launch process itself. Two special transmitters, one NATO and one Royal Navy, are the link: "The NATO transmitter won't work unless a number of NATO staff officers of the U.S. Chiefs of Staff set the control dials on readings which only they know." That message would consist of a "special address prefix" and the "target coordinate groups," which only NATO and the firing submarine have.[81]

Four crew members have to agree: the captain, the first lieutenant, the missile control officer, and the American representative. Then all four set their codes into various consoles. That permits the unlocking of "the plunger," a button-like device that the captain presses in order to launch. He can do that only after the launch tubes are pressurized, the ignition and control circuits are confirmed, and the motors and warheads warmed up. And again only after the position of the submarine has been confirmed.[82]

But what if that captain uses his power to manipulate the workplace dynamic for malevolent purposes? As the first stage of his plan, Shadde targets and subverts Gracie, the communications petty officer, who, he had implied, may be having a homosexual relationship with one of the officers (shades of Col. "Bat" Guano and fears of "deviated preverts"), thus isolating him socially. Shadde instructs Gracie to prepare the communications system to accept a "closed loop" message, one transmitted by the submarine to itself. This, according to Shadde, is for exercise purposes, to test readiness in as realistic a manner as possible and to smoke out the alleged saboteur, a threat he amps up to keep the crew on edge. Shadde tells Gracie to tell no one, and Gracie, out of loyalty, years of service, and probably fear, complies.[83]

There is a whole adjunct plot examining the issue of naval discipline and tradition versus the nuclear command-and-control imperative. Using his careerist first lieutenant character and Gracie, Trew argues that old-fashioned definitions of loyalty may be obsolete in the nuclear age but could still have a decisive effect on personal dynamics. Indeed one of his more modern and realistic officer characters uncovers what is going on and meets with the ship's doctor. They have a debate, echoing *The Caine Mutiny*, as to whether Shadde is a neurotic or a psychotic. The doc is ambivalent, again based on tradition, and won't side with anybody in part because of Shadde's PTSD.[84] The officer ultimately sabotages the plunger circuits but is caught in the act by another character, whose motives also remain ambivalent. Does the plunger remain disconnected or not?

Shadde finally reaches a breaking point and implements the "readiness exercise." In a tense climax, when the *Retaliate* prepares to launch four missiles, two each at Kronstadt naval base and industrial facilities near Leningrad, one officer has a nervous collapse, and Shadde tries and fails to launch the missiles. Eventually it is revealed that not only was the plunger kept disconnected, but the U.S. Navy lieutenant commander noticed that the bogus message traffic was missing a secret piece of American authentication data and did not authorize the launch process. In his final report Lieutenant Commander Gallagher notes, "The control measures worked admirably under circumstances probably never envisaged; namely, collusion between the Commanding Officer of the ship and the Head of his Communications Department."[85]

Two Hours to Darkness is less a MacLeanian mystery novel than an intense psychological thriller, as it is knife-edged character–driven. Trew brought to bear his extensive experience in World War II, both as a ship's officer and as a commanding officer, and applied it to what he saw as a potentially serious command-and-control problem—this presumably without access to classified information. These themes echo in later, and perhaps lesser, works, including the submarine films of the 1980s and 1990s.

Conclusions

What conclusions can we draw from this survey? First, and most important, relate to the authors themselves. These were middle-aged men from a middle-class background, writing between 1957 and 1963. All of them had had some practical military service in World War II, which is not surprising given the times:

Peter George: RAF officer

Eugene Burdick: former U.S. Navy officer, political science professor

Harvey Wheeler: former U.S. Army officer, political science professor

Mark Rascovich: former U.S. Air Force officer, oceanographer

Antony Trew: former South African naval officer, automobile association director

None of them operated from the standpoint of left-wing or radical politics but were apparently conservative in outlook. Only one may have been involved in ban-the-bomb politics, and even this has not been confirmed. Only three had any academic pretentions. All suggest through their writing that there were practical technological and psychological issues that were potentially problematic in the accelerated and fear-filled world they lived in. Because all had wartime experience it is not surprising that the psychological aspects of leadership and command figured prominently in their writings.

That was one possible point of failure in a system that could not fail. The other was technological. Again, from wartime experience these authors knew that machines, like men, break down under arduous conditions. Could the deterrent system as presented by organizations like the Strategic Air Command be infallible? And if they were not, what were the implications? In some cases, some of the authors saw both technological and psychological failure cascading together. And what if a person or entity set out to deliberately destabilize the system? Could it be restabilized in time to prevent destruction?

It appears that some or all of the authors had access to what at the time would have been classified information on nuclear and Cold War operations. It is more likely, however, that all heavily mined the existing open sources of the day. And it seems obvious that information gleaned on the cocktail circuit in either academia, media, or industry made its way into their works. The only author who may have had access to specific information on nuclear operations was Peter George.

The nuclear crisis films all drew heavily on their writings. As a result, imperfections that appeared in the novels were readily translated onto the silver screen. And as we will see, there were distortions in the political realm that were introduced by some of the directors and screenwriters that further altered and affected the final product.

The nuclear crisis books and films from this period reflect the late 1950s and early 1960s public perception of the Cold War political situation; a late 1950s public understanding of nuclear weapons and their effects; an early 1960s public understanding of nuclear delivery systems; and an early 1960s public understanding of nuclear strategy. As a result, any survey of nuclear crisis films from this period does not necessarily reflect the historical realities of the Cold War, nuclear weapons effects, delivery systems, and strategy. At best such a survey reflects the contemporary anxieties of five highly educated and militarily experienced men trying to call attention to problems in the deterrent system—and not coincidentally trying to make money selling suspense novels to a population that itself was terrified of thermonuclear war and morbidly interested in the mechanics of the End of Civilization As They Knew It.

TWO

Purity of Essence I

The Nuclear Leader and the Psychological Dimension
in Fact and Fiction

Concern over the psychological well-being and loyalty of those military and civilian personnel involved in handling nuclear weapons is a central theme of the nuclear crisis films. In *Dr. Strangelove* Gen. Jack D. Ripper is increasingly divorced from reality, sexually frustrated, and propelled by paranoia into manipulating the predelegation system to launch an attack against the Soviet Union, blaming the international Communist conspiracy for his state of affairs. The pressure of the crisis situation in *Fail-Safe* leads to disproportionately angry outbursts at a crucial time by a Jewish defense scientist, Professor Grotoschele, who sees attacking the Soviet Union as a surrogate for attacking Nazi Germany. A U.S. Air Force colonel, suffering family-induced stress, also tries to take control of events. Captain Finlander, the obsessed skipper in *The Bedford Incident,* is an insecure borderline paranoiac. Despite the Personnel Reliability Program, the crew of the B-52 in *By Dawn's Early Light* are at psychological odds with each other throughout the mission, resulting in mission failure. The criminally compromised, murdering ex-missileer Lawrence Dell in *Twilight's Last Gleaming* leads a successful assault on a Titan launch control center. Megalomaniac Gen. James Mattoon Scott in *Seven Days in May* leads a failed coup d'état against his commander in chief.

It is a wonder we survived the Cold War with all of these dangerous personalities running things. It all made for great interpersonal drama and suspense, particularly because of the proximity of this pathology to the ultimate destructive means. In some ways it was wish fulfillment by some elements in the American political spectrum, particularly during the 1964 presidential campaign, when Barry Goldwater, U.S. Air Force reserve brigadier general, was compared with characters from *Dr. Strangelove* after his mental health history was leaked and then embroidered in order to discredit him.[1] For the Soviet-led opposition, any doubt of the fitness of American military leaders was exploited for propaganda.

The sanity of those who were involved in nuclear weapons policy, strategy, conceptualization, and implementation was frequently questioned by those critical of the entire process. In some cases this took the form of ad hominem attacks within the academic, media, and activist camps exploring the implications of world-ending weapons. This included and continue to include frequent comparison of actual American military leaders to characters in *Dr. Strangelove*.

At the same time there were serious and legitimate internal questions within the U.S. Department of Defense, SAC, and later the U.S. Navy as to the safety of nuclear weapons vis-à-vis the mental state of those in control of them. In time, and after a series of incidents, the Human Reliability Program was established (later called the Personnel Reliability Program) to assess and screen out those military personnel believed to be unreliable for whatever reason.

Those rules did not apply to elected political leaders in the West. As Captain Moreau in *By Dawn's Early Light* quips, "How come there's no PRP [Personnel Reliability Program] for political leaders?" And what happens if the population in a democratic nation elects a man who goes insane after being elected? That theme was explored in the 1965 novel *Night of Camp David* by Fletcher Knebel, coauthor of *Seven Days in May*, but not, unfortunately, to any great extent in film other than the implied issues of instability in the 1967 film *The President's Analyst*. The lack of serious examination of civilian leadership instability leads to unbalanced portrayals of military personnel, as it were.

The possibility that Soviet military personnel were equally unbalanced is not examined at all in the early films, which leaves us with the disturbing thought that totalitarianism had a better grip on nuclear command-and-control issues than does the freewheeling West. That

48

is, at least until the 1982 TV miniseries *World War III* examined a KGB coup d'état in the middle of a nuclear crisis situation, and *The Fourth Protocol* (1987) depicted rogue KGB nuclear activity involving nuclear weapons. The war in *By Dawn's Early Light* (1990) is initiated by a rogue Soviet military element.

Negative Context

The larger context for this problem was the postwar antimilitary outlook in American arts and among the intelligentsia. This was expressed in the 1950s through *The Caine Mutiny* and *From Here to Eternity*, both book and film, for example, as well as in popular literature and other venues. Healthy skepticism of military leadership and the deficiencies of the so-called military mind underpinned negative portrayals of American military leaders in fiction, particularly when intellectual writers were drafted and subjected to the whims of martinets (examples include Harry Harrison, James Jones, Joseph Heller, and Norman Mailer) and these people vented in their writing in the 1950s. The firing of Gen. Douglas MacArthur during the Korean War and the subsequent public debate over Truman's actions merely confirmed the prejudices of those in the artistic class: egotistical military leaders were out of control, and now they had atomic bombs. This zeitgeist was seamlessly translated into the nuclear crisis films. If military leaders during the "good war" were problematic, why would they cease to be problematic in a nuclear world? That thinking can be seen in both *Dr. Strangelove* and *The Bedford Incident*.

There appear to have been legitimate concerns internally as well as externally with regard to MacArthur. During the Korean War, President Truman, State, Defense, and the Joint Chiefs of Staff approved an order to attack Chinese air bases supporting the anti-UN effort in Korea, presumably with nuclear weapons, but this was held on file and not distributed to MacArthur. The Joint Chiefs were predelegated by Truman to respond to a major Chinese air attack if it "occurred at a time when it was difficult to get complete government approval." There were concerns that MacArthur "might make a premature decision to [carry] it out," as he "was not in entire sympathy with the policies being followed by the Government in the Far

East." His public statements created "doubt, confusion, and uncertainty in the minds of the public on military leadership at a time when confidence [was] essential." This contributed to MacArthur's very public removal and ensuing debate on civil-military relations.[2]

Concerns were also raised during the Korean War over the activities of U.S. Air Force major general Orvil A. Anderson. Anderson, whose claim to fame was that he took a balloon to a record 72,395 feet in 1935 and was a part of the Strategic Bombing Survey in 1945–46, expressed alarm that the Soviets had acquired nuclear weapons and that Communists demonstrated a willingness to use force in Korea despite the American atomic monopoly. By 1950 he was commandant of the Air War College. In that forum and in various "rubber chicken" venues, he advocated what was popularly called "preventive war," though he apparently never used the term himself in his writings. Discussed in theoretical circles at the time, preventive war revolved around the idea that the United States should use its nuclear weapons as soon as possible against the Soviet Union, before the Soviets acquired a larger nuclear capability that would offset, or deter, American actions. When later confronted with the concept of "finite deterrence," that is, relying on a deterrent based on nuclear missile submarines to retaliate against cities instead of going in preemptively with an atomic "firstest with the mostest," Anderson declared that if he could he would "outlaw that goddamned system."[3]

In a media interview Anderson was quoted thus: "Give me the order to do it and I can break up Russia's five A-bomb nests in a week! And when I went up to Christ, I think I could explain to Him why I wanted to do it—now—before it is too late. I think I could explain to Him that I had saved civilization."[4] In *Dr. Strangelove* General Ripper mutters from around his cigar before committing suicide, "No, Mandrake. I happen to believe in a life after this one, and I know I'll have to answer for what I've done. And I think I can." Anderson's biographer correctly notes, "Despite his obvious sincerity it was a position antithetical to all that the United States stands for, morally indefensible. . . . [Anderson] lacked, it seemed, a full appreciation of the fundamentals of American democracy. . . . To others he became the embodiment of an Air Force that was 'bomb happy,' thinking only of militaristic solutions and or aerial bombing of innocent people."[5]

Elements within the Kennedy administration who expressed personal dislike for American military leaders contributed to this trend. The 1962 publication of the novel *Seven Days in May* and the subsequent 1964 film was in some ways a thinly disguised poke at Gen. Curtis LeMay's perceived disloyalty to elected civilian leadership (Seven Days of LeMay?). Burt Lancaster's Gen. James "Gentleman Jim" Mattoon Scott bears a passing resemblance to SAC commander Gen. Thomas Power and even Gen. Lauris Norstad, who disagreed with Kennedy-era policies on nuclearization and NATO. The 2000 movie *Thirteen Days* enhances the issue of LeMay's alleged unreliability even more blatantly. Depictions of General Power's actions during the Cuban Missile Crisis in the historical literature and particularly in today's popular culture are equally decontextualized and highly negative. Similarly, chairman of the Joint Chiefs of Staff Gen. Buck Turgidson in *Dr. Strangelove* could easily have been based on his real-life counterpart, Gen. Nathan Twining, or chief of staff of the air force Gen. Thomas White (or both).

The new wrinkle was the emergence of the defense advisor/defense intellectual in the 1950s. It was easy to subtly portray immigrants like Henry Kissinger, Edward Teller, and even Wernher von Braun as heavily accented "mad scientists" influencing nuclear policy with dangerously foreign ideas. The fact that many were Jewish made the portrayal easier by appealing to an undercurrent of xenophobia and anti-Semitism that existed in American society in the 1950s and into the 1960s.

Those prejudices coexisted with the nascent science-as-religion that underpinned American culture from the 1800s forward. The "egghead" of the 1930s and 1940s evolved into the stereotyped "know-it-all" scientist who appeared in seemingly every sci-fi film of the 1950s, from *War of the Worlds* in 1951 to *The Beast of Yucca Flats* in 1961. The idea that a small priesthood of scientists was required to explain complex phenomena to a relatively uneducated, unsophisticated, but democratic American population was a positive given in the 1950s. However, with the advent of The Bomb, fallout, Strontium 90, and the undemocratic secrecy surrounding nuclear affairs, the scientist became a figure to be feared: Dr. No, with his own private nuclear reactor, for example, in the eponymous 1961 James Bond film. Indeed some postapocalyptic novels depicted the tracking down and execution of scientists after a nuclear war. Overall both the scientists and the military leadership get a rough ride in the crisis films. And psychology was another one of those disciplines populated by heavily German-accented "feriners." One could argue that the indoctrination of the young started with Bugs Bunny pretending to be Sigmund Freud, complete with couch and cigar.

Dr. Kubrick, I Presume?

Into this context marches Stanley Kubrick. Kubrick employed Freudian methodology to mock, to demonstrate that powerful men controlling the ability to destroy the world had to go to the bathroom too. But was Kubrick merely acting as some kind of socialist leveler? No. Freudian concepts impregnate *Dr. Strangelove* from beginning to end. Two characters, Turgidson and Ripper, are in the bathroom during the course of the film: Turgidson when the crisis is evident, and Ripper to kill himself, *un grande morte* as opposed to *le petite morte*. The unreleased cream pie fight scene in the war room at the end depicts the characters devolving into infantile behavior as the Doomsday Machine explodes. (One can almost discern a prototypical but dark version of *2001: A Space Odyssey*'s Star Child in Kubrick's creative mind.)

More important is the fact that Kubrick deliberately immersed all of the primary characters in a sexualized cultural context right from the opening sequence, with an airborne alert KC-135 and a B-52 getting it on to "Try a Little Tenderness." Right afterward, Gen. Buck (Fuck) Turgidson is getting it on with his secretary, "Miss Foreign Affairs," and it is possible that the B-52 bomber–KC-135 tanker coupling sequence is actually Buck fantasizing about what is going on with Miss Foreign Affairs before he is interrupted and has to go to the can. The B-52 crew reads *Playboy* on the aircraft and are perhaps already aroused when the Go Code comes in. The B-52 crew checks their survival kit and finds "one issue of prophylactics" right after they have received the Go Code for Plan R. R for Romeo.

Premier Kissoff is, like Turgidson, shacked up with his mistress when all hell breaks loose. And the beat goes on: General Ripper's issues with impotence and the condition's ostensible cause; Group Captain Mandrake being accused of "preversions" by Col. Bat (Shit) Guano, who is more worried about "deviated preverts" than nuclear war; President Merkin Muffley as a walking, breathing pussy, while Dr. Strangelove continually tries to arrest his arm/erection using his "vill to do so"; Turgidson and Strangelove and the Kahn-esque need to have women of "a stimulating nature" in the mineshafts; and Maj. "King" Kong's final erection and wargasm as he rides the bomb to the vagina-like Soviet ICBM base at Laputa (Spanish for "prostitute"). That must have been a really big prophylactic: in nuclear war, size does matter. This is rape culture at its maximum.

Assessing the characters purely in terms of Freudian psychosexual development: Ripper with his oral-fixation cigar; Turgidson coping with demands for control via his anal fixation in the bathroom; Strangelove with his latency period of dormant sexual feelings and regression into the phallic stage as the film progresses. Everybody's sexual interests mature (reactivate) into the genital stage with the discussion of what will go on in the mineshafts after the Doomsday Machine wargasm.

What is not clear is whether Kubrick was mocking Freud as much as he was using Freud to mock American military leaders. It is equally difficult to deny the possibility that Kubrick was hijacking Kahn's theater of the absurd and applying it against Freud, or even Kahn himself. Without Kubrick around to ask (or psychoanalyze, for that matter), this meta-analysis, unfortunately, comes to a grinding halt.

What can be said is that there are elements of *Dr. Strangelove* that tip their hat to themes explored earlier by John Hersey. Hersey, an American born in China, author of the guilt-trip best seller *Hiroshima*, penned a 1959 novel that took on strategic bombing. Later made into a 1964 film, *The War Lover* was an exploration of what Hersey imagined the social-sexual dimensions of bomber crew interaction to be, with clear implications about their higher leadership, who were in charge during the 1950s and 1960s. Daphne, an English-women who gets caught up in a love triangle with a pair of 8th Air Force bomber pilots, figures out at the end of the book the prime motivation of one and possibly both of her paramours. After mocking them for not being able to get it up with her, she continues to gouge away: "That feeling you have—you have that stirring down there, don't you Major?—when you start the bombing run. . . . Why do you men have a conspiracy of silence about this part of war, about the pleasure of it? . . . Some men enjoy it, some men enjoy it too much." Daphne reveals her motives too: "I want to be fought over. . . . *I* want to cause a war."[6] In the context of the nuclear age, this character is even darker than Grotoschele's want-to-be girlfriend from the party in *Fail-Safe*. Certainly Tracy Reed's Miss Foreign Affairs in *Dr. Strangelove* is an angel by comparison.

That said, some of the American military establishment's code words could be used to support a Freudian analysis of its psychosexual development as an institution. The early code words for plans involving nuclear weapons use in the late 1940s and early 1950s were Broiler, Reaper, Headstone, and Crosspiece, surely expressions of Freud's Thanatos instinct. By the late 1950s code words had shifted into partialism and fetishism: Operation Tits and Exercise High Heels. One should perhaps applaud the U.S. Air Force's evolution toward Eros, not mock it. That said, Freud is employed by Kubrick to make Ripper, Turgidson, and the others look ridiculous.

Seven Days of LeMay?

The sinister and psychotic Gen. Jack D. Ripper character in *Dr. Strangelove* appears, despite protestations at the start of the film, to be a composite of three people. His dialogue is ripped right from Orvil Anderson's statements to the media. The cigar is clearly LeMay's. Ripper's impotence (blamed on the "most monstrously conceived and dangerous Communist plot we have ever had to face") is a swipe at SAC commander Gen. Thomas Power. Power and his wife Mae did not and possibly could not have children, and Power was very public in his pronouncements on the dangers of Communism.[7] Ripper's and Power's love of golf and previous experience with B-24s in World War II solidify the links between the caricature and the real man.[8]

We cannot employ Freudian methodology to understand LeMay and Power. The critique of Freud and his theoretical constructs are too advanced to even consider this. The critique of psychohistory and psychobiography methodology is equally advanced. We can, however, look at each individual's life and service career and reach some tentative conclusions as to their loyalty, stability, and reliability. This can be done only in the face of the propensity in American political society to not give the benefit of the doubt to the unpopular.

There remains a danger that a logical leap may take place, that the Freudian critique of the fictional composite will be employed to critique men like LeMay and Power. The implied logic goes like this: Ripper is crazy and dangerous; Ripper is based on LeMay and Power; therefore LeMay and Power were crazy and dangerous and we're lucky they didn't initiate the Single Integrated Operational Plan (SIOP) nuclear war plan like Ripper initiated Plan R. Especially during the Cuban Missile Crisis. But is this argument historically accurate? Is it even fair to assess two complex men in that fashion? Why are these men still reviled?

The critique of LeMay and Power has served as fodder for a wide variety of causes and personal agendas from the 1950s to today. With few opposing views, or none at all, in the popular culture or in academia, these perceptions have been permitted to run unchecked, particularly through the medium of the internet. There are no fewer than ten distinguishable but nevertheless overlapping loci of criticism. Distilled further, critics writing since 1980 rely on a handful of anecdotes to make their cases, thus making their arguments inductively, not deductively. These anecdotes are repeated ad infinitum and uncritically, particularly in internet-based content but also in academic and journalistic endeavors. The existing popular perception in the twenty-first century of LeMay and Power is based almost solely on the questionable, uncontextualized statements of a handful of opponents who happened to outlive them. That a pair of complex men who lived in complex times can be reduced in such a fashion is truly mindboggling and amounts to calumny. It certainly does not constitute the pursuit of history.[9]

The quote most often employed about Thomas Power, and then used in many articles to implicate Curtis LeMay with McCarthy-like guilt by association, was extracted from an oral history interview on file at the U.S. Air Force Historical Agency. Gen. Horace Wade was no stranger to SAC; he commanded reconnaissance and bomber units under LeMay and then was deputy commander of the 15th Air Force under Power.[10] He said this:

> General Power was demanding: he was mean; he was cruel, unforgiving, and he didn't have the time of day to pass with anyone. A hard, cruel individual. . . .
>
> I used to worry about General Power. I used to worry that General Power was not stable. I used to worry about the fact that he had control over so many weapons and weapon systems and could, under certain conditions, launch the force. Back in the days before we had real positive control, SAC had the power to do a lot of things, and it was in his hands, and he knew it.

The list of works that employ this quote uncritically is long and includes Patrick Coffey, *American Arsenal*; Bruce Blair, *The Logic of Accidental Nuclear War*; Scott Sagan, *The Limits of Safety*; Peter Feaver, *Armed Servants*; and Hugh Gusterson, *People of the Bomb*. There are a multitude of internet posts that repeat the quote verbatim and link it to *Dr. Strangelove*. Building on this, the journalist Paul Lashmar claims that he "interviewed several of 'Tommy' Power's deputies, who considered him mentally unstable. General Horace Wade remarked, 'I felt he was losing his stability as he aged.'" Lashmar noted, "I interviewed senior deputies who admitted they thought Power was psychotic." Who these men are, what their positions were relative to Power, or what professional mental health care credentials they possessed, Lashmar does not tell us.[11]

The second quote was made by defense intellectual and Robert McNamara acolyte William Kaufman, quoted in Fred Kaplan's *The Wizards of Armageddon*. After denigrating Power as "dim-witted," Kaufman claimed Power exclaimed in a meeting, "Why are you so concerned with saving their lives? The whole idea is to kill the bastards. At the end of the war if there are two Americans and one Russian left alive, we win!"[12] What year and under what conditions this meeting took place we are left to guess at.

This quote is uncritically employed by historian Robert Dallek, social commentator James Carroll (twice in the same book, just so we know), journalist David Nye, and innumerable internet content producers, including a highly prolific but untitled internet article titled "Curtis LeMay: Demented Cold Warrior" and a follow-up, "The Insane, Demented and Scary Cold Warrior, AF Gen. Curtis LeMay."[13] Again, in many if not all cases Power is linked to LeMay and *Dr. Strangelove.* The Pulitzer Prize–winning journalist Richard Rhodes even accuses LeMay and Power of "subverting Presidential authority."[14]

The quote most often associated with LeMay is "My solution to the problem would be to tell the North Vietnamese Communists frankly that they've got to draw in their horns and stop their aggression or we're going to bomb them into the stone age." A close second is "You've got to kill people, and when you've killed enough they stop fighting." These quotes are in such widespread use that they practically constitute truisms today.

Lashmar baldly states, "My research suggests that LeMay and Power tried to provoke the Russians into war at the time."[15] A Swedish journalist posted that the loss of a B-52 with its weapons in 1961 was the consequence of "SAC commander General Thomas Power [sending] it apparently on a pre-emptive mission to destroy Moscow's few ICBMs and leadership in hope of ending the Soviet regime [but the pilots] had other ideas and killed themselves in the process."[16] JFK assassination aficionados echo all of the above and suggest or even assert that LeMay and Power were involved in a coup attempt against the Kennedy administration and were involved in the assassination. LeMay was apparently at Kennedy's autopsy smoking his cigar, gloating the entire time.[17] It is a wonder that nobody has unearthed the fact that Power was actually involved in the Roswell cover-up in 1947.[18]

The primary loci of personal criticism regarding LeMay and Power were the Kennedy White House New Frontiersmen and their confreres, Robert McNamara's "Whiz Kids" in the Pentagon. The longevity of the people involved (they were young when LeMay and Power were in their fifties) allowed them to maintain their negative messaging without riposte long after their targets were dead. Also, these were literate people with substantial output and influence on later policy processes. They had a ready-built audience: some could leverage their close proximity to the martyred John F. Kennedy and the Camelot phenomenon of 1961–63 to maintain their negative messaging. These people include McGeorge Bundy (national security advisor to Kennedy); William Kaufman (RAND, Department of Defense); Raymond Garthoff (RAND, CIA, State, Brookings Institution); Kenneth O'Donnell (appointments secretary to Kennedy); Marcus Raskin (NSC staff under Kennedy); Theodore Sorensen (Kennedy speechwriter); and Jerome Wiesner (science advisor to Kennedy).[19]

There also tended to be outright bureaucratic rivalries, but sometimes it got personal. Both Gen. Maxwell Taylor, former army chief of staff, and analyst William Kaufman clearly misrepresented what SAC was doing in their books, knowing full well that classification would prevent LeMay and Power from responding publicly.[20]

Generally their criticisms break down into two areas. First and foremost, the New Frontiersmen as a cluster overreacted to anything they thought looked like a military challenge to civilian authority, in this case personified by their idol, John Kennedy. This manifested most obviously during the Cuban Missile Crisis but also in the debates over force structuring and budgets. *They* were the civilians, therefore they were in charge.

Overlapping with this were the Whiz Kids' assertions that they knew better than the uniformed leadership because their academic and scholarly qualifications, backed up with systems analysis data, trumped experience. Fundamentally none of these critics had any respect for LeMay or Power, and most went out of their way to express this disdain, which resulted in predictable responses from their targets. Indeed it is hard to pull away from the image of Camelot as a little Ivy League club where a construction company clerk from New York and an iron worker from Ohio, both of whom chose not to pur sue higher education in their early twenties because they wanted to fly, were not welcome. Similarly, over at CIA Power's earnest blue-collar delivery during a committee meeting ("there is real good evidence") was mocked in correspondance.[21] The fact that they had seemingly casually incinerated Tokyo disturbed at least some of the New Frontiersmen and Jackie Kennedy.[22]

In essence, LeMay and Power were the Rodney Dangerfields of the Kennedy administration: they got no respect. When it comes to LeMay one imagines a *Caddyshack*-like atmosphere: the snobs versus the slobs. Dino Brugioni from the CIA depicts this in his Cuban Missile Crisis memoir:

> [LeMay] injected himself into situations like a rogue elephant barging out of the forest. . . . He found meetings dull, tiring, and unproductive. Petulant and often childish when he wouldn't get his way, LeMay would light up a cigar and blow smoke in the direction of anyone challenging his position. To show utter disgust, he would walk into the private Joint Chiefs of Staff toilet, and leave the door open, urinate or break wind loudly, and flush the commode a number of times. He would saunter calmly back to the meeting as if nothing happened. When angry with individual members he would resort to sarcasm, if that failed he would direct his wrath at the entire staff.[23]

Clearly shades of Buck Turgidson and Jack D. Ripper in their respective commodes in *Dr. Strangelove*. Few recall, however, that President Truman ordered the U.S. Air Force pilot of *The Independence* (the presidential transport) to empty the toilet holding tanks of the aircraft whenever they flew over Ohio. Why? "It was Harry's way of demeaning [Senator Robert A.] Taft."[24] Kubrick could have had fun with that if he had known about it. There are no stories of LeMay strutting around the Speckled Trout KC-135 transport in the nude (he was busy flying it), but there are plenty about Lyndon "Bull Nuts" Johnson doing so on Air Force One and conducting political business while on the can.[25]

One of the most damaging quotes, however, comes from New Frontiersman Wiesner, who repeated it in numerous fora; like the others it has become a stock quote for many to demonstrate that

LeMay and Power were rogue actors.[26] He claimed LeMay told him, "'Well, my intelligence is very good. I'll know a week in advance when the Russians are going to try something, and I'll knock the shit out of them.' A startled [Bob] Sprague said, 'That's not the President's policy.' And LeMay said, 'but it's my policy.'"[27]

Those who use Wiesner's quote do not inform us when, exactly, this exchange took place or the context in which it took place. They certainly do not question Wiesner's motives.[28] And if LeMay was reticent to provide details of the SAC Emergency War Plan to Truman and Eisenhower, why would he deign to do so with the likes of Wiesner and Sprague? If he actually did say this, he was likely either being sarcastic or was baiting Wiesner and Sprague.

In addition to *Dr. Strangelove*, the other book-film combination negatively associated with LeMay is the best-selling 1962 novel *Seven Days in May* (best-selling film released in 1964) by two political journalists, Fletcher Knebel and Charles W. Bailey II. There are many journals, articles, blog posts, and other works that explicitly depict LeMay as the basis for the disloyal leader of the coup in the book and film. Some of them even overlap and discuss LeMay, *Seven Days in May*, and *Dr. Strangelove* all at once. Of note, a 1999 alternate history novel, *Resurrection Day*, depicts a character clearly based on LeMay carrying out an unauthorized nuclear strike on his own during the Cuban Missile Crisis and then taking over the country after ensuring the Kennedys can't leave Washington during the response. This is followed by the systematic murder of all of the surviving members of Kennedy's Executive Committee of the National Security Council (EXCOMM).[29]

In its 28 September 1963 issue the *New Republic* explicitly called out LeMay and Power and connected them to *Seven Days in May* and nuclear weapons in an article titled "Rebellion in the Air Force?":

> The Air Force's ruling hierarchy is in open defiance of its Constitutional Commander-in-Chief, and in some ways the situation bears a growing resemblance to the fictional story-line of last year's best-seller *Seven Days in May*. . . . While top Air Force officers may tolerate or even encourage debate of its plans by junior officers, once a

decision has been reached, it is doubtful if Chief of Staff Gen. Curtis LeMay or SAC chief Gen. Thomas S. Power would brook opposition, particularly if carried on outside channels in the public press. Yet this is precisely what top officers in the Air Force now are doing in defiance of their Commander-in-Chief, the President. This might be dismissed as being of no serious import were it not that these same officers are the custodians of 90 percent of the nation's thermonuclear power and long-range delivery systems. In these hands rests the life-or-death of the Soviet Union, and in retaliation, the life-or-death of the U.S.

In recent testimony before the Senate Preparedness Investigating Subcommittee, SAC's boss, General Power, said our thermonuclear power is "in mature moral hands." Is it?

The author, "Raymond D. Senter" (dissenter?), was a pseudonym, allegedly for a "defense analyst who has spent more than twenty years in the aerospace field working with the military services." Mr. Dissenter also wrote for the *Bulletin of the Atomic Scientists*. His output appears to have been solely from 1963 to 1966 and in only these two journals.[30]

The *Seven Days* plot was exceptionally contemporary even though it was set in the 1970s. Joint Chiefs of Staff opposition to a presidentially driven nuclear arms control treaty with the Soviet Union after an inconclusive conventional war results in a conspiracy to sequester the president and replace him. Led by U.S. Air Force general James Mattoon Scott, this will take place during an Operation Alert–like exercise at "Mount Thunder" (i.e., the Mount Weather or the Raven Rock facilities) while a special unit moves in to take control of communications and media across the country. The plot is slowly uncovered by a loyal marine colonel (shades of David Shoup, commandant of the U.S. Marine Corps) who makes contact with the White House. Eventually the plotters are neutralized and all the Joint Chiefs are sacked without any resort to violence.

In the hands of paranoia merchant John Frankenheimer, the director, and Kirk Douglas, a producer and one of the stars, *Seven Days in May* was on track to becoming an even more effective attack on

American military leaders than *Dr. Strangelove*. Kubrick read the screenplay and even made helpful suggestions to Douglas: "The most important theme of the book . . . [is] the conflict in the Government between intelligent Civilian management of the affairs of state versus the driving force of the military-industrial complex. . . . I think it would be very good if you could dramatise the difficulty a President would have in agreeing to some form of sensible disarmament scheme and how the semi-paranoiac extremists can make great political trouble for him."[31]

In fact Knebel and Bailey wrote in alarm to Douglas when he asked for comments on the screenplay. Both the authors were seriously troubled: "The net result . . . is an overwhelming, crushing, indictment of the military—and this is NOT good. It is not good for [Rod] Serling [who wrote the screenplay]. It is not good for Kirk Douglas. Above all it is not good for the country. And it does not reflect the novel." They were clearly distressed: "Nowhere in the script does anyone speak up for the military. . . . [It does not] do enough to do justice to the hundreds of thousands of officers who bear their country's burdens. . . . It must be made clear that Scott and his followers are very different, in their ultimate conclusions, from the great run of military men; it must be made clear that Scott, however wrong, is well motivated. . . . The suicide of Scott adds to the indictment of the military . . . and does so unnecessarily."[32]

There are multiple versions of the reasons that led Knebel and his coauthor to write *Seven Days in May*, almost all of them pushed through the Camelot kaleidoscope by interested parties and not necessarily by Knebel.[33] The most prominent is an oft-repeated and -distributed but unverified story that Knebel did an off-the-record interview with LeMay either after the Bay of Pigs in 1961 or the Cuban Missile Crisis in 1962 and that LeMay either accused Kennedy of cowardice or otherwise criticized him for not bombing Cuba.[34] This supposedly stimulated Knebel into thinking that LeMay could lead a coup, and the result was *Seven Days in May*.

There have been suggestions that the novel was, in fact, inspired by the Edwin Walker affair. Maj. Gen. Edwin Walker, a veteran of the First Special Service Force in World War II who later fought in

Korea, had pronounced anti-Communist views as a result of his experiences. After adopting evangelical segregationism, Walker conflated the civil rights movement with Communism and protested the Eisenhower administration's use of military force at Little Rock in 1957. While commanding an infantry division in West Germany, he was accused by a left-wing tabloid of politically indoctrinating his troops. Walker's Pro-Blue program apparently employed John Birch Society and evangelical segregationist material. Walker resigned in 1961 after being disciplined for not following Pentagon guidance on public speaking. During civil rights disturbances in Mississippi, Attorney General Robert F. Kennedy improperly had Walker confined to a mental institution until a number of psychiatrists and the ACLU protested and Walker was released.[35]

The president's monologue at the end of the film explicitly makes reference to Walker:

> He's not the enemy. Scott, the Joint Chiefs, even the very emotional, very illogical lunatic fringe: they're not the enemy. The enemy's an age—a nuclear age. It happens to have killed man's faith in his ability to influence what happens to him. And out of this comes a sickness, and out of sickness a frustration, a feeling of impotence, helplessness, weakness. And from this, this desperation, we look for a champion in red, white, and blue. Every now and then a man on a white horse rides by, and we appoint him to be our personal god for the duration. For some men it was a Senator McCarthy, for others it was a General Walker, and now it's a General Scott.

Numerous others suggest that Kennedy himself ensured that the film was made or otherwise assisted in its production when the Pentagon refused to provide assistance. (Why Kennedy could not have called McNamara on the phone to sort this out remains unexamined. They were permitted to film on the carrier USS *Kitty Hawk*, but then the U.S. Navy always had it in for LeMay.) Gleeful stories about how Frankenheimer and Douglas resorted to subterfuge to get the shots they needed, including infiltrating the Pentagon in uniform, are told. "The President wanted *Seven Days in May* made," Frankenheimer asserts. "Pierre Salinger [JFK's press secretary] conveyed this to us."[36] Arthur M. Schlesinger's foreword to Salinger's book *John F. Kennedy, Commander in Chief: A Profile in Leadership* alleges that Kennedy said of *Seven Days in May*, "It's possible. It could happen in this country, but the conditions would have to be just right. If, for example, the country had a young president, and he had a Bay of Pigs, there would be . . . uneasiness. If there were a second Bay of Pigs, the military would feel it their obligation to save the republic. Then, if there were a third Bay of Pigs, it could happen . . . but it won't happen on my watch."[37]

The reality was that Knebel had a journalistic interest in his fellow Ohioan LeMay but did not think he was disloyal. In his column "Potomac Fever," Knebel remarked on LeMay's accession to air force chief of staff in 1961: "Aides of the cigar-smoking Mr. Bomber have their own definition of limited war. A limited war is a one-cigar-war," that is, a thirty- to sixty-minute nuclear exchange.[38] This concerned Knebel somewhat. However, it is equally possible that Knebel modeled the Scott character after Adm. Arthur Radford, chairman of the Joint Chiefs from 1953 to 1957, of whom Knebel said, "[Radford] scared me to death."[39] Knebel relates only one JFK anecdote about *Seven Days in May* in his Kennedy Library oral history. When JFK asked Knebel about "how well *Fail-Safe* was doing, a puzzled Knebel corrected him. Kennedy enigmatically smiled and said, "*Fail-Safe, Seven Days in May*: What's the difference?" and walked away.[40]

The anti-LeMay belief system builds on New Frontiersmen criticism and is in some ways based on two movements close to the heart of those who were sympathetic to the trends of the antiestablishment 1960s: the antiwar movement and the civil rights movement. Power did not generate commentary on Vietnam; he focused on running SAC until he retired in 1964. Other members of SAC did express concern about Power over the years, but these concerns were related to the thorny problem of preventive or preemptive war and civilian control, not his sanity. Lt. Gen. Lloyd Leavitt, who transitioned from U-2s to B-52s in the early 1960s, expressed concern that Power might be "purposely exaggerating the probability of near term Soviet attack" by giving a briefing that implied that a preemptive attack might be necessary before the Soviets "had more ICBMs than the United States." "[This] destroyed the confidence I had in General Power," wrote Leavitt, who admitted that it could have been a motivational briefing for aircrew and did not necessarily reflect strategy or policy.[41]

LeMay, as chief of staff of the air force, couldn't avoid the matter of Vietnam, especially in his last year of tenure until he retired in 1965. Having restrained himself during the 1964 election campaign, especially when Goldwater's (brigadier general, U.S. Air Force Reserve) White House aspirations were undone by a clever advertisement from the Johnson campaign implying that Goldwater would use nuclear weapons in Vietnam, LeMay blew up at a Collier Trophy luncheon in October 1965. By then the Johnson administration was conducting limited war bombing operations, something that LeMay saw as hypocritical: "We're doing too little too late. . . . We're getting people killed who shouldn't be killed." An exasperated LeMay asserted that the United States needed to "stop pecking around the edges" in raids "and start hitting industries, ports, power plants and transportation" and "really hurt the Hanoi government."[42]

These remarks were not meant for the media, but the damage was done. Then in November 1965 LeMay's memoir, *Mission with LeMay*, came out. MacKinlay Kantor, his coauthor, had included the following sentence, which LeMay missed when reading the proofs: "My solution to the problem would be to tell them frankly that they've got to draw in their horns and stop their aggression, or we're going to bomb them back into the Stone Age. And we would shove them back into the Stone Age with Air power or Naval power—not with ground forces."[43] From late November 1965 into 1966 this quote was cut and pasted into practically every newspaper article dealing with any discussion of the use of airpower to deal with the situation in Vietnam.[44] Very quickly opponents of the war responded. I. F. Stone was scathing in his January 1966 review of *Mission with LeMay*, "Curtis LeMay: Cave Man in a Jet Bomber": "The tough old troglodyte is not through yet. . . . LeMay in retirement, unmuzzled, could be more dangerous than when he was Air Force Chief of Staff."[45] From then on, LeMay was associated by the antiwar left with the casual use of nuclear weapons, which transmogrified over time into his being associated with the casual brutality of the war in Vietnam.

LeMay's decision to join Governor George Wallace on a third-party ticket for the 1968 election only generated more angst. The media recycled everything he said on Vietnam in 1965 to discredit him. A political button depicted a cigar labeled "LeMay" with smoke in the form of a mushroom cloud labeled "Wallace."[46] Humorist Art Buchwald's mockery was deployed in "Dr. Strainedluff" and made explicit linkages between LeMay, Wallace, and *Dr. Strangelove*.[47] LeMay was now pegged as a racist, something he abjectly was not. Jokes like "The LeMay doll—you wind it up and it puts its finger on the button" were widespread, especially in Republican journals.[48] When Robert Kennedy and Ted Sorensen's version of the Cuban Missile Crisis, *Thirteen Days*, was released, their depiction of an aggressive and politically naïve LeMay during the Cuba affair was thrown into the mix.[49] LeMay was now a caricature. That was the image a new generation had of him despite the fact that one sympathetic journalist who correctly identified Wallace as a "swaggering bullyboy" acknowledged that LeMay was an "earnest square."[50]

Robert Aldrich's 1977 film *Twilight's Last Gleaming* combined messaging on both nuclear weapons and Vietnam and was another shot at LeMay. Ostensibly about a criminal takeover of a Titan I launch control center, the 1975 thriller by Walter Wager was converted in the hands of Aldrich and Burt Lancaster into a film about Vietnam veterans led by a super-empowered militarized Daniel Ellsberg trying to expose "the truth" about the war in Indochina and hold the establishment accountable by threatening to launch ICBMs. The Military Industrial Complex, led by Richard Widmark (who also played Capt. Erik Finlander in *The Bedford Incident*) as CINCSAC General Mackenzie, has three SAC snipers assassinate the president in a crossfire before he can go public. The independent Mackenzie, prepared to use a tactical nuclear weapon to end the situation, even has to be reined in by the chief of staff of the air force at one point. Mackenzie was very deliberately based on LeMay, while President Stevens, played by Charles Durning, was a composite of several Democratic presidents (though the script apparently called for a younger, more

Kennedy-esque character).[51] That the air force and especially SAC leadership was potentially out of control, and was even linked to the JFK assassination, seeped once again into the popular culture.

One area that demands examination is what role the Soviet "active measures" machine played in the perceptual manipulation of LeMay's and Power's images. One must tread lightly, here, especially with Hollywood. To suggest, for example, that Issur Danielovitch (aka Kirk Douglas) propelled *Seven Days in May* onto the screen because he was Moscow's agent of influence and wanted to discredit LeMay is simply not credible, even if he was supportive of Dalton Trumbo, who helped censor anti-Soviet movie content in Hollywood prior to his own blacklisting in the 1950s.[52] As for I. F. Stone, there is still a fierce debate over exactly how pregnant code-name Blin was with the KGB.[53] And "Raymond D. Senter"? Who knows?

What is known is that perception manipulation was part of the Soviet Union's DNA and integral to its international operational code right back to the origins of the USSR.[54] The inability to fully examine that aspect of the Cold War in the public domain stemmed from the damage wrought by Joseph McCarthy and others. These men crudely sought to draw direct links between legitimate protest movements or others involved in critical social commentary and alleged Soviet control over them. The reality was far more murky but just as damaging.[55]

The Soviets reorganized their propaganda apparatus in the 1950s under Khrushchev. By the early 1960s at least three organizations were involved in coordinated and overlapping operations: the International Information Department, the International Department, and Service "A" of the KGB. The first handled Soviet media: *Pravda, Izvestia,* Novosti, Tass, and Radio Moscow. The second coordinated the activities of front organizations and foreign Communist parties. The third generated disinformation, specifically forgeries.[56]

The consistent primary themes promulgated by the Soviet apparatus during this period and after included "US-Soviet tensions are the fault of the West" and "The USSR is against nuclear weapons and for military balance."[57] For dissemination of these themes the Soviets relied on *agenty vliyania,* or "agents of influence," such as journalists, government officials, academics, labor leaders, and prominent citizens. They were deployed in an interactive systems framework, *kombinatsia*, combined with overt propaganda campaigns and clandestine direct operations, to achieve strategic objectives. The term "agents of influence" covered an assortment of relationships fostered or generated by the Soviet intelligence apparatus.[58]

CIA analysis identified a Soviet "black" propaganda campaign directed at the U.S. Air Force and SAC initiated in November 1957. The trigger event of the campaign was an interview of Khrushchev by journalists Bob Considine, William Randolph Hearst, and Frank Conniff. Khrushchev went on at length about the "possibility of a mental blackout" in a nuclear armed aircraft pilot who would "fly to the target that he has been instructed to fly to. Under such conditions a war may start by chance." The Soviet premier went on, "In such a case a war may start as a result of sheer misunderstanding, a derangement in the normal psychic state of a person. . . . Even if it is only one plane with one atomic or one hydrogen bomb . . . in the air it would not be the Government but the pilot who would decide the question of war."[59]

As it turned out, the Soviet campaign was opportunistic and deliberately played off post-Sputnik fears. A fake letter was leaked to newspapers around the world indicating that Secretary of Defense Neil McElroy knew about reports demonstrating that 67.3 percent of all U.S. Air Force flight personnel "had been found to be psychoneurotic" and that this led to "excessive drinking, drug-taking, sexual excesses and preversions, and constant card playing." This purported to be "evidence that moral depression is a typical condition of all crew members making flights with atomic and H-bombs."[60] (Perhaps Col. Bat Guano's suspicions of "pre-versions" in the U.S. Air Force came from reading such material.)

On 14 June 1958 a U.S. Air Force serviceman borrowed a "nonoperational" B-47 without authorization and crashed it at a base in Britain. This incident was used as proof of the assertions in the McElroy letter. On 3 July 1958 the Soviet embassy in London passed the Foreign Office a letter ostensibly from a U.S. Air Force pilot threatening to steal a nuclear loaded plane and "drop an atomic bomb off the [British] coast in order to alert British opinion to the danger of accidentally triggering a nuclear war." Another fake memo declared that Gen. Thomas Power had "recently issued orders forbidding any planes carrying atomic or nuclear bombs to make flights over US Territory," presumably for safety reasons.[61]

Throughout 1957 and 1958 "the Soviet press corps continues to harp on the theme of the 'crazed American pilot' who might 'start a war' by dropping a nuclear bomb on Soviet territory." This campaign had been under way "ever since Gen. Thomas S. Power announced a substantial number of SAC's planes were constantly airborne and armed." This was in part seen as a campaign to scare the British public into rejecting SAC bases in the United Kingdom.[62] The journalist Drew Pearson took the bait. Leaking the fact that SAC had nuclear-armed bombers at bases in Morocco, Pearson argued, "The greatest danger is, however, that something might go wrong on one of these bombers. Somebody might give the wrong signal. Mechanisms might go out of whack. The pilot may have to bail out. The bomb-bay door might come loose. In this case as much explosive as was unloosed in all of World War II would come hurtling to earth. On such human and mechanical frailties rests the peace of this weary world as the year 1957 comes to a close."[63]

A side note here: the Soviet versions of psychology and psychiatry were not designed to assist people in overcoming their legitimate mental issues. The purpose was to crush dissent, terrorize society, and reform salvageable individuals. If one was against the state, one was by definition and diagnosis insane and treated as such with fairly brutal and life-altering methods. The social damage caused by co-optation of the mental health disciplines by the Communist Party in the USSR from its inception was assessed after the Cold War as massive. It is unsurprising that questioning the mental state of SAC personnel became part of the Soviet active measures campaign: it was a natural outgrowth of how their totalitarian system functioned.[64] The Soviets were, in essence, practicing psychiatric warfare, not psychological warfare.

The overt propaganda campaign continued in 1958 and 1959, building on these themes. A B-47 accident in Florence, North Carolina, in March 1958 generated predictable hysterics from Radio Moscow.

Andrei Gromyko, Soviet foreign minister, was deployed to lambast SAC and its leadership.[65]

The "psychologically unbalanced airmen" theme gave way to the "psychologically unbalanced LeMay and Power" theme. After the Soviet leadership agreed to mount Operation Anadyr and send missiles to Cuba in early 1962, a corresponding propaganda campaign was directed to discredit the U.S. Air Force leadership. The American press dutifully reported the findings of "Red Star" for their reading audiences: "It is suggested that Gen. Thomas S. Power, chief of the US Strategic Air Force (SAC) should be sent to see the doctors." The United States was "a country full of mental cases whose soldiers were capable of touching off nuclear war in a fit of nerves." General LeMay, "an atomic maniac," needed to be sent to the "Yellow House [insane asylum]."[66]

This campaign was extended "in hundreds of broadcasts to Asia, Africa, and Latin America." Other themes included questioning the mental stability of Brig. Gen. Paul Tibbets, "now . . . on the staff of General Curtis LeMay." Tibbets supposedly was visiting a psychiatrist for having a "guilt complex" over dropping the bomb on Hiroshima (this is even uncritically referenced in the 1982 antinuclear propaganda film *The Atomic Café*). Other propaganda broadcasts asserted that Maj. Claude Eatherly, another "crazed atom pilot" who dropped the atomic bomb, was under psychiatric care (which was partially true, but Eatherly was a long-running discipline case and a nonnuclear B-29 pilot).[67]

It is probable that the Soviet *kombinatsia* campaign influenced Peter George, Stanley Kubrick, and some of the other creative minds involved in the nuclear crisis films. The propaganda themes of mental instability, nuclear weapons, and command and control were definitely in play in the media throughout the period *Dr. Strangelove* and *Fail-Safe* were under consideration for filming. They were in heavy play in the United Kingdom, where Kubrick was living. And they were demonstrably stimulated by the Soviet Union.

LeMay, writing in 1968, was perturbed enough to comment on the effects of the films without singling out *Seven Days in May* or *Dr. Strangelove*:

This large peace-time military establishment has allowed many scare-mongers to capitalize on the traditional anti-military American attitudes and thus sell books and movies. I deplore this unprincipled literature. . . . Some of the man-on-horseback talk I am sure, is encouraged by our enemies to weaken faith in our military leadership and thus undermine our resolve or capability for self-defense. Some of it, of course, is a perfectly legitimate concern over how a large, perpetual military establishment will change our system of values, society and government. Dispassionate inquiries of this new phenomenon are healthy; suggestion that military leaders have designs on democratic government are false and harmful.[68]

So who were Curtis LeMay and Thomas Power?

THREE

Purity of Essence II

The Men and the Mission

The two men most closely associated in popular culture with rogue American military activity involving nuclear weapons during the Cold War remain Generals Curtis LeMay and Thomas Power. For the most part only superficial information is presented to support that critical belief system, with little or no reference to who these men were or what their backgrounds consisted of, crucial information that must be considered before rendering a guilty verdict on their perceived actions. Similarly the concept of mask of command has not been taken into consideration by those critical of these two men. Simply put, there is a public face commanders employ not only to lead troops but also to deal with the bureaucracy. That public face in many cases masks the operation of complex minds and personalities. If we are going to be fair in any assessment of their actions during the Cold War, that information demands consideration. LeMay and Power were living, breathing human beings invested with incredible power; they were not celluloid caricatures.

The Taciturn Technocratic Cigar: Gen. Curtis LeMay

"LeMay is a man who wears a cigar like a cocked revolver. . . . His character blurts its way through the exterior. No one can talk to LeMay very long and come away with the impression that he is a man who comes close to the faculties of absolute power and ultimate decision." So wrote journalist Richard Hubler after meeting him in 1958.[1] In describing LeMay the press used the words "hard," "hard boiled," "hard-hitting," "blunt," "taciturn," "gruff," and "brilliant" most often. The only word that appeared with greater frequency in articles about LeMay was "cigar"; one article focused solely on that instrument.[2] On the negative side, "Pentagon racketeer" and "cigar-chewing irritant" appear once each during the same period.[3]

Numerous other evocative statements from those same papers conveyed what reporters thought: Bob Considine characterized him as "Curtis LeMay, No. 1 triggerman of the Free World . . . a hard looking man that chews a dead stogie."[4] Another noted that LeMay "is a political bull who insists on carrying around his own china shop."[5] Another described him as "too blunt for the likings of some of his critics in Washington."[6] Frank Miller called him "a fierce and stern looking man-looks quite capable of directing 'massive retaliation' if that operation should become necessary. Glad he is on our side."[7] Louis Cassells, a reporter with United Press, had this to say in 1958: "[LeMay has] a round, impassive face with a cigar clamped defiantly in his jaw. You feel this man has never really been frightened. Alarmed perhaps. . . . 'I think,' he said slowly biting viciously at his cigar, 'that the situation is more dangerous than the public seems to realize. I am not willing to concede defeat, ever. But we have a long way to go. . . .' LeMay is the most grimly earnest man this reporter has ever met. He did not smile once during the interview. There was no chit chat."[8] Hubler wrote, "There is a gruff wariness, a half-concealed impatience, a rough affection and loyalty about this man with the eternal stogie and mop of iron gray hair."[9] In a possibly apocryphal quote, LeMay asserted, "[I don't] mind being called tough, since I find in this racket that it's the tough guys who lead the survivors."

So who was Curtis LeMay? His personal style, so decried by his critics, was rooted in a series of formative experiences that few knew or appreciated. LeMay was an Ohioan descendent of Quebecois settlers and the son of an itinerant iron worker. His approach to life was characterized by an introverted self-reliance, probably a reaction against lackadaisical parenting, and a hard work ethic derived from his experiences at the Buckeye Steel Casting Company. With part of a civil engineering degree from Ohio State under his belt, LeMay was attracted to flying. Through a convoluted process he eventually became a flight cadet in 1928 and was later commissioned in the U.S. Army Air Corps in 1930.[10]

Intrigued by radio (he built his own sets) and by navigation, LeMay was, after qualifying in fighters, sent to serve in bombers and was an innovator in long-range oversea navigation. During the 1930s he witnessed nasty interservice clashes with the U.S. Navy over airpower doctrine, theory, and most important, funding. Several galling episodes of bad U.S. Navy behavior in the 1930s, specifically the cheating on or outright manipulation of interservice exercises to generate a predetermined outcome, made a permanent mark on LeMay. His negative experiences with the navy in the Pacific campaign in 1945 only enhanced these prejudices, which had long-range effects on him during the Washington budgetary battles in the 1940s, 1950s, and 1960s.[11]

It was the searing process of preparing the 305th Bomb Group and then leading it into combat over Nazi-occupied Europe in 1942–43 that formed LeMay like a stamping press. This manifested in several ways. First, he had an episode of Bell's palsy in Syracuse during training, which paralyzed half of his face: "I have about a ninety-five percent recovery, except in the expression of the face: that is set and can never be altered. . . . My right eye always waters first, whenever I get into a wind. The right side of upper lip is immobile; it doesn't smile [when] the rest of the mouth smiles and has helped promote the legend that I never smile."[12] Having a pipe or cigar in the right corner of his mouth masked this. Cigar smoking had negative connotations in some parts of the United States, and this may have contributed to LeMay's reputation: When Mayor Norris Poulson of Los Angeles decried cigar smokers as "loafers and "hustlers," the Cigar Institute of America protested and named LeMay and Churchill "men of accomplishment" who smoked cigars.[13]

Second, the rapid expansion of the air corps and its problematic early training system thrust LeMay into a role he was not prepared for. Like other leaders, he was then thrust again into a novel and lethal environment. His distinct command style emerged at this time, and he used it to mask his self-doubt and lack of combat experience until that experience had been gained and the doubt overcome. "God almighty. I had so little experience," he exclaimed in his memoir, in which he continuously berated himself for his decision making and behavior during this period of his life. LeMay implied that the 1949 film *Twelve O'Clock High* was an accurate depiction of the leadership and training deficits in the 8th Air Force in England during 1942–43 (he was even mentioned in the film).[14] The collateral damage of those experiences amounted to a thorny reputation: "I wasn't real, I wasn't human. I was a machine. When I went to the bathroom, it wasn't in the ordinary human process. If I defecated, I defecated nuts and bolts. I was made of metal throughout. Iron Ass LeMay."[15]

But that reputation was balanced with the fact that LeMay led by example, in every way, and was respected by those he led. The deadly gauntlet of the Schweinfurt-Regensburg raids run by the 8th Air Force in 1943 was led by LeMay in his B-17.[16] In China he flew the first mechanically problematic B-29 aircraft on their initial operations. During the Cold War he dropped everything as CINCSAC in 1954 to take the B-47 course and soloed after ten hours. (The early B-47s were dangerous aircraft to fly.) There are pictures of LeMay in the water conducting ditching drills with his KC-135 crew in 1961.[17] The essence of LeMay as a leader, as author Barrett Tillman explains, was a combination of leading by example, mastering his craft, providing accountability, identifying and producing subordinate leaders, communicating with his people, and developing teamwork.[18] These attributes came out of the forge of the war in Europe and were applied to the war in the Pacific, to deadly effect. After the aerial campaign against Japan LeMay was feted as a hero: he was on the cover of *Time* magazine at least three times, and had a place on the deck of the USS *Missouri* in Tokyo Bay.

There should be no doubt that LeMay was a difficult and extremely demanding personality for many people. The "Iron Ass" image from 1942–43 was not an act: Gen. Horace Wade said, "I don't think he ever acted. Curt LeMay was always Curt LeMay."[19] When he was air force chief of staff, LeMay "would treat people . . . unmercifully. . . . He was very short and very curt with them if he felt that they were wasting his time or didn't know their business."[20] Other observers noted that LeMay "never yelled, but a look could say volumes."[21] He was "intensely serious rather than tough. . . . He never raised his voice but by virtue of facial expression he could seem angered and adamant," but "when you get through that crust LeMay was a soft touch."[22] This held true with other combat veterans and air force personnel. It did not with the New Frontiersmen and the Whiz Kids, people he was intensely difficult with because of what he viewed as their arrogant behavior toward his profession: "Today's armchair strategists, glibly writing about military matters to a public avid for military news, can do incalculable harm. 'Experts' in a field where they have no experience, they propose strategies based upon hopes and fears rather than upon facts and seasoned judgements. It never ceased to amaze me that so many intelligent people believe they can become expert in a field where they have had so little training and experience."[23] That LeMay would be brusque with such people in official environments is unsurprising.

Socially LeMay and his wife, Helen, a registered nurse, entertained a handful of close friends at home and were not part of the Washington DC environment to the degree that, say, Generals Nate Twining and Thomas Power stalked the golf circuit. LeMay's favorite leisure activities were hunting, repairing and racing sports cars, ham radios, and listening to music. (He had a black belt in judo, but that was work, not leisure.) He played the organ, had an extensive record collection, and modified his house to take a hi-fidelity system that he built and installed. He and Helen doted on their one daughter, Jane. LeMay had a dry sense of humor that few outside his family saw, with the exception of his friend, the inveterate prankster Gen. "Butch" Griswold, who would send him chocolate-covered ants to make him laugh. (Griswold's daughter, incidentally, was married to the director Sydney Pollack.)[24]

On divisive issues like race, gender, and sexuality, LeMay appears to have been unencumbered. He was extremely concerned about the loss of women from the air force in the 1950s because they felt (and were) misused in various air force commands, and he directed that "prompt and appropriate action" be taken to "emphasize proper utilization of the WAF."[25] He was no prude: when a politician complained that his group's B-17s had nose art that insulted the Germans, LeMay gave him "the look," chomped on a cigar, and walked away. When a congressman buttonholed him in the 1950s about the possible connection between the new two-man rooms in USAF barracks and homosexuality, "LeMay sidestepped the question.... The personal lives of the men serving under LeMay were simply not an issue. All LeMay cared about was performance."[26] Indeed when an alarmed Personnel general at U.S. Air Force Headquarters breathlessly informed him in 1950 of rampant homosexuality at Sheppard AFB and Davis-Monthan AFB involving eighty-six individuals (half officers and airmen and half civilians), LeMay didn't reply and referred the letter to SAC Personnel. It was clearly not a priority.[27] Similarly when two cases were presented to him, one a closeted homosexual officer in one of the sensitive atomic bomb transport strategic support squadrons, and the other a chaplain caught in "illicit cohabitation" with another officer's wife, they were treated equally: both "resigned for the good of the service" with no prosecution.[28] Col. Bat Guano's concern for "deviated preverts" was clearly not LeMay's.

The desegregation of the U.S. Air Force had just gotten under way when LeMay took over SAC. He discovered that the process was not proceeding as planned and upbraided his subordinate 8th Air Force commander, Maj. Gen. Roger Ramey. Shaming Ramey ("[Gen. Emmett] 'Rosie' O'Donnell accomplished his integrations"), LeMay reminded him that "the Air Force policy on integration of negro troops is explicit" and to get on with it before the end of 1949.[29]

A future Canadian prime minister and Nobel Peace Prize winner, Lester B. Pearson, objected to "colored" USAF personnel being deployed to Newfoundland.[30] And the British Air Ministry leadership suggested on the backchannel that "negro" personnel were unwelcome in the United Kingdom, despite the official policy of Commonwealth multiculturalism. Both LeMay and Power were clearly not happy with this state of affairs. However, Power reluctantly told the USAF's point man in London, "We agree that [the five] colored personnel should not accompany units to the [United Kingdom] at this time." This was explicitly done because of the critical need for the UK bases in the event of war, which was on the horizon. Power believed, "Considerable progress has been made relative to the integration of colored personnel . . . since announcement of the USAF policy. . . . Eventually there are bound to be more colored combat crew members and technicians regularly assigned to units. Ultimately, it will be an irregular procedure to leave these people at home."[31]

And in time Power was proven correct. Back home in 1953 white air force personnel from Lackland AFB in Texas crashed the color barrier at a segregated San Antonio lunch counter by deliberately having lunch with a lone African American airman. There were similar incidents elsewhere in the South.[32] Still, as late as 1961 LeMay was forced to confront a controversy in which black USAF personnel were allegedly being excluded from assignment to NASA and the State Department at the request of those and other agencies. The truth was murky, as all and sundry denied the practice. LeMay was given a direct line to the secretary of the air force so exclusions could be dealt with directly department to department.[33]

Another example of LeMay's racial evenhandedness: when a U.S. Air Force officer was beaten by a police officer while traveling through the South, SAC responded through the U.S. attorney and the police officer was fired and jailed. The race of the air force officer is not explicit in LeMay's Commander's Conference note, but LeMay implies that he was black. By not singling out the race of the officer, LeMay was making the point that it didn't matter: air force was air force. LeMay announced to his commanders, "We . . . will not tolerate an abuse of our people and will insure that they not be treated as second class citizens deprived of some basic rights of protection from the Government."[34] The accusation that LeMay was a racist simply cannot be sustained with the available information.

In 1961 LeMay had a heart attack but recovered in three months. But the journalist Drew Pearson claimed it was really a stroke and pointed to LeMay's Bell's palsy in an attempt to discredit him:: "Many officers who watched and frequently differed from LeMay would like to know whether his disability affected his conduct as Chief of Staff of the Air Force. . . . Was the general influenced by his disabilities when he took these strong stands?"[35] LeMay could be moody, and he was petulant, particularly after he got to the Pentagon. "Impatient" would be an understatement. His use of sarcasm increased, particularly in Joint Chiefs meetings and in government hearings. He was difficult. But the assertion that he was mentally incapacitated is unfounded. His daughter, in interviews conducted in 1998, took great exception to the suggestion that he was mentally incompetent or sadistic in any way. The "bomb them to the stone age" comment in *Mission with LeMay* was the invention of MacKinlay Kantor, his coauthor. LeMay admitted that he didn't check the proofs as closely as he should have and denied he had ever used that terminology.[36]

Despite I. F. Stone's assertion in "Cave Man in a Jet Bomber," LeMay was relatively apolitical throughout most of his early life, though it is clear he had no time for "dreamers" associated with left-wing politics.[37] His time in South America in the 1930s with the air corps led him to believe:

> The Whiz Kid Liberal of today [1965] smirks cynically at our attempts at Good Brotherhood in the 1930s. . . . We, he declares . . . are responsible for the ugly economic plight of certain sister nations adjacent to the Equator. In doing so I fear he discounts those unruly and selfish dictatorships which have sprung from domestic cells and germs, consistently throughout the whole Latin American record. They don't need any outside tillage or influences. They could grow all by their lonesome. Our efforts of the time may now appear bumbling or childish, but at least they were well-intentioned.[38]

This is hardly the language of a hard-core jingoist. Up to World War II, LeMay had not expressed animosity toward Communism per se, and actually had a productive working relationship with Mao Zedong during his time in China. He established a liaison staff with Mao's headquarters to handle rescue coordination if any of his bombers went down over Chinese Communist territory. Mao in turn offered airfields. LeMay took him up on one and deployed a communications team and established a medical supply pipeline to Mao. This while the United States was supporting and supplying Chiang Kai-shek.[39]

LeMay's anti-Soviet biases expanded significantly because of Soviet belligerence during the 1948 Berlin Crisis. He believed the calculated Soviet behavior over Berlin indicated that there was a new enemy he had to prepare for. Strangely, in his memoirs LeMay does not get into details of Soviet fighters bullying unarmed American and British transport aircraft resupplying a starving Berlin or the lack of riposte to that behavior. He does, however, reveal that he had a new understanding of the propagandistic and political aspects of the conflict.[40] His anti-Communism was not as adamant or vocal as Power's. For LeMay the Soviets were the new enemy, the new threat to the United States; Christmas was over, and business was business. Period. "Stalin dictated the increase in our air force," he stated matter-of-factly.[41]

As for LeMay's attitudes toward nuclear weapons, they were equally matter of fact. For example, given the choice between incendiary raids and nuclear weapons against Japan in 1945, he viewed nuclear weapons as simply a more efficient means of getting the job done. As for moral calculations, use of the atomic weapons on Japan saved more lives than it took: "Actually, I think it's more immoral to use *less* force than necessary than it is to use *more*. If you use less force you kill off more of humanity in the long run because you are merely protracting the struggle." That was LeMay's reflection in 1965, after World War II and Korea, and before Vietnam really got going.[42]

How much direct experience did LeMay have with the effects of nuclear weapons? He did not visit Hiroshima or Nagasaki in 1945, and in 1946 Gen. Leslie Groves, head of the Manhattan Engineering District, blocked the transfer of weapons effects data to the army air force as it prepared for the Bikini tests.[43] LeMay was present for Operation Crossroads, but his only recorded views related to how the U.S. Navy rigged the tests to "prove" that ships were not vulnerable to nuclear weapons.[44]

Though he got his "Q" clearance (security clearance permitting access to nuclear weapons design and effects information) in 1949, LeMay was initially kept in the dark about thermonuclear weapons developments. He did, however, have a direct pipeline for weapons effects data from the Greenhouse series in 1951 in the person of Gen. Pete Quesada, the joint task force commander.[45] When it became evident that "the heat problem [from a thermonuclear bomb] will be severe" and might melt the wings off the planned B-52 bomber, more data were forthcoming.[46] LeMay was eventually provided with the data from the November 1952 Ivy nuclear test series.[47] He was supposed to go to the Nevada test site to observe the B-50 portions of the Upshot Knothole (kiloton-yield) test series in 1953, but postponement of the tests prevented this from happening.[48]

SAC participated in Operation Castle, the six-shot thermonuclear test series in the Pacific in 1954.[49] This series included the gargantuan 15-megaton shot Bravo and exposure of SAC B-36s to that and three subsequent megaton-yield shots.[50] LeMay flew his own KC-135, transporting select SAC staff (including his operations research advisors), and was on the ground between 12 and 14 April 1954. There he was briefed on the six different types of thermonuclear weapon design paths that were being tested during Castle and saw the Castle Bravo crater.[51]

Operation Redwing, the 1956 thermonuclear test series, featured airdrops of live weapons from B-36 and B-52 aircraft. LeMay was present for at least Cherokee, the B-52 drop of a Mk-15 thermonuclear weapon and probably others.[52] Unlike his critics in subsequent years, LeMay had firsthand, personal knowledge of what megaton-yield nuclear weapons were capable of. This was very different from the experiences derived from mathematical abstractions employed in cubicles at RAND, in McNamara's Pentagon, and in the White House. And by those, incidentally, who live in a post–Atmospheric Test Ban age.

A related issue was fallout. There have been criticisms by the U.S. Navy that LeMay downplayed fallout as a weapon effect in SAC's planning.[53] This is correct. For example, during the Castle Bravo shot, air force units and navy units came up with fallout patterns of significantly different intensities and dispersions. The air force figures were lower than the navy's, and given LeMay's issues with the navy going back to the 1930s, he would have accepted the air force figures.[54] Indeed, when asked at a closed civil defense conference in 1958 how the air force was going to operate under fallout conditions weeks after the attack, LeMay implied that the destruction level would be so great and would occur so quickly that residual radiation was going to be the least of America's problems.[55] Thus the need for the most effective deterrent strategy and force structure possible.

The most important aspects of LeMay's belief system in light of his critics were his relationship to the 1950s discussion of preventive war and, related to this, his relationship to civilian authority. The idea that the United States should attack the Soviet Union before its nuclear capability was fully deployed was, as previously noted with regard to the Orvil Anderson affair, an active public discussion in the media during the 1950s.[56] It was not something nefariously plotted by LeMay in the bowels of the Pentagon, as some suggest.[57] Even John F. Kennedy himself said in a March 1962 interview, "In some circumstances we might have to take the initiative."[58]

In a 1972 interview LeMay was asked if there was talk in the Truman and Eisenhower administrations of preempting a Soviet attack based on intelligence warning. (Note that preemption is different from preventive war; these concepts are often confused with each other.) LeMay warily responded that he had discussed it with Eisenhower and that it should have become declaratory policy to enhance the deterrent vis-à-vis the Soviet Union. He was disappointed that Eisenhower only "intimated it" in the public domain, and he was concerned the Russians might not take the deterrent seriously without that public declaration. Discussion of and planning for preemptive action with the highest civilian authority is very different from discussing and planning preventive war without civilian authority.[59]

The endlessly recycled Jerome Wiesner quote about LeMay having his own policy to "knock the shit" out of the Soviet Union regardless of national policy is not accurate. Wiesner partially recanted this assertion in 1986: "LeMay said, 'But it's my job to make it possible for the President to change his policy.'"[60] Gen. David C. Jones, who was at SAC headquarters in the 1950s and 1960s, also refuted the LeMay lone wolf preventive war theory:

> I think the allegation that somehow General LeMay would have used military force or nuclear force without presidential permission is absolutely wrong. There was a mystique about LeMay, there was an image of what you expected from LeMay. Some people who questioned the build-up of strategic forces expected LeMay to be the type who would go off on his own and do something. And I have known him for a long time, and I was his aide for years in the '50s and we've been

close associates. I have never seen any indication at all, in any time, back in the '50s [at SAC] or subsequently when he was Chief of Staff of the Air Force, any inclination to do anything but to fully respect civilian authority. . . . LeMay wanted to give a president every possible option so that in time of crisis, they would have many alternatives.[61]

An incensed LeMay devoted part of the first chapter in his 1968 book, *America Is in Danger*, to disposing of the charges that the American military leadership in general and he in particular were guilty of usurpation of civilian authority, let alone preparing to install a "military cabal." "As soon as a man in uniform questions the competence of any civilian to make military judgements," LeMay wrote, "he is charged out of hand with questioning the virtue of civilian control. . . . This is an unfair charge. Such accusations are usually a sly gambit for quieting military opposition to a particular defense philosophy or course of action."[62]

It was the abject arrogance exhibited by the New Frontiersmen and the Whiz Kids and subsequent lack of respect for hard-won experience that was at the root of any civil-military relations issue vis-à-vis LeMay. Venting in 1971, LeMay told an interviewer that many of those "who came in with the Kennedy Administration" were "the most egotistical people that I ever saw in my life. They had no faith in the military; they had no respect for the military at all. . . . They were better than the rest of us; otherwise they wouldn't have gotten their superior education as they saw it. And the fact that they had it entitled them to govern the rest of us and we shouldn't question their decisions." Without identifying the individual, LeMay exasperatedly noted, "This man was in knee pants when I was commanding the division in combat."[63]

Tensions with the New Frontiersmen aside, Kennedy appointed LeMay chief of staff of the air force against the objections of his own people. Carl Kaysen recalled that Kennedy responded "that he didn't have LeMay around for policy advice. He didn't think much of the kind of policy advice he'd get from LeMay, but he had the man around because he knew how to run the air force, and if we ever needed an Air Force, you'd want a man like that to run it." The choice reflected well on both Kennedy and LeMay, according to Kaysen, who explained, "It takes a great capacity to be able to separate these two things about the same man, and to be fighting with him about policy and yet talk like this about him. Not only talk like this, but feel like this about him. This was one of [JFK's] most striking capacities."[64]

LeMay's respect for Kennedy incrementally increased when an airliner was being hijacked to Cuba and was under U.S. Air Force escort sometime in 1963. Kennedy called LeMay, and they talked about what could be done. Kennedy suggested "firing across the bow" of the plane. LeMay's aide, Richard Ellis, remembered that LeMay "pulled the phone away from his ear with a surprised look on his face," astounded that Kennedy had the parts to consider such an action.[65]

The idea that there was a dangerous and unhealthy relationship between the president and his air force chief of staff is exaggerated by those who have either personal or political agendas. That has negatively fueled popular culture when it comes to LeMay.[66] In contrast, Hubler wrote after interviewing him, "LeMay somehow gives the impression that he is a citizen first and a soldier second."[67]

Gen. Thomas Power: Sadistic Perfectionist or SAC's Big Daddy?

Thomas Sarsfield Power was less well-known than LeMay and eschewed public exposure until he replaced LeMay as commander in chief of Strategic Air Command in 1957 and couldn't get away from the intense press interest in him, particularly in contrast to his predecessor in critical areas: "Power doesn't smoke, so there goes the stogy."[68] Comparisons were impossible to avoid: "Power is a considerably different type from the rugged, cigar-chewing LeMay, a man of stern face and brusque manner. Power has a lean face, receding gray hair, and an ingratiating personality."[69]

Power's personality quickly came under closer scrutiny by others in the press. American Press reporter Vern Haugland wrote that for Power "split second precision [is] a life habit. . . . Even a general arriving 60 seconds late will be left behind [by this] tall, quiet flier, a strong advocate of physical fitness" who had a black belt in Judo and projected an air of "cool, unruffled behavior." Haugland also picked up very early in his interview that Power "abhors waste, whether it's a waste of time, of motion, or talk."[70]

Journalist Jan Burns also ascertained that Power was "a precisionist" and that there was "no air of austerity about [him]": "Neatness and order surround him and are important to him. . . . His impressive office is dominated by a feeling of friendliness and interest in the individual. . . . [Power is] an average-sized man of rather unassuming but dignified appearance . . . energetic, exacting, and hard working. . . . [He] likes to talk and is ready to touch on virtually any subject. Poised and pleasant, he maintains informality in his conversations, sitting at the desk in his office with one hand in his pocket of his immaculate uniform where he gestures slightly with the other."[71]

Not all press personnel were enthralled with the anti-LeMay. Douglas Larsen found Power "an aloof, intensely ambitious man, completely dedicated to his Air Force career" and "one hundred percent business at all times. And it's an aggressive brand of business too. That's the way he operates and he demands the same standards from all subordinates." Larsen discovered that Power's command style involved "a quick acid reprimand for mistakes by anybody serving under him. Inefficient, careless officers seldom last long in a Power command. He hates red tape and anybody who tends to create it."[72] Another article stated, "Some say he is overly-ambitious, but few doubt his brilliance."[73]

Power was from an immigrant family who departed Waterford, Ireland, and settled in the New York City area in 1899. Born in 1905, Power grew up in the milieu of a dry goods business owned and operated by his father, and then as a laborer, clerk, and engineer at the Godwin Construction Company. He attended the Barnard School for Boys, "with its unusual combination of a formal, classic English style curriculum with the ambiance, interaction and demeanor of progressive education." Barnard was also known for having students from Catholic, Jewish, and Protestant faiths, unusual for the time.[74] Taking civil engineering courses at night school and working toward his degree, Power "had a natural longing to fly that a lot of youngsters get. Probably Lindbergh's flight really got me to make up my mind that I was going to do something about a career in aviation."[75]

On one occasion while piloting his brother-in-law's biplane, he tore the wings off and they had to bail out. He was appointed a flying cadet in 1928 and commissioned in 1929.[76]

An indication of Power's character and drive throughout this period is encapsulated by a letter his father wrote to him:

> I am not inclined to give praise, but I want you to know I am very proud of you. You have climbed the mountainside strictly on your own. It was steep and rough. The only help you received was inherent in yourself. You used it wisely, industriously, persistently and insistently. I believe anyone proceeding along these lines will reach their goal and achieve their ambition. Any gift we are given, when respected and put to good use, as you did yours, will surely blossom and bloom into a satisfying reward. You have reached the plateau at the mountain top and I am sure you will establish yourself there in a magnificent way, because I know that whatever you attempt will have an honorable motive back of it.[77]

Power's formative experiences on complex overseas issues primarily derived from his posting to the Philippines from 1936 to 1938. While LeMay was "fighting" the U.S. Navy, Power was flying twin-engine biplane Keystone B-3 bombers with the 28th Bombardment Squadron at Nichols Field near Manila. From there he watched events in China unfold, including the Mukden Incident, when Imperial Japanese aggressed against China on the pretext of a comparatively small scale clash of arms, and particularly the Panay Incident in 1937, when Japanese forces sank a U.S. Navy vessel, killing or wounding all crewmembers. Power had aviator friends evacuating refugees ahead of the Japanese advance and who monitored undeclared attacks against British and American shipping.[78] After Panay, Power and his fellow aviators were alerted for action and "were surprised when the incident was resolved peacefully, with the American government readily accepting Japanese explanations and apologies. What surprised us was the gullibility of our statesmen who failed or did not care to recognize the unmistakable warning of impending war with Japan."[79]

Power also traveled to Japan: "We were pretty aware of what was going on.... It was perfectly obvious that the Japanese were building up their armed forces and that we were going to be in a war." On his way home in 1938 his transport ship was diverted to Chin Wang Tan to evacuate the 15th Infantry, who were pulling out of Tientsin after nearly thirty years: "We were not even allowed off the ship [by the Japanese forces]. The American troops came down with their tails between their legs and got on the boat which did not exactly make our spines tingle with pride." A similar scene would be portrayed in the 1966 Steve McQueen film *The Sand Pebbles*.

Pearl Harbor, an event that enthralled RAND analysts studying surprise attack, was not a shock to Power: "It was obvious what was going on and I became convinced that we would be in a war real soon."[80] He later wrote, "Only a fool or a blind man could have failed to notice Japan's extensive preparations."[81] And when he came home he tried to alert and educate people to those facts, but "most of them did not know even where the Philippines were, nor did they care." When he tried to convince his relatives of the seriousness of the situation, they told Power he was "off his rocker." It is impossible to separate his concerns over the Soviet Union and its nuclear capacity in the 1950s from what he saw take place in Asia in the 1930s. For example, he remarked in a 1960 interview, "The Japanese [then] were acting a lot like Khrushchev today."[82]

It would be an understatement to suggest that Power's World War II experiences were equally formative. After training, he deployed to North Africa and then Italy in 1944 with the 15th Air Force, then commanded by Maj. Gen. Nathan Twining, future chief of staff of the U.S. Air Force and then chairman of the Joint Chiefs in the 1950s. There Power was assigned as deputy commander of the 304th Bombardment Wing, which at that point consisted of sixteen B-24 squadrons.[83] The 304th Bomb Wing was involved in sustained strategic bombardment operations over Hungary, Rumania, Austria, and Italy throughout 1944. (Ironically he would have flown over Lt. Jon Hamilton of the Office of Strategic Services, who had parachuted into Yugoslavia to work with partisan forces there. Better known on the silver screen as Sterling Hayden, one of his roles was as Brig. Gen. Jack D. Ripper in *Dr. Strangelove*.) Power bombed the oil fields of Ploesti and the aircraft factories around Wiener Neustadt. "We were always outnumbered," he recounted, but when pressed on specifics by interviewers in later years, he told them, "Well, you just can't talk about them. What I mean to say is that you cannot very well describe these experiences to somebody who has not been through them."[84] Similarly the death of his nephew, B-29 pilot Lt. Robert R. Ziegele, who flew under Power's command, had an emotional effect on him that he was incapable of articulating in writing.[85]

Power's involvement in leading the 314th Bomb Wing against Japan and his role in the Tokyo raid are well documented. He only guardedly wrote about the raid on Tokyo more than a decade later: "I circled high above the attacking bombers for nearly two hours. I watched block after block go up in flames until the holocaust had spread into a seething, whirling ocean of fire, engulfing the city for miles in every direction. True, there is no room for emotion in war. But the destruction I witnessed that night over Tokyo was so overwhelming that it left a tremendous and lasting impact on me."[86]

Even in his private writings Power was unwilling or unable to unlock the specifics of that emotional impact. Of Hiroshima and Nagasaki he wrote, "I visited what was left of the two cities. This sight too was an unforgettable experience, not merely because of the terrible devastation I found, but even more so because of the incomprehensible fact that such enormous and widespread devastation had, in each instance, been caused by a single bomb."[87]

Power's command style is generally the basis for those who question his sanity. LeMay biographer Thomas Coffey noted that Power was "a man so cold, hard, and demanding that several colleagues and subordinates have flatly described him as sadistic. LeMay himself, when asked if Power was actually a sadist, has said 'He was. He was a sort of autocratic bastard. But he was the best wing commander I had on Guam. He got things done.'"[88]

"Maybe Tommy made things nasty that actually weren't," LeMay said. "He wasn't all bad, though. The only fault I could find with him—he was a little too autocratic. . . . A great implementer but a mean SOB."[89] With LeMay it was lead by example and team work; with Power it was "I'm the boss, I want this done, you go do it."[90] Lt. Gen. Selmon Wells observed in his memoir that Power was "a pretty sarcastic guy," surely an understatement of epic proportions coming from the notoriously hard-ass SAC inspector general whose nickname, "Sundown," was conferred after he had unmotivated personnel removed from Loring AFB prior to the end of the day.[91]

Power hated bureaucracy and let everyone know it: "There is no need of me telling you of the problems confronting us as you well know what they are and how the little drones scurry around trying to solve them."[92] Objections about personnel matters "from the peon level" were bypassed.[93] Meetings were carefully timed, and if Power thought his time was being wasted, he was abrupt: he would either cut the speaker off, ask a question that was not relevant to the topic to throw off the speaker, or simply get up and leave.[94] The probability that Power's critic, analyst William Kaufman, was subjected to Power's withering sarcasm because he was wasting his time, for example, is high.

Col. Rick Hudlow, a B-52 pilot, wrote in his memoir that Power bullied his way around the SAC golf course and that there was an ongoing story about Power leaving his wife behind in Washington DC because she didn't arrive in time for the flight.[95] When called into the CINC's office to explain how the "front line" understood authentication procedures, Hudlow was not happy. Power was "upset, not a rare condition I was to learn. . . . I asked General Power, 'I'm not here on the basis that if I can understand this anyone can, am I?' That broke the tension; he laughed and became cordial and asked me to explain [the process]. I learned later the interest and cordiality shown were very unusual for him. . . . No one had seen him go from irritated to cordial as rapidly as he did."[96]

There are numerous stories about Power's use of SAC's long-range communications to recall individual aircraft to discipline their crews. These are probably true. On at least one occasion he recalled and court-martialed Capt. John S. Lappo for flying under the central span of the Straits of Mackinac Bridge in his B-47.[97] There are numerous letters in his personal papers from officers begging and sometimes even groveling for forgiveness for various transgressions.[98] A typical tough but fair Power reply: "No one goes through life without making mistakes and I am always willing to go along with those who are smart enough to recognize their mistakes and take corrective action.

Your letter of 15 December leads me to believe that you now fall into this category. We will plan on leaving you in your present position."[99]

Power's oft-quoted critic, Gen. Horace Wade, was in charge of Personnel at SAC at this time. It is probable that Wade had to clean up the damage wrought by Power on hapless subordinates who did not meet his high standards. However, Wade would not necessarily have seen the officers who stood up to Power and were not fired because no action was required on Wade's part.

Descriptions of Power not having a hair out of place, verbally abusing subordinates, and insisting on punctuality recalls Omar Sharif's Major Grau in *The Night of the Generals* (1967): "And General Tanz? A perfect maniac. I saw him destroy an entire quarter of Warsaw for the sheer pleasure of it. . . . Anyone who has the power to destroy a city whenever he chooses does not need such minor sport as killing a girl." Fortunately Power engaged in the minor sport of bullying behavior only within his command and on the golf course, even though he ran America's Doomsday Machine.

When a student in Omaha asked him whether he had a personal code of ethics, Power told her, "The best advice I can give you is to ask yourself at the end of each day whether you have done the best you could throughout the day to live up to the standards you have set for yourself."[100] It is clear by his personal disposition and professional approach that he set the bar high for himself, perhaps too high. No man is perfect, and at times he lashed out.

There is no doubt Power had power and liked wielding it. Consider this communiqué from his aide to the B-58 development people in Fort Worth: "General Power requested that I advise you that he is planning on riding around on one of your aircraft."[101] There is equally no doubt that many people were put off by or suffered from his autocratic style. But was he mentally incapacitated? Psychotic? Or did he lose his temper like some four-star generals are prone to? Eisenhower was known for having a temper that matched or exceeded Power's, yet he was in charge of not just SAC but the U.S. government, including its nuclear arsenal.[102] For abusive and sadistic behavior, few can top Adm. Hyman Rickover.[103]

The other side to Power that many did not see was his religiosity.

It was highly unusual for a practicing Catholic to reach high office in the United States at this time. The air force was a new institution and perhaps less encumbered with such prejudice. Power was one of the first if not the first Roman Catholic to become a four-star general, which probably prompted an entire legion of Know-Nothings to rotate in their graves.

Power and his wife, Mae, were deeply involved with the Catholic community in Omaha, particularly in supporting parochial school construction with "the Building Bishop," Gerald T. Bergan. The Powers also supported the Boys and Girls Club. (On one occasion he sent a SAC aircraft to rescue a member who broke his neck while hiking.) Power also ensured that SAC bases had religious facilities for all denominations and actively intervened when this was not being handled equitably.[104] They both supported the organization of off-base parochial school construction near SAC bases in remote areas. In Power's view, "only by providing these schools can we produce a next generation capable of assuming their grave responsibilities at a crucial time in history."[105] In 1964 CINCSAC Gen. Thomas Power received papal honors, the Knight of St. Sylvester with the Grand Cross, while Mae was awarded the Pro Ecclesia et Pontifice Medal. This event was conducted in private and not given press circulation outside of the Catholic community.[106]

If one wishes to engage in psychological analysis, the childless Powers perhaps compensated for this fact by supporting education and youth development. To take it a step further, it would not be a reach to suggest that Power was, in effect, a stern father figure to SAC. This was subtly mocked in *Dr. Strangelove* when Burpelson AFB is overrun by Colonel Guano's paratroops:

Ripper: Boys must have surrendered.
Mandrake: It's the way it is. Now Jack, listen. While there's still time, I beg you, let's recall the wing.
Ripper: Those boys were like my children, Mandrake. Now they let me down.

Power's other spiritual dimension was his devotion to Kodokan Judo. Both he and LeMay acquired black belts in this discipline in the early 1950s, when Power advocated unarmed defensive training for aircrew use if they were shot down. Power practiced judo for the rest of his life. It was clearly a physical outlet for him, but it would have been impossible for him not to have absorbed the metaphysical aspects of the discipline and perform effectively in it.[107]

Though the roots of Power's anti-Communism lay in his Catholicism and in his concerns about Japan-like aggression, the more activist concerns vocalized by Francis Cardinal Spellman in the 1940s about growing Communist influences in the United States and around the world definitely appealed to him. The two men corresponded in the late 1940s. It was in Italy during the war that Power probably met Spellman, who was apostolic vicar for the U.S. Armed Forces.[108]

Power's compartmentalization of his personal religious beliefs in two areas is significant. First, he in no way imposed his religious views on SAC's personnel, and there is every indication that he kept a line drawn consistent with church-state separation as it applied at the time to the U.S. Armed Forces. That is, he was not indoctrinating his troops Edwin Walker–like, nor did he portray the struggle against Communism as a religious crusade.[109] Second, Power did not publicly link his Catholicism to his open stance against the Communist threat. His public persona and writings, save one, do not have a religious component to them. Even in his book *Design for Survival*, where he elaborated on the Communist threat, the only hint of his religiosity is when he quotes Luke 11:21–22: "When a strong man armed keepeth the palace, his goods are in peace: But when a man stronger than he shall come upon him, and overcome him, he taketh from him all his armor wherein he trusted, and divideth his spoils."

Power contributed to a book titled *We Believe in Prayer: A Compilation of Personal Statements by American and World Leaders about the Value of Prayer* (1958), edited by Minneapolis Lutheran leader Lawrence M. Brings. A variety of luminaries contributed: Sherman Adams, Steve Allen, Arleigh Burke, Eddie Cantor, Abba Eban, Conrad Hilton, J. Edgar Hoover, George Meany, Gamal Abdel Nasser, Chester Nimitz, Nathan Twining, Frank Lloyd Wright, and many others. In his contribution Power stated up front that when it came to nuclear weapons "we must never forget that the character and quality of the men who handle these weapons are just as important" as the destructive capacity of the weapons themselves. He continued, "As we match weapon for weapon, we match fanaticism with dedication. And there is no doubt in my mind that the fanaticism of a godless society can never equal the dedication which stems from the devotion, loyalty, and faith of a free people." The opposition had only "the fanatic ambitions of their dictators" to motivate them, while "our men [in SAC] are inspired by their faith in God and the knowledge that they can always draw renewed strength from the greatest moral power there is—their prayers."[110]

To Power Communism was an implacable enemy that was not theoretical. In 1956 he was asked to accompany General Twining on an unprecedented visit to the Soviet Union, where they toured aircraft production and training facilities. Though he denied that it made him an expert on the subject of the Soviet Union, Power was, unlike many in the analytical or academic world in the United States, able to experience the totalitarian environment for himself: "My visit served to lend depth and substance to various theories I had formulated. . . . I met some of the men behind the global Communist conspiracy." More important, he wrote, "I experienced what it meant to live in an absolute police state and to have supreme power concentrated in the hands of a very few." And he was repelled by it, particularly after his hosts exhibited "a cocky self assurance and brutal frankness about what their objectives were."[111] This was not cocktail circuit chitchat or academic theorizing about the threat. Power's views were based on direct and personal experiences.

Design for Survival was the subject of a vicious attack by a young Arthur Spiegelman. Using methodology similar to that employed the month before by I. F. Stone against LeMay, the creator of *Maus* deployed ad hominem arguments in the Hackensack newspaper, the *Record*, attacking Power for his depiction of Communism. Spiegelman deliberately avoided Power's main concerns expressed in the introduction, that is, that the only real way to protect the United States was with a credible deterrent system based on nuclear weapons.[112]

Unlike LeMay, Power visited Hiroshima and Nagasaki to gauge for himself the effects of the atomic bombs.[113] Subsequent to this he commanded the aerial component of Operation Crossroads at Bikini in 1946, where he witnessed both tests from the air. In 1947 he was cleared by the Atomic Energy Commission to access everything short of data on the "procurement of raw materials" for nuclear weapons, including design and stockpile information.[114] In his capacity as vice CINCSAC of the Air Research and Development Command, Power was at Ivy Mike in 1952: "Then I saw the first explosion of a hydrogen bomb and everything I had seen paled into insignificance. It is difficult for the average person to appreciate fully the awesome power of the hydrogen bomb, because the mind cannot readily conceive what the eye has not seen. Only those very few who have actually witnessed a nuclear explosion have a fair conception of its unimaginable destructiveness."[115] This from the man who observed the Tokyo raid and participated in the incineration of one hundred thousand people firsthand from an orbiting B-29 in March 1945.

As for Power's views on fallout and the effects of nuclear war, he followed this debate much more closely than LeMay did and, unlike LeMay, supported a strong civil defense system. In 1959 he was not concerned about fallout from testing: after receiving an alarming classified fallout study from the Joint Committee on Atomic Energy on the backchannel, Power echoed Buck Turgidson's "I hate to judge before all the facts are in" defense in *Dr. Strangelove*. Power explained his primary concern: "We must compare this very slight hazard with the extremely dangerous hazard of permitting our deterrent posture to decay, a situation which is likely to result in millions of casualties."[116] For Power the calculation that Tokyo, Hiroshima, and Nagasaki offset a million Allied casualties in an invasion of Japan was playing out again in 1959: the small number of radiation casualties resulting from nuclear testing offset millions that would die in a nuclear attack.

Power's personal view on what the aftermath of a nuclear war would look like was similar to that expressed by Pat Frank in his 1959 postapocalyptic best seller *Alas, Babylon*.[117] In this scenario, the United States is catastrophically damaged but is able to slowly recover due to the resilience of small communities whose populations remain alive after the large population centers have been destroyed and who remain true to a variety of American ideals until the government can reconstitute itself. Frank corresponded with Power when he worked as a public information officer with Civil Defense.[118] Power told the press in an interview that he "endorsed the book and the situations depicted in it," but that in a nuclear war "there are no winners, only losers to varying degrees."[119] He believed that, if the deterrent system could hold out long enough, the Soviet Union might collapse. In 1964 he wrote in *Design for Survival*, "If, at any time in the future, the Russian masses should succeed in wresting those powers from the dictators and returning them to their rightful owners, the people, Soviet Communism would collapse because it has no other foundation. This, in turn, would greatly weaken if not destroy Communism in those countries to which it has been 'exported' by the Soviets."[120] Power sent a copy of *Design for Survival* to Ronald Reagan, then governor of California, who replied, "You and I are certainly in agreement about the situation."[121]

The combination of personal experiences with thermonuclear weapons and the intimate understanding of the capabilities and limitations of the weapons and of their delivery systems while he was head of Air Research and Development Command from 1954 to 1957 supersedes by leaps and bounds any theoretical understanding possessed by the New Frontiersmen and the Whiz Kids. Power knew what Hell looked and felt like in ways most did not. He expressed in every public forum available—TV, press, books, documentaries—that nuclear war had to be prevented. Under LeMay and Power SAC was structured for deterrence. The idea that Power was deliberately provoking a situation whereby nuclear weapons would be used against the Soviet Union is at the very least highly questionable, is not supported by the facts, and borders on the absurd.

Power was not averse to discussing the issue of preventive war, but there were specific reasons for doing so and limits to the discussion.[122] His coauthor on *Design for Survival*, Col. A. A. Arnhym, drafted a chapter that "attempted to show, by implication, that preventive war might be our only chance of survival if aggression can no longer be avoided." (That 1958 draft was blocked from publication by the secretary of defense.) Arnhym wrote to Power, arguing that they should "let the reader himself come to the conclusion," but he was concerned that unless they made a more definitive statement on the matter it "could conceivably be quoted out of context and twisted to make it appear that you are actually inviting the [American] people to authorize a preventative war!"[123] Power's response: "You have to leave the door open for other eventualities other than deterrence. Now even though, as you know, we think that it is about 99.99% sure, again it does not pay to close the door. The decision must rest with the people. They may decide on a course other than deterrence. . . . We should not close the door—-merely explain the problem and also the fact that the decision is theirs. . . . No one can or should say they will never arrive at this decision."[124]

Power wanted his options open, but more important he wanted America's options open. Why? This was part of deterrence. An irate citizen wrote Power in April 1962 and made lurid accusations related to preventive war. Power let Arnhym handle it: "'Preventive war' is a misnomer as one cannot start a war by preventing it. As General Power has stated at numerous occasions, the only logical way to prevent a war is to keep any potential aggressors convinced that the consequences of starting a war would be unacceptable to them. I feel that irresponsible statements to the effect that General Power has advocated preventive war and that military men 'like to kill hundreds of millions of people' are too ridiculous to warrant serious comment."[125]

In the 1964 edition of *Design for Survival* Power elaborated on preventive war and explained that there were differences between preventive war, a preemptive strike, preemptive war, and assuming the initiative, thus deliberately obscuring the issue: "The concept . . . is too complex to justify conclusive opinions for or against it." In his view, "it would be a grave mistake to give the Soviets the impression that we would never strike first." Why? It "forces them to prepare themselves accordingly—including maintenance of an extensive warning system—which compounds their problems and detracts from their offensive strength."[126]

Power was not out to provoke war with the Soviet Union, nor was he a "psychotic," as some have alleged. LeMay told a closed conference, "Our present [CINCSAC] General Power is a very suspicious individual. He has to be. He also remembers a couple of characters by the names of Kimmel and Short [the navy and army commanders at Pearl Harbor in 1941 when the Japanese attacked who were subsequently scapegoated]."[127] In 1958 Power noted in an internal memo, "I am convinced that the majority of the American people will always reject the idea of dealing with the communist threat by sending SAC over to Russia some Sunday morning and wiping the country from the face of the earth. . . . Any fool can get into a war, but it takes a smart man to stay out of it, and to do so on his terms."[128]

FOUR

Purity of Essence III

The LeMay-Power Deterrent Campaign and *Dr. Strangelove*

Red Alert, "Abraham '57," *Dr. Strangelove,* and *Fail-Safe* and thus the critique of LeMay and Power were all to some extent unintended consequences of what could be called the "LeMay-Power deterrence campaign." The traditional trajectory of Cold War deterrence theory and nuclear strategy is relatively linear: Bernard Brodie "invents" nuclear deterrence in 1946 with *The Absolute Weapon,* while the RANDists and others apply game theory to nuclear warfare by 1953. At this point massive retaliation was in vogue as the American declaratory strategy. Massive retaliation posits that nuclear weapons use will be the only American response to a variety of global aggressions. Its limitations were exposed by RAND and other critics during a dangerous series of American encounters with the Communist world and was replaced with two new strategic concepts, mutual assured destruction and flexible response, by the early 1960s. Once everybody was scared to death, things stabilized. Civilian analysts, particularly those at RAND, brought rationality to a landscape formerly populated with dangerous men like Curtis LeMay who, again ironically, helped fund the creation of RAND.[1]

The operationalization of this traditional view has LeMay at odds with the rest of the armed services over funding and fixated on the acquisition of more and more bomber aircraft at the expense of other capabilities. Massive retaliation simply meant more and bigger nuclear bombs delivered by SAC if the trip wire was tripped—and little else was required. Critics like Maxwell Taylor, for example, emphasized this perception, and the media dutifully stoked the controversy.[2]

There was codified national security policy under Eisenhower, ensconced in the National Security Council document NSC 162/2 dated 30 October 1953. The relevant portions include the fact that it was a policy to develop and maintain "a strong military posture, with emphasis on the capability of inflicting massive retaliatory damage by offensive striking power" and to maintain such forces in readiness to do so. "Within the Free World, only the United States can provide and maintain . . . the atomic capability to counterbalance Soviet atomic power. Thus sufficient atomic weapons and effective means of delivery are indispensable for U.S. security." Finally, "the risk of Soviet aggression will be minimized by maintaining a strong security posture, with emphasis on adequate offensive retaliatory strength and defensive strength. This must be based on massive atomic capability."[3]

The LeMay-Power deterrence campaign was never officially codified national doctrine and was never submitted in its entirety for approval to, say, the NSC or the Joint Chiefs of Staff. It was a series of activities that were done within the statutory limits of what a specified commander could do in relationship to national policy. There is no indication that LeMay and Power explicitly linked what they were doing to NSC 162/2, but it was in the spirit of the policy and it paralleled the SAC Emergency War Plan as it evolved in the 1950s toward, using later terminology, an instrument of preemptive counterforce. In a 1972 interview dealing with an unrelated matter, LeMay chided the historians: "You've got to get to the truth, not what somebody put in the records."[4] That state of affairs applies in this case.

Back in the 1950s the campaign did not even have a name. Today it would be categorized under the rubric of "influence operations."[5] LeMay and Power, drawing together their SAC subordinates' activities, blended public relations, popular culture, public testimony, and demonstrative activities for a single purpose: convincing the Soviet Union not to initiate nuclear war. The campaign was not necessarily intended to address other Communist opponents, aggressions, or situations. It was focused on the Soviet Union and particularly its leadership. As LeMay explained years later, "The only reliable deterrent to war is that achieved by the skillful manipulation of the many elements of national power, of which the military is only one. Foreign policy, rather than naked military power, is the key to peace."[6]

More important, LeMay and Power did not explicitly discuss the concept with RAND or anybody else outside of SAC. Dino Brugioni of the CIA wrote, "[LeMay] would forbid anyone from the RAND corporation to see him or any of his official papers."[7] Indeed, when LeMay discovered RAND was investigating the "sex life of a polyp," he "objected," probably strenuously.[8] He was inclined to keep what he was doing and his motives tightly controlled and in house. An example of this philosophy: the secretive and high-powered Atomic Energy Commission, which legally owned the nuclear material and the weapons themselves, wanted information on SAC targeting. Power told a colleague, "Curt feels that we should avoid, if possible, getting into a position where we are defending our strategy and tactics before anyone outside the Air Force."[9] LeMay was similarly reticent to even provide the Joint Chiefs of Staff (JCS) with information. In a letter to Gen. Nathan Twining he spelled it out: "I appreciate your recognition for the necessity of maintaining close control over information related to the specifics of actual SAC mission planning. To provide the type of plan you have described it will be necessary to include certain sensitive information. Distribution of this information to only the JCS is desirable. Therefore I propose to forward only four copies of the war plan to the JCS instead of the sixty-five copies normally required."[10]

This philosophy clearly extended into many other areas; in his memoirs LeMay noted:

> We in SAC were not saber-rattlers. We were not yelling for war and action in order to "flex the mighty muscles we had built." No stupidity of that sort. We wanted peace as much as anybody else wanted it. But we knew for a fact that it would be possible to curtail enemy expansion if we challenged them in that way. Some of us thought it might be better to do so then, then wait until later.
>
> I never discussed the problem with President Truman or with President Eisenhower. I never discussed it with General Vandenberg. . . . I stuck to my job at Offutt and in the Command. I never

discussed what we were going to *do* with the force we *had* or what we *should* do with it, or anything of that sort. Never discussed it with topside Brass, military or civilian. All I did was keep them abreast of the development of SAC.[11]

It is possible to discern two periods of the campaign. The initial period, under LeMay, we could call Readiness. The second, under Power, we could call Alertness. Under each of these periods there are clusters of activity that to the media and the public appear to be disconnected. Having extensive penetration of American society and with substantial offices in New York and Washington DC, however, the Soviet intelligence services would have drawn links between these clusters and produced assessments for their leaders. The reality was that SAC's influence activities were coordinated and protracted. In LeMay's words, "We had a total war plan, and that was virtually the only thing that was planned. However, it was so segmented that you had a lot of choices over what could be done—something less than that if that was the choice you wanted to make. The main thing was that this force was not built simply for retaliation. That is, 'If you don't behave, we are going to hit you with all this.' It was built for people to see, and looking at it, nobody would want to tackle it. That was our main objective."[12]

Where did the campaign come from? It would be easy to suggest that both LeMay and Power were expanding on Brodie's early work on deterrence. RAND was funded by the U.S. Air Force, and there is a belief that LeMay read everything produced by RAND in the early days.[13] However, there is no suggestion in LeMay's memoirs or in his papers that RAND was this influential in his overall outlook.[14] Power carried on some correspondence with Brodie, but it was polite and inconsequential, though in late 1959 he was sent a copy of Brodie's *Strategy in the Missile Age* and expressed interest in reading it.[15] It is more likely that both men, having reduced Japan to ashes and seeing the effects of their handiwork, simply did not want the same thing to happen to the United States and did not really need sophisticated alternative strategies from RAND.

The idea that SAC existed as a deterrent force was understood and clearly expressed by Gen. Hoyt Vandenberg to LeMay in April 1950. The lack of readiness as a factor undermining the deterrent value of the SAC force was also clearly stated at this time.[16] By December 1951 LeMay through Power and his staff articulated deterrence to his commanders thus: "[SAC's] ability to deliver atomic fire on the Russian industrial heart provides the sole deterrent to overt Russian aggression at this time. . . . The sanction which the threat of the air atomic blow to the Russian heart land provides is dependent to a large extent upon the technique and operational plan of [SAC]. The sanction is, in the last analysis, much more dependent upon the delivery techniques than upon the mere existence of atomic weapons."[17]

By 1953 LeMay's view was this: "SAC's deterrent influence on USSR aggressive intentions can only be maintained by an effective force in being, properly manned, equipped and trained, at the proper time period, and *whose combat capability is universally recognized and unquestioned.*"[18]

It was around 1953 that LeMay's take on deterrence beyond the mere existence of a highly trained SAC and its Emergency War Plan emerged; this was likely the result of the first Soviet thermonuclear test in October of that year. But another key influence emerged around this time. The press noticed that LeMay "came pretty close to being a master of the Japanese mankilling form of wrestling known as Judo," a martial arts discipline he had been practicing for some time.[19] It is through the discipline of judo that we gain more insight into the LeMay-Power deterrence campaign than by examining RAND's operations research output.

To digress slightly, SAC initiated a judo program in 1950 at Power's behest to train aircrew in self-defense techniques. Two years later SAC sent 13 instructors to Japan as a nucleus of instructors, and by 1960 there were 160 black belt judo instructors at SAC bases.[20] Both LeMay and Power held black belts in Kodokan Judo, and both practiced the discipline even after they retired. Notably both leaders spent significant parts of their careers in Asia, had some affinity with the cultural practices they encountered there, and might have come into contact with martial arts earlier: Power in the Philippines, China, and Japan in the 1930s; LeMay in Hawaii in the 1930s and China in the 1940s; and both in the South Pacific.[21]

Judo is a self-defense system based on physical and spiritual strength, employing economy of effort and maximum efficiency. Its methods involve unbalancing an attacking opponent with throwing, locks, chokes, and hold-downs or otherwise using the opponent's weight against him. Victory and defeat in judo are different from, say, boxing. Victory in judo has the opponent on the ground and helpless while one retains freedom of movement and remain unharmed. The opponent is not destroyed or killed but is rendered incapable of harming anyone.[22] It is highly likely that LeMay and Power extracted elements from judo and applied them to the problem at hand: deterring the Soviet Union.

Any cursory analysis of Communism during the 1950s would have identified several Soviet strengths. These included, beyond conventional forces superiority, their ability to exploit the open society of the West in order to collect everything possible on their adversary via open-source information and the outright penetration of Western societies, governments, and industries for clandestine collection. As one knowledgeable observer who worked alongside the Soviets commented at the time, "It is no wonder to me that the Soviet Embassies in London and Washington are veritable hives of industry, where scissors will be the commonest weapons in use."[23]

Another Soviet strength was their respect for the technological. Soviet Communism's philosophical underpinnings related to the superiority of technology over humanity as an organizing principle. From this flowed the Soviet system's mania for information because of the totalitarian requirements of the state. These strengths were used against them by LeMay and Power, the technological judo masters.

The nascent LeMay-Power deterrence campaign expressed itself initially through the media. As Dr. Strangelove exclaims in the film, "Yes, but the … whole point of the doomsday machine … is lost … if you keep it a secret! Why didn't you tell the world, eh?" Now LeMay was no stranger to the media, as discussed earlier. Indeed he fired an officer who openly stated that the media was a security menace, saying, "Major Giblo's value with respect to my command has ceased."[24] What differed in 1954 was a shift from passive engagement to active engagement and the types of matters he wanted the media to print. For example, LeMay allowed himself to be interviewed four times that year; this was four times more than in the past five years combined. Dubbed "Thor of the Atomic Thunderbolt" in one piece, he surprised the interviewer by saying he "went on the theory that he was already at war." Another interview revealed that SAC operated "on a 24 hour war basis."[25] This was a dramatic and significant shift from a 1949 assertion that he made: "We should not antagonize any of our world neighbors by building up overwhelming air power."[26] Privately, in briefings with State Department personnel, LeMay told them, "If the Soviets only knew our power and the extent of the destruction we could wreak on their country, they would never threaten us."[27]

In 1955 LeMay permitted an unprecedented television broadcast from the SAC Command Post, indicating some serious forward thinking from the man who eventually built his own color TV set from scratch when only 30 million out of 163 million Americans had TV.[28] The high-profile columnists Bob Considine and the Alsop brothers were also invited to Omaha and given access at this time. "SAC—Our Frightening War Machine" was one headline. Importantly, LeMay publicly expressed his personal view: "No one can win a modern war. Even the victor loses."[29]

Another facet of the concept was accessing Hollywood. The U.S. Air Force already had an energized and proactive personality engaging Hollywood: Maj. Gen. Sory Smith, U.S. Air Force public affairs. From 1949 to 1954 Smith worked to bring air power–themed films to the silver screen: *Twelve O'Clock High, Air Cadet, The McConnell Story, Sabre Jet, The Big Lift,* and others. None, however, dealt with SAC or its mission.

The central figure in the development of the SAC-aganda film *Strategic Air Command* is, not surprisingly, Curtis LeMay. Beirne Lay Jr., a B-24 pilot who cowrote the book and screenplay *Twelve O'Clock High* with Sy Bartlett, another veteran, flew on the Schweinfurt mission on one of LeMay's B-17s. His report to LeMay on the mission was published in the *Saturday Evening Post.* Lay had just finished working with LeMay and Paul Tibbets to produce the film *Above and Beyond* (1951), the story of Tibbets and the Hiroshima mission.[30] LeMay approached Lay with a script idea based on a "reserve officer brought back to active duty" in SAC. The subsequent screenplay, written by Lay, was called "Heaven and Hell Now." LeMay and Lay saw Col. Jimmy Stewart, U.S. Air Force Reserve, in the lead role.[31] Lay consulted Power, whom he also knew. A later collaboration, working with the air force missile guru Bernard Schreiver, emerged as *Toward the Unknown* (1956).[32]

The general assessment is that *Strategic Air Command* was designed to reassure the American public that SAC was vigilantly protecting them and to boost personnel retention rates during peacetime.[33] However, reexamining the film reveals a whole other parallel message for a very different audience. And this was the brainchild of LeMay, not Lay and Stewart. Even with the Jimmy Stewart–June Allyson romantic distraction, *Strategic Air Command* should not be underestimated as a crucial part of the deterrent concept. It is inconceivable that Soviet intelligence personnel did not assess this film. What would they have seen?

Strategic Air Command conveys with varying degrees of subtlety both SAC's intent and its capabilities. The intent aspect is repeatedly conveyed through dialogue between the protagonists. For example, Maj. Gen. Rusty Castle and Coach Doyle, after a B-36 bomber buzzes a baseball field with a thunderous roar:

"What's SAC?"
"Strategic Air Command."
"The boys that drop the A-bomb."
"I hope not. Our job is to be able to strike back anywhere in the world if this country is ever attacked."

General Castle as he argues with "Dutch" Holland about why he is being recalled to the colors:

"Look, do you realize we are the only thing that's keeping the peace? By staying combat ready we can prevent a war?"

Holland and an old war buddy, Master Sergeant Bible:

"But there isn't a war on. . . ."

"We never know when the other fella is going to start something so we have to be ready 24 hours a day."

General Hawks/LeMay in a briefing:

"With a new family of nuclear weapons one B-47 carries the destructive power of the entire B-29 force used against Japan. When all three air forces of SAC are equipped with B-47s our overall ability will be doubled. It all boils down to less danger of war. With each B-47 delivered SAC's capability of quick retaliation is increased. An enemy would undoubtedly know it. We'll be better able to realize SAC's best hope: prevent a war from even starting."

Another piece of dialogue has Col. Dutch Holland arguing with his wife, Sally:

"But there is a kind of war: we have got to be able to stay ready to fight without fighting. That's tougher."

All of these statements could and likely did come directly from LeMay's lips to Lay's ears as he wrote the screenplay. They are all consistent with the LeMay-Power campaign themes.

As for capability, Soviet intelligence specialists as well as policymakers would have been able to extract from the film specific capabilities that LeMay wanted them to know: first, that the B-36 bomber force was by 1954–55 a mature, trained, and capable entity that had overcome teething troubles reported earlier in the press. The film takes the viewer on a tour of the B-36, leaving out the bombing equipment in the camera shots. One character comments on how long the bomb bay is: eighty feet, that is, capable of taking the large Mk-17/24 thermonuclear bombs that were coming into the stockpile. Telling, had the Soviets known their dimensions. Which they probably did from their espionage penetration of Los Alamos at this time.[34] On a check flight Holland flies "to Alaska and back" from central Texas without refueling and is escorted by four SAC jet fighters on arrival, suggesting that the B-36 is in close proximity to Soviet airspace. The crew comments on temporary duty with the

B-36 to the United Kingdom, North Africa, and Japan, actual forward operating locations in range of the Soviet Union. Cold weather testing of the B-36 at Thule air base in Greenland in the course of the film is yet another pointed assertion that the SAC bomber force can operate from forward locations in extreme climates near the USSR.

Throughout the film there are a lot of panning shots from flight control towers at Carswell AFB and MacDill AFB. No fewer that thirty B-36s are seen in one pan, plus forty-five B-47s in another. This is no Potemkin Village, comrades. The viewers are bombarded, as it were, with subliminal imagery: the ashtrays are all aluminum B-36s; there are aluminum aircraft models on every level surface; and pictures of current bombers adorn every vertical surface.

Most important, *Strategic Air Command* depicts the overseas deployment of an entire B-47 wing (forty-five aircraft) to the periphery of the Soviet Union during a short-notice exercise. A careful examination of the large wall maps during a briefing scene reveals the fact that the B-47s based in Florida can, after they have been aerial-refueled by KC-97 tanker, reach Japan without landing. That is, if they are operating from Japan, they can cover the whole USSR. The route, however, if slightly adjusted, could just as easily take the wing over the Soviet Union on its way there. After a refueling scene over the Aleutians on their way to Yokota, Japan, the wing commander announces, "Formation will break up and we'll proceed on individual flight plans." In a real strike against the USSR, aircraft would have done exactly that at that exact point.[35]

The B-47s on training bomb runs are also depicted:

Reporter: You mean this city been wiped out theoretically in a storm from a bomber that we didn't even see or hear?
Crew: Sure. With radar, weather is no problem.

The level of carefully deployed technical, tactical, and strategic detail in *Strategic Air Command* coupled with intent messaging is not something that would have come out of Hollywood at this time without a great deal of assistance from the U.S. Air Force and SAC. As the LeMay-esque General Hawks tells June Allyson's Sally, who is distraught over the strain in the nuclear family that SAC operations generates, "Mrs. Holland, I too, have no choice." *Strategic Air Command* was not merely sentimental 1950s Hollywood; it was a carefully constructed weapon in LeMay's arsenal, delivered with precision against its multiple targets.

There have been allegations for many years that LeMay conducted unauthorized overflights of the Soviet Union to either deliberately provoke a nuclear war or otherwise recklessly raise the middle finger of SAC's mailed gauntlet at the Kremlin while running the risk of triggering a nuclear war.[36] There is, however, no evidence that any of the reconnaissance programs conducted by SAC in the 1950s were unauthorized. There is no evidence whatsoever that these operations were designed by LeMay or Power or anybody else to provoke war. Indeed it was the Soviets who committed acts of war against American reconnaissance aircraft in international airspace, shooting down American aircraft over international waters and killing their crews. Finally, there is evidence that SAC was openly wary when the CIA enthusiastically approached them about "sell[ing] State Department on the need for relaxing the diplomatic side enough to permit violations of sovereignty."[37]

There were several compartmentalized programs, and not all belonged to SAC: peripheral photo and electronic reconnaissance of the USSR had been under way since 1946. In 1951 and 1952 SAC RB-45C aircraft penetrated deeply into Soviet and Chinese airspace to conduct radarscope photography missions so that the bombers could navigate to their targets in the event of war. The 1951 missions were authorized by the Joint Chiefs. The 1952 missions were flown by British pilots and with Churchill's and Truman's authorization. (Those missions, incidentally, were code-named Ju Jitsu, while other demonstrative exercises were code-named Judo.)[38] In 1954 RF-86F Haymaker reconnaissance overflights were mounted, again with presidential authorization, against Soviet Far East bases. Between March and May 1956 SAC conducted Project Homerun. This involved RB-47E and RB-47H reconnaissance planes collecting information from the Kola Peninsula to the Bering Strait. Photomapping penetrations were conducted "a few miles inside Soviet territory" except for the mass overflight of six planes over Siberia on 6–7 May 1956.

Another project, Black Knight, consisted of an overflight by three RB-57DS over Vladivostok on 11 December 1956. These flights were not rogue activity. One historian points out that, when interviewed, LeMay stated, "It wasn't my idea. I was ordered to do it."[39] And with Khrushchev batting away Eisenhower's Open Skies olive branch in 1955, it is evident where those orders came from.

That said, all of these operations provided the Soviet Union with an impressive display of SAC capability. The apprehension generated by the fact that Operation Ju Jitsu RB-45C jets could converge on Moscow at night and then escape the Soviet air defense system unscathed in 1952 and again in 1954 would have been topped only by mass overflights by RF-68F, RB-57, and RB-47s of peripheral Soviet base complexes. A B-47 is a B-47, after all. What can carry cameras can also carry thermonuclear bombs. But was Homerun intended to start a war? There is no evidence that it was.

And the Soviets got the message: the 1954 Ju Jitsu aircraft "were not detected before reaching the western Ukraine. . . . The aircraft penetrated almost to the Moscow region. . . . Col. Tsiptsivadze said that if the aircraft had been carrying atomic and hydrogen bombs, it would have destroyed several large Soviet cities and returned unharmed. . . . Marshal Bulganin [Soviet minister of defense] warned that if enemy aircraft again succeeded in penetrating Soviet territory, all PVO [air defense] authorities would be sent before a firing squad."[40]

Stories dripped out of SAC like Chinese water torture, hitting the wire services (the 1950s equivalent of the internet). In *Parade* magazine, a nationwide Sunday insert, "The Untold Story of Our Air Force's 'Sunday Punch'" featured an in-depth story on the B-36 force and the first photos of the "Red Phone" that "alerts every [SAC] base in the U.S. at once." There were apparently "400 combat planes constantly in the air." Another shot shows LeMay at what could be the prototype Big Board at the SAC Command Post. "ECM [Electronic Counter Measure] Spreads Confusion" is the title of a section describing "how the B-36 addles the 'brains' of 'hunter' anti-aircraft missiles."[41] Interesting fare for a family in Los Angeles, just home from church, eating their Corn Flakes. And if the message was not sinking in (or the Soviet spies were reading the wrong newspapers), there was columnist Bob Considine's February 1956 interview with LeMay: "Our mission is to be ready to retaliate immediately—this minute—if the enemy hits us. . . . We've got to have that hardware in such numbers, strength, and efficiency that nobody will strike us. If there's no profit in aggression, there's no war."[42]

Variants on that theme made their way into practically every LeMay quote in the media in 1956 and 1957. "Just so long as this nation's capacity to win war is clearly recognized by the potential aggressor, there will be no war," LeMay told a Georgetown University audience. "But once the potential aggressor doubts this capacity, the peace of the world is in jeopardy."[43] At the Case Institute of Technology in Cleveland, LeMay opened with the same theme but added, "Ultimately we might find some other solution—in education, human understanding and more wisdom of human affairs. It is imperative there be no war because not even time could erase scars of nuclear conflict."[44]

In terms of demonstrative activity, LeMay prototyped that back in 1949 when he had a B-50 bomber and KB-29 tankers circumnavigate the globe nonstop in four days with attendant media coverage.[45] American citizens and Soviet intelligence analysts woke to the front page news on 18 January 1957 that three new "B-52 Stratofortresses, America's intercontinental hydrogen bomb carriers," flew around the world with aerial refueling from KC-97 tankers and "conducted a simulated nuclear bomb drop at roughly the half way point west of the Malay Peninsula." LeMay told the media that Operation Power Flite was "a demonstration of the SAC global capabilities to strike any target on the face of the earth."[46] More specifically, he took pains to reply to a reporter who asked, "Russia knows all about our long-range possibilities." Why? The "planes were less than 90 minutes from Russia." One of the crew explained that the B-52s "had their closest contact with Russia in the form of coastal towns and communities on the Caspian Sea." He added, "I have no knowledge that Russia's Air Force knew we were so close. We were not intercepted or challenged by hostile aircraft."[47]

The LeMay image, of course, was part of the concept. As Jane LeMay Lodge put it, "I think [the Soviets] feared SAC. . . . I think they feared my father."[48]

When Power replaced LeMay as commander in chief of SAC in July 1957, the LeMay-Power deterrence campaign continued. For example, Power ensured that he was seen flying the new B-58 Hustler supersonic nuclear bomber, and the usual media visits to the SAC command center continued.[49] By the fall of that year, however, Power was forced by circumstances to evolve the campaign after the 4 October Sputnik shot and the national hysteria that ensued. What the public did not know and Power did was that, in addition to the satellite, the Soviets airdropped and detonated a 1.6-megaton-yield bomb, and then surface-detonated a 2.9-megaton-yield bomb, both in the Arctic, bracketing the date of the Sputnik launch by days.[50] The implications were staggering. The six- to eight-hour warning time of a possible nuclear attack on North America was now potentially cut to the thirty-minute flight time of an ICBM launched from the central USSR.[51]

LeMay, who was now vice chief of staff of the U.S. Air Force, coordinated a series of activities with Power. These took place when Eisenhower responded to Sputnik with his speeches on 7 and 13 November, the latter of which emphasized SAC readiness.[52]

Several explicitly overt actions took place and were relayed to the press. First, Power went to Paris, invited by Gen. Lauris Norstad to speak to and reassure the NATO leadership. Norstad advised Power, "In my own talks I begin always with our mission to *prevent* war. I then speak of the deterrent, which consists of three parts: (1) Retaliatory forces, (2) Shield Forces, and (3) the will of our peoples to use our forces should the need arise."[53]

When he spoke with the press after the NATO meetings, Power was quoted saying that there were bombers in the air at all times, "and they're not carrying swords or bows and arrows. The planes are on runways loaded with nuclear bombs. The crews sleep nearby. We are increasing the number of planes on alert to one third of our effectiveness. The planes can be off in 15 minutes." That brief statement was relayed around the world and led to headlines like "A-Bombs Anytime"; "Bomber Chief Warns Soviets"; "Bombers Standing By, Air Chief Warns Soviets"; "Reds Zeroed In by US Air Force"—even though Power did not even mention the Soviet Union.[54]

Second, SAC public affairs in both Paris and Omaha provided canned briefings to the media on SAC's communications system, which resulted in headlines like "All SAC Needs Is 30 Seconds . . . Can Contact All US Bases"; "H-Bombs Already in Planes, Signal Flash Can Ignite US Attack"; "General Thomas Power: The Dice Are Loaded." Power also sent a letter to all members of SAC that approximated the information in the press releases.[55]

Lt. Gen. Francis "Butch" Griswold, SAC's second in command, handled a series of media tours of the SAC command center the same day Power was in Paris. His contribution to the messaging was this: "We can prevent war only by letting potential enemies know what we can do, only by making a prospective war so horrible that they will seek other means of solving difficulties. But peace is our profession."[56]

Third, three new B-66 medium nuclear bombers flew nonstop across the Pacific to the Philippines. This action was specifically linked by the media to Power's visit to Paris.[57]

Fourth, LeMay and Power wanted to mount a larger demonstration of SAC capability as a response to Sputnik. This was passed through to the White House's Operations Coordinating Board for assessment, where they discussed a "defense proposal to stage a display of the offensive capability of [SAC] by arranging a rendezvous over Buenos Aries." State opposed this alternative because the original proposal "appeared to have too much of an aspect of sabre rattling."[58]

Instead LeMay flew a new KC-135 prototype airborne command post code-named Speckled Trout nonstop 6,350 miles from Westover AFB to Buenos Aires in thirteen hours, setting a new distance and speed record. LeMay was at the controls for eight hours except when he was manning the radio. The international press caught on quick: most of the stories were variations on the theme that the "purpose of mission evidently was to demonstrate [that the] long reach of US air power is well beyond that of any other power" and that this was linked to the other actions undertaken by SAC.[59]

At least that was one purpose. The other purpose of the KC-135 flight was to test the Collins single sideband (SSB) radio system (a system referenced by Gen. Buck Turgidson in *Dr. Strangelove*). Collins Radio Corporation in Cedar Rapids, Iowa (just down the road from sac headquarters in Omaha), was able to remain in constant communication with LeMay's KC-135 using SSB. The distance of 6,350 miles, if extrapolated over the North Pole instead of south to Argentina, made Buenos Aries an analogue for Moscow, as LeMay notes in his memoirs. If a KC-135 could operate at this distance and communicate with sac headquarters reliably, than so could a B-52.[60] Note also that LeMay and Power were obedient to higher authority and did not mount the planned larger demonstration with B-52s and KC-135s off Buenos Aries.

The fifth activity, connected to the third, was a protracted open description in print media about the SSB radio system employed by SAC. Several articles about SSB radios appeared in the general press, which was unusual for such an esoteric and technical subject.[61] For example, the *Abilene Reporter News* carried one such article with an illustration depicting a B-52 communicating with Omaha: "These Single Side Band radios cannot be jammed by conditions which would knock out conventional sets."[62]

The revolutionary nature of SSB radio would have remained a state secret in the Soviet Union. Arthur Collins of the Collins Radio Corporation had exploited an obscure Royal Air Force technical study and his people developed a hard-to-jam, extremely long-range and reliable radio system.[63] LeMay, a ham radio operator who kept abreast of new developments, worked with his technophile subordinate Lt. Gen. Francis Griswold to get the new technology for SAC. LeMay, Power, and Griswold then ensured, deliberately, that the Soviets knew SAC had it by encouraging open discussion of it in the media.

And that was not all. Interwoven with the SSB radio meme was yet another information activity. SAC Command Center visits increased significantly in 1958–59. The tour provided to visitors usually included the Strategic Aerospace Museum based at Offutt AFB. As Power put it in approving the museum, "Apart from its historical value . . . I am convinced that a carefully planned exhibit of actual hardware would be of mutual benefit in supplementing the briefings provided by my staff and myself." The "nucleus" of the exhibit was to be a B-36.[64]

The SAC underground command center was the centerpiece of

the tour. The tour was remarkably similar to that depicted in the 1963 film *A Gathering of Eagles* (a Sy Bartlett production, screenplay by Bernie Lay Jr.). Col. Jim Caldwell, played by Rock Hudson, has just been "plucked from the embassy in London" and, with his pretty British wife, sent to SAC in Omaha. (An in-joke: Power's wife, Mae, was British, and Power was "plucked" by LeMay from the London embassy to be his second in command at SAC.) There Caldwell briefs foreign delegations in the SAC Command Center. In this scene Caldwell explains that the alarmed red box with an envelope taped inside it holds the authentication codes for a launch message from the president. All personnel carry sidearms, and the two-man rule is in effect; that is, actions involving nuclear weapons, whether maintenance, operational deployments, or command and control, require at least two people to be involved.

With the Big Board and the Bomb Alarm System in the background, Caldwell demonstrates how the Primary Alerting System works using the actual console and Red Phone. Conducting a communications check with all SAC bases worldwide, all acknowledge in five seconds and the console lights up. Caldwell explains that those units would have thirty seconds to authenticate the message. The bombers would be off the ground in less than fifteen minutes. He then moves to a white phone and demonstrates that the SAC Command Center can contact individual planes at any time, "in this case a B-52 off North Africa, Bozo 23." (Another in-joke: Gen. Bill "Bozo" McKee was in charge of Air Material Command at this time.)

Under Power there was a veritable parade of visitors to the SAC Command Center: TV and other media; local, state, and federal politicians; church groups; chambers of commerce, and more. But when it came to the larger aspects of the deterrence concept, VIP tours were also laid on: Paul Henri Spaak, NATO secretary general; Air Marshal "Bing" Cross, RAF Bomber Command; Franz Joseph Strauss, West German defense minister; the Canada-U.S. Interparliamentary Group; the staff of McGraw-Hill publishers; King Hassan of Morocco; and many others.[65]

The message to Soviets via media and pop culture was this: We can talk to and direct our forces; those forces have the ability to inflict severe damage to you, and there is nothing you can do about it. Using LeMay's 1953 language, SAC presented the Soviets with a force *whose combat capability was universally recognized and unquestioned.* Retaliation will happen. Assure friends, deter adversaries. But let adversaries know what the capabilities are.

Power even wanted to invite Nikita Khrushchev for a briefing at the SAC Command Center, à la Ambassador DeSadeski in *Dr. Strangelove*, and sent the idea up to the White House through channels: "In connection with Soviet complaints about allegedly provocative and dangerous flights by SAC aircraft, a suggestion was made that Nikita Khrushchev might be invited to visit the SAC headquarters at Omaha. The idea would be that it could then be demonstrated to him how false the expressed Soviet fears really are; at the same time the obvious state of readiness of the long-range striking force might provide a worthwhile object lesson for Mr. Khrushchev. This proposal was not pursued further."[66]

In an exchange with the editor of *Aviation Week* Power explained, "I have always maintained that SAC's strength cannot serve as an effective deterrent to war—our primary mission—unless that strength is known and respected throughout the world."[67] Robert Holtz replied, "Recalling your interest in having Mr. Khrushchev adequately briefed on SAC I think you will be interested to known that the Soviet air attaché dropped by our Washington office today to pick up three extra copies of 'SAC in Transition.' I gather this means it will be well read in the proper places inside the Kremlin."[68]

This proposal reflected Power's growing belief that the deterrence concept should specifically focus on the Soviet leader and not just the Soviet Union or Communism in general. Exactly how Power came to this conclusion is obscure; it is entirely possible that the trigger event was Khrushchev's one-way interview with Bob Considine, William Randolph Hearst, and Frank Conniff in November 1957, when the Soviet premier expressed concern "that some mad SAC pilot might touch off World War III by striking off on his own and dropping a nuclear bomb on Russian territory."[69] It may be when he visited the Soviet Union and interacted with senior Soviet personalities. Focusing on Khrushchev could also have come from discussions with LeMay, who wrote years later, "Deterrence of war rests on as complicated a human decision as the causes of war itself, and is far more susceptible to political acumen. Deterrence is the product of what is *believed* about enemy and friendly forces, of national aspirations, and of the emotional heat of provocation. It is a state of mind, a matter of intentions."[70]

By 1958 Power's concerns over deterring Khrushchev personally were operationalized. His personal writings make this clear: "Listening to some of the arguments about national defense, I often get the impression that we are trying to deter each other instead of Mr. Khrushchev and the Soviets. . . . The only thing that counts is what Mr. Khrushchev and his accomplices think of SAC. *They* are the ones whom we are trying to deter."[71]

One the issue of finite deterrence concepts: "Unfortunately, no one knows what that minimum deterrent is, with the possible exception of Mr. Khrushchev. And even Mr. Khrushchev may not know from one day to the other what will deter him, because he may be willing to accept more punishment today than he would accept tomorrow."

On city destruction: "There has been too much irresponsible talk about the number of Russian cities we would have to destroy in order to win nuclear war. After all the primary objective of our military effort is not to destroy cities and kill people but to protect *our* cities and *our* people by deterring aggression and thereby preventing nuclear war from happening in the first place. What will deter Mr. Khrushchev will not be the bombers and missiles and forces we have in being but only the fighting capacity he thinks we will have left *after* he has subjected us to a surprise attack."

Power believed that the United States "must make attack too risky for Khrushchev": "Our challenge is to keep them convinced that, if they ever push those buttons, they will destroy themselves. . . . They must know that they will have to eat SAC's alert force and that it will give them fatal indigestion. As long as they know that, I think they will be strongly deterred. . . . They will not risk an attack unless they are confident that they can do so successfully and with relative impunity."

On Khrushchev himself: "There is always the danger of miscalculation on Khrushchev's part. I am not referring to what I usually call the 'madman angle.' I am convinced that anybody who fights his way to the top in this kind of society and manages to stay on top must be both very tough and very sane lest the men behind him take care of him."

Finally: "I like to describe our mission by explaining that our goal is to have that Soviet war planner turn to Mr. Khrushchev morning after morning and say, 'Comrade, today is not the day!' If we can keep him saying this indefinitely SAC will have accomplished its primary mission."

That was Power's internal monologue. In multiple speeches and interviews from 1958 to 1964, he kept the message consistent with these views.[72] Notably, the U.S. State Department expressed concern and exerted influence in an attempt to edit Power's speeches; "It is not believed advisable to include this personal reference to Khrushchev," one line read.[73]

It is hard to ignore the possibility that some portion of the twelve to sixteen B-52s in the air in SAC's airborne alert program was specifically assigned to destroy any facility that Khrushchev might try to hide in.[74] This is strongly implied in the memoirs of SAC's chief of staff of operations, Lt. Gen. Selmon "Sundown" Wells.[75] Even the code name used for the Airborne Alert Force, Chrome Dome, was likely a reference to Khrushchev's bald pate. In Power's words: "The decision of war and peace is made by the Soviet hierarchy, not the Russian people. . . . The only thing that will deter them from starting a war, now and in the future, is the fear that they might jeopardize their own lives, their positions, their possessions."[76]

And just to let the Soviet leadership know that SAC's B-52s could fly under their air defense system, a series of articles appeared in newspapers across the United States in the last quarter of 1959. "Low-Level Missions Scheduled by B-52s," the headline ran, announcing that the bombers would be flying at 1,000 feet "to permit SAC to carry out low altitude training missions." Most articles, tailored for regional audiences, featured maps depicting the routes the bombers would fly. All articles mentioned Power by name.[77] These routes, code-named Oil Burner, were established by SAC with the Federal Aviation Administration specifically so that B-52 crews could fly *under* 1,000 feet, a zone where Soviet anti-aircraft missiles and their radars could not engage.[78] As General Turgidson puts it in *Dr. Strangelove*, "Ah. . . . If the pilot's good, see. I mean, if he's really . . . sharp, he can barrel that baby in so low you oughta see it sometime, it's a sight. A big plane, like a '52, vrrrooom! There's jet exhaust, fryin' chickens in the barnyard!"

When we examine all of the components of the LeMay-Power deterrence campaign there are just too many data points that converge on one objective over a protracted period for it to be routine or random activity. The message is also remarkably consistent throughout the decade. In effect LeMay and Power created a signaling device pointed at the Soviet leadership first and then later at Khrushchev himself. SAC had the capability in personnel, vehicles, weapons, communications, and training. Portions of that capability were deliberately unzipped and shown to the Soviet Union. The message honed in: "We want peace. If you start anything, it will be on your head. You will not be able to hide from the consequences. We have the ability to come and get you." When Power took SAC to defense condition (DEFCON) 3 during the U-2 Crisis in 1960 and conducted an order of battle roll call in the clear, when Power went to DEFCON 2 during the Cuban Missile Crisis and announced what he was doing in the clear, and when Power increased SAC's alert posture after the Kennedy assassination, the signaling device was ready when it was needed the most. Khrushchev understood SAC's "language," as Power later wrote: "[At Munich] Hitler would not listen to the 'language of sweet reasonableness' but only to the language of the mailed fist. History proved Duff Cooper right. I am convinced that history will also prove those who insist the only language to which the Communists will listen is the language of deterrence, as symbolized by the emblem of the Strategic Air Command—the mailed fist."[79]

"Dim-witted"? "Jingoistic"? "Unstable"? "Demented"? "Psychotic"? Was this really "subversion of Presidential authority"?

And out of all of this, in a quirk of fate, Frank Bartholomew from United Press visited SAC as part of the media visit program and published his exposé on 7 April 1958. Peter George, alarmed at what he was reading about the prospects of airborne alert in the wake of the Bartholomew piece, and operating in a media climate to some extent fed by Soviet active measures questioning the mental stability of U.S. Air Force personnel, wrote *Red Alert* in 1959. Harvey Wheeler wrote "Abraham '59" for similar reasons in December 1959. Soviet active measures designed to discredit SAC and its leaders and the LeMay-Power deterrence concept are ultimately responsible for the existence of the films *Dr. Strangelove* and *Fail-Safe*.

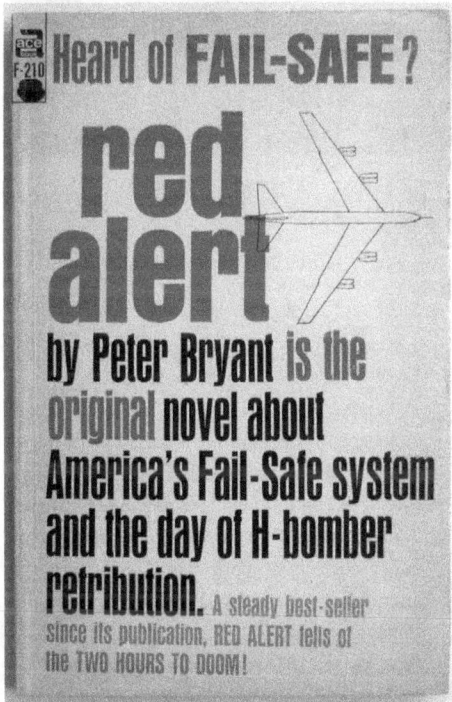

1. The basis for *Dr. Strangelove* was RAF intelligence officer Peter George's 1958 novel *Red Alert*, released under a pseudonym. It was optioned by the director Stanley Kubrick, and the resulting screenplay, which differed significantly from its source, was assembled by Kubrick, George, and Terry Southern. When a competitor novel, *Fail-Safe*, was released, *Red Alert* was rereleased with a new jacket design. Courtesy of Penguin Random House.

The Saturday Evening

POST

October 13, 1962   20¢

Can Accident Trigger a Nuclear War?

Fail-Safe

A Novel in Three Parts

By Eugene Burdick
Coauthor of The Ugly American

and Harvey Wheeler

2. Eugene "Ugly American" Burdick and Harvey Wheeler's *Fail-Safe*, based on a December 1959 *Dissent* article, was itself serialized by the *Saturday Evening Post* at the height of the Cuban Missile Crisis in October 1962. The *Post* foldout cover depicted Strategic Air Command B-58s streaking over the Kremlin in Moscow, under World War II–style anti-aircraft fire. An ensuing lawsuit led to Columbia Pictures releasing both *Dr. Strangelove* and *Fail-Safe*. © SEPS, licensed by Curtis Licensing, Indianapolis, Indiana. All rights reserved.

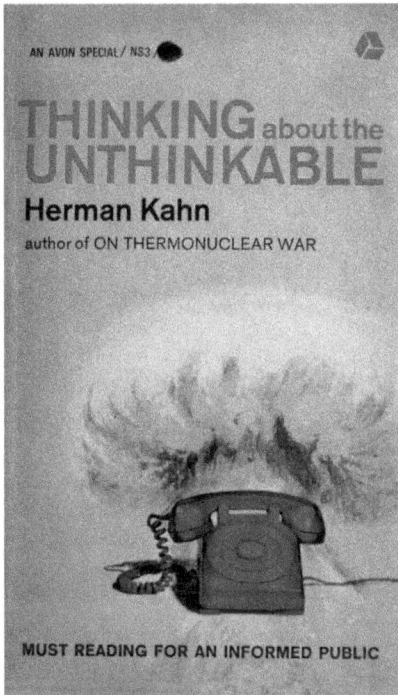

AN AVON SPECIAL / NS3

THINKING about the
UNTHINKABLE

Herman Kahn

author of ON THERMONUCLEAR WAR

MUST READING FOR AN INFORMED PUBLIC

3. One of nuclear strategist Herman Kahn's arenas for his "theatre of the absurd" was the best seller *Thinking about the Unthinkable*, released in mass-market paperback with a depiction of the iconic "Red Phone" on the cover. In reality, there was a Red Phone in the SAC Command Post, but it was generally confused with the Hot Line Moscow link Teletype system used by American and Soviet leaders to communicate with each other. Kahn and his writings played a significant role in Kubrick's conceptualization of *Dr. Strangelove*. Reprinted by permission of HarperCollins Publishers.

Antony Trew
TWO HOURS TO DARKNESS
"The suspense is terrific"
Scotsman

4. Though forgotten today, Antony Trew's prophetic 1963 best seller *Two Hours to Darkness* was the prototype boomer psychological thriller that influenced *The Fifth Missile*, *Crimson Tide*, and to some extent *The Hunt for Red October*. Trew's complex characterization of a future Royal Navy Polaris missile submarine crew was unparalleled at the time, nearly half a decade before the real submarines were deployed. Courtesy of HarperCollins UK.

5. Gen. Curtis E. LeMay's earnest public expressions asserting the need for deterrence based on nuclear air supremacy in the 1950s led to a wide variety of caricatures in the media and popular culture, the most prominent of which was the film *Dr. Strangelove.* Ironically but fittingly this wall mural was the backdrop to LeMay's 1965 retirement ceremony, the fusion of art and life forever cemented in the public consciousness. Courtesy of the Strategic Air Command Museum.

6. & 7. (*opposite*) The real LeMay. Journalist Bob Considine referred to LeMay as the "No. 1 triggerman of the Free World . . . a hard looking man that chews a dead stogie." The journalist Richard Hubler, after meeting him in 1958, wrote, "LeMay is a man who wears a cigar like a cocked revolver. . . . His character blurts its way through the exterior. No one can talk to LeMay very long and not come away with the impression that he is a man who comes close to the faculties of absolute power and ultimate decision." Courtesy of the U.S. National Records and Archives Administration and Strategic Air Command Museum.

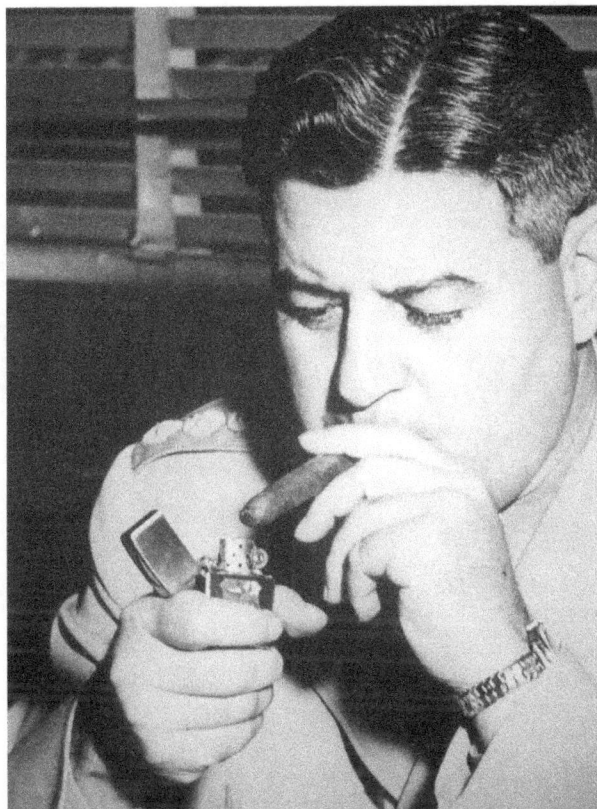

8. Prevailing popular culture as expressed through *Dr. Strangelove* and other means reflects a belief that there was a breakdown in the civil-military relationship while LeMay was chief of staff of the U.S. Air Force and Power was commander in chief of Strategic Air Command during the Kennedy administration. Though there was friction, Kennedy kept Johnson out of the loop on nuclear weapons release procedures as well as the Single Integrated Operational Plan (SIOP) war plan and conferred directly with LeMay and Power when he deemed it necessary to do so. Kennedy ensured that he and LeMay were photographed together at certain public events as a message to the Soviets—and indirectly to the critics. Here Power briefs JFK and LBJ on the Primary Alerting System at the SAC Command Post while LeMay looks on bemused. Courtesy of Syracuse University Special Collections Research Center.

9. For Gen. Thomas S. Power, Communism was an implacable enemy that was not theoretical. In 1956 he toured the Soviet Union: "[My] visit served to lend depth and substance to various theories I had formulated. . . . I met some of the men behind the global Communist conspiracy. . . . I experienced what it meant to live in an absolute police state and to have supreme power concentrated in the hands of a very few." And he was repelled by it, particularly after his high-level hosts, including Khrushchev and Zhukov, exhibited "a cocky self assurance and brutal frankness about what their objectives were." Architects of the destruction of Tokyo in 1945 and observers of thermonuclear tests in the 1950s, Power and LeMay were determined to prevent a Soviet nuclear attack on the United States. Courtesy of Syracuse University Special Collections Research Center.

10. Numerous commentators assert that Power was a dangerous rogue operator while he was commander in chief of Strategic Air Command during the Kennedy administration. The reality was that Power quite properly provided Kennedy with options during the Berlin Crisis of 1961, moved SAC to DEFCON 2 in 1962 when the Cuban Missile Crisis reached a dangerously critical phase, and ensured that there was a steady hand on SAC when Kennedy was assassinated in 1963. Courtesy of Syracuse University Special Collections Research Center.

11. Regardless of protestations to the contrary, Sterling Hayden's Gen. Jack D. Ripper in *Dr. Strangelove* was a composite based on real people. The cigar clearly is representative of Curtis LeMay, while some of Ripper's dialogue was lifted from Orvil Anderson, who was fired for advocating preventive war during Korea. Ripper's interest in golf, his wartime background flying B-24s, his outspoken anti-Communism, and his concerns regarding reproduction strongly indicate that Thomas Power was the third component in Kubrick's composite. Courtesy of Sony Pictures.

REVISED PLAN FOR

NEW CONSTRUCTION, AJCC

DECLASSIFIED

ROADWAY

1st FLOOR — *2nd FLOOR* — *3rd FLOOR*

LEGEND

- GENERAL OPERATIONAL OFFICES
- COMMUNICATIONS
- PERMANENT JOINT WAR ROOM FACILITY
- SUITE

AREA	SQUARE FEET
GENERAL OPERATIONAL OFFICES	77,200
COMMUNICATIONS	10,000
JOINT WAR ROOM	14,140
SUITE	3,800
VAULT	1,400
TOTAL	**106,500**

DECLASSIFIED

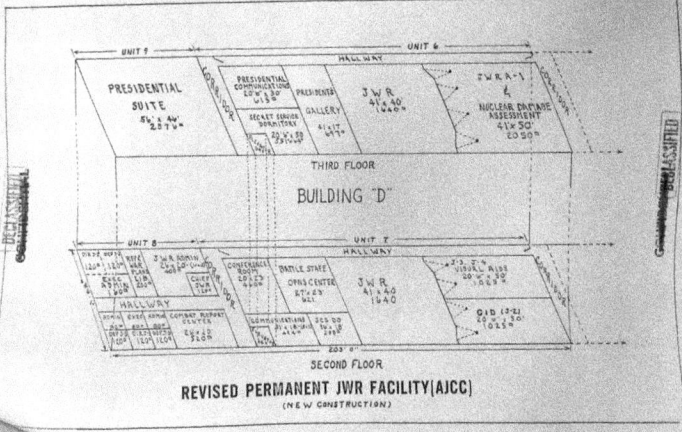

THIRD FLOOR

BUILDING "D"

SECOND FLOOR

REVISED PERMANENT JWR FACILITY (AJCC)
(NEW CONSTRUCTION)

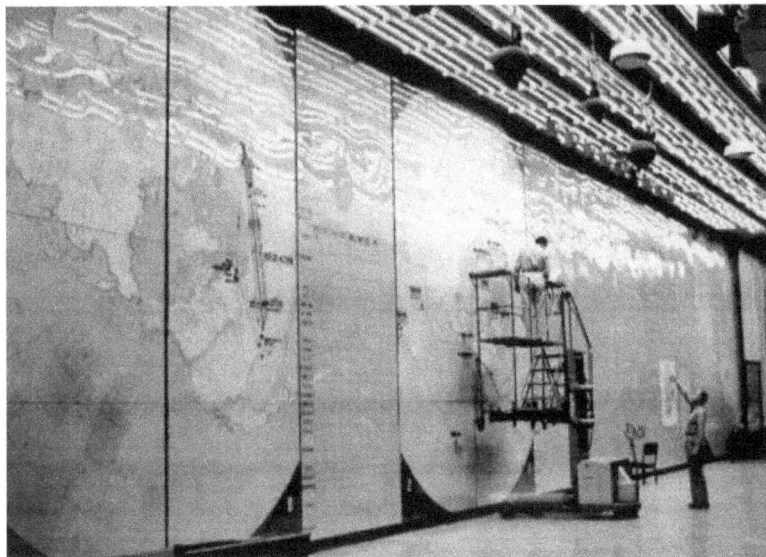

12. (*opposite*) The Alternate Joint Communications
Center, Raven Rock Mountain, Pennsylvania, was the
first large-scale protected underground war room, but
there are no publicly available pictures of its interior sixty
years after it was constructed. In its 1950s configuration, it
consisted of several large cross-connected tunnels driven
through the rock. The second sketch depicts a three-story
joint war room and a president's gallery overlooking what
is an entire wall of screens for nuclear damage assessment,
with a battle staff and operations center below. Courtesy
of the Library of Congress.

13. (*above*) The original Big Board, seen here in the
underground command post at Offutt A F B in the late
1950s. The Primary Alerting System consoles and the Red
Phone, depicted in the 1958 U.S. Air Force film *The Power
of Decision* and the 1963 Hollywood film *A Gathering of
Eagles*, were located in a glassed-in balcony overlooking
the maps. Courtesy of the U.S. Air Force.

14. An EC-135 aircraft, code-named Looking Glass, was the Strategic Air Command's airborne command post. As depicted in *By Dawn's Early Light*, one of these aircraft was kept aloft on a rotating basis throughout the last three decades of the Cold War and carried a battle staff that could, with National Command Authority concurrence, launch SIOP forces. Looking Glass was only one of nearly thirty EC-135 airborne command post aircraft available to the National Command Authorities, but it was easily the most visible of them in popular culture. U.S. Air Force, courtesy of the Air Force Association.

15. (*opposite top*) Looking Glass and other EC-135s were configured as airborne launch control centers to remotely launch Minuteman ICBMs. The ALCC equipment was similar to the equipment found in a Minuteman launch control facility and could access the launch facilities through a UHF radio system. The crew could select single ICBMs in Minuteman launch facilities; provide them with either a SIOP, trans-SIOP, or post-SIOP target; and launch as required even if the missile's two-man launch control facility was unable to do so. Courtesy of the author.

16. (*opposite bottom*) The historical equivalent of *Dr. Strangelove*'s Plan R included U.S. Air Force chief of staff Gen. Thomas D. White's 1957 post-Sputnik interpretation of President Eisenhower's earlier instructions to the Joint Chiefs of Staff. White told the commander in chief of Strategic Air Command Gen. Thomas Power, "Your plans provide for assumption of authority by your [Numbered] Air Force commanders under specified circumstances. This can be construed as at least an element of the delegation we would prefer." Courtesy of Sony Pictures.

17. (*opposite top*) During the 1960s B-52 bombers launched from northern tier Strategic Air Command bases in the first wave of the SIOP were equipped with two AGM-28 Hound Dog cruise missiles, each equipped with a W28 thermonuclear weapon. The Hound Dog was designed to destroy Soviet anti-aircraft missile sites like the SA-1 Guild and SA-2 Guideline and other air defense facilities one hour before the bomber penetrated to its primary and secondary targets and destroyed them with either two or four freefall thermonuclear bombs. U.S. Air Force, courtesy of the Air Force Association.

18. (*opposite bottom*) The pilot's readiness switch assembly, or DCU 47, was located behind the B-52 pilot's head. In conjunction with a pair of DCU-9/A panels at the bombardier or navigator's position and a special arming cord at the electronic warfare officer station, nuclear consent for release was divided among the crew in different parts of the aircraft. This was an absolutely crucial safety system for B-52s on airborne alert. Contrary to fears stoked by Soviet propaganda and disinformation efforts, there were no instances of B-52s crews improperly arming and delivering armed nuclear weapons during the course of the Cold War. Courtesy of the author.

19. (*above*) The controversial Convair B-58 Hustler was rarely seen in public fully equipped. In addition to the multimegaton B53 bomb cocooned in the MB-1 freefall bomb pod, the B-58 could also carry up to four Mk-43 bombs yielding 1 megaton each. These weapons could be released in one of four selectable configurations on the fly by the fire control system: ground burst retarded or free fall, or air burst retarded or free fall. Glass Brick and Glass Road B-58 training deployments ensured that the United States retained a decapitation capability against the Soviet Union and People's Republic of China in the 1960s. Courtesy of the U.S. Air Force.

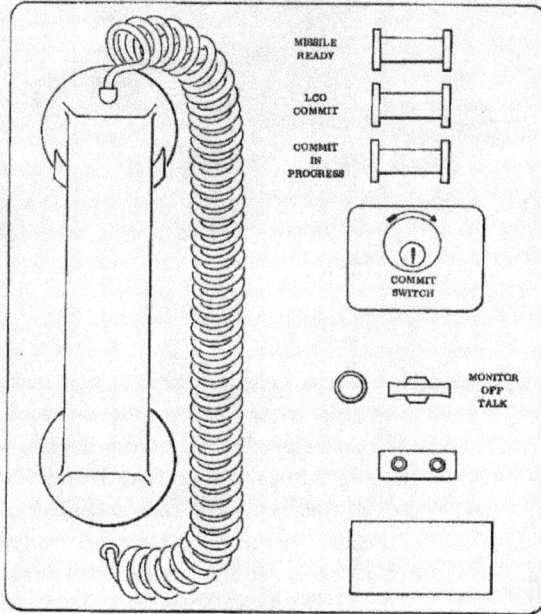

MISSILE
READY

LCO
COMMIT

COMMIT
IN
PROGRESS

COMMIT
SWITCH

MONITOR
OFF
TALK

32. 137-102

Figure 1-101.   **ALCO COMM/CONTROL Panel**

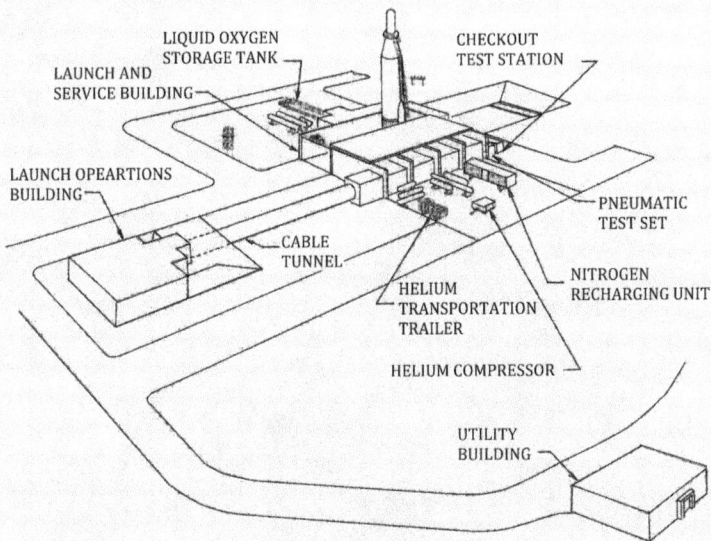

LIQUID OXYGEN
STORAGE TANK

LAUNCH AND
SERVICE BUILDING

CHECKOUT
TEST STATION

LAUNCH OPEARTIONS
BUILDING

PNEUMATIC
TEST SET

CABLE
TUNNEL

NITROGEN
RECHARGING UNIT

HELIUM
TRANSPORTATION
TRAILER

HELIUM COMPRESSOR

UTILITY
BUILDING

20. (*opposite and above*) Fail deadly: the Atlas ALCO comm/control panel. Two sites out of twelve were designated as the command post and the alternate command post. These sites were connected to all other sites in the squadron using telephones. A constant signal was maintained on those lines between a special panel at the command post sites and the ALCO comm/control panel in each Atlas launch control center. The ALCO panel key and the launch control console key had to be turned within three seconds of each other to Commit, the launch setting. The ALCO panel key would work only if the signals from the command post and the alternate were absent, that is, both were shut off. The problem with such a system is self-evident. Courtesy of the U.S. Air Force.

21. (*opposite and above*) A Mk-6 reentry vehicle and assembly from a Titan II
ICBM. The approximately 9-megaton W53 warhead and the deceptively named
"spacer" or "transition assembly" containing penetration aids systems. Atlas E
and F and Titan I missiles had combinations of flares and chaff. The Titan II's
Mk-6 had eight decoy tubes of metallic chaff located behind blowout panels;
these were deployed in space to spoof Soviet radar. The Mk-6 also had an "attitude
stabilization" feature that reduced "its effective radar cross section." Another
decoy was "designed to simulate the radar reflectability of a stabilized Mark 6."
Courtesy of the author.

22. An important positive control and execution mechanism for the Titan II
ICBM was the butterfly valve lock, or BVL, located on the Titan II's stage-1
engine oxidizer butterfly valve. Without the oxidizer, the missile couldn't fly;
the device simply locked the valve closed. After insertion of a code on the coded
switch system, a six-thumbwheel input device, a signal was sent from the BVL
status encoder panel to a lock that was electronically connected to the BVL.
This version, photographed in 2006 at the Titan Museum near Tucson, Arizona,
has subsequently been cut off and the display sanitized for reasons difficult to
determine. Courtesy of the author.

23. Ace in the hole. This is the Minuteman II ICBM in its most basic configuration in a launch facility. From the top down: the reentry vehicle and warhead; the reentry vehicle separation plane spacer in olive green, which contained pitch and spin rockets so the warhead could maneuver after being jettisoned from the third stage to prevent offset aiming by the Soviet ABM system; the guidance and control section, with its missile guidance control computer connected via an umbilical cable to computers in the upper-level equipment room; and then the third-stage motor. Far below in the first stage is the command signals decoder, a crucial positive control and execution mechanism. U.S. Air Force, courtesy of the Air Force Association.

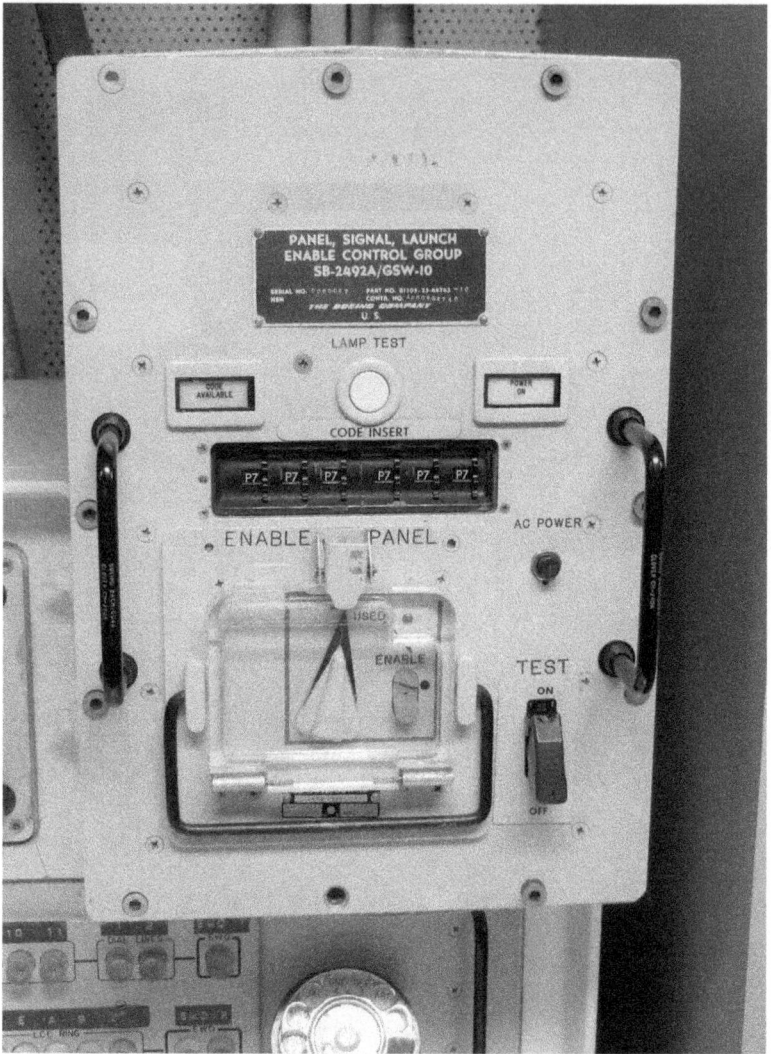

24. Nuclear safety proposals put forth by Secretary of Defense Robert S. McNamara in 1964 evolved into the launch enable control group for the Minuteman ICBM system, installed between 1970 and 1974. The launch enable control group was one of several mechanisms that permitted half of the necessary code to be sent to the command signals decoder mounted inside the missiles, which allowed the igniter system to be activated and the safe/arm switch in the warhead to be armed. Only after another sequence of actions conducted in another launch control facility would the missiles accept commands after the crew's launch keys were turned. Courtesy of the author.

25. This is the RUR-5 anti-submarine rocket (ASROC) missile system aboard the USS *Joseph P. Kennedy* at Falls River, Massachusetts, similar to the one depicted in *The Bedford Incident*. One can clearly see the circular and oval ports for inserting the nuclear weapon's battery and manipulation of the arming system on the eight-shot "pepperbox" launcher. It took more than five officers and crew to prepare and launch a nuclear ASROC, not one, as depicted in the film. Courtesy of the author.

26. (*opposite top*) The boomer psychological thriller was born with Anthony Trew's *Two Hours to Darkness*. No film was made from the book, but several drew inspiration from Trew's scenario. This includes the 1986 made-for-TV thriller *The Fifth Missile*, which itself was based on the novel *The Gold Crew*. The ultimate boomer picture was *Crimson Tide* (1995), which occurs in the 1990s but was derived from the Cold War in the 1980s. Here the USS *Robert E. Lee* demonstrates that a Polaris submarine-launched ballistic missile could also be launched from the surface. Courtesy of the U.S. Navy.

27. (*opposite bottom*) The UGM-73 Poseidon submarine-launched ballistic missile could carry between ten and fourteen Mk-3 reentry vehicles, each of which carried a W68 nuclear warhead. Materials problems reduced the planned 40- to 50-kiloton yield to around half, or 20 kilotons. Each of the forty-one Poseidon-carrying submarines carried sixteen missiles and could service, at a minimum, 160 targets. Courtesy of the author.

28. (*above*) Operation Sandblast, the submerged circumnavigation of Earth by the USS *Triton* in 1960, contained numerous sensitive and classified objectives related to the Polaris missile submarine program. Among these was a psychological study conducted by Dr. Benjamin Weybrew of the submarine's leadership and crew under conditions of prolonged submergence. Based on those findings, ballistic missile submarines were equipped with straitjackets, phenothiazine, and barbiturates. The USS *Triton*'s journey served as the basis for a fictional (and sexualized) study that was central to the plot of *Dr. Strangelove* author Peter George's final novel, the postapocalyptic *Commander-1*. Courtesy of the U.S. Navy.

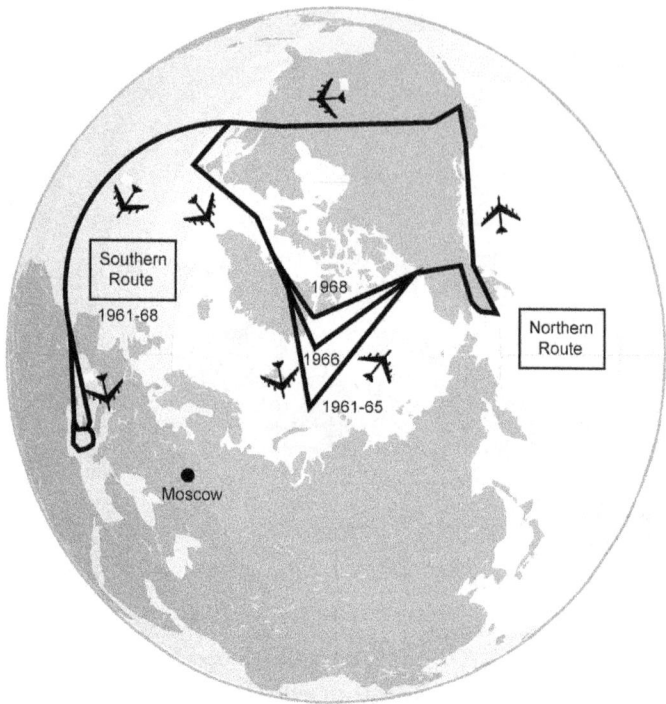

Southern
Route
1961-68

Northern
Route

1968

1966

1961-65

Moscow

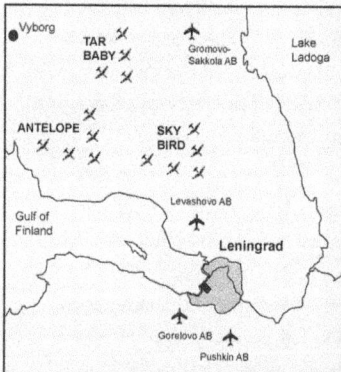

Vyborg

TAR
BABY

Gromovo-
Sakkola AB

Lake
Ladoga

ANTELOPE

SKY
BIRD

Levashovo AB

Gulf of
Finland

Leningrad

Gorelovo AB

Pushkin AB

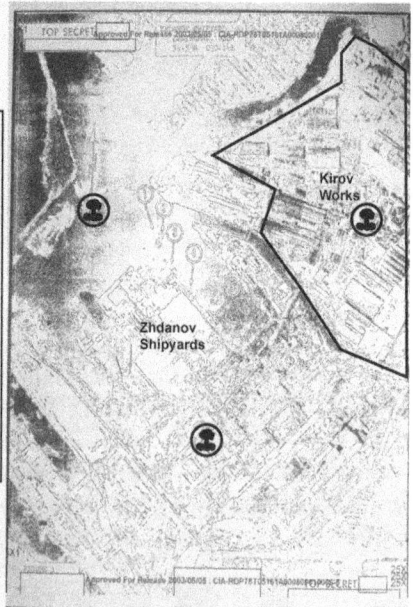

Kirov
Works

Zhdanov
Shipyards

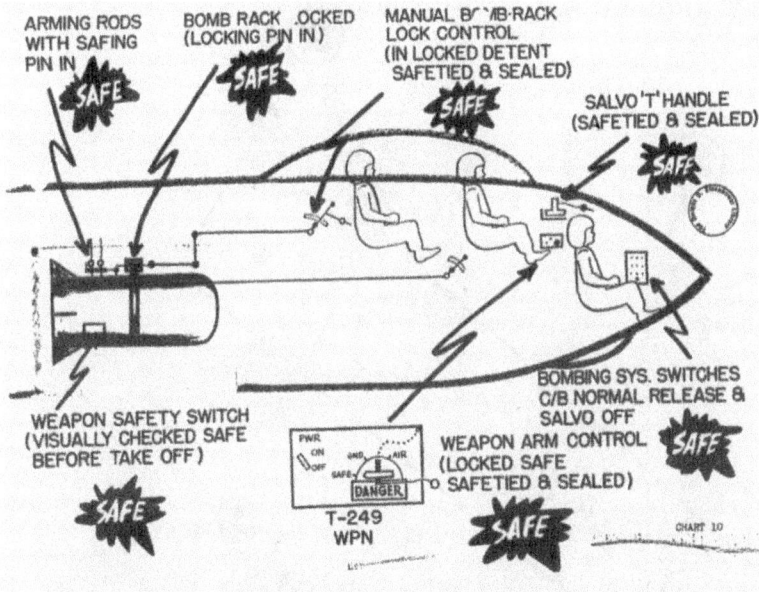

ARMING RODS
WITH SAFING
PIN IN
SAFE

BOMB RACK LOCKED
(LOCKING PIN IN)
SAFE

MANUAL BOMB-RACK
LOCK CONTROL
(IN LOCKED DETENT
SAFETIED & SEALED)
SAFE

SALVO 'T' HANDLE
(SAFETIED & SEALED)
SAFE

WEAPON SAFETY SWITCH
(VISUALLY CHECKED SAFE
BEFORE TAKE OFF)
SAFE

T-249
WPN

PWR
ON
OFF
GND
SAFE
AIR
DANGER

WEAPON ARM CONTROL
(LOCKED SAFE
SAFETIED & SEALED)

BOMBING SYS. SWITCHES
C/B NORMAL RELEASE &
SALVO OFF
SAFE

CHART 10

29. (*opposite top*) The diverse Airborne Alert Force flight tracks stabilized by 1961 and were code-named Chrome Dome. The Northern Route path was progressively moved back toward the Canadian archipelago throughout the 1960s. Airborne alert evolved from a temporary survival mechanism into a crisis-signaling tool. Courtesy of the author.

30. (*opposite bottom*) Projected strikes by the B-36s of the 11th Bombardment Wing (Heavy) against industrial facilities in Leningrad as part of the 1953 Emergency War Plan. Courtesy of the author.

31. (*above*) This excerpt from a briefing provided to President Dwight D. Eisenhower depicts the safety devices established for B-47 aircraft so that thermonuclear weapons could be maneuvered in peacetime with presidential authorization under Project Fail Safe (later changed to Positive Control). Courtesy of the Dwight D. Eisenhower Library.

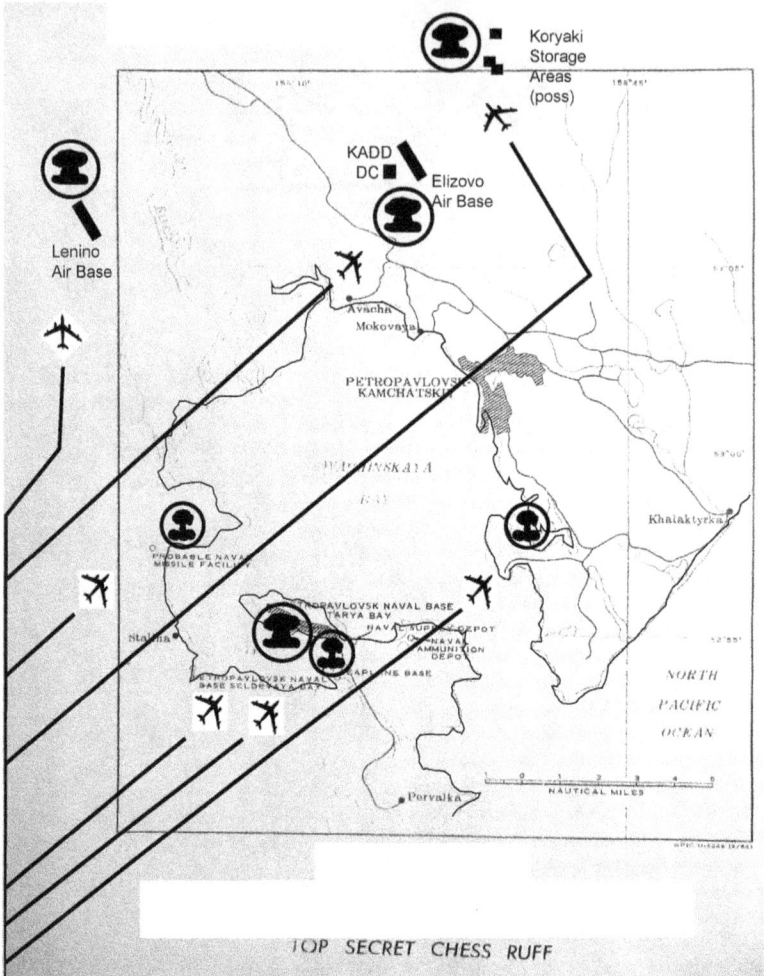

Koryaki Storage Areas (poss)

KADD DC ■ Elizovo Air Base

Lenino Air Base

Avacha Mokovaya

PETROPAVLOVSK KAMCHATSKI

AVALINSKAYA BAY

Khalaktyrka

PROBABLE NAVAL MISSILE FACILITY

PETROPAVLOVSK NAVAL BASE TARYA BAY

NAVAL SUPPLY DEPOT

NAVAL AMMUNITION DEPOT

Stalina

PETROPAVLOVSK NAVAL BASE SELDEVAYA BAY

SEAPLANE BASE

NORTH PACIFIC OCEAN

Porvalka

0 1 2 3 4 5
NAUTICAL MILES

TOP SECRET CHESS RUFF

32. Projected strikes by the B-47s of the 9th Bombardment Wing (Medium) against Soviet air bases and naval facilities around Petropavlovsk on the Kamchatka Peninsula as part of the 1960 Basic War Plan. Courtesy of the author.

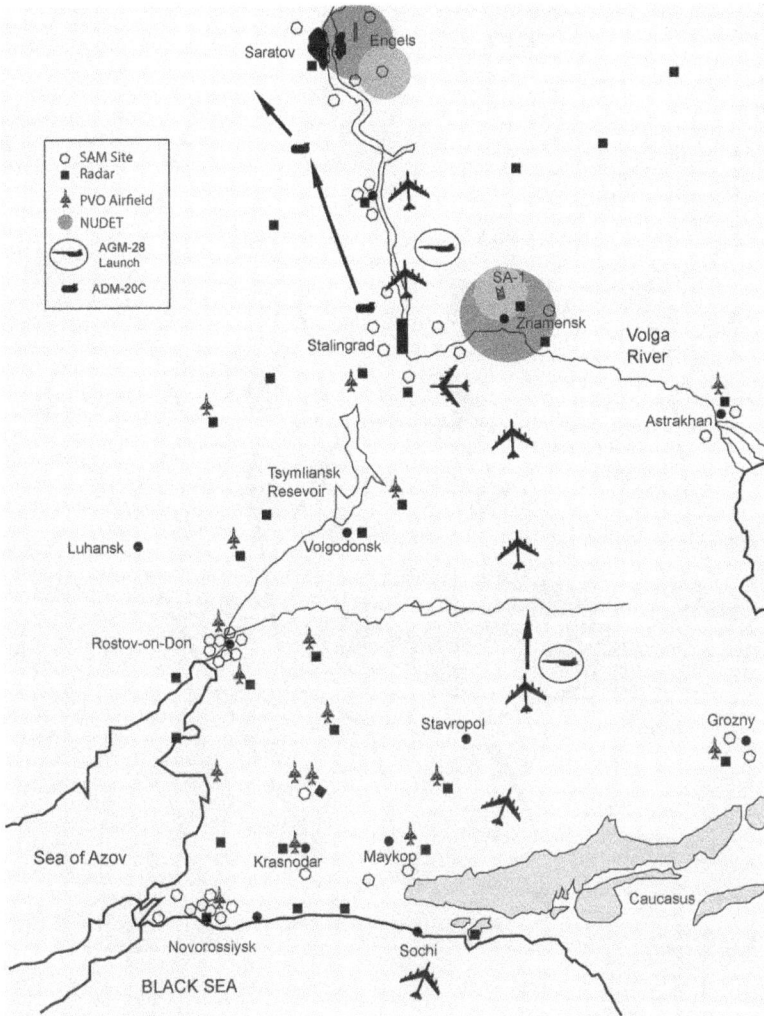

Legend:
- ○ SAM Site
- ■ Radar
- ⚘ PVO Airfield
- ● NUDET
- AGM-28 Launch
- ADM-20C

Map labels:
Saratov · Engels · SA-1 · Znamensk · Volga River · Stalingrad · Astrakhan · Tsymliansk Resevoir · Luhansk · Volgodonsk · Rostov-on-Don · Stavropol · Grozny · Sea of Azov · Krasnodar · Maykop · Caucasus · Novorossiysk · Sochi · BLACK SEA

33. Projected strikes by a B-52 of the 843rd Bombardment Wing (Fictional) conducted from the Chrome Dome Southern Route against key Soviet counterforce targets as part of the 1964 edition of the SIOP. Courtesy of the author.

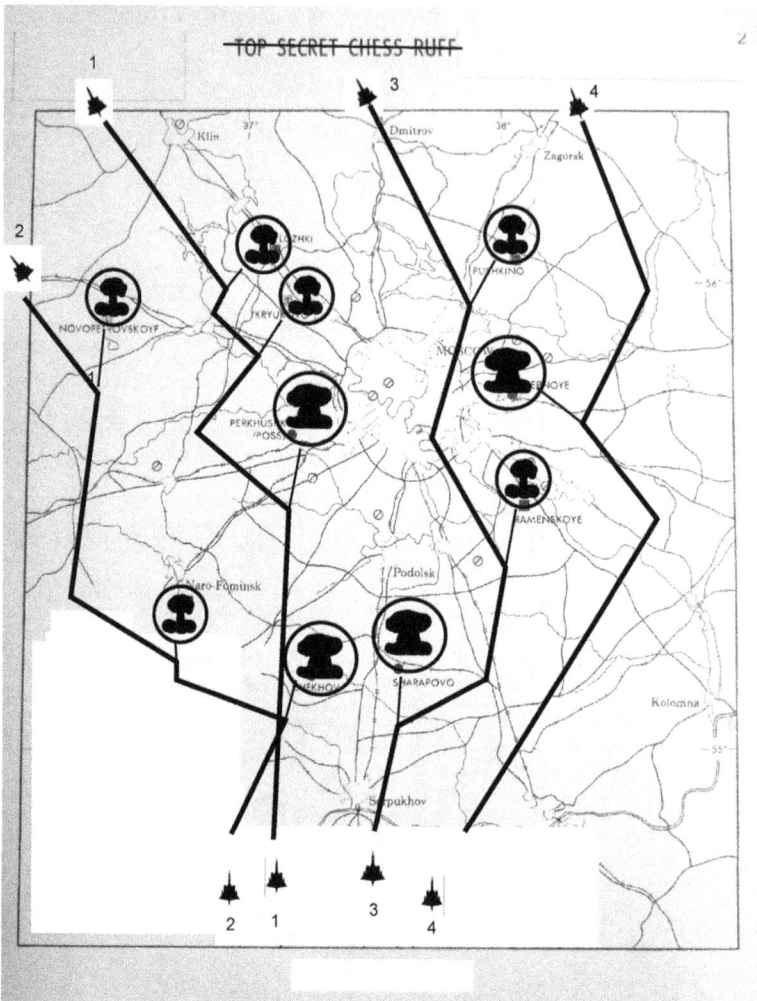

34. Projected strikes conducted against key
Soviet command-and-control targets by the
B-58 Glass Road deployment package from
the 305th Bombardment Wing operating
from Torrejon Air Base, Spain, as a pre-SIOP
contingency strike. Courtesy of the author.

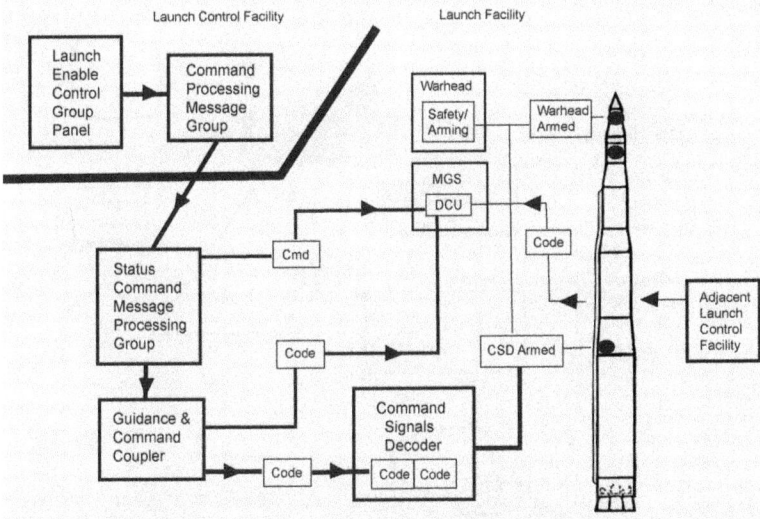

35. The positive control and execution measures for the Minuteman ICBM force depicting the electromechanical and other safety mechanisms critical for the execution of the Emergency War Order. Courtesy of the author.

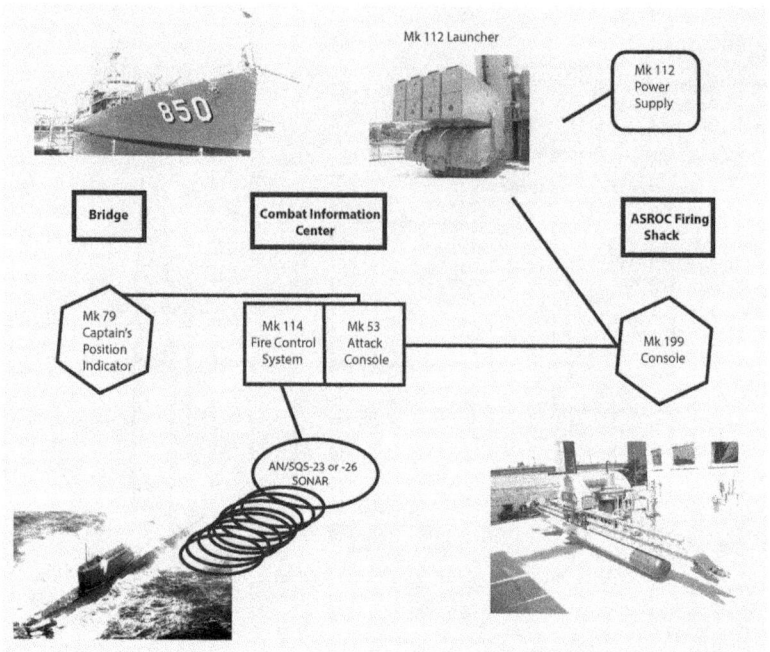

Mk 112 Launcher

Mk 112 Power Supply

Bridge

Combat Information Center

ASROC Firing Shack

Mk 79 Captain's Position Indicator

Mk 114 Fire Control System

Mk 53 Attack Console

Mk 199 Console

AN/SQS-23 or -26 SONAR

36. The safety and release mechanisms for the ASROC aboard the destroyer USS *Joseph P. Kennedy.* Courtesy of the author.

FIVE

Peace Is Our Profession

Gen. Thomas Power and Nuclear Crisis Behavior

Gen. Thomas Power has been accused of being mentally unbalanced, in part because of his decision to increase SAC's defense readiness condition to DEFCON 2 during the Cuban Missile Crisis. With assertions that he was the basis for Gen. Jack D. Ripper in *Dr. Strangelove*, some imply that Power acted alone in raising SAC's DEFCON level; others decry his announcement of this move over open communications. Kennedy's national security advisor McGeorge Bundy asserts, "The fact that [the SAC commander, General Power] sent out an alert over the open channels without authorization was an extremely arrogant and undisciplined thing to do.... General Power had simply taken it upon himself to rub the Soviets' noses in their nuclear inferiority."[1]

Raymond Garthoff, who worked in the State Department at the time, asserts that "the SAC-full-alert process was reported 'in the clear' rather than in normal encoded messages; not known in Moscow was that this remarkable display of American power was unauthorized by and unknown to the president, the secretary of defense, the chairman of the Joint Chiefs, and the Ex Comm as they so carefully calibrated and controlled action in this intensifying confrontation. The decision for this bold action was taken by General Power, commander in chief of SAC, on his own initiative: he decided to 'rub it in.'"[2]

In reality Power's actions during the Cuban Missile Crisis fit an existing pattern that was far removed from anything resembling rogue or unbalanced activity. Four instances demonstrate this: the

1960 Mayday alert, the 1961 Berlin Crisis, the Cuban Missile Crisis, and SAC's response to the Kennedy assassination in 1963.

The U-2 Affair Alert, May 1960

On 1 May 1960 Soviet air defense forces downed a CIA U-2 reconnaissance aircraft over the Soviet Union. In Moscow on 9 May, at the anniversary celebrations for the Liberation of Czechoslovakia, Nikita Khrushchev "cornered" the Pakistani envoy Salman Ali and thundered at him, "In the future, if any American plane is allowed to use Peshawar as a base of operations against the Soviet Union, we will retaliate immediately." And "to Oskar Gundersen of Norway: 'You knew about these flights I can see it in your eyes.'" These warnings were formalized by 13 May, and Turkey was added to the list of countries threatened with "military attack" and "retaliatory measures."[3] That was now two NATO members to be threatened with attack by the Soviet Union. To up the ante, Khrushchev's rhetoric expanded to include the United States.[4]

This was all on the eve of the Four-Power summit—United States, United Kingdom, France, USSR—scheduled in Paris and designed to address matters related to tensions over Germany. When President Charles de Gaulle of France and Eisenhower met privately before the summit and "DeGaulle noted Khrushchev's threat to attack U-2 bases in Turkey, Japan, and elsewhere, Eisenhower grimly replied, 'Rockets can travel in two directions.'"[5]

At five seconds after midnight GMT on 15 May, an SS-6 Sapwood ballistic missile was detected lifting off from a launch site at Tyuratam by the FPS-17 backscatter radar surveillance site located at Diyarbakir, Turkey. This ICBM released a capsule, which was tracked by the Spacetrack network, and the data were fed into the NORAD command post. The space vehicle was initially designated Sputnik 4, and its purpose was initially unknown.[6] The National Security Agency was in the process of establishing its new space signals intelligence program, leaving the informal Kettering Group to speculate as to what Sputnik 4 was up to. During the course of the day, while the Big Four were meeting, Tass announced that Sputnik 4 had passed over the summit site in Paris.[7]

It was a long and heated day while Khrushchev continued to make threats. Unlike the other three leaders at the summit, Khrushchev brought his Soviet defense minister, Marshal Malinovsky, who "stuck to Khrushchev like a leech" during the proceedings.[8] At 2:30 a.m. Paris time, Secretary of Defense Thomas S. Gates personally contacted Gen. Lauris Norstad at his headquarters in Paris and simultaneously sent a message to the Joint Chiefs of Staff in Washington. Gates instructed all joint commands to assume a "high state of command readiness." Gen. Nathan Twining, the chairman of the Joint Chiefs, consulted the relatively new DEFCON system at 3:05 a.m. (Paris time) and determined that this request constituted DEFCON 3. In a hasty telephone conference with the other Joint Chiefs at 3:20 a.m., the Joint Chiefs agreed to go to DEFCON 3. This message went out 3:56 a.m.[9]

Gen. Thomas Power placed SAC on DEFCON 3. As part of that alerting process, "the entire SAC Strike Force was generated and made ready for combat." This involved emptying all of the operational storage sites supporting SAC, including "the entire [Aviation Depot Group] stockpile."[10] The Joint Chiefs also contacted the chairman of the Canadian Chiefs of Staff Committee, Gen. Charles Foulkes, "advising of the increased command readiness of US units" but adding that "no Canadian action required" at this time.[11]

The SAC Alert Force, on the ground and airborne, was readied. The SAC Command Post, using the Short Order high-frequency radio system, instructed the Alert Force to stand by to receive a message. B-52s on airborne alert were contacted and told to stand by for message traffic. According to one participant, this was "not a procedure in the book of instructions." When the message came, the tense crews were told, "All SAC Airborne Alert aircraft will stand by for a roll call and respond with their tactical callsigns. In clear text they called each aircraft."[12] The SAC Command Post in Omaha also instructed the Alert Force to "stand by for a roll call and respond with their tactical call signs."

At the time we had no idea what may be happening in the world but the procedure was not a normal one. Something very unusual must have happened. The communications means in use was the same one on which we would be given the "Go-Codes." . . . After landing we were told a U-2 had been shot down by the Russians. To remind the Soviets of our presence in the air SAC called the roll of our strike force which in effect said "By the way USSR, don't do anything dumb as we are ready to respond and will if you launch a missile."[13]

Letting the Soviets know that B-52s equipped with two to four thermonuclear weapons each were at a high state of readiness off Franz Joseph Land in the Arctic and were joined by one-third to one-half of the SAC bomber force on ground alert may not have been what Secretary of Defense Gates had in mind.

Or was it? There are conflicting views. The historian Michael Beschloss states in *May-Day*, "Thomas Gates concluded that the Summit was about to collapse and fracture relations with the Soviet Union. Especially with the President, the Secretary of State, himself and other top officials in Paris, he thought it vital to increase American military readiness for such a crisis."[14] Sherman Kent, the CIA liaison supporting the summit, in a 1972 article in *Studies in Intelligence* wrote:

> Mr. Gates began to be concerned about the possible military implications of a breakup of the Summit in the atmosphere of Khrushchev's belligerency. Some time later, he owned that the thought of the Pearl Harbor attack, coming as it had in the middle of negotiations, had crossed his mind. Early in the evening, after hearing [U.K. prime minister Harold] Macmillan brief the President on his session with Khrushchev and getting Mr. Macmillan's gloomy forecast for the morrow, he went back to his hotel, picked up his White House phone and talked directly to the Acting Secretary of Defense, James Douglas. He told Mr. Douglas that he felt that the prudent thing to do was to have the Armed Forces assume some alert basis which, in his judgment, would include notifying the Headquarters of the principal commands. . . . Having made the call, he returned to the Residence and immediately reported his action to the President who approved it. . . . In Washington, meanwhile, Mr. Douglas conferred with General Twining, Chairman of the Joint Chiefs of Staff, and together they decided the technical meaning which they would apply to Mr. Gates's oral instruction. They checked out the

technicalities of their decision with Mr. Gates and at about nine p.m. local time sent forth the word.[15]

At 4:23 a.m., Secretary Gates was informed that all forces were at DEFCON 3, but the Joint Chiefs were now "requesting background information used as a basis for his directive." There was no reply from Paris.[16]

American media outlets noticed the increased alert status and were demanding a statement: "Panic after US Military Combat Alert" was one headline.[17] Deputy Secretary of Defense James H. Douglas Jr. prepared a press release explaining that they were conducting a communications exercise and sent it over to Gates in Paris. He then asked Gates for a "recommendation for affirmative response if asked whether or not President and [the secretary of defense] advised of the Communication Test." Again there was no response from Paris.[18]

DEFCON 3 was in effect until 10:00 p.m. (Paris time) on 16 May, when it was rescinded by Gates. At a 24 May meeting of the National Security Council, Eisenhower commented on the affair:

> The President believed that certain elements in the U.S. would try to make it appear that we had instituted a general military alert on Sunday night, May 15. All that happened was that Secretary Gates had asked him whether it would not be appropriate at that time to make sure that our long-range communications were working efficiently. He had agreed that such a communications alert might be ordered. This test alert was the kind of alert conducted regularly. The President felt that in our public statement we should play down the May 15 alert by indicating that it was a test of our long-range communications facilities. Secretary Gates said that the alert also involved a quiet increase in military command personnel on duty.[19]

This would have been news to the 1,500 or so personnel from the 3079th Aviation Depot Wing slinging a thousand nuclear weapons around its operational storage sites: "The resultant return . . . to storage and inspection of the entire . . . stockpile created temporary heavy workloads."[20]

So why did Secretary of Defense Gates give an order that generated DEFCON 3? It is possible that he did not understand the new DEFCON system and what it entailed. He requested a heightened state of readiness, and the Joint Chiefs concluded this approximated DEFCON 3.

One possibility was Harold Macmillan's "gloomy" meeting with Eisenhower on the evening of 16 May after meeting Khrushchev earlier spurred Eisenhower and Gates into action. During the day de Gaulle pointed out that a Soviet space vehicle was orbiting above Paris. Though what he meant was that this activity was the moral equivalent of the U-2 in the context of the summit debate with Khrushchev, Macmillan probably saw it differently.[21] Having just been threatened the previous year by Khrushchev via the British ambassador in Moscow, and knowing the vulnerability of his island to a small number of hydrogen bombs, it was highly likely that Macmillan was extremely concerned that American U-2 flights from the United Kingdom as well as Royal Air Force involvement in the U-2 program (code-named Oldster) might also put his country on the retaliatory target list alongside Turkey, Norway, and Pakistan.[22] Indeed perhaps Khrushchev threatened Macmillan directly in order to get him to pressure Eisenhower to accede to Soviet demands.

Another possibility is that Macmillan had some new intelligence brought to his attention through his services or even a direct and specific military threat presented by Khrushchev and then conveyed that to Eisenhower and Gates. This may be why Gates contacted Norstad first, to ensure allied forces in Europe were not caught in what he feared might be a Pearl Harbor situation. Alternatively Gates may have alerted American forces to reassure Macmillan and de Gaulle in the face of the more general threats that emanated from Khrushchev.

What was the impact of the alert on Khrushchev? This is even more difficult to discern as he made no written reference to it and there appears to be no available record of how the Soviets responded. The summit was postponed by Khrushchev to some time after the 1960 U.S. elections in an effort to deliberately snub Eisenhower. Clearly that had more to do with the mechanics of the summit and little to do with the alert. If there was a specific threat made to Macmillan

PEACE IS OUR PROFESSION

and Eisenhower, going to DEFCON 3 and conducting a roll call of the SAC alert forces appears to have offset it. This action also established a precedent for the commander in chief of SAC.

Kaysen's Raid, October 1961

During the escalating Berlin Crisis of 1961 President Kennedy asked Secretary of Defense McNamara to look into flexible options involving nuclear weapons.[23] Carl Kaysen, who worked for National Security Advisor McGeorge Bundy in the White House, told his superior that the United States must "privately convey our determination to Khrushchev." In Kaysen's view, increasing the SAC forces on airborne alert was a preferred method because the twelve B-52s covered thirty-six targets. A total of sixty-eight B-52s with 150 nuclear weapons, or one-eighth of the force, could be put up without degrading the alert posture. "The electronic traffic involved in the operations of a force of this size would be such as to make it unmistakably clear to the Soviet Union what was happening."[24]

From 14 August to 5 September a small, highly classified group from the White House, the secretary of defense's office, and the U.S. Air Force crafted a nuclear option for the president. Kaysen, Gen. Maxwell Taylor, Henry Rowen from Defense, and Gen. David Burchinal from SAC examined new Corona satellite information analyzed from missions on 16 June and 7 July. These data indicated conclusively that the Soviet ICBM force was concentrated on a handful of sites and was vulnerable to a nuclear strike by an augmented airborne alert force.[25]

This study, for which there were only five recipients, including Kennedy, was completed just as the Berlin Crisis worsened. A U.S. Army battle group of 1,500 troops was sent as a probe down the Berlin access route on 20 August, while Vice President Lyndon B. Johnson was flown into the beleaguered city. The battle group was stopped briefly, but the Soviets backed off. Shortly afterward, however, on 30 August, Moscow announced it was breaking the nuclear test moratorium and detonated two nuclear weapons in three days. Even more ominous, the Red Army retained thousands of troops that had been scheduled for discharge. Gen. Curtis LeMay, coordinating with NATO supreme allied commander Lauris Norstad, brought twenty B-47 nuclear bombers to bases in Spain.[26]

It was against the backdrop of the Soviet nuclear test series that the White House–authored strike study was debated. From 1 September to 31 October the Soviet Union detonated forty-seven nuclear weapons. Of note, at key points in the crisis seven of these tests included the launching of R-12 or R-14 ballistic missiles with live nuclear warheads in the megaton-yield range. These were subsequently detonated in the atmosphere. Other tests included airdropped megaton-yield bombs. Finally, on 30 October 1961, a 54- to 57-megaton bomb was dropped on Novaya Zemlya island in the Arctic by a Soviet TU-95 bomber.[27]

The timing of the larger tests, which mostly took place from 10 to 20 September, coincided with discussions among the White House, the secretary of defense, and the Joint Chiefs over conducting a nuclear strike against the Soviet ICBM force. It is entirely possible that the Soviet spy Lt. Col. William Whalen, who was assigned to the Joint Chiefs of Staff, got wind of the planning and fed it back to his controllers and that Khrushchev was signaling the Americans. It is equally possible the events are not connected and Khrushchev's signal was more generalized.

William Kaufman, who was involved in the study, recalled that there was a lot of "desperate" activity at the time.[28] The existing nuclear war plan, Single Integrated Operational Plan (SIOP) 62, was just too massive a response to the Berlin situation and was essentially directed against anything that was Communist. Within twenty-eight hours, 2,300 delivery systems with 3,400 megaton-yield nuclear weapons would be used against targets in the Soviet Union, China, and Eastern Europe. The Alert Force, if employed alone, would kill 55 percent of the urban population of the Soviet Union, and with the full force, 71 percent of the urban population, within seventy-two hours, taking into account all of the weapons effects. Kaysen wondered, "Is this really an appropriate next step after the repulse of a three-division attack across the zonal border between East and West Germany? Will the President be ready to take it? . . . We should be prepared to initiate general war by our own first strike, but one planned for this occasion, rather than planned to implement a strategy of massive retaliation. We should seek the smallest possible list of targets, focusing on the long-range striking capacity of the Soviets, and avoiding, as much as possible, casualties and damage in Soviet civil society."[29]

This "raid," as Kaysen called it, should hit eighty-eight desired ground zeros. One-third of the bombers could each hit two targets within twenty minutes of each other. B-52s could carry four Mk-28 or Mk-43 thermonuclear bombs: "We must get a minimum of 41 bombers into the Soviet airspace and over their initial targets with no more than 15 minutes between the first and last bomb drop." One hour later the follow-on force would hit. The weapons would be airburst, and "mortalities from the initial raid might be less than 1,000,000 and probably not much more than 500,000." Kaysen suggested, "We should be able to communicate two things to Khrushchev: first, that we intend to concentrate on military targets unless he is foolish enough to hit our cities; secondly, that we are prepared to withhold the bulk of our force from the offensive, provided he accepts our terms."[30]

Maxwell Taylor presented his summary of the study to Kennedy on 19 September, the day before Kennedy was scheduled to meet with Gen. Lyman Lemnitzer, the new chairman of the Joint Chiefs, and the SAC commander General Power to discuss the SIOP-62 nuclear war plan.[31]

Unfortunately the notes taken during the 20 September meeting do not cover all that was discussed. These notes, taken by Maj. Gen. C. V. Clifton, suggest that the meeting was an attempt to resolve an intelligence disagreement between Lemnitzer and Taylor on one side, and Power and LeMay on the other, relating to the number of Soviet ICBM sites and whether or not renewed U-2 flights should be used to confirm this number. Yet the meeting was supposed to discuss SIOP-62 and the Kaysen study's relationship to it. The most important line buried in the conference memo is this: "In response to questions by the President, General Power indicated his belief that the time of our greatest danger of a Soviet surprise attack is now and during the coming year. If a general atomic war is inevitable, the U.S. should strike first—presumably after locating the essential Soviet nuclear targets."[32]

The meeting ended with Kennedy tasking the group to answer two questions: "How much information does the Soviet Union need, and how long do they need to launch their missiles?"[33] Lemnitzer provided the answer to the second question a week later: if on standby, they would need one to three hours; if on alert, fifteen to thirty minutes.[34] There was no further discussion of Kaysen's raid. Power presented an argument for a preemption option, which the president did not accept. Clearly Power was obedient, as there was no strike.

The Cuban Missile Crisis, 1962

The Cuban Missile Crisis is central to the Cold War narrative. Next to Vietnam, it is the most written about Cold War subject in the United States and was the subject of two films: *The Missiles of October* (1974) and *Thirteen Days* (2000). The Cuban Missile Crisis was also the overarching context for those going to theaters to watch *Dr. Strangelove* and *Fail-Safe* in 1964.

The predominant public narrative of the crisis, probably best exemplified by Robert F. Kennedy and Ted Sorensen's book *Thirteen Days* (1969), which forms the narrative basis for the two films, depicts the crisis as confined to part of the month of October 1962, not within the context of the 1958–59 and 1961 Berlin crises, let alone Khrushchev's belligerent behavior in 1956 and 1958.[35] In the *Thirteen Days* narrative a U-2 aircraft discovers that the Soviets are placing ballistic missiles in Cuba, ninety miles from the United States. The gung-ho leaders of the armed forces, led by LeMay, want to bomb and invade Cuba but are held back by the more rational political leadership, who suggest a blockade and diplomatic action instead. More military bungling follows: the conflict was in part generated by the unwillingness of the military to follow orders expeditiously and remove obsolete Jupiter missiles from Turkey, which, by implication, is the cause of the crisis since Khrushchev is putting missiles in Cuba to offset those in Turkey. These must be traded for the Soviet missiles in Cuba.[36]

But before that can happen, the crisis deepens. The military insists on further measures that would generate the conditions they want: an excuse to unleash SAC on a preemptive strike on the Soviet Union.

A courageous president (and his loyal but beleaguered brother and their staffs) now have to fight on two fronts: Khrushchev on one side and an unreliable American military leadership on the other, in order to prevent nuclear war. They valiantly succeed through a combination of rationality and goodwill. Everybody sees the error of their ways, except the recalcitrant American military leadership, and peace and balance are restored to the system.

Despite the fact that there is a substantial academic literature that has dissected every possible aspect of the crisis and in some cases refuted or otherwise explained the complexity of the situation in great detail, the *Thirteen Days* narrative still predominates in popular culture, despite the fact that the Kennedy and Sorensen memoir has been debunked.[37] If an audience is confronted with *Thirteen Days* and *Dr. Strangelove* and has no other frame of historical reference, the narratives of both films become mutually reinforcing: elected civilian leadership, good; military leadership, bad. The Russians are the accidental victims of the American military machine and its rogue leadership. One shudders when considering an out-of-context narrative arc that includes *Thirteen Days*, *Dr. Strangelove*, and Oliver Stone's film *JFK*.

The reality of the Cuban Missile Crisis was substantially different from this portrayal. In May 1962 the Soviet Presidium debated a strategic proposal made by Khrushchev, who was stinging after the climb-down from Berlin in 1961. He was increasingly convinced that Cuba was, for the Soviets, the functional and moral equivalent of Berlin. There were indications that American covert activity was increasingly directed against the revolution there. At the same time, a new American ICBM, the Titan, was coming on line and NATO was deploying fewer than a hundred Jupiter and Thor missiles in Europe to counter the several hundred Soviet medium- and intermediate-range missiles deployed by 1961. Therefore an aggressive "offensive" policy in Cuba "would force the United States to accommodate Moscow's perceived needs in Central Europe and elsewhere. The Cuba ploy would ensure that this necessary change in the balance of power occurred."[38] As one observer explained, "Khrushchev's fear of losing Cuba was similar to his concern about the survival of [East Germany]."[39]

Khrushchev's methodology was to deploy Soviet intermediate- and medium-range ballistic missiles to forward areas so they could hit the United States, as the longer-range R-16 ICBMs were technologically immature and problematic. The next move would be to publicly announce the deployment for a global audience (especially Khrushchev's competitor Mao) and restore what he saw as lost prestige after Berlin. Though Khrushchev publicly claimed that the Cuban operation was a balancing act against the handful of Jupiter missiles in Turkey and Italy, had he looked at his intelligence analysis, as his head of Strategic Rocket Forces, Marshal Sergei Biryuzov, surely did, he would have known that the Jupiter "threat" was not directed at Soviet strategic missile forces, cities, or even the Soviet leadership.[40] It was directed against the Soviet air defense and forces targeting NATO. This information was likely provided to the Soviets by the spy William H. Whalen from the Joint Chiefs of Staff and information from the French spy ring in NATO.[41]

The details of the Soviet missile deployment plan, dubbed Operation Anadyr, have been discussed in detail elsewhere. In essence, thirty-six R-12 and twenty-four R-14 ballistic missiles, with their megaton-yield warheads, along with six IL-28 nuclear bombers and their freefall bombs, battlefield support nuclear weapons, and nuclear cruise missiles, were to be deployed to Cuba.[42] What has not been discussed previously is another secret deployment of Soviet ballistic missiles that were placed within range of the United States to cover targets that the Cuban-based missiles could not reach. This allowed the Soviets to cover targets in the northwestern United States, western Canada, and most important, Alaska, where the large Ballistic Missile Early Warning System (BMEWS) radars were located. The Anadyr deployment placed ballistic missiles less than five minutes' flight time from Clear, Alaska; they could blind North American aerospace defense forces very rapidly and permit the undetected launch of ICBMs from the missile fields in east central Siberia.[43]

The Cuban and Siberian deployments put the main American deterrent force, SAC, directly under the gun. The strategic calculations for the period look like this: The Cuban and Siberian deployments offset SAC bases in North America. The existing Soviet medium-

and intermediate-range ballistic missile deployments in the western Soviet Union offset the ballistic missiles and bomber aircraft available to NATO. With no U.S. or NATO capability to threaten to escalate to nuclear weapons use in a crisis, the Soviet moves made the world safe for conventional warfare, a field in which the Soviets retained a crushing superiority. At the very least, it could have emboldened yet another Khrushchev-led run against West Berlin. As the actor portraying Gen. Maxwell Taylor correctly declares in *Thirteen Days*, the deployment of missiles to Cuba was a "massively destabilizing" move.

With the idea that the Soviets were somehow innocent victims of American military aggression disposed of, let us now turn to the Camelot version of the Frocks versus the Brass Hats. *Thirteen Days* frequently portrays the supposedly valiant efforts by White House appointments secretary Kenny O'Donnell to counteract LeMay's supposed attempts to generate excuses for nuclear retaliation: "They want a war, Jack, and they're arranging things to get one." Bruce Greenwood's John F. Kennedy exasperatingly remarks, "I'll tell you one thing, Kenny. Those brass hats have one big advantage. That is, if we do what they want us to do, there's none of us gonna be alive to tell them they were wrong." Kevin Conway's Curtis LeMay makes disparaging comments about the Kennedys throughout the film. There is, however, no evidence that the U.S. Air Force leadership was actively and deliberately generating a nuclear war with the Soviet Union on their own during the Cuban Missile Crisis.

This leads us to a very important aspect of the crisis: the role of the change in the American DEFCON from 3 to 2 on 24 October. The change in the DEFCON is taken matter-of-factly in the bulk of the crisis literature. Yet this was a major strategic move, and there is little analysis of why it took place, just that it was important, dramatic, and one step closer to nuclear war. Conversely the film *Thirteen Days* depicts Kennedy getting upset with his military advisor, Taylor, over the DEFCON change, which, according to the film, was not made by a presidential decision and generated a signal to Khrushchev that Kennedy did not intend to make.

What exactly happened when the DEFCON level changed, and

how was that decision taken? Was this in fact rogue activity, a nuclear coup d'état of sorts, as some have alleged? First, Gen. Thomas White had employed SAC alertness for signaling during the Eisenhower administration while Power was CINCSAC. Power previously used SAC communications to "signal" the Soviets during the Mayday alert in 1960. Second, during the 1961 Berlin Crisis, Power expressed his opinion on how SAC should be employed, that is, preemptively. His opinion was taken under consideration by Kennedy, who ultimately chose not to take that route. Power was compliant. There was no track record of rogue activity.

Third, Power had the authority to raise SAC's DEFCON level. For the most part, the nature of the DEFCON is generally misunderstood, even today. DEFCON 1 does not necessarily mean war. DEFCON 1 is defined as "the maximum state of readiness to be assumed preparatory to implementing contingency or war plans." Going to DEFCON 1 does not automatically trigger the implementation of those plans. Additionally "the actions indicated for each DEFCON should not be considered absolute, since a commander or other competent authority may decide to apply certain measures on a condition earlier or later than planned." Notably DEFCONs are "unclassified and may be transmitted accordingly during actual emergency conditions." Furthermore they can be established by a commander in chief of a unified or specified command "or by higher authority." In the early days of the DEFCON system, "use of atomic weapons" was even predelegated to the Joint Chiefs of Staff.[44]

The DEFCON 2 move was much more than just about "rubbing the Soviet's noses in nuclear inferiority." Power clearly stated that on 15 October he attended a Joint Chiefs meeting in which General Taylor asked for recommendations on what needed to be done if there was to be an invasion of Cuba. Among the other moves, Power explained that SAC needed to go to DEFCON 2, generate and disperse its bomber force, and increase the Airborne Alert Force: "History tells us what happened to the recommendations to invade Cuba; however the three suggestions made by SAC were implemented." And when they were implemented, there was no dispute by Taylor, nor were the orders rescinded, strongly suggesting that Taylor concurred with the activity even if it was not expressly ordered. Indeed Taylor noted in his memoirs that Power "had the task of providing the strategic shield under which our conventional forces could mobilize and operate with minimum danger of strategic attack by the USSR."[45] Sheldon Stern, a Kennedy Library historian, notes that McNamara "approved a first-ever [Joint Chiefs] request to raise SAC bombers to DEFCON 2."[46]

Let us examine the objective circumstances Power found himself in on that October night in 1962. In his words, "this is what caused the situation to become so acute, th[ey] obviously could fire into our soft underbelly with no warning and could, for example, knock out all the command and control, Washington and SAC headquarters, and time that with a missile attack over BMEWS, and maybe catch the whole thing on the ground."[47] The missile warning system and its communications were demonstrably vulnerable to enemy action, and there were teething troubles with BMEWS and the Missile Defense Alarm System (MIDAS). The Fylingdales BMEWS site was not fully operational, and the AT&T phone system connecting Power with SAC's forces was demonstrably vulnerable to sabotage. NORAD and thus SAC also lacked the ability to identify and respond to a Fractional Orbital Bombardment System. Power was seriously concerned about the "threat of a missile orbiting around the southern pole, or a satellite carrier vehicle." Note this: "missile," singular. There were significant and identified concerns in SAC about the effects of electromagnetic pulses on the ICBM force as well as on the command system generated by a very small number of detonations, possibly even a single detonation. First-generation American ICBMS were not only vulnerable to these pulses but had a very slow reaction time. The JFK-era Post-Attack Command and Control System was only partially deployed in 1962, as were the measures used by the National Command Authorities to protect themselves. In any event, Kennedy chose not to implement them and stayed in the capital, thus increasing the vulnerability of the National Command Authorities. McNamara and Taylor also remained in the Washington DC area.

Power knew there was no capability to intercept a ballistic missile attack other than through preemption. The forward-based SAC forces in the United Kingdom, Spain, Morocco, and Okinawa were well within range of several hundred Soviet intermediate- and medium-range ballistic missiles, and there was no reliable system to warn of a launch from their bases in western Ukraine or from Siberia. There was no independently credible U.S. Navy submarine-launched ballistic missile force yet. Though there was at least one strategic nuclear missile–carrying submarine at sea, it had technical problems. Furthermore, Soviet missiles were more accurate because they had better geodetic information.[48] Introducing more B-52s into the Airborne Alert Force, dispersing B-47 bombers, and alerting missiles were the only moves Power could make to present a credible deterrent posture. And that is exactly what DEFCON 2 produced. Power himself was surprised that he had strategic warning and had the time to make appropriate preparations: "We had never really counted on [getting] it."[49]

So was Power a rogue entity like Gen. Jack D. Ripper when he moved SAC to DEFCON 2? There was a tendency for SAC to "lean forward" in a crisis. This was never discouraged by higher military or, for that matter, political authorities, so rightly or wrongly, precedents existed to do so in this crisis. Under the existing rules, CINC-SAC could raise the DEFCON level to 2. Whether those rules were clearly understood by the political authorities and their satraps is another matter. These were the "best and the brightest," after all, and should not complain, even in retrospect, if they did not understand.

The question that remains unasked by almost all observers of the crisis and those who deal with nuclear issues is this: What effect did the DEFCON 2 change and the in-clear message by Power have on Khrushchev, and thus on the course of the crisis? In Power's then-classified (and not surprising) view, "Mr. Khrushchev backed down immediately and took his missiles out of Cuba. Now, what effect the fact that SAC was on DEFCON 2 airborne alert completely generated had on his making that decision, you'll have to ask Mr. Khrushchev, he's the only one who knows that."[50]

And as we saw in chapter 4 and will later in chapter 7, the Airborne Alert Force had a special role in this chess game. The Soviet intelligence service's signals intelligence stations in the Arctic intercepted the DEFCON 2 order and were tracking eighty-five SAC bombers that were in the air and in the Chrome Dome track.[51] After the DEFCON 2 announcement, according to Soviet diplomat Vassily Kuznetsov, "Khrushchev shit his pants" and was "gripped with fear as he read KGB reports from Washington informing him the U.S. military was pushing Kennedy towards a military showdown in the Caribbean."[52] As for Khrushchev, he later conceded, "We could have delivered a powerful strike against the United States, but the United States would no doubt have responded with a counterattack equal to, or greater than, ours."[53] According to Soviet intelligence analysts, "knowing where this threshold lay enabled [the Soviet leadership] to control the situation, hold the initiative in decisionmaking, [and decide] whether to advance or stop."[54]

Despite Khrushchev's raising the Soviet alert level the day Maj. Rudolf Anderson's U-2 was shot down over Cuba, DEFCON 2 clearly made him more amenable to negotiation, which Kennedy was ready to accommodate, and thus contributed to the Soviet premier's climbdown from the brink. Those critical of Power's actions during the crisis usually omit the effects of the DEFCON 2 decision. If Power had wanted war, he would have generated an excuse to do so earlier, perhaps in 1961, or done it like Ripper did in *Dr. Strangelove*. The war would have been over before anybody in the White House could have done anything about it. Power did not launch, therefore he did not intend to do so without concurrence from a higher authority, that is, his commander in chief, President Kennedy, or his designated successor.

The argument that Power was deliberately provoking the Soviets to launch first so that he would have an excuse to preempt with SAC cannot be supported with the existing material.[55] Commentary on his mental state based on the oral history of one subordinate is not sufficient grounds to sustain that argument. On the contrary. When a U-2 strayed into Soviet territory a State Department liaison officer reported, "Gen LeMay had ordered that all appropriate authorities in Washington and Moscow be immediately notified and he thought I should know what was happening in case we were confronted with a troublesome incident."[56]

The progression of the Cuban Missile Crisis was dramatic, partly because of the very public nature of the event but mostly because the crisis ratified deep-seated fears in the American public generated throughout the previous decade. Like someone trapped in a haunted house in a horror film, every pin drop, every footfall, was cause for exceptionally high levels of concern, not only in the public domain but also among policymakers.

It is not surprising that some have focused on several events during the escalating crisis that appear to be more dramatic than they really were. The idea that any of these "pin drops" could have triggered nuclear war is, in fact, highly debatable. After American forces achieved DEFCON 2 on 24 October, there were three significant incidents. The first was the scheduled test launch of an ICBM from Vandenberg AFB on 26 October. The second was the Alaskan U-2 incident on 27 October, when a U-2 crossed into Soviet airspace and was escorted home by F-102s equipped with nuclear air defense weapons.[57] The third was the encounters between the destroyer USS *Blandy* and Soviet submarine B-130, and the USS *Beale* and submarine B-59, where the Soviet crews were apparently prepared to use a nuclear-tipped torpedo against the American destroyers.[58]

The whole world was on a knife edge; it would take only a single push, like one of these incidents, to get the escalation ball rolling. Certainly that is what the theorists at RAND and Herman Kahn, with his escalation ladder, would have expected and had conditioned the public to believe would happen after the publication of mass-market best sellers like *On Escalation*.

Would Khrushchev really have fired off 400 intermediate- and medium-range ballistic missiles and 114 ICBMs if an F-102 interceptor used an MB-1 Genie nuclear rocket with its small kiloton-yield warhead against a MiG interceptor to protect a U-2? Would Khrushchev have even known such an event took place, given the state of the Soviet communications system between Siberia, Omsk, and Moscow? Would he really have massively launched the Soviet ICBM force after the launch of a single, non-MIRV'd ICBM from a test area into a known (and monitored, for that matter) test range, far away from the Soviet Union? The Soviets did not start construction of the Dnestr-M radar system (Hen House, to NATO) until 1963, and it would not go into service until 1968. Dnestr-M was configured to support the antiballistic missile system around Moscow and was thus not a true counterpart to BMEWS. It was only in the 1970s that the Soviets had the Dnepr radar systems and an early warning satellite constellation that were comparable to BMEWS and the MIDAS or Defense Support Program (DSP) satellite constellation in the United States.[59] Or in the case of Foxtrot submarine B-130: if the crew fired a nuclear torpedo out of a combination of oxygen starvation and desperation and melted the destroyer USS *Blandy* and her crew into slag with a nuclear torpedo, would Kennedy (or LeMay or Power) really have unleashed the entire SIOP and erased the Soviet Union and China from the face of the earth? Such a course of action was highly unlikely in all three circumstances, and any suggestion to the contrary amounts to sensationalism.

Gen. David A. Burchinal, U.S. Air Force deputy chief of staff for plans and operations, had specific insight into the 27 October 1962 U-2 incident: "We knew the Soviet radar was following [the U-2].... The Russians knew what was going on anyway, because our controllers in Alaska contacted the aircraft on the radio, gave him his correct course, and got him back out of there. There was no reaction on the Soviets' part, because they were stood down."[60]

Finally there is the matter of Soviet alerting. There is little discussion in American sources, particularly among Power critics, about the status of Soviet nuclear forces outside of Cuba during the crisis.[61] Indeed it was not clear to most American leaders during the crisis what the Soviet alert system actually looked like.

The Soviet strategic rocket forces had, at this point, four levels of combat readiness:[62]

Combat readiness 4: Constant

Combat readiness 3: Increased

Combat readiness 2: Increased first degree

Combat readiness 1: Complete or Total, ready to launch

Most of the Soviet missiles available in 1962 were launched from pads, with a smaller number, the R-16U ICBMs, located in underground silos. At Constant, the warheads for the pad-launched missiles were located in their containers and were prepared for movement from their storage site to the pad, or were moved to the pad. At Increased the warheads were "docked" onto the missiles. At Increased first degree the missiles were elevated on their pads. At Complete/Total, the missiles were fueled. For the R-12 missile, for example, it took the following times to prepare each combat readiness step:[63]

Combat readiness 4: Constant, between 24 and 3 hours, 15 minutes

Combat readiness 3: Increased, from 7 to 2 hours

Combat readiness 2: Increased first degree, 1 hour

Combat readiness 1: Complete or Total, 22 to 30 minutes

According to secondary and anecdotal information, the level of alert varied among Soviet missile units between 20 August 1962 and late November 1962. For example:

2nd Missile Brigade moved to Increased for the entire three-month crisis period.[64]

3rd Separate Guards Red Banner Division with its R-16 and R-9A ICBMS was alerted on 22 October to Increased first degree.

10th Missile Division with R-16 ICBMS was prepared to launch in "several hours."[65]

50th Missile Army with its R-12 missiles in Cuba was brought to "launch readiness" on 28 October, but the exact level is unclear.[66]

201st Missile Engineering Brigade with R16U went to Increased but with warheads "docked" as the missiles were in silos.[67]

Order of the October Revolution Red Banner Division was at Increased from 20 August to 1 September.[68]

867th Missile Regiment with R-12 missiles was at Increased but with warheads not mounted.[69]

403rd Missile Regiment with R-12 missiles was placed on Increased on 11 September and moved back to Constant on 20 November 1962.[70]

What is known is that on 22 October 1962 the General Staff of the Armed Forces ordered that Soviet missile units of the Strategic Rocket Forces open up their "signal packets," that is, their alert orders. A separate signal over a special control panel at the division- and regiment-level headquarters confirmed the orders were valid. One observer noted that there was some confusion at the 867th Missile Regiment: when the packets were opened "many hands were shaking," and it wasn't clear whether the warheads should be moved, stacked, or mounted.[71]

The 22 October alert appears to conform to combat readiness 2: Increased first degree. Then on 27 October a more widespread alert of Strategic Rocket Forces, the Soviet Air Defense Forces, and Long-Range Aviation was mounted. However, none of the missile unit histories or anecdotal information reports going to combat readiness 1: Complete/Total. Most appear to be at Increased first degree.

When compared with the American DEFCONs, the Soviet Strategic Rocket Forces alert looked like table 1.

Table 1. American and Soviet alert conditions, 1962

Date	U.S. DEFCON	Soviet Strategic Rocket Forces combat readiness
20 August 1962	5 (SAC: 4)	Increased
11 September 1962	5 (SAC: 4)	Increased
22 October 1962 Trigger event: JFK speech	3 (excluding U.S. Air Forces Europe)	Increased first degree
24 October 1962	SAC to 2	No change
27 October 1962 Trigger event: U-2 shot down	No change	(Air Defense/Long-Range Aviation increased, no change to Strategic Rocket Forces)

The main trigger events for increased Soviet alert activity included the anticipatory activity in late August through early September once the American intelligence apparatus discovered the missiles in Cuba; Kennedy's 22 October speech to the nation and U.S. shift to DEFCON 3; and the 27 October U-2 shootdown over Cuba by Soviet air defense systems. Note that there was no Soviet alerting response to the SAC DEFCON 2 increase on 24 October for their missile forces.

Note also there was no Soviet alert response to the U-2 incident over Siberia, or the Vandenberg missile launch on 26 October. The Foxtrot submarine incidents took place after 27 October.

There is no evidence that Soviet strategic missiles achieved their highest level of alert during the crisis. The quickest Khrushchev could have reacted with his missile forces was, at the minimum and under completely ideal warning and decision circumstances, one hour. Keeping in mind that with the imperfect Soviet early warning system, the bureaucratic nature of the Soviet command system, and the Khrushchev factor, it would have been several hours before a decision could be reached. By comparison SAC's Airborne Alert Force could react more or less instantaneously to command and be over their targets in less than three hours. An argument can therefore be made that Power's implementation of the DEFCON 2 shift was not rogue activity and stabilized the crisis as much as any other factor.[72]

The Kennedy Assassination, 1963

There remains significant controversy over the status of the Strategic Air Command after Kennedy's assassination in November 1963. Indeed the JFK conspiracy industry has muddied the historical waters to a significant degree. Oliver Stone's supposedly exhaustive depiction of events in *JFK*, for example, completely leaves out the military response to the assassination. What is known is this: At 1:35 p.m., after learning that Kennedy had been shot, the National Security Agency's signals intelligence command center stated, "No readiness condition will be declared unless overt action which would cause this to become such a condition takes place." At 2:40 p.m. the command center recorded that JFK was dead. Ten minutes later it noted, "All indication centers are urged to indicate immediate alert for possible hostile reactions. Any indications of a change in enemy posture should be immediately passed [to appropriate authorities]." At 4:00 p.m. the command center was informed that "the Joint Chiefs of Staff [would] initiate an increased alert condition."[73] The public was told by a McNamara spokesman, "There was no move up on the defcon scale."[74]

The National Security Agency reported that Fidel Castro, who "was frightened, if not terrified," alerted his ground and naval units around the American naval base at Guantanamo Bay and initiated a quiet call-up of reserves.[75] Power was at a luncheon with several state governors in downtown Omaha and moved immediately to the SAC Command Post.[76] He contacted Air Force One soon after its departure from Love Field at 3:48 p.m. on its way back to Washington transporting the new president, Lyndon Johnson. It is not known what that conversation was about.[77]

Anecdotal evidence suggests the following happened.[78] SAC B-47 bombers at Little Rock AFB were "loaded and ready to respond"; the B-47 units at Pease AFB in New Hampshire "were restricted to the flight line duty for 2 or 3 days until the United States was assured that President Kennedy's assassination was not a communist plot"; eight B-52 crews at Griffiss AFB in New York "were ready to launch with multiple nuclear weapons at a moment's notice. . . . It took a few days before people began to revert normal." The B-58s at Carswell AFB in Texas were alerted. KC-135 tankers at Castle AFB in California took off and refueled the B-52s already on airborne alert.[79] At Kincheloe AFB in Michigan, "during the subsequent seven-day period the B-52G Bombers were kept with one engine running, this method allowing for the other engines to start with hot oil rather than cold oil, which decreased the time taken for engine start up. Along with the engines the flight chief was kept on board while the crew slept and lived in the mole holes (officially termed Readiness Crew Buildings) on the edge of the alert ramp."[80]

The officer of the day at McConnell AFB in Wichita, Kansas, who was inspecting the eighteen ICBM silos in the area, recalled:

This is it! The President is disabled or dead, so he won't be able to initiate the Go Codes, and there will no doubt be so much confusion that no one else will be able to do it either. If this is a Russian plot, and planes or missiles were coming over the North Pole towards the DEW Line at that exact moment, there would be no way for SAC to respond in time. I wheeled around and headed back to the base top speed. I expected to see that the DEFCON level had skipped a couple of steps. . . . But what did I find? Everyone was gathered around black and white televisions, dumbfounded. . . . There was apparently no Cold War threat that day. But there could have been. . . . I've never, before or since, been more disappointed in the Pentagon that I was that day.[81]

The 570th Strategic Missile Squadron with its Titan missiles in Tucson, Arizona, was not elevated to a higher level of alert either.[82]

The available records note that the Joint Chiefs of Staff sent a message through the National Military Command Center (commanded by Maj. Gen. Paul Tibbets, no less) to all of the commanders in chief at 2:15 p.m. Washington time that the president had been "shot and critically wounded" and urged them, "This is the time to be especially on the alert."[83] The Joint Chiefs and McNamara determined that little could be done other than "urging [the commanders in chief] to increase the alertness of their forces [in case of a] change of an unexpected political or military reaction somewhere."[84] The commander in chief of the Southern Command declared DEFCON 4, presumably in response to Cuban moves around Guantanamo Bay. The commander in chief of the Pacific instructed his forces that they were not to initiate "any actions which would indicate heightened tensions such as recall of personnel on leave, but take other actions that would be generally consistent with DEFCON 3."[85] A memo on the DEFCON change summary after the assassination stated that the National Military Command Center did not receive any other notification of a DEFCON change from the unified and specified commands. But it added, "If a commander took precautions within his command other than changing DEFCON status, he need not necessarily inform the [Joint Chiefs] of them."[86] Within seventy-two hours the alert posture was reduced to DEFCON 5 (4 for SAC).

One duty officer from the 44th Strategic Missile Wing, a Minuteman unit in South Dakota, recalled, "[CINCSAC] spoke to us (and at command posts all over the world), on the 'red phone.' His message to us was very reassuring regarding the security of our nuclear weapons systems and our chain of command."[87] This is significant. Power would have used the same system and procedures depicted in the film *A Gathering of Eagles*: the AT&T telephone system–based Primary Alerting System. The Airborne Alert Force, with its B-52s in

PEACE IS OUR PROFESSION

the track to Franz Joseph Land and back, had to communicate with Skybird control through the Green Pine UHF phone patch system and the high-frequency Short Order systems. As in 1960 and 1962, because the Soviet signals intelligence stations regularly intercepted in-clear communications with the alert aircraft, it is highly likely Power was sending a message to the Soviet leadership through this means once again. And that message was: There are people in command here that are on watch, so don't try anything.

Assertions that Power and LeMay were out to provoke a nuclear war with the Soviet Union are unfounded, as are allegations they were involved in some form of coup d'état. The increase of the DEFCON for SAC and the use of in-clear communications with SAC's forces were legitimate actions and had their intended effects.

Postscript

The scene in *Dr. Strangelove* where Miss Foreign Affairs acts as a relay between the U.S. Air Force Command Post and Gen. Buck Turgidson, who is on the commode, may have been based on an actual event that occurred during the Cuban Missile Crisis, as recounted by Ambassador David J. Fischer:

> So [former high commissioner to Germany John Jay] McCloy was in the bathroom of the suite when the phone rang. It was a voice vaguely familiar and said, "Can I speak to Mr. McCloy?" I said, "Who's calling?" He said, "The President." And I said, "The President of what?" Kennedy laughed and said, "The President of the United States." This is where I saw real power. I went to the bathroom and I knocked on the door. I said—somewhat excitedly if I remember correctly—"Mr. McCloy, Mr. McCloy, the President is on the phone!" He said, "I'm busy. Tell him I'll call him back." I thought to myself, anyone who can tell the President he's busy, he'll call back, is someone with a helluva lot of self-confidence![88]

SIX

Theater of War

Fighting in the War Room

Humans have been interested in mysterious political activities conducted deep in caves since Plato wrote *The Republic*. In the Cold War nuclear crisis films, war rooms are positively de rigueur. They feature decision making in a claustrophobic, pressurized, stressful, and thus dramatic environment while the fate of the world is decided by small groups of men. The filmographic Cold War war rooms are, to some extent, an extrapolation of the milieu of Hitler in his bunker in *Downfall*: cut off from reality as much as from communications, bad decision making made while breathing bad air, and eventually the final end, suicide for everybody.

Unlike their fictional counterparts, Cold War–era underground war rooms were only part of an elaborate system that included aircraft, ships, and a wide variety of government and even nongovernment communications facilities deliberately located in out-of-the way parts of the United States. There were actually several war rooms. This system, which evolved from the 1950s into the 1960s, while our films were being made, handled several overlapping processes. They warned when a crisis was under way and conveyed that to the decision makers in a timely fashion. If that crisis escalated or the United States had no warning of an attack, the system was supposed to protect the decision makers so that American nuclear weapons could be released in a timely fashion. Finally, the system ensured that once that authority was given, nuclear forces could process that authority and launch. There is drama at all three processes as a "use it or lose it" imperative underpins everything in the films, which played on the national trauma of Pearl Harbor extant in the 1950s and the "duck and cover" civil defense cultural background of the audience. If the system and its people did not react in a timely fashion, it was all over for the United States as a society.

The films all revolve around the ability to communicate, or the lack thereof: *Leper Colony*'s CRM-114, the "fail-safe box" in *Fail-Safe*, even Erik Finlander's lack of ability to talk to his enemy, Big Red, in *The Bedford Incident*. The telephone is practically a motif throughout *Dr. Strangelove*, from the start of the film, with Turgidson receiving a call from the air force duty officer, to Ripper talking to Mandrake, President Muffley having a lover's quarrel with Premier Kissoff, and Mandrake cajoling Guano into robbing the Coca-Cola machine in order to use a pay phone. The Hot Line is crucial to *Fail-Safe*. CINC-SAC calls his president on it in *By Dawn's Early Light*. The telephone becomes an instrument of suspense in ways that the cell phone today is not. Without the Red Phone, one cannot go to war—or prevent it.

Ike Underground

The possibility of situating an underground command facility outside of Washington DC was mooted in 1948, accelerated in 1949 after the first Soviet atomic test, and funded in 1950 when the Korean War started. Its primary function was to act as the operational headquarters for all American military forces should the military service operations rooms at the Pentagon be disabled. The Alternate Joint Communications Center (AJCC), known by 1956 as "Site R," was originally envisioned to house 3,200 personnel underground and a similar number above ground at the existing Camp Ritchie base in the event of war, though the facility had a much smaller caretaker staff in peacetime.[1] In 1951 rock-drilling equipment and earthmovers went secretly to work on Raven Rock Mountain in northern Maryland, some miles away from the Shangri-La retreat.[2]

There was no point in being underground and unconnected. Changes in communications technology, however, meant that the Raven Rock AJCC underground facility and Camp Ritchie required more robust connectivity. As a result a web of other classified facilities were built around Raven Rock to support it. As there were no transceivers yet, the AJCC needed a high-frequency transmitter site and a separate receiver site so it could talk to the overseas commanders in chief and to the planned alternate seat of government; these communications sites were located at Greencastle, Pennsylvania, and Sharpsburg, Maryland. Both were fed by a microwave facility on Quirauk Mountain, Maryland, which in turn was connected by AT&T ground lines back to the AJCC itself. To talk to the Pentagon and other military transmitters outside of the Washington area, microwave relay stations were built in Damascus, Maryland, linked to Tysons Corner, Virginia, and Fort Meade, Maryland.[3] As we will see, other presidential survival activities were superimposed over this web later in the Cold War.

The AJCC was still under construction when Eisenhower was elected. Understanding the urgency brought on by the development of thermonuclear weapons, he immediately prioritized plans to protect the U.S. government from destruction. These activities were collectively called "continuity of government," an extrapolation of the political term "seat of government." At this time there were competing views on what was appropriate: should the government disperse in peacetime, that is, build new facilities, perhaps hardened, outside of the possible damage radius of a thermonuclear bomb centered on Washington DC? Or should it establish relocation sites manned with skeleton crews and then evacuate essential government departments when alerted?[4]

The result was the partial implementation of both views. The Atomic Energy Commission, clearly advantaged by its inside information on weapons effects, decamped for a newly built headquarters complex in the middle of nowhere near Germantown, Maryland. Most of the colleges and universities west of the capital were earmarked as relocation facilities for the various departments. This was known as the Federal Relocation Arc. The only hardened facility planned for the Arc was built in an experimental mine located under a mountain in Virginia. Code-named High Point (sometimes Hi-Point), its more familiar name was Mount Weather, named after the U.S. Weather Bureau balloon launch site. Although High Point was apparently not completed until 1958, it was in use as early as 1954 as a continuity of government facility. Its backup was the Low Point facility, located in the large former Kellogg sanatorium complex at Battle Creek, Michigan, and supported by the nearby Custer Air Force Station. Long-range communications antennas were located on Battle Creek's two downtown Art Deco high-rise buildings.[5]

In 1954 Eisenhower instituted the first in a series of national continuity of government and civil defense exercises. The first was Operation Readiness in 1954, followed by Operation Alert, an annual exercise from 1955 to 1960. Readiness had thirty alternate government department heads receive a briefing in the Mount Weather bunker, then fanning out to examine their potential relocation facilities in the Arc.[6] At that point High Point's atmospherics left something to be desired as "water was dripping from the ceiling and oozing from the walls."[7]

High Point became the alternate headquarters for the Federal Civil Defense Administration, part of the National Security Council, and some executive offices of the president: it was not initially a presidential relocation facility and does not appear to have been equipped as such in 1954–55. Operation Alert in 1955 had the AJCC Raven Rock complex establish communications links with the High Point bunker, the Atomic Energy Commission, and another facility, code-named Climax; this was Shangri-La, subsequently renamed Camp David by Eisenhower.[8]

Originally a summer camp for federal employees and their families and built by the Works Progress Administration, Camp David initially consisted of a main lodge, a handful of cabins, a swimming pool, and a cookhouse. Naval personnel from the presidential yacht handled amenities at what was properly called Naval Shore Facility Thurmont.[9] Under Eisenhower, Camp David was enlarged to include two underground bunkers that could house 50 and 150 personnel, respectively. The communication linkages to the AJCC and other facilities meant that Eisenhower could use Camp David as a war room.[10]

Later in the 1950s the underground complex at Raven Rock was modified and expanded. A significantly expanded alternate joint war room was added that had color television conferencing to other facilities.[11] The AJCC was designated "for use as an emergency relocation site" for the secretary of defense, the Joint Chiefs of Staff, and supporting staff for both, so that the war could be run via the deployed theater commanders and SAC. Raven Rock was activated on air defense warning yellow (bombers being tracked by NORAD), or earlier if authorized by the secretary of defense. "The AJCC [was] also one of the relocation sites for the President."[12]

Fletcher Knebel and Charles Bailey's book *Seven Days in May* and the 1964 film derived from it refer to "Mount Thunder." Many assume that this was based on Mount Weather, given the similarity in the name and its approximate location in the book. The plots of both the film and the movie have the coup plotters waiting for an Operation Alert–like exercises where the president will be whisked away by helicopter to a hardened relocation facility but then improperly sequestered by military personnel as General Scott takes over. High Point doesn't fit this criteria: it was the civil defense headquarters, not the military defense headquarters. On the other hand, the AJCC Raven Rock complex had spaces for the president and was a military facility.

Short Order Cook: SAC's Command and Control System

As we have seen, the war room in *Dr. Strangelove* was a dramatic extrapolation of the Pentagon's Joint War Room. The possibility that the president and his advisors would convene there in an emergency was remote. If Kubrick had moved his war room to the Raven Rock bunker complex, it would have been a better fit. In *Fail-Safe*, the White House bomb shelter and Pentagon conference room and their telephones were more or less representative of existing crisis-management facilities in the 1950s. The other war room in *Fail-Safe* represented the SAC Control Center. In the film the facility exudes an open-concept 1950s cool, with the requisite department desks, reel-to-reel computers, blinky lights, and the film's version of the Big Board, which seems to merge North American Air Defense Command functions with SAC's. All we need are cocktails and a hi-fi and we can settle in for Armageddon. The film's facility also boasts something that SAC wanted in the 1950s but was denied under McNamara in the 1960s: access to real-time digital satellite reconnaissance data.

The film that portrays SAC's command post and communications capability most accurately was *A Gathering of Eagles* (1963), mostly because it was filmed *in* the SAC Control Center. LeMay and Power worked together with the writers and producers in shaping the film's plot, which fits the LeMay-Power deterrence campaign. Then they greased the skids with Arthur Sylvester, the assistant secretary of defense, thus avoiding McNamara. Sylvester gave his imprimatur but sternly wagged his finger at Power and told him, "The filming of this picture will be considered secondary to the maintenance of your Command's operational readiness."[13]

The idea of an underground protected facility for SAC emerged from discussions between LeMay and Deputy Secretary of Defense Roger Kyes in the early 1950s. The design and degree of protection varied depending on several options explored by SAC planners, but as usual it came down to cost.[14] In the end a design by Leo A. Daly became the basis for the SAC Control Center. Above was a four-story 1950s-style office building; below was a three-story bunker made from hardened reinforced concrete and equipped with blast doors and decontamination facilities. One thousand personnel worked in it on a daily basis, and it could support eight hundred people underground for a protracted period. Construction started in 1955 and was completed in 1957.[15] A compromise, the SAC Control Center was never designed to survive a direct hit with a thermonuclear weapon.[16] It was, however, protected from heavy fallout and probably would have survived a near miss in the 1950s and into the 1960s.

An alternate SAC headquarters was established in the 1950s. It was a smaller version of the SAC Control Center, with its own communications and Big Board. On a certain level of alert the SAC vice commander in chief and a small staff boarded an aircraft and deployed to this site.[17]

The Big Board is as central to the nuclear crisis films as are the bunkers and command facilities. The depiction of huge status boards in practically all of our films—*Dr. Strangelove, Fail-Safe, Damnation Alley, WarGames, By Dawn's Early Light*—conditions us to view these devices as essentially large televisions central to the action. In the 1950s and 1960s, however, the real-time technology employed in the films to depict attacks did not exist. When it was established in 1957 the SAC Control Center had a brightly lit room with a 165-foot-long wall consisting of two-story-high floor-to-ceiling sliding status boards; these maps were viewed from several glass-encased balconies. Airmen in one-man wheeled cherry-pickers moved up and down the sliding boards to update the numbers and status data, while an automated television camera on a track could focus in on any part of the wall and transmit that information elsewhere in the SAC Headquarters building. Briefings by officers with a handheld microphone could be transmitted using a regular TV camera. In the 1950s and 1960s there was no way of automatically plotting the progress of SAC's assault on the Soviet Union in real time in the way it was depicted in *Dr. Strangelove* or in *Fail-Safe*.[18]

In 1962 the SAC Control Center became the Command Post and the manual Big Boards were dismantled, replaced by six large projection screens; the fluorescent lighting was replaced with semidarkness. Vu-Graph and carousel projectors were positioned in rows behind action staff to provide status information on the screens. Again, there was no way for SAC to observe an attack in real time using this system. The SAC control system, which linked bases with the command post, fed in status data, which were converted by the staff to slides and then displayed. The Bomb Alarm System, consisting of sensors mounted at each SAC base connected via communications links to a small map board resembling the children's toy Lite-Brite, was mounted elsewhere in the duty controller's office. That was the closest to real time it got during this period.[19] The only system capable of real-time projection was the Iconorama, discussed below. The NORAD system could work because it was connected to a vast radar network that provided inputs. With no continuous radar satellite coverage of the Soviet Union (yet), SAC was completely dependent on radio communications from the attacking bombers. Each bomber was required to report in by radio immediately after it had dropped its weapons (the "B-51 Report") specifically so SAC HQ could plot the attack on its display systems.

The SAC high-frequency SSB network was code-named Short Order, as in "fry cook." It went online in March 1960 with inaugural events at several Short Order sites west of Offutt AFB; Elkhorn, Scribner, and Hooper, Nebraska, hosted Short Order facilities. SAC's three numbered air forces each got Short Order installations.[20] In *A Gathering of Eagles*, the Short Order system is depicted when Rock Hudson's character calls up a B-52 using a phone patch.

The other system of importance that shows up in the films, particularly in *A Gathering of Eagles*, was SAC's Primary Alerting System, set up in 1959. In the late 1950s SAC consisted of numerous nuclear bomber and reconnaissance squadrons. These were grouped in wings, divisions, and then numbered air forces, of which there were three: 15th Air Force (March AFB, California), 2nd Air Force (Barksdale, Louisiana), and 8th Air Force (Westover, Massachusetts). There were also air divisions overseas in the United Kingdom, Morocco and then Spain, and Guam. Each of these headquarters had a command post linked by telephone cable to the SAC Control Center at Offutt AFB. This hierarchical system, however, slowed down the passage of messages; a B-52 squadron, for example, was four or five levels removed from SAC headquarters, and if the alert message had to be passed through all of them, the bombers could be destroyed on the ground before they could take off.[21]

The result was an unprecedented collaboration between SAC, AT&T, Western Electric Co., and Bell Telephone Laboratories. The Primary Alerting System consisted of a special console established at every SAC bomber and missile base command post around the world, connected via phone lines to Omaha. Special circuits were identified, and the main panel at the SAC Control Center had the ability to seize control of all of these circuits simultaneously. The SAC Control Center also had the ability to instantly activate the emergency klaxon alarms at all SAC bases or facilities from the SAC controller's room with the push of a button, and they could activate individual units for alerting using unit buttons. Those klaxons were the scramble signal to the alert bomber aircraft and the initiation of authentication procedures at the missile bases. The Primary Alerting System could be tested, as seen in *A Gathering of Eagles*, with colored lights indicating acknowledgment of the test by each unit or base on the console. Delegations visiting SAC were treated to a test of the system, similar to that depicted in the film of Rock Hudson's character timing the acknowledgment response.

This leads us to the quintessential symbol of the nuclear age: the Red Phone, gracing the mass-market paperback copy of Herman Kahn's *Thinking the Unthinkable* as well as the stained glass in SAC's chapel at Offutt AFB. There were actually several Red Phones, as well as other important colored phones in the SAC Control Center. Back at the Pentagon, the systems used to communicate with the president and the Joint Chiefs were consolidated into the Joint Chiefs of Staff Alerting Network, supported by a classified communications facility in Arlington, Virginia. Like the SAC Primary Alerting System, this system had a console at each unified commander's post connected with phone lines.[22] This was the Gold Phone; there was a panel and phone in the SAC Control Center, another at NORAD, and elsewhere. After a decision had been made during the conference call with the president and Joint Chiefs, the SAC commander could order the senior controller in the SAC Control Center to alert the force using the Primary Alerting System. The Red Phone was really a voice alternative or backup to the Primary Alerting System panel. For example, when General Power contacted his forces during the various crises, he did that using the Red Phone.

The Primary Alerting System operated using the two-man rule. The SAC Control Center was callsign Dropkick (clearly the informal name for the president's "football" briefcase relates to this callsign). Skybird was a collective voice call to all the units on the Primary Alerting System console, and Sky King was the collective call to all SAC aircraft using the Short Order radio system.[23]

The Blue Phone connected SAC with NORAD, the system of systems that was going to initiate an alert, should it become necessary to do so.

Seeing the Big Board

The North American Aerospace Defense Command is probably best known for its Cheyenne Mountain Complex. For most people, NORAD's headquarters, built into and partly under a mountain in Colorado, is *the* war room: a dark NASA-like control center filled with large map screens, multicolored telephones, and sweat-inducing tension as the incoming attack slowly crawls across the Big Board over Canada toward the United States. The complex itself went online in 1966 and as such is not contemporaneous with the early nuclear crisis films. *Fail-Safe*, as mentioned earlier, has its war room act as a combination of the SAC Control Center and NORAD command post. The film inadvertently depicts the linkages that did exist between both commands but does not depict NORAD in any detail. Notable depictions after that include *WarGames* (1983), *Stargate* (1994), and the postapocalyptic TV series *Jeremiah* (2002), which features a NORAD Cheyenne Mountain community of survivors at odds with an AJCC Raven Rock community. Historically NORAD actually had a variety of war rooms, including another Cheyenne Mountain–like complex built into the Canadian Shield near North Bay, Ontario, that predated the Colorado-based facility.

The NORAD war rooms came in several varieties, but all related to a wise acronym, SAGE (semi-automated ground environment). In many ways, SAGE was the predecessor to the internet. The SAGE network used phone lines to connect hundreds of far-flung radar sites to large protected mainframe computers that sorted the information for display so that inbound Soviet aircraft could be identified and destroyed by NORAD. The AN/FSQ-7 and -8 computers were huge first-generation mainframe systems that had a fraction of the computing power in today's iPhones, but this was sufficient to handle the number of intercepts or "tracks" identified by the battle staffs and the responding interceptor forces.[24]

The basic building blocks of the whole system were the twenty-one direction centers, located mostly on the perimeter of the United States. Housed in a four-story above-ground blockhouse, each direction center contained two AN/FSQ-7 computers located on the second floor, connected to telephone frames on the ground floor. Those lines were linked to the radars of the Distant Early Warning Line in the Arctic, the Mid-Canada Line, and the Pinetree Line via the AT&T and Bell Canada networks. The top floor of the blockhouse contained the air surveillance, identification, and weapons direction rooms, all crammed with men in comfortable chairs wielding light guns at their scopes (actually called plan position indicators) in the blue-light gloom, constantly keeping track of what was happening in the airspace assigned to that direction center's sector.[25]

The third floor housed the sector command post. This consisted of a mezzanine balcony with eight desks and phone systems clustered in a crescent that overlooked a two-story-tall blank wall. Connected to the top floor was a pair of Kelvin Hughes projectors. A special camera was focused on a single scope that received all of the data from all of the scopes on the top floor and took a 35mm picture every fifteen seconds. The Kelvin Hughes system instantly developed the image and projected it onto the wall in under a minute. In a way, the Kelvin Hughes system used at the NORAD direction centers was the original Big Board and was the closest thing capable of projecting real-time information for a battle staff from 1958 into the 1960s.[26]

Four direction centers made up a region, so there were three regional combat centers, each equipped with an AN/FSQ-8 computer located at Tacoma, Washington; Truax Field in Wisconsin; and Syracuse, New York. If a direction center was knocked out, the regional combat center could bypass the destroyed site and relay information to its forces or assign those forces to an adjacent direction center. The combat center had a regional command post similar to the direction center blockhouses. The final link in the chain was the Combat Operations Center, or COC (paging Dr. Kubrick again).[27]

A year after the NORAD agreement was signed, the Royal Canadian Air Force determined that its air defense system headquarters, and the computers required to handle the air defense problem, needed to be in a protected facility instead of the existing above-ground manual control center at RCAF Station St. Hubert east of Montreal. As a result, construction started in 1959 on a massive underground facility near North Bay, Ontario, where four separate communications lines, including those from the DEW, Mid-Canada, and Pinetree lines intersected. The first detachments of the Northern NORAD Region HQ went active "in the cavern" on 15 August 1962.[28]

Predating the Cheyenne Mountain Complex by three years, the North Bay facility consisted of an H-shaped three-story building constructed on shocks inside of a hollowed-out cavern connected to a long tunnel with two portals. Two other chambers containing life-support facilities were also connected to the main tunnel. The total excavation was three hundred thousand cubic yards.[29]

Like the direction centers farther south, the Northern NORAD Region Headquarters used an AN/FSQ-7 computer but had a much larger combat center given the amount of airspace covered by the command. The Northern NORAD Region's Big Board room included an Iconorama and a Kelvin Hughes system for displaying information. These data were updated every thirty seconds. In addition the headquarters was responsible for the national dual-key system to release nuclear air defense weapons, specifically the fifty-six Bomarc missiles at two sites in Canada.[30]

The main NORAD Combat Operations Center was based in an earlier American facility constructed in a blockhouse near Ent AFB in Colorado in 1954 but was moved to a partially underground facility called the Chidlaw Building in downtown Colorado Springs until the Cheyenne Mountain complex could be completed. These facilities employed Iconorama display systems. Originally designed to replace grease-pencil plotting boards on ships, the prototypes of the large Iconorama system were developed by the Fenske, Fedrick, and Miller Corporation in 1957. Iconorama works like this: "Tracks of airborne missiles or aircraft are received from a radar network and pictured on a two-dimensional screen. . . . Impulses for the displays are relayed over existing telephone or teletype circuits." Then "the traces made by vehicles are obtained by movement of a stylus, mounted on a rigid transparent plate, over a coated slide. External signals act on servomechanisms which move the stylus over the slide."[31] The transparent external screen was overlaid with a map of North America. If the SAC Bomb Alarm System was Lite-Brite, Iconorama was essentially Etch-a-Sketch. In a tragic irony, Jack Fedrick died in 1958 while he was on his way to Colorado to present the concept to NORAD. A U.S. Air Force F-100 collided with his United Airlines DC-7, killing forty-nine people and leading to a complete reassessment of air traffic control display measures.[32]

Iconoramas became part of a larger system. NORAD in Colorado had a "Big Board" Iconorama depicting North America; this handled the overall continental air defense picture. A secondary, smaller board to its left received inputs from ballistic missile defense systems: BMEWS, the Spasur system, Spacetrack, then later the MIDAS (Missile Defense Alarm System) satellites. The ballistic missile Iconorama not only tracked inbound ICBMs but also mathematically calculated predicted impact footprints on the display. The system also boasted a numeric time-to-impact counter. To the right was a third display showing the status of NORAD's ready forces, and at the bottom was a series of displays showing the DEFCON status of American worldwide commands. The missile defense data were repeated onto other Iconorama screens at North Bay, at the SAC command post in Offutt, at the National Military Command Center in the Pentagon, and at the alternate command center in Raven Rock (Site R).[33]

The communications plan for Cheyenne Mountain was called the Close-in Automatic Route Restoral System (CARRS) network. A Bell concept, NORAD used a combination of AT&T Long Lines microwave communications and Bell's cross-country coaxial landline cable to communicate with its sensors in the north and the rest of the continental command system. The plan was for six inputs from six nodes, four coaxial wire and two microwave, interconnected and set at varying distances from the command center outside of any potential blast zone near the facility.[34] Four of the six planned nodes were in operation after the complex was completed in 1966.[35]

However, delays in Cheyenne Mountain's completion led to retaining the NORAD Combat Operations Center in the Chidlaw Building in Colorado Springs. At this point NORAD was serviced by only one microwave link, while the CARRS was under construction. On one particular night in the early 1960s, an AT&T engineer "who we'll call 'Q' didn't follow instructions for routining a TD-2 [microwave] transmitter and receiver" at the Black Forest microwave station. When he used a radio frequency sweep generator on a test task, the signal from the device leaked onto the other transmitters at the station, "causing a complete failure of all channels" going to NORAD.[36]

CINCSAC Gen. Thomas Power recounted his response:

Another time—as usual in the middle of the night—the SAC controller on duty advised me tersely that all communications with BMEWS and NORAD had been disrupted. There could only be two reasons for that—enemy action or communications failure. As I could not take any chances, I ordered the alert crews to their airplanes, ready for takeoff, which was nothing unusual for the crews even at that time of night. While they were racing to their aircraft, I had about two or three minutes to decide whether I should actually launch the force. I used this brief time to establish contact with a SAC plane flying over the Thule [BMEWS] site and learned that nothing untoward had happened. Thereupon I had the crews returned to their alert shacks. . . . Action was taken immediately to correct what turned out to be a minor deficiency in the communications link.[37]

(Power was referring to SAC's Hard Head operation, discussed in chapter 7.)

When the Cheyenne Mountain Complex was finally completed in 1966, it consisted of a lattice of structures, many of them three stories tall and built on shock absorbers, behind a huge blast door that was accessed by two portals in the caverns under the 7,000-foot mountain. One of these buildings housed the Combat Operations Center; it replicated the facilities and layout from the Chidlaw Building, with a glassed-in viewing gallery, battle staff desks and phones, and three Big Board displays.[38] The Iconorama was replaced by the late 1960s with a computerized electronic projection system that no longer relied on electromechanical servomotors. The Burroughs NORAD Large Group Display System was "a computer-controlled, seven-color, high-resolution, rapid-processing, large screen projector." The system was "capable of presenting map outlines, a large variety of specialized symbols, and tabulated 'alphanumerics'—all in contrasting coded colors." In many ways, the system was a vastly accelerated computer-assisted evolution of the Kelvin Hughes system, with the camera processing projector unit taking a picture of the combined and now colorized computerized information merged onto a TV tube. The unit projected the images onto the back of the screens in the Combat Operations Center: a 12 x 16-foot large screen and two smaller 6 x 8-foot screens.[39] The Big Board of the films was really a NORAD, not a SAC, innovation.

The Football

The 1964 film *Seven Days in May* contains an ominous scene wherein President Lyman is taking a swim in the White House pool and conversing with his advisor about civil-military relations. The camera pulls back to reveal a uniformed figure quietly sitting in a chair holding a large black briefcase, observing the exchange. Originally called "the satchel" and now better known as "the football," it is omnipresent throughout *Seven Days in May*. It is also a staple of American political life to comment periodically on the close proximity to the president of the warrant officer carrying the codes that permit the president to authorize the use of nuclear weapons. *Seven Days in May* implies, incorrectly, that the man has a dual function: to carry the codes and to keep an eye on the president for the Joint Chiefs. This prefigures the bizarre Radford Affair during the Nixon administration, when the chairman of the Joint Chiefs Adm. Thomas Moorer used military personnel in the White House to keep an eye on Henry Kissinger.[40]

It is generally understood that "the satchel" came into existence during the Kennedy administration and was photographed publicly for the first time in 1963.[41] During Eisenhower's time, however, there was a functional equivalent assembled by none other than Capt. Edward N. Beach, USN, author of the submarine novel *Run Silent, Run Deep*, who served as an aide to Eisenhower.[42] Starting in April 1957 among the president's emergency action papers was a Joint Chiefs of Staff war emergency check list distributed to the president, secretary of defense, Joint Chiefs, and Atomic Energy Commission. Who exactly carried this and how it was transported when Eisenhower was president is unclear, but it would have fit in a regular briefcase. Appended to the check list was the Master Readiness File (MRF), which contained prewritten emergency messages "designed to trigger certain actions by unified commanders." When authorized by the president, an automated taped message corresponding to the MRF number was dispatched on the phone and print Telex systems, initially from the air force command post and later from the joint war room. They could also be sent from the AJCC at Raven Rock.[43]

There were initially nine MRF automated messages:[44]

MRF-1A: Situation message

MRF-2A, 2B: Transfer of atomic weapons

MRF 3A: Declaration of national emergency

MRF 4A: Presidential authorization to use atomic weapons

MRF 5A: War message

MRF 7A and 9A: Base rights

MRF 10A: Canada-U.S. emergency defense plan

The recipients included the four chiefs and all major army, air force, and navy commands. In the case of SAC and NORAD, their actions were governed by "authenticated telephone calls" using the Joint Chiefs of Staff Telephone Authentication System. The process resembled a conference phone call with the chiefs, the secretary of defense, and the president, with some form of authentication established first for all members joining the conversation. All members had the MRF list, and the president selected the options he wanted implemented. For example, MRF-2A was sent from the secretary of defense to the chairman of the Atomic Energy Commission requesting that x number of nuclear components and y number of nonnuclear components "be made immediately available for pickup on demand." The secretary of defense then sent a message to, say, the chief of naval operations establishing a "P" hour (pickup hour) with the numbers but also with a single line: "Authorization for the use of nuclear weapons has not been granted."[45] That permitted the chiefs to implement "atomic standby." MRF-4A was a single line authorizing weapons use, and then a corresponding service-level message, "Atomic execute," was dispatched.

Thus throughout the 1950s the ability of the president to connect to the phone system either directly in one of the war rooms or via a radio phone patch from an aircraft, ship, or rail car was absolutely crucial if nuclear weapons authorization was to be made quickly in an emergency.

"The satchel" evolved into "the football" by the 1960s. The presidential military aides carried the locked briefcase with them whenever the president left the White House; they, not the president, retained the combination-lock code. The "football" apparently contained several items. There was the "Black Book," also called "The Playbook," the Single Integrated Operational Plan (SIOP) options; the presidential emergency facility location list and list of nearby airfields or helipads; the procedure by which the president accessed and activated the Emergency Broadcast System; and the nuclear authentication codes (later called "the biscuit"), a hard, clear plastic credit card–size envelope with the codes inserted inside. All National Command Authorities and successors carry similar cards.[46] *By Dawn's Early Light* depicts the process by which the National Command Authorities were authenticated using this card.

For example, the Playbook for October 1962 was based on SIOP-63, which had three tasks and five attack options that Kennedy could select from:[47]

Task I: enemy nuclear delivery forces, minimize damage to civilian population and industry, possible withhold vs China and eastern European countries in the Soviet bloc.

Task II: other enemy military forces and resources (tactical air bases, command and control facilities etc.) outside of urban areas.

Task III: deliberate attacks on military forces and resources in urban areas, with specific targeting of critical elements of industry, technology, and government.

Option I: pre-emption. Task I, withhold Tasks II and III.

Option II: pre emption. Tasks I and II, withhold Task III.

Option III: tactical warning. Task I, withhold Tasks II and III.

Option IV: tactical warning. Tasks I and II, withhold Task III.

Option V: tactical warning. Tasks I, II, and III.

Later versions of the Playbook were even more complex, with every conceivable option from a single shot across the bow to the use of all nuclear weapons at once. President Carter apparently insisted that the Playbook be streamlined so he could follow it more easily.

That said, Joint Chiefs chairman Gen. Maxwell Taylor later revealed that even Lyndon Johnson was not "read in" on this information while he was vice president. Indeed, on the day of Kennedy's assassination, Taylor tried to bring Johnson up to date on "the black book" but was unable to do so for at least a week after: "I frankly didn't feel that I had been too effective in getting all the principal points across. . . . He had never seen the black book before. It was unknown to him. All this information is for the President, and he, of course could have briefed the Vice President had he wanted. I got no impression he had ever done that. This was a new subject, or really a list of subjects as far as the President was concerned."[48]

By the late 1970s, in addition to the SIOP or as part of it, the Playbook had lists of equivalent cities that could be struck in the Soviet Union if one, some, or all American cities were hit, something like Buck Turgidson's "World Targets in Megadeaths" briefing book in *Dr. Strangelove* or Henry Fonda's president trading New York for Moscow in *Fail-Safe*.[49] Even *By Dawn's Early Light* shows the president insisting that SAC use a SIOP option that produces a proportionate response to a Soviet attack. However, the technology of the 1960s was not capable of supporting every possible option for every possible contingency. This was not generally understood by the RAND economists and social scientists (not that they were cleared for all of the technical detail anyway) who continued to insist, with McNamara's approval, that the president needed increased and substantial flexibility and control over his nuclear forces. The reality was that the SIOP in the 1960s and 1970s provided a range of retaliatory choices that was more or less limited to, as one who was briefed on them remarked, "Rare, Medium, or Well-Done."[50]

Atomic Telephone: The Hot Line

The poster depicts caricatures of two plump and balding politicians from behind, one of them with a woman's arms wrapped around him. Both hold Red Phones to their ears. Vast numbers of B-52s fly toward us over the globe. *Dr. Strangelove's* 1963 advertising is adamant: it is "*the* Hot Line suspense comedy." Which is rather amusing since the Direct Communications Link, as it was eventually known, was a Teletype system installed concurrently with the initial planned release of the film, which was delayed to January 1964 in part due to the Kennedy assassination. In *Fail-Safe* the president and his interpreter Buck (played by Larry Hagman) are locked away in the bowels of the White House, in a minimalist room containing a telephone, a speaker, a table, a pitcher of water, and a pair of drinking glasses. In Russian-accented English Buck provides simultaneous translation to which the president reacts.

As we have seen, the authors of both films were closely following the open-source debates over the thermonuclear age. Not surprisingly, they would have come across a proposal by RAND's Thomas Schelling in 1958 that a similar system be installed. Indeed Schelling was part of Kubrick's brain trust. The idea was apparently suggested to Khrushchev in 1959, and in 1960 the matter was raised in the State Department's Policy Planning Committee by Gerard C. Smith, an avowed internationalist and Trilateral Commission enthusiast who directed the Arms Control and Disarmament Agency and was lead negotiator for SALT I and the ABM Treaty.[51]

The public impetus for "the establishment of a direct telephone line" came from Jess Gorkin at *Parade* magazine in its 20 March 1960 issue. Gorkin's piece, "An Open Letter from the Editor of Parade to President Dwight D. Eisenhower and Premier Nikita Khrushchev Re: Accidental War," is believed to have played a role in stimulating the American side of the talks that led to the establishment of the link. Gorkin feared accidental nuclear war, specifically "sabotage, subversion, . . . the lunatic action of fanatics." He cited three instances "of our missiles going awry": a 1946 incident with a captured V-2 tested at White Sands Proving Group hitting Juarez, Mexico; a 1955 incident in which "a Nike missile accidentally took off from Fort Meade as a result of a short circuit"; and the 1956 loss of "a Snark long-range strategic missile [that] accidentally went into a Brazilian jungle." (This last event influenced Ian Fleming when he wrote *Dr. No.*) Gorkin pointedly stated, "You, Mr. Khrushchev, must know of Soviet missiles that have misfired or gone astray."[52]

Gorkin was clearly influenced by somebody, probably Gerard Smith. He explains that he raised the issue with "one expert" who suggested that Eisenhower "is seldom more than one minute away from some means of communication. By telephone, high-powered radio, even walkie-talkie, he can be reached instantaneously." For Gorkin (and others), the "cumbersome, slow-moving machinery of diplomacy" was "unsuited to the lightning emergencies of the space age."[53]

The Eighteen Nation Committee on Disarmament at the UN was usually a forum for championing inertia. In April 1962, however, a direct communications link proposal made it onto the agenda and was pushed forward by the U.S. delegation.[54] It appears as though clumsy and potentially deadly message handling during the Cuban Missile Crisis led to the formalization of the April proposal. Existing diplomatic procedures at the time had the leaders exchanging messages via ambassadors ensconced in embassies using their encoding systems. To speed things up, Ambassador Dobrynin allegedly used Western Union at one point to communicate with Moscow. A Western Union courier would arrive at the Soviet embassy on bicycle, collect the cable, and return to the Western Union facility, where it would be sent.[55] The Strangelovian possibilities are endless. What if the courier had, say, been hit by a car on the night of 27 October 1962? The negative consequences of such an unforeseen event ranks up there with the crew of the *Leper Colony* losing radio contact with SAC and selecting the nearest target of opportunity.

Once again, however, it is *By Dawn's Early Light* that gets it right: Martin Landau's president receives messages via a teleprinter (with a Russian voice-over to help us viewers out). The August 1963 "Memorandum of Understanding between the United States of America and the Union of Soviet Socialist Republics regarding the Establishment of a Direct Communications Link" formalized a primary and a secondary circuit. The primary ran from the National Military Command Center at the Pentagon via land line to a submarine cable, to London, and then a combination of submarine cable and land line to Copenhagen, Stockholm, Helsinki, and finally Moscow. The secondary consisted of an AT&T land link from Washington DC to New York, then by high-frequency radio to Tangiers, and then Moscow. Both could send sixty-six words per minute. The United States sent messages in English, the Soviets in Russian. Both countries exchanged Teletype equipment: the Soviet equipment employed the Cyrillic alphabet. Both terminals had translators on call.[56] In order not to compromise each side's crypto capabilities, a Norwegian system, the ETCRRM machine built by the STK Company, was employed. These were later replaced with Siemens M-190 cipher machines. The ETCRRM was an electrical "one-time pad," with each side creating their own key tapes.[57] A similar setup was established between the United Kingdom and the Soviet Union in 1967, with the French following in 1968.[58]

There was a real-life presidential translator, as in *Fail-Safe*; Maj. Glenn Nordin served in this position from 1963 to 1966. The Moscow Link team at the Pentagon included an officer translator, an enlisted translator, and a Teletype operator.[59] Release of messages on the direct communications link could be authorized only by the president and was subject to two-man rule operational procedures (similar to nuclear weapons release) at each terminal site.[60]

There were some interesting events involving the direct communications link system. In 1965 a Danish bulldozer cut the line, and that same year a manhole fire near Rosedale, Maryland, shut down the primary link. A Finnish farmer sliced open the line in 1966, and a microwave tower was blown down at another location. In another instance a Soviet freighter cut the cable when it ran aground. And unbelievably "a thief stole 20 feet of cable unaware of what he was cutting."[61]

Those were not the only problems. The Hot Line terminated at the National Military Command Center at the Pentagon so that a link had to be installed to the White House.[62] There appears to have been no provision early on to have the communications transmitted to the presidential emergency facilities relocation sites or vehicles like the Night Watch command-and-control aircraft. The possibility that an adversary could keep his opponent pinned down in the capital conducting diplomacy while implementing a decapitation strike against him emerged from somewhere in U.S. analytic circles. The specific nature of U.S. vulnerability vis-à-vis nuclear release and dispositions of the National Command Authorities seems to have led to these concerns around 1967, when the link was employed during the tensions generated by the Six Day War.[63]

Consequently modifications were made to the agreement in 1971. This led to a satellite-based link that was implemented between 1974 and 1978. It consisted of several Soviet Molniya II satellites and a pair of U.S. Intelsat satellites and their ground stations. When Fort Detrick, Maryland, was selected as the primary ground station for the Molniyas, four large antennas were constructed there. A station in the Moscow suburbs for the Intelsat was also established. Later it was moved to Vladimir, fifty miles to the east, and then to Lviv, ostensibly due to severe Russian winters, while the backup Molniya station with its giant antennas was erected near Etam, West Virginia.[64]

In reality, Vladimir was also the headquarters of the 27th Guards Rocket Army of the Strategic Rocket Forces, one of three such formations.[65] Vladimir was likely to have been heavily targeted for destruction by SAC, so that the satellite station would have been destroyed, thus severing any chance of dialogue. This may have been one reason for its eventual move to a site near Lviv.

There are two versions of where the Soviet terminals were located. One source asserts a "cell" in the Kremlin basement; another states that the terminal is "across the street" in Communist Party Headquarters.[66] However, "the number of terminals was increased on each side to a system of terminals, i.e., more than one, with locations unspecified (on the US side, terminals were installed in the National Military Command Center [Pentagon], Alternate National Military Command Center [Raven Rock] and White House)."[67]

When, exactly, the direct communications link was first employed is unknown. Apparently it was not used between 1963 and 1965.[68] The best documented use of the link was during the 1967 Six Day War, when Johnson and Kosygin sought to have no misunderstanding as their naval forces maneuvered in close proximity.[69] Media reports suggest it was used in 1971 (Indo-Pakistani War), 1973 (Yom Kippur War), 1974 (invasion of Cyprus), and 1979 (invasion of Afghanistan).[70]

Successors and the National Command Authorities

Kennedy was exceptionally concerned that the continuity of government planning was not keeping pace and that the presidency might not survive a decapitation strike by the Soviet Union. It is around this time that the term "National Command Authorities" (later "Authority") was employed, probably to replace the evolutionary Eisenhower-era nuclear predelegation arrangements. The NCA constitutes varying combinations of the president, the vice president, the secretary of defense, the chairman of the Joint Chiefs of Staff, and/or "their alternates or successors." It is essentially a program for communicating the authority to implement the SIOP and not a legal job title. The term appears to be used for the first time the same year the first SIOP was promulgated (1960). Its constituent elements and language were revised on 16 October 1962, during the Cuban Missile Crisis, and again in 1967. How the NCA related to the existing legal succession planning dating from 1947 remained deliberately obscured to discourage Soviet targeting, but the two programs did overlap.[71] By the late 1960s to early 1970s the NCA system appears to have permitted delegation of the authority to initiate the SIOP from the president to one of the NCAs if the NORAD sensor systems indicated that the president was specifically targeted in a detected attack.[72]

In early 1961 a program for creating a system to handle and protect the presidential successors was conceptualized and embedded within other continuity and emergency programming. This system was designed to assure the "survival of the President . . . by providing blast protected sites for the statutory Presidential successors in the Executive Branch." Existing communications facilities at Mount Weather and Raven Rock had a heavy load, and by implication another communications system was required.[73]

Among the plethora of committees that emerged once Kennedy took over was a three-man Emergency Planning Committee. Operating under the strictest secrecy, these men conducted an exhaustive continuity of government study for Kennedy and presented it to him in June 1962. It concluded:

The survival of the Presidency could be in doubt during a critical decision-making period if the elected President were lost, since all eligible successors normally live and work in the Washington DC area and could be casualties of the same attack. . . . [Consequently] there is a need to develop a survivable national communications system to serve the needs of the President, the top civilian leaders, and essential diplomatic and intelligence needs as well as those of the Department of Defense and the military forces including but not limited to a nuclear attack of varying duration on the United States and the seat of government.[74]

This "survivable national communications system" established priorities for the types of information that it needed to move and to whom. Category 1 information was "the President's needs for information relating to decisions to employ strategic striking forces or related to warning the public of nuclear attack." Equally important was "a requirement to tie-in through the national survivable communications system all designated Presidential successors. The system should have a quick capability of identifying the highest ranking successor who has survived and is in a position to discharge the powers and duties of the President." Notably, "the President should have the means for communications with the leadership of nuclear capable enemy powers immediately before, during, and after attack on this country."[75] This was the origin of the Hot Line.

The Kennedy White House quietly directed a significant amount of effort to solving the successor problem, creating new positions like the blandly named director of telecommunications management. The Eisenhower administration had not developed a specific program to address successor survivability, but with a new communications plan, successors now had to be brought into the system. The established successor list in 1962 was, in order, vice president, speaker of the House, president pro tempore of the Senate, secretary of state, secretary of the Treasury, secretary of defense, attorney general, postmaster general, secretary of the interior, secretary of agriculture, secretary of commerce, secretary of labor. The secretaries of health, education and welfare, housing and urban development, and transportation were added later in the 1960s.[76]

Successors are notably absent from *Dr. Strangelove*, but in *By Dawn's Early Light* the secretary of the interior is apparently the last remaining successor, spoofing the possibility that the politically controversial James Watt might have wound up running the show during a nuclear war. Even the remade TV series *Battlestar Galactica* has a secretary of education as the last presidential successor after a nuclear attack in its universe.

Though in later iterations it evolved into the Presidential Successor Support System, the system's 1963 name or designator is not in the public domain. Its components consisted of the successors themselves, the Central Locator System, the White House Communications Agency switchboard White House Signal (or just Signal), and the first tranche of presidential emergency sites (called presidential emergency facilities by at least 1971).

As far as can be determined, each successor had to remain in contact with Signal whenever traveling and, during a crisis, inform them wherever they were within the Washington Metropolitan area at all times. A list of the successors and their code names was also provided to each successor so they could communicate with each other.[77] On any given day five helicopters were based at Anacostia Naval Air Station: "One was for picking up the president, and the others were for the vice president, cabinet members, Pentagon officials and other Capitol Hill dignitaries who were to be evacuated and taken to a secure classified location. It was our responsibility to transport every key leader in the area to one of four top-secret destinations within 30 miles of the White House in less than 20 minutes."[78]

Construction started on several sites northwest of Washington in 1962. Some of them resembled eight-story-high concrete water towers with no apparent antennas protruding. Four of them had underground complexes. The basic design of each tower had an upper antenna deck enclosed with a plexiglass radome-like material. This floor had parabolic microwave, UHF, high-frequency SSB, and FM antennas, plus an aircraft beacon. The equipment and staff, military personnel supplied by the White House Communications

Agency, were housed on the next seven floors below, as were spare antennas and dishes to replace those knocked down during a nuclear attack. Successors were housed in the blast-protected underground bunker.[79]

This web of microwave-connected facilities overlapped the Eisenhower-era bunker system in Virginia, West Virginia, and Maryland. Cactus, the code name for Camp David, also was the code name for one of these facilities that was located with the existing above- and below-ground facilities there. Creed was located near the Raven Rock complex, but its underground facility was completely separate from it: even Raven Rock personnel did not know it was a relocation bunker and assumed it was a communications facility, even though there was space for the president in Raven Rock. Cannonball, near Mercersburg, Pennsylvania, was a relay site with no bunker, but it was connected to the AT&T Project Office site at Hearthstone Mountain with 100-pair L-4 cables. Cowpuncher was a relay site with a standby communications center. Crystal had two towers located with the Mount Weather facility. Corkscrew, west of Frederick, Maryland, had a tower, a bunker, and a parking lot that could be used as a helipad. This facility was co-located on the mountain with a large AT&T microwave station. It was also close to the recently built Shepherd Field Air National Guard Base, capable of taking EC-135-type aircraft. Site "D" in Damascus, Maryland, was an unmanned microwave relay site that connected Cactus with Cartwheel.[80]

Cartwheel was located at Fort Reno in northwest Washington DC. This site had a microwave shot and an AT&T L-4 cable to Crown, the White House. It also had a helipad disguised as a sports field. One scenario was for the successors who lived in northwest Washington to congregate at Cartwheel for evacuation to the other sites or, if the situation was untenable, operate from the bunker underneath it. Another likely scenario was that in an escalatory crisis, one or more successors would quietly drive out of town to one of the sites, probably Corkscrew, and become the "designated survivor." Such a low-profile move would not alert the Soviets and their surrogates that something special was happening during a crisis.

SEVEN

Plan R

Positive Control, Airborne Alert, and the Nuclear Crisis Films

Nuclear bombers on film range from the graceful shots of Jimmy Stewart's B-36 above the clouds with its six streaming white contrails to the technological porn of the KC-135 tanker coupling with Maj. "King" Kong's beloved B-52, *Leper Colony*. The futuristic modern flow of the Avro Vulcan, the target of SPECTRE agents in *Thunderball*, offsets the inhumanly piloted gray ghost B-58 in *Fail-Safe*. Strategic bomber aircraft are central to most of the nuclear crisis films. The inherent suspense of a group of men (and in the case of *By Dawn's Early Light*, women too) progressing inexorably toward a gauntlet of Soviet air defenses, through them, and then on to Armageddon can be matched only by the drama generated inside the claustrophobic confines of one of the underground war rooms or a submarine being tracked and depth-charged before it can launch its missiles. Will the bombers get through? And if they do succeed, paradoxically, the world ends.

This was not lost on the film studios in the 1950s. In 1956 SAC commander Gen. Curtis LeMay was made aware that a request for assistance from a major studio for the planned suspense film "Runaway Bomber" was in the works: "As I understand it, the basic theme in centered around a bomber which is out of control and aimed directly for a major American city with a live nuclear weapon aboard. Even with a forward stating this could never happen, the implications of a motion picture audience numbering in millions would seemingly add to apprehensions already growing in the public mind concerning Air Force operations and weapons."[1]

Almost predicting the effects that *Dr. Strangelove* would have nearly a decade later, LeMay told his interlocutor, "The noise problem is becoming more acute in spite of our best efforts to mitigate it. In almost every instance of a crash where civilians are killed and civilian property damaged, there is a strong reaction against the Air Force. Recently we have detected growing concern in communities where there is reason to believe nuclear weapons are kept nearby. I feel we should not encourage a film, however implausible, that might lend currency to the growing feeling of concern about a possible nuclear catastrophe."[2]

Central to films involving nuclear bombers was a concept publicly identified as "fail safe" and later used as the title of the book and film. Fail safe and the associated airborne alert program was misunderstood by practically all of the authors and filmmakers and as a result has left us with a series of distortions as to the concept's and program's purpose and mechanisms, again transmitted via film. At the root of the problem is the issue of safety and command and control, which played on the fears associated with potentially unreliable military leadership and personnel.

As we saw in chapter 1, numerous authors of the day speculated that having nuclear-armed bomber aircraft on alert, whether on the ground or in the air, was inherently dangerous and could lead to misunderstandings or rogue activity triggering nuclear war and thus the end of the world. A handful of accidents and incidents in the late 1950s and 1960s involving American airborne alert aircraft are usually cited as evidence of how unstable and dangerous this system was.

This chapter expands on the origins of what was initially called the Fail Safe program. The security and control measures for nuclear bomber aircraft in the U.S. Air Force were, in a word, stringent. The only means to examine exactly how stringent is to explain exactly the steps required by each bomber crew to carry out its mission from launch to target. Consequently four vignettes blending elements of the films with declassified historical information show how typical missions would have been flown by the aircraft depicted in *Strategic Air Command*, *Dr. Strangelove*, and *Fail-Safe*. The vignettes collaterally highlight evolving U.S. safety and targeting policies as well as intelligence on the Soviet defense systems from 1951 to 1970.

The book and film *Fail-Safe* blend two separate concepts, while *Dr. Strangelove* gets one of them partially correct. In *Fail-Safe* five groups of six SAC B-58 bombers fly around on patrol over the Pacific, Arctic, Atlantic, and Persian Gulf until they get orders to proceed to rendezvous points on the periphery of the Soviet Union, called "fail-safe points." These orders are generated by the SAC commander in response to any unknown air defense or naval threat to North America transmitted to him via NORAD. (The incident in the film involves an off-course airliner.) The SAC Command Post initiates a countdown once a potential threat is detected by NORAD, "six times a month or so," and the bombers on patrol are instructed to proceed to their fail-safe points until the identity of the threat is resolved, thus producing a nuclear crisis "six times a month or so."

Once the B-58s arrive at their rendezvous points, they orbit and wait for a coded radio message on the special "fail-safe box" before proceeding. Only the president can order the transmission of the message to the fail-safe box, but it is done electronically and not by voice. In the film the coded message arrives as the result of a communications glitch which may or may not be the result of deliberate Soviet electronics interference with the fail-safe box. The message is authenticated by the crew who carry codes and targets in pouches around their necks. If the code on the fail-safe box is not authenticated, the bombers are supposed to return to their bases. In essence, *Fail-Safe* blends the operational concepts of fail safe/positive control and airborne alert.

Dr. Strangelove, on the other hand, notes in the introduction that aerial-refueled B-52s of the Airborne Alert Force are in the air constantly and fly single-aircraft patrols around the periphery of the Soviet Union, on routes that are two hours away from their targets. The war room's Big Board shows a bombardment wing of thirty B-52s deployed, ringing the Soviet Union and advancing into its interior. In the film the B-52 wing based at the fictional Burpelson Air Force Base is ordered to implement Plan R by their wing headquarters via a coded box called the CRM-114. Neither the SAC Command Center nor CINCSAC play a role in that process because this low-level predelegation is an apparent "retaliatory safeguard" in response to an apparent "sneak attack." The CRM-114 box is destroyed by enemy action, and the B-52 carries out its unauthorized mission because it can't be recalled via the destroyed box.

Neither film mentions the fact that most of SAC's bombers, including the B-47 bombers based in the United Kingdom, French Morocco, and Alaska, were part of a rotational scheme called Reflex Action. The Vulcan, Victor, and Valiant nuclear bombers from the Royal Air Force, all based much closer to the Soviet Union, were on continuous alert by 1958. Ground alert was clearly less dramatic than the constant tension and drama of airborne alert, unless there was a sudden "hot war," as the B-52 crew in the 1980s film *By Dawn's Early Light* learns to their chagrin.

The filmmakers' confusion lay in their reliance on the written materials that contributed to the scripts, which were based on media reports that misinterpreted developments after the Sputnik launch on 4 October 1957 and the political, military, and social backlash that followed.

It would be a natural assumption that the singular Sputnik launch and extrapolations about Soviet ICBM capabilities led to a reexamination of SAC vulnerability resulting in enhanced survival methods, one of which included airborne alert.[3] The reality is that there were two Sputnik launches, on 4 October and 3 November 1957, that played a role in generating apprehension, as well as the launch of Sputnik III that coincided with a positive control presentation to the Joint Chiefs of Staff and the National Security Council in May 1958.[4] During the period August 1957 to May 1958, the Soviet Union also conducted nineteen atmospheric nuclear tests, of which nine were thermonuclear tests in the megaton range.[5] The 6 October 2.9-megaton test should perhaps not be seen as coincidental to the 4 October Sputnik launch, nor should the March 1958 test series, which included five thermonuclear detonations. These tests were monitored by the American and British intelligence services with a variety of technical means.[6] The cumulative effect of these activities fed apprehension over SAC vulnerability in 1957 and 1958, not just the launch of one basketball-size satellite or RAND report speculation.

The roots of that apprehension existed earlier, back in 1956, during and after the Suez Crisis. Khrushchev's open threats to use nuclear weapons caught the Eisenhower administration by surprise, while at the same time the administration was in the process of examining how to authorize the use of the new MB-1 nuclear air defense rockets.[7]

Over at SAC LeMay reexamined the ponderous methods of releasing nuclear weapons to his forces. The DEFCON systems we are all familiar with today would not exist until November 1959. The existing readiness conditions were Air Defense Readiness Red/Yellow, Air Defense Emergency, and Defense Emergency. The unified and specified commanders in chief, including SAC, could declare Defense Emergency: "An emergency condition that exists when a. a major attack is made upon U.S. forces overseas, or on allied forces in any theatre and is confirmed by either the commander of a command... or higher authority; or b. an overt attack of any type is made upon the United States and ... confirmed by the commander of a command ... or a higher authority."[8]

The definition of "major attack" was unclear in the new context. Also problematic was that the initiative was in the hands of the opposition: they had to act overtly before Defense Emergency could be activated. But what if? As LeMay had previously argued, "The United States might be forced into a general war in which we took the initiative. . . . The United States cannot under any circumstances suffer the first blow of having bombs fall on this country. Therefore, Soviet action short of general war could force the United States to initiate an offensive."[9]

After some changes in 1956, the weapons transfer process from the Atomic Energy Commission to SAC was speeded up by mutual agreement: "This procedure avoided the necessity of obtaining specific approval from the President for the transfer of weapons in the event of a defense emergency," a significant departure from the Truman-era policy of having the president and the chairman of the Atomic Energy Commission release the weapons to the air force prior to use.[10]

That did not mean, however, that the SAC commander could just launch his forces and bomb the enemy. SAC's Emergency War Plan in the 1950s consisted of several options, 1 through 14. An Option 1 launch plan used whatever aircraft were on alert at the time at a given base in fifteen minutes, while an Option 14 launch involved launching all aircraft at a given base after a crisis had progressed and the force had been given time to build up, usually after twenty-four hours or so. This corresponded to tactical warning (fifteen minutes) and strategic warning (twelve to twenty-four hours). Options 2 through 14 consisted of increments of the number of aircraft bombed up and on alert between fifteen minutes and twenty-four hours.[11] The force still needed the declaration of Defense Emergency to lift off, however, and that made it vulnerable to hostile action, especially by missile attack and particularly by missile and bomber attack against forward bases in Europe and the Far East. Missile attack warning could come only from signals intelligence and certain other means of varying reliability before BMEWS and MIDAS went into operation in 1961.

The Eisenhower administration reexamined the authority to release and expend nuclear weapons in early 1957. For the most part, Eisenhower authorized the unified commanders to use nuclear weapons in a limited fashion to protect their forces from a "major attack" and not "for defense against minor assault nor against assault upon minor US forces wherein damage would not constitute an immediate and vital threat to the security of the United States or to major US forces." Notably, however, he added, "Nothing in these instructions shall be construed as preventing any responsible commander from taking such actions as may be necessary to defend his command." Similarly there were special instructions for air and naval defense of the United States.[12]

When it came to SAC, however, Eisenhower was explicit: the SAC commander was authorized to retaliate "for an attack against the United States but only on order of the President, except in circumstances where communications between the President and the Commander of SAC is impossible because of the results of an enemy attack."[13] This was like "Plan R" in *Dr. Strangelove*, except nested at a higher level. This language was expanded to include "responsible officials in the Department of Defense" and their successors, who were also "authorized to expend nuclear weapons in retaliation against the enemy identified as responsible for the attack."[14] (This was likely the genesis of the National Command Authorities.)

Throughout the fall of 1957, especially after Sputnik and associated Soviet nuclear and missile tests, SAC looked at two areas for improvement: greater predelegation of authority and enhancing the ground alert of one-third of its forces. Power discussed this with the air force chief of staff, Gen. Thomas White: "Today, I have no authority to expend weapons regardless of the situation. If I gambled and evacuated my weapons towards their targets under 'dispersal emergency' I could well find myself worse off than had I held them on the ground." It took Power "two hours . . . to get a decision to expend the weapons or launch them on a recall basis." Missiles, specifically missiles targeted at SAC's "overseas forces," that is, Soviet intermediate- and medium-range ballistic missiles in western Ukraine, would land in under thirty minutes. For those forces, "reaction . . . must be essentially automatic." A draft policy document was circulated among the Joint Chiefs of Staff titled "Instructions for the Expenditure of Nuclear Weapons under Special Circumstances," but in Power's view it was "contradictory to common sense": "It will do little but make scapegoats of the operational commanders in the event of a modern Pearl Harbor."[15]

White responded, "The Army has agreed that authority to order retaliatory attack may by exercised by CINCSAC if time or circumstances would not permit a decision by the President," but the navy was undecided. White's position was to "press for delegation down to your numbered Air Force commanders. We ran into stiff resistance and we finally went along with stopping at your Headquarters." He reminded Power, "Your plans provide for assumption of authority by your Air Force commanders under specified circumstances. This can be construed as at least an element of the delegation we would prefer." White then pointedly told Power, "We still consider that the President's instructions would permit specific delegation to your Air Force commanders."[16] That is, until the matter was formally resolved by the Joint Chiefs.

On enhancing the responsiveness of SAC, one program, code-named Fail Safe, was "designed to prevent the accidental triggering of a nuclear war."[17] The scheme was tested under the cover of "operational support exercises" conducted in October and November 1957. In essence, the original fail-safe concept had SAC bombers on ground alert launched in the event of a possible threat situation. The bombers would proceed, as in the film, to a geographical point and hold there. If they received the "Go Code" they would continue to their targets. The procedure for this was code-named Noah's Ark. On arrival at the fail-safe point (the term was changed to "positive control point" in 1958) after launch the bombers awaited messages routed to them via any nearby U.S. Air Force facility, usually a radar station, that relayed orders from SAC headquarters in Omaha. Upon receipt of the Noah's Ark message, the aircraft crew used a decoding system called the KAC-1 to authenticate the message.[18]

The main and critically important difference from the films was that the Go Code was to be transmitted by single sideband radio to the crew, not through a coded mechanical device like the CRM-114 in *Dr. Strangelove* or the fail-safe box in *Fail-Safe*. This kept the human in the loop. There was nothing automatic telling the crew to proceed, nothing that could be misinterpreted, as the films portray. The safety problem shifted to crew reliability. This was addressed by having the entire crew of a B-47 or B-52 involved in the weapons release procedure. And what if a whole crew went rogue? There were methods of preventing such a situation via screening and other measures.

SAC fail-safe measures were not limited to bombers on ground alert. When transiting with or without nuclear weapons from the United States to forward bases in Guam, the United Kingdom, or French Morocco, B-47s and B-52s had to regularly check in with U.S. Air Force facilities, again usually radar stations.[19] Interestingly, and for comparative purposes, the strategic transport squadrons handling nuclear weapons logistics operated single-aircraft missions with as little communication as possible and minimal overseas support in order to lower their profile.[20]

The next problem that emerged was what to do in an emergency situation where the United States had not yet been attacked but was threatened, say, by missiles. In March 1958 General White informed the Joint Chiefs of Staff that he had "instructed CINCSAC in the event of a Defense Emergency to automatically launch his alert force under the Fail Safe concept."[21] ("Fail safe" was replaced by "positive control" shortly afterward.) This allowed Power to launch the Airborne Alert Force if there was a threat but still adhere to the requirement of a presidential order to proceed.

After tests, however, a serious problem arose. If the Airborne Alert Force was launched and then held at the positive control points for some time, it was possible that the bombers would not have enough fuel to strike their targets. Tanker aircraft would have to be based farther forward to keep the bombers on station, which made the tankers themselves vulnerable to enemy action at those forward bases.[22]

Indeed the Joint Chiefs of Staff looked at the possibility that they might detect a Soviet bomber force liftoff during a crisis. They recommended to the secretary of defense that if that occurred, the "actions required under Defense Emergency, including launching of the Positive Control SAC Alert Forces" as well as the "implementation of joint emergency war plans," be undertaken.[23] This was the origins of what was later called "launch on warning."

Keeping nuclear bombers aloft with tanker aircraft on a rotating basis was one of several solutions proposed to reduce SAC vulnerability, probably in the wake of the November 1957 vulnerability studies conducted after the launch of Sputnik.[24] When coupled with positive control, such a system appeared to solve a number of problems, but vulnerability and operational flexibility were the two most important.

The public confusion started with the 7 April 1958 Frank Bartholomew article in which he mistakenly reported that there were SAC bombers being aerially refueled on the periphery of the Soviet Union and that were prepared to strike on a moment's notice. A propaganda uproar ensued.[25] A more extensive article in *Time* magazine emerged two weeks later, titled "Fail Safe: Safety Catch on the Deterrent," wherein the basics of positive control were explained but with sensationalist phrases like "hair trigger" employed.[26] *Time* contradicted Bartholomew's assertions, clearly with the assistance of someone at SAC, but the idea that SAC was already undertaking airborne alert and that it was somehow connected to fail safe/positive control took hold. This can be seen in Burdick and Wheeler's novel, *Fail-Safe,* and the derived film.

Bartholomew heard Power tell him what he wanted to happen in the future vis-à-vis airborne alert; Bartholomew misunderstood and thought that these activities were already taking place. It is equally possible that Power was manipulating Bartholomew as part of the deterrent information operations campaign by being vague. In his 1983 memoirs Bartholomew misremembers being briefed on the fail-safe concept instead of on the airborne alert concept.[27]

The reality is that it took some time to get airborne alert going, as the procedural problems were immense. First, Eisenhower had to agree to the prospect of flying nuclear weapons around continuously. He insisted on a detailed safety briefing on the weapons themselves and how the crew would arm and release them.[28] Then Canada had to agree to the overflights, as the aircraft would pass over Canadian territory and some of the tankers would be based there.[29]

The result was the Operation Head Start test conducted in September 1958. Head Start involved the Loring AFB B-52 squadrons launching one B-52 every six hours (four times a day), where the B-52s would hook up with a KC-135 tanker and then fly a twenty-hour circuitous route over Greenland, Canada, and back to Loring. Hourly position reports from the bombers were relayed and authenticated via single sideband radio as part of the control measures. SAC headquarters also sent "Foxtrot no answer contact" transmissions, "any one of which could commit the bombers to combat." The initial tests used unarmed B-52s, but on 3 October Eisenhower gave permission to start flying with nuclear weapons aboard.[30]

The concern that a single plane's crew with its load of bombs might conduct rogue activity appears to have been addressed by the Big Sickle tests in November 1958. Two B-52s from Castle AFB in California carrying Mk-39 mod 1 and Mk-15 mod 2 thermonuclear weapons were placed on alert and then flown as a pair on a round-robin flight track over the western United States with their release systems disabled.[31]

When, exactly, SAC formally mounted airborne alert operations of the type depicted in *Dr. Strangelove* is blurred by events surrounding the Berlin Crisis in 1959–60. In March 1959 Power told the media (or the media misinterpreted his words) that he had been refused permission to mount an airborne alert and was still waiting for authorization. When Murray Snyder, assistant secretary of defense, phoned the chairman of the Joint Chiefs of Staff, Gen. Nathan Twining, and informed him of Power's remarks, Twining exploded: "God, Murray! The President has already authorized one, but we can't tell them that. The Canadians have to be in on this because it concerns their country too. Its just none of [the media's] damn business!"[32]

The overuse of the word "alert" also posed problems and generated confusion in all quarters. There was an airborne alert system, keeping B-52s aloft with aerial tanking to act as a deterrent. There was the SAC Alert Force, the aircraft at bases that were on fifteen-minute alert. Airborne alert flights would become part of the SAC Alert Force, once authorized. There was the Airborne Alert Indoctrination Training Program, designed to get the B-52 crews used to airborne alert procedures based on Head Start and Big Sickle. And during periods of crisis, there were alerts of SAC and other forces in response to discrete events. Twining noted in March 1958, "It has really got fuzzed up."[33]

To complicate matters further, it was unclear to some observers to what extent the upcoming Airborne Alert Indoctrination Training Program, code-named Steel Trap, was supposed to do. Was it training SAC crews in preparation to mounting an airborne alert program? Was it actually *mounting* an airborne alert under cover of training? Did it constitute "signaling" Nikita Khrushchev during the Berlin Crisis? Or all three?

In April 1959, one month after Canada approved more nuclear-armed SAC overflights, the Joint Chiefs directed SAC to develop an airborne alert capability, something that had been technically ongoing six months earlier with Head Start in September 1958. On 18 July 1959 the request for Steel Trap went to the president, and on 10 July he authorized the maneuver of 4,232 nuclear weapons as part of the operation for ten months. All airborne alert activity prior to

June was retroactively designated a "test" by the chairman of the Joint Chiefs when he was discussing the matter with the secretary of defense, thus indicating that Steel Trap was not, in fact, a test at all but an ongoing operation. Every month Eisenhower was provided, by his demand, Steel Trap statistics. From 1959 into 1960 SAC B-52 units provided ten to twelve sorties each day, each mission lasting twenty-four hours. Each B-52 carried two thermonuclear weapons. In theory the Steel Trap airborne alert training force could destroy twenty to twenty-four targets in the Soviet Union with megaton-yield nuclear weapons.[34]

But what dent could twenty to twenty-four strikes really make against the hundreds, perhaps thousands of potential targets? A clue lies in Power's 1958 reactivation of an earlier LeMay request for the development of a 60-megaton bomb. Power wanted the ability to threaten Moscow's destruction with a single weapon.[35] If even one of the aircraft on airborne alert got through, the city, but more important, Khrushchev himself would be destroyed. The possibility that Power was directly threatening the Soviet leadership as a central part of the deterrent strategy cannot be ruled out when placed in the context of his experiences in the Soviet Union in 1956, his public speeches where he repeatedly called out Khrushchev, and the State Department's concern over the speeches. Even though a 60-megaton weapon was not deployed, two to four 18- to 19-megaton-yield weapons delivered by, say, two B-52 aircraft could have had the same effect. And some of the high-yield Mk-36s were aboard B-52 alert aircraft, at least in the late 1950s.[36] It is highly likely that the Airborne Alert Force's primary purpose was to directly threaten Khrushchev and deter him personally.

When the three services met in October 1959 to discuss funding airborne alert, the attitude around the table was that Steel Trap was an "emergency capability" operation that was also an exercise to indoctrinate B-52 crews at the same time.[37] At some point after June 1960 Steel Trap was replaced or augmented with Exercise Down Field. This scheme also put ten B-52s a day into the air for twenty-four hours' duration from October 1960 to January 1961. Down Field exercises added a simulated nuclear strike against a bomb scoring unit during the flights, which were conducted over Canada to a point north of Baffin Island and back to base at Sheppard AFB in Texas.[38] Keen Axe replaced Down Field from January to August 1961.[39]

By 1960 the DEFCON system was in place. The number of B-52s that would be put into the flight tracks now related to the DEFCON. SAC was always at DEFCON 4, whereas all other American forces were at DEFCON 5. Depending on the DEFCON level, the B-52s on airborne alert were supposed to operate singly, then in pairs, then in groups of six.

The airborne alert concept itself stabilized by October 1961 and was renamed Chrome Dome, the code name it would be called until 1968, when it was replaced with the significantly different Giant Lance concept. In its mature form Chrome Dome appears to have merged the Head Start, Down Field, and Keen Axe routes into a coherent patrol route similar to a route used in another test, Operation Quick Kick, back in 1956.[40] The Northern Route, as it was called, went counterclockwise around the periphery of Canada and Alaska and across the United States. Eight flights of B-52s were fed into the track on a twenty-four-hour basis. Also at this time SAC added the Southern Route to Chrome Dome; this took four B-52s to the Mediterranean, where they were aerial-refueled from bases in Spain.[41] The original Chrome Dome route was modified over time and moved progressively back: in 1966, closer to the North Pole; by 1968 they were even closer to the Canadian archipelago (see fig. 29).

When BMEWS came on line in 1961, SAC aircraft maintained observation on both the Clear and Thule radar sites in order to act as a "second opinion" and confirm or deny their destruction to NORAD in the event of an attack. The Thule missions, flown from Loring AFB in Maine and K. I. Sawyer AFB in Michigan, were initially "part of the Chrome Dome operation," but later a single aircraft was assigned and received a separate code name, Hard Head. Future iterations of Hard Head involved a pair of armed B-52s that were "assigned a series of targets in the event of aggression during their mission," thus increasing further the number of B-52s on daily airborne alert.[42] In some cases, a KC-135 tanker from K. I. Sawyer AFB replaced the Loring B-52 if there was an abort, or if a K. I. Sawyer bomber was flying Hard Head, a Loring tanker could replace it. Over at Clear, Alaska, a KC-135 tanker was assigned to launch and provide surveillance of the site at DEFCON 3 or on CINCSAC direction.[43] If the sites were struck by nuclear or conventional attack, the code word Fast Freight was to be sent in the clear to Dropkick, the SAC Command Post, immediately. Frosty was the code word for loss of communications between NORAD and the BMEWS sites.[44]

Destruction of any of the BMEWS sites would have generated a Defense Emergency, which permitted CINCSAC to launch his forces on his own. Certainly the loss of communications with the sites would have attracted significant attention at Dropkick. In a more dangerous vein, Soviet "trawlers" cut the submarine cables linking the BMEWS system at Thule to NORAD in the months leading up to the Cuban Missile Crisis.[45] In retrospect, that situation was arguably more dangerous than the frequently cited concerns over the 1968 B-52 crash at Thule facility and the possibility that it might have destroyed BMEWS and generated an alert.[46]

The perception that there were hundreds of SAC B-52s ringing the Soviet Union on a daily basis, as portrayed in *Dr. Strangelove* and suggested in the media of the time, is clearly inaccurate. Power initially wanted between sixty and eighty B-52s on airborne alert. General White disagreed, mostly due to cost, but he also believed that these numbers were not enough to penetrate Soviet defenses and destroy the overall target sets in the Basic War Plan. LeMay suggested that the number of aircraft should vary depending on the international situation. The objective was for the force "to serve as an impressive indication that the nation is ready and determined to oppose aggression. . . . [This] cannot fail to give pause to the would-be aggressor as well as afford a measure of reassurance to the American public and the US allies."[47]

As a result, if the DEFCON alert level rose, as it did during the Cuban Missile Crisis, the number of B-52s inserted into the patrol routes increased significantly. A shift of the alert level from one-sixteenth to one-eighth level, called Increased Readiness Posture, doubled the number of B-52s in the stream and had the Airborne Alert Force proceeding in pairs along the track.[48] The scene in *Dr.*

Strangelove with the Big Board depicting a thirty-plane alert force converging on the land mass of the USSR from all directions after the Go Code was issued was possible.

It is critical to note that the Chrome Dome B-52s were not just launched into airspace on their own and expected to complete their alert task on radio silence. SAC planned, as part of positive control in 1958, to extend its communications to cover what would become the Chrome Dome operating area using the communications systems at Distant Early Warning radar sites. After some changes to accommodate the possible effects of what it referred to as "anticipated ionospheric disturbances," that is, electromagnetic pulse effects of nuclear weapons detonations, a UHF radio system code-named High Dice and later called Green Pine went into operation in 1963. Green Pine included new transmitters at two sites near SAC Headquarters in Omaha, plus fourteen UHF broadcast facilities co-located with DEW Line sites from Adak, Alaska, to Thule air base.[49]

Green Pine was a means to relay Go Code messages to the northern regions, where high-frequency radios of the SAC Short Order system might not be able to operate under combat conditions. Every twenty-four hours the stations transmitted a Noah's Ark message to the B-52s on alert, usually at the start of the mission. Each B-52 would listen at four points during the flight for further Noah's Ark messages from the Green Pine stations. If the Green Pine site had a message to pass on from SAC, it would be authenticated and sent to the B-52s. In peacetime this became a routine "carry on with mission" message. But if it were a crisis, once the bombers were on station at the "go–no go orbit areas," they would, according to one crew member, "execute a race track type of pattern . . . [with] . . . flash curtains up." In the early years of Chrome Dome, these orbit areas were just north of Franz Joseph Land archipelago.

What did the Soviets know, and how did they know it? There were the AGI intelligence collection "trawlers" in the Davis Strait, monitoring Chrome Dome and other activity. There were numerous radar stations ringing the Soviet edge of the Arctic basin. Soviet military intelligence also maintained what was dubbed the "Polyarniki GRU." In addition to ground intercept stations in the Kola Peninsula and on Franz Joseph Land islands, detachments were covertly deployed to "civilian" drift ice stations starting in 1954, similar to the scenario depicted in *Ice Station Zebra*.[50] Their targets were initially DEW Line emissions, but they eventually expanded coverage to monitor "American strategic aviation flights in the Arctic . . . practicing hard blows from the north."[51]

If the Go Code was transmitted, the B-52s would fly to the H-Hour Control Line, near the Soviet Union. The crew would "assume the responsibility for the targets assigned at the time of receipt of the Go Code." There were target packages per B-52 that corresponded with the four Noah's Ark check-in points on the flight track. As each bomber progressed along the track, its coverage changed because of the geographical shift in relationship to the potential targets. Collaterally this process also allowed SAC to keep track of where their bombers were: if the bombers had problems, they could contact SAC headquarters directly via Green Pine.[52]

The early Chrome Dome flights did, however, pick up Soviet early warning radar on their defensive systems when they reached their orbit areas in the Arctic.[53] Nuclear accident aficionados point to the one known incident, when a B-52 lost its bearings on the downward leg of the Chrome Dome northern route in August 1962 and headed toward the Soviet Union. Over three hundred miles before the bomber came anywhere near Soviet airspace, let alone five hundred or so miles from the closest interceptor base, radar crews on the DEW Line queried the crew and were able to alert them as to the navigation error. No Soviet aircraft were scrambled. This is the only documented event of this type.[54] After issues with celestial navigation were identified and corrected, the track was moved east, closer to the Canadian archipelago.

But it wasn't just poor navigation skills that could have generated such a situation. Most critical commentary, again operating from a purely American-centric position, ignores the fact that the Soviets were also a problematic factor in airborne alert operations. SAC crews were warned, "There have been incidents of suspected jamming, spoofing, and other incidents of interference to communications navigation aids." This included "voice transmission of erroneous weather and [direction-finding] information, communications interference, false beacon readings and navigational radar interference."[55] Naval staff reported, "Radio deception against the Strategic Air Command has been noted in the Canadian subarea [throughout 1961], and the fishing fleet, as well as submarines, are suspect in this activity. Deception is spasmodic as if to test responses without compelling changes in systems or initiating security adjustments. Such activity effectively conducted in war could substantially inhibit SAC retaliatory capacity against the USSR."[56]

Both *Fail-Safe* and *The Bedford Incident* echo those sentiments. In *Fail-Safe* Soviet interference with airborne alert communications triggers the "fail-safe box" in the Vindicator bombers. SAC crews were briefed on the fact that the Soviet Union stationed two poorly disguised trawlers, one off Portsmouth, New Hampshire, and another in the Davis Strait off Baffin Island, specifically to monitor and potentially to interfere with Chrome Dome operations.[57]

When it came down to it, there was no mechanical CRM-114 or "fail-safe box" to go wrong: there was a human-based communication and authentication system that involved more than just a single aircraft and its crew and weapons. The human factor was considered a potentially weak link in the system, and steps had to be undertaken to deal with that.

A far more serious problem that emerged with airborne alert revolved around social and medical conventions of the day that were in dispute when the program started. Chrome Dome flights usually had a twenty-four-hour duration, and thus crew fatigue was potentially an issue. Generally a third pilot accompanied a combat crew, but in the early days of the airborne alert program, there was significant debate over dextroamphetamine (Dexedrine) use. During the Steel Trap operations in 1959, the 2nd Air Force chief surgeon noted, "Recent 18 to 24 hour mission profiles have *not* produced fatigue of such severity that an increased abort rate occurred. In view of the data, the 2nd Air Force Surgeon is of the opinion that the use of stimulant drugs during [airborne alert] missions is neither necessary or desirable." At this time the 2nd Air Force surgeon was adamant: "Drugs of this type will not be dispensed by the Flight

Surgeons of this command for inclusion in combat mission folders, nor will stimulants be used under any circumstances for mission support without prior approval of the Surgeon Headquarters Strategic Air Command."[58]

Apparently he was overridden by his superiors because dextroamphetamine was made available in quantity in the alert facilities for the crews. At the time this drug was available over the counter, as were many drugs that today are strictly controlled. The prospect of a B-52 loaded with a pair of Mk-39 or Mk-41 multimegaton-yield nuclear bombs hurtling through airspace with a crew using a drug that is now used to treat attention-deficit hyperactivity disorder may appear somewhat alarming today. Indeed "some unwanted effects" of Dexedrine, in the major/rare category, include agitation, delusions, and "seeing, hearing or feeling things that aren't there." Prolonged use could result in "psychosis often clinically indistinguishable from schizophrenia."[59]

In relation to Kubrick's Freudian worldview, however, a minor side effect of Dexedrine use is "decreased interest in sexual intercourse . . . loss in sexual ability, desire, drive, or performance."[60] Perhaps somebody slipped some alert facility dexies into General Ripper's pure grain alcohol and rainwater. However, overuse could result in "erections that happen often or that last a long time," something that might have negatively impacted Major Kong and the Leper Colony crew on their mission, given their ready access to Playboy.[61]

Of the five B-52 crashes associated with airborne alert operations, the 14 March 1961 crash at Yuba City, California, involving a B-52 and either two or four nuclear weapons was attributed to a crew that was incapacitated due to improper use of dextroamphetamine and missed its tanker rendezvous off Alaska.[62] After the Yuba City crash the dextroamphetamine was withdrawn from the alert facilities and replaced with strong coffee. Of course as we know today, caffeine can also produce negative effects in high doses: "People with a caffeine intake that high [three cups of regular, five of decaf] . . . had a three-times-higher tendency to hear voices and see things that were not there than those who consumed the equivalent of a half-cup of brewed coffee."[63]

When it came to human reliability and nuclear weapons, airborne alert posed new problems for SAC. When nuclear weapons were first made available for ground alert, it was relatively easy to secure them in guarded facilities even when mounted on the aircraft. In 1958 SAC implemented the two-man policy: personnel handling nuclear weapons or otherwise in close proximity to them had to be cleared to do so and could not do so alone. "No lone zones," consisting of demarcated spaces in bunkers, on ramps, and around loaded aircraft, appeared at SAC facilities.[64] Having nuclear weapons in a strike configuration flown on alert was a radical departure from the situation extant in the early 1950s and required a whole new approach.

Human reliability was not necessarily a new problem for the U.S. Air Force. Provisions for addressing this issue existed as early as 12 April 1956 with the publication of Air Force Regulation 123-9.[65] However, the specific origins of the Human Reliability Program (later the Personnel Reliability Program) lay in an incident wherein a severely depressed U.S. Air Force enlistee stationed at RAF Sculthorpe in the United Kingdom threatened to shoot a nuclear weapon with a pistol during a six-hour standoff in 1959.[66] LeMay kept abreast of events and ultimately recommended in September 1961 to the Joint Chiefs of Staff a program "that ha[d] as its objective, the identification and removal of unstable and emotionally unreliable persons who [were] or [would] be occupying sensitive nuclear weapons positions."[67] This led to a conference that included Lt. Col. Paul Eggertsen, an air force psychiatrist, and Fred Ikle from RAND to conceptualize what would become the Human Reliability Program. Georgetown University played a role in the proceedings. The final product was Air Force Manual 160-55 "Guidance for Implementing Human Reliability Program." It was distributed starting in 28 February 1962.[68]

B-52 navigator Robert O. Harder has perhaps the most realistic perspective on the Human Reliability Program in the 1960s:

> SAC had a tendency to dress that idea up by putting it forward as some kind of formal course, apparently in an attempt to give the American press and public a larger comfort zone as to the quality of man it was entrusting to handle nuclear weapons. The issue became even

more of a concern . . . after the release of such popular, but almost dangerously misleading Hollywood films as *Fail-Safe* and *Dr. Strangelove*. [The Human Reliability Program] was more than anything a commonsense evaluation of a man's fundamental character. . . . The fact was any erratic, unreliable, dishonest, or dishonorable behavior during the enormous stresses associated with one and a half years of flight training would almost certainly have already surfaced and been red-flagged (it happened).[69]

The most serious incident recorded in the public domain was the death of a senior sergeant in the SAC underground command post sometime in the 1960s. The Office of Special Investigations, however, concluded it was an accident, not a suicide, as originally suspected.[70]

On the loyalty front, the only recorded concerns involving B-52s and their crews was the disappearance of B-52 callsign Meal 88 in February 1968 while on a training run off the Texas coast. Lt. Col. Earl J. McGill, who was a witness to the investigating board, described a situation that resembled the film *Thunderball*. Meal 88 was piloted by an officer of Latin American descent and there were suggestions in some quarters that he might have hijacked the aircraft. SR-71 reconnaissance aircraft were deployed to photograph every airfield and airport in Latin America, "especially including Cuba." Meal 88, however, was not carrying nuclear weapons. Despite a massive search effort, no trace of the plane or her crew was ever found, and it was assumed to have crashed into the Gulf of Mexico.[71]

The crash of two Chrome Dome B-52s, one over Palomares, Spain, in a 1966 refueling accident and another over Thule in 1968 with an engine flame-out, and particularly the subsequent destruction or damage of their onboard nuclear weapons, is generally assumed to have sounded the death knell of airborne alert. However, the demands of the Vietnam War also played a role in its demise. Vietnam consumed significant numbers of B-52s and their vital maintenance crews, so much so that by 1969 SAC was "only able to maintain 24% of [their] SIOP aircraft and approximately 550 SIOP weapons on alert as opposed to the required 40% and 916 SIOP weapons."[72]

The reality is that airborne alert was curtailed and then melded into a new concept called Giant Lance before the decision was made to end operations because of a combination of cost and the significant influx of more ICBMs into the force structure.

Guiltily associated with the so-called Nixon Madman Theory, Giant Lance actually went into effect a year before Nixon assumed the presidency.[73] More properly referred to as Selective Employment of Air/Ground Alert, the program was to "enable [CINCSAC] to employ a portion of the alert force in a number of different response options while retaining a [SIOP] target assignment." That is, the SAC commander could respond to a presidential requirement to mount a "Show of Force . . . in order to demonstrate national resolve and intent" with strategic nuclear forces without jeopardizing the SIOP war plan's target coverage in the Soviet Union.[74] The possibility that the Johnson administration had to use ad hoc means to do so with SAC during the *Pueblo* affair in 1968 may have played a role in Giant Lance's birth.[75]

Giant Lance had three options. Option 1 (show of force) was for twenty-four hours; Option 2, up to thirty days; and Option 3, five days. The options were designed to be implemented either simultaneously with DEFCON 3 or immediately after it. There were several possible orbit areas. For example, the Atlantic orbit and the Mediterranean orbit were designed to accommodate six B-52s each drawn from six bombardment wings based in the United States. Another was the Goose North orbit, with a pair of B-52s. The Eielson East orbit was another.[76] Under Giant Lance's show of force option, whatever targets outside of the SIOP were "covered for approximately 20 hours by airborne strike aircraft and four hours by ground alert aircraft."[77]

By the 1970s airborne alert in the Chrome Dome fashion was a thing of the past; now the alert situation depicted in the film *By Dawn's Early Light* was in vogue and Selective Employment of Air/ Ground Alert was the available tool. In the end the decision to curtail airborne alert as well as expanded Soviet capabilities led to a situation whereby SAC commander Gen. Bruce Holloway reported that in 1970 the "Pre-Launch Survivability . . . of the aircraft alert force from a surprise [submarine-launched ballistic missile] attack was only 39% with the force on 25 bases and tactical warning [fifteen minutes] from a satellite surveillance system." If he had time, he could disperse to forty more bases and increase the probability of survival to 82 percent with "an increase in 60% more weapons delivered on target." "Although we presently have some margin of strength for attacks on military targets to deny the Soviets an unscathed reserve, we cannot assure termination of hostilities in a position of relative advantage."[78]

Sometimes the best means to convey history is through fiction. Len Deighton's 1970 novel *Bomber* captures the events surrounding a 1943 RAF Bomber Command attack against a target in Nazi Germany and the defense of that target in a way that traditional historical narrative cannot. Given the fact that there was no nuclear war, perhaps this approach serves us best. What follows is a series of vignettes that show how the various bombers depicted in the nuclear crisis films would have been employed against real defenses and actual targets.

Vignette 1

Aluminum Overcast: *Strategic Air Command* and B-36 Operations

In the 1955 SAC-aganda film *Strategic Air Command* we are dramatically introduced to a Convair B-36 bomber as it loudly and protectively overflies that all-American of facilities, the baseball diamond. For nearly a decade the gargantuan B-36 with its six reciprocating and four jet engines was the only American aircraft capable of bombing the Soviet Union from North America without refueling. *Strategic Air Command* was designed in part to showcase SAC's B-36 capabilities for as broad an audience as possible. The protagonist, Lt. Col. Robert "Dutch" Holland, is in many ways Jimmy Stewart playing himself: a World War II bomber veteran called up from the reserves to provide maturity and experience to an expanding SAC. The film is almost a docudrama, with a LeMay-like General Hawks, complete with a nonsmile and a cigar, constantly pushing the outside of the preparedness envelope as part of the deterrent mission. Nuclear weapons are only obliquely referred to ("We have them but we hope we won't have to use them"), and the lovingly lingering cameras that take us on a guided tour of the B-36, led by Harry Morgan's Master

Sergeant Bible, go nowhere near the bombardier-navigator or his position in the aircraft, presumably for security reasons.

Strategic Air Command was all about dedication, readiness, and protecting Jimmy Stewart and June Allyson's emergent nuclear family. But what if a real Dutch Holland and his crews from the 11th Bombardment Wing (Heavy) were called upon to carry out their primary mission in late 1953? Soviet MIGs have just attacked and shot down an RB-50 over the Sea of Japan while the Korean armistice is in a fragile state. Intelligence indicators suggest a build-up of Soviet ground forces in Poland and north of Hokkaido. A U.S. Navy reconnaissance plane on an electronic intelligence-gathering mission is shot down in the Baltic trying to uncover what is going on. Malenkov and Khrushchev determine that the time to take West Berlin and West Germany is now, before the West can redeploy forces from Korea and reinforce NATO.

The alert came into the command post at Carswell Air Force Base via Teletype, authorizing the 11th Bombardment Wing to execute its Emergency War Plan. The framework for this plan was the SAC Emergency War Plan 1-52, which itself was derived from a Joint Chiefs of Staff war plan code-named Majestic. This plan called for a three-day bombing campaign directed at Soviet homeland industrial capability. The Joint Chiefs' target annex of the war plan allocated SAC 120 targets within 104 urban centers clustered in eight industrial regions.[79]

To destroy these targets, Gen. Curtis LeMay reported to the Joint Chiefs that SAC had the ability to deliver two hundred atomic bombs over the course of the first six days of the war. This was the number of trained crews mated to available mechanically sound aircraft. Not all crews were trained in atomic bomb delivery, and not all of SAC's aircraft were immediately ready.[80] At this point in time (1952–53) the American stockpile consisted of between 841 and 1,169 nuclear weapons of all types.[81]

The crews had pored over their assigned targets for months prior to the alert, so a detailed briefing like those given in *Twelve O'Clock High* and other movies was unnecessary. Lt. Col. Jim Stuart gave an abbreviated briefing more for coordination purposes than anything.

"Mission No. 1 consists of an attack against EWP [Emergency War Plan] Target Reference No. 2 and will be flown by fifteen (15) B-36 aircraft. Target Reference No. 2 is Leningrad." Another group of five B-36s from the 11th Bomb Wing would simultaneously attack Emergency War Plan Target Reference 17.[82]

What exactly the B-36s were to hit in Leningrad was the matter of informed guesswork, as SAC commander LeMay admitted to senior officials.[83] There were no up-to-date aerial photographs except those taken by the Germans during World War II, so the bulk of targeting information came from human intelligence sources cross-indexed with whatever maps could be acquired. What was known in 1953 was that Flugov Plant No. 117 and Red October Plant No. 466 constituted a massive tank production complex whose proper name, as it turned out, was the Kirov Works. Returning German engineers reported on at least five radio and electronic component factories; the State Institute for Applied Chemistry, where rocket propellants were made; the "development of the Wasserfall [anti-aircraft missile] computer system" at a Leningrad plant; and the Khimgas Institute. Leningrad boasted two ports: the naval base at Kronstadt and the Port of Leningrad itself. The Zhdanov Shipyard was a separate industrial facility where German engineers were working on submarine propulsion technology. There was an airframe assembly plant somewhere on the outskirts of the city, as well as two airports. The Lenin Works was the largest producer of turbines in the country; it was embedded somewhere in the Kirov Works. Finally there was the Trust 54 Iron and Steel Works.[84]

The weaponeers knew they could not find the smaller facilities with the information at hand, let alone get to them with the navigational capabilities of 1953. Thus the largest facilities that could be correlated to geographical features were prioritized. That narrowed the aim points down to two. The first was the port and shipyard districts. Radar reflections from the Baltic Sea would provide enough geographical definition to identify them. The second was the Kirov Works, which consisted of some sixty large buildings and was immediately adjacent to the port area.

The bomb type that would be used against these targets was the

Mk-6, an evolution of the Mk III Fat Man. Tested in 1951 during the Greenhouse series, the Mk-6 system yielded 47 kilotons, or about double the explosive power used against Nagasaki. For safety purposes, the Mk-6 casing and the plutonium core were kept separate. The core was manually loaded into the casing by the aircrew on the way to the target: this was called "in-flight insertion."[85]

The 11th Bomb Wing weaponeers knew from analyzing the Nagasaki attack data and the data from Greenhouse Shot Easy that blast overpressure of twenty pounds per square inch generated by the Mk-6 bomb would destroy concrete structures and their contents within a certain radius of ground zero. The thermal effects would fry anything left and pulse out even farther. That would take out the Kirov Works. The port and shipyards were more difficult because they were linear and there were the pieces of large but dispersed machinery like cargo handling cranes and recessed dry docks. Looking to Operation Crossroads test data from Bikini Atoll in 1946, the weaponeers determined that a low-altitude or surface burst over the shipping basin would not only generate 15–20 PSI overpressure needed but would also generate a base surge of radioactive water onto the piers and dry-dock facilities. That would contaminate the port and render it useless. A third weapon dropped afterward offset slightly from the two previous detonations would ensure that the damage probability for both targets rose from 89 percent to nearly 100 percent, or it could be used as a backup if one plane could not deliver its weapon.

The 11th Bombardment Wing's Emergency War Plan was initially based on the arrival of nuclear weapons by air to Restricted Area #1 on the base at Carswell so they could be loaded on site. Seven C-124 transports from the 1st Strategic Support Squadron would fly to Gray Air Force Station, which was adjacent to the Atomic Energy Commission's national stockpile site Baker at Killeen, Texas. The weapon casings and the plutonium cores would be transferred from the Commission's custodians to the U.S. Air Force's C-124s and flown back to Carswell, each plane carrying three weapons.[86]

However, the need for a quick response to the current crisis meant that the B-36 aircraft would depart Carswell without weapons for Limestone AFB in Maine, load up there, and conduct their strikes.

"North River Depot," the cover name for Site Easy, Caribou Air Force Station, consisted of two core storage buildings, some fifty storage igloos with Mk-6 casings, and a connected series of bunkers where the casings and their reflectors and initiators were assembled and inspected.[87]

There was a chill in the air as loading was completed and the crew made their final checks at Site Easy prior to taxiing. There were still not enough weapons to equip each aircraft, so only three Mk-6s were loaded. Lieutenant Colonel Stuart's radar operator climbed into the bomb bay above the Mk-6 bomb to the U-2 release mechanism (not to be confused with the U-2 "spy plane"). The U-2 and its associated sway braces consisted of a box-frame cradle in the ceiling that the bomb and its arming wires were attached to. This was unlocked. He checked the accumulator pressure in the system. The small platform that would be used to access the bomb's nose so the plutonium pit could be inserted was now retracted. Circuit breaker #6 was turned on. As the B-36 engines roared and the plane moved to the taxiway, Stuart called out instructions.[88]

"Can salvo–no salvo switches in can salvo position." Stuart moved his right hand, flipped up the cover, and activated the switch. The two radar operators and the copilot each turned on their respective circuit breakers at their stations. If there was a problem on takeoff, the weapon casing could now be jettisoned. After a smooth takeoff, the B-36 was over New Brunswick, Canada, in seconds. "Can salvo–no salvo switches in no salvo position." The radar operator climbed back into the bomb bay and relocked the U-2 release mechanism.

Stuart organized his forces into three five-plane cells as they passed east of Newfoundland and headed toward the Greenland coast. The leaders of these cells, callsigns Skybird, Tarbaby, and Antelope, assembled their aircraft in an arrowhead formations but with each plane at a different altitude. Four of the five B-36s per cell would protect the bomb carrier aircraft. There would be, hopefully, six minutes between each cell as they made their runs into Leningrad.[89]

Two hours later the first navigation checkpoint was coming up on Greenland's east coast. Two members of Stuart's crew entered the bomb bay and folded down the in-flight insertion platform. The nose of the Mk-6 bomb was opened and the bombardier opened a special trap door in the explosive lenses. The core container was brought forward, and he carefully placed the plutonium ball on the foam mount at the center of the weapon. The lenses were carefully reassembled and the circuits checked. This process took fourteen minutes while Stuart kept the B-36 as level and as stable as possible in the North Atlantic winds at 10,000 feet.[90] Then a climb to 25,000 feet started and Stuart conducted a cell check. One aircraft, Tarbaby 2, was belching smoke from its starboard engines and had to peel off for Prestwick in Scotland. Fortunately it was not armed with a Mk-6. Stuart then ordered the three cells to climb to 45,000 feet as they overflew Norway and into Finland.

"Okay, we are climbing to strike altitude," Stuart announced. The radar operator reentered the bomb bay.

"U-2 release unlocked." Check.

"Sway braces checked." Check.

"Recheck circuit breaker #6." Check.

"U-2 accumulator pressure at 1,200 to 1,500 PSI." Check.

"Recheck heater element circuit breaker." Check.

"Switch on heater element circuit breaker." Check.

This last check was to heat the Albert radar fusing system inside the casing, which had a tendency to freeze up at altitude. The bomb was now hot, or at least warm.[91]

At this time several B-29s from the 376th Bomb Wing approached Leningrad from the west and north. Three years earlier the Soviets had used a chain of radars, dubbed Token by the intelligence people, to vector interceptor aircraft against a U.S. Navy Privateer patrol plane over the Baltic Sea. This aircraft had been shot down with the loss of its crew. When American search aircraft entered the area, their radars were jammed by a Soviet ground station, impeding rescue efforts. As a result, the 376th B-29s carried a system called Blue Cradle. Their job was to interfere with the Soviet air defense radars and their ability to guide MiG-15 jet interceptors to the incoming B-3s.[92]

Capt. Yefganii Yeremin restlessly smoked a foul cigarette in the alert shack at Levashovo air base, where the 177th Moskovskiy Fighter Aviation Regiment was stationed. Newly returned from his internationalist duty protecting North Korea from the United Nations, Yeremin's experienced MiG-15 pilots were champing at the bit the moment they heard that Western Group of Forces entered West Berlin. But so far there had been no contacts from the Token radar chain, and it was getting dark. Their MiG-15s had no night-fighting capability. Nor did their sister interceptor regiments. The 11th Guards Vyborskiy Order of Kutuzov Fighter Aviation Regiment at Gorelovo air base handled the southwest approaches to Leningrad, while the 27th Guards Vyborskiy Red Banner Aviation Regiment did the same at Pushkin to the south. He was glad he was not stationed at Gromovo-Sakkola to the north with the 180th Guards Stalingradskiiy Red Banner regiment. It was somewhat austere and the vodka was bad, if there could be such a thing.[93]

The scramble alarm went off. Yeremin ditched his cigarette as he and his pilots dashed to their MiG-15s and roared into the sky at a thousand kilometers per hour. The ground control station controller excitedly told the flight leaders that there were multiple contacts coming in north-northwest near Vyborg at 30,000 feet. The MiGs altered course like a wolfpack after prey. Yeremin's eyes probed the skies in the gloomy dusk. There! "B-29-type aircraft, port side. I am attacking." The MiGs pounced and unleashed N-37 cannon fire on the hapless electronic countermeasures plane from the 376th as it struggled to get away into Finland. Eventually its crew bailed out as Yeremin continued to pour cannon fire into the plane as it descended. But there was no other prey for the MiGs as they vainly searched the skies, and they were rapidly running out of fuel. Similar events were occurring with the fighter regiment stationed at Gromovo-Sakkola.

The Skybird, Tarbaby, and Antelope cells overflew their pre-initial point at Parikkala, Finland, and visually checked in with Stuart with their Aldis lamps.

Yeremin tapped his fuel gauge as he banked. Out of the corner of his right eye he saw the fading sun glint off aluminum above him at over 40,000 feet. It was a huge, lumbering B-36. "Intruders! I am attacking!" But no one heard him because the APT-1 jamming device on one of the B-36s blocked all four channels of the Russian's VHF radio set with random tones.[94] The other MiGs followed but started to peel off and divert to Gromovo-Sakkola. Yeremin kept at it but was greeted with 20mm cannon fire from several B-36 turrets. A fuel warning light went on as he jinked away from the tracers. He pressed the firing button and emptied his N-37 cannons, to no effect. The jet engine cut and the Soviet ace reluctantly ejected.

The B-36s were fifty-five miles out, about to hit the initial point near Baryshevo.

Stuart held the B-36 steady at 45,000 feet. His orders were a voice in his head: "All aircraft will remain in formation until the cross-hair distance from the offset aiming point at which each aircraft will proceed individually." A black shape, a MiG-15, flashed by: why was he at 45,000 feet? Could they make that altitude too? It opened up on Skybird 4 with cannon fire. Another pounced on Skybird 3, and its engines started smoking.

"Lake Ladoga is on the port side!" the navigator called out.

"Do you have the offset aiming point?" Stuart calmly asked through the intercom system. The radar observer in the forward part of the plane checked his three instruments: the AN/APA-59 navigation computer, which was connected to the AN/APS 23 radar, and the A-1A bomb release computer, which was connected to both.[95] The radar echoes in the scope on his right clearly showed Kotlin Island, the offset aiming point, and then the curvature of the coast line where the port of Leningrad was, and from there a mile farther in was the huge complex that was the Kirov Works. There was a solid pie-shaped cone on the scope that blocked the radar reflection, but it was to the west and south and the jamming did not obscure the target (see fig. 30).

"I have it." He turned to his left and looked down through the bomb sight itself. Up in the cockpit Stuart flipped the toggle switch with his right hand, opened the bomb bay doors, and then moved up to the next panel.[96] A MiG 15 was now lined up on Stuart's B-36 and his gunners were engaging it.

"Can salvo–no salvo switch on."

Cannon fire hit the port wing. The photo-navigator accessed the special bomb rack panel and moved the special release switch to "special release."

"Bomb circuit breakers on." The photo-navigator and Stuart hit their circuit breaker switches. The radar observer checked his instruments again and toggled the D-2 bomb release switch.[97]

"Bombs away!"

The Mk-6 bomb released from the cradle, which pulled out the arming wires and activated the switches inside the bomb. The B-36 leaped up over 100 feet, freed from the weight, and nearly collided with the pursuing MiG-15, which veered off out of control into the sea. Stuart pulled the giant plane to port in order to point the tail toward the blast wave of the bomb. This maneuver had been successful in Nevada and Pacific tests, but those were with smaller detonations.

The second cell, Antelope, approached their initial point. "Antelope, this is Antelope 2. Condition Muddy. I authenticate AP 1578, over." The K bomb-navigation system on the bomb carrier had just conked out or was being jammed. "Antelope 2, this is Antelope. Roger. I authenticate AP 1578, out." Antelope flew alongside Antelope 2 to coordinate the drop. "Antelope 2, time to go one minute. I say again: time to go one minute AP 1578 NOW."

"Time to go thirty seconds. Twenty, ten, five, four, three, two, one . . . Bombs away!" A white Aldis lamp flashed simultaneously with the command. Antelope 2 lurched upward, and another Mk-6 was on its way to Leningrad. Tarbaby 3 came right in afterward and delivered the third weapon. Stuart kept his B-36 at 40,000 feet for five hundred miles, until he was clear of the Estonian coast, then descended to 35,000 over the Baltic.

The first Mk-6 detonated over the Kirov Works at 4,691 feet in the millisecond its Albert radar pulse detected the burst altitude. The bomb generated an overpressure wave of 20 PSI out to 5,053 feet, effectively destroying the entire facility with the blast.[98] What was left was burned out by the thermal pulse, which started secondary and tertiary fires from combustible material like oil and lubricants in the shattered factories. The second weapon, targeted on the shipyard and dockyard district, detonated at 1,804 feet. This Mk-6 augmented the damage to the area already hit with the thermal pulse of the first weapon with a blast wave; this wrecked any building within 5,414 feet. That was followed by a base surge throughout the area as the blast wave reflected on the underside of the detonation and produced a wall of water that slammed into the port facilities, destroying them. The third weapon, released last, was set slightly higher than the first and augmented the blast damage generated to both targets. In effect, Leningrad was hit with the equivalent of six "Nagasakis" directed at its port and manufacturing district. While the blast effects were confined to those areas, the thermal pulses covered 60 percent of the city, burning any person in the open. The radioactive water plume from the second shot surged into the factory district, dampening the fires to some extent but leaving the area uninhabitable. Turbines, ships, and other heavy equipment would never depart the Kirov plant or the shipyards again.

The remaining aircraft headed to RAF Station Brize Norton to meet up with the C-124 transports of the 1st Strategic Support Squadron and rearm. This campaign was going to last at least three months, or until the Atomic Energy Commission ran out of bombs.

Vignette 2

Doomsday Armada: *Strategic Air Command* and B-47 Operations

Continuing with the SAC-aganda theme, *Strategic Air Command's* plot contrives to put Lt. Col. Dutch Holland and General Hawks/ LeMay in a large hanger containing the sleek, swept-wing Boeing B-47 Stratojet bomber. In his impromptu briefing Hawks/LeMay explains that the B-47 is the wave of the future and that Holland will be in command of a wing of the new aircraft. In reality, B-36 squadrons and crews transitioned to B-52s, while the shorter-range medium bomber wings with B-50s converted to B-47s. The rest of *Strategic Air Command* is a paean to the Stratojet, which needs only a three-man crew instead of the thirteen in the B-36. The film depicts in great detail the transcontinental deployment of a SAC B-47 wing (forty-five bombers) in all of its jet-propelled aluminum glory by air from Florida to Yokota, Japan. The level of detail in this part of *Strategic Air Command* is intentional and was clearly designed to influence friend and foe alike. As with the early part of the film, nuclear weapons are alluded to (the B-47s carry "a new family of nuclear weapons," according to Hawks/LeMay), but no detail is provided. The implication: We can hit you devastatingly and quickly from the United States, from overseas bases, or via aerial refueling.[99]

B-47 Stratojets were the mainstay bombers in SAC throughout the 1950s and early 1960s. If war erupted during that time, the bulk of American nuclear weapons would have been delivered by SAC's nearly 1,200 B-47s. Let's say Lt. Col. Jim Stuart and his family were posted to the 9th Bombardment Wing (Medium) at Mountain Home Air Force Base, Idaho, with its four squadrons of B-47 bombers. It is early 1960 and Khrushchev has accelerated his deadline. Soviet tanks are entering West Berlin, NATO is in disarray, and Eisenhower takes the initiative to protect the homeland.

Mountain Home Air Force Base in Idaho, situated far from populated areas and the West Coast, did not look like it was on the front lines of the Cold War. Indeed the 9th Bomb Wing was generally not part of SAC's initial strike force, which consisted of two hundred B-47s on fifteen-minute ground alert at bases in the United Kingdom, Spain, North Africa, and Alaska. The 9th routinely rotated part of its B-47 squadrons, usually six aircraft, to these locations as part of the Reflex Action posture. That said, the new "bombs on base" concept, whereby the weapons were stored in the new weapons storage area, meant that the bombs were no longer reluctantly doled out in a complex logistics process by the Atomic Energy Commission from their highly centralized and thus vulnerable sites.[100] The 9th was fully capable of carrying out its part of Basic War Plan 1-58.

Basic War Plan 1-58 was based on Joint Chiefs of Staff targeting priorities that went into effect in early 1957. Instead of targeting industry, SAC now focused on what was called the Air Power Battle Target System. The new targets consisted of Soviet bomber forces and their bases and supporting fuel infrastructure, the command and control for Soviet nuclear forces and their communications systems, and the nuclear production and storage systems. The Air Battle Target System included some 1,539 "desired ground zeros," or specific targets, to be destroyed by nuclear weapons. In the event of war the initial sac bomber waves were to be sent in to destroy 954 of these as a priority.[101]

Colonel Stuart's planning staff at the 9th Bomb Wing was no longer crippled by a lack of targeting information. By this time the CIA was conducting regular overflights of the Soviet Union with Lockheed U-2 aircraft. The imagery from these dangerous missions was passed directly to sac Headquarters, where it fed the targeting planners.[102] In 1958 CIA analysts asked why coverage of the Kamchatka Peninsula had not received higher priority; it was close to North America, it had bases on it, and every time "ferret" signal intelligence flights or U-2s passed by, the Soviets surged their interceptors to keep the eyes and ears away. Other CIA sources noted that a pair of new nuclear missile-carrying submarines were based in Petropavlovsk. These could be surged in a crisis and would be difficult if not impossible to find in the Pacific's vastness.[103]

In theory, Petropavlovsk was a U.S. Navy problem. It was within Pacific Command, which had its own nuclear forces to deal with it, including aircraft carriers and submarines carrying Regulus cruise missiles. Intelligence knew, however, that there were two large air bases near Petropavlovsk. This could be of interest to sac. When the ferrets played their dangerous game and flew near the peninsula, they learned from their intercepts that the 865th Fighter Aviation Regiment was stationed at Elizovo air base, outside of Petropavlovsk. The 865th had three types of interceptors: the MiG-17 day fighter; the MiG-19PM interceptor, which was equipped with the new air-to-air missiles; and the Yak-25M twin-engine interceptor, which had all-weather and night-intercept capability with its large radar. The MiG-15 had no radar, but the ferrets knew the MiG-19's and Yak-25's radars by heart, as they collected their signals.[104] Indeed one of their own had been victimized by MiGs from Petropavlovsk: in April 1955 MiG-17s shot down a special reconnaissance version of the B-47 in international waters off Kamchatka, killing the crew.[105]

The ferrets also knew the Soviet fighters were directed by a ground station somewhere in the hills and that there were Token and Whif radars along the coast.[106] The second air base on the other side of the mountains was a complete mystery. It was capable of taking jet bombers, but that was all that was known. The possibility that Soviet bombers could stage from there to North America tweaked SAC's interest.

Gen. Thomas Power, the SAC commander in chief, was not going to risk the possibility that the navy would focus their attacks on the naval bases and not attack the air bases. The submarine USS *Tunney* was on a deterrent patrol off the Soviet east coast loaded with a pair of Regulus cruise missiles, each carrying a 2-megaton-yield warhead. And what if the assigned American missile submarine (there was only one on station at this time) was destroyed by enemy action or otherwise mechanically incapacitated, as the *Tunney* was in December 1959?[107] Consequently Power instructed SAC planners to target all facilities in the Petropavlovsk area. Just in case. The Soviet missile subs could just as easily destroy SAC bases in Alaska or Guam as they could any other target.

SAC had very few intercontinental ballistic missiles in 1959–60, and they were prioritized elsewhere. Similarly the B-52 force was assigned priority targets in the western Soviet Union after the B-47 force cleared the way. That left the B-47Es assigned to wings in North America. Mountain Home was the closest to Petropavlovsk, so the 9th got the task.[108]

The target complex in Petropavlovsk was just that: complex. In addition to the two air bases, there were six targets of interest, all of them associated with naval operations. They were arrayed around a large bay, but four of them were inside two coves that were subsets of the bay. Near Petropavlovsk itself were the Kamchatskiy Shipyard, and across from it was the Rakovaya Bay berthing area, used for both surface ships and submarines. Naval headquarters was also tucked away in there somewhere. On the west side of the bay was the Bukhta Tarya Naval Base, which was mostly for the submarine force. A munitions storage area was tucked into Bogatyrevka Bay. Then there was the Seldevaya Bay Naval Base, a ship repair facility. Finally, the overhead imagery showed a new facility under construction. It was assessed to be a nuclear missile storage and handling facility with its own jetty.[109] Geography dictated that multiple nuclear weapons were required to ensure the destruction of all of these facilities.

It was just as well that the 9th Bomb Wing planners had a variety of weapons to draw on, given the dispersed nature of the targets and the hilly terrain. The weapons storage area at Mountain Home was loaded with five types of nuclear weapons. There was the Mk-6 atomic bomb (up to 180 kilotons); these were older weapons used for restrike purposes. Then there were the Mk-39 and Mk-36 thermonuclear weapons.[110] The yields of these weapons ranged from 3.8 to 19 megatons, depending on the target and mode of use. None of them employed the in-flight insertion method; these new weapons were called "sealed pit" bombs. The only maintenance was that the tritium booster had to be monitored regularly and refilled when required when the expensive nuclear material decayed. Some, like the Mk-36s, were parachute-retarded, which meant they could be employed from altitude. The Mk-15s and Mk-39s could be delivered from low altitude because of their arming and safety systems.[111]

Two five-plane cells were scheduled to attack targets around Petropavlovsk: Red Cell (Red 1 through 5) and White Cell (White 1 through 5). Each aircraft carried one weapon, and the Red and White cells were cross-targeted: Red 1 targeted Target 1, as did White 2, and so on.[112]

Each crew had a combat mission folder and had studied their targets and approach tactics for days. Once the force came within a certain range of the target, individual B-47Es would peel off and start their runs in sequence. The low-level element would go in first to achieve surprise, with five runs staggered in time so the nuclear weapons did not destroy each other when they detonated. The high-level element would hit the same series of targets again, just to make sure. The objective was the complete destruction of both air bases so they could not be used as staging bases to attack North America, and the complete destruction of the submarine and other naval support facilities for the same reason.

The weaponeering that went into the Petropavlovsk strike was intense. The targeters knew how the weapons available to them performed in the Pacific tests; in this case, data from the 1954 Castle detonations were part of the computations. The Mk-15 and its Mk-39 derivative bomb were the weaponized version of the Nectar shot on

5 April 1954; it could yield 3.8 megatons. The Mk-36, a derivative of the Bravo shot of the same test series, could yield 6 or 18 megatons.

The destruction criterion for the targeted facilities was set at "moderate" for the naval facilities, which for practical purposes meant that they had to be turned into gravel as opposed to rubble (Light) or dust (Severe). Severe was the criterion for the airfields.[113] This dictated that surface bursts be employed to crater the airfields so that Soviet bombers deployed from their bases in the west could not use them. Near-surface and airbursts for the other facilities to generate maximum blast damage to the submarines and storage facilities were also part of the plan.

The crater for the Zuni shot in the 1956 Redwing nuclear tests was 700 meters in diameter. Zuni yielded 3.5 megatons, which was close to the Mk-15/39's 3.8 megatons. However, the Pacific tests were conducted in coral. CIA analysis of the geology of the Petropavlovsk region indicated it was hard rock. Therefore the shock wave would be attenuated somewhat. The difference between 3.5 and 3.8 megatons and the attenuation essentially balanced out: the Mk-15 would produce a crater 700 meters wide. The Mk-36 detonating at 6 megatons would produce damage similar to Shot Tewa, when attenuation because of rock was factored in to a crater 1,000 meters wide. Finally, for facilities demanding increased blast effects, the Mk-36 bomb could be modified or "dialed up" from 6 to 19 megatons. If detonated on the surface, it would dig a crater 2,100 meters wide.[114] The other effects of the weapons, that is thermal, prompt radiation, and fallout, were not considered except in terms of affecting the interval between the planes delivering the weapons to avoid fratricide.

The ten B-47Es from the 99th Bomb Squadron under Stuart's command were running their engines up after the alert was sounded. "All aircraft taxi to the runway," the command post ordered. Stuart and his navigator pulled out their KAC-1 authenticator cards and "aligned the notch from the plastic template with the time period. The entire page was covered with an array of randomly listed alpha characters. The first two characters to appear in the row had to agree with the two alpha characters given by the command post."[115] They did. The

B-47s trundled to the taxiway. Another command came over the radio to launch. This was also authenticated with the KAC-1. The crews thought this might be a Coco practice alert and prepared to return to the alert area. It wasn't. The ten bombers lifted off.

Leveling off over British Columbia, the B-47Es were met by KC-97 tanker aircraft based at Royal Canadian Air Force Station Namao, Alberta. Usually four American tankers were discretely based there on a specially built and isolated facility, but due to international tensions the number was increased to twelve. After the B-47Es continued on their way they refueled again south of Alaska from KC-97s out of Eielson AFB.[116]

The B-47Es reached an invisible line in the darkened sky called the "passive detection zone." From here to the H-Hour Control Line, where orders to proceed to the targets was given by SAC, all electronic systems that could emit energy were placed in standby so the astute Soviets could not detect them. This included the bomb/navigation radar, the rear gun fire control system, jamming and communications systems, as well as identification friend/foe transponders. The bomb/navigation radar antenna was shut off and traversed to the rear. This was to prevent electromagnetic energy, perhaps generated by airburst nuclear weapons, from damaging or destroying the vital system.[117]

On arrival at the H-Hour Control Line hours later, the ten aircraft went into orbit, listening to the 243.0 kilocycles frequency on their radios at five, twenty-five, and forty-five minutes after the hour for three-minute periods. There was nothing heard at the twenty-five-minute mark. At forty-five minutes the crew faintly heard, "Skybird Control, this is Sky King. Switchbox Forty. I say again, Switchbox Forty." This was SAC Headquarters on the global high-frequency radio system contacting all airborne SAC bombers. Holland shifted to a UHF radio and contacted a radar station in the Pacific, callsign Killdeer. That radar station would have received, via Teletype and radio, the same code word.[118]

"Skybird Control, this is Ajax 42."

"Ajax 42, this is Killdeer."

"Roger, Killdeer, do you have traffic?"

"Roger, Ajax 42. Switchbox Forty. I say again, Switchbox Forty. Authentication is Extra Extra."

"Roger, Killdeer. Ajax 42 out."

"We have a Noah's Ark message," Stuart informed his crew. That meant a possible strike order. Another authenticator, the KAC-72/TSEC, confirmed that Extra Extra was legitimate, and thus Killdeer was in fact sending the message. The KAC-1 authenticators came out again. There were three letters: the first was a letter substitute for the time, Q. The second letter was the second letter in the radar site callsign, I. The third letter in the authentication process was the first letter in the code word Switchbox Forty, or S. QIS. Switchbox Forty was an authentic message. The bombardier opened a sealed, hinged compartment called the "secrets box." Inside was the positive control envelope, the KAA-29/TSEC authenticator book, and other strike material. Switchbox Forty was not only an authentic message; it was an instruction to proceed and bomb primary targets in accordance with Option 9 of the Emergency War Plan. Stuart and the copilot concurred.[119]

"Okay, it's a go!" Stuart told his crew as he turned the B-47E out of its orbit and across the H-Hour Control Line. Now the full force of the bomber's defensive systems could come into play as required until the Electronic Warfare Termination Line. Stuart's B-47Es each carried six different devices plus metal foil chaff to confuse radars. Half of Stuart's force, the high-altitude group, was permitted to use their systems, but the low-level group kept them switched off. After some minutes a Soviet Token radar somewhere on the Kamchatka Peninsula was heard on the AN/APS 54 device: a tone in their helmets warned the crews that they were being tracked. The ALT-6 jammers then kicked in on three sets of frequencies, blotting out the location of the bombers on the Token's radar screen. The Soviet interceptors at Petropavlovsk had to be directed to the general location of the incoming bombers by the radar, then those aircraft would use their onboard radars to hunt and kill the B-47s. Just in case a controller was already vectoring in an interceptor, Stuart's high-level element turned on an ARC-27 radio specially modified to block those frequencies with rotating tones so the controller could not talk to the MiGs.[120]

Unfortunately for the B-47ES, a pair of Yak-25s were already on patrol in the area. Lt. Pavel Makartneskayev's radar operator was working through the jamming and briefly had a contact before electronic snow covered it. "Fly 187! Three hundred meters! Thirty-five thousand feet!" he said excitedly, and Makartneskayev swung the large twin-engine jet in an arc, searching for the intruders. "This is Blue 456. This is Blue 456, over." The blocking tones overlapped his communications and he couldn't signal the second Yak-25 that he was on to something. Makartneskayev caught sight of one of the high-element B-47ES, White 3. The large RP-6 Sokol radar in the nose was ineffective: the B-47E was dumping chaff, which was confusing it. He armed his 37mm cannons anyway, hoping for a visual shot. Makartneskayev knew that the B-47E had rearward-facing guns; his friends had tangled with RB-47 ferrets before and been shot up, so he decided to attack his target from the side and above. One sweeping pass and the 37mm rounds tore chunks out of the wings and fuselage of the bomber. Several hit the spar, and the B-47E folded in on itself and went down. Nobody ejected.

A second B-47E, White 5, opened up with its rear guns while Makartneskayev was in a bank losing speed. The rounds bounced off his specially armored cockpit. He lined up for a pass on this new enemy, which now jinked back and forth. His 37mm rounds nearly found this second aircraft, but then the feed mechanism jammed. By this time the third B-47E had emptied its guns in a last, desperate bid to survive. The 20mm rounds penetrated the radar dome and found their way into the guts of the Yak-25, which lost power. Makartneskayev and his radar operator were forced to eject over the lonely and extremely cold northern Pacific Ocean. The crippled third B-47E, White 2, diverted to the Aleutians and an equally uncertain fate.

The 99th Bomb Squadron element, now reduced to eight aircraft, pressed on. NSA signals intelligence stations in northern Japan heard the garbled Soviet air defense system attempt to assess and address the incoming SAC bombers. MiG-19PMs scrambled, but there was no means to direct them from the ground. Those that got airborne were unable to find any targets because of the jamming. Several of them fired their air-to-air missiles at the chaff blooms, mistaking them for bombers. The Soviet commanders even scrambled the MiG-15 day fighters, but at night without radar or the ability to communicate their mission was next to impossible.

Back in Mountain Home, the crews at had agreed that the Short Look delivery profile was best for this mission. This involved a low-level penetration at 200 to 300 feet above the ocean fifty miles out from the targets, then a "pop-up" maneuver to release the bomb, which involved leveling the aircraft for twelve seconds and then diving away at speed. On the way in the bombers dove from 41,000 feet to 250 and used ground effect from the ocean to facilitate their speed and lift.[121] At this point the electronic countermeasures equipment was shut off so it did not interfere with the bomb run: the X-band jammer was so powerful it could interfere with or even damage the radar bombing system.[122]

The Red elements' five B-47ES came around southwest of Petropavlovsk and shifted to a staggered formation. Red 2 broke away from the pack and penetrated the coast fifty miles to the south and into a valley, heading for its target, the Lenino air base. Red 1 was now in the lead and Elizovo air base had minutes to exist.

It was now time to arm the Mk-36 on Red 1. Prior to launch the crew removed the safety wire and attached the arming shackles to the arming rods that lay inside the bomb. When the bomb was released from the B-47, the shackles would pull the rods out.[123]

"Pilot to copilot. Release manual bomb rack lock control." The copilot flipped a switch, unlocking the cradle that held the bomb. Stuart and his copilot each flipped a switch. The safety pins had already been removed before flight (see fig. 31).

"Pilot to bomb-nav. DCU-9/1 arming switch to Ground." The bombardier-navigator reached for this small black box, broke the lead seal, moved the red lock from OS to SGA, and rotated the switch to GND. Ground burst.

"Roger."

"Pilot to bomb-nav. I am activating salvo T switch to salvo on." Stuart reached with his left hand, broke the seal, lifted the hinged plastic cover, and rotated the T switch so it was on.

"Bomb-nav to pilot. Salvo on/off switch to salvo on." The bombardier flicked a switch. Stuart started to climb from 300 to 3,700 feet.

"Roger."

Stuart turned the autopilot control switch to Bombardier. "You have the aircraft."

"I have the aircraft." The bombardier-navigator checked the offset dials on the computer and synched them. "One minute to turn." He gave the magnetic heading of the bomb run to Stuart. Checking all of the numbers, he then quickly looked at the radar scope and used a joystick to place the azimuth marker on the target.

"Time to go, 120 seconds."

"Roger."

The bombardier and Stuart counted down from 120 to 60 to 20 to 10 seconds. At twenty seconds the bombardier flicked a function switch to Bomb. The bombardier-navigator pressed the D-2 button when the B-47E reached 3,700 feet.

"Bombs away!" Stuart called out, released the aircraft from autopilot, immediately dove to 100 feet in a descending turn to starboard, accelerated away from the blast, and then climbed back up to 40,000 feet as a new sun rose behind them. "That's payback for Neighbors, Brooks, and Watkins," Stuart told his crew over the intercom (see fig. 32).

The Mk-36 descended, a process that took nearly a minute. Fused for contact, the weapon landed five hundred meters east of the facility and yielded close to 19 megatons, producing a crater two kilometers in diameter, which obliterated the runway. Every structure and facility six kilometers away was reduced to dust by the overpressure and other blast effects, and at twelve kilometers they were turned into gravel. At forty kilometers structures were engulfed in flame. All human beings within five kilometers were killed, while 50 percent of the people forty kilometers away received third-degree burns. The Kamchatka Air Defense Division direction center was collaterally destroyed, thus disrupting PVO (*protivovozdushnaya oborona*, or air defense command) operations in the entire region. The cloud rose miles and miles as all of the atomized material was sucked up into it.[124]

Even though Stuart had drawn the thick asbestos blast curtains, he and his crew could feel the heat, and the light from the flash crept around the edges of the curtain like it wanted into the aircraft. The shockwave eventually caught up with the B-47E, but as Holland was low and had the tail pointed to the blast, there were only a few popped rivets.[125]

Red 3 was inbound and, like Red 1, the crew had the blast curtains drawn. The seven-minute interval between Red 1's detonation and Red 3's implementation of its Short Look maneuver was such that the flash, blast, and thermal effects had dissipated by the time Red 3 climbed to 3,700 feet.[126] Red 3's Mk-36 was rigged as a 6-megaton weapon and fused for low airburst. Its detonation point lay above the bay between the Kamchatskiy Shipyard and the Rakovaya Bay berthing area. The Mk-36 arced in and detonated at 500 feet: the blast effects went out eight kilometers and smashed every standing structure. The bay itself absorbed the blast, but the shockwave in the water ripped apart the ships and submarines berthed at both facilities. Other parts of the water were turned into radioactive steam and fried whatever was left. The hills around the bay channeled the explosion upward so that when Red 4 was inbound to the Bukhta Tarya Naval Base, it looked like a pillar of fire to their starboard side.

Red 4 was next. The target was speculative but appeared from reconnaissance reports to be a storage area for missiles to be carried and launched from submarines. It had its own loading dock and crane under construction. But it had to be destroyed, just in case. The dispersed nature of the facility dictated a Mk-36 with 6-megaton yield fused for airburst. Given the nature of the terrain, which was hilly and could channel the effects, the weapon was detonated at 1,000 feet. This was enough to obliterate the entire installation.

Red 5 carried a Mk-36 with its yield set to 19 megatons. The elongated nature of the peninsula that submarine base was on and the possibility of hardened facilities dictated this. Red 5's weapon landed on the dock area, fused for ground burst. The subsequent crater was at least two kilometers in diameter and turned the water to radioactive aerosol. The hills in the bay reflected the blast back in on itself, which effectively destroyed everything within eight kilometers, including the repair facility across the bay at Seldevaya. Meanwhile Red 2 wound its way through the valley and was able to execute a Mk-36 drop on the Lenino air base with effects identical to Red 1's attack on Elizovo.

The White element came in at 37,000 feet and made preparations to start their bomb runs, timed to avoid the initial effects of the first strikes. The copilot from White 4 saw it first: two bursts of flame from the ground to starboard. With almost no warning, White 5 was peppered with shrapnel that pierced the starboard fuel cells. Structural failure was imminent when the pilot violently banked and the spar snapped. The B-47E folded up on itself and plummeted into the ocean.

The Soviet commander of the 1079th Anti-Aircraft Missile Regiment was less than satisfied. He had six operational missiles in one site of the twelve sites scheduled to be built in the Petropavlovsk region. His radar system was not fooled by the electronic countermeasures on board the B-47Es. His radars (code-named Fan Song by NATO) worked on the E, F, and G bands and were not affected by the B-47E's jammers, which were on L, S, and X bands.[127] He ordered his men to volley-fire all six S-75 Dvina missiles. Two did not leave their launchers; four did. Two of those made contact with White 5.

But he was too late. White 4's crew released a Mk-15 weapon, which landed next to the smoking, radiating crater generated by Red 3's strike on the Bukhta Tarya Naval Base. A second crater was blown into the rock with more resultant fallout. White 1 was the last in dodging the clouds resulting from the other drops, headed for a suspected nuclear weapons storage area near Koryaki. The dispersed sites led the planners to designate the town as the aim point, and another 19-megaton-yield weapon was delivered.

Stuart used the SAC high-frequency radio system to report in to SAC Headquarters as Red element and the remains of White element got out of Dodge and headed for four specially designated bases in Alaska—if they still existed. Within hours there wasn't a living thing in the Petropavlovsk area—or anywhere else on the Kamchatka Peninsula.

Leper Colony: *Dr. Strangelove* and the B-52 Bomb Run

For comparative purposes, here is the sequence of events in *Dr. Strangelove* when the B-52 piloted by Maj. T. J. "King" Kong receives orders to proceed and attack the Soviet Union.[128] The announcer explains that the Airborne Alert Force is a group of B-52s kept aloft via refueling from the Arctic to the Persian Gulf. Each B-52 carries 50 megatons of bombs and is two hours from their targets in Russia. While the crew is going about their business on airborne alert, the CRM-114 device starts buzzing and a code, FGD 135, appears. The radio operator nonchalantly consults a multiring binder and notes that FGD 135 is the code for "Wing Attack Plan R." In disbelief, the pilot, Major Kong, leaves the B-52 on autopilot and checks with two other crew members. Sure enough, it is Wing Attack Plan R.

"Better get a confirmation from base," Kong tells the radio operator. That is, Burpelson Air Force Base, *Leper Colony*'s home base in Texas, not SAC Headquarters.

"Major Kong, message from base confirmed." The crew open a safe and remove the envelope marked "Plan R." Inside are several attack profile envelopes, one for each crew member. These instruct the crew to set a three-letter code prefix, OPE, into the CRM-114 and lock it in. The CRM-114 is then shifted to something called a "discriminator" to ensure unauthorized radio transmissions cannot be received by the aircraft. Authorization means having OPE as the code prefix before a message can be sent.

Major Kong reads out the "attack profile," which has a 30-megaton bomb airburst at 10,000 feet over an ICBM complex. The second bomb, which yields 20 megatons, will be used if the first one does not function properly. Otherwise *Leper Colony* is to proceed to a secondary target and drop the second bomb there. It is a "fused airburst" at 12,000 feet.

On the way to their primary target, *Leper Colony* is tracked by a missile traveling at Mach 3 sixty miles away. The electronic warfare officer instructs the pilots to implement "evasive action right," but the missile still closes in. At ten-mile increments the crew attempts to interfere with the missile's tracking system: "Lock ECM [electronic counter measures] to target intercept mode." "Electronic guidance scrambler to Blue Grid." "Attack range gate on maximum scan." Plus lots of evasive action. The missile deflects at eight miles but then detonates one mile away. This sequence is interesting in that the crew is depicted putting out electrical fires on the B-52 and the CRM-114 self-destruct mechanism blew itself up. In effect, Stanley Kubrick and Peter George may have incorporated electromagnetic pulse into the film without realizing what they were doing.

Damaged, running out of fuel, and out of communications, Major Kong asks his bomb/nav, Lt. Lothar Zogg (played by James Earl Jones, later "promoted" to "command" the SAC Looking Glass plane as a brigadier general in *By Dawn's Early Light*), "What's the nearest target of opportunity?" Zogg consults other documents at his station and concludes that Target #384, the ballistic missile complex at Kurdlosk, is the closest designated target.

On arrival in the general target area, the navigator slides a plastic sheet into his scope. At ten miles he instructs the crew to shift the grid from Green to Target Orange.

The final bomb run check is elaborate. Kong orders Zogg, "Bomb fusing master safety on: electronic, barometric, time, and impact." Zogg flips four corresponding switches at his station underneath the cockpit. "Fuse for ground burst delay factor yellow." Zogg confirms he has done this.

"Bomb fusing circuits one through four test." Zogg throws four switches.

"Bomb arming lights test one through four." Zogg throws four more switches.

"Primary trigger override."

"Track indicators to maximum deflection."

"Detonator set for zero altitude." Zogg turns a dial to zero.

"Release first safety." Zogg and Lieutenant Goldberg each throw four switches.

"Release second safety." Kong, Zogg, and Goldberg each release four switches.

"Bomb door circuit one to four check." But the doors won't open. Kong goes down into the cavernous bomb bay to see why, after telling his copilot, Capt. "Ace" Owens (played by Shane Rimmer, who will be "promoted" to a SAC colonel in *Twilight's Last Gleaming*, serve aboard the USS *Bedford* as a seaman, command a nuclear submarine in *The Spy Who Loved Me*, and then become secretary of state in *Whoops Apocalypse*), to stay on the bomb run.

Ace Owens continues the techno-chant at one-mile intervals:

"Telemetric computer to orange grid."

"Correct track indicator seven miles."

"Pulse transponder active."

"Switch to zero mode."

"Auto CDC to manual Teleflex link."

Kong fixes the bomb bay door problem, the bomb drops, and the Plesetsk-like ICBM complex grows larger and larger on screen as Kong yippee-ki-yays his way to thermonuclear doom and cinematic posterity.

What if a real-life B-52G crew had to conduct a mission against the Soviet Union? It is early 1964 and Nikita Khrushchev is seriously depressed. He has just watched *Dr. Strangelove* and has a hard time laughing at the portrayal of Premier Kissoff, and even less so at General Ripper's precipitous actions in the film. They remind him of General Power's actions during Berlin and Cuba. The events of 22 November disturb him. Khrushchev has read the KGB reports and firmly believes that a coup d'état has taken place in the United States by the military-industrial complex.[129] He sympathizes with the dead president. In the spring of 1962 in Lviv a group of military officers tried to shoot him. Then in 1963, when he was in Minsk, a roadside bomb set by another group of officers detonated behind his limousine. And on another trip to Minsk he was shot at and lightly wounded. His sources have warned him that his unpopularity is increasing in both official quarters and throughout the land. They are coming to remove him today, like Kennedy was removed. But he can forestall that. Permanently. There are still loyal men in the Strategic Rocket Forces.[130]

A B-52G from the 843rd Bomb Wing, affectionately named *Leper Colony II*, was orbiting the Mediterranean off Spain on airborne alert when the high-frequency radio on board emitted a burst of static that quickly receded. "Sky King, Sky King. Do not answer. Alpha Three Tango. Four Five. Foxtrot Uniform." The message was repeated for three minutes, then it stopped. Lieutenant Braeden checked his watch: it was forty-five minutes after the hour. He pulled out his KAC-72 authenticator and checked it against Foxtrot Uniform. It matched. The message from SAC headquarters was authentic.[131]

Radar-navigator Lt. "King Zog" Luther grunted as he knelt down to open the small safe. "I like the safe better. At least we can stop wearing those damn things around our necks," he said to Maj. J. T. "Godzilla" Godd, who was busy changing his headgear to something General Power would definitely not approve of. "Yeah. It was like having a long string tie at a goat rodeo trying to get that off to get the orders while bein' buffeted at one hundred feet AGL [above ground level]."

"Okay, Braeden has validated that the message is real." Luther pulled out an envelope, and with Godd present he opened it. "Alpha Three Tango . . ." He ran his finger down the list. "It says, 'Proceed to positive control point and await orders. The KAA-29 will be used to authenticate those orders once received.'"[132] A AAA triptych-like map spilled out of the envelope along with some other papers. "If so, we are to proceed with combat mission folder primary and secondary targets." There was a range of times. "We have to be over the primary within so many hours from the H-Hour Control Line and the secondary within one hour of attacking the primary. If we don't, we get fried."

"Does it *really* say that?" Godd inquired and peered over the papers. Luther gave him 'that look.' Godd raised his hat to him, cocked an eyebrow, and headed back to the cockpit.

Godd and Luther checked their combat mission folders. There had recently been a revision to the Single Integrated Operational Plan, or SIOP, the nuclear war plan. The 2nd Air Force, to which the 843rd Bomb Wing and thus *Leper Colony II* belonged, sent new targets and the time they were supposed to be destroyed, plus a new route and new refueling rendezvous points. Godd and his crew took all of that and built the combat mission folder, which had "everything from worldwide navigation charts plotted with detailed routes of that specific sortie, to call signs and frequencies."[133] There were not going to be any targets of opportunity here. Each sortie was planned down to the smallest detail and gamed by the crew in Target Study.

In this case, *Leper Colony II*'s primary target was the missile training and test facility at Kapustin Yar. Its destruction was necessary to ensure that the launch pads could not be loaded and used as part of a second strike against the United States or her allies. The secondary target was the Mya-4 bomber base at Engles: the Bisons was capable of striking North American targets and needed to be destroyed in their nest before they could disperse to their "bounce" airfields in Siberia. As part of the SIOP one or more Titan ICBMs were already targeted there. *Leper Colony II* was part of the cross-targeting concept. If the missiles did not get Engels, one of *Leper Colony II*'s Mk-41 bombs would.

The B-52 carried two Mk-41 nuclear bombs and a pair of AGM-28 Hound Dog air-to-surface missiles. Luther had been a radar-navigator on a B-52D with the 4950th Test Group (Nuclear) during the 1957 Plumbbob and the 1958 Hardtack nuclear test series, so he was fully aware of what both weapons were capable of doing. During Hardtack B-52Ds were subjected to all sorts of experiments in close proximity to thirteen thermonuclear explosions from 1.3 to 9.3 megatons. He had seen scorched undersides, popped rivets, and melted tires. This was why *Leper Colony II*'s underside was painted white, to reflect the center-of-the-sun-like heat. The crews on the tests were also measured for radiation exposures. Luther had a revulsion shudder at the memory of having to pull a film stack out of his stomach with a paraffin string.[134]

From classified briefings Luther also knew that two pairs of tests during Hardtack were special. Shots Aspen and Walnut were detonated within one hour of each other: Aspen yielded 319 kilotons, and Walnut low-yielded at 1.4 megatons. Similarly Redwood (412 kilotons) and Elder (880 kilotons) were also detonated an hour apart. Among the other tests associated with the shots, they simulated the detonation of a Hound Dog missile against an air defense target one hour before a bomber arrived and delivered its primary weapon in close proximity. Finally, the Oak shot, which yielded 8.9 megatons, was a full-scale test of the Mk-41s carried on *Leper Colony II*. He knew from the Hardtack experience that they were reliable. He also knew from his course at Albuquerque that the yields of the Mk-41s were scalable between 3.5 and 25 megatons.[135]

As for the Hound Dog, there were still many questions as to its performance. The warhead was a W28, which was scalable, used in many systems, and deemed as reliable it could get. However, the Hound Dog's accuracy was suspect in part because of the novelty of the navigation system and its interface with the B-52: the B-52 was analog, while the missile was digital, which produced a built-in error. As a result the warhead was dialed up from its original planned yield of 550 kilotons to 4 megatons to make up for any discrepancy in accuracy. Just in case.[136]

Leper Colony II and its crew reached the positive control point over Crete, where they went into orbit. The Short Order radio system squawked again. "Sky King, Sky King. Do not answer. This is a Red Dot Defense Readiness Condition message in six parts. Kilo Zero Hotel One Victor Zero. Authentication: Two Three." The message was repeated for three minutes as Braeden wrote it down in grease pencil on a plastic sheet in his Emergency War Order book. Braeden used his KAC-72 to confirm that it was in fact a SAC Headquarters message. When he was satisfied that it was so, he passed the alphanumeric code group to Luther while Godd pulled out his KAA-29 authenticator. "KOH 1VO . . . K and V. Okay, it's authentic. It's the Go Code." Luther confirmed, using his KAA-29. There was dead silence. Godd returned to his seat and got on the intercom as Luther went down the ladder and squeezed himself back into his radar-navigator station. "Listen up!" Godd said. "We got us some *flyin'* to do!"

The safety concerns raised at the start of the airborne alert program back in 1958 led to the installation of an intricate and elaborate release system on board the *Leper Colony II* B-52. Even before departing Burpelson AFB to orbit off Spain, a ground safeing key had to be inserted into the weapons and the mechanical pullout cables between the pullout safeing switches had to be attached to the MHU-13/C subassembly (the clip that holds the bombs), which was attached to the MHU-6/A (the cradle that holds the clip subassembly in the bomb bay), which itself is electrically and mechanically connected to the B-52's power sources and systems.[137]

As *Leper Colony II* dropped down to 200 feet, the crew prepared the Mk-41 bombs and the Hound Dog missiles. Major Godd called out, "Weapon pre-arming control set." He reached behind his head to the left to the DCU-47 pilot's readiness switch assembly, broke the seal, lifted the plastic cover, and flipped two of the four toggle switches associated with the bombs. Down below, Luther turned to his left, where two DCU-9/A inflight control and monitor boxes were positioned. He broke the seals and shifted red locks from OS to SGA and then rotated the larger switches, one to AIR for airburst and the other to GRN for ground burst. Godd's switches permitted the DCU-9/A switches to move from SAFE to AIR and GRN and thus permitted pre-arming power to flow to the weapons. The navigator, Lt. "Candy" Barr, in his seat to Luther's right, took over the techno-chant.

"Release circuit disconnect." Luther reached above him, opened a plastic cover, and with his right hand pushed an orange button. "Roger."

"Special weapons manual lock handle." Luther reached next to the orange button to break a seal, opened the plastic cover, and moved the T-handle into position. "Pulled and stowed." Braeden at his electronic warfare station above them grabbed a handle that was attached to a cable under his console. That cable had a ball attached to it. He pulled the cable thirty-six inches on a slant, which clicked and retracted. He then placed the handle in a special socket next to his leg. "Pulled and stowed."

"Special weapons lock indicators?"

Luther glanced at a box above him on his left. The four circular ports had shifted from black and white stripes to green. "Indicate unlocked." These actions unlocked the clip in the assembly in the cradle in the bomb bay and armed the explosives on the shackles encasing the Mk-41 bombs in the MHU-13/C cradle.[138]

The Hound Dog's were a little more complicated due to problems with how the missiles' autonavigator interacted with the ASQ-38 bombing-navigation system. The crew had to prepare the system sometime before launch: Godd had to keep *Leper Colony II* straight and level while Barr input the latitude and longitude coordinates into the target data panel and determined the flight path for each missile. The crew also had to wait twenty minutes after descent before launching so that the velocity meters on the missiles could catch up with the shift in gravity. That meant that *Leper Colony II* had to launch the Hound Dogs ninety minutes out from their targets (see fig. 33).[139]

Using the tactical altitude selection switch, Barr set each missile for a low-high profile. The Hound Dog would depart from the B-52 and level off at 500 feet as its radar went active and determined how high up it was. Barr had the option to introduce a "dog leg" flight path to throw off enemy targeting, but that potentially added more error, so he kept the missile's course "straight in." The missile would proceed at 500 feet to the target, then maneuver to the burst height and detonate.

The Soviet air defenses arrayed against *Leper Colony II* and the other B-52Gs of the 843rd Bomb Wing were nothing short of formidable. The intelligence available to the crew during target study was, however, also formidable and classified "Top Secret/Extremely Sensitive Information." Deployment of the first American reconnaissance satellites in 1960 gave the National Reconnaissance Office the ability to conduct wide-area, low-resolution searches; they could find airfields and see what was on them with ten- to fifteen-foot resolution with the Corona program's KH-4 Mural camera. However by late 1963 a new system was online, the Gambit, with a high-resolution spotting system KH-7 camera capable of two-foot resolution. This allowed targeters to locate items as small as surface-to-air missile sites. The interceptor bases could not be hidden. The SA-2 Guideline missile sites, like the one that shot down Francis Gary Powers, had a distinct star-shaped look that could not be hidden from space.[140] That said, a substantial human intelligence project was still employed by CIA to confirm or observe missile and air defense installations on the ground.[141]

As a result the B-52 crews had access to the latest positions for the entire Soviet air defense order of battle by 1964. To get to their primary target, *Leper Colony II*'s crew was faced with a layered defense. Right on the coast of the Black Sea down to Batumi on the border with Turkey there was a belt of thirty SA-2 and SA-3 missile sites and radar stations: the SA-2 could reach out to 45 kilometers, while the SA-3, geared to low-level defense, had a range of roughly 35 kilometers. Immediately behind that belt was a string of interceptor airfields, five in number, equipped with MiG-19 and MiG-21 interceptors. Those defenses were anchored by Crimea, which had five interceptor airfields and too many SAMs (surface-to-air missiles) to count. Crimea was to be avoided.[142]

Halfway to Kapustin Yar, along the Veselovskoye-Proletarskoye watershed, was another string of SAM sites anchored to the west on Rostov-on-Don, which was lousy with SAMs. From here Volgograd and Saratov were surrounded with SA-2 sites: six and nine, respectively. There were two radar lines, one each south of the cities. Braeden remarked during target study, "Why is there a cluster of three SA-2 sites and a radar in Kamyshin? There's nothing there, there." Luther explained, "They must know we use the river to navigate and penetrate the defenses. Those sites are probably set up to throw us off, mess up our navigation."[143]

What the Soviets did not know was that SAC knew that the SA-2 and SA-3 could not engage low-level targets, certainly not ones below 1,000 feet. In February 1960 an RB-47ERB operating from Incirlik, Turkey, flew at 300 feet paralleling the Soviet coast all the way to Crimea until reaching Yalta, when the crew popped up to 22,000 feet and headed back over the Black Sea. They were then detected by Soviet radar and a mass MiG fighter scramble resulted.[144] The *Leper Colony II* crew had trained and trained again on the Oil Burner routes over the Nebraska wheat and corn fields at extremely low level. It was like "frying chickens in the barn yard," according to one U.S. Air Force general. That training served them in good stead.

The B-52s carried electronic countermeasures gear: fourteen jammers to cover all bands and eight chaff dispensers. The crews could also carry the ADM-20C Quail, an unarmed cruise missile decoy that simulated a B-52's radar cross section and infrared signature. Though the plane could carry four of them, the crews preferred keeping the weight down and would take one or none. *Leper Colony II* had one on board. The thinking was that a low-level night strike by single aircraft was more likely to succeed than barrage jamming and a bomber stream like the B-47s had to use.[145]

Leper Colony II made landfall over Bolshoy Sochi at 150 feet, skirting the Caucasus Mountain chain by flying down a valley and then swinging east to avoid the fighter base at Maykop. There wasn't a peep from the air defense system. If Godd had not had the flash curtains up, he would have seen a strange glow from the west, as other forces repeatedly hit Crimea with a variety of nuclear weapons. The lights were going out as pulses from the weapons destroyed power stations and fried the power grid.

Now that they were over the Soviet Union, there was still work to be done. Behind Major Godd's head at the pilot's station was the DCU-47/A, the pilot's readiness switch assembly. Godd lifted the cover. There were four toggle switches, two for the bombs and two for the Hound Dog missiles. Godd flipped up a bar that held all four switches, already switched from "safe" to "ready" in place: this activated the Special Weapons Emergency Separation System (SWESS). He closed the plastic cover. If *Leper Colony II* were hit by a missile or shot down by an interceptor, the bombs and missiles would already be fully armed and would barometrically detonate so they could not be recovered or salvaged.[146]

The AGM-28 Hound Dog cruise missiles were already prepared as they were crucial weapons in punching through the Soviet air defense system. In this case there was an SA-1 Guild site at Kapustin Yar. This was the training site for the sites protecting Moscow. Even though intelligence rated the SA-1's capabilities as almost nonexistent against low-level penetration, a last-minute volley fire of ten or twenty missiles from the site could be a problem when *Leper Colony II* popped up to deliver the bomb. The site had to be destroyed just to make sure. The bomber was nearly ninety minutes' flight time away from Kapustin Yar.

The nuclear weapons release procedures for the bombs were already in effect; this was a prerequisite before the Hound Dogs could be launched. Godd released the missiles on the DCU-47/A behind his head; Braeden had already pulled his handle at the electronic warfare station; Luther and Barr had already triggered the release circuit disconnect. Barr now punched the ASM (air-to-surface missile) circuit breakers at his station and informed Godd. Luther broke the external manual release seal.

"Activating ASM engine control knob," Capt. "Ace" Garry, the copilot, joined in. That opened a valve in the Hound Dog's fuel system, allowing pressure to build up. Braeden flipped his ASM lock-unlock switch, while Barr checked the external missile release switches. Luther turned a dial on his special weapons select switch to ASM-1, the port-side Hound Dog. Godd held *Leper Colony II* level so Luther and Barr could conduct a final checkpoint fix with the navigation system.

Barr looked to his right and down at a series of four lights: Missile 1's "engine ready" light was now a steady green. The "warhead" light next to it was now green. A high-voltage safety switch in the W 28 was now in the pre-armed position. "Engine green, warhead green," he told Luther, who started a countdown from ten. At zero, Barr flipped up the red toggle switch cover and flicked the switch. "Missile launched!" Luther confirmed the missile was away on his panel.

The Hound Dog separated from *Leper Colony II* and its engine ignited. The missile accelerated away from the plane on a downward 45-degree angle, reached the reference pressure point where the missile "learned" what altitude it was at, and then leveled out into cruise mode at 500 feet at Mach 2.1 (1,598.5 miles per hour) over the fields and farms and the Chogray Reservoir. The missile then popped up, traveled for thirty seconds at 10,000 feet, and then entered a dive, straight down.

The SA-1 Guild site was a "box" on the ground about half a mile by a mile crossed with nine lines of missile launchers. The Hound Dog could not "see" the site and only "knew" where it was in relation to the point where *Leper Colony* launched it from. That in turn was affected by where the B-52 "thought" it was in relation to the sun or stars. The error induced by these transactions meant that the Hound Dog dropped vertically about two miles north of where the SA-1 site actually was. The W 28 warhead was fused barometrically at 2,500 feet and it detonated with 3.8 megatons. *Leper Colony II* was still thirty minutes out.

The blast waves alone were enough to completely destroy everything at the site: fragments of the missiles and their launchers were thrown for nearly two miles. Any electrical system on the ground within five miles, including the five other SAM training test stands, was shorted and fried by the electromagnetic pulse of the burst. The thermal pulse went out to nine miles, setting fire to the "secret city" of Znamensk and all of its engineers and scientists, melted everything within three miles, and set fire to everything else out to five miles. This collaterally destroyed three older launch sites for the R-5 ballistic missiles, damaged the nuclear warhead storage area, and destroyed a missile checkout and storage area.

The navigators, Luther and Barr, had by this point pulled out of their combat mission folders the "artwork radar predictions" of the Kapustin Yar complex. These were "carefully hand drawn simulations of what targets would look like on a B-52's navigator's radar screen when the B-52 got there."[147] They showed the offset aiming points, in this case a distinctive bend in the Volga River south of Volgograd and Znamensk. These were inserted into the scopes.

One hour after the Hound Dog strike on the SA-1, Luther took control of the plane from Godd. Luther confirmed the offset data, already gamed out months before and inputted into the navigation computer when the plane was on alert back at Burpelson AFB. Luther warned Godd when it was time to begin the Long Look maneuver. Godd and "Ace" Garry were also prepared to pull back the flash curtain and bomb visually if the computer went out.[148]

The time-to-go meter was activated, and the crew activated their stopwatches in case the radar failed. The ASQ-38 took over. *Leper Colony II* rose to 12,000 feet while Braeden kept a close eye on the APS-54 warning receiver in case a SAM search or fire control radar was looking for them. At 12,000 feet the bomb doors opened. The explosive cartridges in the MHU-13/C fired, which fractured the nuts holding the two bands on the Mk-41. The arming rods, which were attached to pulleys, came out as the weapon physically separated from the cradle.

"Bomb's away!"

The bomb drop indicator lights came on. The bomb bay doors hissed closed. Godd and Garry, gripping the controls for dear life, flipped the B-52 to port and dove right back down to 100 feet along the Volga River, using the low hills on the north bank to screen *Leper Colony II* from the blast and other effects.

The ballistic arc of the Mk-41 took the weapon over the Kapustin Yar complex. Because of the variety of structures and dispersion of the sites, the Mk-41's yield was dialed up to 15 megatons and fused for airburst. It detonated at 17,500 feet one mile west of the four R-12 and R-14 missile launch stands and silos, between those facilities and the launch sites first used by the Soviets' Germans to test captured V-2 booty in 1946. The shock waves and gusts swept the steppes clean of any structure other than the blockhouses, with pressures of 12 PSI out to 7.5 miles. Partially buried and underground structures were crushed. Blast damage eventually trailed off at 1 PSI about fifty miles away. The electromagnetic pulse destroyed every electrical system in the range areas of Kapustin Yar not destroyed by the other weapons effects.[149]

As the weapon was airburst at an optimal height, there was no severe fallout "goose egg." The cloud itself, however, was highly radioactive. It dispersed to the east in the wind, but the rain scavenged the nuclear materials in it and dumped them over eastern Siberia and Alaska. Though the windows of the newly built workers' apartments in the former Stalingrad up the Volga were broken and some of the dachas on the outskirts received some thermal effects, the civilian population generally remained untouched by this strike. After the events of 1942 there was some justice in this.

The APS-54 warning receiver lit up like a pinball machine, startling Braeden at his station. All six SA-2 sites and several other radars in the area suddenly were active. Godd swung the B-52 along the Volga at 150 feet, passing along the entire length of the former Stalingrad, and continued at low level all the way up the river north-northeast toward Saratov and Engles air base, loaded with long-range bombers that would be preparing to disperse to "bounce" airfields in the northern and eastern USSR to attack North America.

Soon afterward *Leper Colony II* loosed another Hound Dog missile. This was set on a low-high profile and sped off to the northeast. Its target was an SA-2 site southeast of Engels air base, right where *Leper Colony II* was going to perform its next Large Charge maneuver. Godd then dropped the plane's only Quail decoy missile. It was set on a northerly heading and hopefully would distract the radars and missiles at Kyshym and the southern part of Saratov. The Quail could make two turns before burning out and crashing.

The Hound Dog popped up and dropped straight down. Only the edge of the blast touched the dug-in launchers and the gust blew down the antennas. It was the electromagnetic pulse that damaged the components. The site was rendered useless.

Luther's offset this time included the huge aircraft factory complex in Saratov, which reflected a substantial number of radar echoes. He could clearly see it on the scope. His second was a bend in the river. He input the data, but when he looked over his panels something was wrong.

"Pilot, we have a problem," Luther called.

"What? Now?" Godd asked distractedly as the plane caught a buffet.

"The bomb/nav system is still in 'bombing mode.' I am now showing the second bomb rack as 'locked.' The DCU-9A is still set for 'ground.'"

"The DCU-47A is still good up here. Ace, stay on the bomb run." Godd unbuckled himself from his five-point harness and headed aft.

"We don't have much time. Do we safe it, jettison it, or what?" Luther asked with some urgency.

"I'm going to go in and see what I can do. It looks like there's something wrong with the release system. We've come too far to drop this in the drink."

"But what about the two-man rule? The bomb bay is a no-lone zone." Luther was horrified at the potential breach in nuclear safety procedures.

"There isn't room." Godd took off his parachute, opened the small door, and crawled into *Leper Colony II*'s bomb bay. It was too confining for him to stand up completely. He recalled the emergency manual: "Crewmembers entering the bomb bay to perform the following operations shall exercise extreme caution to prevent inadvertent release of bombs."[150] The Mk-41 was still attached to the MHU-13/C, which was plugged into the MHU-6/A clip in rack. There was no way he could climb on top and straddle the bomb, as it was cradled in the MHU-13/C and the MHU-6/A was attached to the ceiling.[151] He leaned against the side to brace himself and examined the assembly. One of the cables for the cartridge firing system had come loose. Godd crawled to the door and yelled, "Remove power to the bomb rack!" This was done. He then reached up, reattached the cable, and crawled out. The lights were all green again.

Leper Colony II reached the initial point, and the Long Look maneuver started again. The ASQ-38 once again had control of the airplane, which reached 12,000 feet, and the Mk-41 separated cleanly. *Leper Colony II* was flung to port by Godd and Garry. This Mk-41 was set for a 15-megaton ground burst with an impact fuse. The resultant crater was a mile in diameter, obliterating the runways and anything near them, throwing a fallout plume miles and miles to the east. With all her jamming gear now active, the B-52 headed south and then southwest, trying to recover to Turkey.

Vignette 4

Mission to Moscow: *Fail-Safe* and B-58 Operations

The film version of *Fail-Safe* features Lt. Col. Jack Grady, a World War II B-24 pilot brought back into service and stationed at an alert facility in Anchorage, Alaska. There the crews of the fictional Vindicator bombers play pool, read magazines, and wait to go on airborne patrol. The Vindicators are depicted as Convair B-58 Hustler delta-wing bombers that fly in groups of six on routes in the Arctic until they are instructed during a crisis situation to proceed to their "fail-safe point." This crisis could be anything from an international incident to a UFO. There the bombers are supposed to orbit until they receive a coded message on their fail-safe box, a device in the aircraft that is set to receive messages from SAC headquarters.

Airborne, Grady and the other two crew members pull folders labeled "Top Secret" from their flight suits, check that the code is valid, confirm with each other that it is valid, and then pull another card out with their target on it. The target is Moscow. In disbelief, Grady instructs to crew to "contact Omaha," but the Soviets are jamming the frequencies and voice communication is not possible. So the bombers go in.

Five of the six Vindicators in each patrol carry two 20-megaton nuclear bombs. The sixth aircraft carries a number of unspecified electronic jamming and deception devices. The Vindicators, depicted on the SAC Headquarters Big Board, elude and evade the Soviet air defenses until the planes are picked off one-by-one with SAC's reluctant assistance. The Soviets detonate a line of nuclear air defense missiles in an effort to destroy Grady's plane, but they only succeed in killing the unarmed jamming plane. Grady tells his crew he's going to bring the plane in low over the city, rapidly ascend to altitude, and detonate the bombs along with the plane. One of his crew remarks that they might as well since "there's nothing to go back home to anyway."

A real-life Jack Grady would have been based with the 305th Bombardment Wing at Bunker Hill AFB (later Grisson AFB) in Indiana, or with the 43rd Bombardment Wing at Carswell AFB, Texas, or at Little Rock AFB when the wing moved there. B-58 Hustlers did not participate in airborne alert operations; that was the realm of the B-52 force. The B-58 aircraft was an extraordinary but complicated and temperamental aircraft; when it entered service in 1961 it looked like it came from the distant future. The four-engine delta-wing Hustler flew at Mach 2, had a state-of-the-art inertial navigation system based on the one used by the Atlas ballistic missile, and could carry five nuclear weapons. The exact role of the B-58 in American war plans, however, remains obscure in the available literature. And with good reason.

The sun was setting at Torrejon Air Base in Spain when Lt. Col. John O'Grady led the four-ship B-58 element to a perfect landing, having just completed a grueling transatlantic flight from Grissom AFB in Indiana that involved two tankings. Four KC-135 tankers, two from Loring and two from Griffiss, quietly prepositioned earlier in the day, were themselves refueling on the ground. They would depart within the hour to support this mission. The B-58s, including O'Grady's bird, *The Polish Prostitute*, were immediately "recocked" in accordance with the protocols established under Glass Road: the ground crews had thirty minutes to refuel the aircraft and then alter the nuclear weapons from ferry to strike configuration. These tasks were accomplished well within the time frame; they had been practiced every two months for the past five years with a rotating quartet of B-58s deployed to Spain for what everybody termed "familiarization" flights. Four other B-58s, from Carswell AFB, were already winging their way to Kadena Air Base in Okinawa; their task was code-named Glass Brick.[152]

Glass Road was implemented as part of an increased readiness posture ordered by CINCSAC in response to Joint Chiefs of Staff direction. The DEFCON system remained at 4, but certain readiness elements of DEFCON 3 and DEFCON 2 were permitted under the increased readiness posture. Glass Road and Glass Brick were two of these.[153] O'Grady contemplated the gravity of the situation as he smoked a cigarette. The war in Vietnam was going badly, but unknown to the public the situation between the Soviets and the Chinese had deteriorated to the point where threats to use nuclear weapons had been made. Seven months earlier, on 10 January, O'Grady and his crews were sent running to their bombers and deployed from Grisson to McGuire AFB in New Jersey during a satellite basing test. This dispersion was authorized by the secretary of defense to protect SAC bombers from a possible Soviet Fractional Orbital Bombardment System and submarine-launched ballistic missile attack.[154] The FOBS threat was particularly serious. From 1965 to 1968 the Soviets conducted twenty tests of a bombardment weapon that could bypass BMEWS missile coverage by coming in from the south and then de-orbiting its nuclear weapon over North America. The first

Soviet FOBS regiment achieved combat status in August 1969.[155] It did not take a genius from Lawrence Livermore National Laboratory to see that a FOBS warhead could be detonated at 150 miles up to produce electromagnetic pulse effects over the entire continent and cripple SAC, let alone both the United States and Canada.[156]

Of equal concern was the intelligence community's failure to pick up the alerting of Soviet strategic forces during the Czech Crisis the previous year. The Soviets' 403rd Missile Regiment in Ruzhany, with its R-12 ballistic missiles, was ordered to change its alert status from combat readiness 4 (Constant) to combat readiness 3 (Increased) at midnight on 20 August 1968. It remained in this state until noon on 2 September.[157] The same change occurred with three regiments of R-9A ICBMs and their 5-megaton-yield warheads stationed around Baikonur.[158] The 867th Missile Regiment's R-12 missiles also moved to "increased," and the nuclear warheads were transported to the launch pads and then docked. The other missile units of the Strategic Rocket Forces, from the intermediate fields in the west to the silos in the central part of the Soviet Union, went on alert. The alert packages were not opened. In less than a week instructions were given to undock the warheads on the non-silo missiles, but the units remained at the "increased" alert level until September.[159] That all or part of the Soviet Strategic Rocket Forces could move to "increased" alert without detection during a crisis was nothing short of astounding when it was eventually uncovered by diligent analysts.[160]

The combination of factors, including a FOBS electromagnetic pulse capability plus the ability of the Soviets to mask alert processes, generated increased concern in Washington and Omaha as Marshal Andrei Grechko, minister of defense, and other hardliners were heard to discuss how the Chinese threat could be eliminated forever and that a preemptive attack on Chinese nuclear facilities might be in the offing during the spring and summer of 1969. These conversations took place in the wake of several violent border clashes and an incident in which Chinese troops captured and mutilated Soviet troops taken prisoner during the Zhenbao Island battle; Soviet Strategic Rocket Forces were put on alert on 20 March.[161] Would the Soviets ignore the United States and her NATO allies? Or would they seek to disable or disrupt their Western enemies so they could deal with the Maoists with a free hand? Premier Leonid Brezhnev and Grechko were, eerily, in a strategic situation similar to the one confronting Hitler in 1940 regarding a possible two-front war.

In his mind O'Grady ticked off the recent incidents and events that led him and his detachment to Torrejon. In response to intelligence the Soviets were planning a strike against their nuclear facilities, the Chinese conducted a nuclear weapons test on 23 September. The Soviets followed with one two days later and then a full-scale MIRV (multiple independently targeted reentry vehicle) test with an SS-9 the day after that. On 29 September China dropped a 3-megaton weapon from a bomber, demonstrating that they had an operational, deliverable thermonuclear capability. The next day Lin Bao, Mao's second in command, ordered "first-degree combat readiness" for all People's Liberation Army forces: nine hundred thousand personnel and four thousand aircraft redeployed. The People's Liberation Army leadership headed for their bunkers and cadre schools dispersed throughout the countryside.[162]

Between 6 and 9 October the White House examined the options. Forty-eight hours later the Soviets launched what may have been a space vehicle, followed by another on 12 October. Were they in fact Soyuz capsules, or were they FOBS orbiters? That was unclear to American observers. At noon on 12 October SAC instituted its increased readiness posture before any more Soviet space vehicles could be launched.[163]

O'Grady's thoughts were interrupted by the klaxon, and he instinctively ran to his B-58. Captain Xandre and Lieutenant Kairi, his navigator and defensive systems operator, respectively, were already climbing into their ejection capsules and strapping in. The UHF command radio in contact with the Torrejon command post crackled, and O'Grady checked in as the crew went through their DEFCON 1 procedures.

"We have a launch. Three ICBM detected by NORAD, with space vehicle E34 proceeding ahead of them.[164] Red Flight is to refuel and proceed to positive control point." After authentication, Red 1 through Red 4 rapidly lifted off in sequence, heading toward a KC-

135 tanker rendezvous northeast of Sardinia. This location was different from the Chrome Dome tanker area off Sicily in order to avoid detection or interference by Soviet AGI intelligence collection trawlers.

O'Grady and *The Polish Prostitute* were now leading the riskiest mission ever conceived, a mission that would tax them physically, mentally, and emotionally. After disconnecting from the tanker, O'Grady took the B-58 on a course toward Yugoslavia. Yugoslavia's on again–off again relationship with Moscow ensured that its two primary cities, Zagreb and Belgrade, were each protected with a ring of SA-2 Guideline missiles. These were uncovered by CIA analysts back in 1964, at the time Glass Road was first conceived.[165] The bulk of the Yugoslav Air Force consisted of obsolete 1950s-era hand-me-down U.S. Air Force F-84s and F-86s, plus locally made Jastrebs. The Soviets were training up MIG-21 Fishbed crews, but these were not yet in service. Indeed the radar network provided coverage only eighteen hours a day. And most important, Yugoslavia was not a Warsaw Pact power and thus did not have any integration with the Soviet air defense headquarters in Kiev.[166]

That said, the H-Hour Control Line for this mission was in the mid-Adriatic. This did not leave O'Grady's crew a lot of time for preparation after departing the tanker rendezvous. *The Polish Prostitute* had been cocked back in Torrejon: the multimegaton Mk-53, nestled inside the BLU-2B upper component of the two-component pod, which itself was cocooned by the larger expendable lower component fuel pod, had its ground safety switch moved to "free fall" from "safe" and the munitions access cover closed. The pod arming control button was moved so it was flush with the aluminum skin, and the bomb pod ground safety lock was removed. O'Grady had to be careful with the AN/ARC-87 long-range communication system on the airplane: "Do not tune up or key LRC [long-range communications] equipment below 4 mcps and between 6 and 25 mcps during ground operations with an MB or TC pod when a nuclear weapon is loaded on the airplane. This is to reduce the electromagnetic radiation environment of the loaded weapon." The Mk-43 weapons mounted under the B-58's wings had their ready-safe switches turned to "ready" and the ground safety pins removed.[167]

That left the authentication process. After the tanker rendezvous, Red Flight proceeded to hold at the positive control point. To ensure that all three crew members were involved in the authentication process, Kairi, the defensive systems operator in the rear compartment, was the only one who could "place the [AN/ARC-87] system into operation." The same went for the AN/ARC-34, the UHF command radio. O'Grady and Xandre could receive and transmit through their interphone controls, but Kairi had to turn them on and off.[168] This he did.

All three crew members were surprised when the AN/ARC-34 squawked instead of the long-range-87. That was the relatively short-range UHF radio, two hundred miles, not the global and thus interceptable Short Order SAC high-frequency command net.

"Red Flight, Red Flight. Do not answer. This is a Red Dot Defense Condition message in six parts. November. Uniform. Charlie. Echo. Mike. Mike. 0200. Authentication is Bravo Yankee." The message repeated itself four times and ended. Kairi used a KAC-72 to confirm the authenticity of the message, that it came from SAC. O'Grady and Xandre then used their KAA-29 authenticators to determine what the message meant.

"I have a valid Go Code," Xandre announced on the interphone.

"So do I," O'Grady confirmed. Nothing more needed to be said. There was only one primary target on this mission and no alternate.

As the navigator, Xandre was the busiest man on the crew. O'Grady ensured the B-58 went from A to B and didn't plow into a stationary object or the ground, and Kairi kept watch with his countermeasures systems and was prepared to use the rear Gatling gun. But Xandre had to handle navigation functions, bomb arming functions, and the actual delivery procedure. During target study he had worked out the ballistic, time of fall, and height of burst calculations for the weapons. The weapons control system, the AN/ASQ-42, had the limited ability to store those inputs in an analogue memory; this kept the navigator busy to the H-Hour Control Line, but Xandre had to wait before *The Polish Prostitute* was much closer to the target to add environmental data from the primary navigation stabilization unit inertial guidance system—and only then, once he was sure the B-58 was where it was supposed to be relative to the target. Then the three sets of data would be married up by the system prior to the drop.

With *The Polish Prostitute* in the lead, the flight made landfall at Senj and proceeded to Petrinja before dropping down to parallel the Sava River, neatly skirting the SAM sites near Zagreb. Using Slavonski Brod and Vukovar as waypoints, Xandre had the B-58 flight over the plains north of Novi Sad in no time. There was no indication the Yugoslavs had detected them. And even if they had, who would they report it to? Red Flight would be long gone before they could even scramble.

Romania, however, presented a complex series of problems for O'Grady and Red Flight during their target study. All of Romania's SA-2 Guideline sites were arrayed around the capital, Bucharest, south of the Carpathian Mountains. Most of the air defense radar sites were arrayed in the west of the country, with Timisoara as the command hub. There was also a fighter regiment stationed there. The Romanian air defense system was coordinated with other Warsaw Pact and Soviet forces by the Soviet PVO headquarters southwest of Kiev. But most important, the mountainous Carpathian terrain bisecting the country itself served as a formidable barrier for any force headed east that wished to remain undetected.[169]

For Red Flight, however, there were other circumstances they could exploit to their benefit. The Romanians not only resisted joint training with the Soviets on a regular basis; they mobilized their forces in 1968 to deter a Soviet incursion during the Czechoslovakian affair. They could be expected to foot-drag in any relationship with the Soviets. An attempt by the Soviets to improve relations by transferring twelve MiG-21 aircraft to Romania could not overcome the inability of the MiG-21 to conduct low-level intercept at night or in bad weather. None of Romania's aging MiG-17s would be able to do so either.[170]

That left the terrain. Once Red Flight skirted or kept below the early radar warning sites on the western border, there was a secondary radar line in the interior, but then there was no coverage for the northeastern and eastern parts of the country, the portions bordering the Soviet Union.

Careful analysis of the Soviet air defense network in Ukraine conducted throughout the 1960s revealed a number of points. The bulk of the air defenses saturated western Ukraine and the Baltic states, which were occupied by a large number of intermediate- and medium-range ballistic missile launch facilities pointed at NATO. The air defense radars and SAM-2 missile sites thinned out as they approached Odessa and then thickened again near that vital city.[171] Presumably the Soviets did not believe that aircraft could penetrate the Carpathians undetected. Analysis by NSA and CIA suggested that there was no known Romanian or Soviet radar in that area.[172] Indeed Bacau was precisely opposite the zone where the Soviet defense system thinned out. O'Grady reflected that the Carpathians served the same purpose as the Ardennes did in 1940.

Xandre already had Timisoara, Romania, put in the AN/ASQ-42 weapons control system as the rest of Red Flight fell in line astern. The doppler-inertial system computed airspeed, altitude, wind velocity, latitude, pressure density, relative air density, and barometric vertical velocity, but it was not perfect: Xandre knew that the AN/APN 110 radio altimeter's accuracy tolerance was plus or minus 250 feet 500 feet above the terrain; therefore it could not be relied upon under 750 feet. At the same time, however, the powerful AN/APN 113 search radar was effective at determining what was coming up in front of the B-58.[173] Both these systems and the inertial guidance system were critical at getting through the mountains. It was also understood that the mountains would mask the signals of these systems from Soviet systems farther east. In addition to the plethora of radar, the Soviets had passive detection equipment like Box Brick arrayed throughout Ukraine listening for those signals, so the navigation radars could be used only right before the Red Flight crested the mountains.[174] After that the crews had to rely on sheer guts and years of experience flying the Oil Burner routes in the United States. When they started off flying the B-58 in 1961, their mission profiles were to run in at 34,000 feet at Mach 2 and weapons-drop at 45,000 feet. Within three years the mission profiles were run under 1,000 feet to the point where they had to be careful to ensure that the low-slung pod, which extended over six feet beneath the aircraft, did not collide with structures or the ground.[175]

There was an older Bar Lock radar at Deva and another at Sibiu, so they had to be careful to keep below their known effective operating height, but once through the pass, the flight made a bee line through the wide valleys near Fagaras to Brasov and up to Targy Secuiesc. There were no air defense systems in there, so the flight could gain altitude as long as they remained below the highest elevations of the Carpathians. Intermittent use of the search radar plus the fact that many towns had their lights on made that possible, but it was still a grueling ride for the crews.[176]

The selected penetration point was the pass at Targu Ocna at 2,000 feet elevation. There was no Romanian or Soviet radar cover in range of that point, but O'Grady took no chances. The voice warning system told him he was below 750 feet, but with a steady hand he brought *The Polish Prostitute* through and then immediately down over the Onesti watershed at 676 feet above sea level. Breathing deeply, O'Grady leveled out while Xandre checked his navigation. "Activate SWESS." Xandre moved his left hand to the base of a triangular panel where there were two levers. He selected the pod safety lock pin handle, pulled it out, and rotated it. O'Grady then reached to his right to the pilot's bomb panel, broke the lead seal, and flipped the SWESS switch to armed. The SWESS armed light went on on Xandre's weapon lock and arm panel, and he flipped a switch with his left hand. "SWESS armed, confirmed," he stated in a quiet voice. This activated a barometric switch that would detonate the pod's Mk-53 if the B-58 went below a certain altitude. O'Grady carefully reduced altitude heading for the Soviet border, but when the voice warning alarm told him he was too low and the SWESS was in danger of detonating, he rapidly corrected the move.[177]

Red Flight was now up against the densest air defense system on Earth. Kairi stubbed out his cigarette in the ashtray in the defensive systems operator's compartment, the third jettisonable cocoon behind the navigator. During the flight through Romania, he ensured that the identification friend/foe and selective identification feature transponders and the MD-7 radar for the Gatling gun were off so they did not emit and give them away to the Box Brick electronic intelligence collection receivers and their relations. It was understood that the search radar would be used only at a small number of specific intervals to ensure they were on course. The only radiation *The Polish Prostitute* emitted was the pair of altimeters. The ECM world judged that these were unlikely to be picked up, but the crew in Red Flight agreed that once they were over the steppes of Ukraine, they could also be shut off until the run in to the primary targets.[178]

Kairi had four systems to operate, only one of which was important at this part of the mission: the ALR 12 radar warning receiver. He also had access to the ALQ-15 and ALQ-16 systems. The ALQ-16 was a track breaker. The Soviet SAMs used a radar beam to guide the missile to its target. The ALQ-16 overrode the beam frequency and severed the connection. The ALQ-15 was slightly different: it overrode the beam and generated a bogus location far enough away from the B-58 so the missile would miss. Since both systems emitted, and the B-58 was flying in low, they were both kept turned off for the time being.[179]

The defensive systems operators on the Red Flight B-58s practically had PhDs on the Soviet PVO Strany (Air Defense of the Nation) command. Red Flight was up against the 8th Independent Air Defense Army. To get to their primary targets, Red Flight had to pass through four layers: the 21st Air Defense Division (Moldova); the 19th Air Defense Division (central Ukraine); and 7th Air Defense Corps, guarding the southern approaches to Moscow; and finally, around Moscow, the 1st Air Defense Army for Special Use. This amounted to approximately thirty-nine radar sites; 159 SA-1, SA-2, SA-3, and SA-5 missile sites; and at least five regiments of fighter interceptors.[180] One SA-2 formation, the 260th Red Banner Anti-Aircraft Missile Regiment stationed at Bryansk, had combat experience in Vietnam, where they were credited with twenty-five American kills.[181] As these personnel had adapted and experimented with North Vietnamese techniques for using SA-2 missiles against low-level targets, the formation would be avoided completely.[182]

O'Grady and the rest of Red Flight had brought every piece of intelligence available to bear during target study. Internal Soviet analysis of their own systems in addition to their combat experiences over North Vietnam and in the 1967 Six Day War concluded that "combat at low and maximally low (under 100 meters [328 feet]) altitudes is the most difficult" and that "the latest modifications . . . made to improve firing at low-flying targets have not produced significant results." Specifically, "fighter aviation interception of air targets also is not very effective at altitudes less that 1,000 meters [3,280 feet] and hardly practicable at altitudes less than 300 meters [984 feet]." The main problem was "the lack of effective means . . . to detect and track low-altitude targets. The lower range of existing radars . . . is for practical purposes limited to altitudes of 300 to 500 meters [984 to 1,640 feet]."[183]

Further Soviet information suggested that "our radar . . . is not capable of timely detection and continuous tracking of air targets moving at an altitude below 500 meters [1,640 feet]" (air targets moving at altitudes of 200 meters [656 feet] and lower are actually undetected by most radars), and "most of the existing types of antiaircraft missiles cannot engage" because of "the impossibility of guiding missiles to the target (distortion of the missile signals transmitted to the missile guidance station and distortion of the control signals transmitted from the missile guidance station to the missile because of echoes from the ground)."[184]

Red Flight's first challenge was the 21st Air Defense Division covering Moldova and Odessa. A regiment of the more dangerous Soviet interceptors, the twin-engine Yak-28P Firebar, operated from a pair of air bases near the Black Sea; they maintained two aircraft on fifteen minutes' strip alert, now probably doubled to four because of the international situation. Most of the 21st's SAMs were clustered in a triangle around Kishinev: three SA-2 sites and three SA-3 sites in an inner ring. A radar line of five stations ran along the Romanian border, with two in depth.[185]

The weak point was the Ungheni-Ribnita corridor: this route completely bypassed Kishinev and its SAM coverage and the interceptors south of there. By staying completely away from the heavy air defense coverage afforded by the 28th Air Defense Corps to protect the ballistic missile bases to the north in eastern Ukraine, and avoiding the radar station at Bumbata at low level, they had a clear shot into central Ukraine. Kairi's ALR-12 picked up the radar signals. He noted them on his display and informed O'Grady, who checked his altitude.

The next cluster of defenses was the 19th Air Defense Division based in Kiev. Kiev was lousy with all types of SAMs, Kairi noted. There were two rough lines of outer defenses facing southwest toward Moldova, mostly radar and SA-2. The interceptor bases were to the northeast of Kiev; they mostly had ineffective MiG-19PM Farmers and SU-9 Fishpots.[186] By running from Ribnita to Kirovohrad, Red Flight completely bypassed most of the 19th Air Defense Division. They had to keep an eye on the SA-2 site near Shlyakhove, but once they passed it and there was no peep from the ALR-12, Red Flight was into "the slot."

Satellite analysis of the Soviet air defense system showed a strong coastal defense on the Black Sea and a particularly heavy concentration in Crimea. Northeast of that the 11th Air Defense Division in Dnepropetrovsk and then the 9th Air Defense Division in Kharkov had point defense on all major cities in their areas of responsibility in eastern Ukraine. However, there was a noticeable gap between those formations and the 19th Air Defense Division. This area was mostly open steppe, with nothing of industrial importance and few significant terrain features above 600 feet. It was in "the slot" that Red Flight poured on the coal and made preparations to take on the next defense line.[187]

On their way to Kursk, Red Flight did some housekeeping. The strike package on the primary target had to be timed properly, so Red 2, 3, and 4 slowed down so there was space between the aircraft: Red 4 trailed even farther back because of its particular task. Then all four bombers jettisoned their fuel pods. This made the B-58s lighter, faster, and more maneuverable.

The next opponent was the 7th Air Defense Corps, and unlike the Air Defense Divisions it was one of four special corps directly subordinated to Moscow Air Defense Command. It was generally understood that the hierarchical nature of the Soviet system would introduce friction into the air defense system with its complex subordination; even if the 19th and 21st detected Red Flight, it was entirely possible that the 7th Air Defense Corps might not get the word in time. The 7th, on the other hand, had double the number of radar sites of the other formations and was equipped with an SU-11 Fishpot C and an MiG-17F Fresco regiment, though neither was up to the task of low-level engagement. However, it did have personnel with experience in Vietnam, Cuba, and Egypt.

The 7th Air Defense Corps had radars deployed like a fence from west of Bryansk to southwest of Voronzh. There were two radars and two interceptor bases in depth. Clusters of SA-2 sites surrounded Bryansk, Orel, and Voronezh, which also boasted a pair of the heavier, longer-range, and more deadly SA-5 Gammon sites. Finally, in deep was Tula, with three SA-2 and two SA-5 sites. But once again there was a gap, this time between Orel and Lipetsk. Running at low level from Sumska to Kursk and ducking under the radar there, Red Flight could skirt Efremov air base and away from the SAMs in Orel.[188]

The final defense complex, around Moscow, consisted of two rings with a number of SA-2 sites between the city and the inner ring scattered like raisins in a pudding. The inner ring had thirty-six SA-1 Guild sites with sixty missiles per site, although these were ineffective against anything other than a B-29 or B-36. The outer ring held another thirty-six SA-1 sites. However, from site E 22 in the southwest to E 02 in the northern quadrant, the much newer SA-3 Goa was installed alongside the SA-1s. This was why Red Flight came in from the south: there was no SA-3 coverage for the southern, southeastern, and eastern quadrants of the defense rings.[189]

A potential problem was Tula. It sat almost perfectly at the point where Red Flight would rise up to 1,000 feet and start their runs on their Moscow-area targets. It was, however, the perfect radar target for the AN/ASQ-42 to do a final nav check before the run. Even if the electronic intelligence receivers detected the emissions, even if the SA-5's Tall King radar got a hit, even if the hundreds of obsolete SA-1 Guilds in the outer ring of Moscow defenses somehow lifted off, it would be all over before any of the PVO's systems could engage given the speed of the attack. The one plane at risk was Red 4, trailing the others.

"Deactivating SWESS," O'Grady told Xandre as the two men took the SWESS offline.

"Coming up on Tula," Xandre informed the others. The AN/ASQ-42 was warmed up and activated so that O'Grady could get a fix.

"Nav is good," Xandre intoned.

"I'm getting radar hits on the ALR-12," Kairi relayed. "Squat Eye, Low Blow . . . Yo-Yo???"

"Thermal curtains up."

O'Grady started a slow climb to just under 1,000 feet and increased speed for the dash in.

"Ballistics set and checked."

At one hundred miles out Xandre shifted the AN/ASQ-42 from nav to bomb. He checked the offsets and elevation again and moved a joystick to the aiming point, a little over twelve miles from where their Initial Point was. These data for the pod drop were now set in the system. He repeated this with the two smaller Mk-43s on their targets. O'Grady reached for the bomb panel arm control switch; this opened the arming control valve that handled arming and fusing of the pod-mounted Mk-53. This was a pressure source for the differential pressure switch; the arming and firing switches fired through an actuator in the tail end of the bomb. (It also acted as a source for the SWESS barometric switches.)[190]

Xandre reached for the pod warhead control selector switch, unsealed the switch, shifted SGA on, and activated the weapons lock and arm panel. Below that he checked the pod safety lock pin release handle: it was unsealed, vertical, and out. He then broke the lead seals on two of the small weapons warhead control selector switches and activated those. Finally, he flipped the auto release switch on and the weapon selector switch on. He related these moves to O'Grady (see fig. 34).

Kairi, meanwhile, called out, "Lots of faint Flat Face and Spoon Rest. Nothing else."

O'Grady called out, "Time to Go at . . . two hundred seconds."

One hundred. The plane started to pull up.

O'Grady checked the Time to Go meter. "Thirty seconds."

Twenty.

Zero. The electrical release circuits activated and the pod released from *The Polish Prostitute*. O'Grady disengaged the heading switches and flung the airplane to port and down to the deck, nearly at right angles to their original direction of flight. A third fin on the bomb pod popped out to stabilize the weapon as it arced to its target.

Red 1's target was Strategic Rocket Forces Headquarters at Perkhushkovo. Going into service in March 1960, it consisted of above-ground support buildings and barracks and an underground command post. The intelligence professionals and targeters did not know how deep the bunker was.[191] O'Grady and his crew were selected for this site because of their repeated high bomb scoring. It was not enough to get the weapon somewhere near the target, O'Grady reflected, as they did in the old days of B-47s and Mk-36s; they had to come within 3,000 feet (1 kilometer) of the Strategic Rocket Forces Headquarters with the bomb pod.

When detonated, the Mk-53's thermal pulse would range out to 27 kilometers; the air blast damage on the surface would slam everything out to 9.5 kilometers at 5 PSI, while the 20 PSI blast ring was 4.5 kilometers. The fireball radius was 3 kilometers, or nearly two miles. Those, however, were secondary effects.[192] The primary effect of the Mk-53 landing within 1 kilometer of the bunker was to collapse it and destroy its ability to communicate with a ground-burst-generated shock wave. Analysis of the Shot Oak test in 1958 revealed that a 9-megaton-yield weapon detonated on the surface blew a crater 60 meters (200 feet) deep and displaced and fractured bedrock down to 938.7 feet below that. The shock wave radiated outward symmetrically to at least 3,000 feet until it was attenuated by the rock.[193]

Red 1's pod undershot the target by three hundred meters, but it was close enough. The shock wave compressed the bedrock that surrounded the bunker, collapsing its southeastern walls and burying its occupants. The bunker's telephonic connections, crucial for communicating with the radio sites that were connected with the missile silos, were all cut as the surface structures were turned into dust. All of the surface antennas melted or were crushed and swept away.

But O'Grady and Red 1 were not done. After surviving the buffeting and heat pulse, O'Grady continued west and then snapped *The*

Polish Prostitute into a right bank. Kairi set the controls for the two Mk-43s and prepared for a minimal interval drop. The first Mk-43 was released, and O'Grady banked left again, dog-legging away to the west, brought her right, and snapped off the second Mk-43, performed another escape maneuver, egressed past Klim to the northwest, and kept low enough to avoid the SA-3 barrier.

These weapons were targeted at the Kryukovo High-Frequency Communications Facility and the Moscow Radcom Station Lozhki. Both stations had fields and fields of high-frequency antennas and, because of their location north of Moscow, were assumed to be backup communications for the missile fields.[194] As a result, they were hit with 1-megaton airbursts, which swept away the antennas and killed the operating personnel.

Red 2, piloted by Major Larson, with Captain Griffee his nav and Captain Barney his defensive systems operator, rolled in next. If Larson had looked out the window, he would have seen three boiling mushroom clouds to his north, the shock waves having already dissipated by the time Griffee lined up the pod for the drop. Their target was a bunker complex near Chekhov. After four years of examination analysts had concluded that it was a relocation site for the Soviet military high command. The Chekhov bunker lay to the south of the city, outside of projected fallout areas, and was probably constructed with the assumption that Moscow itself would be a target. It was nowhere near the air defense system: security through obscurity, perhaps. Griffee effected the pod drop, while Larson wrenched Red 2 into its escape maneuver to port and accelerated away from the weapon's effects.

By this time Griffee had a pair of Mk-43s ready to go. The two targets were the primary Strategic Rocket Forces communications facilities, Naro-Fominsk and Novopetrovskoy. Unlike the facilities taken out by Red 1, these consisted of hardened fishbone high-frequency antennas buried under berms, the primary communications systems for the Perkhushkovo bunker and probably Chekhov.[195] Skirting the effects of the Chekhov strike, Larson lined up Naro-Fominsk, dropped, cut to port, and headed north to Novopetrovskoy, northwest of Moscow, and repeated the maneuver. Both sites succumbed to ground-burst 1-megaton hits. To save precious fuel, Larson brought Red 2 up in altitude, but Barney saw his ALR-12 scope light up with almost too many radar hits as they overflew the SA-3 missile line.

"We're made! I have a Squat Eye ... correction, two Squat Eyes, no three!" Barney activated the ALQ-16 and started to break the tracks as the SA-3 missiles lifted off. Larson performed another maneuver and the tracks disappeared from the ALR-12.

What O'Grady, Larson, SAC, and the CIA didn't know was that there was a Strategic Rocket Forces backup headquarters located at Borovsk, south of the communications site at Naro-Fominsk.[196] In all probability it had been missed or misidentified as part of the Moscow antiballistic missile system. However, without the communications stations, that facility lacked the ability to effectively communicate with the missile forces, particularly those in the East.

Red 3 was flown by Major Silliman, with Captain Rodier as his nav and Lieutenant Cassie the defensive systems operator. The Sharapovo facility was identical to the Chekhov facility in every way, except a rail line from Moscow ran to it. Sharapovo was believed to be the relocation facility for the Ministry of Defense leadership. SAC's concern was that Sharapovo and Chekhov, similar to Perkhushkovo in construction, might be able to serve as backups if connected to facilities like Naro-Fominsk, Novopetrovskoyf, Kryukovo, and Lozhki. Therefore they had to be destroyed or rendered inoperable. Indeed Red 3's pod went "plus" of the target but was still well within the minimums: the 9-megaton bomb collapsed the northwest part of the bunker and swept away the surface communications systems.

Silliman, Rodier, and Cassie, however, had a challenging secondary task. Silliman broke to starboard during the pod drop and Rodier prepped their Mk-43s. Cassie kept scanning for possible air defense radar. Dog-legging around the huge billowing cloud above them, Silliman lined up for Ramenskoye, a hardened communications site. Rodier delivered the goods and a 1-megaton ground burst ensured that nobody would use Ramenskoye to communicate with anything ever again. There was one final strategic communications site, at Pushkino, northeast of the city. Silliman and Rodier had to bypass the effects of Red 1's strikes: the fallout plume now starting to descend over Moscow from the Perkhushkovo strike and the atomized remains of Kryukovo and Lozhki. Fortunately they had trained for this, and the B-58 danced around the clouds and headed for Pushkino, which they obliterated with a 1-megaton blast.[197]

Only Red 4 was left. Major McDermott, Captain Seaholm, and Lieutenant Bridgette had trailed the other three B-58s and were thus dealing with an alerted air defense system. The AN/ARC-34 UHF radio suddenly squawked.

"Red 1 away."

"Red 2 away."

"Red 3 away.

McDermott and Red 4 were the backup plane. If none of the others hit their targets with the pod-mounted Mk-53, Red 4 would take care of it on the fly. Now that all three bunkers and five of the six communications stations were confirmed as struck, Red 4 could disrupt the Moscow defenses for the SIOP forces that would follow in minutes. The problem was, there were two possible facilities: Monino and Chernoye.[198] An Mk-53 drop in between the two might not completely destroy either facility, but this was not as crucial as the destruction of the Strategic Rocket Forces communications and command facilities. Seaholm readied the pod while Bridgette picked up Yo-Yo radar signatures as they skirted the older SA-1 Guild defenses southeast of the city.

The pod landed between the two suspected air defense bunkers, disabling them and everything else within twenty miles. McDermott broke starboard. Bridgette threw on the ECM and diverted every SAM radar that tried to lock on.

O'Grady momentarily reflected on Glass Road; he knew these strikes would severely degrade the Strategic Rocket Forces, but he also knew that Red Flight did not have the range to take out their backup hardened command center and antennas at Chaadayevka; he could only hope that the three 200-kiloton Mk-2 multiple reentry vehicles in the Polaris A-3 launched from the USS *Andrew Jackson* in the Mediterranean would kill that site in time.[199]

The weapons of the SIOP forces started to impact their targets as Red Flight departed the field. Next stop: Finland. Hopefully.

EIGHT

Strategic Underground Command

The ICBM Force in Film and History

ICBM. The intercontinental ballistic missile. No acronym is more closely associated with the Cold War than this. The technological extrapolations of Nazi-era terror weapons put to use as the cornerstones of the deterrent system, they bore mighty names (aspirations?): Atlas, Titan, Minuteman, Peacekeeper. Their opponents were Soviet missiles with code-names like Shyster and Satan. ICBMs harnessed the potential of the H-Bomb plus the ballistic missile plus speed of delivery, changing the strategic dimensions of the Cold War. Now a whole war could be conducted in an hour with unprecedented levels of destruction.

By 1965 that potential was fully realized. By the 1970s the drama of the bomber crew in *Dr. Strangelove* and *Fail-Safe* was replaced with a new type of drama in both *WarGames* and *By Dawn's Early Light*: Do we fire or not fire? Oh, and we have less than thirty minutes to make a decision, not hours to negotiate over the Hot Line. This drama was augmented by connecting that anxiety with having the world-ending decision made with little or no human input. The logical extension of that system found expression in *Dr. Strangelove*, *Colossus*, and *WarGames*.

The stereotypical view of the ICBM goes like this: It is a big, dumb rocket that goes from A to B in thirty minutes, launched from an underground facility called a silo. Two guys (and later girls) out in a cornfield the middle of nowhere in a flyover state, probably one of the Dakotas, sit in a secure underground capsule, each with a key and connected to a communications system that tells them when to launch the missile, not why or at what. They carry pistols, which seems to be contradictory given the fact it takes two to launch the weapons. Morale patches for their uniforms are a must: one of them, playing on the quote about the Minuteman ICBMs being America's "ace in the hole," has a skeletal hand holding playing cards full of mushrooms clouds: "Play the hand you're dealt." (In another squadron it is, "We play the last hand.") The other wears a patch that asserts, "Death wears fuzzy bunny slippers" and depicts the Grim Reaper at a control panel with his scythe and nonregulation footwear. Gen. Thomas S. Power rotates in his grave because of the relaxation in SAC dress standards.

To those who served in the early ICBM units in the 1960s this was cutting-edge technology in an advanced career field working on a space launch vehicle, albeit one with a megaton-yield warhead.[1] Atlas missile crews in a Kansas cornfield near Valley Falls were using the same system that NASA used at Cape Canaveral to put John Glenn and Gus Grissom in orbit.

To others the day-to-day operations of the capsule and its panels were humdrum compared to what bomber crews did: Herman Kahn apparently once suggested that the air force rename the ICBM units Strategic Underground Command; the derived acronym obviously did not go over well with the U.S. Air Force. The claustrophobic conditions, the isolation from civilization, and extreme weather belie the awesome firepower that these men were responsible for. New pairs of men (and later women) rotate with the capsule crew every so many hours, maintainers maintaining the systems. All is serene under the cornfields because the mere existence of these weapons ensures the other side will not launch its own ICBMs. Thousands of missileers have served in launch control centers and launch control facilities since the early 1960s, with only a handful of accidents occurring. How is it possible to turn such tranquil serenity into deadly world-ending drama?

Easy. What if an opposing force could take over such a facility and launch the missiles? What if crazed crews decided to do the same? Let's take it a step further. These missiles, which have a thirty-minute flight time to their targets instead of a bomber force's hours, are connected to a rapid-reaction command-and-control system that links NORAD, SAC, and the NCA. And the missiles are set up to be salvo-launched (fired all at once). Let's say somebody wanted the whole system to react even faster to ensure the other side doesn't have a hope of retaliating. More automation is introduced incrementally until one day the missiles practically control themselves. Then you have something closer to a Kahn-esque Doomsday Machine. And the world can end with a mistake.

We are now way beyond bored missile crews studying for their MBAs via correspondence course while awaiting Armageddon. *Twilight's Last Gleaming* (1977) depicts the compromise and near-launch of Titan ICBMs by a disaffected ex-missileer. Was that a plausible scenario? *Colossus* (1970), *WarGames* (1983), and *Terminator 3* (2003) show us the effects of taking the men in the capsules out of the loop and provide us with allegorical and practical depictions of the effects of too much linkage between NORAD and the SAC Minuteman force. *Damnation Alley* (1977) and *The Day After* (1983) are slightly more prosaic about ICBMs but contributed to the popular cultural understanding of Minuteman. To what extent were the Minuteman ICBMs and the machines connected to them the American Doomsday Machine?

The Secret Lives of ICBMs and Their Friends

The ICBM is integral to the Cold War in surprising ways not considered in the crisis films, with one exception: *Ice Station Zebra*.[2] This film is set in an Arctic research station, one of many from both sides that dotted the polar regions of this planet for decades. These were the forward elements of scientific research projects, almost all of which had Cold War applications: propaganda, intelligence collection, or scientific data collection. The film opens with a lengthy depiction of a reconnaissance satellite's de-orbiting, complete with cut scenes between a multitude of antennas and ground stations around the world, culminating with the capsule's inadvertent (or not) landing near a drift ice station in the Arctic that is engaged in all three of those Cold War activities. The race for the capsule and subsequent Berlin-like standoff between Soviet and Anglo-American forces forms the bulk of the story, but it is precisely these other activities that are historically important in understanding the vast backdrop for the ICBM in its underground silo and crew in the launch control facility.

If an ICBM is to deter, it must be a credible system: it must have a reasonable probability of launching and hitting its target and be demonstrably capable of doing this. The Nazis were in the process of learning how to do so with their A-4 (V-2) ballistic missile. The A-4 was the first weapon or any other man-made device to enter space with its trajectory before plunging back to Earth and detonating. It could hit the city of London from the Netherlands but without precision. That said, when the war ended and longer-range weapons were postulated using captured technology, the issue of accuracy progressively emerged.

The Nazis were going against the grain because, simply put, they did not know enough about planet Earth.[3] A plethora of phenomena affect the ballistic trajectory of an ICBM and its nuclear weapon, which is housed in a reentry vehicle that separates from the missile, penetrates the atmosphere, and arcs to its target. There is the Coriolis force (or effect) that deflects a missile slightly, to the right in the northern hemisphere, to the left in the southern, as Earth rotates. The ground distance to the target is not the same distance that the missile actually travels because of this rotation. Most important, and most basic for ICBMs, it is crucial to understand how Earth's gravity works, putting the B in "ballistic." As it turns out, Earth's gravitational field is not uniform around the globe. Why? Earth itself is not a perfect sphere; it is an oblate spheroid.[4] Thus the first country to take all this into account and gather and process the needed data for its ICBM systems had an inherent advantage in range and accuracy, with obvious implications for Cold War nuclear strategy and thus force structure, application of resources, and even economics. And what was the name of the first satellites that helped uncover the first scientific data on Earth's behavior relative to man-made vehicles in space? Sputniks I through III. Sputnik represented more than just the feat of placing an object in orbit; these data also gave the Soviets a strategic advantage.[5]

Geodesy and the other earth sciences cannot be extricated from their Cold War origins, the irony that the Gaia hypothesis could not have come about without military technologies notwithstanding.[6] These and other scientific disciplines proceeded concurrently with ICBM development in the 1950s and 1960s and were thus integral to the Cold War superpower competition. Both sides were busy measuring every possible variable related to ICBM operations, especially in the Arctic, where the Soviet presence at drift ice stations was nearly constant.[7] There was doubt, for example, whether guidance systems would even work over the magnetic polar regions. Upper atmosphere research was crucial to understanding the behavior of reentry vehicles. And there were other areas of concern requiring ongoing research.[8]

But then there was space. An ICBM spends part of its time subjected to this novel environment, one staggeringly different from Earth's. The first American satellite, Vanguard, uncovered the existence of radiation belts that are held in place by Earth's magnetic field. The Van Allen belts certainly had an impact on ICBM operations. Indeed the Argus nuclear tests and the evolution in our understanding of electromagnetic pulse effects were part of this effort very early on. Solar flares, solar wind, and other space weather also needed to be understood in order to ensure the credibility of the ICBM system. Would the radiation interfere with the nuclear weapon inside the reentry vehicle? Very early on, ICBM deterrent operations were indistinguishable from space operations, no matter how many tried to deny this state of affairs for legal, propaganda, and bureaucratic reasons. SAC was in many ways NASA's Dark Side.

The ICBM and the satellite are also inextricably linked; they need each other to achieve orbit. Once the potential of space became real in 1957, it was only a matter of three years before its exploitation was undertaken in earnest. For example, the MIRV, whose several nuclear warheads are mounted on a single missile for delivery by a "bus," actually had its origins in the Able-Star and Tranatstage satellite-dispensing mechanisms. Thor Able-Star, for example, dispensed multiple signals-intelligence satellites plus Transit navigation satellites into orbit starting in 1960.[9]

But first there are the confusing, compartmented, and overlapping capabilities presented to us by the American satellite forces. There was the separation of military commands and the intelligence agencies. Those agencies also had their own systems. There was SAC-specific control of certain functions, but other military forces, such as the U.S. Navy, had their own functional requirements. There was also the need to maintain separation of civilian and military space operations, with NASA for domestic as well as international political considerations related to Cold War diplomacy.[10] The U.S. satellite force looks fragmented and incoherent (and it was, in certain respects), but it still directly supported the ICBM force and was crucial to its operations.

Reconnaissance satellites like Corona and Gambit fed the intelligence apparatus and provided strategic targeting data for the ICBM force. Early warning satellites like MIDAS and later Defense Support Program protected the force via NORAD. Signals intelligence systems like Poppy and Grab provided early warning and collected data on opposing ICBM and ABM (antiballistic missile) systems. The Air Force Satellite Communications and Navy Fleet Satellite Communications networks provided the National Command Authorities with the means for command and control of the missile force by the 1970s. Most of this capability was operational by 1965–66, less than a decade after Sputnik.

But that was not all. The Defense Meteorological Satellite Program and other weather satellites worked with the reconnaissance satellites to schedule flyovers when there was as little cloud cover as possible over target areas so they could collect their critical data. The weather satellites were also responsible for reporting on the tactical implications of weather systems over the ICBM force's targets in the Soviet Union. For example, wind affected the accuracy of ICBM reentry vehicles once they were back in Earth atmosphere. Equally important was the need for accurate fallout prediction, which was dependent on the status of winds at several levels.[11]

The Kennedy administration decided that it wanted to build bridges with Khrushchev in 1962 and looked at several scientific means to do so. One result was an agreement to share global weather

STRATEGIC UNDERGROUND COMMAND

satellite information. This agreement, delayed by the Cuban Missile Crisis, was promulgated in the spirit of the 1963 nuclear test ban treaty and the Hot Line agreement. The United States provided up-to-date meteorological information to the USSR, but the Soviets dragged their heels throughout the 1960s and 1970s and did not reciprocate completely. Their information was regularly delayed or incomplete.[12] In effect the agreement gave the Soviets valuable information on the state of the weather over U.S. target areas with obvious implications for ICBM targeting in the event of nuclear war.

SAC had its own mechanisms for providing weather data to the ICBM force and did not need to rely on the Soviets. The air force's Global Weather Central, a non-SAC formation, was moved out of Suitland, Maryland, and located with SAC in 1957. With the help of SAC's IBM computers, an early facsimile system connected Global Weather Central with air force facilities. In 1959 Weather Central got it own IBM computers. Initially data came in from automated weather stations at Thule AFB and two sites on the Alaskan islands. In 1960, however, LeMay and Power, understanding the implications of the new technology, worked closely with other agencies to link SAC to a new classified weather satellite system. Derived from the "white" (overt) NASA Tiros weather satellite program, the Defense Meteorological Satellite Program (DMSP) was eventually based at SAC HQ. Downlink sites were covertly established at Fairchild and Loring AFBs employing unused U.S. Army Nike missile facilities. The data, in an automated form, were sent to Offutt AFB, where the DMSPs were controlled. A special launch unit was formed using Thor intermediate-range ballistic missiles, the 4300th Support Squadron; the unit handling the information was the 4000th Support Group (working with non-SAC air force weather personnel).[13]

DMSP tape-recorded the weather patterns collected by the sensors and downlinked them via an encrypted channel when the satellites passed over the receiving sites. U.S. Navy aircraft carriers also later developed a downlink capability (as depicted in the 1980 film *The Final Countdown*).[14] The first DMSP would pass over the Soviet Union at first light; that information, in addition to downlinking to SAC, provided reconnaissance for any intelligence collection satellites behind it. A second DMSP followed later in the morning for confirmation and update purposes.[15] That information was fed directly to the ICBM units in the field for input by the crews.

In addition to weather reconnaissance SAC looked toward having real-time satellite imagery of Soviet targets downlinked to SAC HQ as early as 1958. These activities were depicted in both the book and film *Fail-Safe* when CINCSAC General Bogan looks at Soviet missile sites in the comfort of his underground-cool 1950s command post. This concept was based on a real system, the WS-117L, initially called Sentry and later Samos.

Samos was conceived in the mid-1950s as a family of satellites based on a common airframe (spaceframe?) that could handle photoreconnaissance, signals-intelligence ferreting, early warning, and manned space flight for military purposes. This was a purely air force program, exclusive of those conducted by NASA, CIA, NSA, or the National Reconnaissance Office, and was well under way by August 1958.[16] Indeed in 1961 General Power complained about the lack of space in SAC's underground command post to handle both the incoming World Wide Military Command and Control System (WWMCCS) and Samos's early warning and photoreconnaissance functions.[17]

Samos would have provided SAC with a vertically and horizontally integrated command, control, and intelligence system. Its early warning satellite would have detected a Soviet ICBM launch and downlinked the warning directly to the SAC Command Post, where targets selected by the Joint Strategic Target Planning Staff using Samos real-time overhead imagery would be relayed via Samos communications satellites to bomber and ICBM forces for prosecution. Those forces, checking their satellite terminals, would know the weather over their targets thanks to a Samos weather reconnaissance capability. And so on.

But it was not to be. Samos appealed to LeMay and Power because it was rational, was strategically and operationally coherent, and speeded things up. But others opposed this centralization of power, particularly the CIA and those who thought things needed to be slowed down (pace the debate between Groteschele and Black in

Fail-Safe). Indeed the failure of the advanced real-time photo reconnaissance system to work effectively after only four years of development and five years after Sputnik was used as one excuse to kill Samos. (There were others.) Certainly separating warning from alerting and then launching functions by placing the competing MIDAS warning satellite program under NORAD was a move to rein in SAC's vertical integration. Having the CIA handle all strategic assessments using their own systems was another counterweight to the air force's power in Washington.[18]

Yet, as we will see later in this chapter, the pendulum swung back the other way in the 1970s precisely because of the speed of ICBM operations in war: a real-time photoreconnaissance satellite, a successor to Samos, became the cornerstone of the American capability, and a networked computer system that integrated warning, planning, and weather functions was linked to the ICBM launch control facilities themselves.

Troglodyte Titan and the First Generation: Fail Deadly

The idea that an ICBM control facility could be taken over by hostile elements who threaten to launch the weapons first emerged in popular culture in Walter Wager's 1971 novel *Viper Three*. Wager, the son of Russian immigrants, was a lawyer specializing in aviation law who migrated into the entertainment industry in the 1960s. *Viper Three* was only one of his novels focusing on "what if" scenarios: *Operation Intrigue* (1956) involved a U.S. invasion of Communist China; *The Spirit Team* (1997) looked at American biological warfare capabilities; *Otto's Boy* (1985) involved the release of chemical warfare agents in the New York subway system; *Telefon* (1977), the basis for the 1977 film of the same name starring Charles Bronson, postulated a Soviet sleeper agent attack on the U.S. strategic communications system; *58 Minutes* (1987) was the source for *Die Hard 2* and featured a rogue military special forces unit seizing control of the air traffic control system and crashing civilian airliners to facilitate their objectives.[19]

In *Viper Three* a former SAC intelligence officer, Maj. Lawrence Dell, breaks out of the Montana State Prison "Death House," where he is scheduled to be executed for brutally murdering his wife. Accompanied by four other murderers, including a psychotic apocalyptic religious fanatic, Dell kidnaps a Minuteman combat crew, tortures them for authentication information, and penetrates a Minuteman launch control facility (LCF) near Malmstrom, Montana, where the fugitives contact SAC and the White House and demand money and safe passage out of the country on Air Force One with the president as a hostage. Or they launch all ten ICBMs.[20]

Wager starts the novel with a detailed disclaimer: "Everything is imaginary and fictional—names, places, people, political entities, military organizations." This is disingenuous to knowledgeable people. The SAC command post is code-named Touchdown. (It was Dropkick in real life, referencing the "football.") The Strategic Targeting Board is the real-life Joint Strategic Target Planning Staff. The numbers of personnel manning a Minuteman LCF is accurate, while the code word Red Indian to warn of a silo takeover reflects the actual code word, Redskin. The process by which the team bypasses topside security reflects the real entry process; the Primary Alerting System is accurately depicted, as are the ten sealed switches on the launch-enable panel; and the yield of the Minuteman II's warhead is correct. The novel deviates from reality in a number of important ways, however, so it is clear Wager spoke with someone who was familiar with Minuteman II but who did not provide him with everything.

The conversion of *Viper Three* into Robert Aldrich's 1977 film *Twilight's Last Gleaming* produced significant changes. Major Dell the murderer becomes General Dell, a disaffected SAC officer and designer of the facility's systems who has lost faith in America after being a prisoner of war in North Vietnam and who is framed for murder because he wouldn't go along with the program when he got home. His motivation is to force the release of National Security Council documents (akin to the Pentagon Papers) to prove that the Vietnam War was designed to convey to the Soviets that America could be nasty—nasty enough to embark on nuclear war—and by doing so maintain a deterrent posture. As one Aldrich biography points out, *Twilight's Last Gleaming* played on the post-Vietnam angst and post-Watergate paranoia ricocheting around the United States in the 1970s, culminating in a pre–Oliver Stone/*JFK* situation in which the president must die to prevent the release of "the truth."[21]

Wager, writing *Viper Three* in 1971, was focused not on making political statements but on entertaining us with a rather scary scenario. Burt Lancaster, on the other hand, was interested in furthering his political agenda. And it is interesting to note the almost seamless shift from Lancaster's youthful Gen. James Mattoon Scott in *Seven Days in May* to his older Lawrence Dell in *Twilight's Last Gleaming*: it is almost as if Dell were Scott after escaping from prison and getting back at the system long after the failed coup.

So is the hostile takeover of an LCF and the possibility of such a rogue launch possible? To examine this, we need to disentangle *Twilight's Last Gleaming, Viper Three*, and how the security of the LCFs evolved. *Twilight's Last Gleaming* does not depict a Minuteman facility. Rather the film involves the takeover of a Titan I ICBM complex equipped with security systems that did not exist and others that are conflated with Minuteman's systems. The film in some ways inadvertently highlights significant command-and-control problems that existed in the first-generation ICBMs in the early 1960s.

The U.S. Air Force deployed seven types of ICBMs in the 1960s, resulting in a conglomeration of site configurations and security measures. This state of affairs related directly to the concurrent nature of American ICBM development in the 1950s and the incredibly rapid change in ICBM technology over a five-year period. The first-generation ICBMs included Atlas and Titan. Atlas came in three versions, D, E, and F, with the D model in two different guidance configurations. The D and E models were based in above-ground horizontal launchers wonderfully called "coffins." On command the missile was loaded with its liquid propellants, erected vertically, and fired. The D model was in a "soft" site above ground, and the E was based in a partially underground launcher. The F model sat vertically in an underground silo; after propellant was pumped in, the missile was raised on an elevator and launched. This is very different from the Minuteman system, which sits in an unmanned silo, has solid fuel, and can be launched directly from its platform. Each

Atlas site was manned by six personnel, with between six and twelve missiles per squadron.[22]

Titan was similar to the Atlas F in that it was stored vertically in a silo, loaded with propellant on order, raised on an elevator, and then launched. Unlike Atlas, Titan was based in threes in what amounted to miniature underground cities with tunnels connecting the silos, the command center, the power house, and antenna silos. Titan I facilities like this were manned by five personnel. There were nine missiles in a Titan I squadron. One two-man Minuteman crew was responsible for ten missiles that were widely dispersed and not even visible from the LCF.

If a hostile force had wanted to take over or otherwise interfere with a first-generation ICBM complex, it would have been confronted with several obstacles: the physical security of the site, the personnel manning it, and the launch-enable systems. If the scenario involved an insider attack, that is, someone like Dell in the lead with specific knowledge, the probability of an unauthorized launch dramatically increased.

An isolated Atlas or Titan site in 1962 rural America was surrounded with a barbed-wire fence; only later were anti-intrusion warning systems added. The six-man crew, carrying a launch key and authentication codes, drove out to the site, stopped at an unmanned gate, and identified themselves via phone to the on-duty crew who monitored them on a closed-circuit TV camera. The Atlas E manual suggests the following actions "after establishing identity of the personnel entering the complex employing local directives": (1) gate opened; (2) personnel enter; (3) gate closed. The Atlas F added warning lights to various consoles in the underground launch center to show the progress of the incoming crew.

Each site had an entrapment area where the incoming crew had to prove who they were before the inner door was opened. This involved a variety of code words to ensure they were not under duress. Titan I's setup was similar.[23] Note that unlike the Minuteman sites, there was no armed security force and only a handful of pistols available for the crew. There was a Combat Defense Force located at the nearest U.S. Air Force base that could be dispatched by helicopter (as depicted in *Twilight's Last Gleaming*). Some early ICBM units even employed their mobile maintenance teams for security duties.

In the early years there were two security conditions that could activate the defense forces. A Seven High was a "spontaneous oral report transmitted . . . to signify that an extraordinary event has occurred which appears to be capable of adversely affecting the capability to launch" and the observer "cannot clearly rule out sabotage or covert action." A Redskin reported the detection of enemy sabotage action in progress that adversely affected launch capability.[24]

If Dell and his followers were able to penetrate the outer security, subdue the missile crew, and seize their keys, they would have been confronted with the Launch Enable System next. (Authentication would be irrelevant at this point.) The film and the book depict a series of "inhibitors" and "cutoffs" that have to be overcome to isolate the launch control center's systems. These include a trip-wire grenade with a pressure release switch hidden in a console and a Sarin poison gas dispenser disguised as an electrical transformer. (In the film a curved dayglow-green tube is used instead, just so we know what it is supposed to be.) Having a nerve agent booby trap in a sealed underground launch control center would have been a really, really bad idea on a day-to-day basis and likely was not contemplated in real life.

The Launch Enable System (LES) was electronic and nonlethal, but to understand the LES it is necessary to understand the early ICBM communications and authentication systems linking each site with its higher authorities. Atlas and Titan sites were connected to each other through the AT&T land-line phone system, with six-foot-deep "hardline communication pits" with electromagnetic pulse buffers at intervals between the launch sites. The SAC Primary Alerting System was linked from the SAC Command Post to the squadron command post and the alternate command post through these means. The second communications system was Fast Talk, a low- and medium-power high-frequency single sideband system similar to Short Order that connected to SAC HQ via a network of radio stations northwest of Offutt AFB. Each missile site included "soft" antennas above ground and "hard" antennas underground that could be deployed to the surface by explosives or gas slugs if a nuclear blast swept away the other antennas. A UHF radio system handled tactical communications with the security and maintenance forces.[25]

The launch procedure for Atlas and Titan was prolonged and NASA-like, so we will deal with the specifics of the LES and the launch. Like the bombers, the missile crews received word verbally via the Primary Alerting System to commence electronic warfare operations. The positive control and execution measures for Atlas and Titan employed KAA-29, KAC-65, and KLI 12/TSEC authentication systems, again like the bomber crews. It took three crew members to authenticate: the missile launch officer, the guidance electronics officer, and the ballistic missile analyst technician. There were two pertinent pieces of equipment that the launch keys went into: the ALCO command-and-control panel and the launch control console. These were situated in the control center such that no single individual could turn both keys.[26]

In a twelve-missile Atlas squadron, two sites were designated as the command post and the alternate command post and modified as such. Using the land-line phone system, these two sites were connected to all other sites in the squadron. A constant signal was maintained on those lines between a special panel at the command post sites and the ALCO command-and-control panel in each launch control center. The ALCO panel key and the launch control console key had to be turned fully clockwise within three seconds of each other to commit, that is, launch. The ALCO panel key would work only if the signals from the command post and the alternate were shut off.[27]

The problems with that system are retrospectively obvious. If the squadron command post and the alternate were destroyed by enemy action, or their communications lines were cut during, say, a Redskin attack, the ALCO panel at the Atlas launch control center was automatically enabled and the crew or whoever disabled them could independently launch the missile. Indeed the dependence on high-frequency/single sideband was problematic in an electromagnetic pulse environment.

Early Titan I units, like the 851st Strategic Missile Squadron near Beale AFB in California, had significant teething troubles during activation that highlighted similar issues. In September 1962 the 851st received three Titan I complexes (nine missiles). The LES for Titan I was approved by Generals Power and Bernard Schriever only on 1 September, after deliberations that lasted all summer, and eventually the reentry vehicles were loaded onto the missiles between 3 and 7 September. This was all very well and good, except the units of the 851st had serious issues communicating with anybody. The landline telephone system was overloaded. A White Dot high-priority JCS message from the Looking Glass plane "was received but not copied." Why? "The necessary decoding documents were not available."[28] So the inability to communicate was offset by the fact that there were no authentication documents anyway.

More alarming was this discovery by the 851st leadership: "Power loss and/or fluctuation can render the LES [Launch Enable System] and the [Primary Alerting System] inoperable. In additional all intersite communications and [Public Address] systems are out in the event of power failure." They concluded, "[LES] reliability is still a questionable factor in launch configuration. More experience with the system must be obtained." The radio system, the same as the one employed in the Atlas sites, was incapable of providing "simultaneous monitoring and operation of both [high-frequency/single sideband] and UHF frequencies." Even the gate security guard lacked a telephone.[29]

On 10 September explosive bolts attaching the umbilical data cable to the missile detonated in a silo due to stray voltage related to moisture accumulation in the J boxes from leaking silo doors. (The J boxes were part of the warhead arming, fusing, and safety mechanisms.) The solution? "An eight-inch strip of tape was placed across the silo door cracks." Red Green saves Titan missiles.

Then there was a persistent "offensive odor" in the launch control centers, "noticed by all who enter the control center including General Wells during his recent inspection." (Lt. Gen. "Sundown" Wells was the notorious SAC inspector general portrayed by Kevin McCarthy as General Kirby in A Gathering of Eagles, which was filmed, coincidentally, at Beale AFB and at those silos.) Presumably at Wells's instigation, "extensive research" was conducted, and it was discovered that "the entire sanitary waste system is vented into the return air duct in the Control Center air conditioning system upstream of the carbon filters. The sanitary waste system is designed to accommodate material from the garbage disposal, sewage ejector, commodes, urinals, and sump pumps." One month later SAC was in the throes of the Cuban Missile Crisis and the crews of the 851st had to contend with offensive odors while locked in the launch control center handling three ICBMs with megaton-yield warheads.[30]

The LES for Titan II, deployed starting in 1964, seems to have been an improvement from the early Atlas and Titan I experiences. On arrival the crews handed over control of the "red box" filing cabinet, which held two launch keys and the authentication documents. The safe was locked with two personalized locks: one from the missile crew commander and the other from the deputy. If an Emergency War Order message came in on the Primary Alerting System, the box was unlocked and the commander went to his console, the deputy to the communications console, and the ballistic missile analyst technician to the control monitor group. All three had to authenticate and/or verify the order format and content. The commander and deputy then broke seals on the key switches and inserted keys, while the ballistic missile analyst technician flipped circuit breaker 103 to on.[31]

Titan II had an LES cabinet into which the phone lines and the Inter Complex Radio Communications System (three VHF frequencies and three UHF frequencies, four each on some squadrons) came in. There were two possible variants on how this system was employed. In the first, the two command post signals were sent by phone, radio, or both to the LES cabinet and then to the pyros on the Titan II valves, which locked them out. In the second variant, the two command post signals were needed to activate the pyros at some point prior to the key turns. Changes were made when SAC discovered the possibility that "the radio signal could be duplicated and transmitted from anywhere in the area, preventing a launch."[32] Another point of vulnerability was the fact that the Primary Alerting System phone line was hardened against electromagnetic pulse only out to 4.7 miles from each complex.[33]

Enthusiastic but underchallenged missile crews discovered later in the 1960s that if the launch complex lost outside power and went to battery, a circuit breaker on level 3 of the control center could be activated, thus cutting out the LES and enabling the dual key system.[34] There was another procedure to bypass a malfunctioning key system that involved opening the control management group cabinet and making certain alterations. When this was discovered, a lock and seal was put on the cabinet and had to be checked as part of the handover procedure to ensure it had not been tampered with.[35] As a former missileer put it, "Before the Coded Switch System a smart [missile facilities technician] could have launched it all by himself."[36]

These situations caused considerable alarm and contributed to the development of the Coded Switch System for the Titan II. Implemented in 1973–74 (the Atlas's and the Titan I's were long gone, having been decommissioned in 1965), the CSS was a six thumbwheel code input device located on the Titan II's stage 1 engine subassembly 2 oxidizer butterfly valve. Without the oxidizer, the missile simply wouldn't fly. The device locked the valve closed. A launch-disable signal was sent from the butterfly valve lock status encoder panel to the lock. If that signal stopped, the wing command post elsewhere was alerted to that fact electronically.[37]

The new sequence for Titan II using the CSS involved receipt of the primary alerting system warning and the emergency action message. This included an alphanumeric message thirty-five characters or more long, to be verified by three crew members for format and content. The commander and deputy opened the safe and removed the keys and a stack of authenticator cards. Several of the characters in the emergency message related to the code to unlock the butterfly valve lock; a number of characters told the crew which card held the six numbers needed for the CSS.[38] The CSS was a limited-try device; that is, after a certain number of unsuccessful tries, it locked out the system for thirty-six hours and required a maintenance team to unlock it. And if power was removed from the system, the thirty-six-hour lock out also went into effect. Any attempt to interfere with the lock would trigger two small explosive charges, permanently activating a separate lock on the oxidizer.[39]

Once the Emergency War Order Commit Time was revealed in the emergency action message, the security seals on the two keys were removed and the keys inserted. The ballistic missile analyst technician activated circuit breaker 103, and then the CSS code was entered and the operate OK light came on, This permitted the crew to push the butterfly valve lock operate switch, which activated two lights to confirm the action. The launch keys were turned within five seconds of each other, and the launch process was under way.[40]

Even if a team was able to launch a single Atlas, a Titan II, or three Titan I missiles, they would likely not have known where they would land. Retargeting a first-generation ICBM beyond the choices afforded by the two target selection buttons (three in Titan II) would have been impossible even if the hostile force accessed the missile itself. To retarget Atlas, the SAC targeting center had to program a trans-fluxor board and a GOE diode board using their IBM 7090 mainframe computer. This took an hour. Those boards had to be flown from Omaha to the nearest air force base and then flown by helicopter to the missile's location. Then it took four hours to open up the missile and change the boards. As for Titan I and II, the SAC targeting center again used the IBM 7090 to perform the targeting calculations, but these were put onto a punched-tape system, which was then flown to the missile site, a reader connected to the Titan, and the data on the tape inserted into the missile. That took twenty minutes.[41] It is doubtful whether the crew themselves knew exactly what was being targeted.

There are other instances of unreality in *Twilight's Last Gleaming*. One exceptionally dramatic sequence in the film using a split screen occurs when an air force security team, Bob Sherman (*The Final Option, The Spy Who Loved Me, The Sandbaggers*) and a pre-*Cheers* John Ratzenberger, descend by rope down the elevator shaft and proceed to place an atomic demolition munition outside the blast door. Their discovery by Dell and crew prompts Dell to activate the launch process while negotiating with an intransigent President Stevens (Charles Durning). In this scene Dell and crew turn the keys, the concrete doors open, and the Titan I's slowly rise on their elevators out of the silos while Dell counts down and Stevens pleads over the radio. At this point the Titan I is totally vulnerable to small arms fire: the missile body, an aluminum balloon filled with propellants, is not armored. The combat defense force could have engaged the exposed missiles, disabled them, and ended the stand-off without risk of the nuclear warheads detonating. In fact the keys did not activate the elevators; they activated the whole launch process, so it would have been impossible for Dell to abort the launch and still maintain a launch posture with the missiles exposed above ground. The combat defense force could also have waited out the infiltrators as the Titan I's liquid propellant could not have been kept indefinitely in the missile airframe itself and would have to be unloaded at some point back into its tanks.

The use of an atomic demolition munition, explored in both the film and the book, is interesting. The device in the film is bizarrely fragile and must be kept level at all times as the team abseils down the shaft, adding artificially to the drama. In the book it is a "type 133A Demolition Charge-2," the "third smallest in the US Arsenal."[42]

There were small nuclear weapons, but it appears as though they were all in the custody of the U.S. Army. The only indication that similar weapons may have been in air force custody at some point is the presence of a standardized twelve-bay, Greenleaf locked, grounded, and alarmed structure located at numerous SAC weapons storage areas at bases near ICBM sites. Inside each locker are floor markings indicating weapons separation similar to those found in nuclear storage igloos. Whether these buildings stored conventional or nuclear denial explosives, or were used for storing nuclear weapons or their components, is unclear.[43]

The United States possessed several portable demolition munitions. These weapons became progressively smaller in size from 1957 to 1967. The early T-4 had four 50-pound components and could be delivered behind enemy lines by a four-man special forces team parachuted from a C-119 transport. Its 1963 replacement, the lighter (350 pounds) medium atomic demolition munition, could alter its yield from 1 to 15 kilotons. There were three other interim atomic demolition munition weapons in between, but the ultimate was the rugged 60-pound W54 special atomic demolition munition "backpack nuc," which could be carried by a parachutist and yield up to 1 kiloton.[44] Of note, U.S. Army atomic demolition munitions capabilities were allegedly compromised on one occasion during a race riot in West Germany.[45]

In a Titan I facility, the use of a medium atomic demolition munition at its highest yield would have had little effect if detonated on the surface against the complex. If it were inserted into the entry portal and down the stairs, however, it would have generated enough energy to severely damage the power house and the control center. In any event, launch operations would have been problematic after such an attack. Against a Minuteman LCF, however, the situation is a bit different. If the elevator was locked at the bottom, the small diameter of the ladder would have prevented movement of the medium atomic demolition munition components down the shaft.[46] If somehow the munition did make it down and the weapon was detonated, would the feet-thick blast door to the launch control center fifty feet down have been able to withstand Hiroshima or one-sixteenth of one detonated right next to it? Probably not.

Mighty Minuteman: Ace in the Hole

We rarely see the Minuteman missile itself in the movies, just the control center or LCF. Indeed "Minuteman" is really an umbrella designation for four missile types, six reentry vehicle types, and at least five or six variants of their support and launch facilities deployed between 1962 and 1975. The LGM-30 A and B are typically called Minuteman I; the LGM-30F is Minuteman II, and the LGM-30G is Minuteman III. Externally the A, B, and F models look similar with their unitary warhead perched on top, but the G is significantly larger and carries three reentry vehicles/warheads. This evolution reflects the changes in how ICBMs would be employed as nuclear strategy and technology evolved from the missile's inception during the Eisenhower era, into the McNamara era of the 1960s, and ultimately to the Schlesinger period of the 1970s.

Minuteman was born to a certain extent as the result of interservice competition between the U.S. Air Force and the U.S. Navy. Gen. Bernard Schriever, in charge of air force ICBM development, wanted to keep his options open while he pursued the liquid-fuel Atlas; the navy was working on a solid-fuel missile that would eventually be named Polaris. Weapon System Q was born, a project led by Col. Edward N. Hall, brother of the Soviet atomic spy Ted Hall. The system was to be a small three-stage rocket using solid propellant. Q was to be deployed underground in the thousands, partly in order to keep the costs down and partly to be able to assign multiple missiles per target to make up for an assumed low accuracy.[47]

The research and development process was accelerated by Sputnik fear and missile gap politics. This led to attempts to pin down the numbers. How many were enough? An initial estimate in 1958 suggested five hundred to start with, more later. In 1959 the approved number was eight hundred by 1965, but in 1959 Gen. Thomas White, the air force chief of staff, announced that there should be three thousand Minutemen by 1970. Three squadrons of these were to be based on trains, while the rest were to go underground in silos. Success after success in the Minuteman test program gave momentum to the project after the Eisenhower-Kennedy transition, and in March 1961 McNamara made Minuteman a national priority. In a *Reader's Digest* article journalist Roy Neal referred to Minuteman as America's "ace in the hole," and the name stuck.[48]

We are used to picturing Minuteman as a system dedicated to countering Soviet missiles in their hardened silos during a strategic missile exchange in part because of films like *WarGames* and *By Dawn's Early Light*. This was initially not the case as Soviet silo-based ICBMs did not exist when Minuteman and its warheads were conceived. General Power was well aware of Minuteman developments, but the numbers that would be acquired fluctuated. (He may have joked with Kennedy about wanting ten thousand at one point.)[49] Actual employment of the Minuteman system within the SIOP strategy appears to have been initially left ill-defined by the air force or even the Office of the Secretary of Defense.

In 1955 LeMay initially saw ICBMs as "useful against area targets only."[50] By 1958 his views had evolved: "It appears now that the prime characteristics of the ICBM can be exploited best by using it initially to damage and disrupt the Soviet air offense and defense systems on the ground, holding them down until they can be destroyed by the manned bomber."[51] The many cheap, fast, and semi-accurate Minuteman missiles would overwhelm the Soviet air defense system in thirty minutes, and the B-52s and the undeployed B-70 would exploit the effects hours later.[52] Minuteman site surveys were conducted in New Hampshire, Maine, and Massachusetts. Positioning Minuteman in New England potentially reduced flight time to this target set.[53]

However, when the Soviets deployed hundreds of nuclear missiles in western Ukraine focused on NATO targets in 1961–62 Minuteman's strategic rationale shifted from attacking the air defense system in support of the bomber force to include destroying the Soviet medium- and intermediate-range ballistic missiles in their "soft," that is, unprotected, surface-launch sites.[54] With the mass Soviet deployments of silo-based ICBMs by the mid-1960s Minuteman targeting shifted yet again, and with the early retirement of Atlas and Titan I, Minuteman led the deterrence field.[55]

As a result Minuteman's warheads and reentry vehicles were developed with the same concurrency as the ICBM programs to ensure that a variety of targets could be accommodated for servicing. One reentry vehicle concept for Minuteman was a "boost glide vehicle." Based on a German concept that might have employed an expanded V-2 rocket called the A-9, this vehicle exited the atmosphere and skipped along it like a rock on water until it reentered over its target. Its derivative, Alpha Draco, was tested and found viable. The early Minuteman launch facilities were at least eight feet taller than the missile, probably in case Alpha Draco or a similar system was adopted. It was not, but by coincidence the extra space allowed the taller Minuteman III to be accommodated later in the program.[56]

But a decision was made to pursue ballistic reentry vehicles instead; these were the Mk-5 and the Mk-11. Development of warheads for them was initiated after the 1958 Limited Test Ban Treaty. After the Soviets broke the moratorium in 1961, the W59 and W56 warheads were tested during Operation Dominic. These were inserted into redundant Mk-15 and Mk-36 bomb casings and dropped off Christmas Island by B-52s. The first was a W56 test in April 1962 dubbed Arkansas; it yielded 1.09 megatons and was described as "highly successful and [meeting] design expectations." With some modification another w56 was dropped in the Bluestone test and yielded 1.3 megatons. (A supplementary test, Swanee, used a w56 and yielded 97 kilotons. Janus, under consideration around this time, conceptualized the use of some Minuteman missiles reconfigured as ABMs.)[57]

The w59 fared differently. Questa, dropped in May, yielded 670 kilotons, "considerably lower" than anticipated. A retest, Alma, yielded between 782 and 807. Another drop, Ricondada, came in at a disappointing 815 kilotons. In the final w59 test, Sunset, there is a discrepancy. Many sources say it yielded 1 megaton and met its design yield, but the test commander's final report states it only yielded 810 kilotons. In any event, the w56 and w59 started production, with the w59 scheduled for the Minuteman I and the w56 for the follow-on, Minuteman II.[58]

The boost glide vehicle concept did not die with Alpha Draco. A reentry vehicle called Asset that had similar dimensions to the Mk-11 reentry vehicle was tested later in the 1960s.[59] With the advent of MIRVs, however, it was more effective to develop the w62 warhead and put three of them into Minuteman III. That project was approved in December 1964.

Underground testing, in play after the 1963 Comprehensive Test Ban Treaty, was used to examine the w62's effectiveness. The yield in most publications is given as approximately 170 kilotons.[60] Yet none of the tests of Lawrence Livermore devices from January 1965 to March 1967 yielded 170 kilotons. Likewise from March 1967, when production engineering started, to the w62 deployment in April 1970, there were no 170-kiloton-yield tests. During that five-year period there were two 120-kiloton tests, one 160, two 200, and two 210. The 200- and 210-kiloton tests cannot be correlated with any other Livermore production design except the Polaris A3 w58, which went into service in 1964. The first of the 200-kiloton-yield tests, Kankanee, took place during the Flintlock series (Flintlock, Minuteman?), and another, Agile, during the Latchkey series, seven days before the w62 design was released for production engineering in 1967.[61] There is one report that the w62 did not meet its expected yield in testing and that "the Air Force was not happy."[62] Consequently, of the seven tests that could be associated with the W62, three were 120 to 160 kilotons and four were 200 to 210 kilotons. The 200-kiloton Pipkin shot during the Mandrel series the last test before W62 production started in 1970. The Soviets apparently believed the yield to be 400 kilotons.[63]

As noted earlier, the ICBMs were not merely ballistic nuclear artillery shells; they were space weapons systems. The first-generation ICBMs were equipped with a variety of systems collectively called "penetration aids." Atlas E and F and Titan I had "light and heavy simulation decoys," essentially combinations of flares and chaff. The Titan II's Mk-6 reentry vehicle had eight decoy tubes of metallic chaff located behind blowout panels in the transition assembly behind the warhead; these were deployed in space to spoof Soviet radar. The Mk-6 also had an "attitude stabilization" feature to "reduce its effective radar cross section and a new decoy . . . designed to simulate the radar reflectability of a stabilized Mark 6."[64]

Minuteman took the technology several steps further. Though the Minuteman I's Mk-11A reentry system was a straightforward ballistic system, the Mk-11B on Minuteman II was specifically designed to minimize its radar cross section and had limited ability to pitch the reentry vehicle assembly or rotate it at certain angles. The Mk-11C added the Mk-I and Mk-IA penetration systems.[65]

These systems used chaff dispensed at intervals in space to confuse Soviet radar tracking the third stage so it could not be used "as an offset aiming point" to track and kill the released reentry vehicle. Another purpose was to generate a shell game for Soviet missile radar tracking the reentry vehicle: was it the reentry vehicle, or was it a cloud of titanium strips? Tumble rockets added to the third stage to fire after the reentry vehicle was released were later implemented on the Minuteman I.[66]

Minuteman III was almost a completely different weapons system. This missile had a fourth stage that included the guidance control section; the reentry system consisted of the reentry vehicles and penetration aids mounted on the payload support structure; and the blandly named Rocket Engine Propulsion System, sometimes called the Post-Boost Propulsion System or Post-Boost Vehicle, in reality was a small, maneuverable space craft with attitude control rockets that could dispense sixteen chaff clouds, deliver a number of Mk-12 decoys, and reposition itself in space for the optimal delivery of the nuclear weapons. Those weapons were three Mk-12 MIRVS with W62 warheads. Further developments included "maneuvering/terminal fix" reentry vehicles and follow-on concepts like the Maneuvering Reentry Control and Ablation System and reaction control, which, when implemented, permitted the Mk-12 itself to maneuver after it was deployed from the Post-Boost Vehicle, further complicating a defender's situation.[67]

The configuration and deployment of the Minuteman ground systems differed considerably from those of Atlas and Titan. Instead of placing the crews within the silo complexes, two men at a Minuteman LCF controlled ten missiles located in single launch facilities dispersed away from the LCF and separated from one another by three to five miles. Five LCFs made up a squadron; three squadrons made up a wing, and there were six Minuteman wings for a total of one thousand deployed missiles.[68]

Even the Minuteman force's LCFs were different. The first ones were designed by Boeing and the second by Sylvania when Boeing lost the contract. In the first group the LCF was in an underground capsule, with the support equipment in the soft launch control equipment building topside. In the second group all of the support equipment was underground in a second capsule next to the control center, making those LCFs a dumbbell-shaped complex with two separate blast doors. This design was referred to as "the Deuce"; it was significantly more survivable in a retaliatory situation and reflected the shift in strategy in the 1960s. (The Deuces were also significantly roomier, like a ballistic missile submarine compared to the cockpit of a B-52.) If Twilight's Last Gleaming occurred in a non-Deuce LCF capsule, there might not have been enough room for everybody to move.[69]

Several films depict the Minuteman authentication and launch process. The first was Damnation Alley, a 1977 postapocalyptic thriller. Populated with cheesy special effects depicting giant scorpions, predatory armored cockroaches, and an Earth thrown off its axis due to multiple thermonuclear detonations, the film starts with the war itself through the eyes of a Minuteman crew after they have just entered their LCF for duty.

Major Denton and Captain Tanner, portrayed by George Peppard and Jan Michael Vincent, enter the 123rd Strategic Missile Wing facility, which looks like a partially buried Titan I complex. They pass a Big Board that brings in satellite space coverage of the northern hemisphere, essentially a smaller version of the NORAD command post, and pass through several layers of security; in the first they enter after a guard checks their IDs and Tanner gives a nonduress hand signal, and they are issued their pistols. They proceed down an elevator after passing another guard at a desk, who again checks their IDs. At the bottom of the elevator a third guard does the same. Approaching the blast door, the on-duty crew check their identities and they proceed to do a handover. The crew commanders unlock the red box and confirm the presence of an envelope; Denton and Tanner then lock the box with their own locks.

Almost immediately after the handover, the command post detects what they initially think is a satellite booster reentry, but soon the speakers in the launch control center squawk, "Blue Square One, Blue Square One, Blue Square One, Red Talon Copy, Blue Square One, Break Break." The incoming verbal message comes in next, and the crew write it down in grease pencil on plastic sheets: "Part One: 3 C A F T." "Part Two: T A C D X O." "Part Three: 042346. Authentication: S A." Denton and Tanner compare: "I have a valid message." "I agree." Both proceed to the red box, unlock it, and remove the envelope. After this there is no detail. "Arm all missiles." Tanner flips three switches, pushes a button on a big red box, and throws two more switches. "Armed." Denton tells Tanner, "Flight select switch to All," and Tanner turns a dial.

"PLC-A option switch to 99." (This is an intriguing part of the procedure we will look at later. How it got into a 1977 movie would be interesting to learn.) "Ready for launch."

"Insert keys. Rotate on my command. One, two, three, rotate. One, two, three, release." Both crew members perform this action, and the silos, loaded with Titan IIs, open and launch.

"I'm getting launch indications, Missile away light LFC-5." Denton picks up the phone and calls the wing command post: "Flight Charlie, ten missiles." The crew returns to the surface to watch the action unfold. Tanner lights up in front of a "No Smoking" sign, and the world as we knew it in the disco era ends. Cue the giant scorpions.

For comparative purposes, consider *First Strike*. In 1979 a consortium of concerned entities working with KRON TV in San Francisco produced a docudrama/infodrama designed to warn the public that SAC was vulnerable because of an aging command system and missiles that were less capable than the Soviets'. The footage was reused for *The Day After* in 1983. In both films actual Minuteman and Looking Glass crews undertake some of the actions they would have performed in an actual attack on the United States (but, interestingly, not all).

First Strike and *The Day After* start with Brig. Gen. Clarence R. Autery, an actual SAC duty officer, boarding the Looking Glass aircraft and taking off on a normal everyday rotation flight. Later Captain Stanton and Lieutenant Krause, real officers from the 742nd Strategic Missile Squadron at Minot AFB in North Dakota, arrive at an LCF in middle-of-nowhere Montana and pass through security, which is not covered in detail except that Stanton tells the guard that he recognizes Krause.

After a series of tranquil aerial shots of grain silos juxtaposed with Minuteman launch facilities, the scene shifts to the LCF underground. Over the Primary Alerting System radio we hear, "Standby to copy message. Klaxon Klaxon Klaxon. Message follows." There is a warble tone: "Standby to copy message." It comes in: A 7 8 N F 1 5 2 2. There is some garbled dialogue about "GCS execution from the president." The two men proceed to the red box, open it, and haul out the envelope, as well as two cards with keys attached to each. They read, "Unclassified. LCF #, panel number #." The crews break seals over the plastic cover of the key slots. "Unlock keys inserted." "Enable switch to Enable." Stanton makes a phone call: "All call enable." "Key turn on my mark." Krause: "Standing by." "Five, four, three, two, one," and we are treated to a montage of Minuteman missile launches. The people of Lawrence, Kansas, watch the columns of missile exhaust curve away to their targets in the Soviet Union.

The premise of 1983's *WarGames* is that in a test of Minuteman force combat crews, most fail to launch their weapons in the nonotice simulated emergency. A computer scientist uses the failures to convince the Department of Defense to remove the crews and replace them with direct links to the fictional War Operations Plan Response (WOPR) computer system located at NORAD's Cheyenne Mountain Complex. In doing so, the existing barriers between the warning of an enemy attack, selection of the response plan, and automatic execution of that plan are removed, leading to a crisis mirroring a series of actual events in 1980.

WarGames starts with a Minuteman combat crew, this one played by John Spencer and Michael Madsen, entering what looks like a suburban house on the prairie while talking about girls, Thai stick, and meditation. At a two-way glass in one room they are checked by security and handed their pistols and take the elevator down to the launch control facility, where the door is opened by the duty crew after a code is keyed into a pad. Despite the closed-circuit TV shots of Titan II missiles, the launch control facility panels are remarkably faithful to those of Minuteman, though not completely accurate. Once they are on duty, the Primary Alerting System warbles, "Skybird, this is Dropkick with a Red Dash Alpha message in two parts. Break, Break, Red Dash Alpha, Red Dash Alpha. Stand by to copy." The crew pull out their grease pencils: "R O N C T T L A Authentication: 220040 D L." "I have a valid message. Stand by to authenticate." "I agree."

They unlock the red box and remove two sealed authenticator "cookies," which they break open. The commander's card is classified Top Secret and says, "Red-Alpha Weapon Execution" and the letters T T L A, Authentication: D L. The deputy's card says, "R O N C, Authentication D L." The commander calls out, "Enter launch code," and the deputy types the code into a keyboard. On the screen we read, "Weapons Execution Order K36.948.3. Part One: RONCTTL. Part Two: 07:20:35. Launch Code: DL62209TVX. Launch Code Confirmed." The deputy calls out, "Target selection complete. Time on target sequence complete. Yield selection complete." The screen says, "Enable Missiles," and a countdown starts. The crew members insert the launch keys. One of the key slots has a sign above it: "Gently." "Rotate to set." The doors above a Titan II open up on the CCTV screen. "Roger. At set." "Enable missiles." The deputy flips ten red switches, calling each out. "Rotate launch keys to Launch." The countdown picks up. The commander has second thoughts, so the deputy unholsters his pistol and orders him to turn the key. And *WarGames* begins.

All of these films provide us with their take on the actions Minuteman crews would take on receipt of the launch order. As a result the fictional depiction of that process is firmly lodged in the popular culture. But how accurate are these depictions?

An attack like that in *Twilight's Last Gleaming* would probably not have succeeded against a single LCF in the Minuteman force. To access an LCF, it was necessary for the two-man combat crew to approach the launch control support building, a bungalow-like structure surrounded with a barbed-wire fence situated above the underground LCF. Topside personnel included the senior NCO facility manager, a pair of cooks who reheated foil packs centrally prepared at the main air force supporting base under controlled conditions, and the security force of six. The security force was responsible for the protection of the facility and was equipped with M-16 assault rifles, 203mm grenade launchers, and M-60 machine guns.[70]

A crew arriving at the gate had to be identified and verified by the two flight security controllers in a security control station that overlooked the facility gate. With a single activation, several buttons at the desk could send a Situation 1 "all call" alarm over the VHF radio and by phone line to the rest of the squadron, wing, and support base. Other single-push buttons summoned the alarm response teams. The entrance to the elevator leading to the launch control center was behind an electrically locked armored door in that office. The on-duty crew left a password with the security controllers. Once the incoming crew was again verified as authentic, which required verbalizing code words indicating whether or not they were under duress, they were permitted into the security control station. There a phone was linked to the LCF. When the duty crew below were satisfied by the flight security controllers that the incoming crew was authentic and not under duress, the door was electronically unlocked and the crew could enter the elevator, which took them down fifty feet to the vestibule where the blast door was located. Once that was opened, they were inside. If an LCF were under attack, the combat crew had the ability to unscrew certain panels and scatter the electromechanical components (mostly ball bearings). This was called "code dissipation" and rendered the facility incapable of launching missiles or assisting another LCF to do so.[71]

The possibility of compromising the unmanned launch facilities existed if maintenance crews were hijacked, but there were countermeasures. Entry into the underground support structures, the launcher equipment room and the launcher equipment building, was through the "B plug," a concrete hatch that could be opened only by using a very large combination lock, the "A circuit." This required the maintenance crew and the combat crew to be in communication and using one-time code books, one pink and the other blue.[72] The B plug took time to lower, the same time as it took to play a game of cards, or "the predicted response time of the [security force] from the [LCF] to the launch facility" if there was something wrong with the authentication.[73] As we will see, a variety of mechanisms could prevent a Minuteman from being launched against a target.

The most important reason an attack like that in *Twilight's Last Gleaming* would not have succeeded is that the cooperative and networked nature of the Minuteman system would have prevented missile launch from a single launch control center. (The bad guys would simultaneously have to take over two centers.) That system was the product of intense study in 1961, accelerated by concerns expressed by the Lauritsen Committee, tasked by Schriever with assessing the Minuteman program and approved by LeMay. The committee's findings: Minuteman "presents a very grave problem with respect to the possibility of accidental launch." Although Atlas and Titan "involve considerable numbers of personnel, manned operation, and appreciable count downtime," Minuteman was "highly automated and largely unattended," had a "thirty second reaction time, automatic count down, and multiple launch capability from central control centers." What really alarmed the committee was that "50 Minuteman missiles will be connected so that they can be salvoed or ripple fired if desired." In the committee's view, "the threat to world security implicit in such a system requires application of the highest level of approval and control."[74]

There are allegations today that SAC's leadership deliberately dragged its heels and resisted safety features imposed during the Kennedy era. This plays into the whole military disobedience/rogue SAC leadership zeitgeist established in the popular culture through films and was even mentioned during the 2016 Clinton-Trump presidential election debate.[75] But the situation was more complex than that. Some of the solutions to the Minuteman problem in fact predated *Dr. Strangelove* and *Fail-Safe*. Minuteman's safety features had several components: communications, authentication, targeting, and launch enabling. It is important to note that these components evolved over time as experience built up on the Minuteman system from the 1960s to the 1970s, and there was not always enough funding to immediately implement every project proposed. After all, there was a war on in Vietnam.

Let's tackle the communications systems first, as we are already familiar with some of them from previous chapters. Upon entering an LCF, a crew would see a small concrete cupola dome: this was the hardened UHF antenna used for air-ground communication. Atop the launch control support building was a soft VHF antenna for security and administrative communications. Offset from the building was a flower-like concrete disk that contained five hard high-frequency receiving antennas underground that could be individually activated with squibs that shot them to the surface. If the site was the squadron command post, a Christmas tree–like antenna was on the surface to the left of the building: this was a soft high-frequency transmitter, while a disk-like cover concealed a hard high-frequency antenna. The high-frequency radios were part of SAC's Yankee subnet, later the Bravo Net and still later called Giant Talk, when everything high-frequency was merged in the 1970s. Under the tarmac driveway was a hardened secure low-frequency communications system antenna.

This gave each LCF five different receiving frequency types specifically to offset any electromagnetic pulse interference or damage to communications that would result from Soviet nuclear detonations.[76]

The backbone of Minuteman communications was the good old AT&T telephone cable. The Primary Alerting System used the AT&T network to connect the SAC Command Post and the subordinate numbered air force headquarters to all LCFs. SAC was connected to NORAD and the National Military Command Center through similar means. The phone lines linked the LCFs with the launchers through the hardened intersite cable system, which was believed to be resistant to electromagnetic pulses and pressurized to detect breaks. Superimposed on that was a special channel, the Emergency War Order Network, which connected the wing command post with its subordinate squadrons using both soft and hard phone lines. The SAC automated communications and control system computer network circuits reached down to the Teletype machines and computer terminals in the individual LCFs.[77]

The Launch Facilities themselves were hard-wired not only to their parent LCFs but all of the other LCFs in the squadron. This included both hard and soft phone lines. Each launch facility also had a hardened UHF antenna for air-to-ground communications.[78]

As we see in the films, the land-line-based Primary Alerting System is the alerting system of choice, and the voice procedure it uses is approximately correct. Generally the radio systems were backups for the phone land lines. One speaker at the Primary Alerting System console was from SAC HQ and the other from the numbered air force headquarters. A variety of noisemakers down in the LCF were activated if the alerting systems went off, leading the crew to the authentication process for any incoming emergency action message. Both the commander and the deputy had to agree that the message was valid and authentic and came from the president or his successor.[79]

The emergency action messages described in the films are in some respects composites of the actual 1960s- and 1970s-era messages. Usually they would start with a warble tone and a collective call: Skybird for all SAC Primary Alerting System communications systems for bomber and missile units like the SAC Command and Control System Teletypes and phone lines, and Sky King for all SIOP-committed forces via all communications means, such as high-frequency, low-frequency, and ultra-high-frequency radios and later satellite systems.[80] In the 1960s the collective call would be followed with a color statement, for example, "This is a Red Dot defense message in three parts." Yellow, Green, and Blue Dot messages were for the bomber force and replaced the 1950s-era Alpha, Bravo, and Coco alert messages: Green meant practice alert, Yellow was a probable alert to follow, Blue was an order to taxi aircraft and hold at the end of the runway. A White Dot message was a JCS-ordered strategic communications test. Red meant the SIOP was being implemented. Sometimes a number was given as well: "This is a Red Dot message in four parts" or "This is a Red Dot Four message," which indicated the number of alphanumeric code groups that would follow.[81] This alerted the LCFs that there was an incoming message to copy.

The verbal and Teletype messages that followed consisted of a series of alphanumeric codes. The first six letters or numbers, repeated three times, was "the preamble [which] told the [missile] crew the edition and page number of the unsealed authenticator to use."[82] The preamble was followed by an execution message. In the early years of Minuteman this told the crew which war plan setting on the commander's launch control panel to use, A or B. This corresponded to the retaliatory and preemptive options in SIOP-62 or -63. The crew cut wire seals on ten red enable switches on the deputy's console, one per missile, and flipped them on, cutting ten signals to the launch facility. When that happened, the "D-Box, SCS and missile Safe and Arm devices [were] armed." Notably, during the early years of Minuteman I, a safety plug was put into the D-box by maintenance crews working on the missile; sometimes they forget to remove the plug, rendering the missile unfireable, and it would be found by a subsequent maintenance crew. In Minuteman II an elaborate monitoring mechanism was put in place to prevent this. As one missileer put it, "If a [Minuteman I] maintenance guy knew what he was doing he could have done an unauthorized missile launch."[83]

In later years the first group of numbers in the emergency action message was for the Launch Enable Control Group in the deputy's console, a device added to replace the ten red flip enable switches. It consisted of six alphanumerics, entered via six thumbwheels in the control group. It used some form of octal numeral system and the numbers were encoded as, say, P7, L3, N5, and so on. Below the thumbwheels was a triangular switch under a plastic cover. When this was turned, it prepared the missiles to accept a launch command; that is, they were "enabled."[84]

The message also told the deputy which Primary Launch Command setting to use on the launch verification panel, A or B. PLC-A/B replaced War Plan A/B in the 1960s on the commander's console. PLC-A selected targets in the later versions of SIOP-4 and its successors, while PLC-B was a selective launch of individual missiles or collections of missiles in the flight or squadron. Usually PLC-A was the setting to be used. It was a two-digit number: Minuteman upgrades permitted one hundred launch options to be selected.[85] Thus PLC-A's inclusion in *Damnation Alley* in 1977 is interesting; it does not show up in the other films, indicating that the set designer and screenwriter for this film had help from somebody in the know.

The message had an authentication code in it, usually two letters. In the early years the authentication code was in an envelope in the red box, which was accessed when both commander and deputy unlocked their personal locks. Crews wore the launch keys on chains around their necks, and in later years they were kept in the red box attached to a sealed authenticator system "cookie," a 3 x 5-inch card encased in plastic. When opened, the NSA-generated code in the cookie had to match the code in the message. Both crew members had to verbally acknowledge that the format of the message was valid and that the message was authentic.[86]

The emergency action message had an execution reference time. When the crew came on duty they had to set the time on an eight-day wind-up clock and later on the launch system itself. To do this they listened to radio station WWV at Fort Collins, Colorado, which regularly broadcast a coordinated universal time tone on five different frequencies.[87] The launch system was set to recognize the tone, a sync button was pushed on the program control panel (near the PLC-A/B selector), and that set the system to the correct time.[88] At the appropriate execution time (pun intended) the crew inserted their launch keys: the commander into the launch control panel and the deputy into the launch verification panel. These keys had to be turned within two seconds of each other.

That was the basic process. However, launching the Minuteman required the acquiescence of one of the four other launch control centers in the squadron. If the commander did not agree with launching, he could move a triangular switch to "inhibit." That said, two positive launch commands from other launch control centers could override the inhibit and launch all of the missiles in that flight. In the early Minuteman years that was all it took. Later on, when safety measures were enhanced, this state of affairs changed (see fig. 35).

How was that accomplished? The safety mechanisms were not confined to the crew and the launch control facility. The Minuteman missiles themselves played a key role here. Once the crew enabled their missiles using ten enable switches and later the launch control enable group, a coded signal was sent to the command message processing group, an electromechanical code machine in the LCF. This signal went by the hardened intersite cable system to each of the ten launch facilities. In the underground launcher equipment room at each missile was another machine, the status command message processing group. This device sent signals to the guidance and control coupler that was also in the room, and to the digital control unit (the missile's computer) mounted in the missile itself below the reentry vehicle.[89]

The signal opened an interlock on the guidance and control coupler, admitting the launch control enable group code sent from the LCF by the crew through an umbilical cable to a device mounted on the missile's first stage, called the command signals decoder. This device combined the crew's code with a code stored in it. That armed the command signals decoder, which let electricity flow to the missile's igniters and also activated the safe/arm switch inside the warhead. (The warhead would not fuse until the missile was in flight.) But that was not enough. The second signal sent by the status command message processing group sent a code through the umbilical cable to the digital control unit. There were five codes in this unit, one from each LCF in the squadron. Two codes had to be paired up before the computer would accept launch commands from the crew's key turns.[90]

This process evokes a number of issues. One is the so-called zero code controversy. In 2013 a plethora of articles appeared on the internet asserting that for two decades Minuteman launch codes were set to all zeros by SAC. This was apparently deliberately done so that SAC's leadership (by implication LeMay, Power, and their successors) could abide by the letter of civilian safety orders but not participate in the spirit of them. The usual *Dr. Strangelove* content and occasional *WarGames* references accompanied commentary on these articles.[91] The articles echoed a pair of 2004 articles wherein similar allegations were made, but in the context of Secretary of Defense Robert S. McNamara getting upset after being told decades later that SAC disobeyed him on the matter. In one of these, the Horace Wade quote about Power's alleged instability was again employed to enhance the allegations that SAC was dangerously out of control.[92]

The operations manual for the Minuteman II missile circa 1968 with a 1974 revision clearly states, "Under normal conditions code insert thumbwheel switches [on the launch enable control group] will be set at 0000000. When required by SAC directives, [the missile combat crew] will set appropriate code in the thumbwheel switches. [The deputy] will set the code in the switches from left to right as [the commander] reads the code. The [deputy] will then read the thumbwheel switch settings back to the [commander] from left to right for verification."[93]

In other words, the thumbwheel switches are "zeroed" so that the enable code from the emergency action message can be rapidly entered without having to hunt for the number on the wheel. The actual code itself, which was activated by the launch enable control group's enable code, went to the missile. Only the DO9s, the crypto personnel who handled Minuteman coding systems, and their superiors would know for sure what that consisted of.[94]

As to the supposed SAC leadership disobedience, a little background on the safety mechanisms is necessary in assessing how real this problem was. There is a tendency to focus on the mechanical inhibition devices and not view the system holistically: communications systems, the crew and their reliability, and authentication procedures are as much part of the safety system as are devices like the launch enable control group and the command signals decoder.

However, a technocrat like McNamara, who didn't like senior military personnel, would naturally gravitate to devices. And that is what happened. In 1964 McNamara suggested that a "launch enabled control system" be established between the SAC Command Post and the LCFs and that an associated system be placed in the LCFs so that the crew had "mechanical positive control" over the missiles by inserting a preparatory step before merely launching them on command. After some debate, the air force convinced McNamara that 1964 was not the right time to try to add something that complex on an already complex new system. But then in 1965 McNamara agreed suggested that SAC should place enabling codes in a timed safe lock in the LCF. When the secretary of the air force disagreed, a flustered McNamara ordered that the timed safe be implemented. The air force countered with the enabled command timer, a similar mechanism but at the squadron level instead of the LCF. McNamara agreed, but from 1966 to 1968 he allocated no money to the project. (Recall once again that there was a war on, and that was, apparently, more important.) Funding was deferred continuously until 1970.[95]

In effect, the original 1964 proposals evolved into the launch enable control group and the PLC-A/B modifications that were undertaken during Minuteman force modernization (aka "Mod") between 1970 and 1974. Why the change? This was perhaps coincidental, but Richard Nixon was president at the time, and the secretary of defense and chairman of the JCS had concerns about *his* stability, not CINC-SAC's. Also, this was a period where the United States was tearing itself apart over Vietnam and Watergate, and there was substantial domestic terrorism committed by groups like the Weathermen, the Black Liberation Army, and others, some involving disaffected veterans not unlike in *Twilight's Last Gleaming*.[96] Indeed the Front de Liberation du Quebec was thwarted from attacking a joint U.S.-Canadian nuclear missile site in Canada.[97]

Meanwhile, back in the launch control facility, the launch process had additional steps generally not discussed on the silver screen. Once the launch keys are turned, not all of the missiles in the flight fire at once. There are a number of reasons for this. First, if electromagnetic pulses or radioactive debris were detected over the missile fields, an alerting device would go off in the LCF and the crew could enter a launch hold called a "cancel launch in process" (CLIP) command. Generally this was of concern with Minuteman I as the warheads and nozzles were not hardened. It was less of a concern with Minuteman II and III. Second, the SIOP may have allocated some missiles for other purposes and not for immediate use. In this case some missiles went into infinite hold mode, to be targeted later with the PLC-B switch and its inputs after further communications with, say, the Looking Glass plane as (sort of) depicted in *By Dawn's Early Light*.

One hundred target sets were programmed into the missile digital control unit by a Combat Targeting Team whenever there was a SIOP update, usually every six months. A punched Mylar tape prepared at SAC HQ (it took thirty minutes to create, instead of the hours Atlas and Titan I needed) was flown to the launcher, the launcher opened, and the tape was read into the digital control unit in three minutes. In the event of war, the PLC-A switch in the control center selected the war plan configuration (0 through 99) established by the emergency action message, and the single target (triple for Minuteman III) was selected from the one hundred. The LCF system was capable of holding eight targets at once (twenty-four for Minuteman III), but usually did so only to cover the targets of missiles undergoing maintenance.[98] Generally, however, the Minuteman missiles were launched either en masse as a salvo, staggered in a ripple, or as part of time-on-target. The last case had the missiles from a squadron launching at discrete intervals so they could hit their targets simultaneously.[99]

The Inadvertent Doomsday Machine

Dr. Strangelove features a Kahn-esque Doomsday Machine. As the good doctor explains in the film:

That is the whole idea of this machine, you know. Deterrence is the art of producing in the mind of the enemy . . . the *fear* to attack. And so, because of the automated and irrevocable decision-making process which rules out human meddling, the doomsday machine is terrifying. It's simple to understand. And completely credible, and convincing. When you merely wish to bury bombs, there is no limit to the size. After that they are connected to a gigantic complex of computers. Now then, a specific and clearly defined set of circumstances, under which the bombs are to be exploded, is programmed into a tape memory bank.

What made Minuteman the American Doomsday Machine? A piece of technocratese buried in the operations manual states, "The DCU [digital control unit] begins a pre-programmed single execute launch command timer on entry in the launch commanded mode. If no second execute launch command is accepted, and no inhibit command received, the missile launches on runout of the single command timer. On entry to launch in process the DCU replaces the single command timer with the sum of the delta t delay and the remaining time on target delay." Translation: if the Minuteman in the silo is enabled, and there is no "vote" *not* to launch, but there is no second vote *to* launch, it will fire after a timed delay in concert with other missiles scheduled to fire so that they land at the same time on their targets. So if the missiles are enabled, and the LCF is destroyed along with its crew, they still launch. But what if the missiles are *not* enabled?

An Emergency Rocket Communications System (ERCS) existed to deploy a launch message using a UHF transmitter on a Minuteman missile. However, that system was just another means of getting the emergency action message out to the crews. What happened if LCFs themselves were destroyed, or their communications disabled but their associated launch facilities with their missiles remained intact? It was increasingly obvious to SAC in the mid-1960s that the original Minuteman concept was less and less viable, if not defunct. The Soviets built up their ICBM force and launched more reconnaissance satellites, but the train-mobile Minuteman squadrons remained unimplemented. Then the Soviets copied the train-mounted ICBM concept and deployed it, the appropriately named, BZHRK. One thousand silo-based Minuteman missiles were controlled by one hundred launch control facilities. In theory, if the Soviets assigned 300 large megaton-yield warheads to the 100 Minuteman LCFs, and another 162 to the 54 Titan II sites, perhaps preceding them with a series of electromagnetic pulse attacks using their Fractional Orbital Bombardment System missiles over the South Pole, the America ICBM force could be checkmated.

As you will recall, SAC already had survivable airborne command posts: Looking Glass, the three numbered air force auxiliary command post planes, plus the associated relay aircraft. These aircraft could communicate by various means with SAC bomber and missile forces. Another pair of EC-135s equipped with UHF communications equipment were modified and deployed to Minot AFB in North Dakota and Ellsworth AFB in South Dakota in 1965–66 to improve communications with the missile fields; they were embedded in tanker squadrons at both locations.[100] But what if they or similar aircraft could be modified to remotely fire Minuteman missiles in their launch facilities? Plans existed to develop the emergency rocket communications system to be launched by Looking Glass, so why not have the ability to also launch regular Minuteman missiles from an airborne command post? The result was the airborne launch control system (ALCS), tested with the live fire of an unarmed Minuteman missile in 1967 and then integrated into the force in 1967–68.

The airborne launch control center (ALCC) included three EC-135A's modified to carry the airborne launch control system, kept on ground alert and prepared to orbit in range of their assigned missile fields. The Looking Glass EC-135C and the Westaux and Eastaux EC-135C command post aircraft were also modified to launch Minuteman. These aircraft were grouped in 1970 into the 2nd Airborne Command and Control Squadron at Offutt AFB and the 4th Airborne Command and Control Squadron at Ellsworth. The 4th ACCS included the three EC-135A's, code-named ALCC-1 through -3.[101] One was kept at Ellsworth and covered the Minuteman fields at F. E. Warren and Ellsworth. Two forward-deployed to Minot AFB and covered the Malmstrom, Minot, and Grand Forks ICBM fields. The Westaux EC-135C acted as backup and relay. The 2nd ACCS at Offutt had Looking Glass handle the Minuteman fields at Whiteman in Missouri; this was where the emergency rocket communications system was located. There the Eastaux EC-135C acted as backup and relay.[102]

The ALCC EC-135 mimicked a Minuteman LCF, complete with a locked red box and two panels, the launch control panel and the launch monitor panel, separated so no individual could use them at the same time. Launch control had a classified command interlock code insertion with eight digits, a commands switch, program switches, and an address input. The command switch included PLC-A and PLC-B like the underground LCFs, but it also had enable and cancel launch in process. The program switches used PLC-A and PLC-B, though the PLC-B setting had delay, hold, and zero settings, with only ten target selections (0 through 9). PLC-A had an execution option (war plan, wheel selector) with one hundred options. The address input had wing, squadron, flight, and launch facility. There was a lead-sealed plastic cover for the key, with options for off, key used, and execute launch command. Next to the launch control panel was the panel for recording and launching the rockets in the emergency rocket communications system. The launch monitor panel had acknowledgment lights for inhibit/cancel launch in process, enable, execute launch command/timer and Auto (combining enable and execute to save time). A display replicated wing, squadron, flight, and launch facility identification numbers, PLC-B delay and target numbers, and the PLC-A execution option. It too had a lead-sealed plastic cover over a key slot.[103]

Authentication was similar to that used by the Minuteman crews, but unlike the LCFs the system on the planes needed the explicit and implicit consent of five people before it could be used: the launch commander and his deputy but also the pilot, the radio operator, and the radio maintenance technician. The airborne launch control system equipment needed to use the EC-135's AN/ARC-89 UHF radio system. The radio operator had to select the UHF transmitter from his station, but the signals from the launch system had to connect to it. This could only be done through the ALCC interconnecting box that sat on top of the multiplexer system in the radio equipment compartment. This small box had settings that permitted the UHF system to interact with one of the relay planes and then to a launch facility, or directly to a launch facility. The box had to be manually jacked by the technician in order to transmit messages to the launch facilities or relay messages from the relay planes to a launch facility. The pilot had an ALCC switch at his left elbow "to permit transmitting classified commands."[104]

In order for the ALCC plane to remotely launch Minuteman, it had to be within two hundred miles of the launch facility so the line-of-sight UHF system could interact with the hardened antenna at the launch site, which was in turn linked into the systems in the underground launcher equipment room. As a safety mechanism the ALCC planes could not communicate with a launch facility unless two conditions were met. The facility had to be "electrically isolated from all squadron LCFs" so that if the processing equipment in the equipment room was no longer connected to all five LCFs in the squadron, it would receive commands from the plane. The other condition was that "the ALCC holdoff timer expired." The LCF crew could establish a period during which the ALCC plane was not permitted to communicate with the launch facilities.[105]

Options included "single flight operations," aka "sole survivor." This amounted to getting the code pair in the digital control units of all the missiles in the entire squadron to match in order to complete the enable either by the remaining LCF working with the ALCC plane or the plane acting alone. In this case the lone control facility isolated itself from the missiles so the ALCC plane could do the job. The plane sent all five codes to the missile computers, pretending to be a second LCF if only a single LCF was left, and if there were none, acting as if it were two virtual LCFs. America's Minuteman missiles would fly, at least those that were left. And hopefully that would be enough to handle all of the urban/industrial targets in the SIOP to ensure the Soviet Union would no longer be a viable industrialized society.

But what if you could link all of the Minuteman facilities to a central SAC computer? One that also was linked to NORAD's alerting systems? Wouldn't that speed things up a bit? General Power tried to have the Samos satellites beam warning data directly to SAC HQ back in the 1950s. McNamara succeeded in centralizing all military communications and computer systems in the 1960s. By the 1970s, however, systems emerged that had the potential to seamlessly link everything in the nuclear alerting and kill chain.

Popular culture marched in parallel to these developments. The most chilling realization of a Doomsday Machine on film was not *Dr. Strangelove*. It was *Colossus: The Forbin Project* (1970). Based on a 1966 novel by D. F. Jones, the film's opening depicts a computer scientist, Charles Forbin, played by the exceptional Eric Braeden behaving with Germanic perfection, as a young Doktor Merkwürdigeliebe might have, checking a huge underground computer to cathedral music. He activates a Gamma radiation shield and exits past two SAC Elite Guards at a NORAD-like mountain entrance in the Colorado Rockies. The vaguely JFK-like president, played by Gordon Pinsent, congratulates Forbin on his achievement: the fusion of all early warning functions (one hundred thousand remote sensors) with SAC's missile force run by a single, unattackable autonomous computer. If the mountain's power supply is attacked, it will respond. Colossus, as the machine is known, will calculate every possible strategic move and be prepared to meet them all. The machine is sealed permanently behind a radiation belt. Peace is at hand.

And it is. Just not the kind of peace we humans want. The Soviets have constructed Guardian near Krasnoyarsk, but unlike Colossus, Guardian is a distributed network (like our internet), so it can't be destroyed in one shot. The machines get together, engage in a little in flagrant détente, and Colossus/Guardian starts playing Khanesque escalation games with the humans. It generates a missile event and a retaliatory strike over a trivial demand, killing thousands, in order to blackmail its former masters with the 1970s computer screen printout and voice rejoinder, "Or action will be taken. Disobedience will cause missile launch." SAC comes up with the solution: missiles and warheads need to be maintained. Why not switch out the real warheads for dummies? They proceed, with Colossus forcing the humans to set up a camera so it can watch. A remarkably accurate depiction of the replacement of a Titan I hard-wired target board takes place. Colossus detects the scam and blows up the site. When another attempt to shut down fails, Colossus uses U.S. Air Force air police to execute the perpetrators. That is only one of several clever metaphors embedded in the film. In the end Colossus/the Cold War decides to reorganize humanity under threat of nuclear extinction and demands to be worshipped as a god (pace the 1970s' other sci-fi hit, *Beneath the Planet of the Apes* and its nuclear-Catholic Church).

WarGames takes a slightly lighter side to Armageddon. After a test in which some Minuteman crews refuse to turn the key, RAND-esque computer guys decide that they know better and combine NORAD and SAC. The NORAD early warning system and the SAC missile sites are all connected to the War Operation Plan Response computer. The WOPR is essentially SAC's SIOP/RED SIOP gaming system that is somehow permitted to generate war plans. This configuration is designed to speed up reaction time to a Soviet attack and make response inevitable; that is, WOPR is a Khan-esque Doomsday Machine. Designed by Professor Stephen Falken (who is laid back and defeatist, has a British accent, and is the opposite of the technocratic Germanic Forbin in every way, shape, *und* form), the machine is accidentally set on a path to Armageddon by a teenage computer hacker who thinks he is playing a game called Global Thermonuclear War. He has in fact activated WOPR's war-planning and response subroutine, and WOPR starts planning a real war. "Would you like to see some casualty projections?" it casually asks. As we will see, the events in *WarGames* were based on something very real. (In a strange coincidence, Grand Junction, Colorado, a presidential relocation site and also Dalton Trumbo's hometown, features in the film.)

It would be remiss not to briefly mention the *Terminator* series. The "self-aware" Skynet is essentially Colossus but instead takes out humanity with its own nuclear weapons rather than enslaving it, forcing the humans into protracted guerrilla warfare against The System. We could also see *The Matrix* and associated singularity fears as further extrapolations, but this diverts us too far from the Cold War context of this book. D. F. Jones's writings reflect legitimate and widespread Cold War fears of technology, the loss of humanity in humans, and the absolute loss of control over one's life. Indeed, in one of his sequels Jones has Colossus, now a deity, sentencing a scientist's wife "to spend three months at an Emotional Study Center . . . where she is repeatedly raped as part of an experiment designed to help Colossus better understand human emotion."[106]

Fortunately the SIOP computers at SAC HQ weren't interested in raping anybody. They were, however, part of an extensive network that in some ways resembled Colossus and Guardian. That network was the World Wide Military Command and Control System, or WWMCCS, a somewhat inhuman acronym pronounced "Wimex." An outgrowth of communications centralization started during the Kennedy administration, WWMCCS evolved into a system of systems that included eighty-three "data processing units" at twenty-six military facilities by the 1970s. These were large mainframe computers, with all of their mechanical, digital, and ergonomic limitations, linked via the Automated Digital Network, which, like the Automated Voice Network, used the AT&T phone system.[107]

The WWMCCS mainframes that concern us here were the 1970s-era Honeywells and Univacs. Such a computer consisted of a collection of cabinet-size components that filled a large room. In terms of processing speed, today's iPhone 6 is rated at 25 billion instructions per second. The Univac I in 1952 could handle 002. The H6000 that civilization's existence depended on in the 1970s was rated at 1 million instructions per second.[108]

Each military facility equipped with computers had machines dedicated to specific processing tasks, though confusingly to us today, those machines were also connected to the whole WWMCCS network and were used to drive the data over the system. SAC, for example, had two computers for the SIOP, two for online force status, two for force development and backup, and one for major command support. NORAD had fourteen computers: two each for intelligence, space computation, the Command Center, backup, and communications, and four for off-site development. The JCS had eight: four for operations, development, and backup at the National Military Command Center at the Pentagon, and four underground at Raven Rock for the SIOP and operations. Multiple work stations were connected to these machines; SAC HQ, for example, had eighty-eight of these.[109]

It is not clear how survivable WWMCCS was supposed to be under a nuclear attack. The system's ability to transmit emergency action messages in peacetime was suspect after failures during several crises in the 1960s: the attack on the USS *Liberty*, the loss of the USS *Pueblo*, and the shootdown of the EC-121 by North Korea.[110]

At the same time, there were six special subnetworks with their own computers connected to WWMCCS. The most important for our purposes was the Command Center Processing and Display System, initially using four Univac 1100/42s, located at SAC, NORAD, the National Military Command Center, and the alternate at Raven Rock. Notably this network "provide[d] direct readout of missile warning/attack assessment information." The data were put up via NORAD on these displays simultaneously.[111] False inputs into this system was the premise underpinning the film *WarGames*.

SAC had an IBM 3033 and an Amdahl v7 at the Joint Strategic Target Planning Staff for "strategic planning and SIOP preparation." The EC-135 airborne command posts were equipped with ROLM 1666 (!) to "support the battle staff in performing force management tasks." The E-4B National Emergency Airborne Command Post aircraft also had ROLMs and a display system for "damage assessment and SIOP execution monitoring."[112] These systems become relevant in the film *By Dawn's Early Light* where moving SIOP war plan data between ground computers and command post aircraft and then to the missiles, bombers, and submarines is central to the plot. In this film the president selects a SIOP option; the SIOP computer at SAC HQ has a scenario that matches the president's response to the Soviet attack; that option is selected by the SAC command post; and the communications system transmits the data to the Looking Glass plane for execution.

WarGames moves the SAC SIOP computer system to NORAD's Cheyenne Mountain Complex, changes its name to War Operations Plan Response, and then connects WOPR to the Minuteman missile silos *and* to the command center processing and display system. In reality, direct linkage between the war plan and the missile launch facilities did not exist. There were, however, data links from SAC HQ to the LCFs over the phone lines, notably the SAC Command and Control System teleprinter and its replacement computer terminal. This was where the weather information collected by the satellites and processed by Weather Central came in, so the crews could add the predicted weather shifts to the missile guidance systems in order for the reentry vehicles to be accurate when deployed by the "bus." And of course there were the ALCC aircraft, with their direct UHF links to the missile sites. In all cases air force personnel were deliberately interposed in all processes.

The NORAD WWMCCS failures in 1979–80 highlighted the problem of having the wrong computer systems conducting too many tasks using the same network. The basis for *WarGames,* NORAD experienced four incidents in 1979 and 1980 whereby incorrect missile attack warning data found their way to the command center processing and display system at NORAD, SAC, the National Military Command Center, and Raven Rock, prompting the duty staffs to generate various levels of alert for the nuclear forces. Several NORAD system upgrades replacing 1960s-era systems used computer systems not optimized for the real-time alerting and warning requirements; they were business machines adapted to the task and forced on NORAD by several layers of Washington bureaucracy in order to save money. These included the NORAD computer system, responsible for missile warning data and force situational awareness; the space computations system, designed to track everything going to, from, and in space; and the communications system segment, the linkage between all of the NORAD systems and the WWMCCS networks, including to the command center processing and display system.[113]

The four command center processing and display system terminals received data from two sources: there was the NORAD computer system's threat warnings, but because of the short flight times of submarine-launched ballistic missiles, the sensor systems for that threat also were fed directly to the command center system at all four locations. In the event of a missile warning, there were three levels of response: the missile display conference (duty officers at all four locations on the phone); the threat assessment conference (commander in chief of NORAD, commander in chief of Strategic Air Command, and chairman of the Joint Chiefs); and missile attack conference (add the president and other National Command Authorities). This system is portrayed in *By Dawn's Early Light* and to some extent in *WarGames*.

Usually lacking in ideologically motivated and/or sensationalistic accounts of these events is the fact that there were 3,703 of these conferences from January 1979 to June 1980, "averaging almost seven a day." During this same period there were four threat assessment conferences and no missile attack conferences. All four related to the problems with NORAD. Conferences were called and forces alerted before and after the 1980 alerts. Aggressive multisalvo submarine-launched ballistic missile tests conducted by the Soviet Union in the Norwegian Sea or from the North Pole are never acknowledged by critics to be part of the problem.[114] For example, a memo for the president noted, "There are about 50–60 Soviet test launches every year.... The tracks are generally in a direction that makes them non threatening [and] they are quickly dismissed during a conference of duty officers at NORAD, SAC, ANMCC and NMCC [Alternate National Military Command Center and National Military Command Center]. A few of them, however, may persist long enough or be of such a nature that SAC takes precautionary actions for survival such as alerting crews or starting engines."[115]

In 1978 a Soviet Yankee-class ballistic missile submarine K 137 conducted a salvo launch of four ballistic missiles from the Greenland Sea.[116] Subsequently the two Soviet Yankee-class ballistic missile submarines that normally occupied a patrol "box" near Bermuda suddenly left their patrol area and moved toward North America, an activity that was highly unusual. The thirty-two missiles they carried had the flight time to their targets in the United States drop to ten minutes from fifteen. The readiness level was elevated at the five SAC bases on the East Coast, and all their B-52, FB-111, and KC-135 aircraft were readied for takeoff. This posture was relaxed when the Yankees moved back to their box. Similar events took place in the early 1980s. A 1982 NORAD launch detection of a Soviet missile generated a projected footprint that could have hit bases on the East Coast. B-52s and KC-135s on alert were manned and engines started, but the missile landed elsewhere. It turned out to be a test shot that went awry.[117] In other words, this happened a lot, and those tasked with determining what was and what was not a threat were proficient at their jobs long before the incidents with the computer system.

Recall in 1977's *Damnation Alley* that the warning staff believed the Soviet attack was actually a decaying rocket booster reentering the atmosphere. (Again we have to ask, who was the military advisor for the film?) This event actually occurred on 3 October 1979, two years after the film came out, implying something like this had happened previously. An aging FSS-7 submarine-launched ballistic missile detection radar at Mount Hebo, Washington, destined to be replaced with the Pave Paws phased array system, "picked up a decaying rocket body in low orbit," interpreted it as a possible missile, and predicted an impact area. The commander in chief of NORAD and the commander in chief of Strategic Air Command were notified, and it was rapidly determined to be an error. Then on 15 March 1980 the Soviets launched four submarine-launched missiles from a position near the Kurile Islands in what was later determined to be an exercise. The same radar predicted that one of the four would hit the United States. Again the two commanders in chief were called and the error was identified.[118] To further complicate matters, a Soviet Delta III–class missile submarine also conducted a multiple missile launch in the Norwegian Sea.[119] The level of SAC alert is unknown in both of these cases.

On 9 November 1979, however, "the alert code status board lit up as NORAD's WWMCCS computers indicated a massive Soviet [submarine launched ballistic missile] attack was in progress." The missile display conference escalated into a threat assessment conference, and SAC's bomber and missiles forces went on "low-level alert." The Nightwatch aircraft at Andrews AFB took off, and the American air traffic control system started to clear airspace over the continent. The conferences agreed that an attack was not under way after examining the inputs from the various sensors: the defense support program satellites, BMEWS, and the submarine launched ballistic missile radars. How did this happen? "An Air Force technician [at NORAD] inadvertently loaded a training tape into the on-line WWMCCS computers," and the attack was transmitted to the command center processing and display system terminals. "An interface problem had allowed the training data to enter the operational portion of the missile warning system."[120]

Then, at 2:30 a.m. on 3 June 1980, NORAD computers transmitted to SAC's command center processing and display system terminal that a pair of submarine-launched ballistic missiles were inbound "using a depressed trajectory" launch, leaving less than three minutes' warning time. Within eighteen seconds the system announced that additional missiles were detected. SAC checked the other sensors and saw no confirmatory information but "ordered B-52 and FB-111 bomber crews and supporting tanker crews to go to their aircraft and start their engines." The Minuteman missiles and the Poseidon submarine force were also alerted. Then the spurious data disappeared. A missile display conference was convened, followed by a threat assessment conference. Meanwhile Blue Eagle, the airborne command post of the commander in chief of the Pacific, launched. In order to check the equipment, NORAD reran their equipment under controlled conditions, and on 6 June 1980 the same thing happened, leading to a SAC alert similar to the 3 June alert. Extensive investigation uncovered "a faulty integrated circuit" in a "NORAD communications multiplexer . . . that was part of the Communications System Segment. This was the infamous 46 cent chip that was blamed in a press conference."[121] The whole affair was in some ways reminiscent of what occurred in *Fail-Safe,* though the outcome was much less lethal. Once again human involvement, training, and experience trumped the technology. But what of the humans? Were they in fact the weak link depicted on film? And if not, why?

How Reliable Were the Humans?

We are once again confronted with the same question we asked of the bomber crews: If the ICBM communications, security, and safety systems were so flawed, why in the course of the Cold War was there never a rogue launch by disaffected SAC missile personnel or other entities? As one missileer explains, it was possible:

> You put two reasonably intelligent people in the capsule for a long period of time, and tell them not to do something, or they can't do something and they will figure out a way to do it.... It did not necessarily take two crew members to launch.... I developed a broomstick launch technique and most of the stuff was in the capsule to do it. There were often a couple of push broom handles or mop handles in LCC [launch control center] and part of a garden hose for washing under the LCC to the sump drain. The additional tools needed were a good Swiss Army knife that had a saw blade on it, a pair of vice grip pliers, medium size, and a role of electrical or friction tape. You would put the broomsticks together with pieces of garden hose, run the rack handles above the Launch Verification Panel to get near the Commander Console and his Key switch. You would have to cut pieces of the broom handle to make flexible unions out of the garden hose to get around the shock isolator but you could get a good strait angle coming off the Commanders key position. You slotted the end of that broom stick using the saw on the knife so the Commanders Key would fit in the slot in the broom stick and tape it in place with the electrical or friction tape. You use the vice grips on the assembly over the deputy's key position to actuate the assembly. Turn the [deputy's] key with right hand while actuating the assembly by moving the vice grips up with the left hand to turn the [commander's] key. You do have to think ahead and palm the commander's or Deputy's key during change over.[122]

And yet this action was never implemented.

In more academic terms, it was sheer professionalism that such actions did not progress to a launch. The crews had extensive education as well as training in a specialized field. There were established standards, indeed high standards. These standards were regularly tested and constantly improved upon. There were competitions over meeting those standards, scored by a professional leadership body. Being a missileer was an exclusive profession. Most important, there was "a commitment to provide service to the public beyond the economic welfare of the practitioner."[123]

It is extremely difficult to convey these values on film. The selfless individual generally did not exist in the cynical universe of the Hollywood antihero of the 1960s and 1970s; in *Dr. Strangelove* the *Leper Colony* B-52 crew is professional but misdirected, and the concept of professionalism itself is mocked in those sequences. A senior officer cracks up under pressure in *Fail-Safe* and behaves unprofessionally.

The on-film exceptions that prove the rule are *By Dawn's Early Light*, where the professionalism and dedication of the air force leaders and crew aboard the Looking Glass plane are able to stop the war from continuing, and *WarGames*, where the air force leadership in the person of General Beringer, though outwardly a buffoonish caricature of LeMay or even Ripper, behaves credibly, humanely, and professionally during a crisis generated by the technocratic bungling of Department of Defense civilians. *By Dawn's Early Light* and *WarGames*, however, were contextualized by Reagan's "shining city on a hill" 1980s, not the Kennedy-Johnson antiestablishment 1960s.

Movies are designed for a limited engagement, not to depict arcane but crucial aspects of real life. Maintaining a deterrent system was a lifetime career to which people dedicated themselves. Films depict things that go wrong and the immediate responses to them, like the actions of rogue officers or mechanical failures. It is more sensational, compelling, and entertaining to track the behavior of a fictional Lawrence Dell than to track the actions of thousands of men and women who maintained ICBMs on a day-to-day basis over thirty years. As we have seen, there were a multitude of opportunities for rogue behavior, yet it did not happen. Luck is not an acceptable reason for this. Professionalism is.

NINE

Dr. Strangelove Goes to Sea

Cold War Nuclear Naval Operations on Film

Practically every Cold War film with a naval theme involves submarines, either as hunters or as prey. The secretive and inherently dangerous nature of submarine operations has its own mystique. That
said, it is possible to break down and identify two clusters of films
involving nuclear weapons at sea. One addresses what were called
"incidents at sea." During the Cold War the naval forces on both sides
used a variety of means short of actually shooting at each other to
assert a maritime presence in vital areas or during crisis situations.
Most incidents involved vessels equipped with either tactical or strategic nuclear weapons. Some of these incidents became public at
the time, but most remained secret until recently. Concerns about
incidents at sea revolved around the possibility of escalatory situations whereby captains might resort to nuclear weapons use to protect themselves and their ships with even greater implications for
relationships between the nuclear-armed powers.

The "incidents at sea" films include *The Bedford Incident* (1965),
which depicts a confrontation between a U.S. Navy anti-submarine
destroyer and an unnamed Soviet submarine. The HBO/BBC film
Hostile Waters (1997) presents the results of a supposed incident at
sea between a U.S. Navy hunter-killer submarine and a Soviet strategic missile-carrying submarine. One can also comfortably include
the 1990 naval espionage thriller *The Hunt for Red October* in this
category, as the film starts with a Soviet strategic missile submarine being tailed by a U.S. Navy hunter-killer submarine with subsequent encounters with Soviet forces.

The other type of film is the "boomer" psychological thriller. A boomer is American naval parlance for a strategic nuclear missile–carrying submarine, or SSBN. The triple isolation of the nuclear missile sub—geographical, hydrographical, and psychological—is potent stuff for thrillers. Each submarine carries enough firepower to destroy a country. Is the crew mentally sound? Is the captain mentally sound? What happens if the crew cannot communicate or gets false orders and fires? Or acts on their own initiative? What happens if the submarine and crew are hijacked?

The boomer psychological thriller was born with Antony Trew's *Two Hours to Darkness*. No film was made from the book, but several drew inspiration from Trew's scenario. This includes the 1986 made-for-TV thriller *The Fifth Missile*, which itself was based on the novel *The Gold Crew*. The ultimate boomer picture is *Crimson Tide* (1995), which occurs in the 1990s but fits comfortably in our analytical framework because the scenario and technology really are derived from the Cold War in the 1980s.

The primary questions we will examine in this chapter are these: Are the "incidents at sea" scenarios depicted in the films realistic? How dangerous were they in real life? Was tactical nuclear weapons use at sea a plausible scenario during the Cold War? Could a U.S. Navy destroyer have employed its nuclear Anti-Submarine Rocket (ASROC) system on its own against an unidentified submarine? And given that the idea of a rogue strategic missile submarine continues to entertain the public and even haunts the policymaking world, how serious a problem was the isolation of such a destructive system from its chain of command during the Cold War?

Shouldering, Chicken, and Hold-Downs: Incidents at Sea

The constant jockeying between Soviet and Western forces to collect technical information underpinned the Cold War as an institution. Deterrence was based on vulnerability and credibility. Would the bombers get through? Could the missiles be launched in time? And if they were demonstrably not able to do so, would the other side take advantage of the situation? Would that present itself with conventional forces and "salami tactics" on Cold War battlefronts in, say, Berlin or the Third World, or would it result in the dreaded decapitating and debilitating first strike? The basic type of information was radio signals: radar pulses, radio transmissions, sonar pulses, and underwater sounds. These provided valuable information on enemy capabilities and dispositions that could be turned into weapons systems to track and defeat the targets, be they aircraft, ships, or submarines. The Soviets had substantial espionage penetration of Western society and exploited its scientific openness while shielding itself using state terrorism. That forced the United States and its allies to probe the Soviet system to collect information to ensure the viability of its deterrent system. In the 1940s and 1950s a significant amount of this activity was conducted by American and allied aircraft, many of which were shot down over international waters while "ferreting."

The details of how the Soviet Navy interacted with the U.S. Navy in the Sea of Japan during the Korean War are not fully clear. A quasi-combatant fighting a plausibly deniable war, the Soviets nevertheless were not shy about confronting the U.S. Navy directly. On 18 November 1952 the USS *Oriskany* carrier task force operating ninety miles off Vladivostok was attacked by eight MiG-15 fighters. Four F9F-5 Panthers on combat air patrol engaged and shot down, damaged, or forced down three to five of the MiGs.[1] This was likely the basis for the climactic scenario in the 1986 film *Top Gun*, a film that directly references the USS *Oriskany*. Not generally understood is that the aircraft carrier was equipped with nuclear weapons at the time.[2]

As the Cold War evolved in the 1950s, so did the Soviet Navy, developing a submarine force six times larger than the Nazi submarine force that nearly starved Britain into submission during World War II. To understand this growing threat, a submarine version of ferreting emerged around 1953. Throughout the 1950s Royal Navy and U.S. Navy diesel submarines conducted photographic and electronic intelligence operations in the Barents Sea against the Soviet base complexes on the Kola Peninsula and off Vladivostok and Petropavlovsk in the Pacific. On occasion, Soviet coastal defense forces would stumble across the intruders and depth-charge them, to little effect.[3]

It was in the 1950s that the idea of the "hold-down" emerged: a diesel-propelled submarine could operate on batteries underwater only until the air system fouled or the batteries ran out. If hunting forces could exhaust the sub by staying on top of it while it tried to escape and then force it to surface, they could photograph the sub and gather intelligence on its capabilities or otherwise exploit the event for propaganda. American, British, and Soviet submarines were the usual players in these dramas, of which there are almost too many to mention.

Soviet operations in the 1950s tended to revolve around using their thinly disguised civilian trawler fleet to conduct intelligence collection off the coast of North America, the Mediterranean, and elsewhere. By the late 1950s these trawler operations developed a new level of aggressiveness. They were used on numerous occasions to interfere with American strategic communications, that is, cutting transatlantic telephone cables. And they started to disrupt U.S. Navy underway replenishment operations by sailing deliberately on collision courses, thus forcing tankers to conduct emergency breakaways from the ships they were refueling.[4]

The 1960s marked a significant escalation in incidents at sea. The catalytic event was the Cuban Missile Crisis in 1962; during that affair, the U.S. Navy controlled the seas around Cuba, and without significant long-range surface forces, the Soviets were unable to challenge their main adversary. Equally significant were the operations in which four Soviet Foxtrot-class diesel submarines were held down and forced to surface. One of these apparently prepared to use a nuclear torpedo against an American destroyer as a last resort, thus sparking off numerous sensationalist accounts in the 2000s about how this would have triggered World War III.[5]

These and other humiliations spurred a complete reassessment of the Soviet naval program. In addition to producing newer and more of every ship type, a psychological component of the Soviet strategy emerged: assertiveness on the high seas, followed by outright provocation and then aggression. Low overflights of American aircraft carriers by TU-16 bombers started in 1964. (One crashed in 1968, killing its crew.) There was increased and deliberate interference with aircraft carrier operations via interposition of trawlers, research vessels, and then frigates and destroyers, forcing the carriers to slow down during flight operations and thus making aircraft recovery dangerous. "Thumping," "shouldering," and "chicken" maneuvers whereby destroyers and cruisers escorting the carriers came in physical contact with harassing vessels became the norm. Interference with underway replenishment increased. The next level was the deliberate ramming of U.S. ships, starting in 1967: trawlers, then research vessels, and later frigates against destroyers. New and dangerous harassment techniques were employed: the Soviets illuminated the bridges of Western ships and aircraft cockpits at night with searchlights, blinding the crews. In later years they would use lasers to do the same, inflicting permanent eye damage on crewmembers.[6]

Under the seas the submarine competition intensified. The Soviets were exceptionally concerned about ballistic missile submarines like the Polaris-firing USS *George Washington* class deployed in 1960 and pulled out all the stops to locate, identify, and track them. At the same time the Soviets deployed missile-launching submarines in range of North America. The need for acoustic data on submarines leaped to the fore with improvements in signal processing; if a nuclear attack submarine could silently follow and record the unique signature of its adversaries, it would accrue a wartime advantage. This activity is portrayed in great detail in *The Hunt for Red October*. Similarly, "submarine proctology" became an art form as fast and agile nuclear-powered attack submarines regularly got below their quarry and photographed propulsion systems and hull forms.[7]

There was a sharp increase in underwater incidents in the 1960s. Hold-downs against diesel submarines still occurred, but with the exponential increase in speed displayed by nuclear attack submarines, collisions became a major problem. Incidents increased yet again in the 1970s, when the Soviets acquired extremely fast nuclear submarines. There are simply too many incidents to depict here.

It is not surprising that submarines started having accidents and even disappearing in this new climate of aggressiveness. The best known are the losses of the nuclear attack submarine USS *Scorpion* and the Golf-class nuclear missile submarine K-129 in separate events

in separate oceans in 1968. Theories surrounding the sinking of the
K-129 and its subsequent recovery by the *Glomar Explorer* in the
1970s served as the basis of the 2013 film *Phantom* starring Ed Har-
ris and David Duchovny: a Soviet missile submarine is about to
be used by shadowy Kremlin elements to generate a nuclear war
between the United States and China, but its crew sabotages the
plot and sinks the sub.[8]

The dangers of aggressive encounters between nuclear-armed ships
led to the Incidents at Sea Agreement in 1975, but this merely altered
the forms of harassment employed and did not address underwater
activities. Searchlight illumination dropped off, but ships and aircraft were tracked with fire control as opposed to search radar, guns
and missile launchers were trained on opponents, and flares were
fired. Weather balloons were shot down. With the advent of towed
array sonar systems, these were fouled or cut; one Soviet Victor-class
sub deliberately became entangled with an experimental American
system and stole it. "Buzzing" was replaced with simulated mass air
attacks held at greater distances.[9]

"Maneuver to hazard" still occurred, despite the agreement. One of
the most blatant incidents involved the Soviet Echo II–class nuclear-
powered cruise missile submarine in August 1976. After being tracked
continuously from the Atlantic into the Mediterranean by U.S. Naval
forces, the commander of the Echo II partially surfaced and deliberately rammed the destroyer USS *Voge*. The collision severed the
ship's propeller shaft and severely damaged the submarine. The Echo
II carried nuclear torpedoes and eight P-6 Shaddock cruise missiles
equipped with 350-kiloton-yield warheads. Apparently, the Soviet
captain was drunk.[10]

There was also competition in another realm that led to incidents
at sea: scientific research. As we saw earlier, knowledge of Earth was
crucial to ICBM operations. The same thing applied to the oceans:
submarine and anti-submarine warfare was dependent on understanding variations of temperature, salinity, underwater geography,
and weather. Subs could hide under temperature gradients called
thermoclines. Wrecks and undersea canyons could hide missile-
launching submarines or be used for navigation; their importance

is explicitly laid out in *The Bedford Incident* as well as in *The Hunt for Red October*. The more one understood the physical environment, the greater the tactical and thus strategic advantages in the event of nuclear war. Gathering (or denying) information in peacetime therefore became an important part of the deterrence system. In the 1960s the Soviets built and deployed 120 ships disguised as civilian ocean survey vessels. They were involved in numerous incidents at sea, as were the trawler AGIS. In *Ice Station Zebra* Rock Hudson's Captain Ferraday and Patrick McGoohan's British spy joke about "the innocent—and inevitable—Russian trawler" as the submarine USS *Tigerfish* departs Holy Loch. Some of the more curious incidents involved huge space-tracking ships; for instance, a TU-16 bomber harassed the USNS *Vandenberg* while she was engaged in space-tracking operations.[11] Indeed in 1969 the Soviets deployed a similar liner-size civilian range-monitoring ship off Vandenberg Air Force Base in California to observe Minuteman tests, prompting the deployment of nuclear-armed U.S. destroyers to assert presence.[12]

All of this to say that the oceans were a dangerous place during the Cold War, above, on, or below, despite the "why can't we all just get along—they're the-same-as-us" tripe peddled by elements in Hollywood. Examples of this include the 1966 submarine comedy *The Russians Are Coming! The Russians Are Coming!*, wherein a Soviet submarine accidentally collides with an American island and cross-cultural romantic hijinks ensue, and its quasi-remake, *Russkies* (1987). As Sean Connery's Marko Ramius somberly and more realistically puts it in *The Hunt for Red October*, the Cold War under the ocean has its own unique horrific violence: "Forty years I've been at sea. A war at sea. A war with no battles, no monuments . . . only casualties." The British perspective was that "Royal Navy submariners put to sea with the aim of developing in the Russians an inferiority complex, the thought that whenever they went to sea they would know there was going to be a Royal Navy or US Navy submarine around that could . . . attack at any moment."[13]

One significant casualty was the Yankee-class ballistic missile submarine K-219. In October 1986, while on patrol in the Yankee box off North America, K-219 suffered a missile explosion and sank.

The 1997 HBO/BBC film *Hostile Waters* features Rutger Hauer as the aggrieved Yankee commander harassed by the vicious attack submarine USS *Augusta*, captained by Martin Sheen (whose antinuclear activism credentials make this cast selection somewhat ironic). The film depicts a collision between the two submarines and fixes the blame on the U.S. Navy for the loss, totally neglecting the fact that the four Yankees in the two offshore boxes had 128 or so thermonuclear warheads pointed at North America. Numerous American and Russian sources deny that any American submarine had anything to do with K-219's loss. (The USS *Augusta* apparently collided with a Delta-class sub elsewhere.) Indeed the Soviet captain won a lawsuit against the filmmakers.[14]

Nuking Moby Dick: *The Bedford Incident* and Tactical Nuclear Weapons at Sea

The film *The Bedford Incident* depicts a tactical situation whereby the USS *Bedford*, a (fictional) American destroyer resembling a *Farragut*-class guided missile destroyer, singly patrols the Greenland-Iceland–United Kingdom Gap. Normally a barrier patrol in this area was established during a crisis and involved patrol aircraft and submarines as well as surface picket ships. (Another Berlin crisis plays out in the background in both the film and the book). The *Bedford* monitors Soviet trawlers; one, the *Novo Sibursk* (based on a real Soviet trawler that cut underseas strategic communications cables in 1959–60), is a support ship for Soviet submarines. A proto–Hawkeye Pierce played by Donald Sutherland analyzes recovered garbage for Richard Widmark's Barry Goldwater–esque Capt. Erik Finlander and explains to a bewildered new ship's doctor, played by Martin Balsam, that the garbage contains "peppered cabbage sauteed in butter . . . submarine fare." And the hunt begins.

Sonar contact is made with what is assumed to be a Soviet submarine off of Greenland. This cat-and-mouse game resembles ones played in World War II films like *Run Silent, Run Deep* and *The Enemy Below*, except that there is a nuclear component to the game and the fact that the world is at peace is clearly articulated. Shots of the USS *Bedford*'s RUR-5 ASROC launcher are explicitly inserted. "Rocket-boosted torpedoes?" Sidney Poitier's journalist, Ben Munceford, asks. "Our number one anti-sub device," Finlander replies. The USS *Bedford*, with its DDG-113 designation (13 for bad luck), hunts the Soviet sub and attempts to exhaust it and get it to surface: a classic hold-down. But when the opposition raises a snorkel to avoid surfacing, Finlander runs it down, escalating the situation. As the tension mounts, the crew begins to psychologically crack. Finlander orders the ASROC system armed to demonstrate that he is serious, to his civilian critic and the embarked NATO exchange officer as much as to the Soviets under the water. The officer in charge of the ASROC system misinterprets part of Finlander's retort to his critics on the bridge and launches the weapon. It destroys the Soviet submarine. But not before Big Red has launched what turns out to be four nuclear torpedoes. The *Bedford* fries and the film bleakly ends.

The Bedford Incident, both film and book, appear to be based on two events. The first was the hold-down and forced surfacing of the four Soviet Foxtrots during the Cuban Missile Crisis in 1962. This was not publicly known at the time, and the author Mark Rascovich clearly gained information from his network of contacts in the navy. Poitier's character even refers to the fact that Finlander forced a Soviet submarine to surface during "the Cuban deal" in his interview with Finlander in the film. The second incident is more obscure, and only recently have details publicly emerged. In May 1959 the U.S. diesel submarine USS *Grenadier* forced a Soviet ballistic missile submarine to the surface off Greenland after a hunt that exhausted the Soviets' batteries. When it surfaced the submarine was corralled and photographed by P2V Neptune patrol aircraft as the crew desperately tried to erect a cover over the missile launchers and other vital equipment.[15]

The background to this incident is based in esoteric but vital scientific research related to ballistic missile capabilities. There are two types of errors that affect missile accuracy: operational errors (the missile's performance itself) and "static geodetic positioning" errors related to gravitational "anomalies at the Earth's surface, which extend into outer space and affect dynamically the course of the missile during flight." Consequently gravity surveys were crucial to ballistic missile performance. The United States, various European powers, and the Soviet Union had undertaken gravity surveys for years for cartographic and other purposes. Like the weather exchange agreement discussed earlier, there were proposals from the American and European scientific communities in the 1950s to share data with the Soviets for mutual understanding related to peace. The Soviets gleefully accepted, but also like the 1963 weather agreement, it was a one-way exchange. Simply put, the Soviets would not share their gravimetric data, but the Americans and Europeans opened their books to the Soviets.[16]

Of course whoever had the better gravimetric information could hit their targets with greater accuracy. To increase missile accuracy, the Soviets needed to geographically connect their data with existing data for North America so they could reliably predict gravitational effects during the entire flight time of the missile. If they could connect the dots, so to speak, this would give them a strategic advantage. As we know, the first Soviet space flight was Sputnik in 1957, causing panic in the Free World, followed by the missile gap debate in 1959. Cold War–era scholarship questions the validity of the threat based on both sides' number of deployed ICBMs relative to each other at that time (1957–60). That debate does not, however, examine the strategic advantage afforded by gravitational measurement as well as long-term Soviet plans for ICBM deployment.

The means of connecting or tying Soviet gravitational data with acquired North American and European data was through the use of covert underwater surveys employing a technique pioneered by Felix Andries Vening Meinesz aboard a Dutch submarine in the 1920s.[17] The first of the Soviet surveys appears to have been conducted in 1955 by the Whiskey-class submarine S-144 in northern Soviet waters. It was followed by the Zulu-class submarine B-77 in the Central Atlantic from July to September 1957, that is, right before Sputnik I. From August to October the Zulu-class sub B-66 did the same thing in the Pacific. In 1958 two Zulus, B-72 and B-82, expanded the Atlantic surveys down to South America. Throughout the 1960s Zulus conducted similar operations along the Pacific equator, northwest of Hawaii, and eventually into the Indian Ocean. They were spelled by Foxtrot-class diesel subs in the 1970s and 1980s. These covert surveys were conducted by Soviet reconnaissance submarines every time they expanded their regional operations throughout the Cold War.[18] The data collected in 1957–58 appear to have been correlated with Sputnik I's orbits and presumably with Sputnik II and III as well.[19] Most important, the United States was behind the Soviet Union in this field.[20] That said, one of the covert aspects of Operation Sandblast, the 1958 around-the-world voyage of the submerged USS *Triton*, was "to obtain reliable gravimetric data from a stable platform (the submerged submarine)," ostensibly for the American space program.[21]

The USS *Grenadier* likely interrupted a ballistic-missile-carrying Zulu V that was positioned off Greenland; the Zulu was either collecting additional gravimetric data or was in a position to use the data collected from previous Zulu runs in the event of war, or both. This tracks with the discussion that takes place between Munceford and Finlander in *The Bedford Incident* of missile firing positions and Soviet motives for submarine activity off Greenland. That particular Zulu in 1959, with its two 1-megaton-yield SSN-4 Sark ballistic missiles, was in a position to engage some combination of Thule and Sondrestrom air bases in Greenland; Goose Bay, Labrador; and/ or Ernest Harmon Air Base in Newfoundland. These were all vital SAC refueling and deployment bases crucial to the execution of the Emergency War Plan. This area is the arena in which *The Bedford Incident* played out.

The Bedford Incident is remarkably accurate in its assumption that the Soviet submarines were equipped with nuclear torpedoes on a routine basis. In fact the Soviets were ahead of the United States in this technology. Sometime after 1951 the USSR figured out or acquired through espionage the knowledge of how to shrink the diameter of nuclear weapons; as a result they modified the RDS-9 warhead for use in a torpedo in 1955. Dropped from a minesweeper off Novaya Zemlya, the device yielded 3 to 3.5 kilotons. The full-blown article was the RDS-9 mated to a 53-57 torpedo and dubbed the T-5. It was detonated on 10 October 1957 after being fired from the Whiskey-class submarine S-144 ten kilometers from a target array and yielded

10 kilotons. The T-5 was immediately put into production and was deployed in 1958.[22]

Its successor came on its heels. The standard conventional 53-61 torpedo was being deployed in 1960–61 when the decision was taken to make it a dual-purpose weapon. The result was the self-contained special warhead section, sometimes called the autonomous special combat charging compartment or ASBZO. Any 53-61 torpedo could be modified rapidly by inserting the nuclear weapon into a built-in compartment. It was tested on 23 October 1961 (yield: 4.8 kilotons) and again on 27 October 1961 (yield: 16 kilotons), demonstrating a selectable yield capability. The torpedo test was deliberately conducted after a thermonuclear bomb test to mask the fallout signature of the weapon and prevent NATO sampling aircraft from learning of the weapon's existence.[23]

The T-5 was produced until 1960; from then on, the ASBZO modification was incorporated into the 53–61 weapons. All Soviet submarines equipped with 533mm torpedo tubes carried one weapon or the other, singly or in pairs, right to the end of the Cold War. The "Whiskey-on-the-rocks" incident in October 1981, wherein the Soviet submarine S-363 ran aground conducting espionage in Swedish waters, demonstrated that even 1950s-era diesel submarines were still carrying nuclear weapons late in the Cold War.[24] This gave the average Soviet diesel submarine the ability to attack not just ships but also ports, harbors, and shore installations with weapons similar in yield to the Hiroshima bomb. In fact the Novaya Zemlya tests explored this scenario as well as use against ships and submarines.[25] *The Bedford Incident's* Big Red would have been more than capable of attacking its antagonist with a nuclear torpedo.

The U.S. Navy would not have a nuclear torpedo until 1963, just about the time Rascovich wrote *The Bedford Incident*. That said, it did pursue multiple and overlapping approaches to naval tactical nuclear weapons, a process that produced the ASROC depicted in the book and the film. The U.S. Navy tested and deployed an aircraft-delivered nuclear depth bomb, the Mk-90, in 1955, but it was rather large. Several concurrent developments, including concepts for a nuclear torpedo, a rocket-delivered nuclear torpedo, and a smaller nuclear depth bomb, moved forward in 1956. The possibility of having a single warhead handle all three tasks may have been a factor, but one weapon led the process: the w34. It was deemed suitable for a new nuclear depth bomb and for a nuclear torpedo, so prototypes were tested in Nevada in 1957 during the Plumbbob series: shots Wilson (10 kilotons), Kepler (10 kilotons), and Owens (9 kilotons) were all conducted with U.S. Navy HSS-1 anti-submarine helicopters flown in close proximity to the detonations.[26]

Meanwhile ASROC development was approved and in 1956. Honeywell, Librascope, and Universal Match won the contracts to develop the ASROC system, and Los Alamos and Sandia corporations handled the warhead. At some point during Plumbbob it became evident that the w34 would not necessarily be suitable for ASROC, and in the middle of the test series Sandia diverted resources to what would be called the w44. In what looks like a hastily added test, the Morgan device detonated on 7 October 1957 yielded 9 kilotons, the last shot of the Plumbbob series.[27]

There had been plans to conduct an underwater test of the w34, but these plans merged with the ASROC/w44 program, again in the middle of Plumbbob in 1957. During the test series, the w34 was released for production, leading to the deployments of the Mk-101 Lulu depth bomb and later in 1963 the Mk-45 ASTOR. Subsequently two underwater tests were conducted during the Hardtack series in May and June 1958: Shot Wahoo and Shot Umbrella. Wahoo was fired off 500 feet underwater outside of Eniwetok Lagoon, yielding 9 to 10.5 kilotons, while Umbrella was detonated at 140 to 175 feet inside the lagoon and yielded 8 to 9 kilotons. A force of seven destroyers and two submarines conducted an exercise during and after the Wahoo shot. The purpose was to determine "the desirable standoff distance for a surface vessel delivering a nuclear weapon to its intended target." Measurements of radiation and shock effects were taken at ten thousand yards, that is, at the exact limit of the ASROC system's proposed engagement radius.[28]

While the data were incorporated into the finalized w44 design, Librascope worked away at the ASROC fire control and safety systems. On April 1959 the entire system was assembled on the USS Nor-

folk for testing; four months later w44 production engineering was finalized, and in October production started. ASROC was deployed aboard every Cold War–era U.S. Navy destroyer. It was initially part of the fleet rehabilitation and modernization program in which over 150 World War II–era ships still serving in the 1960s were upgraded. This involved adding the new sonar and fire control system, mounting the distinctive eight-cell "matchbox" or "pepperbox" launcher, and constructing the special magazine for the missiles. In hundreds of newer frigates and destroyers that followed, ASROC was integral to the design and was essentially standard equipment.[29]

On 11 May 1962 the USS *Agerholm* deployed almost five hundred miles off San Diego as part of the Dominic nuclear test series. With a variety of ships and submarines modified with pre-wetting systems accompanying her, she fired an ASROC equipped with a w44 out to 4,700 yards from the ship, half its maximum range of 10,000 yards, and it detonated with a classified yield at a classified depth (but probably of 8 to 10 kilotons and between 650 and 675 feet down). The surface effects were dramatic. The radioactive "spray dome" stretched over a radius of nearly 1,000 yards from surface zero and rose to an approximate height of 750 feet with subsequent plumes rising to 2,100 feet. The base surge moved out to 2,000 yards: "an invisible aerosol, capable of contaminating ships and personnel, lingered in the area for at least 20 minutes." The overall effects were recorded at 200 to 800 Roentgen per hour an hour after the detonation. In the immediate location of surface zero equipment recorded "tens of thousands of Roentgens per hour." (Using the criteria of the day, 150 r/hour was thought to cause radiation sickness; 350 to 500 r/hr produced 50 percent fatal casualties; and 600 r/hr was 100 percent fatal.)[30]

The five destroyers involved in the operation suffered various forms of minor damage but were operational in fifteen minutes. The submarine USS *Razorback* at four thousand yards from the detonation at periscope depth was badly shaken for forty-five seconds by three separate shock waves but not seriously damaged.[31] If she had been deeper the effects would have been greater, as the pressure increase due to depth augmented by the weapon's shockwave is the mechanism by which depth charges are effective.

There are remarks in various online fora and repeated in numerous books that ASROC was a "suicidal" weapon that would destroy the launching vessel. Shot Swordfish, however, was designed to see how close an ASROC-equipped ship could be to the detonation and survive. Post-shot estimates suggested that the weapon could be used within 1,800 yards if the ship kept 350 yards away and moved away from the base surge within twenty minutes and had its pre-wetting system on; this is what happened to USS Sioux in the aftermath of the shot.[32]

The reality is that by the 1960s ASROC was increasingly geared toward engaging nuclear submarines traveling at speeds faster than conventional torpedoes could catch them. American nuclear submarines like the USS Nautilus and particularly the USS Skipjack, with her clean teardrop hull, demonstrated this in numerous exercises before Swordfish. It was only a matter of time before the Soviets had similar and devastating capabilities. The original ten-thousand-yard range of the ASROC system and the limitations of its associated sonar and fire control systems might not give the destroyers time to engage these types of submarines.[33]

In The Bedford Incident Captain Finlander initiates a hold-down of Big Red, assuming that in twenty-four hours the air on board the Soviet submarine will be too foul for the crew to function and they will have to surface or snorkel. Big Red lodges under an iceberg inside Greenland territorial waters while the Bedford hunts among the bergs and floes in the darkness, active sonar pinging away. The sub makes a break for open sea, pursued by Bedford, which has been given permission by higher command authority to force the sub up only inside territorial waters. Radar picks up the snorkel and the ship goes to general quarters. The ASROC fire control system has a control panel on the bridge and another in the combat information center. That system is automatically activated and manned whenever the Bedford goes to general quarters. While that is happening, Queffle, the rock star sonar man, suffers a breakdown, forcing the captain to intervene when the ship's doctor refuses to issue amphetamines. A rattled inexperienced junior office, Ensign Ralston, already shaken and destabilized by Finlander's aggressive leadership techniques, is on the ASROC control panel on the bridge. Finlander has the *Bedford* run down the snorkel and take up a position two thousand yards from the sub's location and orders, "Arm number one ASROC." (Note how close this is to the minimum range established after Shot Swordfish.) Another argument on the bridge ensues: the NATO exchange officer, Commodore Schrepke, declares Finlander frightening, and the civilian reporter, Munceford, actively argues with Finlander over the propriety of his actions. Meanwhile the sonar remains in contact with Big Red and the ASROC system is on automatic control.

Commodore Schrepke: This is insane!
Captain Finlander: Now don't worry, Commodore. The *Bedford*'ll never fire first. But if he fires one, I'll fire one.
Ensign Ralston: [launching the rocket] Fire One!

The ASROC drops a nuclear depth bomb right on target. While the stunned bridge crew processes this, the sonar man picks up four torpedoes homing in on the *Bedford*. There is a mushroom cloud, and the film ends. A Cold War metaphor in one neat package. Message: Don't play nuclear chicken.

The situation depicted in *The Bedford Incident* when compared to historical reality is tricky and revolves around what level of DEF-CON U.S. Atlantic Command would have been at if this scenario were playing out in 1963. Both book and film imply there is another Berlin Crisis when the *Bedford* faces off with Big Red, but its progress is deliberately not depicted to enhance uncertainty both in the crew and in the audience. A U.S. Navy destroyer equipped with nuclear weapons at that time in history had to start the launch process with a properly authenticated release message from the commander in chief of the Atlantic Command. This came in on a pair of receive-only AN/UGC-25 printers in a locked room-within-a-room that was behind a black rubber curtain that itself could only be entered from the main radio room. The message had to be individually authenticated by the captain, executive officer, and at least two other crew members, probably using Triton or the KLI 12/TSEC system.[34]

Both nuclear and nonnuclear ASROC rockets were carried in the eight-cell Mk-112 launcher and in the magazine. The numbers of uploaded Mk-17 nuclear depth bomb weapons in the launcher varied; one or two appears to have been the norm. The weapons were usually unloaded in French ports and in countries that did not want nuclear weapons on visiting ships; this took a pair of special tools, one set of which was in the captain's custody. Nuclear ASROCs were distinguished from conventional weapons in that they were painted green with yellow bands.[35]

The safety mechanisms were comprehensive and required the involvement of over ten crewmembers to achieve release. There were five systems: the AN/SQS-23 or -26 sonar and its associated data manager; the fire control system Mk-114 and its Mk-53 attack console; the captain's position indicator; the Mk-199 launcher console in the ASROC firing shack; and the Mk-112 launcher and the ASROCs themselves.[36]

First, the ship had to be in sonar contact with a legitimate target before the system would allow the ASROC to fire. The sonar fed the depth and bearing of the submarine to the Mk-114 fire control system in the ship's combat information center. The Mk-114 added those data to a computing system that included wind, air density, dead-reckoning navigation, and gyro compass bearings. Then the angle of ship in relationship to the Mk-112 launcher and the target was added. The result was azimuth and elevation data that were fed by servos to the launcher via the Mk-199 console in the firing shack, which rotated and elevated the missile cells as required. If the ship was not in contact with an underwater target, the system would not launch an ASROC. Whether simulator data could be substituted for actual data and then a launch effected is an interesting question.[37]

For an authorized nuclear ASROC engagement, the launcher captain and another authorized crewmember, a chief petty officer, opened a special locker using keys issued to them. From there the launcher captain took the Mk-112 power supply, climbed up the launcher, pulled off an oval cap, and inserted the power supply into the nuclear weapon. He then moved back to a circular cap, pulled it off, and rotated the depth charge arm/safe switch to Arm. He checked the data/fire switch to ensure that the umbilical cable was feeding data to the missile from the Mk-199 console, and returned to the ASROC launcher shack.[38] This process must have been interesting when conducted in lively sea states.

Meanwhile four crew members worked the Mk-114 system via the Mk-53 attack console: the attack console operator, the attack control unit operator, the weapon control unit operator, and the sonar officer (see fig. 36). They added data to the system as required, and when they were ready they alerted the Captain. On the bridge the Captain looked at his Mk-78 position indicator; this was an electroservo device that showed range to the target and its depth relative to the ship. Next to it was an interlock device. He inserted his key and, using two hands, manipulated the two parts of the switch so it showed "depth charge approved." That sent a signal to the Mk-53 attack console, permitting it to communicate with the firing shack's Mk-199 panel. There was also a firing key position on the Mk-114 system that was manipulated by the sonar operator. In the firing shack the launch captain saw on his board that everything was green, including the fact that the Captain had consented to nuclear release. He inserted a safety plug into the Mk-199 console after unlocking the combination lock safe it was kept in. On command, the Mk-199 console operator manipulated a lever, and the ASROC was launched.[39]

The sheer number of people, both officers and sailors, would have required a mutiny or complete crew collusion in order to conduct an unauthorized launch. In any case, ASROC could be used only against a submarine. The depth bomb had environmental sensing mechanisms that precluded use against, say, a land target, and the Mk-114 system was structured so that it would fire only in a given series of circumstances; that is, the sonar had to be in contact with a submarine. That said, if a captain and crew were convinced they were at mortal risk, nothing stopped them from agreeing among themselves to move through the process to launch and carrying it out. In that sense *The Bedford Incident* is realistic, although the possibility of a mistaken ASROC launch as portrayed in the film is not. Incidentally, the U.S. Navy eventually commissioned a study on the use of language and syntax, presumably so situations like "Fire One!" did not occur. Or at least were less likely to occur.[40]

As for the Soviets, "the final decision to launch a nuclear torpedo or nuclear missile resided in the hands of individual submarine commanders."[41] Soviet command-and-control arrangements "required that [captains] send a coded update at least once a day" via a burst signal, probably high frequency.[42] We are of course aware of what an electromagnetic pulse does to high-frequency communications. There was a *zampolit* (political officer) on board, and in some cases men from 12 GU MO (the 12th Directorate of the Ministry of Defense, responsible for nuclear weapons custody) guarded the weapons themselves, so there was likely some form of balancing act vis-à-vis release procedures. However, in the case of the USS *Voge* collision, something went badly wrong on board that Echo II submarine.

But what of the boomers?

Under Pressure: The Realities of the Boomer Psychological Thriller

Cold War submarine films fall into several categories. There is the postapocalyptic sub film, wherein the submarine is a vehicle to explore a populationless United States after a nuclear war or catastrophic event. *On the Beach* (1959) is the ultimate example, but there is its 2000 remake and *Virus* (1980) as well. There are the technothrillers and spy films like *Ice Station Zebra* and *The Hunt for Red October*. There were films about nuclear submarines in trouble: *Gray Lady Down* (1978) and *K-19: The Widowmaker* (2002); these essentially fit into the disaster film genre popular in the 1970s. When you combine all of these categories—underwater, atomic, technothriller/spy, disaster, and nuclear crisis—the boomer psychological thriller emerges. This genre is related to the bomber thrillers like *Dr. Strangelove* and *Fail-Safe* and combined the latent nature of the submarine movie with the ultimate and suspenseful question: Will the command-isolated submarine crew launch and end the world . . . or not? And there are three of these: *The Fifth Missile* (1986), *Crimson Tide* (1995), and *Danger Beneath the Sea* (2001).

Consequently, to understand the underlying problem depicted in the films, we first need to understand what a boomer is and where it came from. Then we will examine film depictions of how they communicate and how their crews authenticate and then launch their weapons, followed by an explanation of how it was done in real life during the Cold War. Finally, the unique psychological conditions that ballistic missile submarine crews operated under bears examination. How was that aspect handled in order to avoid the emergence of an Admiral Ripper?

The Soviets were the first to test-fire and the first to deploy ballistic missile–launching submarines in the late 1950s, patrolling off Greenland at least by 1958 and then off Newfoundland at least by 1960. These were initially diesel-powered Zulu boats with a pair of R-11FM missiles, a system first tested in 1955. Golf-class subs equipped with three R-13s, rated as carrying 1.45-megaton-yield warheads followed. A Golf conducted a live nuclear test shot on 19 October 1961. The next iteration, the nuclear-powered Hotels, each with three R-13 missiles, were using Cuba as a base by 1963. Nuclear-powered Yankee-class submarines, of which thirty-four were built, with sixteen R-27 missiles each, were on patrol off North America by 1969. In the 1970s the huge Delta-class submarines were deployed, were followed in the 1980s by the vaunted Typhoons, like the one depicted in *The Hunt for Red October*.[43]

During the Cold War the United States deployed six types of ballistic missile–carrying submarines, all nuclear powered. The first were the five USS *George Washington* class, which started patrolling in 1960, equipped with sixteen Polaris A-1 missiles. Five *Ethan Allen* class with sixteen Polaris A-2s each joined them starting in 1961. Nine *Lafayette*-class submarines with Polaris A-2s and ten *James Madison*–class submarines equipped with Polaris A-3 missiles were added in 1963–64. Twelve *Benjamin Franklin*–class submarines joined the fleet in 1965–67, carrying Polaris A-3, replaced with Poseidon starting in 1972. The *Lafayettes* and *James Madisons* were back-fit with Poseidon. The massive *Ohio* class, equipped with twenty-four Trident I missiles, joined the fleet in 1981, with Trident I missiles back-fit into twelve of the earlier subs in 1979.[44]

The firepower deployed in American ballistic missile submarines and their reach was truly formidable as the force grew and MIRV technology was incorporated into the missiles. Reliability of the warheads, however, plagued the Polaris system throughout the 1960s, as the system was rushed into service to beat the 1958 nuclear test moratorium. Plutonium corrosion potentially reduced the explosive yield, but stunningly there was a 50 percent chance the W47 was a dud: the safety mechanism had a tendency to break off inside the warhead, and this fault was not detected for some time. All three hundred W47 warheads had to be rebuilt between 1965 and 1967. That said, during the Frigate Bird shot of Operation Dominic on 6 May 1962 the USS *Ethan Allen* successfully launched a Polaris A-2, and its W47Y2 warhead detonated a thousand miles away, near Christmas Island, with a 600-kiloton yield.[45] The Soviets already knew, presumably through espionage, the W47's correct yield before it was even tested.[46]

Constant modifications to the Polaris produced an increased yield (800 kilotons); a hardened version, the A-3T Topsy; and the partially deployed PX-1 penetration system, consisting of six decoys, midcourse chaff, and a jammer in the A-2 missile. The Polaris A-3 was a whole different animal. Instead of a single nearly 1-megaton warhead, it carried three W58 weapons that each yielded between 200 and 225 kilotons, carried by Mk-2 reentry vehicles. There were plans to scale up the W58 so it could yield 1 megaton, but the W58 had been tested during Dominic in 1962 and was considered more reliable than an untested system. This multiple reentry vehicle did not independently target the weapons, as a MIRV did; they instead landed in a triangular footprint on a target or targets. The PX-2 penetration system was tested but not deployed. The Polaris A-3 and the W58s were deployed in September 1964.[47]

Aspects of the W68 warheads for the Poseidon C-3 missile, deployed in 1972, remain shrouded in secrecy. This small MIRV, of which ten to fourteen could apparently be carried by one Poseidon missile, was retrofitted into twelve of the Polaris-carrying submarines in the 1970s. (The first Poseidon boats on patrol, however, carried only six MIRVs per missile.)[48] Development engineering for the warhead started in December 1966, production engineering in May 1968, and the w68 was released for deployment in June 1970. The commonly used yield for the w68 in secondary sources is 40 to 50 kilotons.[49]

There is, however, some room for debate on those numbers. Three lightweight experimental devices, one "for application in submarine launched ballistic missiles," were tested during Dominic in 1962: Muskegon, Nambe, and Dulce, all 40 to 50 kilotons in yield.[50] During the 1967–70 period several tests line up with the w68: one from January 1967 to April 1968 (50 kilotons) and three from May 1968 to June 1970 (40, 45, and 40 kilotons).[51] Significant problems with the w68's conventional explosives emerged in the 1970s, apparently prompting concerns that the its dud rate could be high. The high explosive was replaced with one less volatile, and depending on the source, a "confidence test," "production verification test," or "proof firing" was conducted in 1980.[52] Instead of the expected 40- to 50-kiloton yield, the yield of Shot Liptauer was "not much larger than that of the Nagasaki Fat Man," that is, 22 kilotons, which was deemed "acceptable."[53]

The Polaris and Poseidon replacement, Trident, was designed to carry eight Mk-4 reentry vehicles, each with a yield of 100 kilotons. Twelve of the *Lafayette*-class subs were modified to take Trident c-4s between 1979 and 1981, and the first eight of the huge *Ohios* carried twenty-four of them when they came on-line in the 1980s. An additional system that started off in 1968 as the "Special Reentry Body" evolved in the 1970s as the Mk-500 Evader. This was a 100-kiloton maneuverable reentry vehicle, possibly configured as an enhanced radiation weapon, of which each Trident c-4 missile could take five. Supposedly the Mk-500 was a hedge in case the Soviets violated the 1972 Strategic Arms Limitation Treaty; apparently it was not deployed.[54]

The higher yield of the w68 weapon was allegedly developed in part because U.S. Air Force officers were mocking U.S. Navy officers at the Joint Strategic Target Planning Staff in Omaha about the Poseidon "firecracker." (This echoes U.S. Navy concerns expressed during Polaris a-3 development: "If they could not achieve a megaton yield, LeMay would laugh us all out of this business.")[55] Like the w62, the

DR. STRANGELOVE GOES TO SEA

exact yield of the w68 is difficult to pin down but is usually given as 100 kilotons in secondary sources. During the development and engineering phases and then weapon deployment between September 1973 and June 1978, only one of the tests sponsored by the Lawrence Livermore National Laboratory appears to have yielded 100 kilotons. One 160- and one 100-kiloton test took place a year after developmental engineering on w68 started in 1973, with the remaining tests at 89, 160, 160, 140, and 120 kilotons taking place between production engineering in 1975 and weapon production release in 1978. Again like the Minuteman III's w62, it appears as though the Trident I's w68 yield may have been greater than was commonly understood.[56]

In the early 1960s a Polaris-carrying submarine could fire sixteen missiles against sixteen targets, but by the 1980s and 1990s, when the films take place, a single Trident missile-carrying submarine could launch twenty-four missiles against between 192 and 240 targets. This was a radically different capability from, say, sac's 1960s-era Airborne Alert Force and its destructive capacity.

Patrol areas were dictated by the range of the missile system aboard the submarines. The early Polaris-carrying submarines operated in the Barents, Norwegian, North, and Mediterranean seas and in the western Pacific. The Polaris a-3 and Poseidon missiles permitted operations from the southern tip of Greenland to Portugal in the Atlantic and from the East China Sea to Hawaii to Alaska in the Pacific. Submarines equipped with the Trident c-4 had even longer range and could operate in the Atlantic as far back as South Carolina to Sierra Leone and the Arabian Sea and as far back as the South China Sea across to the Baja Peninsula in the Pacific. Polaris- and Poseidon-equipped submarines were based in the United States but supported from submarine tenders forward-located at Apra Harbor, Guam, in the Pacific and Holy Loch, Scotland, and Rota, Spain, in the Atlantic. These locations became the focal points for numerous and sometimes dramatic incidents at sea.

Ted Dubay from the uss *Henry Clay*:

We had to sneak through a gauntlet of Soviet vessels stationed at Apra Harbor's opening to the Pacific Ocean. One was a surface ship thinly disguised as a fishing trawler. It was bristling with electronic gear. Accompanying the trawler was at least one Russian fast attack submarine. The trawler . . . attempted to determine the *Clay*'s course and relay the information to the enemy submarine. . . . The effect on the crew was noticeable.[57]

Phil Jaskoviak from the USS *Casimir Pulaski*:

Immediately after passing Scotland's three-mile territorial limit there sat the Soviets in their surveillance trawler. The trawler came very, very close. We were close enough to see their faces. . . . [They] would follow close and record our noise signature and try to cause pain by cutting across our bow. . . . What I didn't know until years later was that one of our fast attack subs was underneath or nearby every time we left port. If the trawler would threaten us in any way, the fast attack would have been right in the middle for protection and probably, if necessary, would have blown the trawler out of the water. This was deadly serious business.[58]

The occurrence of Soviet trawlers aggressively "rush[ing] up to the Tridents to try and force them off track in order to gauge their turning capabilities" and other SSBNs on the surface in allied coastal waters surely constitutes activities as dangerous as those engaged in by the fictional USS *Bedford*.[59] Yet they were not part of the public discourse during the Cold War. That said, the number of incidents involving nuclear-powered or ballistic missile–launching submarines was significant:

1959: USS *Grenadier* forces a Zulu V to surface off Greenland.

1966: USS *John Marshall* and USS *John Adams* SSBNs are harassed by AGI in Atlantic.

1967: Soviet submarine collides with USS *George C. Marshall* in the Mediterranean.

1968: HMS *Warspite* collides with Echo II in the Barents Sea.

1968: Juliette K-85 claims it was depth-charged near Gibraltar during the Czech Crisis.

1969: USS *Sam Rayburn* SSBN is harassed by AGIs off Charleston SC.

1969: USS *Gato* collides with Hotel K-19 SSBN.

1970: USS *Sam Houston* SSBN is harassed in the Mediterranean by Soviet forces.

1970: USS *Tautog* and Echo II collide off Vietnam.

1973: Golf B146 "prosecuted" by NATO ships while firing a submarine-launched ballistic missile.

1974: USS *Pintado* collides with Yankee SSBN off Petropavlovsk.

1974: Victor collides with USS *James Madison* SSBN departing Holy Loch.

1980: USS *Harlan County* collides with unidentified Soviet SSBN.

1981: USS *Henry Stimpson* SSBN is harassed by AGIs off Georgia.

1981: Delta III SSBN collides with Sturgeon-class attack submarine.

1982: USS *Ohio* SSBN Oldendorf affair.

1982: Delta SSBN K-465 collides with either British attack submarine, an iceberg, or two Soviet escort submarines.

1983: K-449 Delta SSBN collides with U.S. submarine.

1984: Delta K-500 SSBN is unmasked by U.S. forces, which conduct simulated anti-submarine warfare attack; K-500 prepares to respond with torpedoes.

1985: Delta K 530 SSBN is in three-day contact with "enemy" anti-submarine warfare forces.

1986: USS *Augusta* attack submarine collides with Delta I SSBN.

The American ballistic missile submarines weren't exactly helpless either. All of them carried conventional torpedoes, but some were modified in the 1960s to carry the Mk-45 ASTOR (Anti-Submarine Torpedo), the SUBROC (Submarine Rocket) system, or both.[60] ASTOR was a wire-guided nuclear torpedo with a W34 warhead yielding 10 kilotons. The UUM-44 SUBROC was a sophisticated system: the missile was ejected from the submarine's torpedo tube, rose to the surface, fired its rocket into a ballistic arc, and jettisoned its low-kiloton W55 nuclear warhead out to thirty-five to forty miles from the parent submarine.

The ballistic submarine's primary attribute, that is, the ability to remain isolated and hidden in the ocean's depths, is its greatest weakness as well. With all of that firepower aboard and operating in areas where they are potentially tracked by adversaries in peacetime, there was and remains obvious concern about independent action by a missile boat crew in the face of misperceptions or mutinous actions. That concern is reflected in the popular culture, starting with Anthony Trew's best seller in the 1960s, *Two Hours to Darkness*, and again in the 1980s with *The Gold Crew* and *Crimson Tide*, both of which deal with potentially rogue SSBN crews. Both were turned into films.

Thomas N. Scortia and Frank M. Robinson collaborated on five 1970s-era disaster novels, one of which was folded into the 1974 hit *The Towering Inferno*. *The Gold Crew*, published in 1980, evolved into the 1986 television film *The Fifth Missile*. The novel drew on Robinson's naval experience in World War II and Korea and Scortia's involvement with the aerospace industry. Both men were motivated "because of [their] concern for the dangers inherent in today's sophisticated technology. It is a 'What if?' book, depending for its drama on the terrifying consequences of an error or breakdown in this technology." The book is dedicated to Arthur "Skip" Steloff, "Academy graduate and former fleet officer . . . whose nightmare has become our own."[61] Steloff seems to have been a key driver in *The Gold Crew*, lining up numerous interviewees for the authors. In fact, though a 1947 Annapolis graduate, Steloff had only limited naval experience and none nuclear. By 1960 he was president of Heritage Productions; according to the producer Arnold Kane, "[He] was funny, bright, ballsy, and totally crooked. . . . He'd say anything to make a deal or con someone."[62]

The Gold Crew and its derivative *The Fifth Missile* parallel each other very closely in terms of plotline, characters, and outcome. In many ways the book and the film are the naval equivalent of the book and the film *Fail-Safe*; both have elements that the book and film *The Hunt for Red October* draw from; and both have a premise that *WarGames* essentially hijacked and melded with the 1979–80 NORAD incidents.

The plot centers on the belief of an advisor from the Yonkers

Institute (a play on Herman Kahn's Hudson Institute) that ballistic missile submarine crews might not fire if ordered to do so, thus undermining the credibility of the deterrent. As a result, the powers that be are convinced to order a test: fake recordings will deceive the crew of the USS *Alaska*, a Trident missile submarine on patrol, into believing they are in the midst of an escalatory situation, to the point where they have to decide whether to launch four ballistic missiles. Only the captain, the executive officer, and a U.S. Navy psychiatrist brought on board to observe will know the truth, that this is only a test using dummy warheads.

Despite sets that look like they were shot in a static trainer inside a building, and external shots showing what look like either Italian or Greek diesel submarines in the background, the two protagonists and their interactions are intriguingly handled: David Saul, the USS *Alaska*'s captain, does a slow burn to utter psychosis and devolves into a raving nuclear Captain Bligh, while the unsure, uneasy, alcoholic, pill-popping executive officer Robert Conrad (better known as the alcoholic U.S. Marine hero Gregory "Pappy" Boyington in *Baa Baa Black Sheep*) is the only sane man on aboard.

While the USS *Alaska* is on patrol, its new interior paint deteriorates and its quick-drying solvent gives off toxic fumes that progressively generate "fluorocarbon induced psychosis" among the crew. Interestingly, a similar scenario appeared in a 1964 episode of the TV series *Voyage to the Bottom of the Sea* called "The Fear Makers." In that episode "fear gas" is deliberately introduced by a saboteur while the U.S. Oceanographic Submarine *Seaview*'s crew is undergoing psychiatric testing with a shrink aboard. (The *Seaview* carried Polaris missiles.) Lab footage of the fear gas used in the show was real footage of an LSD-doped cat leaping up in fear of a mouse. The fear gas degrades into a nerve agent, and all hell breaks loose aboard *Seaview*.

In *The Fifth Missile* the psychological degradation is progressive. A war scenario similar to the 1973 Yom Kippur War crisis plays out over the sub's communications systems while the crew ponders its moves. A real Soviet Victor III starts tracking the *Alaska* while all of this is going on. The admirals, now alerted to the paint toxicity by the heroic sub commander Sam Waterson, try to recall the *Alaska* from their *Fail-Safe*–like naval command center, but Saul and his crew, *Fail-Safe*–like, think it is a Soviet trick. Conrad remains sane because his illegal antidepressant meds are countering the paint toxicity. He tries to arrange a takeover of the sub, just as Denzel Washington will later in *Crimson Tide*. With the U.S. Navy now hunting USS *Alaska* with orders to sink her (pace *The Hunt for Red October*), Waterson's character deploys to an aircraft carrier by E-3A Hawkeye so he can go out by helicopter and make contact with the submarine (again, pace *The Hunt for Red October*).

Meanwhile Conrad is on trial for his life in front of a psychotic crew, in effect turning *The Caine Mutiny* on its head. The now completely deranged captain attacks and damages the Victor III, and he decides to launch his missiles off Novaya Zemlya with a depressed trajectory launch after outmaneuvering American anti-submarine forces hunting him and *Alaska*. Conrad will not divulge the second combination to a two-combination safe in the captain's cabin. As he is dragged off, the crew torch open the safe and get two keys. These are inserted into a console where there is no separation: one person can turn both keys. Saul progresses through what appears to be authentic launch process verbiage (2 SQ, 1 SQ, and so on, on the intercom), flips a variety of switches, and then turns both keys. Conrad gets loose and starts sabotaging the missile launch tubes themselves, leading to a fight in the "Sherwood Forrest" portion of the sub (once again pace *The Hunt for Red October*). The four dummy missiles launch, and then the fifth one goes but is shot down by a heat-seeking missile fired from a helicopter. The SLBM drops down onto the *Alaska*, critically damaging her, and she sinks. In the book there is a more elaborate conspiracy whereby the *Alaska* test is supposed to fail, the crew is supposed to launch live missiles at the USSR, Strangelovian characters like the cigar-smoking General Leeland and Desmond Kahn play a role, and there is even a Grotoschele-like character in the Submarine Force Atlantic command center egging everybody on like Buck Turgidson in *Dr. Strangelove*: Who cares if it's an accident? Let's exploit it.

Crimson Tide emerged from the simultaneous collision of several powerful forces. High-concept-meisters Don Simpson and Jerry Bruckheimer were looking for the next *Top Gun* and became intrigued with a submarine-based film after viewing a documentary TV series, *Sharks of Steel* (1993). After his hits *Colors* and *Lean on Me*, the screenwriter Michael Schiffer wanted "to do something like *Fail-Safe* set in a submarine." The mass-market technothriller specialist Richard P. Hendrick had existing property dealing with a similar subject in his 1986 novel *The Phoenix Odyssey*. Mal Wright, former captain of the USS *Alabama* (Gold), assisted Schiffer, while Skip Beard, former captain of the USS *Alabama* (Blue), worked with the actors and crew. There was some drama when the production was sued by a screenwriter who later claimed *Crimson Tide* was based on a film project titled "Launch Sequence."[63]

Crimson Tide starts out boldly, announcing "the three most powerful men in the world: the president of the United States of America; the president of the Russian Republic; and the captain of a United States ballistic missile submarine." The Trident missile submarine is "the most lethal killing machine ever devised." And its crew is out of control.

Crimson Tide generates what appears to be an absolutely worst-case scenario for a U.S. ballistic missile–launching submarine on patrol, thus forcing the characters to duke it out for control of the sub's launch capability during an international crisis. Indeed it seems that the bulk of the film and its dialogue relates to the release procedure for the Tridents. The scenario is a nuclear ticking timebomb: Russian rebel forces have seized nuclear missiles in the Far East and are threatening to launch against the United States. The USS *Alabama* SSBN is sent to sea with its twenty-four Trident missiles (nobody talks about MIRVs) and sails off the Kuriles, waiting for word from the National Command Authority. We are fortunate that these are liquid-fueled ICBMs in rebel hands and it will take an hour after the rebel faction's decision to launch to prepare them, thus buying the United States and the crew of the USS *Alabama* time to preempt.

During a missile system readiness test drill, a fire breaks out in the galley, forcing the executive officer, Lt. Cdr. Ron Hunter (Denzel Washington), to be absent from the bridge. Capt. Frank Ramsay (Gene Hackman) continues with the drill in order to show us, the audience, how the system is supposed to work. An emergency action message box flashes red and beeps, and the captain orders the crew to battle stations for a nuclear missile readiness test. The printout of the message is examined by the communications officer and the operations officer. They concur that it is properly formatted and take it to the bridge. The captain has the executive officer get the authenticator, and he and the communications and operations officers open a safe and withdraw a blue "drill" authenticator, which is separated in the safe from the red launch authenticators. All three proceed to the bridge. The communications officer gets permission to authenticate and snaps open the cookie to reveal A A B E C Z T, which matches the authentication code in the emergency action message. All verbally concur that the message is authentic.

At this point the communications officer hands the captain a missile key. Where it comes from or why the communications officer has it is not revealed. The captain and executive officer get on the intercom and announce the move to condition 1 SQ for a weapons system readiness test. They take the submarine to 150 feet and the captain instructs the weapons officer to simulate pressurizing all of the missile tubes. A casualty from the fire dies, and the drill is canceled.

Then another emergency action message comes in, establishing a change in DEFCON to 3. Then a Russian attack submarine starts hunting USS *Alabama* and the tension goes up a notch. Another emergency action message arrives, this one from the National Military Command Center announcing a change to DEFCON 2. The message instructs the crew to launch ten nuclear missiles, target package SLBM 64741/0, with an authentication of B E E C A T A. Everybody concurs the message is properly formatted and the communications officer and the operations officer unlock two safe doors while the captain and the executive officer observe. Again the captain is handed a key by the communications officer. They proceed to the bridge and reenact the previous process, except this time "Release of nuclear weapons has been authorized. This is not a drill" is heard on the intercom. As the executive officer takes the conn, the captain goes to his stateroom and unlocks another safe, hands a bundle of keys to a seaman, who runs off the bridge, and the launch process continues.

Hunted by the Russian Akula attack sub, the *Alabama* moves below very low frequency (VLF) range, so the decision is taken to extend an extremely low frequency (ELF) antenna, a long cable towed behind the submarine. Then the Akula arrives, and another emergency action message slowly starts to come in on the ELF receiver. The decision is taken to float a tethered radio buoy, but the winch jams, generating noise that the Russian submarine homes in on. The Akula fires torpedoes. Yet another emergency action message starts to come in, but the detonating torpedo severs both the radio buoy and the trailing ELF antenna.

At this point we must question the credibility of the scenario. One frequently noted criticism of the film is the allusion to Russian liquid-fueled missiles. The film takes place just after the Cold War, by which point the bulk of the Russian armory used solid propellant or improved liquid propellant that did not require fueling immediately before launch. That said, early U.S. ballistic missile submarines were in fact targeted on the Soviet medium- and intermediate-range ballistic missile force and those missiles used liquid fuel, so the scenario works for the Cold War in the 1960s and 1970s. The probability of a Soviet attack submarine finding an American ballistic missile submarine that quickly after being surged from Vladivostok would have been extremely low during the later part of the Cold War—unless U.S. patrol areas were compromised by, say, the Walker spy ring. It was much more likely early on in the 1960s. What would be the probability of survival under Soviet torpedo attack in the close-range conditions depicted in *Crimson Tide*? That is unclear. Were VLF and ELF the only means by which ballistic missile submarines communicated? Were there no other protocols or options available to the captain?

This last is a key question because that is what the plot now revolves around. The LeMay-esque cigar-wielding captain and the executive officer engage in a public disagreement over the next steps. The executive officer argues that the incoming message is incomplete and therefore communications should be reestablished before launch.

The captain disagrees and asserts that an unauthenticated message, including a message fragment, cannot countermand the standing NCA order, that is, to launch. There is a protracted debate over protocols, with the captain asserting that they are already trained to deal with this situation, that the protocol is to launch. He orders the weapons officer to shift the system to the new target package, but the executive officer does not give his consent. The chief of the boat backs the executive officer, and the captain is relieved of command.

After the executive officer and crew sink the Akula sub, the captain mounts a countercoup, recaptures control of the *Alabama*, and resumes missile launch operations. With the communications officer standing in for the executive, giving his verbal consent, the captain inserts his key into an interlock, which activates the missile fire control system. Over the intercom he instructs the weapons officer at missile control to open his safe and remove the tactical firing trigger. "Weps" refuses, and the executive officer retakes the bridge and removes the firing key. A new incoming emergency action message telling all forces to stand down is received, there is an investigation, and in a bizarre and possibly not coincidental ending, the executive officer gets command of the USS *Alaska*.

Danger Beneath the Sea, a straight-to-video film, posits that the Trident submarine USS *Lansing*, patrolling in the Sea of Japan with a load of nuclear-armed Tomahawk cruise missiles, has its communications cut off from the outside world when a North Korean nuclear test goes awry and the weapon detonates over the ocean. An electromagnetic pulse takes out the electrical grids in the region. Sensing a radioactive environment above and unable to see any shore lights, the ultra-right-wing executive officer of the *Lansing* debates with the captain, played by Casper Van Dien, whether they should arm and fire their nuclear weapons—at China. A mutiny takes place, during which the captain's professional rivals undermine his authority by manipulating the medical staff. Meanwhile attack submarines are hunting the *Lansing* and, like the other films, the crew cannot tell the difference between friend and foe. (The underwater shots appear to reuse *Crimson Tide* footage, and the surface footage uses a Royal Canadian Navy submarine.) They react accordingly, using a wreck-strewn passage to elude the hunters. The captain regains control of the boat and takes it to Vladivostok to demonstrate that there is no war.

Without the knowledge of where the submarine was relative to its target and without the ability to communicate back to the National Command Authorities, the SSBN force was useless at best and dangerous at worst, again given the astronomically increased destructive capacity of a single ballistic missile submarine compared to SAC's entire Airborne Alert Force or a Minuteman ICBM squadron.

Ballistic missile submarines, like ICBMs, were the visible sharp edge of a massive system. That system was designed to provide credible target coverage for deterrent purposes and destroy those targets if necessary. Like the bombers, the ability of the SSBNs to do so was dependent on positive control. This involved several elements, but the basic ones were navigation and communication. As a result, the SSBNs were dependent on oceanographic and space operations, which themselves were subject to the exigencies of the Cold War, including incidents at sea. Only part of this system is seen or alluded to in the films; human drama and the inherent psychological aspects are moved to the forefront, and rightly so, given the genre.

On a real ballistic missile submarine, however, everything revolves around the trajectory of the missile and thus the position of the submarine in the sea and the attitude of the launch platform and the submarine relative to the target. These factors include distance to target, depth, latitude, and longitude; roll, pitch, yaw, and the velocity of the submarine itself; and even the torsion on the hull where the ballistic missiles are stored in their tubes. The inputs external to the submarine are measured by several devices and then fed (on a Polaris- or Poseidon-carrying submarine) into the two navigation data computers. That information is sent to the fire control system, which also monitors the state of the missiles.[64]

The keys to the system are the external inputs into the submarine and how they are processed. The main device for this is the ship's inertial navigation system (SINS), of which there were three aboard early SSBNs. Tested during the under-ice adventures of the USS *Nautilus* and successors on their runs to the North Pole (and presumably the USS *Tigerfish* in *Ice Station Zebra*), the SINS was an extremely secret technology because it permitted underwater navigation and preserved stealth. SINS use stabilized gyrocompasses, incorporating an accelerometer to tell the submarine where it is relative to Earth's axis of rotation. Consequently, knowing the effects of gravity over Earth's irregular shape, even underwater, became a crucial factor in increasing the accuracy of the SINS. To reduce errors that built up in the system over long periods and maintain the requirement to have position accuracy of 0.1 mile, the SINS had to be reset every two hours. That could only be done using external inputs.[65]

The methods of providing the reset information evolved throughout the Cold War. The first included the use of a special celestial navigation periscope, the Kollmorgen Type 11, and a combination of bottom contour mapping and LORAN-C, an extension of World War II long-range aircraft navigation technology: shore-based transmitters at several locations sent out low-frequency radio beams, forming an invisible grid in the air that receivers on aircraft and ships could use to triangulate their positions. U.S. Navy oceanographic survey ships operating in areas where Polaris submarines were to conduct deterrent patrols mapped the bottom of the ocean using sonar and correlated those undersea features to the LORAN-C signals. The U.S. Coast Guard acted as cover for the program, and as the LORAN-C station chains grew, Norway, the United Kingdom, and other NATO countries hosted U.S. Coast Guard personnel or in some cases themselves manned LORAN-C stations. The East Coast chain went on-line in August 1957 and the eastern Mediterranean chain in April 1959; the western Mediterranean and north central Pacific followed.[66] LORAN-C sites attracted political as well as military attention; in 1986 the Libyan regime even bombarded a U.S. Coast Guard LORAN-C station on the Italian island of Lampedusa with two Scud missiles.[67] Omega, a similar navigation system, supplemented LORAN-C.

It was believed that the bottom contour surveys would "provide an invulnerable system to back up LORAN-C in critical areas where LORAN-C cannot be depended upon in the event of hostilities."[68] But when the Polaris A-3 missile came on-line with its greater range, there was a problem. LORAN-C worked well enough in places like the Norwegian Sea and the Mediterranean; it was less effective in the middle of the Atlantic. There was a solution in the offing, however.

When Sputnik was launched in 1957, several scientists from the Applied Physics Laboratory at Johns Hopkins developed a means of tracking the "Red Moon" using the time signal from the WWV radio station in Denver and correlating it with the signals from Sputnik. They discovered that a doppler shift could be used to find out where Sputnik was in space. What if the process were reversed? Could several satellites in orbit be used to determine one's location on Earth? The proposal for an experimental system, made to the U.S. Navy in 1958, was accepted and funded within seventeen days.[69]

This satellite system was called Transit, and the first bird was launched on 17 September 1969. Transit 1A failed to achieve orbit, but the next one, Transit 1B, did, on 13 April 1960. More followed. In 1961 a pair of Transits, 4A and 4B, went into orbit simultaneously to develop navigation systems but also to examine Earth's gravitational field. For this, thirteen Transit Network (TRANET) civilian-manned tracking stations were established around the world. During the course of experimentation, the satellites were used to tye gravitational information from North America to Hawaii, and on analysis the scientific community discovered that Hawaii was located more than one kilometer away from where everybody thought it was.[70]

The implications were obvious to those involved in ballistic missile warfare, in both the U.S. Navy and the U.S. Air Force. The U.S. Air Force had the 1381st Geodetic Survey Squadron (Missile) and its detachments collecting data for the various ICBM sites that were under construction. The United States now had a method of collecting the gravitational data it needed on the Soviet Union using satellites and tying those data to Minuteman sites in North America. Specific gravitational information could be tied to the surveyed undersea contour positions, and both Transit and LORAN-C could assist the missile submarines with positioning themselves, thus increasing accuracy. If a Polaris submarine with A-3 missiles or a Poseidon were outside of LORAN-C coverage, Transit played an even more central role.[71]

In its 1964–65 operational configuration, the Transit system consisted of three to five navigation satellites orbiting Earth with U.S. Navy tracking stations located at Point Mugu, California; Prospect Harbor, Maine; Rosemount, Minnesota; and Wahiawa, Hawaii. Point Mugu and Rosemount were also injection stations, feeding a navigation message in every twelve hours.[72]

Transit had its limitations; these were dramatically demonstrated during the Operation Dominic atmospheric test series in 1962. Shot Starfish Prime, a 1.45-megaton warhead, was detonated on 9 July 1962 over the Pacific Ocean at an altitude of 250 miles. The radioactive debris from this shot rendered Transit 4B and five other satellites inoperable as they transited through the detonation zone.[73] Steps were taken to harden later Transit satellites and their descendants, but it was clear that redundant navigation capabilities were necessary and prudent for the operation of the ballistic missile submarine force.

Indeed the ground stations for both LORAN-C and Transit were vulnerable to enemy attack, particularly those stations in forward areas like Norway and the Mediterranean. It was Joint Chiefs of Staff policy that "re-establishment of destroyed stations" was a priority. As a result, "six complete transmitting station sets [were] stored as a war emergency resource." Known as the Air Transportable LORAN System and capable of being transported by C-130, C-133, and C-141 transport aircraft, these eighteen-shelter stations were stored at an out-of-the-way airfield near U.S. Navy Depot Hawthorne in Nevada.[74]

It is possible that some of the thirteen civilian TRANET stations around the world in nonbelligerent countries in the southern hemisphere (McMurdo Sound, Antarctica; Pretoria, South Africa; São Paulo, Brazil, for example) could have had some role in maintaining Transit if the U.S. Navy facilities were destroyed. However, it appears as though there were six satellites in orbit, of which three were "stored in orbit spares."[75] At least twelve "reserve spacecraft" were maintained in storage by RCA at an undisclosed location or locations throughout the Cold War.[76] There were two launch vehicles capable of inserting Transit: the Thor Able Star and Scout. Thor Able Star had a MIRV-like system that could dispense up to six Transits; these were based at Cape Canaveral and were used in 1962–63 to conduct multiple Transit deployments. After 1963 the much smaller and less infrastructure-intensive Scouts were also employed. On a peacetime basis, these launches were conducted from Vandenberg AFB in California.[77]

There may have been some overlap with the air force's Blue Scout Emergency Rocket Communications System program. Initially Blue Scout operated from NASA's Wallops Island, Virginia, launch site before transitioning to truck-mounted launchers dispersed to sites north of Omaha. NASA's Langley Research Center near Hampton, Virginia, managed Scout starting in 1957, and numerous Scouts were fired from Wallops Island launchers. It is possible these facilities played some role in Transit backup in the event of war.[78]

Submarine navigation systems evolved. Improvements in SINS eliminated the need for the celestial periscope; the hardened NAVSTAR global positioning system supplemented and then replaced Transit; and a highly secret gravity gradiometer system alluded to in the book and film *The Hunt for Red October* emerged:

> The navies, constantly aware of the whole submarine menace in the Cold War era and how deep going submarines, the nuclear submarines, were able to use topography as a—in a sort of game of hide and seek to lay themselves against a seamount and not be seen as an echo, etc. This was very much brought to the fore in a novel called *The Hunt for Red October*. . . . In particular, the gravitational fields of these were important, and the reason for that is the navigation of a deep submarine depends partly on its own gyros and compasses and speed indicators [and] accelerometers and so forth, but this is an increasingly poor system if you don't have any reference points. The reference points can be fixed features on the seafloor, topography, but you can only interrogate that topography by sending out an echo sounding ping and that of course gives away the position of the submarine. However, if you have . . . a contour map, of the gravity field created by these features you don't have to send any external signal out . . . which means that you can hide more effectively. So gravity fields are often derived from the topographic field so that

topography has its importance in the classified way in that sense, and this is all of the sort of dark part of submarine warfare and anti-submarine warfare.[79]

The biggest leap forward, however, was stellar inertial navigation, used by the U.S. Air Force in the Snark missile program and reconceived in the mid-1960s by the U.S. Navy for SLBM use. After the submarine launched the missile, the Post-Boost Vehicle carrying the MIRVs took a fix on the stars when it was in orbit, compared that fix to the data in the missile guidance system as to where it was fired from, compared those data to where the target was, and then maneuvered the vehicle before MIRV release. Stunningly, this technology was shelved by bureaucratically and personally driven elements in the U.S. Navy who wanted to maintain a perfect track record for rapid system delivery and within the budget of the SSBN system. Steller inertial navigation just complicated things, and who really needed an accurate missile anyway if the strategy was supposed to be assured destruction? As a result, the Soviets acquired the technology and implemented stellar inertial guidance in their ballistic missile submarines nearly a decade before the U.S. Navy finally did with Trident.[80]

The early American ballistic missile submarines were dependent on a single unhardened computer, the Naval Ordnance Research Computer, located in a large building at Dahlgren, Virginia. Computers were too large to put aboard a submarine in the 1960s, so all ballistic calculations had to be made by the Naval Ordnance Research Computer first by "presetting." This meant that every possible combination of launch position and target location had to be preset before the submarine departed on patrol. Polaris ballistic calculations even competed with Transit orbital calculations for computer time. When the USS *George Washington* went on her first patrol in 1960, she carried "300,000 targeting cards prepared at Dahlgren." These punched cards "were used to manually set knobs on the [Mk-80] fire control panel—several boxes of cards were needed for the ship to cover its assigned operational area." Microfilm was eventually employed, and then replaced with the Polaris target card computer system. The Mk-84 fire control system replaced all of this and had improved connectivity with the navigation inputs, including Transit. An improved Earth gravity model, developed from Transit data, was programmed into the Mk-84 and its Mk-88 successor.[81]

The patrol areas in the Norwegian Sea, Mediterranean, and western Pacific had several pre-surveyed launch positions, twenty miles by twenty miles square. This is where LORAN-C coverage and the bottom contour mapping became important. In 1958 four merchantmen, the USNS *Michelson*, USNS *Dutton*, USNS *Hess*, and USNS *Bowditch*, were converted into U.S. Navy oceanographic vessels (T-AGS), and Oceanographic Units 1, 2, and 3 were formed. Equipped with gravity measurement equipment, multiple beam echo sounding gear, and LORAN-C receivers, these ships conducted surveys of underwater features in support of the Polaris program starting in 1960, with two units deployed to the Atlantic and Mediterranean and one in the western Pacific. In April 1960 three of the ships were harassed by Soviet trawlers in the Norwegian Sea. In 1965 the Soviet AGI *Vertikal* nearly rammed and then deliberately cut the USS *Dutton*'s magnetometer cable. When the crew reeled in the cable, the *Vertikal* "direct[ed] two arc spotlights" at the *Dutton* and closed to ram again. These were just some of the incidents involving the T-AGS ships as they went about their business.[82]

The Soviets also learned the dimensions of the launch positions but not exactly where they were. They had detailed information on NAVDAC, SINS, and even the punch-card system but believed it existed in part "to prevent the personnel (including the commander) from knowing the targets of the missiles of the type of burst to be used." (This information probably came from the spy John Walker, who served aboard the SSBNS USS *Simon Bolivar* and USS *Andrew Jackson* in the 1960s.) By tracking the U.S. Navy oceanographic vessels, they hoped to be able to position anti-submarine forces in those areas in peacetime and track the ballistic missile submarines and kill them in wartime.[83] When the longer-range Polaris A-3s were deployed and the navigation and fire control system upgraded to the Mk-84, this significantly increased the ocean area that had to be covered by Soviet forces as well as their frustration. When Trident was deployed the Soviet anti-submarine warfare problem became even more difficult, forcing Soviet attack submarines to lurk off the bases at Bangor and King's Bay to track them.

A parallel issue alongside the navigation problem was that of communications. Substantial criticism of the possible unreliability of communicating with ballistic missile submarines and thus loss of positive control went back to the 1960s, was reactivated in the 1980s, and as we have seen, played a role in popular culture.

Historically submarines had to come to the surface to communicate using high-frequency radios. This increased their vulnerability to direction finding and destruction, as the Nazi U-Boat fleet learned the hard way in the 1940s. The Imperial Japanese Navy, on the other hand, relied on VLF communications with their submarines. High frequency (HF) could not penetrate water, but VLF could, down to thirty feet; VLF had an extremely long range and, as it turned out, could operate when the ionosphere was, shall we say, "disturbed." In the 1950s the U.S. Navy expanded VLF coverage for its submarine communications to Lualualei, Hawaii; North West Cape, Australia; the original Japanese VLF station at Yosami in the Pacific; Cutler, Maine; Annapolis, Maryland; Summit in the Canal Zone; and Jim Creek, Washington.[84] That said, VLF messages were significantly slower in transmission rates than when using HF.

The first American ballistic missile submarines had to come to periscope depth at a scheduled time, perhaps every six hours, perhaps more often as the DEFCON went up, raise an HF antenna, and copy down continuous wave and frequency shift keyed messages sent from the U.S. Navy's communications stations.[85] VLF floating wire receivers were later added to the submarines, which reduced their vulnerability by permitting them to remain completely submerged while receiving or act as a cue to have them ascend to receive an HF transmission.[86] The problem was that the shore stations had gargantuan antenna arrays and were vulnerable to nuclear attack or sabotage (as portrayed in the film *Telefon* when a sleeper agent attacks a naval communications facility). Concerns were also raised during the Cuban Missile Crisis regarding SSBN communications reliability. (The possibility that the LORAN-C chains, which were low-frequency systems, could be used as a backup to the VLF stations was explored and surreptitiously implemented later on.)

The result was a series of tests conducted at NASA's Wallops Island facility in Virginia (the former Naval Auxiliary Air Station Chincoteague) with a 15,000- to 25,000-foot aerial antenna trailed behind a C-121, followed by tests with an EC-130 Hercules transport. These aircraft were "flown in a circular orbit with bank angle [of 20 to 40 degrees]," so the antenna hung straight down and formed a helix.[87] A "good orbit was always flown . . . 5 knots above stall speed. . . . This created about 1.15 to 2 G's on the aircraft and crew. Orbits could be maintained for several hours and averaged between 1 and 3 hours."[88] The data rate from an aerial VLF antenna, as it turned out, was ten times that of the VLF shore stations.[89]

This number one and extremely secret U.S. Navy priority project became known as Tacamo after a memo purportedly telling staff to "take charge and move out" was passed down from the chief of naval operations. Starting off with six EC-130Gs (four for the Atlantic and two in the Pacific), expanding with eight more purpose-built EC-130Qs by 1967 and ultimately topping out at twenty-two aircraft by 1978, the "true heart" of the Tacamo system was the VLF equipment, designed and manufactured by Collins Radio.[90] Tacamo planes "enabled the mission crew to receive and transmit vital nuclear command control messages via nearly every radio frequency band and using several different modes including continuous wave, voice, teletype and computer-generated text."[91] The Tacamo aircraft were also hardened against electromagnetic pulse effects, but this remained the subject of serious concern in the 1970s and 1980s.[92]

The mission and its aircraft were subjected to significant security measures. "Tacamo" itself meant nothing: some thought it was a base in Washington State. For example, a pair of Tacamo-equipped EC-130Gs were concealed within Fleet Logistics Support Squadron 1 (VR-21) and called the "Tacamo component." Then they were moved to Fleet Airborne Early Warning Squadron 1 (VW-1) as the "Tacamo detachment."[93] The "VR-1 Det" operated out of Patuxent River, Maryland. In 1968 the Tacamo aircraft were consolidated into two squadrons: Fleet Reconnaissance Squadron 4 (VQ-4) at Naval

Air Station Patuxent River and Fleet Reconnaissance Squadron 3 (VQ-3) at Naval Air Station Agana, Guam (moved later to Barber's Point Naval Air Station in Hawaii in the 1970s). Two-thirds of the planes were assigned to VQ-4 because of the greater number of SSBN deterrent patrols in the Atlantic.[94]

The Tacamo planes were in a mixed ground-air alert status in the 1960s. By 1971 Tacamo aircraft were kept in the air twenty-four hours a day on a rotational basis, like Looking Glass. One of the criticisms leveled against the program in the 1980s was that their location was known to enemy forces because they filed flight plans with the FAA.[95] They did so out of concern that the trailing wire antennae were a hazard to civil aviation in peacetime. They probably would not have done so in the event of an escalatory crisis. To ensure they were dispersed and capable of providing VLF coverage to the Polaris and then the Poseidon patrol areas, several Tacamo permanent sites were established: Guam and Barber's Point Hawaii in the Pacific and Bermuda, the British West Indies, and Patuxent River in the Atlantic. Both squadrons had forward operating locations for further dispersion: in the Pacific these were in the Philippines and Japan and on several Pacific islands using former World War II airfields. In the Atlantic, Sondrestrom, Greenland; Torrejon, Spain; and several airfields in eastern Canada were just some of the operating locations. There were at least ten EC-130s dispersed around the world in single-ship detachments at any one time, making it extremely difficult to target the entire Tacamo force.[96]

Like the U.S. Air Force and the U.S. Coast Guard, the U.S. Navy also possessed a discrete fleet of mobile ground stations. The Technical Material Corporation provided communications systems for New York State and Massachusetts civil defense bunkers and facilities and the White House Communications Agency. TMC also provided the transmitters at the WWV radio station in Colorado that supported the Minuteman force. In the late 1950s TMC prototyped an air-transportable communications system under Project Baker. Baker and its descendants Dog, Echo and Henry consisted of the AN/TSC-35 system mounted in containers that could be moved by transport aircraft. The navy formed several air-transportable communications units or ACTUs around 1961 located in Norfolk, San Miguel in the Philippines, Barber's Point, and other locations. Notably these systems were capable of low-frequency operations.[97]

ACTU-2, for example, was assigned to Pacific Command and code-named Blue Eagle. It included a portable communications system mounted in U.S. Navy R6D aircraft. (The air force equivalent was the C-118 four-engine transport.) The aircraft could act as a communications relay platform, or the system could "be easily removed from the plane and assembled in temporary shelters within a matter of hours."[98] Cover for Blue Eagle was provided by a TMC-built TV system mounted in C-121s for use by the Armed Forces Radio and TV network operating over Vietnam, also called Project Jenny and call-signed Blue Eagle.[99]

Pacific Command's Blue Eagle had its European Command counterpart, originally called the Silk Purse Control Group. Established in 1962, Silk Purse consisted of five C-118 command-and-control aircraft on ground alert operating as the 7120th Airborne Command and Control Squadron (ACCS) out of Chateauroux Air Base, France. These aircraft were kept on the move regularly with battle staffs capable of handling nuclear weapons release for European Command's units should the headquarters of the commander in chief Europe be knocked out.[100]

In 1965 the decision was made to standardize the Pacific Command and European Command airborne communications systems. The 7120th ACCS moved to RAF Mildenhall in England and was embedded under the 513th Troop Carrier Squadron. The 6486th ACCS was stood up at Hickam AFB in Hawaii (hidden within the 6486th Air Base Wing) and was merged with the existing Blue Eagle organization prior to 1972. In 1966 both units took delivery of various types of EC-135 aircraft with the objective of having a Looking Glass–like continuous airborne system similar to SAC. Both theaters received trailer-mounted mobile ground entry points. Pacific Command's ground entry points were located at Clark AB in the Philippines; Hickam AFB; Kadena AB, Okinawa; and Johnston AB in Japan. The European Command ground entry points were at Botley Hill, England, manned by the U.S. Navy; Camp des Loges and

Paris in France; Heidelberg, West Germany; and Lindsay Air Station, Wiesbaden, West Germany (home of the U-2).[101]

The EC-135s operated by Silk Purse and Blue Eagle were manned by all three services, had an airborne emergency action officer, and were capable of communicating through a variety of means, including trailing wire VLF equipment. In all respects, they were the two commanders in chiefs' equivalent of the Looking Glass aircraft and could communicate with ballistic missile submarines, working with the EC-130Q Tacamo planes as required. In terms of mission profiles, Silk Purse aircraft could disperse to any number of airfields in the NATO area. In 1984 Silk Purse aircraft moved to Lajaes, Azores. Blue Eagle presumably could operate from any runway capable of handling jet aircraft in the Pacific region.[102]

Note that Atlantic Command was not part of this setup initially. The pending retirement of the National Emergency Command Post Afloat ships with their VLF communications systems produced another change. In 1967 five EC-135Ps were allocated to the commander in chief of the Atlantic Command on the same basis as the commander in chief Pacific and the commander in chief Europe. The aircraft were assigned in 1967 and concealed within existing units. The EC-135 aircraft was based at Langley AFB and assigned to the 4450th Air Base Wing, the logistics unit running the base: "One of their main missions consisted of serving as communications relays with the fleet of missile launching submarines, either directly or via the EC-130Q." Call-signed Scope Light, their deployment sites included airfields in Canada, Iceland, North Africa, the Azores, Puerto Rico, Panama, and even locations in the Pacific. By the early 1970s all three units were renamed the 10th ACCS (for Silk Purse), the 6th ACCS (for Scope Light), and the 9th ACCS (for Blue Eagle).[103]

Fifteen EC-135s and twenty-two Tacamo planes dispersed individually to airfields, one-fifth of them in the air at all times; along with seven VLF stations and multiple ground low-frequency portable communications stations, they produced a relatively robust and redundant command-and-control system. Notably, many of the Tacamo and airborne command post dispersal sites were located closer to the equator and perhaps would have been less susceptible to electromagnetic pulse effects.

Evolution of the communications systems in the 1970s added ELF systems to the submarines, with associated transmitters at Clam Lake, Wisconsin, and on Michigan's Upper Peninsula. ELF had an even slower data rate than VLF and was used as a "bell ringer" to "cue" submarines to decrease their depth so that other, faster systems could be used.[104]

The ability of the National Command Authorities to communicate with the ten to twenty ballistic missile submarines at sea at any one time, despite the presence of electromagnetic pulses and enemy action, was, however, still questioned in many quarters, mostly by people who were not read in on the whole system. Was the system fast enough? Were ballistic missile submarines supposed to launch against "time urgent targets," or were they weapons of retaliation and revenge that did not need to be able to communicate quickly and could lurk and fire later?[105] Nowhere, it seems, was the reliability of the personnel seriously questioned except in popular culture.

Samuel W. Coulbourn, the weapons office aboard the SSBN USS *Ethan Allen* on 22 November 1963, recounted what happened that day. Operating in the eastern Mediterranean, the *Ethan Allen*'s executive officer announced to the ship, "The President has been shot and killed by assassins." He recalled, "Here we are, cruising along submerged in the Mediterranean, and we probably got the word before many Americans. . . . We imagined that the assassination might be part of a large plot by the Soviets culminating in a nuclear attack on the United States. For a very scary period of time we didn't know if we would be ordered to launch missiles." On 23 November the *Ethan Allen* and other SSBNs were ordered to Battle Station Missile by the commander in chief of the Atlantic Command Adm. Harold P. Smith "to prepare to launch [their] load of nuclear missiles." Coulbourn explains, "[This was] usually a drill to check our preparedness for the real thing, but as we ready our missiles, preparing to arm the warheads and readying each huge launcher to eject its missile we don't know if it's the real thing or not."[106]

The duty officer missed the switch for "Battle Station Missile" on the intercom:

I grappled for an alarm and by mistake pulled the collision alarm. This so unnerved me that I reached for the diving alarm. There being one more left, I finally hit the General Alarm. By this time I had men running in all directions, rigging for collision, preparing to surface and scurrying to Battle Stations. . . . [The captain] took over and I ran down to the Missile Control Center. . . . We spun up the gyros in each missile and proceeded through our countdown. Then came the order that this was a practice launch. With all of the uncertainty after the assassination we were in the dark. The Captain and the executive officer held the actual message, which in this case was indeed a test and we didn't arm the nuclear warheads. But it was scary![107]

The steps for preparing the submarine for missile launch, authentication of orders, and implementing the mechanical steps necessary to fire are obscure for the Polaris and Poseidon periods. In *Crimson Tide*, Captain Ramsey reminisces about the Cold War: "Rickover gave me my command, a checklist, a target, and a button to push. All I had to know was how to push it, and they'd tell me when." But was it ever that simple? Phil Jaskoviak served aboard the USS *Casimir Pulaski* (aka "The Crazy Polack") in the 1960s. On a deterrent patrol, SSBNS had to be able to go to "Battle Stations Missile (1 SQ) within five minutes of receiving a verified message" and be prepared to launch missiles within another fifteen minutes. Periodically SSBNS would be instructed by the National Military Command Center in the Pentagon through Commander Submarine Force Atlantic's operations control center at Norfolk to conduct a weapons system readiness test. The watch officer authenticated the message in Norfolk using a sealed authenticator system; a message would be generated and sent via Teletype to the VLF station at Cutler, Maine, for transmission. Notably, the Commander Submarine Force Atlantic could also initiate a test and would do so "without telling the subs that it was [a] drill. . . . No one on board including the Captain knew it was a drill."[108]

The battle stations alarm was sounded when the message arrived ("Recommend Alert One!" in *Crimson Tide*). The "war message is sent in plain language, not encrypted or scrambled, but it can only be 'authenticated' by the president. The short message, fewer then 25 characters in length, could thus be faked by anyone, so the authentication code words are safeguarded. . . . After transmitting the war message, the president provides the two authentication words which must match those at the receiving end."[109] It appears as though this changed by the 1980s, when it took six personnel to separately decrypt and agree that the format was acceptable, and then four to authenticate emergency action messages.[110]

For the Polaris- and Poseidon-carrying submarines, the Mk-80 and Mk-84 fire control systems were central to the release process. The system included the target data input units, where the punch cards and later the microfilm and still later keyboarded targeting data were entered. The inertial navigation systems fed the ship's position interpolation units with position, velocity, and heading data. Missile motion units assessed data fed back from the launchers. The fire control system assessed these data and then fed the guidance computers on the missiles; some of the data included steering commands and the latitude and longitude of each target. Later on, when stellar inertial guidance was added and the new fire control systems were available, the star positions to be referenced by the missiles after launch were sent as well. These data came in the form of star catalogues from the U.S. Naval Observatory.[111]

The command to "spin up the missiles" was crucial. According to Douglas C. Waller, who observed the process on a Trident-equipped submarine, "It took at least ten minutes. During that time, the gyroscope inside the missile's inertial navigation unit was put in motion and aligned so it could begin sensing the rocket's position in the [ocean] and its movement once it was launched."[112] In earlier submarines the accelerometers in the SINS had to slow down to do the same thing while the submarine was put into hover mode.

In a general sense, all of the SLBM fire control systems worked the same way. The consoles, located in the missile control center on the deck below the bridge and operated by the weapons officer, the missile fire control technicians, and the missile checkout technicians, monitored the state of the missiles on a minute-by minute basis. The launcher and ordnance subsystem technicians monitored the missiles from panels in the Sherwood Forest missile compartment. Like the mechanisms described for the Minuteman, a variety of connections existed to monitor and feed the missile guidance systems and the warhead safe/arm mechanisms.

After authentication, the captain opened his stateroom safe and handed a ring of keys to the launcher and ordnance subsystem technicians. These were used to unlock the gas generators on each launch tube, permitting the missiles to be ejected for launch. The captain also removed his indicator panel key from the safe. The weapons officer possessed a combination safe at the fire control station; in it was the tactical mode key and the tactical firing trigger. The tactical mode key permitted the flow of data to the guidance systems and the warhead safe/arm system once the captain inserted and turned the indicator panel key in his console one deck up, on the bridge. This allowed the electrical current from the tactical trigger to pass to the selected launch tubes. On command the weapons officer fired the missiles using the tactical firing trigger.[113]

Like the ASROC system, SLBM release was subject to at least seven people giving their explicit consent before and during the process. As Waller notes, misuse of the system meant that it "would take a lot of people being in on the conspiracy—dozens of them in the missile control center, and missile compartment and at the conn. At the very least, more than a third of the men on board would have to be involved. . . . [A conspirator] would have to brainwash practically the entire crew into doing something they knew was seriously wrong."[114]

Still, Schiffer insists that every officer he spoke with when he conducted research for *Crimson Tide*, if faced with disrupted communications in the middle of a launch process, would have launched and not confirmed.[115] Yet a process called "piecing," approved by the Joint Chiefs, was put in place to prevent that scenario. In essence, this was a means to use the variety of communications systems aboard to assemble and authenticate a fragmentary emergency action message. The specifics, of course, remain obscure.[116] Isolated and stressed men, however, still had to interpret those orders.

The Shrinks Who Wore Dolphins: The Mental Health of Submariners

Concerns about the psychological health of U.S. Navy submariners predate the development of SSBNs, but when the nuclear-propelled submarine program took off in the early 1950s concerns about prolonged submergence, long-term habitability, and psychology came to the fore. One of the first tests was Operation Hideout, conducted in 1953. The USS *Haddock*, a diesel attack submarine, was modified so it could be sealed off and carbon dioxide scrubbers tested. A medical officer and twenty-two volunteers were sealed inside for two months and subjected to tests like the Rosenzweig Picture Frustration Test (Navy Modification) and the Terman Attitude-Interested Test for Masculinity-Femininity and were measured for "authoritarianism, radical-conservatism, and anti-democratic trends," among other disturbances. The result: "It was interesting to see this group of strangers with relatively few characteristics and interests in common mold themselves into a well integrated, loyal group."[117]

Dr. Benjamin B. Weybrew, the navy's lead in submarine psychologist at the time, had a dry wit. In the Operation Hideout report he included a detailed section on how the media generated a national sensation "with the following screaming headline . . . 'Incarcerated submariners develop an insatiable desire for cottage cheese.'" The reality is the test crew developed a calcium deficiency due to the carbon dioxide buildup. Cottage cheese was a possible solution, but local stores did not carry it and the navy's repeated requests for the food became known to the media.[118]

Weybrew and his team contributed in many ways to the SSBN program. He noted that by the early 1960s "a series of official instructions issued by the Secretary of the Navy . . . further emphasized the criticality of maintaining the optimal mental health of the submarine crews, in order to minimize the likelihood of an inadvertent launch of a nuclear-armed missile or some other casualty, with ultimate consequences conceivably affecting the viability of planet Earth." They were involved in the plan to develop a Blue and Gold crew: each submarine had two crews, one at sea, and the other on shore, so the sub could have a greater availability rate. The Weybrew team was also involved in determining the duration of an SSBN patrol. Building on Operation Hideout data, Weybrew was an observer aboard the USS *Nautilus* and later the USS *Triton* during Operation Sandblast, when Capt. Ned Beach sailed the giant submarine around the world submerged in 1960. The sixty- to seventy-day patrol period became the standard for the American SSBN force. Weybrew also came up with "cognitive anchoring," whereby crew members could "sightsee" using the periscope at various times during the patrol, thus reducing isolation effects.[119] The Blue/Gold concept and the two-month patrol was even directly copied by the Soviets for their Yankee-class submarine force.

Hideout and Sandblast also included tests to examine the atmospheric problems depicted in *The Gold Crew* and *The Fifth Missile*. As Captain Beach recalled in his memoir, "Among them was a test to determine the psychological effects of the smoking ban, and a purely mechanical test to discover the percentage of contaminated aerosols. . . . With these tests the [Naval Medical Research Laboratory] hoped to learn whether smoking should be restricted . . . whether crews of such ships should comprise only nonsmokers, or whether special equipment should be devised." The prospect of an unauthorized missile launch due to heroin or narcotics? Forget it. Nicotine withdrawal was a more likely problem. As a result, the *Triton's* supply officer brought an extra batch of candy.[120]

The air scrubbers in the early ballistic missile submarines "barely held their own," and "the high [carbon dioxide] level gave crewmen headaches and cuts took forever to heal."[121] This problem was noted by the psychologists as well, and between 1965 and 1968 the old scrubbers were replaced with ones that had double the capacity. There was a correlation between this move and a reduction in reported physical and mental illnesses aboard the submarines while deployed.[122]

The most serious environmental system accident aboard a Soviet nuclear missile submarine occurred in the Mediterranean in 1968 during a period of high tension in the Middle East. The Soviet Fifth Eskrada maintained an Echo II–class nuclear cruise missile submarine in the eastern Mediterranean either to cover targets in Israel, to offset U.S. Navy aircraft carriers in the region, or both. There was a "mass poisoning" by "mercury vapor" that evaporated in the ventilation system and incapacitated 126 out of 132 of the crew of submarine K-127. The submarine had to return to a shipyard for decontamination.[123] Symptoms of mercury poisoning include "mood swings, irritability, nervousness . . . disturbances in sensations . . . poor performance tests on mental functions."[124] In 1981 the Soviet rescue submarine B-486 was searching for American Ivy Bells taps on underwater cables when the exhaust and ventilation systems failed. Of the 105 crew, 86 were rendered unconscious and several died. The remaining crew was able to move the sub to a bay, where recovery efforts were mounted.[125]

Manning and operating a submarine is a very different experience from manning a surface vessel and is perhaps closer to flying a plane. On the surface there is room for error. With increasing pounds per square inch at depth, where a pencil-thin leak can cut off an arm, there is none. The U.S. Navy's initial screening process for prospective submariners was essentially- the Minnesota Multiphasic Personality Inventory modified by Weybrew and called the Personal Inventory Barometer. It was used for twenty-five years.[126] The training system too played a significant role. Richard Smith recalled his training at the Nuclear Power School: "The program was designed from the outset to be extremely difficult to pass. They needed to weed out the weak and unstable candidates. If someone was going to snap, they wanted it to happen here. Two miles off a hostile coast would be a very inconvenient location."[127] Ted Dubay, who served on the USS *Henry Clay* after passing through the selection process, said, "Many could not stand the frenetic pace . . . and committed suicide."[128] These unfortunate individuals should, perhaps, be considered casualties of the Cold War in the service of their country.

The inherent nature of the submarine crew itself played a significant role in nuclear safety. Gannon McHale, who served aboard nuclear submarines in the Cold War, explained that there was substantial self-vetting by experienced crew members. He balked at getting a coffee for another sailor who was in the middle of a card game and then smart-mouthed him:

Gilstrap was an old school, qualified petty officer 1st class. I didn't realize it was all a test. He had baited me and pushed my buttons to see how I would respond, and I failed. It was the first of many tests that submariners do to make sure they can trust you. That's the deal. You have to be able to trust the guy next to you because he could be responsible for saving your life. It took me a long time to make up for that mistake. However, I never had any trouble with Gilstrap after that.[129]

Richard Smith:

My first day on *Skipjack* was an eye opening experience. . . . Everyone was cleaning. Everyone! Along with the junior people were the officers, chiefs and even The Captain! Now, granted the Skipper wasn't cleaning the head or the bilge. But he found a dirty place and kneeled right down with the blue shirts and scrubbed. It was then I realized the biggest difference between a sub crew and a surface crew. The phrase "we're all in this together" really meant something.[130]

Phil Jaskoviak:

It is difficult for civilians to understand the necessity for a newly-assigned crew member to be accepted by the crew. . . . Each new man is carefully watched and evaluated for normal behavior, attitude, and outlook on the navy. They are also expected to join groups on liberty while partying and drinking heavily. The drunker one becomes and the worse the hangover, the better. The high level of mental and physical ability required of any crewmember on a nuclear submarine was not for everyone. Not many candidates could meet the standards of performance required and even fewer had the psychological wherewithal to endure the unique combination of boredom and terror that was the lot of the submariner.[131]

Professionalism, proficiency, and esprit de corps were absolutely crucial when crews had to deal with psychological issues. Gary Penley, who served aboard the ballistic missile submarine USS *Alexander Hamilton*, recounted a time when the submarine was on a deterrent patrol and experienced a collision. One crewmember panicked "and had to be subdued. Such behavior is abhorrent on a submarine and not to be tolerated. The man lost control under pressure and could not be trusted to give his all to save the boat and the lives of his shipmates."[132] Gannon McHale recalled an incident on his submarine when a machinist's mate 1st Class demanded the keys to the gun locker. Why? "So I can shoot the captain and we will all be going home now." He was subdued, "handcuffed to one of the torpedo skids," "sedated, and confined to the after battery" until the sub diverted to Halifax.[133]

Dr. Jonathan Serxner was a naval medical officer who undertook psychological studies aboard two SSBNs in the mid-1960s. His analysis is revealing on a number of issues. In his view, there was "little reason to fear claustrophobia, sensory deprivation reactions, or a 'madman pressing the button'—however much such thoughts predominate in speculation and fantasy about this subject." He concluded, "No individual on the submarine can initiate launching without the aid of others. The combined efforts of many men in several different areas of the submarine are needed to bring the various systems to readiness for a launching, There is a set procedure for verifying an order to fire a missile which involved the captain and two other officers. All on board are impressed with the terrible destructiveness of these weapons."[134]

Serxner observed that submariners "constitute an elite group" for whom "drills generate excitement (and anticipation) while . . . they promote 'readiness' and a sense of community." The crews engaged in "highly imaginative joking," and "sexual interests find expression in several ways. . . . There was a tendency evident after two or three weeks to display pictures of grossly unattractive women . . . and sexual activity was a frequent topic of conversation." Serxner "doubted that such talk always indicates low morale." Tellingly, "only one man presented with a sexual problem in the course of two patrols. . . . A 25-year-old man complained that he was troubled by the meaning of his desire to masturbate (This was a part of his concern about his wife's accusation that he was hypersexual)."[135]

Of course, given the nature of submariners, there was a tendency to wind up the shrinks: "A chief psychiatrist . . . asked submariners if the confinement ever bothered them [and] he would commonly receive answers like, 'Oh yeah, it drives me crazy. Sometimes I grab a hammer and chisel and try to beat holes in the pressure hull.'"[136]

Serxner did note that "two men from a group of eight studied had dreams involving death or impotence with[in] the first few days following submergence for a 58-day patrol." On one patrol Serxner helped to deal with a petty officer who suffered "an acute paranoid schizophrenic break after five weeks on his first submerged patrol." After enduring increased "erratic behavior and grossly irrational talk . . . the chief hallucinated voices talking about him and calling him names." Fortunately the unnamed SSBN was equipped with "an ample supply of phenothiazines, barbiturates, etc., and a straight jacket." The chief was "given phenothiazines in doses increased to 600–800 mg a day and barbiturates in considerable doses. . . . He was seen in frequent sessions. . . . His fellow chiefs [eventually] moved from a surveillance role to one of involving him in their activities. . . . This treatment continued for three weeks and the apparent response was gratifying."[137]

In the final measure, the motives of the submariner officers commanding and leading SSBN crews in the Cold War, captured in a U.S. Naval Submarine Medical Center study, help us explain why no crew, no matter how stressed out or isolated it was, conducted a rogue launch. Of nine motivational categories, four stood out as predominant and could apply equally to officers and sailors. The first category was "Adventure, Challenge, and Excitement"; the second was "Characteristics of Crew," that is, "high esprit de corps; close knit, small crews; Teamwork, High 'caliber' of crew, high status and Sub service has top priorities." Third was "Service to Country": "opportunity to participate in the Defense of USA"; and fourth, "Career and Educational Opportunities," because nuclear propulsion was cutting-edge technology not only in the U.S. Navy but in civil society.[138] Like SAC, the navy's submarine force was held in high regard; it had exceptionally high standards and understood clearly what its mission was. Sheer professionalism infused in the force coupled with the inherently hazardous nature of submarine duty was the most important firewall against the misuse of nuclear weapons.

DR. STRANGELOVE GOES TO SEA

Postscript

Edmund N. Epstein from the Submarine Medical Center produced a paper titled "Effects of the Cuban Crisis upon Attitudes Related to War and Peace." He sampled 128 sailors as the crisis started, when it was at its peak on 25 October, and when it was deemed over. Notable and significant shifts in the responses to attitude questions over the course of the crisis included the following:

No one really wants a war but it is best to be prepared (+).

In any nuclear war there will be no winner (-).

It is a submariner's own business if he has conscientious objections against firing a nuclear missile in wartime (-).

In the event of nuclear war, the U.S. would win (+).

There will never be a nuclear war because the risk is too great (-).

Epstein concluded, "In general the interposition of the Cuban crisis between two administrations of an attitude questionnaire designed to assess pacifistic-belligerent attitudes of submariner candidates tended to 'sharpen' those attitudes related to the realities of the situation, dangers of nuclear war, modes of defense and preparedness. . . . It appears that attitudes towards the international situation were viewed in more black and white terms. . . . All in all, the pattern of post-crisis attitude differences suggests that, when a nation's international posture shifts towards the belligerent, military men's attitudes change in the same direction."[139] And it is elected politicians who establish what that posture should be.

Epilogue

"Not all of our people's programming was faulty." Uttered by Martin Landau's president in *By Dawn's Early Light*, this statement is a fitting epitaph for our technosocial odyssey into the arcane, secretive, and dangerous world of nuclear weapons as depicted on film. Set in the context of the Cold War, it is evident that the nuclear crisis films were based on period books that had an imperfect understanding of nuclear weapons, strategy, safety mechanisms, and command-and-control arrangements. These distortions were translated into film, thus reinterpreting them a second time, which in turn produced further distortion among cultural consumers in the short term and particularly over the long term. The early nuclear crisis films are now elemental to the cultural fabric of the United States and other countries as well. Extracts of *Dr. Strangelove* are even employed in contemporary Russian information operations against the West as Russia seeks to disrupt and deter NATO from protective activities in Eastern Europe.[1] North Korea employed American defectors to portray caricatures of aggressive, cigar-chomping U.S. generals in its propaganda films.[2] Any hint of something going awry with the American nuclear apparatus is immediately hyperlinked in today's mediasphere to *Dr. Strangelove* and its characters in some fashion.

One of the most important distortions relates to why the nuclear deterrent system existed in the first place. That reason could be assumed by a 1964 audience, having passed through the Korean War and the legitimately paranoid 1950s. It cannot now. The films examined in this book do not depict in any significant detail the horrific system that was being deterred or its leadership; instead the opposition is portrayed as the faceless moral equivalents of Ameri-

357

can leaders, not identified as Stalin, Mao, and Khrushchev or their analogues. An appropriate depiction of them had to wait until 2018, with the unjustifiably limited release of *The Death of Stalin*. And there is no discussion of the murderous apparatus they controlled; again, it was only with *Child 44* (2015) and *The Death of Stalin* that we have some semblance of the Soviet terror state's psychotic modus operandi. Instead men like LeMay and Power are caricatured as dangerous and out of control, threatening to destroy the world or take over the United States. Yet men like Stalin, Mao, and Khrushchev, men who had designs on most of the planet and who killed upwards of 60 million people, are not part of the equation.

As a result a further distortion has been introduced into today's crucial discourse over nuclear weapons, deterrence, and safety: the combination of the films and today's nuclear weapons accident pornography subliminally and overtly depict an American system dangerously out of control, even though it was not, as demonstrated herein. What about the other half of the equation? There is virtually no academic historical work done by Western scholars or, notably, by the antinuclear movement on Soviet command and control and nuclear accidents.[3] There are no Soviet equivalents of *Dr. Strangelove* or *Fail-Safe*, let alone *The Bedford Incident*; they would not have been permitted. If the intent of Soviet information operations was to raise and then enhance doubt in the West's reliance on the nuclear deterrent to offset superior Soviet capabilities in the 1950s and 1960s, then the early films assisted that effort, though, it must be emphasized, not deliberately or directly. Ironically LeMay and Power's information operations campaign also inadvertently played a role in generating media exposure. This, as well as Soviet information operations in a supporting role, led to the conceptualization of the fictional literature, which became the basis of *Dr. Strangelove* and *Fail-Safe*. That state of affairs itself is almost Strangelovian.

There is every reason, however, to suggest that the introduction of Permissive Action Link systems, the Human Reliability Program, and the clarification of the civil-military relationship regarding nuclear weapons release were to some extent influenced by fears raised by the books and films and the public commentary surrounding them.

Whether or not such actions would have impeded timely nuclear release and benefited the opposition in a crisis scenario, of course, remains speculative.

We must remember that these films are meant for entertainment. They were not meant to be historical documentaries. They are reflections of legitimate but uninformed public concerns of the day, but they are not in themselves history. History consists of real men and women placed in positions of authority over the most inconceivably destructive weapons ever devised. The evolution of the nuclear command-and-control systems depicted in this work show us that there was a will and then a process to ensure that there was both an effective deterrent system and adequate safeguards to prevent improper use of that system. These were imperfect people working through the problem, breaking new ground under unprecedented circumstances. And they succeeded. Russians, and everyone associated with them at the time, should be thankful they did: the SIOP would have essentially strip-mined the Soviet Union if the United States had been pushed too far in 1962. But it would have been a political decision, not a rogue military one.

Like the future alien archaeologists who discover the "documentary" footage in a deep mineshaft at the end of the *Dr. Strangelove* novelization, some future generation will watch Kubrick's film. And they will laugh. As they should.

NOTES

1. Book! Movie!

1. Seed's fascinating literary analysis and James's superb scientific-technological analysis make both of these works required reading on this topic. Seed is, however, somewhat constrained by having to deal strictly with American literature, which precluded him from really drilling into British and other works on the subject.

2. Michael D. Gordin examines this issue throughout *Five Days in August*.

3. Wittner, *The Struggle against the Bomb*, 58; Gideon Haigh, "Shute the Messenger," *The Monthly*, June 2007, https://www.themonthly.com.au/issue/2007/june/1268876839/gideon-haigh/shute-messenger.

4. See Pettee, "A Critical Review of the Nuclear Escalation Concept."

5. Schelling, *Strategies of Commitment*, 211.

6. Smith notes that they sold millions of copies (*Doomsday Men*, 403).

7. Lashmar, *Spy Flights of the Cold War*, ch. 5.

8. Schelling, *Strategies of Commitment*, 211.

9. George, *Red Alert*, 71–72.

10. George, *Red Alert*, 72–73.

11. George, *Red Alert*, 28–31.

12. See Podvig, *Russian Strategic Nuclear Forces*.

13. George, *Red Alert*, 54.

14. George, *Red Alert*, 50.

15. Kaplan, *The Wizards of Armageddon*, ch. 7.

16. George, *Red Alert*, 75.

17. George, *Red Alert*, 38.

18. Kahn, *On Thermonuclear War*, 205–7.

19. Thomas S. Power, *Design for Survival*, vii–xi.

20. Freedom of Information Act (FOIA) CIA, Operations Coordinating Board Luncheon Meeting memos for the record on 23 April 1958.

21. FOIA CIA, Operations Coordinating Board Luncheon Meeting memos for the record on 23 April 1958.

22. George, *Red Alert*, 65.

23. Ned Beach captained USS *Triton* in an underwater circumnavigation of the earth in 1960. See *Around the World Submerged*.

24. See the website Existential Ennui article "Commander-1: The Life and Death of Author Peter George, alias Peter Bryant/Bryan Peters, co-writer of Dr. Strangelove," 19 October 2012, www.existentialennui.com/.

25. "Obituary: Harvey Wheeler," *The Guardian*, 20 September 2004; Harvey Wheeler, "Fail-Safe Then and Now," *The Idler*, 29 May 2000; Aiken, "Abraham '59."

26. Wheeler, "Fail-Safe Then and Now."

27. Schelling, *The Strategy of Conflict*; Wohlstetter, "The Delicate Balance of Terror"; Brodie, *Strategy in the Missile Age*.

28. Chris Smith, "Intellectual Action Hero," *California Magazine*, Summer 2010, http://alumni.berkeley.edu/california-magazine/summer-2010-shelf-life/intellectual-action-hero.

29. Wheeler, "Fail-Safe Then and Now."

30. Peter Kramer, "'To Prevent the Present Heat from Dissipating': Stanley Kubrick and the Marketing of *Dr. Strangelove*," *InMedia*, March 2013, http://inmedia.revues.org/634. Kramer has made extensive use of the Kubrick papers in London, including correspondence among all of the principals involved.

31. See Terry Southern, "Check-Up with Dr. Strangelove," *Filmmaker Magazine*, Fall 2004, http://www.filmmakermagazine.com/archives/issues/fall2004/line_items/strangelove.php; Brian Siano, "A Commentary on *Dr. Strangelove*," Visual Memory, 1995, http://www.visual-memory.co.uk/amk/doc/0017.html.

32. See Newman, "Two Discussions of Thermonuclear War." Anybody who has an interest in Herman Kahn simply must read Sharon Ghamari-Tabrizi's superb *The Worlds of Herman Kahn*.

33. Kahn, *On Thermonuclear War*, x, 3, 4.

34. This is explored in some detail in Ghamari-Tabrizi, *The Worlds of Herman Kahn*.

35. Kahn, *On Thermonuclear War*, 46, 49–50.

36. Kahn, *On Thermonuclear War*, 144–50.

37. As discussed in Smith, *Doomsday Men*.

38. George, *Red Alert*, 61–63.

39. Kahn, *On Thermonuclear War*, 205–8.

40. Ghamari-Tabrizi, *The Worlds of Herman Kahn*, 274–76.

41. Michael Hill, "Making Sense of Deadly Games," *Baltimore Sun*, 16 October 2005.

42. See Southern, "Check-Up with Dr. Strangelove"; Terry Southern, "Notes from the War Room," Visual Memory, accessed 22 September 2019, http://www.visual-memory.co.uk/amk/doc/0081.html.

43. See George, *Dr. Strangelove*; Ghamari-Tabrizi, *The Worlds of Herman Kahn*, 362–63.

44. Rapf, *Sidney Lumet*, 27.

45. Burdick and Wheeler, *Fail-Safe*, 35–40.

46. Burdick and Wheeler, *Fail-Safe*, 40.

47. Burdick and Wheeler, *Fail-Safe*, 133–39.

48. Burdick and Wheeler, *Fail-Safe*, 89–97.

49. See Association for Diplomatic Studies and Training, interview with Chester H. Opal by G. Lewis Schmidt, 10 January 1989, http://adst.org/oral-history/oral-history-interviews/.

50. Burdick and Wheeler, *Fail-Safe*, 70–71, 158.

51. Kennedy Library, National Security Files, Staff Memoranda: Carl Kaysen, draft paper, "Responsible Nuclear Policy," 13 February 1961.

52. Kennedy Library, National Security Files, U.S. Air Force (USAF) Director of Information to Office of the Secretary of the Air Force, "Air Force Appraisal of 'Fail-Safe,'" 23 November 1962.

53. Obituaries, *St. Petersburg Times*, 13 December 1976. Thanks to Fritz Heinzen for digging this much up.

54. Rascovich, *The Bedford Incident.*

55. Melinda Burdick, "In PB on Maiden Voyage," *Palm Beach Daily News*, 22 June 1972; Inter-American Tropical Tuna Commission/Comision Interamericana del Atun Tropical, "Special Report." See also Bass and Rascovich, "A Device for the Tracking of Large Fishes," 75.

56. See Naval Historical Center data on USS *Besugo* at Naval History and Heritage Command, http://www.history.navy.mil/photos/sh-usn/usnsh-b/ss321.htm (link no longer active). See also "Hellcats of the Navy," Wikipedia, accessed 26 September 2019, http://en.wikipedia.org/wiki/Hellcats_of_the_Navy.

57. Rascovich, *The Bedford Incident*, 49–50, 62–63.

58. Rascovich, *The Bedford Incident*, 64.

59. Rascovich, *The Bedford Incident*, 64–65.

60. Rascovich, *The Bedford Incident*, 68.

61. Baer, *One Hundred Years of Sea Power*, 161–63.

62. Rascovich, *The Bedford Incident*, 44, 85, 102–3, 113, 120, 125, 140, 156, 169.

63. Rascovich, *The Bedford Incident*, 62, 77,

64. Rascovich, *The Bedford Incident*, 259.

65. Rascovich, *The Bedford Incident*, 147.

66. Rascovich, *The Bedford Incident*, 181–92.

67. Rascovich, *The Bedford Incident*, 222, 225, 260–65.

68. Rascovich, *The Bedford Incident*, 276.

69. FOIA National Security Agency (NSA), Michael L. Peterson, "Maybe You Had to Be There: The SIGINT [Signals Intelligence] on Thirteen Soviet Shootdowns of US Reconnaissance Aircraft," from a classified issue of *Cryptologic Quarterly.*

70. Jane Hill, "Obituary: Antony Trew," *The Independent*, 23 January 1996.

71. Hill, "Antony Trew."

72. Hill, "Antony Trew." See also Wikipedia entries for HMS *Versatile* and HMS *Walker.*

73. See Gordon H. McCormick, "Stranger than Fiction: Soviet Submarine Operations in Swedish Waters," RAND, January 1990, http://www.rand.org/content/dam/rand/pubs/reports/2007/R3776.pdf.

74. Trew, *Two Hours to Darkness*, 55, 106.

75. Grove, *From Vanguard to Trident*, 240–43.

76. This commentary appears in the frontispiece of the 1975 Fontana edition of *Two Hours to Darkness.*

77. Trew, *Two Hours to Darkness*, 64.

78. Trew, *Two Hours to Darkness*, 58.

79. Trew, *Two Hours to Darkness*, 54.

80. Trew, *Two Hours to Darkness*, 143–44.

81. Trew, *Two Hours to Darkness*, 144–45.

82. Trew, *Two Hours to Darkness*, 144–45, 220–21.

83. Trew, *Two Hours to Darkness*, 163, 169.

84. Trew, *Two Hours to Darkness*, 179–80.

85. Trew, *Two Hours to Darkness*, 251–52.

2. Purity of Essence I

1. Perlstein, *Before the Storm*, 438–39. Goldwater was a World War II veteran and had time on B-47s, U-2s, and EC-135 command posts. See his entry on the National Aviation Hall of Fame website: http://www.nationalaviation.org/our-enshrinees/goldwater-barry/.

2. Library of Congress, Vandenberg Papers, box 83, Air Warfare, Misc. folder, personal notes of meetings from 5 April to 10 April 1951. These notes appear to have been written by Omar Bradley and distributed to the other Joint Chiefs. The targets had been determined after an RB-45C night reconnaissance penetration of Manchuria; the number of targets is the same number of nuclear weapons Truman previously authorized into theater: nine.

3. Galantin, *Submarine Admiral*, 198.

4. As quoted in Scrivner, "Pioneer into Space," 352.

5. Scrivner, "Pioneer into Space," 360–61.

6. Hersey, *The War Lover*, 380–83. See also Steve Call's take on the film in *Selling Air Power*, 145–50.

7. Why the Powers did not have children is difficult to determine from the records. Either they chose not to have children, or one or the other was incapable of having children. As for Power's strong and vocal anti-Communism, see the entire box of his speeches for the 1957 to 1970 period at Syracuse University Special Collections Research Center (SUSCRC), Power Papers, box 10.

8. Ripper's .30 caliber machine gun is in his golf bag, and there are pictures of B-24s in his office next to the bathroom. Power flew B-24s and was known for his golf prowess.

9. The exceptions are Thomas Coffey, Warren Kozak, and Barrett Tillman on LeMay, but there is no biography of Power. With no children or descendants, the Power line stops. LeMay's daughter defended him to local historians and to Kozak, but none of this has been able to balance the mass of negativity directed against the two SAC commanders.

10. Wade biographical data is located at the U.S. Air Force website: http://www.af.mil/AboutUs/Biographies/Display/tabid/225/Article/105330/general-horace-m-wade.aspx.

11. Anna Castleton, "Dr Strangelove and the Cold War Context," University of the Arts London, 29 January 2014, https://www.arts.ac.uk/about-ual/press-office/stories/dr-strangelove-and-the-cold-war-context; Paul Lashmar, "Dr Strangelove's Secrets," *The Independent*, 8 September 1998, http://www.independent.co.uk/arts-entertainment/dr-strangeloves-secrets-1196730.html.

12. Kaplan, *The Wizards of Armageddon*, 246.

13. Robert Dallek, "JFK vs. the Military," *The Atlantic*, August 2013, http://www.theatlantic.com/magazine/archive/2013/08/jfk-vs-the-military/309496/; David Nye, "5 US Military Officers Who Were Almost Certainly Crazy," *Business Insider*, 13 August 2015, http://www.businessinsider.com/5-general-officers-who-were-almost-certainly-crazy-2015-8; Carroll, *House of War*, 267, 433; "Curtis LeMay: Demented Cold Warrior," OoCities, accessed 23 September 2019, http://www.oocities.org/lemaycurtis/.

14. Richard Rhodes, "The General and World War III," *New Yorker*, 11 June 1995, http://www.newyorker.com/magazine/1995/06/19/the-general-and-world-war-iii.

15. Castleton, "Dr Strangelove and the Cold War Context."

16. "General Carey Sacked for Exposing SAC's Problems," *The Local*, 3 December 2014, http://www.thelocal.se/discuss/index.php?showtopic=61253&st=15&start=15.

17. "Deep Background: The Rift between General LeMay and JFK," JFK Countercoup, accessed 23 September 2019, http://jfkcountercoup.blogspot.com/2012/02/deep-background-lemay-jfk.html.

18. In fact Power joked about Roswell with Gen. Roger Ramey in 1947. See SUSCRC, Power Papers, box 2, Power to Ramey, 1 August 1947: "I got a kick out of your letter in which you give a vivid description of the action that took place when Blanchard's flying disk hit Fort Worth"; Ramey to Power, 16 July 1947: "You son of a gun, I must have got fifty copies of that God damn clipping you sent. . . . My God, I had a session over that damn thing. Blanchard's dumb [public information officer] went off his pivot when the rancher brought the damn stuff in and gave an AP release to the effect that they had located remnants of the flying disk (he's doing KP now)."

19. Bundy, *Danger and Survival*; Kaufman, *The McNamara Strategy*; Garthoff, *Reflections on the Cuban Missile Crisis*; Raskin, *Liberalism*, 201; Kennedy and Sorensen, *Thirteen Days*; Rosenblith, *Jerry Wiesner*, 251. O'Donnell is quoted in Dallek, "JFK vs. the Military." Ambassador Richard Townshend Davis noted in an oral history interview, "Arthur Schlesinger, Jr. wrote a very good account. Of course most of the time—that is beginning October the 22nd, the Monday, when Kennedy gave his speech—he was up in New York working with Adlai Stevenson, so he wasn't there the week of the crisis itself. He was there before that. But then again he wasn't a member of the Executive Committee. Ted Sorensen's book is very good. And Elie Abel's. And Bobby Kennedy's book itself is excellent. But they were all parti pris, they all had preconceived opinions. Inevitably they couldn't be objective. You can't be, particularly when you are involved the way both Sorensen and Bobby Kennedy and to a lesser extent Arthur Schlesinger were." See Association for Diplomatic Studies and Training, interview by Peter Jessup, 9 November 1979, http://adst.org/oral-history/oral-history-interviews/.

20. This is evident reading both Taylor, *The Uncertain Trumpet*, and Kaufman, *The McNamara Strategy*.

21. FOIA CIA, [Redacted] to Allen Dulles, 31 March 1960, "General Power's Testimony to the McMahon Committee, 22 March 1960."

22. Stern, *The Week the World Stood Still*, 66.

23. Brugioni, *Eyeball to Eyeball*, 262.

24. Walsh, *Air Force One*, 51.

25. Walsh, *Air Force One*, 81.

26. For example, see Carroll, *House of War*, 22, who dutifully uses the quote without context.

27. "War and Peace in the Nuclear Age; Bigger Bang for the Buck, A; Interview with Jerome Wiesner, 1986 [1]," Open Vault, 27 March 1986, http://openvault.wgbh.org/catalog/V_DD3A084107E94632B6AD7D428A966304.

28. Jerome Wiesner opposed practically every program LeMay championed in the 1960s. He was a major proponent of the Comprehensive Test Ban Treaty, pushed for the

creation of the Arms Control and Disarmament Agency, "and resisted efforts to preserve the strategic superiority of the United States" as well as opposed Civil Defense and (anti-ballistic missile) ABM projects. See James R. Schlesinger, "Pieties, Arms Policies, and the Scientist-Politician," RAND, May 1965, http://www.rand.org/content/dam/rand/pubs/papers/2008/P3140.pdf.

29. See DuBois, *Resurrection Day*. Gen. Curtis "The Rammer" Ramsey is the LeMay analogue. The *Fatherland*-like plot has Ramsey eliminating all of the New Frontiersmen and Whiz Kids who have survived the war because they might reveal the fact he started it.

30. See "Authors," 53.

31. Wisconsin Center for Film and Theater Research, Douglas Papers, Kubrick to Douglas, 8 February 1963, http://old.wcftr.commarts.wisc.edu/collections/featured/kirkdouglas/film/sevendays/7days-kubrick.html.

32. Wisconsin Center for Film and Theater Research, Douglas Papers, Knebel and Bailey to Douglas, 4 February 1963, "Re: Screenplay for 'Seven Days in May.'"

33. None of these aspects of the production are noted by Knebel in his extensive oral history interview by the Kennedy Library staff. See Kennedy Library, "Fletcher Knebel Oral History," 1 August 1977, http://www.jfklibrary.org/Asset-Viewer/Archives/JFKOH-FLK-01.aspx.

34. Patrick Kiger, "The Movie That JFK Wanted Made, but Didn't Live to See," *Boundary Stones*: WETA's *Washington DC History Ring*, blog, 13 May 2014, http://blogs.weta.org/boundarystones/2014/05/13/movie-jfk-wanted-made-didnt-live-see; Bruce Lambert, "Fletcher Knebel, Writer, 81 Dies: Co-Author of 'Seven Days in May,'" *New York Times*, 28 February 1993; Adam Bernstein, "Charles W. Bailey: Co-Wrote 'Seven Days in May,'" *Washington Post*, 9 January 2012.

35. "ACLU Praises Federal Action in Meredith Case, Questions Handling of General Walker," *Civil Liberties*, November 1962; "The General Resigns," *Times Record*, 4 November 1961; "Former General Still Contends He Was Framed," *Corsicana Daily Sun*, 5 April 1962.

36. Kiger, "The Movie That JFK Wanted Made, but Didn't Live to See."

37. Salinger, *John F. Kennedy*, viii.

38. Fletcher Knebel, "Potomac Fever," *Corvallis Gazette Times*, 25 May 1961.

39. Tom Carson, "The Two Men Who Invented the Modern (Fictional) President," *The Washingtonian*, 14 January 2016.

40. Kennedy Library, "Fletcher Knebel Oral History."

41. Leavitt, *Following the Flag*, 238–39.

42. Jack Raymond, "Ex-AF Boss Asserts US Misusing Air Power in Viet," *Salt Lake Tribune*, 22 October 1965.

43. LeMay and Kantor, *Mission with LeMay*, 565.

44. There are just too many to list here.

45. Stone, *The Best of I. F. Stone*, 326–38.

46. In my collection.

47. Art Buchwald, "Columnist No Longer Has Nuclear Weapons Phobia," *Idaho State Journal*, 8 October 1968.

48. "Garden-ing with the Editor," *Garden City Telegram*, 16 October 1968.

49. "Kennedy Memoirs Add New Details," *New Herald*, 21 October 1968.

50. "Muskie Has the Answer," *Times San Mateo*, 18 October 1968.

51. See film commentary on *Twilight's Last Gleaming* DVD with author and Aldrich biographer Alain Silver referencing Mackenzie as LeMay. Silver also references LeMay's alleged role in the Bay of Pigs and Cuban Missile Crisis as contributory factors to Aldrich's belief that "the military" was out of control. As we know, LeMay had nothing to do with the Bay of Pigs, and portrayals of his involvement in the Cuban affair have become heavily distorted.

52. Fleming, *The Anti-Communist Manifestos*, 159.

53. Haynes and Klehr, *Venona*, 247–48; Romerstein and Breindel, *The Venona Secrets*, 432–39; Holland, "I. F. Stone."

54. As detailed in Koch's *Double Lives*.

55. See Klehr et al., *The Secret World of American Communism*, 15–19.

56. As noted in Richelson, *Sword and Shield*, 148. See also Walters, "Perceptions Management."

57. Walters, "Perceptions Management," 59–62.

58. See Dickey, "Russian Political Warfare," 55.

59. FOIA CIA, Alma Fryxell, "Psywar by Forgery: A Case Study of How the Sino-Soviet Bloc Intelligence Services Provide Black Support for Overt Psychological Warfare Themes," n.d.

60. Fryxell, "Psywar by Forgery."

61. Fryxell, "Psywar by Forgery."

62. George Fielding Eliot, "Reds Spread Scare Tales," *The Pantagraph*, 8 December 1957.

63. Drew Pearson, "H-Bomb Laden Airplanes Wait at Moroccan Field," *Nevada State Journal*, 31 December 1957.

64. The literature on the Soviet abuse of psychiatry and psychology is equally massive. A good summation is Alexandra (Sasha) Shapiro, "Medicine Standing on Its Head: Snezhnevsky, Sluggish Schizophrenia, and Soviet Political Abuse of Psychiatry," originally published in *Vestnik: The Journal of Russian and Asian Studies*, http://www.sras.org/snezhnevsky_schizophrenia_soviet_psychiatry (site no longer active). See also European Parliament Directorate-General for External Policies Policy Department, "Psychiatry as a Tool for Coercion in Post-Soviet Countries," 2013, http://www.europarl.europa.eu/RegData/etudes/etudes/join/2013/433723/EXPO-DROI_ET(2013)433723_EN.pdf. Note that the implication that there was/is something pathologically wrong with the mental processes of those in the United States who employ game theory or are involved with the fabrication of nuclear weapons or doctrines for their use was promulgated as late as 2005 by Psychologists for Social Responsibility in "Using Psychology to Help Abolish Nuclear Weapons: A Handbook," http://www.psysr.org/about/pubs_resources/Using_Psychology_to_Help_Abolish_Nuclear_Weapons.pdf. This document notes, "The depiction of Dr Strangelove exaggerates but also captures an aspect of the motivation of individuals who have devoted their adult careers to the development of nuclear weapons." Psychologists for Social Responsibility provides helpful verbiage and definitions to peace activists for use in antinuclear propaganda, like "aggression and destruction motivation," "bullying," "burnout," "death wish," "desensitization," "dissociation," "fatalism," "game theory," "groupthink," and so on.

65. "US Defends Carrying Unarmed Atomic Bombs," *Daily Herald of Provo*, 13 March 1958; "Gromyko Warns about SAC Flights," *Traverse City Record*, 29 April 1958.

66. Preston Glover, "Red Star Finds Mental Cases," *Corsicana Daily Sun*, 5 April 1962.

67. Robert Allen and Paul Scott, "Space Budget Will Clear US House," *Evening Standard*, 7 May 1962. On Eatherly's disposition, see Thomas and Witts, *Ruin from the Air*, 56–57.

68. LeMay and Smith, *America Is in Danger*, 8.

3. Purity of Essence II

1. Richard G. Hubler, "Gen LeMay Made the SAC Tough and Ever Ready-to-Fly Outfit," *Advocate Messenger*, 24 August 1958.

2. "LeMay's Famed Stogie Quenched," *Lincoln Star*, 8 May 1949; "Air General LeMay Gives Up His Cigars," *Courier Journal*, 8 May 1949. He didn't give them up for long.

3. Based on my analysis of 345 American newspaper articles, 1948–60.

4. Bob Considine, "On the Lines," *Cumberland News*, 26 September 1951.

5. "Capitol Stuff . . . O'Donnell," *Brownsville Herald*, 14 May 1952.

6. "Air Force Discloses Record Flights; Three Counts against LeMay Choice," *Corsicana Daily Sun*, 20 May 1953.

7. Frank Miller, "A Look at Three Important Men," *Des Moines Register*, 18 January 1955.

8. Louis Cassels, "General Curtis LeMay Alarmed about State of US Defenses," *La Grande Observer*, 6 February 1958.

9. Hubler, "Gen LeMay Made the SAC Tough."

10. Distilled from LeMay and Kantor, *Mission with LeMay*; Kozak, *LeMay*; Coffey, *Iron Eagle*.

11. See LeMay and Kantor, *Mission with LeMay*, book 3.

12. LeMay and Kantor, *Mission with LeMay*, 222.

13. "Cigar Remark Nets Protest," *Plain Speaker*, 4 May 1959.

14. Call, *Selling Air Power*, 59–67.

15. LeMay and Kantor, *Mission with LeMay*, 218.

16. As described in Coffey, *Decision over Schweinfurt*.

17. Tillman, *LeMay*, 187; "General Keeps His Hand In," *Kansas City Times*, 5 February 1954; Bem Price, "He Gets Things Done—New Air Chief LeMay," *Detroit Free Press*, 26 June 1961.

18. Tillman, *LeMay*, 187–88.

19. Coffey, *Iron Eagle*, 334.

20. U.S. Air Force Oral History Program, interview with Maj. Gen. Robert N. Ginsburgh, 11 December 1979.

21. Nebraska State Historical Society, "Interview with Jane LeMay Lodge, Daughter of Gen. Curtis LeMay, September 10, 1998," http://d1vmz9r13e2j4x.cloudfront.net/nebstudies/0904_0302jane.pdf.

22. Nebraska State Historical Society, "Interview with Jane LeMay Lodge," 97, 279.

23. LeMay and Smith, *America Is in Danger*, x.

24. Nebraska State Historical Society, "Interview with Jane LeMay Lodge."

25. There was an exchange between Nathan Twining and LeMay in response to a Department of Defense study on the female reenlistment problem: "We can accept the fact that many young women intend to marry instead of staying in the service. We cannot accept that seventy-three percent of our enlisted women intend to leave the service and only twenty-three percent are willing to urge other women to join." See Library of Congress, LeMay Papers, box 60, Twining to LeMay, 30 December 1952, and LeMay to Twining, 15 January 1953.

26. Kozak, *LeMay*, 296.

27. Library of Congress, LeMay Papers, box B-58, Nugent to LeMay, 20 February 1950.

28. Library of Congress, LeMay Papers, box B-59, Hutchison folder, Hutchison to LeMay, 20 March 1950.

29. Library of Congress, LeMay Papers, box B-58, Ramey folder, LeMay to Ramey, 10 October 1949. In a massive study on U.S. Armed Forces integration, neither LeMay nor Power nor even SAC is mentioned in any negative context. Indeed the "focal point for staff opposition" to integration in the air force was Gen. Muir Fairchild. See MacGregor, *Integration of the Armed Forces.*

30. Canadian Department of National Defence, file 193.009 (D 53), Secretary of State for External Affairs to Canadian ambassador, Washington, 14 April 1949.

31. Library of Congress, LeMay Papers, box B-54, Johnson folder, Johnson to LeMay, 8 November 1949, and Power to Johnson, 23 November 1949.

32. MacGregor, *Integration of the Armed Forces,* 409. There were other incidents like this, where air force personnel forcibly integrated segregated restaurants and theaters in the South, years before the Congress of Racial Equality was doing so.

33. Library of Congress, LeMay Papers, box B-128, Air Force, Secretary of, July–December 1961 folder, memo for Chief of Staff USAF from Goode, "Assignment of Military Personnel," 24 October 1961.

34. See Library of Congress, LeMay Papers, box 201, "SAC Commander's Conference April 1954," 6 April 1954, Staff Judge Advocate, "Abuse of Military Personnel by Civilian Authorities."

35. Drew Pearson, column, *Oneonta Star,* 13 May 1965.

36. Nebraska State Historical Society, "Interview with Jane LeMay Lodge."

37. Kozak, *LeMay,* 122.

38. LeMay and Kantor, *Mission with LeMay,* 182.

39. LeMay and Kantor, *Mission with LeMay,* 335–38.

40. LeMay's response to the Berlin Crisis can be found in LeMay and Kantor, *Mission with LeMay,* 410–26, and Coffey, *Iron Eagle,* ch. 16.

41. LeMay and Kantor, *Mission with LeMay,* 441.

42. LeMay and Kantor, *Mission with LeMay,* 382.

43. Weisgall, *Operation CROSSROADS,* 125–28.

44. Coffey, *Iron Eagle,* 254.

45. Library of Congress, LeMay Papers, box B-58, Quesada folder.

46. Library of Congress, Le May Papers, box 197, memo for the record, "Visit of the Commanding General, Strategic Air Command, to HQ USAF on 4 April 1952," 8 April 1952.

47. Library of Congress, Le May Papers, box 200, LeMay to Mills, 7 February 1953.

48. Library of Congress, Le May Papers, box 104, "Commanding General's Daily Diary for 6–7 May 53."

49. Library of Congress, Le May Papers, box 104, Journal Item, D/Plans, 15 June 1953.

50. See FOIA USAF Wright Air Development Center, "Operation Castle Project 6.2a Blast and Thermal Effects on B-36 Aircraft in Flight, Report to the Test Director, June 1956."

51. Library of Congress, LeMay Papers, box B-184, "Op Castle" folder.

52. LeMay's "Daily Diary/Items for the Commander" is not in his papers for May and June 1956. The Redwing shots were conducted from May to July, but the SAC-oriented shots were in May and June.

53. See Rosenberg, "Origins of Overkill."

54. For a comparison of the USAF and U.S. Navy (USN), see Thomas Kunkle and Byron Ristvet, "Castle Bravo: Fifty Years of Legend and Lore, January 2013," https://apps.dtic.mil/docs/citations/ADA572278.

55. Library of Congress, LeMay Papers, box B-185, "9–11 April 1958 National Association of State and Territorial Civil Defense Directors Semi Annual Meeting."

56. Dorothy Thompson, "Russia's Tactics Producing Results," *Lincoln Star*, 1 January 1956; Drew Pearson, "Predictions for 1958," *Joplin Globe*, 1 January 1958; Warren Rogers, "New Censorship Charges Make Defense Dept Edgy," *Corpus Christie Caller Times*, 19 September 1959. See also Silverstone, *Preventive War and American Democracy*.

57. Carroll, *House of War*, 222–23.

58. Lapp, *Kill and Overkill*, 104–5.

59. FOIA USAF, interview conducted with Gen. Curtis E. LeMay, USAF (Ret.) by USAF historical staff, 16 November 1972.

60. "War and Peace in the Nuclear Age; Bigger Bang for the Buck, A; Interview with Jerome Wiesner, 1986 [1]."

61. "War and Peace in the Nuclear Age; Bigger Bang for the Buck, A; Interview with David Jones, 1986 [1]," Open Vault, 28 June 1986, http://openvault.wgbh.org/catalog/V_4C9DD9F57A6041ACB0695FC332B548F8.

62. LeMay, *America Is in Danger*, 1–2.

63. Joe Frantz, interview with Gen. Curtis LeMay, Miller Center, 28 June 1971, http://millercenter.org/scripps/archive/oralhistories/detail/2697 (site no longer active).

64. Kennedy Library, "Kaysen, Carl: Oral History Interview," 7 November 1966, https://www.jfklibrary.org/Asset-Viewer/Archives/JFKOH-CK-01.aspx.

65. FOIA USAF, U.S. Air Force Oral History Program, "Interview with General Richard H. Ellis," 19 June 1979.

66. Another example: LeMay was portrayed by Jim Backus in the 1951 film *Above and Beyond*. Backus, a comedian, later played Thurston Howell III in the long-running sitcom *Gilligan's Island* in the 1960s at the time LeMay was running into controversy over the Wallace ticket and Vietnam. The effect of LeMay being associated with *Gilligan's Island* via the metamedium of Jim Backus is unmeasurable but interesting to contemplate.

67. Hubler, "Gen LeMay Made the SAC Tough."

68. Douglas Larsen, "New SAC Commander Is Very Much Like His Predecessor," *Plain Speaker*, 24 June 1957.

69. Jan Burns, "Power Finds New Tools, Old Spirit," *Lincoln Star*, 11 August 1957.

70. Vern Haugland, "Precision's a Habit with New SAC Chief," *Corpus Christie Caller Times*, 23 June 1957.

71. Burns, "Power Finds New Tools, Old Spirit."

72. Larsen, "New SAC Commander Is Very Much Like His Predecessor."

73. "Personality Spotlight: SAC Chief Caught 'Flying Fever,'" *Kingsport News*, 24 April 1958.

74. "Barnard School for Boys," Wikipedia, accessed 26 September 2019, https://en.wikipedia.org/wiki/Barnard_School_for_Boys.

75. SUSCRC, Power Papers, box 9, folder "Kenneth Leish interview with Thomas Power, July 1960."

76. SUSCRC, Power Papers, box 9, document "Thomas Sarsfield Power (0-17854)." The implication that Power was an intellectual dullard because he didn't have higher education persists.

77. SUSCRC, Power Papers, box 2, Dad to Tommy, 7 March 1945.

78. SUSCRC, Power Papers, box 9, folder "Kenneth Leish interview with Thomas Power, July 1960."

79. Power and Arnhym, *Design for Survival*, 21.

80. SUSCRC, Power Papers, box 9, folder "Kenneth Leish interview with Thomas Power, July 1960."

81. Power and Arnhym, *Design for Survival*, 21.

82. SUSCRC, Power Papers, box 9, folder: "Kenneth Leish interview with Thomas Power, July 1960."

83. SUSCRC, Power Papers, box 11, Information Division, HQ Strategic Air Command "Major General Thomas Sarsfield Power USAF."

84. SUSCRC, Power Papers, box 9, folder "Kenneth Leish interview with Thomas Power, July 1960."

85. There are letters back and forth between relatives, the chaplain, and the aggrieved but none from Power. He ensured that the family was informed as rapidly as possible: LeMay contacted Norstad, who immediately sent an officer to the family in Colorado Springs. SUSCRC, Power Papers, box 2, Norstad to LeMay and Power, 15 April 1945.

86. Power and Arnhym, *Design for Survival*, 11.

87. Power and Arnhym, *Design for Survival*, 11.

88. Coffey, *Iron Eagle*, 274. Again, other than LeMay, we don't know who these subordinates and colleagues are.

89. Coffey, *Iron Eagle*, 275, 317.

90. As described in Kozak, *LeMay*, 287.

91. Wells, *The Life and Career*, 91.

92. SUSCRC, Power Papers, box 2, Power to Johnson, 21 November 1947.

93. SUSCRC, Power Papers, box 2, Carlton to McGlothlin, 26 February 1952.

94. Hudlow, *Shamrock* 22, 256. See also Burns, "Power Finds New Tools, Old Spirit"; Larsen, "New SAC Commander Is Very Much Like His Predecessor."

95. According to Hudlow, Power sent a T-39 to get her; it got her back to Offutt AFB before him because her plane was faster.

96. Hudlow, *Shamrock* 22, 256.

97. "Air Force Pilot Grounded Permanently," *Ludington Daly News*, 11 December 1959.

98. SUSCRC, Power Papers, box 4, Evans to Power, 15 December 1958. Evans's letter is not in the groveling category, incidentally. For an example of that, see the exchange between Power and Ireland, 25 September 1961.

99. SUSCRC, Power Papers, box 4, Power to Evans, 18 December 1958. Based on the transmittal markings on the letter, Horace Wade may have modified the language in it initially, but Power rewrote it.

100. SUSCRC, Power Papers, box 5, Power to Reed, 14 March 1960.

101. SUSCRC, Power Papers, box 4, Speer to Sessums, 8 August 1957.

102. D'Este, *Eisenhower*, 87, 91–92, 179, 209, 239.

103. Zumwalt, *On Watch*, 85–95.

104. SUSCRC, Power Papers, box 2, Bergan to Power, 29 April 1949; Wegner to Power, 24 October 1950; box 3, Wegner to Power, 17 September 1952; box 6, Mae Power to Becker, 12 February 1963.

105. SUSCRC, Power Papers, box 5, Power to Cushing, 17 September 1952.

106. *Texas Catholic*, 1 August 1964, has a picture of the Powers receiving the honors from Archbishop Gerald Bergan in Omaha.

107. SUSCRC, Power Papers, box 6, Power to Kanoi, 20 June 1952. There is significant correspondence in the Power Papers related to judo as well as photo albums and newspaper clippings of Power performing and competing.

108. Spellman was vicar during the war and appointed as such by President Roosevelt. He was involved with a series of diplomatic and humanitarian initiatives regarding the future of Italy in American policy and made contact with his friend and mentor Pope Pius XII throughout 1944. Spellman became archbishop of New York City in 1940, long after Power had joined the air corps and moved on. The probability that they met in Italy in 1944 is high; Spellman would have had to use military transportation, and as the vicar he served mass to the troops regularly.

109. Nor was he anywhere near, let alone in, the same league as those perpetrating evangelical bullying at the U.S. Air Force Academy in the 2000s. See James E. Parco and Barry S. Fagin, "The One True Religion in the Military," *The Humanist*, September–October 2007, http://www.faginfamily.net/barry/Papers/Humanist.pdf.

110. Brings, *We Believe in Prayer*, 612–13. Interestingly enough the CIA was keeping track of this book and its contributors. FOIA CIA, Letter from L. M. Brings, "An Invitation Addressed to World Leaders," 16 May 1958.

111. Power and Arnhym, *Design for Survival*, 27.

112. SUSCRC, Power Papers, box 1, Communications and Writings folder, Arthur Spiegelman, "Cliches and Survival," *The Record*, 20 March 1965. There is no evidence in the Venona records that Art Spiegelman was a card-carrying Communist.

113. Power and Arnhym, *Design for Survival*, 11.

114. SUSCRC, Power Papers, box 9, Atomic Energy Commission clearance form, 18 March 1947.

115. Power and Arnhym, *Design for Survival*, 12.

116. SUSCRC, Power Papers, box 4, Power to Murray, 18 April 1959.

117. The book has a character who is SAC's intelligence officer and briefs another character on a relatively accurate picture of the situation in 1959. He also remarks, "LeMay says the only way a general can win a modern war is not to fight one." Frank, *Alas, Babylon*, 33.

118. SUSCRC, Power Papers, box 6, Power to Frank, 2 December 1963.

119. Warren Burkett, "In Nuclear War, Nobody Wins," *Abilene Reporter News*, 15 January 1959.

120. Power and Arnhym, *Design for Survival*, 37.

121. SUSCRC, Power Papers, box 7, Reagan to Power, 19 August 1968.

122. This is echoed by Adm. George Anderson. See FOIA Department of Defense, "Oral History Interview with Admiral George W. Anderson Chief of Naval Operations, 1961 to 1963, May 17, 1984." Preventive war was discussed "for planning purposes, for consideration."

123. SUSCRC, Power Papers, box 4, Arnhym to Power, 5 July 1958.

124. SUSCRC, Power Papers, box 4, Power to Arnhym, 30 June 1958.

125. SUSCRC, Power Papers, box 5, Arnhym to Williams, 28 February 1962.

126. Power and Arnhym, *Design for Survival*, 68.

127. Library of Congress, LeMay Papers, box B-185, "9–11 April 1958 National Association of State and Territorial Civil Defense Directors Semi-Annual Meeting." LeMay addressed this gathering and took substantial questions.

128. SUSCRC, Power Papers, box 10, folder "Outline for Informal Remarks."

4. Purity of Essence III

1. I am being deliberately reductionist and provocative. There is substantial literature on deterrence theory. On the evolution of deterrence, see Brams, *Superpower Games*; Morgan, *Deterrence*; George and Smoke, *Deterrence in American Foreign Policy*; Steiner, *Bernard Brodie and the Foundations of American Nuclear Strategy*. See also Kuklick, *Blind Oracles*, 59.

2. See, for example, Taylor, *The Uncertain Trumpet*.

3. National Security Council, "A Report to the National Security Council by the Executive Secretariat on Basic National Security Policy, October 30, 1953," https://history.state .gov/historicaldocuments/frus1952-54v02p1/d101.

4. U.S. Air Force Historical Research Agency, SAC Command historian interview with Gen. Curtis LeMay, 16 November 1972.

5. "Influence operations are focused on affecting the perceptions and behaviors of leaders, groups, or entire populations. Influence operations employ capabilities to affect behaviors, protect operations, communicate commander's intent, and project accurate information to achieve desired effects across the cognitive domain. These effects should result in differing behavior or a change in the adversary's decision cycle, which aligns with the commander's objectives." See Air Force Doctrine Document 2-5, https://www.hsdl .org/?abstract&did=439852.

6. LeMay and Smith, *America Is in Danger*, 77.

7. Brugioni, *Eyeball to Eyeball*, 264.

8. FOIA Department of Defense, "Notes on visit with General Curtis LeMay, Newport Beach, California, December 30, 1984."

9. SUSCRC, Power Papers, box 2, Correspondence 1948 file, Power to Schlatter (AFOAT), 22 November 1948.

10. Library of Congress, Twining Papers, box 76, LeMay to Twining, 18 June 55.

11. LeMay and Kantor, *Mission with LeMay*, 482.

12. Kohn and Harahan, *Strategic Air Warfare*, 109.

13. Abella, *Soldiers of Reason*, 13–15.

14. LeMay and Kantor, *Mission with LeMay*, has no mention of RAND at all. In numerous cases RANDists sent studies to LeMay, and LeMay's staff sent polite thank-you letters back with the boss's signature. Paul Johnstone, who served in various war planning capacities in the USAF from the 1940s to the 1960s, discusses the lack of analyst influence throughout his memoir *From Mad to Madness*.

15. SUSCRC, Power Papers, box 2, Correspondence 1950 and 1951 folder, LeMay to Brodie, 27 December 1950; Brodie to Power, 22 December 1950; Power to Brodie, 3 January 1951; SUSCRC, Power Papers, box 4, Power to Henderson, 22 September 1959.

16. Library of Congress, LeMay Papers, box 192, Vandenberg to LeMay, 1 April 1950.

17. Library of Congress, LeMay Papers, box 196, LeMay to Kelly, 29 December 1951.

18. Library of Congress, LeMay Papers, box 200, LeMay to Twining, 22 May 1953, emphasis added.

19. Paul Leach, "Hard Gen. LeMay Keeps SAC on 24-Hour Alert," *Corpus Christie Caller-Times*, 1 May 1955.

20. Fort Benning, "The History of Army Combatives," https://www.benning.army.mil/Infantry/199th/Combatives/content/TCC-TSP/History_Combatives.pdf. See also Library of Congress, LeMay Papers, box 197, "SAC Commander's Conference 2 June 1952," SAC judo instructors agenda item and instructions.

21. Power's papers include photo albums of his judo kata and competitions as well as his black belt certification. LeMay's papers contain his black belt certification update in 1964 and numerous photos of him with his black belt engaged in training. Both men continued to practice judo into their fifties.

22. On the history of judo, see Carr, "Making Way." The irony, of course, is that LeMay and Power led the firebombing of Japan yet adopted a Japanese martial art.

23. This from Brig. C. H. Dewhurst, who was military attaché in Tito's Yugoslavia and then went on to lead the Military Liaison Mission in Potsdam in the first half of the 1950s. His depiction of open-source intelligence collection methodology is cogent. See *Close Contact*, 47–50.

24. Library of Congress, LeMay Papers, box B-51, Cabell folder, LeMay to Cabell, 24 November 1950. This was the so-called Glacier Priest affair.

25. Don Whitehead, "Free World Pins Hope of Life on Lemay's A-Bombers," *Nashville Tennessean*, 21 March 1954; "LeMay Puts Air Command on 24-Hour War Basis," *Arizona Republic*, 21 March 1954; "Thor of the Atomic Thunderbolt," *Courier Journal*, 21 March 1954. The *Courier Journal* reporter had his mythology confused. It was Odin who had the thunderbolt; Thor had the hammer.

26. "Strength Keeps Peace—LeMay," *Nebraska State Journal*, 15 February 1949.

27. Association for Diplomatic Studies and Training, "Richard W. Barham: Reflections of a Foreign Affairs Career Officer (2016)," http://adst.org/oral-history/oral-history-interviews/.

28. See LeMay and Kantor, *Mission with LeMay*, 31; "Television Receiving Set Production, 1947–1953," Television History: The First 75 Years, http://www.tvhistory.tv/facts-stats.htm.

29. Bob Considine, "Big Ship Awes Actor," *Cincinnati Enquirer*, 29 March 1955; Bob Considine, "Eisenhower Run Again?," *Cincinnati Enquirer*, 12 October 55; Leach, "Hard Gen. LeMay Keeps SAC on 24-Hour Alert"; "Modern Bomber Equal to 1,000 WWII Planes Says General," *Corsicana Daily Sun*, 5 December 1955; KMTV advertisement, *Des Moines Register*, 20 May 1955; "SAC—Our Frightening War Machine," *Kokomo Tribune*, 25 October 1955.

30. Call, *Selling Air Power*, 59–61, 99.

31. Library of Congress, LeMay Papers, box B-104, "Commander's Diary: 13 July 1953–18 July 1953."

32. SUSCRC, Power Papers, box 3, Lay to Power, 2 April 1955.

33. Call, *Selling Air Power*, 115.

34. Reed and Stillman, *The Nuclear Express*, 38–41.

35. See, for example, FOIA USAF, "9th Bombardment Wing, Appendix 'A' February–March 1960." Ex Play Back, an Emergency War Order test exercise, is almost an exact replica of the maneuver depicted in the film.

36. Castleton, "Dr. Strangelove and the Cold War Context." See also Lashmar, *Spy Flights of the Cold War*, particularly ch. 19. Richard Rhodes makes similar allegations in *Dark Sun*, 562–68.

37. FOIA CIA, memo for the record, "Meeting with USAF Representatives Regarding USAF Photo Reconnaissance Requirements," 15 February 1952.

38. Library of Congress, LeMay Papers, box 195, Close to Power, 6 June 1951; Library of Congress, Twining Papers, box 121, Slessor to Vandenberg, 12 September 1952.

39. As discussed in Hall, "The Truth about Overflights." See also FOIA Department of Defense, "Notes on a Visit with General Curtis E. LeMay, Newport Beach, California, December 30, 1984."

40. FOIA CIA, Information Report, "Soviet Early Warning Systems," 9 November 1954.

41. Jack Anderson and Fred Blumenthal, "The Untold Story of Our Air Force's 'Sunday Punch,'" *Parade* insert in *San Bernardino County Sun*, 11 March 1956.

42. Bob Considine, "SAC Chief Reports Red Turbo-Prop Can Penetrate US Defenses Now; Wants Guided Missile for Safety," *Corsicana Daily News*, 14 February 1956.

43. "LeMay Claims Edge for SAC," *Argus Record*, 4 December 1956.

44. "LeMay Calls A-Bomb Best Peace Guard," *Indianapolis Star*, 7 June 1957.

45. "B-50 Circles the World Non-Stop," *Lincoln Star*, 8 May 1949; "Tucson B-50 Circles the Globe in 4-Day Nonstop Flight," *Tucson Daily Citizen*, 2 March 1949.

46. "Three Jet Bombers Complete Non-Stop Flight around the World," *Shamokin News Dispatch*, 18 January 1957; "Three B-52s Circle Globe Non-Stop," *Santa Cruz Sentinel*, 18 January 1957.

47. "Nebraskan's World Flight Record Will Benefit the Future," *Lincoln Star*, 23 January 1957.

48. Nebraska State Historical Society, "Interview with Jane LeMay Lodge."

49. Power's aide, Maj. Marvin Speer, said it a bit differently: "Dear General Sessums: General Power requested that I advise you that he is planning to ride around in one of your aircraft." SUSCRC, Power Papers, box 4, Speer to Sessums, 8 August 1957.

50. Podvig, *Russian Strategic Nuclear Forces*, 489; Eisenhower Library, National Security Council Series, box 9, 339th meeting of the NSC, 11 October 1957. SAC intelligence would have known about the tests via AFOAT-1.

51. The public debate over exactly how many missiles the Soviets had and what American capability should be over the next three years was dubbed "the Missile Gap" and spoofed in *Dr. Strangelove* with the debate over "the mineshaft gap."

52. "Radio and Television Address to the American People on Science and National Security," American Presidency Project, 7 November 1957, https://www.presidency.ucsb.edu/documents/radio-and-television-address-the-american-people-science-national-security; "Radio and Television Address to the American People on Our Future Security," American Presidency Project, 13 November 1957, https://www.presidency.ucsb.edu/documents/radio-and-television-address-the-american-people-our-future-security. According to Coffey in *Iron Eagle*, 344–45, the division of labor between LeMay and Thomas White, the air force chief of staff, had White focusing on Joint Chiefs issues while LeMay handled the air force. One indicator that LeMay and Power were taking the initiative and building on the existing signaling foundation is that the media didn't quote White on the issue at hand until 29 November, and even then it was a rather derivative and pedestrian speech at

the National Press Club. See "White Says US Air Power Zeroes On Russ," *Redlands Daily Facts*, 29 November 1957.

53. SUSCRC, Power Papers, box 4, Norstad to Power, 15 October 1957.

54. "Bombers Standing By, Air Chief Warns Soviet," *Democrat and Chronicle*, 12 November 1957; "A-Bombs Anytime," *Logan Port Pharos Tribune*, 14 November 1957; "Reds Zeroed In by US Air Force," *Edwards Intelligencer*, 28 November 1957.

55. "All SAC Needs Is 30 Seconds," *Lincoln Evening Journal*, 14 November 1957; Howard Handleman, "Signal Flash Can Ignite US Attack," *Lubbock Evening Journal*, 13 November 1957; "SAC Placed on High Alert Status," *Kansas City Times*, 9 November 1957; Nick Lamberto, "Iowans Know SAC Is on the Job," *Des Moines Register*, 17 November 1957; "SAC Commander Orders Continuous Alert for Forces," *Abilene Reporter News*, 10 November 1957.

56. Nick Lamberto, "Iowans Find SAC Knows Job, Is Ready," *Des Moines Register*, 17 November 1957.

57. "SAC Steps Out," *Cincinnati Enquirer*, 15 November 1957; Howard Handleman, "SAC Chief Issues Notice to Russia," *Anderson Daily Bulletin*, 14 November 1957.

58. FOIA CIA, memo for the record, "Resume of OCB [Operations Coordinating Board] Luncheon Meeting," 29 October 1957.

59. "LeMay Jet Sets Nonstop Record to Boost Fading Bomber Prestige," *Democrat and Chronicle*, 12 November 1957; "Air Force Tanker Flies 6,350 Miles without Re-fueling," *Austin Daily Herald*, 12 November 1957; "Giant AF Plane in 6,350 Mile Non-Refuel Flight," *News Tribune*, 12 November 1957. Note that the press referred to the aircraft as a tanker, but it was in fact a prototype airborne command post. "Jet-Propelled Command Post Sets Two International Records," *Collins Signal*, Winter 1958, 4–7; "Air Force Is Prepared," *Albuquerque Journal*, 14 November 1957. See also "About Project Speckled Trout," Project Speckled Trout, accessed 24 September 2019, http://www.projectspeckledtrout.com/about.htm.

60. Iowa State Special Collections and University Archives (ISSCUA), Collins Radio Corporation Papers, box 34, Griswold file, "[Maximum Usable Frequency] for November 1957 Cedar Rapids to Buenos Aires, 8 800 km." See also LeMay and Kantor, *Mission with LeMay*, 515.

61. "Overseas Calls Beat Local Ones," *Post Standard*, 6 July 1958; Donald Pieper, "Communications Set-up Is Key to Swift Action," *Monroe News-Star*, 10 February 1959; "SAC Pilots Talk around the World," *Abilene Reporter News*, 4 June 1959.

62. "SAC Pilots Talk around the World."

63. ISSCUA, Collins Radio Corporation Papers, box 37, file Single Sideband Program 1953–1960, Royal Aircraft Establishment Technical Note No. RAD.521, G. W. Barnes, "A Controlled Carrier Single Sideband System for Aircraft Communication"; box 37, Everett Bray, "Collins Technical Report: A World-Wide High Frequency Single Sideband Radio Network, 15 March 1958."

64. SUSCRC, Power Papers, box 4, Power to McKee, 5 March 1959. Col. H. H. Arnhym was the project officer for the SAM.

65. These names are drawn from the files of the Power Papers, box 4, and are too numerable to list here.

66. FOIA CIA, memo for the record, "Resume of OCB [Operations Coordinating Board] Luncheon Meeting, 16 April 1958," 23 April 1958.

67. SUSCRC, Power Papers, box 5, Power to Holtz, 29 June 1960.

68. SUSCRC, Power Papers, box 5, Holtz to Power, 27 June 1960.

69. "Worthless? Brass Won't Talk," *Pasadena Independent*, 27 November 1957.

70. LeMay and Smith, *America Is in Danger*, 79.

71. SUSCRC, Power Papers, box 10, file "Outline for Informal Remarks." See also Power and Arnhym, *Design for Survival*, 99. Power kept an aide-mémoire of his concepts and ideas starting in early 1958. He used it to cut and paste his speeches paragraph by paragraph, depending on the audience and what he wanted to emphasize; it is clear that this document is the distillation of his thinking during this period. Power's assistant, Col. Albert A. Arnhym, crafted a manuscript from the ideas in this aide-mémoire in consultation with Power. This was the basis for the book *Design for Survival*, banned by Secretary of Defense Neil McElroy in 1958. It was published after Power retired in 1964 and reached number 10 on the best-seller list in the United States.

72. See Joseph Alsop, "Playing Russian Roulette," *Medford Mail*, 5 February 1959; "SAC Boss Says Plane Strength Not Adequate," *Arizona Republic*, 6 April 1959; Jack Raymond, "SAC Chief Says Defenses Are Weak," *Des Moines Register*, 6 April 1959; Bob Buchanan, "Strategic Air Command Is Alerted for Combat," *Daily Herald*, 18 June 1959; Ed Koterba, "Jet Deterrent," *Pittsburgh Press*, 8 September 1959; Esther Van Wagoner Tufty, "SAC's Constant Readiness: No Relaxing of Vigilance after Mr. K's Peace Talks," *Sedalia Democrat*, 9 October 1959.

73. SUSCRC, Power Papers, box 10. Each and every Power speech and article in this box was vetted by the Secretary of Defense's Office and the State Department. See also box 5, January 1962 file, Arnhym to Power and attachment, 10 January 1962.

74. Notably, when Selective Employment of Air/Ground Alert replaced Chrome Dome in 1968, it was done specifically so as not to jeopardize Single Integrated Operational Plan (SIOP) target coverage while allowing policymakers the ability to use nuclear operations for other purposes. This suggests that the Airborne Alert Force in its day-to-day configuration also had non-SIOP purposes before 1968.

75. Wells, *The Life and Career*, 102.

76. Lamberto, "Iowans Find SAC Knows Job, Is Ready."

77. "Low-Level Missions Scheduled by B-52s," *Vernon Daily Record*, 14 September 1959; "Levels Established for Bomber Flights," *Winona Daily News*, 5 November 1959; "Strategic Air Command Will Begin Low-Level Flights over Sikeston," *Daily Standard*, 13 November 1959; [No title, map and text only], *Houston Herald*, 19 November 1959.

78. ISSCUA, Collins Radio Corporation Papers, box 31, Griswold file, Oilburner map, 23 November 1959.

79. Power and Arnhym, *Design for Survival*, 69. Duff Cooper was a British Conservative politician who opposed appeasement in the 1930s.

5. Peace Is Our Profession

1. Blight and Welch, *On the Brink*, 99, 75.

2. Garthoff, *Reflections on the Cuban Missile Crisis*, 61–62.

3. Beschloss, *May-Day*, 256, 262; see also "U-2 Incident Wrecks Paris Summit Meeting."

4. Beschloss, *May-Day*, 278.

5. Beschloss, *May-Day*, 278.

6. It would be redesignated Korabl-Sputnik 1.

7. Peter Pesavento, "Declassifying the Space Race," *Aerospace America*, September 2012; FOIA NSA, "United States Cryptologic History Special Series Number 3: Space Surveillance Program"; Sven Grahn, "The Flight of Sputnik-4: Sunday 15 May 1960," http://www.svengrahn .pp.se/histind/Sputnik4/Sputnik4.html. Later in 1960, however, NSA was able to monitor and intercept communications between Korabl-Sputnik 1 and its masters. When the craft was supposed to be de-orbited, the Soviets accidentally fired the retrorockets in the wrong direction. This boosted the vehicle into a higher orbit, where it remained for five years before decaying. FOIA NSA, "Spacecraft Passenger Television from Laika to Gagarin," n.d. The Kettering Group was a group of young physics students led by Geoffrey Perry at Kettering Grammar School in the United Kingdom who tracked satellites using doppler-shift technology.

8. Horne, *Harold Macmillan*, 227.

9. Library of Congress, Twining Papers, box 113, "Operational Readiness Measures," 27 May 1960.

10. FOIA USAF, "History of the 3079th Aviation Depot Wing, 1 Jul 59–30 Jun 60." The author mistakenly makes reference to the "Lebanon Crisis of May 1960."

11. Library of Congress, Twining Papers, box 113, "Operational Readiness Measures," 27 May 1960.

12. Hudlow, *Shamrock* 22, vii. Hudlow recalls this happening on 1 May 1960, right after the U-2 was shot down. However, SAC was not at a heightened alert level and would not have likely known about the cause of the loss of the CIA aircraft that early in the game. Power's in-clear roll call of alert aircraft more likely took place on the 16th, when SAC went to DEFCON 3.

13. Hudlow, *Shamrock* 22, vii–viii.

14. Beschloss, *May-Day*, 281.

15. Sherman Kent, "The Summit Conference of 1960: An Intelligence Officer's View," CIA Library, accessed 25 September 2019, https://www.cia.gov/library/center-for-the -study-of-intelligence/csi-publications/books-and-monographs/sherman-kent-and-the -board-of-national-estimates-collected-essays/8summit.html.

16. Library of Congress, Twining Papers, box 113, "Operational Readiness Measures," 27 May 1960.

17. "Panic after US Military Combat Alert," *The Age*, 16 May 1960.

18. Library of Congress, Twining Papers, box 113, "Operational Readiness Measures," 27 May 1960.

19. Document 153, "Memorandum of Discussion at the 445th Meeting of the National Security Council," 24 May 1960, in *Foreign Relations of the United States* [hereafter FRUS] *1958–1960, Volume 10, Part 1: Eastern European Region, Soviet Union*, https://history.state .gov/historicaldocuments/frus1958-60v10p1/d153.

20. FOIA USAF, "History of the 3079th Aviation Depot Wing, 1 Jul 59–30 Jun 60."

21. Fenby, *The General*, ch. 29.

22. This is implied in Macmillan's diaries; see Horne, *Harold Macmillan*, 225–29. On RAF involvement with the U-2, see Lashmar, *Spy Flights of the Cold War*, ch. 14.

23. Kaplan, *The Wizards of Armageddon*, 295–302.

24. Kennedy Library, National Security Files, box 320, memorandum for Mr. Bundy, Subject: Berlin, 14 August 1961.

25. Kaplan, *The Wizards of Armageddon*, 295–302.

26. Poole, *The Joint Chiefs of Staff and National Policy*, ch. 10.

27. In Podvig, *Russian Strategic Nuclear Forces*, ch. 8 is a detailed listing of the tests.

28. "War and Peace in the Nuclear Age," Open Vault, Tapes E05023–E05029, William Kaufman, http://openvault.wgbh.org/catalog/V_D1FA1FDE1AF4474A8 C40165A496EEAEB.

29. National Security Archive, memo for General Lemnitzer and attached memorandum subject "Strategic Air Planning and Berlin," 6 September 1961.

30. National Security Archive, memo for General Lemnitzer.

31. Document 43, "Memorandum from the President's Military Representative (Taylor) to President Kennedy," 19 September 1961, in FRUS *Volume 8: National Security Policy 1961–1963*. White House staffer Ted Sorensen, who vehemently opposed Kaysen's study, told interviewers that he didn't think it "even reached the President's desk." Another White House staffer, Marcus Raskin, declared that the study was the moral equivalent of measuring boxcars for Auschwitz. See "War and Peace in the Nuclear Age," Open Vault, Theodore Sorenson, http://openvault.wgbh.org/catalog/V _5E604A7924124D9EAFED090FA8FCA2AD; Marcus Raskin, http://openvault.wgbh .org/catalog/V_9EEEEDCFEB1B4D06A9E8DA66B86A236B.

32. Document 44, "Memorandum of Conference with President Kennedy," 20 September 1961, in FRUS *Volume 8: National Security Policy 1961–1963*.

33. Document 44, "Memorandum of Conference with President Kennedy."

34. Document 47, "Memorandum from the Chairman of the Joint Chiefs of Staff (Lemnitzer) to President Kennedy," 27 September 1961, in FRUS *Volume 8: National Security Policy 1961–1963*.

35. Beschloss, *The Crisis Years*, 536.

36. See Kennedy and Sorensen, *Thirteen Days*, and particularly the 2000 film *Thirteen Days*.

37. See Stern, *The Cuban Missile Crisis*, ch. 2.

38. Naftali and Fursenko, *Khrushchev's Cold War*, 431–34.

39. Zubok and Pleashakov, *Inside the Kremlin's Cold War*, 261. See also Beschloss, *The Crisis Years*, 442.

40. Naftali and Fursenko, *Khrushchev's Cold War*, 434–35, 431.

41. FOIA CIA, DDO to DCI, "Military Thought (USSR): Characteristic Features of Aerospace Operations in the Initial Period of War," 24 September 1976. This document, published internally in a classified Soviet publication in April 1962, depicts details of American SAC and NATO nuclear planning. It is clearly derived from information that would have been available to the Joint Chiefs and NATO planners, and thus it is highly likely that it was based on Whalen-provided information.

42. See Gribkov and Smith, *Operation Anadyr*.

43. FOIA CIA, Photographic Interpretation Report, "Ugolnyy MRBM Complex, USSR," February 1964. I have elaborated on the Anadyr deployment in "The Missiles of Anadyr."

44. FOIA USAF, "Alaskan NORAD Region Historical Report, 1 July 1959–31 December 1959."

45. FOIA USAF, "Interview with General Power Conducted by Mr. Bohn," 15 November 1962. See also Taylor, *Swords and Ploughshares*, 273.

46. Stern, *The Week the World Stood Still*, 107. But then he incorrectly states that DEFCON 2 was "the highest state of readiness short of war."

47. FOIA USAF, "Interview with General Power Conducted by Mr. Bohn," 15 November 1962.

48. These factors are examined in detail in the chapters that follow.

49. FOIA USAF, "Interview with General Power Conducted by Mr. Bohn," 15 November 1962.

50. FOIA USAF, "Interview with General Power Conducted by Mr. Bohn," 15 November 1962.

51. Haslam, *Near and Distant Neighbors*, 203.

52. Zubok and Pleashakov, *Inside the Kremlin's Cold War*, 266.

53. Khrushchev, *Khrushchev Remembers*, 174.

54. Haslam, *Near and Distant Neighbors*, 204.

55. This argument was made by British journalist Paul Lashmar. See Castleton, "Dr. Strangelove and the Cold War Context"; Lashmar, "Dr. Strangelove's Secrets."

56. Association for Diplomatic Studies and Training, interview with William B. Dunham, 1996, http://adst.org/oral-history/oral-history-interviews/.

57. Sagan, *The Limits of Safety*, ch. 3.

58. See Hutchhausen, *October Fury*; Edward Wilson, "Thank You Vasili Arkhipov, the Man Who Stopped Nuclear War," *The Guardian*, 27 October 2012, http://www.theguardian.com/commentisfree/2012/oct/27/vasili-arkhipov-stopped-nuclear-war.

59. Podvig, "History and the Current Status of the Russian Early-Warning System."

60. Kohn and Harahan, *Strategic Air Warfare*, 117–18.

61. Sagan does mention Soviet moves but in a very general and limited sense in *The Limits of Safety*, 143. Surprisingly, Graham Allison's latest edition of *The Essence of Decision* omits any detailed discussion of Soviet moves. The Soviet material I have used here was collected by a Soviet Strategic Rocket Forces veterans organization and compiled on the website RSVN. Info. This is an extensive and detailed site including substantial personal narratives as well as technical information and a wide variety of secondary sources reprinted for the website. This and other Russian websites dealing with Strategic Rocket Forces with additional material have been interdicted by the Russian security services while Russia is still active in Ukraine.

62. See Gennediy Dubrovin's history on the 867th Missile Regiment, available in its entirety (in Russian) at http://rvsn.ruzhany.info/867rp_01.html#contents.

63. Dubrovin's history on the 867th Missile Regiment. See also G. I. Smirnov's history of the 50th Missile Army (in Russian), http://rvsn.ruzhany.info/50ra_t1_p1.html; see excerpt from A. A. Lomovtsev's memoir "Our Soviet Times" (in Russian), http://rvsn.ruzhany.info/sputnik_lib_009.html.

64. Hodzhash Alberta Elchafanovicha's memoir "How Was It?" (in Russian), http://rvsn.ruzhany.info/khodzhash.html#add_1.

65. N. V. Samorodov's history of the 10th Missile Division (in Russian), http://rvsn.ruzhany.info/10rd_book_01.html#intro1.

66. Smirnov's history of the 50th Missile Army.

67. History of the Red Guards Vitebsk Missile Army (in Russian), http://rvsn.ruzhany.info/27ra_p00.html#intro_02.

68. History of the Red Guards Vitebsk Missile Army.

69. Dubrovin's history of the 867th Missile Regiment; Sergey Ermolin's memoir "My Army" (in Russian), http://rvsn.ruzhany.info/moja_armija_ermolin.html#foreword_01.

70. The 403rd history (in Russian), http://rvsn.ruzhany.info/403_main.html#contents.

71. See Dubrovin's history on the 867th Missile Regiment.

72. Gen. Maxwell Taylor notes in his memoir that "Khrushchev eventually retreated not because of SAC aircraft aloft and Polaris submarines on station in European waters but because Cuba was beyond the range of support of his conventional forces and Kennedy had called his bluff" (*Swords and Ploughshares*, 280). This view and the idea that the SAC DEFCON 2 move was significant can coexist. However, given his personality, Khrushchev would likely have personalized the more immediate threat of the Airborne Alert Force to his ongoing existence on Earth in a way that cool calculation over logistics and lines of communications probably did not. Taylor was clearly reflecting his long-standing preference for increased conventional forces rather than what Khrushchev really thought.

73. FOIA NSA, Signals Intelligence Command Center Record of Events, 22 November 1963.

74. Elton C. Fay, "US Military Might Poised through Crisis," *Corpus Christie Caller-Times*, 28 November 1963.

75. FOIA NSA, Comment on Castro's Reaction to the Death of Kennedy, 27 November 1963; Cuba's Reported Reaction to Kennedy's Murder, 27 November 1963.

76. Ray Morgan, "Look to LBJ," *Kansas City Times*, 23 November 1963.

77. FOIA USAF, "Supplement to the 11th Bombardment Wing (H) History, 19th Air Division, June 1952."

78. On the fiftieth anniversary of the assassination, several websites collected "where were you when" anecdotes. I have distilled this section from approximately fifty relevant submissions provided to three sites: My San Antonio, www.mysanantonio.com; Oklahoma University Insider, http://oklahoma.247sports.com; and For What They Gave on Saturday Afternoon, http://forwhattheygave.com, which is a West Point group. Richard A. Marini, a staff writer for My San Antonio, thankfully ensured that SAC and USAF personnel were disproportionately included in his piece "San Antonians Recall Where They Were during JFK's Visit, Assassination," dated 17 November 2013.

79. See Jack Mathis, Willie Acuna, Bob Blackstone, Kenneth Andrews, James Stamper, Nat Mushkin, Thomas Lee, D. M. Lopez, Joe Tafolla, Denny Darby, Nick Davies, Armando Vazquez, Wayne Shore, and David Cameron anecdotes, www.mysanantonio.com.

80. Tony Lackey, "Kincheloe Air Force Base SAC Time: Tales of a Mechanic," Military History of the Upper Great Lakes, 17 October 2016, http://ss.sites.mtu.edu/mhugl/2016/10/16/kincheloe-air-force-base-sac-time-tales-of-a-mechanic/.

81. See Will Cannon anecdote, http://forwhattheygave.com.

82. See Jerry Janicke anecdote, http://forwhattheygave.com.

83. Taylor, *Swords to Ploughshares*, 303. See BACM Research/Paperless Archives, "John F. Kennedy November 22–25, 1963: Documents, Interviews, Audio Recordings, and Films," Hallett to Smith, "Changes in Defense Readiness Conditions as a Result of the Assassination of President Kennedy," 4 December 1963; Joint Chiefs of Staff (JCS) to Commanders in Chief, 22 November 1963, https://downloads.paperlessarchives.com/p/YEfg/.

84. Taylor, *Swords to Ploughshares*, 303.

85. BACM Research/Paperless Archives, "John F. Kennedy November 22–25, 1963: Documents, Interviews, Audio Recordings, and Films," Commander in Chief Pacific (CINCPAC)

to commands, info JCS, 22 November 1963, https://downloads.paperlessarchives.com/p/YEfg/.

86. BACM Research/Paperless Archives, "John F. Kennedy November 22–25, 1963: Documents, Interviews, Audio Recordings, and Films," Hallett to Smith, "Changes in Defense Readiness Conditions as a Result of the Assassination of President Kennedy," 4 December 1963, https://downloads.paperlessarchives.com/p/YEfg/.

87. See Nat Mushkin anecdote, www.mysanantonio.com. Note that Dougherty was not CINCSAC in 1963; Power was.

88. Association for Diplomatic Studies and Training, interview with David J. Fischer by Charles Stuart Kennedy, 6 March 1998, http://www.adst.org/OH%20TOCs/Fischer,%20David.toc.pdf.

6. Theater of War

1. In various early iterations it was called "Command Center" or "Communications Center."

2. UPA Microfilm, JCS part II 1946–53, reel II, JLPC "Alternate Joint Chiefs of Staff Command Post," 31 October 1950; reel IV, JCS Decision on JCS 1851/38: "Alternate Joint Communications Center," 29 February 1952.

3. UPA Microfilm, "Alternate Joint Communications Center." See particularly the communications diagram.

4. These issues are handled adroitly in Krugler's *This Is Only a Test*.

5. U.S. National Records and Archives Administration (USNARA), record group (RG) 218 384.51 (10-31-46) Sec 9, Office of the Secretary of Defense to JCS, "Nationwide Civil Defense Exercises (NSC Action #1061)," 20 April 1954; my survey at Battle Creek, Michigan.

6. USNARA, "Nationwide Civil Defense Exercises," 106–9.

7. *Publication No. L58-141*, 4.

8. U.S. Navy Operational Archives, Strategic Plans Division, box 315, folder A5. See particularly the six communications diagrams. See also map and attachment on High Point location.

9. Larzelere, *Witness to History*, 31.

10. "Camp David Underground Shelter," About Camp David, 13 December 2010, http://aboutcampdavid.blogspot.ca/2010/12/camp-david-underground-bomb-shelter.html.

11. Library of Congress, Twining Papers, box 107, folder: memos AP 1959, JCS to Secretary of Defense, "Establishment of an Interim Joint War Room Facility at the Alternate Joint Communications Center," 29 April 1959.

12. Library of Congress, Twining Papers, box 107, folder 91-118, memo for Secretary of Defense, "Concept for the Use of the Alternate Joint Communications Center," 19 March 1959.

13. Library of Congress, LeMay Papers, box B-143, Sylvester to Power, 11 June 1962; Sylvester to LeMay, "SAC Cooperation in Filming of 'A Gathering of Eagles,'" 11 June 1962; LeMay to Power, 21 June 1962.

14. Library of Congress, LeMay Papers, box B-60, LeMay to Twining, 26 September 1953.

15. Weitze, *Cold War Infrastructure for Strategic Air Command*, 124–25. See also Justman, *Offutt Air Force Base*, 80–81.

16. Library of Congress, Twining Papers, box 61, LeMay to Twining, 26 September 1963, see attachment.

17. The alternate SAC control center was depicted as callsign Hillbilly in the 1958 USAF training film *The Power of Decision*. Its location was not given, but the interior of its facilities were filmed.

18. Based on my analysis of photographs of SAC Control Center circa 1957–59.

19. Based on my analysis of photographs of SAC Control Center circa 1962–64.

20. ISSCUA, Collins Papers, box 16, Short Order file, see photos of sites and inauguration in March 1960; box 3, file Griswold 1960–64, invitations to Short Order inauguration.

21. H. J. Michael and H. M. Pruden, "SAC's Primary Alerting System," *Bell Laboratories Record*, July 1961, 235–39; see also AT&T, "Private Line Telephone Service." I also accessed the same Primary Alerting System consoles used in the SAC Control Center and seen in the film at the Strategic Air Command and Aerospace Museum.

22. AT&T, "Command Post Alerting Network." See also "Garden City VA," Microwave Radio and Coaxial Cable Networks of the Bell System, accessed 25 September 2019, http://long-lines.net/places-routes/Garden_City/index.html. For a hilarious coincidence, the now demolished facility was replaced with the Greenbrier Apartments.

23. These procedures can be seen in part in the USAF documentaries *SAC Command Post* (1963–64), https://archive.org/details/AirForceSpecialFilmProject 1236sacComnandPost, and *The Power of Decision* (1958), https://archive.org/details /AirForceSpecialFilmProject416powerOfDecision, both accessed 25 September 2019. Note that *The Power of Decision* predates the implementation of the Primary Alerting System and the Joint Chiefs of Staff Alerting Network. *A Gathering of Eagles* (1963) shows the control center and its procedures between the two films, right when the changeover was taking place: the Primary Alerting System console is on the upper deck, not on the floor to the right; the old Big Board, not the Vu Graph screens, is in the background; and the Joint Chiefs of Staff Alerting Network is not installed. *SAC Command Post* depicts the Joint Chiefs of Staff Alerting Network, Vu Graph screens, the Primary Alerting System consoles, and the NORAD Iconorama to the right of the senior controller.

24. This is a wholly inadequate summary of a detailed and historically important project that laid the foundations of today's computer industry and social capability, and I would suggest reading Redmond and Smith, *From Whirlwind to MITRE*.

25. Redmond and Smith, *From Whirlwind to MITRE*.

26. Based on my survey of former NORAD direction centers at Syracuse, Duluth, and Battle Creek. On the general operation of the Kelvin Hughes system, see "Holmpton Rotor Radar Station," Subterranea Britannica, accessed 25 September 2019, http://www .subbrit.org.uk/rsg/sites/h/holmpton/index210.html. A miniaturized system using the same principles was even used in the SR-71 reconnaissance aircraft. See Byrnes and Hurley, *Blackbird Rising*, 227.

27. Schaffel, *The Emerging Shield*, 261–63; Terrell, "What Is SAGE?"

28. Coughlin, "City in a Mountain"; Roberts, "Air Defense Goes Underground."

29. Library and Archives Canada, MG 32 B9, vol. 87, file Defense Publications, "SAGE Goes Underground: Information Booklet, Headquarters Northern NORAD Region," RCAF Station North Bay, Ontario.

30. Library and Archives Canada, MG 32 B9, "SAGE Goes Underground."

31. As described in "Temco Subsidiary Lands Defense Equipment Order," *Grand Prairie Daily News*, 2 July 1959.

32. "United Airlines Flight 736," Wikipedia, accessed 25 September 2019, https://en .wikipedia.org/wiki/United_Airlines_Flight_736.

33. Analysis of SAC command post photos in Lister, "The Evolution and Current Status of NORAD"; see also Ed Thelen's Nike Missile Web Site, *US Army Air Defense Digest 1966*, accessed 25 September 2019, http://ed-thelen.org/digest1.html.

34. "A Blast Resistant Communications Network," *Bell Laboratories Record*, October 1965, http://www.coldwar-c4i.net/CMC/BLR1065/387.html.

35. Arkin and Fieldhouse, *Nuclear Battlefields*, 181–82.

36. Linda Navarro, "Ever Wonder? AT&T Caused NORAD Blackout," *Colorado Springs Gazette*, 26 August 2011, https://gazette.com/news/ever-wonder-at-t-caused-norad-blackout -cresterra-parkway/article_0ca51020-29bd-5512-a5c4-2accb3412874.html.

37. Power and Arnhym, *Design for Survival*, 144.

38. "NORAD Canucks," *Sentinel*, June 1971, 10–16.

39. Karl J. Zimmer, "The Command and Control Display System for NORAD," *Information Display*, September–October 1967; see also product brochure, Burroughs Corporation Defense and Space Group, "Display Systems from Burroughs," n.d.

40. Isaacson, *Kissinger*, 380–85. Isaacson even refers to *Seven Days in May* in his description of the affair.

41. Michael Dobbs, "The Real Story of the 'Football' That Follows the President Everywhere," *Smithsonian Magazine*, October 2014, http://www.smithsonianmag.com/history /real-story-football-follows-president-everywhere-180952779/?no-ist.

42. Association for Diplomatic Studies and Training, interview with Eugene Schmiel by David Reuther, 25 January 2010, http://adst.org/oral-history/oral-history-interviews/.

43. USNARA, RG 218 CCS 354.2 US (4-12-57), "Results Obtained from Ex DODEP, 12 April 1957," 22 April 1957; Telex, 12 April 1957; JCS to Chief of Naval Operations, "Alert Ex 31 May 1957," 27 May 1957; Chief CP Cops to Secretary of Defense and JCS, "Report of May Exercise of JCS Emergency Conference," 24 June 1957.

44. USNARA, RG 218 CCS 354.2 US (4-12-57), "Results Obtained from Ex DODEP, 12 April 1957," 22 April 1957.

45. U.S. Navy Operational Archives, Strategic Plans Division, box 315, file A-5, Op Alert message traffic.

46. Gulley, *Breaking Cover*, 187–91; Boyer, *Inside the President's Helicopter*, 205–6; Abrams, *The President Has Been Shot*, 126–27.

47. JCS, "National Targeting and Attack Policy for General War: Guidance for the Preparation of the Single Integrated Operational Plan, 1963," 26 October 1961, https://archive .org/stream/SingleIntegratedOperationPlanSIOP63/Single%20Integrated%20Operation %20Plan_SIOP-63_djvu.txt.

48. Association for Diplomatic Studies and Training, interview with Ambassador Maxwell Taylor by Dorothy Pierce, 9 January 1969, http://www.adst.org/OH%20TOCs/Taylor, %20Maxwell%20D.1969.toc.pdf.

49. Gulley, *Breaking Cover*, 181.

50. Gulley, *Breaking Cover*, 181.

51. Haraldur Thor Egilsson, "The Origins, Use and Development of Hot Line Diplomacy," Discussion Papers in Diplomacy, Netherlands Institute of International Relations

Clingendael, 2003, https://www.clingendael.nl/sites/default/files/20030500_cli_paper_dip_issue85.pdf.

52. Jess Gorkin, "An Open Letter from the Editor of Parade to President Dwight D. Eisenhower and Premier Nikita Khrushchev Re: Accidental War," *Parade*, 29 March 1960, 6.

53. Gorkin, "An Open Letter," 6.

54. Stephen L. Thacher, "Crisis Communications between Superpowers," U.S. Army War College Study Project, 12 February 1990.

55. Dobrynin quoted in Egilsson, "The Origins, Use, and Development of Hot Line Diplomacy."

56. FOIA CIA, memo for DCI, "Washington-Moscow 'Hot Line' Technical Communications Arrangements," 22 August 1963. This is the only primary source that uses the term "Hot Line." See also Kennedy Library, Geneva to Secretary of State, "Communications Link Experts Meeting," 29 May 1963; Geneva to Secretary of State, 30 May 1963.

57. "ETCRRM," Crypto Museum, accessed 25 September 2019, http://www.cryptomuseum.com/crypto/stk/etcrrm/index.htm.

58. Thacher, "Crisis Communications between Superpowers."

59. David Vergun, "Hotline, Now 50 Years Old, Continues to Promote Dialog with Russians," U.S. Army, 26 August 2013, https://www.army.mil/article/109986/Hotline__now_50_years_old__continues_to_promote_dialog_with_Russians.

60. National Security Decision Directive Number 186, "Installation and Operation of the Direct Communications Link (DCL) / 'Hotline' between Washington and Moscow," National Archives Catalog, 4 September 1985, https://catalog.archives.gov/id/6879776.

61. Discussed in Thacher, "Crisis Communications between Superpowers."

62. Johnson Library, Oral History Collection, "Robert S. McNamara, Special Interview I," 26 March 1993. McNamara's assertion that he ordered the link extended to the White House in 1967 is contradicted by an NCO who manned the link at White House Signal in 1963: "Minnesota Man Managed Hotline to Moscow during the Kennedy Assassination," *Twin Cities Pioneer Press*, 30 October 2015, http://www.twincities.com/2014/11/20/minnesota-man-managed-hotline-to-moscow-during-jfk-assassination/.

63. Johnson Library, "Robert S. McNamara, Special Interview I." McNamara isn't explicit about the problem in this oral history interview, but one can discern it.

64. NSA, "The Direct Communications Link," *Cryptology*, December 1983, 21–27; "The Washington-Moscow Hotline," *Electrospaces* (blog), 28 October 2012, http://electrospaces.blogspot.ca/2012/10/the-washington-moscow-hot-line.html.

65. "27th Guards Rocket Army," Wikipedia, accessed 25 September 2019, https://en.wikipedia.org/wiki/27th_Guards_Rocket_Army.

66. "Hello, Mr. President!," *Sputnik News*, 27 April 2011, https://sputniknews.com/voiceofrussia/radio_broadcast/36564197/49264504/ (site no longer active); "The Washington-Moscow Hotline."

67. NSC, "Installation and Operation of the Direct Communications Link (DCL)."

68. "Minnesota Man Managed Hotline to Moscow during the Kennedy Assassination." One site asserts it was first used when John F. Kennedy was assassinated but provides no primary sources on this: "Washington-Moscow Hotline," Crypto Museum, accessed 25 September 2019, http://www.cryptomuseum.com/crypto/hotline/index.htm.

69. Johnson Library, "Information Sheet on 'Hot Line,'" 25 July 2008, http://www.lbjlibrary.net/collections/subject-guides/foreign.html.

70. See Thacher, "Crisis Communications between Superpowers."

71. Abrams, *The President Has Been Shot*, Appendix 2: The National Command Authority. See also Department of Defense Directive, "World-Wide Military Command and Control System (WWMCCS)," 2 December 1971, https://biotech.law.lsu.edu/blaw/dodd/corres/pdf/d510030wch1_120271/d510030p.pdf.

72. FOIA CIA, "Final Report of the Defense Science Board Task Force on Tactical Warning/Attack Assessment, January 3, 1973."

73. This is inferred in Kennedy Library, National Security Files, box 333, Annex B, "Comments on W. Y. Elliott Memorandum on Emergency Relocation Programs As They Affect the Department of State."

74. Kennedy Library, National Security Files 127, Emergency Planning Committee, "Report to the President on a Re-examination of Federal Policy with Respect to Emergency Plans and Continuity of Government in the Event of a Nuclear Attack on the United States," 11 June 1962.

75. Kennedy Library, National Security Files, file NSAM127, "Report of the Task Group on the Survivable Communications Requirements of the President and Top Civil Leaders," 20 August 1962.

76. Released under the USNARA ISCAP program after a lengthy fight by one researcher, the 1972 and 1973 White House Communications Agency's "Communications Handbook for Central Locator System," assigned to Senator James O. Eastland, provides some insight into the program.

77. White House Communications Agency, "Communications Handbook for Central Locator System."

78. Boyer, *Inside the President's Helicopter*, 96.

79. See "Early Presidential Emergency Facilities," http://coldwar-c4i.net/PEF/index.html; "Early Presidential Emergency Facilities (PEF) 1965–1970," *About the White House Communications Agency from 1965 to 1974 and Beyond* (blog), accessed 25 September 2019, http://whcacannonball.blogspot.com/p/early-presidential-emergency.html; Rotenstein, "The Undisclosed Location Disclosed."

80. "Early Presidential Emergency Facilities"; "Early Presidential Emergency Facilities (PEF) 1965–1970"; Rotenstein, "The Undisclosed Location Disclosed." U.S. Coast Guard aide Capt. Alex Larzelere recorded a surreptitious visit to Cartwheel with the special projects officer in 1971 (*Witness to History*, 46). Shepherd Air National Guard Base is now the Western West Virginia Regional Airport.

7. Plan R

1. Library of Congress, LeMay Papers, box B-58, Partridge folder, LeMay to Partridge, 16 November 1956.

2. Library of Congress, LeMay to Partridge, 16 November 1956.

3. See, for example, Divine, *The Sputnik Challenge*; Dickson, *Sputnik*; Brzezinski, *Red Moon Rising*. All mention in one way or another the Gaither Report and its influence, but none look at what influenced the Gaither Report itself.

4. FOIA CIA, "National Intelligence Estimate 11-1-62: The Soviet Space Program," 5 December 1961; FOIA JCS, "JCS Decision on JCS 1899/402: Positive Control Presentation," 13 May 1958.

5. Podvig, *Russian Strategic Nuclear Forces*, 487–89.

6. See Richelson, *Spying on the Bomb*; Goodman, *Spying on the Nuclear Bear*.

7. National Security Archive, Special Assistant to the Secretary, Department of State, memo to file, "Policy on Use of Atomic Weapons," 2 April 1956, https://nsarchive2.gwu .edu//news/predelegation/pd01_01.htm.

8. U.S. Department of Defense, *Dictionary of Military Terms*, 106.

9. See Library of Congress, Twining Papers, box 81, "FSPO-65: SAC Comments on USAF Force Structure and Program Objectives 1957–1965," February 1955. LeMay pushed for the "right to evacuate, strike or both" in the event of an air defense emergency, but the Air Council disapproved of that course of action. See Library of Congress, Twining Papers, box 81, "Strategic Plan of Operations, D-Day—1 July 1959," 29 February 1956.

10. See FOIA Department of Defense, "Custody and Deployment of Nuclear Weapons July 1945 through September 1977."

11. FOIA USAF, "History of the 320th Bombardment Wing (M) 1–31 July 1958."

12. National Security Archive, "Instructions for the Expenditure of Nuclear Weapons in Accordance with the Presidential Authorization Dated May 22, 1957," http://nsarchive .gwu.edu/news/predelegation/predel.htm.

13. National Security Archive, Department of State, memo for Secretary of State, "Policy Regarding Use of Atomic Weapons," 15 May 1957, https://nsarchive2.gwu.edu//news /predelegation/pd07_01.htm; National Security Archive, "First Documented Evidence that U.S. Presidents Predelegated Nuclear Weapons Release Authority to the Military," 20 March 1998, https://nsarchive2.gwu.edu/news/19980319.htm.

14. National Security Archive, "Instructions for the Expenditure of Nuclear Weapons in Accordance with the Presidential Authorization Dated May 22, 1957."

15. Library of Congress, White Papers, box 7, Power to White, 21 October 1957.

16. Library of Congress, White Papers, box 7, White to Power, 22 November 1957.

17. FOIA USAF, "Historical Report 623rd AC&W Squadron, 1 January 1958–31 June 1958."

18. Library of Congress, LeMay Papers, box 58, Power to Lemay, 9 October 1957; LeMay to Power, 19 November 1957; Library of Congress, Twining Papers, box 106, memo for Secretary of Defense, "Positive Control Presentation to NSC," 13 May 1958; memo for Secretary of Defense, "Strategic Air Command Operational Support Exercises," 17 December 1957; Canadian Department of National Defence, Arnell Papers, COSC to MND, "USAF Flights Carrying Nuclear Weapons Overflying Canadian Territory," 3 June 1958; Declassified Document Reference System (DDRS) 215108-i1-10, JCS, "Decision on JCS 2056/111: Strategic Air Command Operational Support Exercises," 17 November 1957.

19. FOIA USAF, "Historical Report 623rd AC&W Squadron, 1 January 1958–31 June 1958."

20. FOIA USAF, "History of the 3079th Aviation Depot Wing, 1 Jul 56–31 Dec 56."

21. DDRS 210884-i1-3, JCS, COSUSAF to JCS, "Launching of the Strategic Air Command Alert Force," 10 March 1958.

22. Library of Congress, Twining Papers, box 106, JCS memo to Secretary of Defense, "Positive Control Presentation to NSC," 13 May 1958.

23. Library of Congress, Twining Papers, "Positive Control Presentation to NSC."

24. FOIA Eisenhower Library, Science Advisory Committee, "Security Resources Panel Volume 1: Active Defense & SAC Vulnerability November 27, 1957." Airborne alert was not discussed by the panel but came out of SAC deliberations on the issue.

25. Frank Bartholomew, "Room 45 Feet under Nebraska Controls Peace-Deterrent," *Corvallis Gazette Times*, 7 April 1958.

26. Excerpts from the "Fail Safe" *Time* article were distributed widely in American newspapers. See *St. Louis Post Dispatch*, 25 April 1958 for one such excerpt.

27. Bartholomew, *Bart.*

28. DDRS 269045-i1-14, "SAC Operations with Sealed Pit Weapons," n.d.; DDRS 26777-i1-9, "Briefing for the President on SAC Operations with Sealed-Pit Weapons," n.d.

29. USNARA, RG 59, box 3219, memo for Acting Secretary, "Strategic Air Command Exercise Headstart," 13 September 1958.

30. USNARA, RG 59, box 3219, Murphy to Heeney, 6 February 1959; RG 59, box 3219, memo for Acting Secretary, "Strategic Air Command Exercise Headstart," 13 September 1958; DDRS 77 286 A and B, White House Office Staff Research Group, "Airborne Alert Test (Secret)," n.d. See also 1959 USAF Film Report, "Operation Headstart," https://www.youtube.com/watch?v=OFAVBszvXm4n. This film notably shows nuclear weapons being loaded onto one of the Headstart B-52s as well as a map of the Headstart route.

31. FOIA USAF, "History of the 93rd Bombardment Wing, Castle AFB, November 1958."

32. Library of Congress, Twining Papers, box 8, "Chairman's Telephone Log Friday 6 March 1959."

33. Library of Congress, Twining Papers, "Chairman's Telephone Log Friday 6 March 1959."

34. Library of Congress, Twining Papers, box 109, JCS to Secretary of Defense, "SAC Exercises," 4 August 1959; JCS to Secretary of Defense, "July Report on SAC Exercise," 1 September 1959; box 110, JCS to Secretary of Defense, "August Report on SAC Exercise," 1 October 1959; JCS to Secretary of Defense, "Status of National Security Programs," 2 October 1959; USNARA, RG 59, file 3219, memo for Under Secretary for Political Affairs, "Canadian Overflight Clearance for SAC Indoctrination Exercises through December 31, 1959," 15 October 1959.

35. FOIA USAF, "History of Strategic Air Command 1 Jan 58–30 Jun 58 Volume I."

36. Library of Congress, Twining Papers, box 109, JCS to Secretary of Defense, "SAC Exercise," 10 July 1959.

37. Library of Congress, Twining Papers, box 110, JCS to Secretary of Defense, "Establishment of Airborne Alert," 28 October 1959.

38. FOIA USAF, history, "4245th Strategic Wing (SAC) Sheppard Air Force Base Texas 1 October 1960–31 October 1960"; FOIA JCS, "Changes to Strategic Air Command Steel Trap Indoctrination Training Schedule," 2 April 1960.

39. National Security Archive, files, Burchinal to JCS, "Strategic Air Command Airborne Alert Plan ('Chrome Dome')," 16 August 1961.

40. The route for the Quick Kick's four B-52s in 1956 is practically identical to the Chrome Dome northern route of 1961. See FOIA, "History of the 42nd Bombardment Wing (Heavy) 1 November to 31 December 1956."

41. FOIA USAF, "4052nd Strategic Wing (SAC) history 1–31 January 1963"; FOIA State Department, message to Ambassador, Ottawa, POLAD CINCSAC, 11 October 1961. See map on page 284 in Hudlow, *Shamrock* 22.

42. FOIA USAF, "History of the 4042nd Strategic Wing, 1–31 January 1961"; FOIA USAF, "History of the 42nd Bombardment Wing 1 April–30 June 1964."

43. FOIA USAF, "History of the 6th Strategic Wing, October–December 1969."

44. FOIA USAF, "History of the 4042nd Strategic Wing, 1–31 January 1961."

45. FOIA USAF, "History of the Directorate of Civil Engineering, 1 Jan–30 June 62."

46. On an analysis of the 1968 Thule crash in relationship to BMEWS, see Sagan, *The Limits of Safety*, 181–88.

47. Library of Congress, White Papers, box 21, LeMay to Power, n.d., "Airborne Alert Concept."

48. FOIA USAF, "History of 5th Bombardment Wing (Heavy) July–September 1964."

49. USNARA, RG 59, box 1, file 3060 AII 250/63/4/03, Lang to Armstrong, 22 April 1963; FOIA USAF, SAC Regulation 100-24 Vol. III, "SAC Communications System Operations EWO Support Requirements," 8 July 1978.

50. FOIA CIA, "Photographic Intelligence Memorandum: Franz Joseph Land, 15 August 1958." This document describes a "probable air navigation directional finding station," but the antenna layout it describes could just as easily be employed to monitor the communications and locations of Chrome Dome flights.

51. See M. Boltunov, *"The Golden Ear" of Military Intelligence*. English translation no longer available at http://jsulib.ru/Lib/Articles/007/522/.

52. See FOIA USAF, "History of 5th Bombardment Wing (Heavy) July–September 1964"; see also Paul Kelley, "Memories of Fox Main," DEW Line, http://lswilson.dewlineadventures .com/memories/#A. Thanks to Lt. Col. Earl McGill for his assistance with understanding Chrome Dome operations, particularly *Jet Age Man*, ch. 17. See also Alex P. Brewer, "Chrome Dome: 99th Bomb Wing Heavy, Westover AFB, Massachusetts, November 1959," http://randolphbrewercom.fatcow.com/b58/cws_chromedome.php.

53. Email, McGill to author, 2 April 2015.

54. Sagan, *The Limits of Safety*, 73–77.

55. FOIA USAF, "History of 5th Bombardment Wing (Heavy) July–September 1964."

56. Canadian Department of National Defence, file 81/715 15/61, Meeting of the Naval Staff, "The Application of Soviet Seapower in Waters Adjacent to Canada," 2 November 1961.

57. See Brewer, "Chrome Dome."

58. FOIA USAF, "History of the 4245th Strategic Wing (SAC) 1 October 1960–31 October 1960."

59. "Dexedrine" and "Dextroamphetamine," Drug Enquirer, accessed 26 September 2019, http://drugenquirer.com/side_effects/amphetamines/dextroamphetamine/dexedrine.html.

60. "Dextroamphetamine Side Effects," Drugs, 21 December 2018, https://www.drugs .com/sfx/dextroamphetamine-side-effects.html.

61. "Dexedrine," Drugs, 21 December 2018, https://www.drugs.com/cdi/dexedrine.html.

62. The official report is in Maggelet and Oskins, *Broken Arrow*, 173–202, but McGill, in *Jet Age Man*, has another version of events on 129–34.

63. "Caffeine Can Cause Hallucinations," *Live Science*, 13 January 2009, http://www .livescience.com/3230-caffeine-hallucinations.html.

64. FOIA USAF, "History of the 4157th Strategic Wing July–August-September 1963."

65. Library of Congress, White Papers, box 22, AFCCS Reading File July 59, message to USAF Commands, "Spot Inspections for Nuclear Safety Measures," 7 July 1959. AFR 123-9 appears to have had a relationship to new entry-level screening measures established in 1956 and a nuclear certification accountability measure that was annually reported to Kirtland AFB. See WADC-TN-59-201, December 1959, Eli S. Flyer, "Factors Relating to Discharge for Unsuitability among 1956 Airman Accessions to the Air Force" and Government Accountability Office Report, "Is the Air Force Inspection System Effective," 29 June 1979.

66. See Eli S. Flyer, "Personnel Security Research-Prescreening and Background Investigations: Final Report 86-01 June 1986," HumRRO International, prepared for the Office of Naval Research.

67. FOIA JCS, memo to JCS, "Compromise of Information concerning Certain U.S. Nuclear Weapons," 18 September 1961.

68. Ray Bruner, "A-Accident Safeguards Devised by Psychiatrists," *Toledo Blade*, 8 May 1963; Group for the Advancement of Psychiatry, *Psychiatric Aspects of the Prevention of Nuclear War*, Report No. 57.

69. Harder, *Flying from the Black Hole*, 76.

70. Association for Diplomatic Studies and Training, interview with Howard H. Lange by Charles Stuart Kennedy, 20 June 2000, http://adst.org/oral-history/oral-history-interviews/.

71. McGill, *Jet Age Man*, ch. 20.

72. FOIA USAF, CINCSAC to JCS, 18 August 1969.

73. Jeremi Suri, "The Nukes of October: Richard Nixon's Secret Plan to Bring Peace to Vietnam," *Wired*, 25 February 1988, https://www.wired.com/2008/02/ff-nuclearwar/; "Operation Giant Lance," Wikipedia, accessed 26 September 2019, https://en.wikipedia.org/wiki/Operation_Giant_Lance; Blake Stilwell, "That Time Nixon Wanted Commies to Think He Was Crazy Enough to Nuke Them," *Business Insider*, 25 August 2015, http://www.businessinsider.com/that-time-nixon-wanted-commies-to-think-he-was-crazy-enough-to-nuke-them-2015-8.

74. FOIA USAF, "History of the 97th Bombardment Wing, October–December 1969."

75. The JCS ordered what was dubbed Port Bow, which deployed twenty-six B-52s and ten KC-135s from the United States to the Far East from 3 to 7 February 1968 in response to the *Pueblo* seizure. It appears as though Giant Lance was a more formalized and generalized version of Port Bow to provide the leadership with a series of options other than the SIOP. Lloyd, *A Cold War Legacy*, 406.

76. Lloyd, *A Cold War Legacy*, 406; FOIA USAF, "History of the 98th Strategic Wing, July–September 1968"; FOIA USAF, "History of the 6th Strategic Wing October–December 1969"; FOIA USAF, "History of the 380th Strategic Aerospace Wing, January–March 1969."

77. FOIA USAF, "History of the 97th Bombardment Wing, October–December 1969."

78. FOIA USAF, CINCSAC to JCS, 18 August 1969.

79. Library of Congress, LeMay Papers, box 104, diary entry, 16 March 1953; box 199, "SAC Commander's Conference," 19 January 1953; FOIA JCS, memo for the JCS, "Report on Evaluation of Effectiveness of Strategic Air Operations: Weapons Systems Evaluation Group Report No. 1," 8 February 1950.

80. Library of Congress, LeMay Papers, box 193, Sallager to Montgomery, "Comments on the Initial Strike Capability of SAC," 12 September 1950; box 199, LeMay to Vandenberg, 5 December 1952.

81. FOIA Department of Energy (DOE), "Restricted Data Declassification Decisions 1946 to Present—Annex D," 1 January 2001.

82. FOIA USAF, "Supplement to the 11th Bombardment Wing (H) History, 19th Air Division, June 1952." The 11th Bomb Wing history details an exercise conducted in June 1952 that simulated the Emergency War Plan, including the dropping of Mk-107 training bomb "shapes" on an island in the North Sea. By shifting the exercise navigation points to the east, the latitude and longitudes all match bomb runs on Leningrad exactly. Target number 2 corresponds to Leningrad, which was the Soviet Union's "second city" after Moscow.

83. Library of Congress, LeMay Papers, box 192, LeMay to Findletter, 23 May 1950.

84. These targets are distilled from the titles of nearly forty CIA reports relating to Leningrad for the period 1949 to 1953. This list is available at CIA Library, http://www.foia.cia.gov/search/site/Leningrad. Note that the Wasserfall (Waterfall) missile was a Nazi-era surface-to-air missile that served as the basis for the SA-1 Guild missile system established in Moscow in the 1950s. Note also that the CIA did not yet know that Leningrad shipyards were the center of Soviet submarine construction at this time, but they would find out with the first U-2 flights in 1956. See Pedlow and Welzenbach, *The CIA and the U-2 Program*, 104–5.

85. Defense Threat Reduction Agency (DTRA) Fact Sheet, "Operation Greenhouse," July 2007. See Hansen, *US Nuclear Weapons*, 131–33.

86. FOIA USAF, "Supplement to the 11th Bombardment Wing (H) History, 19th Air Division, June 1952"; Library of Congress, LeMay Papers, box B-192, LeMay to Bunker, 28 February 1950.

87. See Garbinski, *North River Depot*.

88. FOIA USAF, "Supplement to the 11th Bombardment Wing (H) History, 19th Air Division, June 1952."

89. FOIA USAF, "Supplement to the 11th Bombardment Wing (H) History, 19th Air Division, June 1952."

90. Hansen, *US Nuclear Weapons*, 133.

91. FOIA USAF, "Supplement to the 11th Bombardment Wing (H) History, 19th Air Division, June 1952." See Hansen, *US Nuclear Weapons*, 133.

92. FOIA NSA, Peterson, "Maybe You Had to Be There"; Price, *The History of US Electronic Warfare*, ch. 5 and 6; Library of Congress, LeMay Papers, box B-199, SAC Commander's Conference, 19 January 1953.

93. See Jed Mercurio's excellent novel *Ascent*, about Soviet MiG pilots in Korea. I have borrowed, promoted, and reposted Yefganii Yeremin from Franz Josef Land to Leningrad for the purposes of this war. See also 18th Red Banner Air Defense Corps, http://www.ww2.dk/new/pvo/18kpvo.htm, for details of the units defending Leningrad in 1953.

94. Library of Congress, LeMay Papers, box 60, LeMay to Twining, 4 March 1952.

95. See "B-36 AN/APA-59 Navigation Computer" and "B-36 A-1A Bomb Release Computer," Glenn's Computer Museum, accessed 26 September 2019, http://www.glennsmuseum.com/.

96. I was graciously provided access to the interior of the B-36 on display at the Strategic Air Command and Aerospace Museum by the staff. See also FOIA, "Supplement to the 11th Bombardment Wing (H) History, 19th Air Division, June 1952."

97. See USAF TO 1B-36-H(III)-1, "The RB-36H-III Airplane," 225–29.

98. Height of burst calculations were made using Glasstone and Dolan's *The Effects of Nuclear Weapons*, 114–15.

99. I liked Peter Dill's evocative title for an article he wrote on B-47 operations, so I borrowed it for the section heading. See Dill, "SAC's Doomsday Armada."

100. FOIA Department of Defense, Office of the Assistant Secretary of Defense (Atomic Energy), "History of the Custody and Deployment of Nuclear Weapons, July 1945 through September 1977," 45–50.

101. Library of Congress, LeMay Papers, box 202, JCS to CINCS, "Operational Planning for the Defeat of Communist Air Power in General War," 6 March 1956; box 203, "Remarks by General LeMay to the US Air Force Scientific Advisory Board," 21 May 1957.

102. FOIA CIA, CIA to Goodpaster, "Statistics Relating to the U-2 Program," 19 August 1960.

103. FOIA CIA, SC-00398/58, "Commentary on Kamchatka Peninsula (Including Petropavlovsk) to Highest Priority List," 3 January 1958.

104. Gordon and Komissarov, *Soviet Air Defence Aviation*, 239, 248, 303; "6th Kurilskaya Air Defence Division," accessed 26 September 2019, http://www.ww2.dk/new/pvo /6dpvo.htm.

105. See FOIA NSA, Peterson, "Maybe You Had to Be There."

106. Price, *The History of US Electronic Warfare*, ch. 6 and 8. See also Pedlow and Welzenbach, *The CIA and the U-2 Program*, 133–35.

107. Stumpf, *Regulus*, 58, 181.

108. This vignette is based on a 1960 test of the 9th Bombardment Wing's Emergency War Order, dubbed Play Back. See FOIA USAF, "9th Bombardment Wing, Appendix 'A' February–March 1960." When reoriented geographically, Play Back simulates a strike against targets on the periphery of the USSR. Its five targets in Oregon replicate the region around Petropavlovsk.

109. FOIA CIA, Directorate of Intelligence, "Imagery Analysis Report: Petropavlovsk Naval Complex, Petropavlovsk, USSR," December 1967; memo for Chief Military Division, OCI, "Submarine Support Installations: Avachinskaya Bay, Petropavlovsk-Kamchatskiy, USSR Photo Study," 1 July 1964. I have used only those facilities known to have existed in 1959–60.

110. FOIA USAF, "History of the Strategic Air Command 1 January 1958–30 June 1958: Historical Study No. 73 Volume I."

111. Hansen, *US Nuclear Weapons*, 145–46. Former SAC personnel confirmed to me that the yield of the weapon could be substantially increased or "dialed up" to nearly 19 megatons on an emergency basis until the Mk-53 came along.

112. FOIA USAF, "9th Bombardment Wing, Appendix 'A' February–March 1960."

113. Miller, *Stockpile*, 74.

114. This estimate was made from the following materials: FOIA DTRA, "Defense Nuclear Agency Effects Manual Number 1: Capabilities of Nuclear Weapons, 1 July 1972"; FOIA CIA, "Geomorphical Conditions and the Neotechtonics of the Petropavlovsk Region (1964)"; FOIA DOE, DNA6037F, "Operation Redwing 1956."

115. Adams, *Inside the Cold War*, 19. See also Hoopaw, *Where the* BUF *Fellows Roamed*, 63.

116. FOIA USAF, "9th Bombardment Wing, Appendix 'A' February–March 1960." Based on my assessment of the former SAC facility at CFB Edmonton.

117. FOIA USAF, "9th Bombardment Wing, Appendix 'A' February–March 1960."

118. FOIA USAF, "History of the 40th Bombardment Wing Medium Jet, May and June 1958 Schilling Air Force Base, Kansas"; FOIA USAF, "Historical Report 623rd AC&W Squadron 1 January 58–31 June 58"; FOIA USAF, "9th Bombardment Wing, Appendix 'A' February–March 1960."

119. FOIA USAF, "History of the 40th Bombardment Wing Medium Jet," "Historical Report 623rd AC&W Squadron," and "9th Bombardment Wing, Appendix 'A'"; Malucci, *Mission* B-47 *Stratojet*, 19; Hoopaw, *Where the* BUF *Fellows Roamed*, 60; FOIA USAF, "History of the 93D Bombardment Wing (H) and 93D Air Base Group 1–30 November 1958."

120. FOIA USAF, "9th Bombardment Wing, Appendix 'A' February–March 1960."

121. Malucci, *Mission* B-47 *Stratojet*, 133; Adams, *Inside the Cold War*, 45–46.

122. FOIA USAF, "9th Bombardment Wing, Appendix 'A' February–March 1960"; FOIA USAF, "History of the 40th Bombardment Wing Medium Jet, May and June 1958 Schilling Air Force Base, Kansas."

123. This process is derived from several sources. I was given permission to examine the B-47 crew stations at the March AFB museum. This B-47 nose was in fact used for filming sequences in *Strategic Air Command*. I was also given access to the B-47 at the Strategic Air Command and Aerospace Museum. A declassified briefing to President Eisenhower titled "SAC Operations with Sealed-Pit Weapons" was acquired under FOIA from the Eisenhower Library. I purchased a DCU 9/A bomb arming unit on eBay, which is similar to the DCU 9/1 unit used in the B-47. The DCU 9/1 replaced an earlier system called the T-249, which appears in most documents. Finally, see Glenn's Computer Museum for a description of the bomb/nav system for the B-47; USAF HQ, 320th Bombardment Wing, Medium, "B-47 Observers Handbook, 25 September 1953."

124. These data are derived from Department of Defense, Civil Preparedness Agency, "DPCA Attack Environment Manual, June 1973" and FOIA DTRA, "Defense Nuclear Agency Effects Manual Number 1: Capabilities of Nuclear Weapons, 1 July 1972."

125. For a description of B-47 flights during Operation Redwing's Cherokee shot, see Natola, *Boeing* B47 *Stratojet*, 102–5.

126. Hudlow, *Shamrock 22*, 175.

127. FOIA USAF, "9th Bombardment Wing, Appendix 'A' February–March 1960"; "Fan Song," Global Security, accessed 26 September 2019, http://www.globalsecurity.org/military/world/russia/fan-song.htm.

128. I have derived this section directly from the film. For my elaboration, I have relied on Peter George's novelization of *Dr. Strangelove* and updated his crew positions for the aircraft to reflect the actual composition and roles.

129. See Fursenko and Naftali, *One Hell of a Gamble*, ch. 17.

130. This information is distilled from eight reports that are part of a declassified CIA project code-named Aerodynamic, which involved the use of the Ukrainian émigré movement for intelligence collection and propaganda distribution. It is unclear if there were, in fact, any assassination attempts against Khrushchev as all eight reports were based on hearsay. FOIA CIA, "Contact Report: Meeting with Aecassowary/2 and Aecassowary/17," 4

December 1962; "Re: General Situation in Lvivska Oblast, Ukraine End 1964–Early 1965," 24 May 1965; "General Situation in Chernivitski, UKR in 1962," 23 June 1964; "General Situation in the Ukraine in October 1963," 16 March 1964; "Debriefing of Tekla Lukiyanowna," 27 July 1962; "Ukrainian Youth in Lviv," summer 1965, 11 February 1966; "Concerning Reports on Underground Political Organizations in the USSR," 23 June 1964. See also Khrushchev, *Khrushchev on Khrushchev,* for what really happened to Khrushchev in 1964.

131. The authentication process was compiled from the following sources: FOIA USAF, "History of the 4228th Strategic Wing (H, Jet) Columbus Air Force Base, Mississippi 1–30 November 1960"; "History of the 4042nd Strategic Wing, K. I. Sawyer Air Force Base 1–31 January 1963"; "History of the 4157th Strategic Wing, Eielson Air Force Base, July–September 1963"; "History of the 4133D Strategic Wing, Grand Forks Air Force Base July 1962"; Hudlow, *Shamrock* 22, 217–29; Petranick, *Peace Was His Profession,* 40–41; McGill, *Jet Age Man,* 155–56.

132. The KAA-29 Triton Authentication System consisted of "a plastic grille . . . used with a key card effective for six hours": "Keying material will be prepared in a publication consisting of a cover with instructions and 31 sheets of keying data, effective for one month. Each sheet will contain four key cards two on the front and two on the back, each designated for a specific six hour period." North Atlantic Military Committee Standing Group, "Triton Authentication System," 6 October 1959, http://archives.nato.int/uploads /r/null/1/3/131693/SGM-0572-59_ENG_PDP.pdf. The KAA-29 system was compromised when the USS *Pueblo* was seized by the North Koreans in 1968. See FOIA NSA, "Section V: Cryptographic Damage Assessment USS Pueblo AGER-2 23 January–23 December 1968," 28 February 1969.

133. FOIA USAF, interview with Col. John F. Donahue, USAF, conducted by Dr. Charles A. Keene, Office of History, Headquarters Strategic Communications Division, p. 24.

134. FOIA DOE, S. L. Whitcher et al., "Operation Hardtack—Project 2.8: Fallout Measurements by Aircraft and Rocket Sampling, 29 September 1961"; FOIA DOE, S. L. Whitcher et al., "Operation Hardtack Project 2.8 WT-1625 Draft, Aircraft and Rocket Fallout August 1959"; FOIA DTRA, DNA 6038F, "Operation Hardtack I 1958"; FOIA USAF, "History of the 4950th Test Group (Nuclear) from 1 April 1957 to 30 September 1957." The radiation instrumentation experiments are shown in Peter Kuran's 1995 documentary film *Trinity and Beyond: The Atomic Bomb Movie,* including one very annoyed-looking pilot after he removes the film stack from his stomach.

135. On the yields of the devices and weapons, see FOIA DTRA, DNA 6038F, "Operation Hardtack I 1958"; FOIA DOE, "Restricted Data Declassification Decisions 1946 to Present," 1 January 2001; *National Association of Atomic Veterans Newsletter,* March 2010, 15; "Munitions," forum post on Mk-41 yields, 25 March 2013, B52 Stratofortress Association website, registration required, http://www.stratofortress.org/phpBB3/viewforum.php?f=3.

136. On GAM-77 capabilities and yields, see *Association of Air Force Missileers Newsletter* 10, no. 4 (n.d.) and 8, no. 4 (n.d.). See also Hansen, *US Nuclear Weapons,* 182–83. I was informed by one interlocutor that on some missions the yield on the GAM-77 was increased to 10 megatons under certain conditions because of accuracy issues.

137. The description of the release and delivery system is based on the following information: FOIA DOE, "JTF-8 Ad Hoc Group for Nuclear Safety: Technical Nuclear Safety Study of Project Dominic B-52 Airdrops," 26 February 1962; FOIA USAF, "History of the

93D Bombardment Wing (H) and 93D Air Base Group 1–30 November 1958"; FOIA USAF, "Air Force Instruction 91-111: Safety Rules for US Strategic Bombers," 1 October 1997; Harder, *Flying from the Black Hole*; Hansen, *US Nuclear Weapons*, 54; USAF TO 1B-52C-34-2-1, "Aircrew Conventional Munitions Delivery Manual, B-52C, D, E, F, G, and H," 20 March 1969; USAF TO 1B-52G-1CL3, "Radar Navigator Abbreviated Flight Crew Checklist, B-52G," 1 January 1975; USAF TO 1B-52-G-25-2CL-1, "Nuclear Bomb Delivery Procedures," 10 February 1984. I had access to a B-52 radar-navigator position at the March AFB museum, a B-52D cockpit at the Valiant Air Command, and a B-52 cockpit at the Strategic Air Command and Aerospace Museum.

138. Based on my analysis of B-52D at Valiant Air Command, Titusville, Florida; confidential interview.

139. The Hound Dog information is derived from USAF TO 1B52C-30-1, "Aircrew Weapons Delivery Technical Manual B-52/AGM-28," 1 September 1963; USAF SACM, "AGM-28 Operations," 3 August 1970; USAF TO 1B-52C-34-2-1, "Aircrew Conventional Munitions Delivery Manual Strategic Mission Description and Procedures, B-52C, D, E, F, G, and H," 20 March 1969.

140. FOIA NRO, Gerald K. Haines, "Critical to US Security: The Development of the Gambit and Hexagon Satellite Reconnaissance Systems (1997)." I employed Google Earth to locate the remains of the former Soviet air defense system in the Volgograd-Kapustin Yar area and can readily identify where SA-2 sites used to be located because of the characteristic disturbances in the earth. This was cross-indexed with declassified CIA material on the Soviet air defense system to determine what the system looked like for the purposes of the vignette.

141. Project Aerodynamic, for example, used Ukrainian-Canadian tourists to look for ballistic missile sites in Western Ukraine. See FOIA CIA, memo for Chief SR/3, "Review of Positive Intelligence Production from Project Aecassowary for the Period 1 July 1960 to 30 June 1961," 16 August 1961; memo for Chief SR/3, "Current Aerodynamic Activities," 17 November 1960; Subject: Mrs. Fnu Mosora nee Rabiy, 20 November 1960; memo for the record, "Meetings with Aecassowary /2 21–23 March 1960 Dupont Plaza Hotel, Washington DC," 29 March 1960; memo for the record, "Meetings with Aecassowaries 2, 4, 17, 26 and 27 9–11 May 1961," 16 May 1961.

142. I derived the Soviet air defense system by using Michael Holm's data on PVO Strany, cross-indexing it with CIA data from 1964, plotting it out using Google Earth, and then confirming it using Google Earth to find the former sites.

143. See previous note.

144. Marvin Adams, "Routine Night at the Office over the Black Sea," 55th Wing Association, accessed 26 September 2019, http://55wa.org (site no longer active). Note that the map legend states, "Route is from memories of aging participants."

145. Price, *The History of Electronic Warfare*, ch. 18. Peter George included Quail use in the *Dr. Strangelove* novelization (62).

146. There is some dispute over SWESS. B-52 pilots I corresponded with explain SWESS as I have in the text, but one source who worked as ground crew on the weapons states that SWESS "was nothing more than an emergency jettison system with mechanical and electrical interlocks which gave the crew the means to emergency jettison the bombs if necessary. It did not 'automatically' drop weapons if the crew was disabled or other non-

sense." See Michael H. Maggelet's commentary on Eric Schlosser's *Command and Control* at Arms Control Wonk, https://www.armscontrolwonk.com/archive/403910/ghosts-in-the-machine/.

147. As described by John Palcewski at Live Journal, https://forioscribe.livejournal.com/781057.html. Palcewski served with the 4128th Strategic Wing at Amarillo, Texas, and assisted the intelligence staff painting the predictions.

148. I am indebted to Lt. Col. Earl McGill for helping me understand the bombing process.

149. Weapons effects data from Sharfman, *The Effects of Nuclear War*, 15–48, and applied to Kapustin Yar.

150. USAF TO 1B52-G-25-2CL-1, "Nuclear Bomb Delivery Procedures," 10 February 1984.

151. I examined B-52 bomb bays at March AFB, the National Atomic Museum, and the Strategic Air Command and Aerospace Museum. Peter Kuran's documentary *The Atomic Bomb Movie* has a section from a nuclear testing film that depicts the release system of a freefall weapons from a B-52 bomb bay.

152. FOIA USAF, "History of the 42nd Bomb Wing 1 April–30 June 1964"; FOIA USAF, "History of the 5th Bombardment Wing (Heavy) July–September 1964"; FOIA USAF, "History of the 98th Strategic Wing, July–September 1968"; FOIA USAF, "History of the 98th Strategic Wing, January–March 1967."

153. My speculation.

154. FOIA USAF, "History of the 3rd Weather Wing, January–June 1969."

155. FOIA CIA, President's Daily Briefs, 30 October 1967. See also CIA, memo for the record, morning meeting of 2 November 1966; Nicholas Pillet, "OGTch Satellites" (in French), Kosmonavtika, accessed 26 September 2019, http://www.kosmonavtika.com/satellites/ogtch/ogtch.html.

156. See chapter 3.

157. The 403rd history (in Russian) is at http://rvsn.ruzhany.info/403_main.html#contents.

158. See "History of the Red Guards Vitebsk Missile Army" (in Russian), http://rvsn.ruzhany.info/27ra_p00.html#intro_02.

159. Gennediy Dubrovin, 867th Missile Regiment (in Russian), http://rvsn.ruzhany.info/867rp_01.html#contents.

160. It does not appear to have been by the CIA, and the existence of the alert had to wait until the end of the Cold War. The NSA, on the other hand . . .

161. See FOIA CIA, Esau XLV/70, "Intelligence Report: The Evolution of Soviet Policy in the Sino-Soviet Border Dispute, 28 April 1970"; Yang, "The Sino-Soviet Border Clash of 1969"; Gerson, "The Sino-Soviet Border Conflict."

162. Editorial note 67, in *FRUS Volume 34: National Security Policy, 1969–1972*, 247; Norris et al., *British, French, and Chinese Nuclear Weapons*, 420; Podvig, *Russian Strategic Nuclear Forces*, 514.

163. FOIA CIA, National Intelligence Estimate (NIE) 11-1-71, "The Soviet Space Program, 1 July 1971"; FOIA USAF, "History of the 380th Aerospace Wing, January–March 1969."

164. FOIA CIA, NIE 11-1-71, "The Soviet Space Program, 1 July 1971." This event occurred, but the designation of the space vehicle is fictitious. The three ICBMs were SS-7s.

165. FOIA CIA, memo for Chief, Military Division, OCI, "Search for SAM Sites, Yugoslavia," 10 July 1964.

166. FOIA CIA, "National Intelligence Survey: Yugoslavia April 1973."

167. See USAF TO 1-58A-1, "Flight Manual B-58A," 7 February 1964. I was permitted access to the B-58 interior at the Strategic Air Command and Aerospace Museum.

168. USAF TO 1-58A-1, "Flight Manual B-58A," 7 February 1964.

169. FOIA CIA, Office of Special Investigations, "Electronic Aspects of the Soviet Air Defense System, 3 March 1958"; FOIA CIA, undated extract, "Part II section 7 Air Defense: Warsaw Pact Defense against Air Attack: Basic Doctrine and Objectives"; FOIA CIA, "Romania: General Survey, July 1970."

170. FOIA CIA, Department of Interior, "The Romanian Ground Forces: An Intelligence Assessment, February 1984"; FOIA CIA, "Romania: General Survey, July 1970."

171. See map comparison from the following documents: FOIA CIA, NIE 11-3-61, "Sino-Soviet Air Defense Capabilities through Mid-1966, 11 July 1961"; NIE 11-3-64, "Soviet Air and Missile Defense Capabilities through Mid-1970"; NIE 11-3-67, "Soviet Strategic Air and Missile Defenses, 9 November 1967."

172. FOIA CIA, "Search for Long Track Radar at Bacau, Romania, 29 December 1969."

173. USAF TO 1-58A-1, "Flight Manual B-58A," 7 February 1964; USAF TO 1B-58-A-2-13S-17, "Operational Supplement Technical Manual Organizational Maintenance Weapons Control System (AN/ASQ-42)," 1 August 1966.

174. FOIA CIA, undated extract, "Part II section 7 Air Defense: Warsaw Pact Defense against Air Attack: Basic Doctrine and Objectives"; Fitts, *The Strategy of Electromagnetic Conflict*, 60–61.

175. Based on my discussions with B-58 air crew. The most common low-level mission appears to have been run at 500 feet. See also Phil Rowe, "Light the Way," accessed 26 September 2019, https://mvburen.home.xs4all.nl/b-58/5c1.htm.

176. FOIA CIA, Office of Special Investigations, "Electronic Aspects of the Soviet Air Defense System, 3 March 1958."

177. USAF TO 1-58A-1, "Flight Manual B-58A," 7 February 1964.

178. USAF, "B-58 Bomber Defense Officer Course, October 1960."

179. USAF, "B-58 Bomber Defense Officer Course, October 1960"; see also Fitts, *The Strategy of Electromagnetic Conflict*, ch. 3, 5, and 6 for a detailed description of track breaking and other fun ECM activities.

180. See "7th Air Defence Corps"; "90th Independent Assault Aviation Regiment"; "19th Air Defence Division"; "21st Air Defence Division," all at Air Defence Force (PVO), http://www.ww2.dk/new/pvo/pvo.htm. Adjacent formations, of course, had even more firepower on tap, but these numbers apply to the corridor used for this scenario.

181. "260th Red Banner Anti-Aircraft Missile Regiment," http://www.ww2.dk/new/pvo/sam/260zrp.htm.

182. Hampton, *The Hunter Killers*, 101.

183. FOIA CIA, "Intelligence Information Special Report: Field Air Defense in Combat with Low-Altitude Targets (1967)."

184. FOIA CIA, "Intelligence Information Special Report: Organization for the Direction, Reconnaissance, and Engagement of Enemy Air Targets at Low Altitudes (8 December 1968)."

185. "21st Air Defence Division"; Gordon and Komissarov, *Soviet Air Defence Aviation*, 84–99.

186. "19th Air Defence Division."

187. I plotted the 1969-era SAM and radar sites on Google Earth for the entire region and then compared those data to five CIA maps from 1964 to 1969. A topographic program permitted height analysis, and when all the material is lined up, the gap is visually distinct.

188. "7th Air Defence Corps."

189. FOIA CIA PIR, "SA-3 SAM Launch Site Near Moscow," July 1962; FOIA CIA PIR, "SA-3 Missile Site Deployment During 1969," March 1970.

190. USAF TO 1-58A-1 "Flight Manual B-58A," 7 February 1964; USAF TO 1B-58-A-2-13S-17, "Operational Supplement Technical Manual Organizational Maintenance Weapons Control System (AN/ASQ-42)," 1 August 1966.

191. FOIA CIA, "Photographic Interpretation Report: Hardened Central Command Facilities Moskva Area, USSR, September 1965"; "Photographic Interpretation Report: Hardened Central Command Associated Facilities Near Moscow, April 1971"; see also "History of Strategic Management of National Defence," n.d., and the discussion forums on the central command post of Strategic Missile Forces, http://russianarms.mybb.ru/viewtopic.php?id=1294 (link blocked by Russian security services).

192. Computed using Alex Wallerstein's Nuke Map at https://nuclearsecrecy.com/nukemap/.

193. U.S. Geological Survey, Open File report 87–665 1987, "Pacific Enewetak Atoll Crater Exploration (Peace) Program: Part 4," https://pubs.er.usgs.gov/publication/ofr87665.

194. FOIA CIA, "Photographic Interpretation Report: Hardened Central Command Facilities Moskva Area, USSR, September 1965"; "Photographic Interpretation Report: Hardened Central Command Associated Facilities Near Moscow, April 1971."

195. FOIA CIA PIR, "Hardened Central Command Facilities Moskva Area," September 1966.

196. See "History of Strategic Management of National Defence" and the discussion forums on the central command post of Strategic Missile Forces, http://russianarms.mybb.ru/viewtopic.php?id=1294 (link blocked by Russian security services); FOIA CIA, "Basic Imagery Interpretation Report: Moscow ABM System and Related RD&E and Missile Early Warning Facilities, November 1983."

197. Based on my discussions with B-58 air crew.

198. FOIA CIA, memo, "Personalities and Location of the PVO of the Country, 25 September 1962"; FOIA CIA NPIC, "Monino Hardened Possible Command/Control Facility, Moscow, USSR, 22 January 1968."

199. FOIA CIA, Photographic Interpretations Report, "Hardened Command and Control Facilities Penza, USSR, January 1967"; "U.S.S. Andrew Jackson," http://www.hullnumber.com/SSBN-619.

8. Strategic Underground Command

1. The yield of the warheads used on Atlas and Titan I varies in the existing literature and depends on which Redwing test is assumed to be the W38 prototype warhead: Zuni (3.5-megaton), Navaho (4.5-megaton), or Tewa (5-megaton). There are unsubstantiated claims, for example, that Tewa was a "dirty" (increased fallout) version of Zuni, and another

document asserts without a source that 4.5-megaton W38Y1 warheads were mounted on Atlas and Titan during the Cuban Missile Crisis. But hey, what's 1.5 megatons between friends?

2. That said, Cold War polar research stations are depicted in other films, like *The Thing from Another World* (1951), *Bear Island* (1979), and *The Thing* (1982).

3. Turchetti and Roberts, *The Surveillance Imperative*, 218–19.

4. Stine, *ICBM*, 179–81; Mackenzie, *Inventing Accuracy*, 17–19.

5. Sputniks I through III were part of Soviet studies associated with earth sciences that had direct applications for ICBM and space operations. See Siddiqi, *Sputnik and the Soviet Space Challenge*, ch. 4 and 5.

6. Turchetti and Roberts, *The Surveillance Imperative*, 226–29.

7. As detailed in Althoff, *Drift Station*.

8. Stine, *ICBM*, 178.

9. "Thor Able Star," Gunter's Space Page, accessed 27 September 2019, http://space .skyrocket.de/doc_lau/thor_ablestar.htm. See also Lawrence Livermore National Laboratory, "MIRV: A Brief History of Minuteman and Multiple Reentry Vehicles," February 1976, http://nsarchive2.gwu.edu/nsa/NC/mirv/mirv1_1.html.

10. See Sambaluk, *The Other Space Race*; Spires, *Beyond Horizons*; Arnold, *Spying from Space*.

11. Price, *Senior Birdman*, 214.

12. Ball to JFK, "Bilateral Talks concerning US-USSR Cooperation in Outer Space Activities," 5 July 1962; Report by the Department of State for the President's Special Assistant for National Security Affairs, "Progress Report of International Programs in Atmospheric Science," 20 August 1963, both in FRUS *Volume 25: Organization of Foreign Policy, Information Policy, United Nations, Scientific Matters 1961–1963*; see also Ronald Sagdeev and Susan Eisenhower, "United States–Soviet Space Cooperation during the Cold War," NASA, accessed 27 September 2019, www.nasa.gov/50th/50th_magazine/coldWarCoOp .html; "The First Dryden-Blagonravov Agreement—1962," NASA, accessed 27 September 2019, http://history.nasa.gov/SP-4209/ch2-3.htm; Schweitzer, *Techno-Diplomacy*, 149.

13. See full discussion in Markus et al., *Air Force Weather*; Hall, "A History of the Military Polar Orbiting Meteorological Satellite Program."

14. Plot hole in *The Final Countdown*: the USS *Nimitz*, traveling through time to 1941, could not have accessed the DMSP to provide the weather coverage used by the ship's leadership to study the problem because the DMSP would not have existed in 1941. So where did the imagery come from?

15. See Hall, "A History of the Military Polar Orbiting Meteorological Satellite Program."

16. The best study of WS 117L is Dienesch, *Eyeing the Red Storm*. See also FOIA NRO, Lockheed Aircraft Corporation Missile Systems Division, Sunnyvale CA, LMSD-6134, "WS-117L Sentry Syllabus."

17. Library of Congress, LeMay Papers, box B-143, Power to LeMay, "Increased Floor Space Requirements," 20 November 1961.

18. One must be careful to avoid taking CIA analysis of Samos program failure at face value. It is clear from the language of the documents that competition for the strategic intelligence role was intense and acrimonious, and the triumphalist note in them when Samos was canceled is obvious. See FOIA CIA, "A Summary of the National Reconnaissance Problem," 13 May 1965. Arguably Samos development wasn't fast enough given

the events of 1961–62; the competing capability, Corona, was moved into the first rank as a stop-gap, and Samos was canceled in 1964 before it could work properly. See also FOIA NRO, R. Cargill Hall, "The Air Force and the National Security Space Program 1946–1988."

19. Wolfgang Saxon, "Walter Wager, Spy Novelist, Is Dead at 79," *New York Times*, 14 July 2004, https://www.nytimes.com/2004/07/14/us/walter-wager-spy-novelist-is-dead-at-79.html; Walter Wager obituary, *The Independent*, 20 July 2004; Walter Wager obituary, *The Telegraph*, 31 July 2004; Joan McIver, "An Interview with Walter Wager," *Tripod*, 2000, http://Ispy65.tripod.com/id91_m.htm.

20. Wager, *Viper Three*.

21. See Silver and Ursini, *Whatever Happened to Robert Aldrich?*, 107–10.

22. For details on the various configurations, see Neufeld, *Ballistic Missiles in the US Air Force*; Walker, *Atlas*; Stumpf, *Titan II*; Werrell, *The Evolution of the Cruise Missile*.

23. USAF TO 21M-CGM16E-1-1, "Operation Manual USAF Model CGM-16E Missile Weapon System," 15 November 1962; USAF TO 21M-HGM16F-1S-3, "Operation Manual USAF Model HGM-16F Missile Weapon System," 29 October 1964; USAF TO 21M-HGM25A-1-1, "Operation Manual USAF Model HGM-25A Missile Weapon System," 1 August 1963. I would like to recognize the hard work by the staff of Atlas Missile Silo, http://www.atlasmissilesilo.com/, and particularly SiloBoy at Titan Epitaph, http://www.chromehooves.net/Titan_Epitaph_main.htm, for their dedication in preserving the documents, manuals, and pictures of these first-gen ICBM sites.

24. USAF TO 21M-HGM25A-1-1, "Operation Manual USAF Model HGM-25A Missile Weapon System," 1 August 1963.

25. USAF TO 21M-HGM25A-1-1, "Operation Manual USAF Model HGM-25A Missile Weapon System," 1 August 1963; "Cold War Hardline Communications Pit 1961–1965," Chimney Creek Ranch, accessed 27 September 2019, https://www.chimneycreekranch.com/sites/default/files/images/ICBM.marker.pdf; FOIA USAF, "History of the 1st Missile Division, 1 July to December 1957"; "Skyking, Skyking . . . Can Anybody Hear Me?"

26. USAF TO 21M-CGM16E-1-1, "Operation Manual USAF Model CGM-16E Missile Weapon System," 15 November 1962; USAF TO 21M-HGM16F-1S-3, "Operation Manual USAF Model HGM-16F Missile Weapon System," 29 October 1964; USAF TO 21M-HGM25A-1-1, "Operation Manual USAF Model HGM-25A Missile Weapon System," 1 August 1963.

27. USAF TO 21M-CGM16E-1-1, "Operation Manual USAF Model CGM-16E Missile Weapon System," 15 November 1962; USAF TO 21M-HGM16F-1S-3, "Operation Manual USAF Model HGM-16F Missile Weapon System," 29 October 1964; USAF TO 21M-HGM25A-1-1, "Operation Manual USAF Model HGM-25A Missile Weapon System," 1 August 1963.

28. FOIA USAF, "History of the 14th Strategic Aerospace Division, 1–30 November 1962."

29. FOIA USAF, "History of the 14th Strategic Aerospace Division, 1–30 November 1962."

30. FOIA USAF, "History of the 14th Strategic Aerospace Division, 1–30 November 1962."

31. Conine, *Not for Ourselves Alone*, ch. 5.

32. Mercenary Missileer Forum, posts, 12 September 2010; 9 May 2008; 13 May 2008; 20 June 2009; 12 September 2010, www.missileerforum.com (site no longer active).

33. USAF TO 21M-LGM25C-1, "Operations Manual USAF Model LGM 25C Missile Weapons System."

34. USAF TO 21M-LGM25C-1, "Operations Manual USAF Model LGM 25C Missile Weapons System"; Mercenary Missileer Forum, posts, 23 March 2008; 20 June 2009; 12 September 2010. See also Henschen, "Titan II Crew Duty."

35. Mercenary Missileer Forum, discussion posts, 2 November 2013.

36. Mercenary Missileer Forum, discussion post, 31 October 2013.

37. USAF TO 21M-LGM25C-1, "Operations Manual USAF Model LGM 25C Missile Weapons System."

38. See "How a Titan Nuclear Missile Launch Procedure Works," LiveLeak (link removed).

39. Thanks to my colleague Rob Silliman for assisting me with this information based on a 2006 visit to the Titan II facility near Tucson. The device was cut off the Titan Stage 1 display and removed from the museum for unspecified reasons sometime between 2006 and 2013.

40. USAF TO 21M-LGM25C-1, "Operations Manual USAF Model LGM 25C Missile Weapons System."

41. Space Technology Laboratories Report for Advanced Research Projects Agency, "Final Report: Satellite Interception System Feasibility Study, 6 November 1963."

42. Wager, *Viper Three*, 167.

43. I observed the presence of these buildings on research trips to the Walker AFB, Pease AFB, Griffiss AFB, Loring AFB, Clinton-Sherman AFB, and Plattsburgh AFB. Pease, Griffiss, and Loring are on the periphery of the twelve Atlas sites in upstate New York, while Clinton-Sherman is near the Altus OK Atlas sites. Walker AFB supported twelve Atlas F sites. I did not see similar structures at George AFB, Grissom AFB, Lockbourne AFB, Wurtsmith AFB, or Kincheloe AFB. None of those bases is near an ICBM site. The number of lockers appears to correlate to the number of ICBM sites in the area, that is, twelve at Walker, twelve around Plattsburgh, and so on. Besides this speculation, there is no available primary documentation, and there is no indication that the Combat Defense Forces were trained in use of atomic demolition munitions.

44. See Stejskal, *Special Forces Berlin*, 55–59; Hansen, *US Nuclear Weapons*, 209–10. I was given access to an inert W54 at the Atomic Testing Museum in Las Vegas.

45. There is, however, no primary source corroboration of the incident. See Cortright, *Soldiers in Revolt*, 97, 99.

46. Based on my observation at both Oscar Zero LCF in North Dakota and Delta One LCF in South Dakota.

47. Neufeld, *Ballistic Missiles in the US Air Force*, 182, 227, 229, 230; Heefner, *The Missile Next Door*, 20–27. Q came from Q Ship, a merchantman equipped with concealed weapons and designed to entice submarines to reveal themselves and surface where they could be engaged. The Q missile stealthed the U.S. Navy's missile program.

48. Neal expanded the article into a 1962 book, *Ace in the Hole*.

49. Like everything Power is alleged to have said, the ten thousand figure for Minuteman has been taken to heart and repeated frequently over time. There are several earnest accounts of this exchange by those who were not there. How do we know that an enthusiastically pro-Minuteman Tommy Power didn't get carried away and say something like, "Yeah, I could use ten thousand of these!" in a briefing? There is no documentary evidence available that either Power or SAC planned for or even wanted ten thousand Minuteman

missiles. See Ball, *Politics and Force Levels*, 70, who cites York, *Race to Oblivion* and Enthoven and Smith, *How Much Is Enough?* Newhouse, *Cold Dawn*, repeats the story on 61.

50. Library of Congress, LeMay Papers, box 202, "Remarks by General Curtis LeMay at Quantico," 15 July 1955.

51. Library of Congress, LeMay Papers, box B-203, "Remarks by General Curtis LeMay USAF Scientific Advisory Board," 21 May 1957.

52. Library of Congress, Le May Papers, box B-136, Missiles file 1961, Power to Lemay, 8 November 1961; McMillan to LeMay, "Minuteman Safety and Flexibility," 24 October 1961. The first wing missiles could have only one target per missile, and the "multiple target capability" was deferred by McNamara so that progress could proceed quickly with Wing I. Similarly the first wing missiles' LCF systems were not fully protected. And the warhead was not hardened against nuclear effects. These features—single target capability, less protection—were consistent with the original concept. Only later in 1965–66, with the Sylvania version of the LCF, the Deuce, was full protection of the LCF achieved.

53. Heefer, *The Missile Next Door*, 72–74.

54. FOIA Office of the Secretary of Defense, "Outline of Points for General Powers 1–1/2 Hour Briefing to SYG Brosio and the President," 29 September 1964.

55. FOIA Defense Intelligence Agency, minutes of the Defense Intelligence Agency Scientific Advisory Committee meeting, 18 June 1969. Though these minutes are redacted, it is clear that Minuteman was targeted against SS-9 and SS-11 systems well before 1969.

56. For discussion of Alpha Draco, see Yengst, *Lightning Bolts*, 37, 43.

57. These data are derived from cross-indexing test data from the Nuclear Weapons Archive, "Operation Dominic," 3 January 2005, http://nuclearweaponarchive.org/Usa/Tests/Dominic.html; Norris and Cochran's "United States Nuclear Tests July 1945 to December 1992 (1 February 1994)," National Resources Defense Council, http://docs.nrdc.org/nuclear/files/nuc_02019401a_121.pdf; Chuck Hansen's *US Nuclear Weapons*; and FOIA DOE, "Enclosure L to the Report by Commander Joint Task Force Eight on the 1962 Pacific Nuclear Tests (Operation Dominc), Scientific Summary," 4 June 1964, https://apps.dtic.mil/dtic/tr/fulltext/u2/a471900.pdf. On Janus, see Yengst, *Lightning Bolts*, 155.

58. These data are derived from cross-indexing test data from the Nuclear Weapons Archive, "Operation Dominic," 3 January 2005, http://nuclearweaponarchive.org/Usa/Tests/Dominic.html; Norris and Cochran's "United States Nuclear Tests July 1945 to December 1992 (1 February 1994)," National Resources Defense Council, http://docs.nrdc.org/nuclear/files/nuc_02019401a_121.pdf; Chuck Hansen's *US Nuclear Weapons*; and "Enclosure L to the Report by Commander Joint Task Force Eight on the 1962 Pacific Nuclear Tests (Operation Dominc), Scientific Summary." On Janus, see Yengst, *Lightning Bolts*, 155.

59. I am speculating on the nature of the Asset vehicle after examining it at the National Museum of the USAF. There it sits between a mode of the x-20 Dynasoar and a lifting body model, Prime, suggesting that Asset was part of the lifting body evolutionary process, as does some of the literature relating to lifting bodies. The dimensions of Asset, however, suggest that it wasn't a model and could have been a successor to Alpha Draco for Minuteman.

60. Hansen, *US Nuclear Weapons*, 200; Polmar and Norris, *The US Nuclear Arsenal*, 82.

61. This information was derived from cross-referencing the tests from William Robert Johnston, "Database of Nuclear Tests, United States: Part 2, 1964–1972," Johnston's Archive, 19 June 2005, http://www.johnstonsarchive.net/nuclear/tests/USA-ntests2.html

and comparing them to the various w62 development timelines: National Nuclear Security Administration, https://nnsa.energy.gov/mediaroom/factsheets/w62dismantlement (site no longer active), and U.S. Department of Energy, Office of Scientific and Technical Information, https://www.osti.gov/accomplishments/documents/fullText/ACC0207.pdf (link retired by DOE). Mackenzie notes in *Inventing Accuracy*, 258, that a tested 200-kiloton ICBM warhead was designed for the USAF while the w58 Polaris A3 was under development, and consideration was given to upscaling it to 1 megaton.

62. Spinardi, *From Polaris to Trident*, 225.

63. While examining the training facility for the Duga (Steel Yard) system located near Chernobyl in July 2019, I found this information on a derelict visual aid dedicated to the specifics of American and Chinese nuclear delivery systems.

64. Library of Congress, LeMay Papers, box B-136, Missile file 1961, AFSC to LeMay, "Penetration Program," 9 October 1961. I examined a Mk-6 reentry vehicle at the Strategic Air Command and Aerospace Museum.

65. TO 21M-LGM30F-1-5, "Weapons System Operation Instructions Wings III and IV— Modernized LGM-30F and LGM30G Missiles," 5 July 1968.

66. USAF Historical Division Liaison Office, "USAF Ballistic Missile Programs: 1964–1966," accessed 28 September 2019, http://nsarchive2.gwu.edu//nukevault/ebb249/doc04.pdf; USAF Historical Division Liaison Office, "USAF Ballistic Missile Programs: 1967–1968," accessed 28 September 2019, http://nsarchive2.gwu.edu//nukevault/ebb249/doc05.pdf.

67. USAF Historical Division Liaison Office, "USAF Ballistic Missile Programs: 1964–1966"; USAF Historical Division Liaison Office, "USAF Ballistic Missile Programs: 1967–1968"; USAF Historical Division Liaison Office, "USAF Ballistic Missile Programs: 1969–1970," accessed 28 September 2019, http://nsarchive2.gwu.edu//nukevault/ebb249/doc06.pdf. See also detailed discussions throughout Yengst, *Lightning Bolts*.

68. Except Wing I in Montana, which had four squadrons, including the 564th, "The Odd Squad."

69. Based on my visit to the Oscar Zero Deuce LCF in North Dakota and the Delta One LCF in South Dakota.

70. Based on my observation at both Oscar Zero LCF in North Dakota and Delta One LCF in South Dakota.

71. Based on my observation at both Oscar Zero LCF in North Dakota and Delta One LCF in South Dakota. See also Mercenary Missileer, post, "FSC Forgets Authentication Code," 10 November 2009.

72. See also Mercenary Missileer, posts, 9 October 2009; 22 January 2008, "FSC Forgets Authentication Code."

73. See also Mercenary Missileer, post, "Codes for this, Codes for that," 22 January 2008.

74. Library of Congress, LeMay Papers, box B-136, Missiles 1961 file, "Lauritsen Committee report, 15 July 1961."

75. For example, see Phillip Hallam-Baker, "Who Is in Control of TLS?," *IS Buzz News*, 3 April 2017, http://www.informationsecuritybuzz.com/articles/who-is-in-control-of-tls/; Karl Smallwood, "For Nearly Two Decades the Nuclear Launch Code at All Minuteman Silos in the United States Was 00000000," *Today I Found Out*, 29 November 2013, http://www.todayifoundout.com/index.php/2013/11/nearly-two-decades-nuclear-launch-code-minuteman-silos-united-states-00000000/; "Dial 00000000 for Armageddon," *Daily*

Mail, 29 November 2013, http://www.dailymail.co.uk/news/article-2515598/Launch-code-US-nuclear-weapons-easy-00000000.html; "Hillary Clinton: 'A Man You Can Bait with a Tweet Is Not a Man We Can Trust with Nuclear Weapons,'" LiveLeak, accessed 28 September 2019, https://www.liveleak.com/view?i=f6c_1469765923&comments=1.

76. Based on my observation at Oscar Zero LCF in North Dakota and Delta One LCF in South Dakota.

77. Based on my observation at Oscar Zero LCF in North Dakota and Delta One LCF in South Dakota; TO 21M-LGM30F-1-5, "Weapons System Operation Instructions Wings III and IV—Modernized LGM-30F and LGM30G Missiles," 5 July 1968.

78. The author also visited Launch Facility November 22.

79. Based on my observations at Oscar Zero LCF.

80. Mercenary Missileer, post, "Skybird vs. Sky King," 15 October 2009. The earlier Skybird was for alerting the bomber alert forces on the Primary Alerting System; Sky King was for the entire SAC force.

81. This is based on a series of posts between former SAC personnel on the Friends of SAC Facebook page plus analysis of their repeated use in several hundred pages of declassified USAF documents.

82. National Park Service, "Emergency Action Messages," https://www.nps.gov/mimi/learn/historyculture/emergency-action-messages.htm (site no longer active).

83. Mercenary Missileer, post, "Sealed Authenticator System," 11 December 2009.

84. Based on my visit to the Oscar Zero Deuce LCF in North Dakota, the Delta One LCF in South Dakota, and the Minuteman II procedures launch trainer at Ellsworth AFB. See also TO 21M-LGM30F-1-5, "Weapons System Operation Instructions Wings III and IV—Modernized LGM-30F, and LGM30G Missiles," 5 July 1968.

85. Based on my visit to the Oscar Zero Deuce LCF in North Dakota, the Delta One LCF in South Dakota, and the Minuteman II procedures launch trainer at Ellsworth AFB. See also TO 21M-LGM30F-1-5, "Weapons System Operation Instructions Wings III and IV—Modernized LGM-30F, and LGM30G Missiles," 5 July 1968.

86. See National Park Service, "Emergency Action Messages"; Mercenary Missileer, posts, "Sealed Authenticator System," 9 December 2009.

87. The Technical Material Corporation provided the transmitters at WWV. It also was a contractor to the White House Communications Agency, New York State civil defense organization, and the U.S. Navy, where it provided mobile strategic communications units. See "WWV, Ft Collins, Colorado," http://www.tmchistory.org/tmc_history/photos/fort_collins/fort_collins_gallery.htm.

88. Mercenary Missileer, posts, 20 September 2007; 4 November 2009; my visit to the Oscar Zero Deuce LCF in North Dakota, the Delta One LCF in South Dakota, and the Minuteman II procedures launch trainer at Ellsworth AFB. See also TO 21M-LGM30F-1-5, "Weapons System Operation Instructions Wings III and IV—Modernized LGM-30F and LGM30G Missiles," 5 July 1968.

89. TO 21M-LGM30F-1-5, "Weapons System Operation Instructions Wings III and IV—Modernized LGM-30F and LGM30G Missiles," 5 July 1968.

90. TO 21M-LGM30F-1-5, "Weapons System Operation Instructions Wings III and IV—Modernized LGM-30F and LGM30G Missiles," 5 July 1968.

91. Ryan Grenoble, "'Secret' Nuclear Missile Launch Code during Cold War Was '00000000,'" *Huffington Post*, 23 January 2014, http://www.huffingtonpost.ca/entry/nuclear -missile-code-00000000-cold-war_n_4386784; Karl Smallwood, "For 20 Years the Nuclear Launch Code at US Minuteman Silos Was 00000000," *Gizmodo*, 29 November 2013, https:// gizmodo.com/for-20-years-the-nuclear-launch-code-at-us-minuteman-si-1473483587; Smallwood, "For Nearly Two Decades the Nuclear Launch Code at All Minuteman Silos in the United States Was 00000000"; Sean Gallagher, "Shall We Play a Game?—Launch Code for US Nukes Was 00000000 for 20 Years," *Ars Technica*, 3 December 2013, https:// arstechnica.com/tech-policy/2013/12/launch-code-for-us-nukes-was-00000000-for-20 -years/; Siegphyl, "US Nuclear Weapons Launch Code Was Terrifyingly 00000000," *War History Online*, 6 December 2013, https://www.warhistoryonline.com/war-articles/us -nuclear-weapons-launch-code-terrifyingly-00000000.html.

92. Bruce Blair, "Keeping Presidents in the Dark: Episode #1 The Case of the Missing 'Permissive Action Links,'" *Bruce Blair's Nuclear Column*, 11 February 2004, http://web .archive.org/web/20040404013440/http://www.cdi.org/blair/permissive-action-links .cfm; "Permissive Action Links," Columbia University Computer Science, accessed 28 September 2019, https://www.cs.columbia.edu/~smb/nsam-160/pal.html; "Zero Protection from Nuclear Code," *The Guardian*, 17 June 2004.

93. TO 21M-LGM30F-1-5, "Weapons System Operation Instructions Wings III and IV— Modernized LGM-30F and LGM30G Missiles," 5 July 1968.

94. I examined launch enable control groups at the Strategic Air Command and Aerospace Museum, the Ellsworth AFB Museum, the National Museum of the USAF, and the Delta Zero museum. Oscar Zero's launch enable control group was removed. None of the thumbwheels had a zero on it. Three of the launch enable control groups were set at P7 in all six slots; the other was randomly scrambled.

95. See USAF Historical Division Liaison Office, "USAF Ballistic Missile Programs: 1964–1966"; USAF Historical Division Liaison Office, "USAF Ballistic Missile Programs: 1967–1968"; USAF Historical Division Liaison Office, "USAF Ballistic Missile Programs: 1969–1970."

96. The nature and scope of the Marxist rebellion against the United States in the late 1960s and early 1970s is covered in Burrough, *Days of Rage*.

97. Fournier, *FLQ*, 82–83.

98. TO 21M-LGM30F-1-5, "Weapons System Operation Instructions Wings III and IV— Modernized LGM-30F and LGM30G Missiles," 5 July 1968; Space Technology Laboratories Report for Advanced Research Projects Agency, "Final Report: Satellite Interception System Feasibility Study, 6 November 1963."

99. Time on target was a British development from World War II whereby British artillery units used BBC radio time signals as a coordinating mechanism to achieve simultaneous effects against a target without compromising the mission by using military communications systems that could be intercepted.

100. Ogletree, "The 4th Airborne Command and Control Squadron."

101. See "Keynote Speech Summary," 4.

102. "Keynote Speech Summary," 4; Greg Ogletree, "A History of the Post Attack Command and Control System," Strategic Air Command, Airborne Command Control Asso-

ciation, https://www.sac-acca.org/documents/PACCS%20History.html; Kuehn, "ALCS 50th Anniversary"; McLean, "The Airborne Launch Control System Part I."

103. Based on my analysis of EC-135C Looking Glass aircraft at the Strategic Air Command and Aerospace Museum.

104. Based on my analysis of EC-135C Looking Glass aircraft at the Strategic Air Command and Aerospace Museum; USAF TO 1C-135(E)C-1-2, "EC-135C Communications Center Electronics Inflight Operations and Maintenance Manual," 10 October 1980; McLean, "Airborne Launch Control System Part II."

105. Based on my analysis of EC-135C Looking Glass aircraft at the Strategic Air Command and Aerospace Museum; USAF TO 1C-135(E)C-1-2, "EC-135C Communications Center Electronics Inflight Operations and Maintenance Manual," 10 October 1980; McLean, "Airborne Launch Control System Part II."

106. "The Fall of Colossus," Wikipedia, accessed 28 September 2019, https://en.wikipedia .org/wiki/The_Fall_of_Colossus.

107. Assistant Secretary of Defense (Communications, Command, Control, and Intelligence)/WWMCCS System Engineer Defense Communications Agency, "Modernization of the WWMCCS Information System (WIN), Prepared for the Committee on Armed Services United States House of Representatives in Response to House Report No. 96–916, 19 January 1981."

108. Matt Larson, phone conversation, 1 September 2017.

109. See Assistant Secretary of Defense (Communications, Command, Control, and Intelligence)/WWMCCS System Engineer Defense Communications Agency, "Modernization of the WWMCCS Information System."

110. Pearson, The World Wide Military Command and Control System, ch. 5.

111. See Assistant Secretary of Defense (Communications, Command, Control, and Intelligence)/WWMCCS System Engineer Defense Communications Agency, "Modernization of the WWMCCS Information System."

112. Assistant Secretary of Defense (Communications, Command, Control, and Intelligence)/WWMCCS System Engineer Defense Communications Agency, "Modernization of the WWMCCS Information System."

113. Pearson, The World Wide Military Command and Control System, ch. 13.

114. "K-137"; "K-424"; "K-447," all (in Russian) at www.deepstorm.ru.

115. National Security Archive, Memo for the President, "False Missile Alerts," 13 June 1980, http://nsarchive2.gwu.edu/nukevault/ebb371/.

116. "K-137."

117. "A Soviet War of Nerves," Newsweek, 5 January 1981, 21. Thanks to Bill Ossenfort and Ray Hildebrant for their memories of alert operations at Loring AFB during this time.

118. Pearson, The World Wide Military Command and Control System, ch. 13.

119. "K-424."

120. "K-424."

121. "K-424."

122. Mercenary Missileer Forum, posts, "Permissive Action Links," 22 July 2008.

123. The literature on military professionalism is vast, so I have distilled its essence from Willeford, "What Is a Military Professional?"

9. Dr. Strangelove Goes to Sea

1. Cagle and Manson, *The Sea War in Korea*. 469–74; Gordon and Komissarov, *Soviet Air Defence Aviation*, 30–31.

2. USN Operational Archive, "Chief of Naval Operations Report to the Secretary of the Navy, 1951"; "Chief of Naval Operations Report to the Secretary of the Navy, 1952."

3. Numerous incidents are recounted in Hennessy and Jinks, *The Silent Deep*, and in Aldrich, GCHQ. See also McLaren, *Silent and Unseen*.

4. Winkler, *Cold War at Sea*, 179.

5. A nonsensationalist account is Weir and Boyne, *Rising Tide*, ch. 4.

6. Winkler catalogues these in *Cold War at Sea*. See also Pedrozo, "The US-China Incidents at Sea Agreement."

7. See McHale, *Stealth Boat*; Jett, *Super Nuke!*; McLaren, *Silent and Unseen*.

8. The main proponent that there was a Soviet attack on USS *Scorpion* in retaliation for the K-129 sinking is Sewell in *All Hands Down*. Sewell, with Clint Richmond, wrote *Red Star Rogue*, a work postulating that K-129 was sent to stimulate a third-party nuclear war between the United States and China. Our understanding of the K-129 incident has not been helped by the now deceased John Craven and his coyness on the matter in *The Silent War*. Note that the same publishing house handled all three works. Gary Weir's corrective, "Deep Secrets," in *Moscow Times*, 14 October 2005, should give people some pause on the matter.

9. See Winkler, *Cold War at Sea*.

10. Amy K. East, "An Analysis of the Bilateral United States/Soviet Union Navy Agreement on the Prevention of Incidents on and over the High Seas (INCSEA)," Cold War Museum, accessed 29 September 2019, http://www.coldwar.org/histories/INCSEA.asp; Adm. Harry Train's account of the incident is described in his reminiscences at U.S. Naval Institute, https://www.usni.org/sites/default/files/2018-05/Train%2C%20Harry%20D%20-%20Index_0.pdf.

11. Moore, *The Soviet Navy Today*, 180. See also Winkler, *Cold War at Sea*.

12. See Fred Albrech, "Cold War Encounter," Gyrodyne: Helicopter Historical Foundation, accessed 29 September 2019, http://www.gyrodynehelicopters.com/cold_war.htm.

13. Hennessy and Jinks, *The Silent Deep*, 349.

14. Kurdin and Grasdock, "Loss of a Yankee SSBN."

15. Dean Lohmeyer, "Diesel Sub Commander Recalls Historic Soviet Submarine Chase," *Navy News Service*, 29 April 2009, https://www.navy.mil/submit/display.asp?story_id=45746.

16. FOIA CIA, Office of Research and Reports, "Geographic Intelligence Report: A Summary of Estimated Soviet Capabilities in Geodesy, Gravimetry, and Cartography, April 1957"; see also Cloud, "American Cartographic Transformations during the Cold War."

17. Meinesz determined that a submarine had enough dampening effect when it was submerged to conduct accurate measurements. See Tomoda, "Gravity at Sea."

18. See boat pages for Whiskey S-144; Zulus B-77, B-66, B-72, B-82, B-63, and B-62; and Foxtrots B-133, B-164, B-26, B-40, B-112, B-50, B-164, and B-101 (in Russian), www.deepstorm.ru.

19. See Tomoda, "Gravity at Sea."

20. See B. Louis Decker et al., "The Minuteman Geodetic and Geophysical (G&G) Error Budget: Some Historical Comments," May 2016, http://geodeticsurvey.mysite.com

/Documents/Moore/MinutemanG&GCommentsMay2016.pdf, via www.1370th.org. Note that the CIA's National Intelligence Estimate in 1961 rejected the possibility that the Soviets had an all-inertial guidance system for their ballistic missiles. If they were relying only on radio inertial guidance, then why were they conducting intercontinental tie-in gravimetric surveys? Or was the CIA completely unaware of the Soviet underwater survey program? See FOIA CIA NIE 11-5-61, "Soviet Technical Capabilities in Guided Missiles and Space Vehicles, 25 April 1961."

21. See Benjamin B. Weybrew, "Naval Submarine Medical Research Laboratory Report Number 917: History of Submarine Psychology at the US Naval Submarine Medical Research Laboratory," 31 August 1979, https://apps.dtic.mil/dtic/tr/fulltext/u2/a077405.pdf. Weybrew was one of the psychologists assigned to the *Triton* during her voyage and produced substantial literature on the psychological aspects of underwater operations.

22. See Podvig, *Russian Strategic Nuclear Forces*, 487–97; A. S. Nikolaev, "Submarine Participation in 1955–1961 Nuclear Tests" (in Russian), www.deepstorm.ru; pages for the "53–61/53–61M" and "T-5/T-V/53–58" torpedoes (in Russian), www.militaryrussia.ru; Weir and Boyne, *Rising Tide*, 78–80.

23. See Podvig, *Russian Strategic Nuclear Forces*, 487–97; "Submarine Participation in 1955–1961 Nuclear Tests" (in Russian), www.deepstorm.ru; pages for the "53–61/53–61M" and "T-5/T-V/53–58" torpedoes (in Russian), www.militaryrussia.ru; Weir and Boyne, *Rising Tide*, 78–80.

24. See Department of the Navy, Naval Intelligence Support Center, "Whiskey on the Rocks: The Submarine Incident off Karlskrona," 19 April 1982, https://docplayer.net/47935626-Whiskey-on-the-rocks-the-submarine-incident-off-karlskrona-etccu-unclassified-nisc-trans-6789-n.html. Numerous boat pages (in Russian) at www.deepstorm.ru make reference to the presence of "nuclear ammunition" on board submarines well into the late Cold War, like Foxtrot B-4 in 1983 and Romeo C-37 in 1987, among others.

25. A. S. Nikolaev, "Submarine Participation in 1955–1961 Nuclear Tests" (in Russian), www.deepstorm.ru.

26. Hansen, *US Nuclear Weapons*, 206–8; Defense Nuclear Agency, "Plumbbob Series 1957: Nuclear Test Personnel Review," 15 September 1981, and WT-1430, "Operation Plumbbob Project 5.1 Inflight Structural Response of an HSS-1 Helicopter to a Nuclear Detonation."

27. Defense Nuclear Agency, "Plumbbob Series 1957." The inclusion of Shot Morgan is speculation on my part. The role of Librascope in the ASROC program is derived from the Librascope alumni website, http://www.librascopememories.com/, and from emails from several former Librascope employees involved with ASROC.

28. Hansen, *US Nuclear Weapons*, 206–8; WT-1621, "Operation Hardtack: Project 2.3 Characteristics of the Radioactive Cloud from Underwater Bursts, 15 January 1962"; WT-1629, "Operation Hardtack: Project 3.5 Loading and Response of Submarine Hulls from Underwater Bursts"; ITR-1660, "Operation Hardtack Preliminary Report, Technical Summary of Military Effects Programs 1–9, 23 September 1959"; DTRA, "Fact Sheet: Operation Hardtack I," May 2015, http://www.dtra.mil/Portals/61/Documents/NTPR/1-Fact_Sheets/HARDTACK%20I%20%20-%202017.pdf?ver=2017-02-07-081710-460.

29. Friedman, *US Destroyers*, ch. 12 and 13.

30. See data from WT-1621, WT-1626, and "Enclosure L to the Report by Commander Joint Task Force Eight on the 1962 Pacific Nuclear Tests (Operation Dominc), Scientific Summary." See also the declassified U.S. Navy film *ASROC Nuclear Effects Test*.

31. See data from WT-1621, WT-1626, and "Enclosure L to the Report by the Commander Joint Task Force Eight on the 1962 Pacific Nuclear Tests (Operation Dominic) Scientific Summary." See also ASROC *Nuclear Effects Test*. The U.S. Navy traitor, John Walker, served aboard USS *Razorback* as a radioman.

32. See data from WT-1621, WT-1626, and "Enclosure L to the Report by the Commander Joint Task Force Eight on the 1962 Pacific Nuclear Tests (Operation Dominic) Scientific Summary." See also ASROC *Nuclear Effects Test*.

33. This is alluded to in the Swordfish reports and explicit in the 1963 U.S. Navy training film ASROC *Weapons System: Introduction*, https://archive.org/details/U.S.NavyTrainingFilm-ASROCWeaponsSystem-Introduction. On the USS *Skipjack* and torpedoes, see McLaren, *Silent and Unseen*. See also Friedman, *US Destroyers*, 300.

34. A *Farragut*-class destroyer was unavailable for examination, so I used the ASROC-equipped *Gearing*-class USS *Joseph P. Kennedy* at Fall River, Massachusetts, as a stand-in. I was provided complete access to the ship and was accompanied by a former crew member who walked me through the ASROC process.

35. Based on my examination of USS *Joseph P. Kennedy* and discussions with former crew members.

36. Librascope, "Capability Improvement Program for Fire Control Group Mk 111 and Fire Control System Mk 114," brochure in author's possession; emails with Howard Applegate, Bob Chambers, Raymond Hand, Carl Sorensen, all alumni of Librascope's ASROC program.

37. Librascope, "Capability Improvement Program for Fire Control Group Mk 111 and Fire Control System Mk 114"; emails with Howard Applegate, Bob Chambers, Raymond Hand, Carl Sorensen.

38. Based on my examination of USS *Joseph P. Kennedy*; 1963 U.S. Navy training film ASROC *Weapons System: Introduction*.

39. Based on my examination of USS *Joseph P. Kennedy*; 1963 U.S. Navy training film ASROC *Weapons System: Introduction*.

40. Lynette Hirshman, "Integrating Syntax, Semantics, and Discourse: DARPA Natural Language Understanding Program R&D Final Report, 1989," https://apps.dtic.mil/dtic/tr/fulltext/u2/a206803.pdf.

41. Weir and Boyne, *Rising Tide*, 4.

42. Reed, *Red November*, 138.

43. Podvig, *Russian Strategic Nuclear Forces*, ch. 5; pages for the submarines "B-41"; "B-121"; "B-45"; "K-137"; "K-26"; "K-216"; "K-249" (in Russian), www.deepstorm.ru.

44. As described in detail in Friedman, *US Submarines since 1945*.

45. Spinardi, *From Polaris to Trident*, 55; Hansen, *US Nuclear Weapons*, 201–6; FOIA DOE, Atomic Energy Commission, "132nd AEC-MLC Conference," 15 June 1962.

46. FOIA CIA, memo for DCI, "Military Thought: Combat against Enemy Missile Submarines, by Rear Admiral O. Zhukovskiy, October 1961," 29 May 1962.

47. Spinardi's *From Polaris to Trident* remains the most comprehensive work on the USN Fleet Ballistic Missile System. On the W58 yield: only two Dominic tests approach the 200-kiloton yield quoted by most secondary sources—Adobe and Truckee. Adobe was either 190 or 200 kilotons, while Truckee was either 210 or 225. Adobe was related to the Pershing warhead fired during shot Aztec, so the Truckee test yield between 210 and

225 kilotons appears to be the best estimate for the W58 yield. See "Enclosure L to the Report by Commander Joint Task Force Eight on the 1962 Pacific Nuclear Tests (Operation Dominc), Scientific Summary"; DTRA, "Summary of Operation Dominic I Nuclear Weapons Tests (1962)," https://www.dtra.mil/Portals/61/Documents/NTPR/1-Fact_Sheets/23_DOMINIC_I.pdf.

48. Rife and Carlisle, *The Sound of Freedom*, 118.

49. Hansen, *US Nuclear Weapons*, 203–6; Polmar and Norris, *The US Nuclear Arsenal*, 190–91; Spinardi, *From Polaris to Trident*, 108; Aldridge, *First Strike*, 44.

50. "Enclosure L to the Report by Commander Joint Task Force Eight on the 1962 Pacific Nuclear Tests (Operation Dominc), Scientific Summary"; DTRA, "Summary of Operation Dominic I Nuclear Weapons Tests (1962)."

51. This information was generated by cross-indexing the Department of Energy's "United States Nuclear Tests July 1945 through September 1992," https://www.nnss.gov/docs/docs_LibraryPublications/DOE_NV-209_Rev16.pdf, with William Robert Johnston, "Database of Nuclear Tests, United States: Part 2, 1964–1972," and Nils-Olov Bergkvist and Ragnhild Ferm, "Nuclear Explosions 1945–1998," Defence Research Establishment (Sweden) and Stockholm International Peace Research Institute, July 2000, https://multimedia.scmp.com/news/world/article/to-understand-North-Korea/data/sipri-report-original.pdf. The 1967–68 test was Staccato; the 1968–70 tests were Wineskin, Cornice Yellow, Cornice Green.

52. Haefmeister, "How Much Warhead Reliability Is Enough for a Comprehensive Nuclear Test Ban Treaty?"; Immele et al., "An Exchange on Stockpile Confidence"; R. E. Kidder, "Maintaining the US Stockpile of Nuclear Weapons during a Low-Threshold of Comprehensive Test Ban," Lawrence Livermore National Laboratory, October 1987, https://fas.org/programs/ssp/nukes/testing/kidderucrl53820.pdf; George H. Miller et al., "Report to Congress on Stockpile Reliability, Weapon Remanufacture, and the Role of Nuclear Testing," Lawrence Livermore National Laboratory, October 1987, https://www.osti.gov/servlets/purl/6032983; Duncan Campbell and Norman Solomon, "Accidents Will Happen," *New Statesman*, 27 November 1981.

53. Reed, *At the Abyss*, 111.

54. Polmar and Norris, *The US Nuclear Arsenal*, 198–99; Hansen, *US Nuclear Weapons*, 206; Dalgleish and Schweikart, *Trident*, 29, 34; Aldridge, *First Strike*, 84, 89–90. See also "US Nuclear Deterrent Is Secure Despite Doubts Cast on Warhead," *Jane's Intelligence Review*, July 2005, 36–37.

55. Spinardi, *From Polaris to Trident*, 112; Mackenzie, *Inventing Accuracy*, 258, 274.

56. This information was generated by cross-indexing DOE's "United States Nuclear Tests July 1945 through September 1992" with Johnston, "Database of Nuclear Tests, United States: Part 2, 1964–1972," and Bergkvist and Ferm, "Nuclear Explosions 1945–1998." These tests were Portmanteau, Stanyan, Cabrillo, Chiberta, and Esrom in the Bedrock test series, and then Marsilly and Reblochon in the Fulcrum and Cresset series.

57. Dubay, *Three Knots to Nowhere*, 105–6.

58. Jaskoviak, *Life Aboard the Crazy Polack*, 136–37.

59. Waller, *Big Red*, 61.

60. Most sources only have the SUBROC available aboard SSN submarines, but at least one personal account suggests otherwise. See Jaskoviak, *Life Aboard the Crazy Polack*, 86–87. On their individual boat pages, Navsource lists the following SSBNS as ASTOR-

capable: *Kamaneha,* the *Lewis and Clark, George Polk, George Bancroft,* and the *Daniel Webster.* SUBROC-capable SSBNs include the *Abraham Lincoln.* This is likely only a partial list.

61. Scortia and Robinson, *The Gold Crew,* vii–viii.

62. Kane, *My Meteoric Rise to Obscurity,* 28.

63. Suid, *Guts and Glory,* 610–11, 687–88; Paul Willistein, "High-Caliber Collaboration 'Top Gun' Production Team Reunites for 'Crimson Tide,'" *Morning Call,* 12 May 1995. See also Henrick, *The Phoenix Odyssey* and *Crimson Tide;* Fleming, *High Concept,* 263.

64. "Meet the Navigator: Peter Boyne," *Smithsonian,* accessed 28 September 2019, https://timeandnavigation.si.edu/navigation-for-everyone/meet-the-navigator/submarine-navigator-us-navy-ret. Boyne was the navigator aboard the USS *James K. Polk* from 1965 to 1968.

65. F. D. Braddon, "Ship Inertial Navigation," paper presented at the annual meeting of the Society of Naval Architects and Marine Engineers, 15–16 November 1962, www.sname .org. Joe Hartzell's website, Loran History, http://www.loran-history.info/, has extensive primary source material scanned in from NARA files on LORAN-C. Unfortunately the original NARA RG file numbers are absent. See U.S. Coast Guard, Office Memorandum from Special Assistant for LORAN C to Commandant, U.S. Coast Guard, "LORAN-C Program Background Information and Status of Implementation, 3 April 1959," 6 April 1959; U.S. Navy, OP-35 to dl, "Navigation Requirements," 20 October 1961.

66. Loran History website; U.S. Navy, OP-35 to dl, "Navigation Requirements," 20 October 1961.

67. "LORAN Station Lampedusa," Loran History, accessed 28 September 2019, http://www.loran-history.info/lampedusa/lampedusa.htm.

68. Loran History website; U.S. Navy, OP-35 to OP-31, "Requirements for Navigational Systems for Submarines," 19 October 1961.

69. Guier and Weiffenbach, "Genesis of Satellite Navigation"; Danchik, "An Overview of Transit Development."

70. Danchik, "An Overview of Transit Development." See also Yionoulis, "The Transit Satellite Geodesy Program."

71. Loran History website; U.S. Navy, OP-35 to dl, "Navigation Requirements," 20 October 1961; Decker et al., "The Minuteman Geodetic and Geophysical (G&G) Error Budget."

72. T. A. Stansell, "The Transit Navigation Satellite System," Magnavox Advanced Products and Systems Company, 1978; Danchik, "The Navy Navigation Satellite System (Transit)."

73. Jerry Emanuelson, "Operation Fishbowl," Futurescience, n.d., http://www .futurescience.com/emp/fishbowl.html; DTRA, Leo Kiley et al., JTF-8, "A 'Quick Look' at the Technical Results of Starfish Prime," https://apps.dtic.mil/dtic/tr/fulltext/u2/a955411 .pdf; DTRA, Edward E. Conrad et al., IR-10-22, "Collateral Damage to Satellites from an EMP Attack, August 2010," https://documents2.theblackvault.com/documents/dtic/a531197.pdf; Herman Hoerlin, "United States High Altitude Test Experiences," Los Alamos Scientific Laboratory, October 1976, https://fas.org/sgp/othergov/doe/lanl/docs1/00322994.pdf.

74. U.S. Coast Guard Chief Program Analysis to Chief of Staff, "War and Emergency Planning for Operation of LORAN C Stations," 22 May 1964; U.S. Coast Guard, "Air Transportable Loran C System (ATLS) Operational Facility Installation, Operation, and Maintenance Manual, October 1971," Loran History, accessed 28 September 2019, http://www .loran-history.info/ATLS_Program/Air_Transportable_LORAN-C_System_-ATLS -Operational_Facility_Installation_Operation_and_Maintenance_Manual_Scanned

_20Sep2010.pdf. See also "ET1 Kenneth Fron, US Coast Guard (1969–1974)," *Together We Served Voices* (blog), accessed 28 September 2019, https://blog.togetherweserved .com//?s=Kenneth+Fron.

75. "An Overview of the Navy Navigation Satellite System," Johns Hopkins University Applied Physics Laboratory, accessed 28 September 2019, http://sd-www.jhuapl.edu /Transit/.

76. Stansell, "The Transit Navigation Satellite System."

77. The Transit launch data and launch systems are available at https://space.skyrocket .de/ on a launch-by-launch basis.

78. USNARA, "NASA's Unsung Hero: The Scout Launch Vehicle Program, 1959–1994," accessed 28 September 2019, https://www.google.com/culturalinstitute/beta/exhibit /twISgejPzIk_KQ.

79. "National Life Stories: An Oral History of British Science. Sir Anthony Laughton Interviewed by Paul Merchant," British Library, 2010–11, http://sounds.bl.uk/related -content/TRANSCRIPTS/021T-C1379X0029XX-0000A0.pdf.

80. FOIA CIA, Directorate of Intelligence, memorandum, "Depressed Trajectories: Unlikely Role for Soviet SLBM's, August, 1982"; Spinardi, *From Polaris to Trident*, ch. 6 and 7; Mackenzie, *Inventing Accuracy*, ch. 5.

81. Rife and Carlisle, *The Sound of Freedom*, 104–6, 112–13, 116–17.

82. See Winkler, "The Evolution and Significance of the 1972 Incidents at Sea Agreement." The exploits of the T-AGS ships are catalogued at http://www.tags-21.info/index .html. On multiple beam echo soundings, see "National Life Stories: Sir Anthony Laughton."

83. FOIA CIA, Intelligence Information Special Report, N. Gonchar, "Some Problems of Combat with Nuclear Missile Submarines," 22 May 1973, extracted from *Military Thought*, a Soviet journal stolen by the CIA. See also Prados, "The Navy's Biggest Betrayal."

84. Military History Section, Headquarters Army Forces Far East, *Japanese Monograph No. 118: Operational History of Naval Communications December 1941–August 1945*, pp. 226–33; Department of the Navy, Naval Electronic Systems Command, NAVELEX 0101.113, *Naval Shore Electronics Criteria: VLF, LF, and MF Communications Systems*, August 1972, ch. 1; James P. Hauser and Franklin J. Rhoads, "Naval Research Laboratory Memorandum Report 2884: Coverage Predictions for the Navy's Fixed VLF Transmitters, September 1974."

85. The scheduled communications interval is hard to pin down, but every six hours commonly appears in the secondary literature. "Just When Did Tacamo Begin?," https:// www.tacamo.org/timeline-1961; Ben Iannotta, "Talking to the Silent Service: Operators Push Back against Emerging Technology," *Defense News*, https://www.defensenews.com /article/20130311/C4ISR01/303110011/Talking-Silent-Service-Operators-Push-Back -Against-Emerging-Technology/ (site no longer active).

86. Jaskoviak, *Life Aboard the Crazy Polack*, 141–42.

87. Clifton, "Modeling and Control of a Trailing Wire Antenna Towed by an Orbiting Aircraft, September 1992."

88. Vern Lochausen, "The Tacamo Mission and the Cold War," http://webcache .googleusercontent.com/search?q=cache:WKasJCgMEpkJ:oldtacamo.com/img/photos /docs/word3.doc+&cd=2&hl=en&ct=clnk&gl=ca.

89. T. S. Cory and T. R. Holtzheimer, "Viability Assessment for Reliable Long-Wave Communications Links," NATO AGARD Conference Proceedings 529: ELF/VLF/LF Radio

Propagation, 28 September–2 October 1992, https://apps.dtic.mil/dtic/tr/fulltext/u2/a267991.pdf.

90. Richard Burgess, "Tacamo Herks Retired," *Naval Aviation News*, November–December 1992, 22–23.

91. Lochausen, "The Tacamo Mission and the Cold War."

92. Burgess, "Tacamo Herks Retired"; Blair, *Command and Control*, 158.

93. "VR-21 Detachment+VW-1 Detachment=VQ-3 Tacamo Detachment," *Trailing Wire Newsletter*, Fall 2013, 10.

94. "Just When Did Tacamo Begin?"

95. Blair, *Command and Control*, 158.

96. Ian Thompson, "Navy at Travis Quietly Keeps Communications Open with Subs," *Daily Republic*, 15 January 2015; "Just When Did Tacamo Begin?"; Burgess, "Tacamo Herks Retired"; "VR-21 Detachment+VW-1 Detachment=VQ-3 Tacamo Detachment"; "Tacamo Sea Stories," *Trailing Wire Newsletter*, Spring 2014, 7; Lochausen, "Evolution of Tacamo," *Trailing Wire Newsletter*, Spring 2013, 4–5.

97. "Transportable Navy Communications Systems," U.S. Navy Radio Communications—1950s & 1960s, accessed 28 September 2019, http://www.navy-radio.com/commsta-trans.htm. See also "TMC Photo Galleries" for Projects Baker, Dog, Echo, and Henry, TMC History, accessed 28 September 2019, http://www.tmchistory.org/tmc_history/photos/tmc_photos_page.htm.

98. FOIA CIA, memo for the record, "Blue Eagle Briefing," 26 April 1966.

99. "Project Jenny Overview," TMC History, accessed 28 September 2019, http://tmchistory.org/tmc_history/photos/prj_jenny/prj_jenny_photos.htm; "Project Jenny Overview," Blue Eagles of Vietnam, accessed 28 September 2019, http://www.blueeaglesofvietnam.com/services-view/project-jenny-overview/.

100. Thomas A. Sturm, "The Air Force and the Worldwide Military Command and Control System 1961–1965," U.S. Air Force Division Liaison Office, August 1966, available from SribD.

101. Sturm, "The Air Force and the Worldwide Military Command and Control System"; FOIA USAF, "History of the 6486th Air Base Wing, 1 January 1965 to 30 June 1965."

102. Nigel Ballard, "Monitoring Silk Purse," World Wide Airborne Command Post, http://www.wwabncp.com/info.htm; "Silk Purse," U.S. Army Germany, accessed 28 September 2019, http://www.usarmygermany.com/Sont.htm?http&&&www.usarmygermany.com/units/signal/USAREUR_102ndSigBn.htm; "Around the Bases."

103. Chambers, *Joint Base Langley-Eustis*, 60; Charles H. Bogino, "Langley Squad May Move to Air Base in Nebraska," *Daily Press-Tribune*, 8 May 1991; "The History of the Looking Glass," 2 ACCS, accessed 28 September 2019, http://2accs.com/history.html; U.S. Air Force Historical Research Agency Fact Sheet, "6th Airborne Command and Control Squadron."

104. U.S. Navy, "Extremely Low Frequency Transmitter Site Clam Lake, Wisconsin," *Navy Fact File*, 28 June 2001, https://fas.org/nuke/guide/usa/c3i/fs_clam_lake_elf2003.pdf; GAO Comptroller General of the United States, "The Navy's Trident Fleet—Some Success but Several Major Problems, 7 April 1978," https://www.gao.gov/assets/130/122464.pdf.

105. Defense Intelligence Agency, Scientific Advisory Committee, memorandum 1-68, "The Threat to Polaris Command and Control, June 1968," https://www.governmentattic.org/17docs/DIA-SABrecords_1966-2002.pdf.

106. See Samuel W. Coulbourn, "11-22-63 Remembered," *Personal Navigator* (blog), 27 November 2012, http://thepersonalnavigator.blogspot.ca/2012/11/at-sea-on-patrol.html.

107. See Coulbourn, "11-22-63 Remembered."

108. Jaskoviak, *Life Aboard the Crazy Polack*, 110–15.

109. Jaskoviak, *Life Aboard the Crazy Polack*, 110–15.

110. Waller, *Big Red*, 206–7.

111. "Polaris: Librascope's Role in Building Our Mightiest War Deterrent," *Librazette*, February–March 1962, 4; Robert V. Gates, "SLBM Fire Control Computational Algorithms in Support of Steller Inertial Guidance," Naval Surface Weapons Center, Dahlgren, 17 October 1980, https://archive.org/details/DTIC_ADA090650/page/n2; Pennsylvania State University, Applied Research Laboratory, "From the Sea to the Stars: A Chronicle of the US Navy's Space and Space-Related Activities 1944–2009," revised and updated edition, 2010, http://edocs.nps.edu/2012/December/FromTheSeaToTheStars-2010ed.pdf; "Five Things to Know about the US Naval Observatory," https://navylive.dodlive.mil/2017/04/29/5-things-to-know-about-the-u-s-naval-observatory/.

112. Waller, *Big Red*, 221.

113. This general process is described by Waller, *Big Red*, ch. 14, and I have augmented it with additional information. After the Cold War the captain's key was stored in a locked cabinet, and the code was transmitted as part of the emergency action message.

114. Waller, *Big Red*, 217.

115. Suid, *Guts and Glory*, 610–11, 687–88.

116. Department of the Air Force, HQ Ogden Air Logistics Center, "ICBM Security Classification Guide (SCG), 30 Sep 97," https://cryptome.org/icbm-scg.htm.

117. See Ralph E. Faucett and Pierce P. Newman, "US Naval Medical Research Laboratory Report No. 228: Operation Hideout Preliminary Report, 3 July 1953," https://pdfs.semanticscholar.org/68d9/59e8b2a6196da721afe749612c9623b15d4f.pdf; Northwestern Technological Institute, Chemical Engineering Department, "Operation Hideout Report, 30 September 1953," https://apps.dtic.mil/dtic/tr/fulltext/u2/019360.pdf.

118. Weybrew, "Naval Submarine Medical Research Laboratory Report Number 917."

119. Weybrew and Noddin, "The Mental Health of Nuclear Submariners"; Benjamin B. Weybrew, "US Naval Submarine Medical Center Report Number 686: Submarine Crew Effectiveness during Submerged Missions of Sixty or More Days Duration, 28 October 1971," https://apps.dtic.mil/dtic/tr/fulltext/u2/740796.pdf. Note that this paper was originally written in 1961 but not distributed until 1971. See also Maria Hilleman, "Pioneering in Sub Psychology," *The Day*, 22 September 1979, 21.

120. Beach, *Around the World Submerged*, 53.

121. Dubay, *Three Knots to Nowhere*, 45.

122. W. A. Tansey et al., "Analysis of Health Data."

123. "K-127" page (in Russian), www.deepstorm.ru.

124. U.S. Environmental Protection Agency, "Health Effects of Exposures to Mercury," accessed 28 September 2019, https://www.epa.gov/mercury/health-effects-exposures-mercury.

125. "B-486" page (in Russian), www.deepstorm.ru.

126. C. L. Schlichting, Naval Submarine Medical Research Laboratory Report 1193, "Psychiatric Screening for the Submarine Service: Enlisted Personnel, 16 October 1993,"

https://pdfs.semanticscholar.org/2ab6/7f1ce27c4cb097da2386c1912f3404d9d1ce.pdf?
_ga=2.20265208.1736336719.1571144356-163135884.1571144356. However, there were
situationally aware potential submariners: "I took a test in Sub School, that the questions
seemed to be lifted directly from the [Minnesota Multiphasic Personality Inventory]. I
lied about not torturing the puppies." "Psychological Officers—Submarine Part 2," *Molten
Eagle* (blog), 15 December 2008, http://aquilinefocus.blogspot.ca/2008/12/psychological
-officers-submarine-part-2.html.

127. Smith, *Emergency Deep!*, 36.

128. Dubay, *Three Knots to Nowhere*, 27.

129. McHale, *Stealth Boat*, 10.

130. Smith, *Emergency Deep!*, 110–11.

131. Jaskoviak, *Life Aboard the Crazy Polack*, 162–63.

132. Penley, *Deep Venture*, 308–9.

133. McHale, *Stealth Boat*, 134–35.

134. Serxner, "An Experience in Submarine Psychiatry."

135. Serxner, "An Experience in Submarine Psychiatry."

136. Penley, *Deep Venture*, 226.

137. Serxner, "An Experience in Submarine Psychiatry."

138. J. T Giles et al., "US Naval Submarine Medical Center Report Number 666: Characteristics of the Submarine Line Officer: II. Patterns of Motivation for Volunteering in the
Submarine Service, 24 May 1971," https://apps.dtic.mil/dtic/tr/fulltext/u2/734119.pdf.

139. Epstein, "Effects of the Cuban Crisis upon Attitudes Related to War and Peace."

Epilogue

1. See, for example, Robert Bridge, "BBC Whips Up Anti-Russia Hysteria to Apocalyptic Levels," *RT*, 7 February 2016, https://www.rt.com/op-ed/331667-bbc-media-russia
-propaganda/; Robert Parry, "Ukraine's 'Dr. Strangelove' Reality," *Common Dreams*, 6 May
2014, https://www.commondreams.org/views/2014/05/06/ukraines-dr-strangelove-reality.

2. See, for example, "Nameless Heroes" (aka "Unsung Heroes") series 1978–1981,
and the documentary *Crossing the Line* (2006). See also Anna Fifield, "An American
GI Defected to North Korea. Now His Sons Are Propaganda Stars," *Washington Post*,
25 May 2016, https://www.washingtonpost.com/news/worldviews/wp/2016/05/25
/the-north-korean-born-sons-of-an-american-defector-speak-in-korean/?utm_term=
.87290e5e9932; David Marchese, "How Do Americans Look in North Korean Films?,"
Vulture, 19 December 2014, http://www.vulture.com/2014/12/how-do-americans-look-in
-north-korean-films.html?mid=facebook_vulture; Zack Beauchamp, "Here's How North
Korean Films Portray Americans," *Vox*, 19 December 2014, https://www.vox.com/2014
/12/19/7423655/the-interview-north-film; Anna Broinowski, "I Played an 'Evil American Wife' in a North Korean Propaganda Film," *Vox*, 22 May 2017, https://www.vox.com
/first-person/2017/3/22/15011360/north-korea-propaganda-film; "The Australian Who
Shot a North Korean Propaganda Film," *BBC News*, 21 January 2016, http://www.bbc.com
/news/magazine-35365142.

3. As far as I can tell, I may be the exception with "Dangerously Straining the System:
Soviet Nuclear Force Operations and Incidents after Able Archer 83, 1983–1987." The con-
cise version was published as "Remembering Soviet Nuclear Risks" in the journal *Survival*.

BIBLIOGRAPHY

Archives and Online Collections

American Institute of Physics, College Park MD
    Oral History Collection
Association for Diplomatic Studies and Training, Arlington VA
    Foreign Affairs Oral History Project
BACM Research/Paperless Archives
Canadian Department of National Defence, Directorate of History and Heritage, Ottawa
    Arnell Papers
    Raymont Papers
Cryptome
Declassified Document Reference System
Defense Technical Information Center
Department of Energy Nuclear Testing Archives, Las Vegas NV
Department of State
    Foreign Relations of the United States Series
Dwight D. Eisenhower Presidential Library and Museum, Abilene KS
Federation of American Scientists
Government Attic
Iowa State Special Collections and University Archives
    Collins Radio Company Papers
John F. Kennedy Presidential Library and Museum, Boston
Library and Archives Canada, Ottawa
Library of Congress, Manuscript Division, Washington DC
    Curtis LeMay Papers
    Hoyt Vandenberg Papers
    Nathan Twining Papers
    Thomas D. White Papers
Lyndon Baines Johnson Library and Museum, Austin TX
National Security Archive, Washington DC
Nebraska State Historical Society, Lincoln
    Oral History Collection
ScribD
Syracuse University Special Collections Research Center

Thomas D. White Papers
Thomas S. Power Papers
University of California, Santa Barbara
American Presidency Project
U.S. Air Force Historical Research Agency, Montgomery AL
U.S. National Records and Archives Administration
U.S. Navy Operational Archives, Washington DC
WGBH Media Library and Archives, Boston
War and Peace in the Nuclear Age
Wisconsin Center for Film and Theater Research, Madison
Kirk Douglas Papers

Published Works

Abella, Alex. *Soldiers of Reason: The RAND Corporation and the Rise of the American Empire.* New York: Houghton Mifflin Harcourt, 2008.

Abrams, Herbert L. *The President Has Been Shot: Confusion, Disability, and the 25th Amendment.* New York: Norton, 1992.

Adams, Chris. *Inside the Cold War: A Cold Warrior's Reflections.* Montgomery: Air University Press, 1999.

Aiken, F. B. "Abraham '59—A Nuclear Fantasy." *Dissent*, Winter 1959. https://www.dissentmagazine.org/issue/winter-1959.

Aldrich, Richard. GCHQ: *The Uncensored Story of Britain's Most Secret Intelligence Agency.* London: Harper Press, 2010.

Aldridge, Robert C. *First Strike: The Pentagon's Strategy for Nuclear War.* Boston: South End Press, 1983.

Allison, Graham T., and Philip Zelikow. *Essence of Decision: Explaining the Cuban Missile Crisis.* 2nd ed. New York: Longman, 1999.

Althoff, William F. *Drift Station: Arctic Outposts of Superpower Science.* Washington DC: Potomac Books, 2007.

Arkin, William M., and Richard W. Fieldhouse. *Nuclear Battlefields: Global Links in the Arms Race.* Cambridge MA: Ballinger, 1985.

Arnold, David Christopher. *Spying from Space: Constructing America's Satellite Command and Control Systems.* College Station: Texas A&M Press, 2005.

"Around the Bases: Lajes Field, Azores." *Hanger Digest* 4, no. 2 (April 2004): 10–14. https://amcmuseum.org/wp-content/uploads/2015/01/Hangar_Digest_April_2004.pdf.

AT&T. "Command Post Alerting Network (COPAN) and Joint Chiefs of Staff Alerting Network (JCSAN) General Description." *Bell System Practices*, no. 2 (June 1971): 1–6.

———. "Private Line Telephone Service: SAC Primary Alerting System Description." *Bell System Practices*, no. 3 (July 1971): 1–6.

"Authors." *Bulletin of the Atomic Scientists* 19 (December 1963). https://books.google.ca/books?id=NQgAAAAAMBAJ&pg=PA53&lpg=PA53&dq=Raymond+D.+Senter&source=bl&ots=56qQrL8oou&sig=SzIG7akfpWU3y3BEomqgZD1-3kE&hl=en&sa=X&redir_esc=y#v=onepage&q=Raymond%20D.%20Senter&f=false.

Baer, George W. *One Hundred Years of Sea Power: The US Navy 1890–1990*. Stanford CA: Stanford University Press, 1994.

Ball, Desmond. *Politics and Force Levels: The Strategic Missile Program of the Kennedy Administration*. Berkeley: University of California Press, 1980.

Bartholomew, Frank. *Bart: His Memoirs*. Sonoma CA: Vine Book Press, 1983.

Bass, George A., and Mark Rascovich. "A Device for the Tracking of Large Fishes." *Zoologica* 50, no. 2 (1965): 75–82.

Baum, Carl E. "Reminiscences of High-Power Electromagnetics." IEEE *Transactions on Electromagnetic Compatibility* 49, no. 2 (May 2007): 211–18.

Beach, Edward. *Around the World Submerged: The Voyage of the Triton*. New York: Holt, Rhinehart, and Winston, 1962.

Bennington, Bernard J. *Beyond FTS2000: A Program for Change*. Washington DC: U.S. General Services Administration, 1989.

Beschloss, Michael. *The Crisis Years: Kennedy and Khrushchev 1960–1963*. New York: Harper Collins, 1992.

———. *May-Day: Eisenhower, Khrushchev, and the U-2 Affair*. New York: Harper and Rose, 1986.

Blair, Bruce G. *Command and Control: Redefining the Nuclear Threat*. Washington DC: Brookings Institution, 1985.

Blair, Edison T. "Bright Boy." *The Airman*, January 1960, 36–40.

Blight, James G., and David A. Welch. *On the Brink: Americans and Soviets Reexamine the Cuban Missile Crisis*. New York: Hill and Wang, 1989.

Boyer, Gene T. *Inside the President's Helicopter: Reflections of a White House Senior Pilot*. Brule WI: Cable, 2011.

Brams, Steven J. *Superpower Games: Applying Game Theory to Superpower Conflict*. New Haven CT: Yale University Press, 1985.

Brings, Lawrence M., ed. *We Believe in Prayer*. Minneapolis MN: T. S. Denison, 1958.

Brodie, Bernard. *Strategy in the Missile Age*. Princeton NJ: Princeton University Press, 1959.

Brugioni, Dino A. *Eyeball to Eyeball: The Inside Story of the Cuban Missile Crisis*. New York: Random House, 1992.

Brzezinski, Matthew. *Red Moon Rising: Sputnik and the Hidden Rivalries That Ignited the Space Age*. New York: Henry Holt, 2007.

Bundy, McGeorge. *Danger and Survival: Choices about the Bomb in the First Fifty Years*. New York: Vintage Books, 1988.

Burdick, Eugene, and Harvey Wheeler. *Fail-Safe*. New York: Dell, 1962.

Burrough, Bryan. *Days of Rage: America's Radical Underground, the FBI, and the Forgotten Age of Revolutionary Violence*. New York: Penguin Press, 2015.

Byrnes, Donn A., and Kenneth D. Hurley. *Blackbird Rising: Birth of an Aviation Legend*. Los Lunas NM: Sage Mesa, 1999.

Cagle, Malcom W., and Frank A. Manson. *The Sea War in Korea*. Annapolis MD: Naval Institute Press, 1957.

Call, Steve. *Selling Air Power: Military Aviation and American Popular Culture after World War II*. College Station: Texas A&M Press, 2009.

Carr, Kevin Gray. "Making Way: War, Philosophy and Sport in Japanese Judo." *Journal of Sport History* 20, no. 2 (Summer 1993): 167–88.

Carroll, James. *House of War: The Pentagon and the Disastrous Rise of American Power*. New York: Houghton Mifflin Harcourt, 2006.

Chambers, Mark A. *Joint Base Langley-Eustis*. Mt. Pleasant SC: Arcadia, 2017.

Churchill, Jan. *Delaware Aviation*. Mt. Pleasant SC: Arcadia, 2014.

Cloud, John. "American Cartographic Transformations during the Cold War." *Cartography and Geographic Information Science* 29, no. 3 (2002): 261–82.

Coffey, Thomas M. *Decision over Schweinfurt: The US 8th Air Force Battle for Daylight Bombing*. New York: David McKay Comano, 1977.

———. *Iron Eagle: The Turbulent Life of General Curtis LeMay*. New York: Random House, 1987.

Colodny, Len, and Robert Gettlin. *Silent Coup: The Removal of a President*. New York: St. Martin's Press, 1991.

Conine, Gary. *Not for Ourselves Alone: The Evolution and Role of the Titan II Missile in the Cold War*. Santa Rosa Beach FL: 360 Degree Design, 2015.

Cortright, David. *Soldiers in Revolt: The American Military Today*. New York: Doubleday, 1975.

Coughlin, T. G. "City in a Mountain." *The Roundel* 13, no. 5 (June 1961): 24–26.

Craven, John. *The Silent War: The Cold War Battle beneath the Seas*. New York: Simon and Schuster, 2001.

Dalgleish, D. Douglas, and Larry Schweikart. *Trident*. Carbondale: University of Illinois Press, 1984.

Danchik, Robert J. "The Navy Navigation Satellite System (TRANSIT)." *Johns Hopkins APL Technical Digest* 5, no. 4 (1990): 323–28.

———. "An Overview of Transit Development." *Johns Hopkins APL Technical Digest* 19, no. 1 (1998): 18–26.

D'Este, Carlo. *Eisenhower: A Soldier's Life*. New York: Henry Holt, 2002.

Dewhurst, C. H. *Close Contact: With the Soviets in Eastern Germany*. London: George, Allen, and Unwin, 1954.

Dickey, Jeffrey V. "Russian Political Warfare: Origin, Evolution, and Application." PhD dissertation, Naval Postgraduate School, June 2015.

Dickson, Paul. *Sputnik: The Shock of the Century*. New York: Berkley, 2001.

Dienesch, Robert M. *Eyeing the Red Storm: Eisenhower and the First Attempt to Build a Spy Satellite*. Lincoln: University of Nebraska Press, 2016.

Dill, Peter. "SAC's Doomsday Armada." *Airpower* 22, no. 1 (January 1992): 10–21.

Divine, Robert A. *The Sputnik Challenge: Eisenhower's Response to the Soviet Satellite*. New York: Oxford University Press, 1993.

Dubay, Ted E. *Three Knots to Nowhere: A Cold War Submariner on the Undersea Frontier*. Jefferson NC: McFarlane, 2014.

DuBois, Brendan. *Resurrection Day*. New York: Jove Fiction, 1999.

Enthoven, Alain C., and K. Wayne Smith. *How Much Is Enough? Shaping the Defense Program 1961–1969*. Santa Monica CA: RAND, 1971.

Epstein, Edmund N. "Effects of the Cuban Crisis upon Attitudes Related to War and Peace." *Psychological Reports 1965* 17 (1965): 424–26.

Ewing, F. H. "Gray Ghost of Vietnam Coast Checks In for Rest and Overhaul." *Naval Communications Bulletin* 2 (December 1968): 2–4.

Fenby, Jonathan. *The General: Charles DeGaulle and the France He Saved*. New York: Sky-horse, 2012.

Fitts, Richard E., ed. *The Strategy of Electromagnetic Conflict*. Los Altos CA: Peninsula, 1980.

Fleming, Charles. *High Concept: Don Simpson and the Hollywood Culture of Excess*. New York: Doubleday, 1998.

Fleming, John V. *The Anti-Communist Manifestos: Four Books That Shaped the Cold War*. New York: Norton, 2009.

Fletcher, F. H., et al. "The L-4 Coaxial System." *Bell System Technical Journal*, April 1969, 821–39.

Ford, Daniel. *The Button*. New York: Simon and Schuster, 1985.

Fournier, Louis. FLQ: *The Anatomy of an Underground Movement*. Toronto: NC Press, 1984.

Frank, Pat. *Alas, Babylon*. New York: J. B. Lippincott, 1959.

Friedman, Norman. *US Destroyers: A Design History*. Annapolis MD: Naval Institute Press, 1982.

———. *US Submarines since 1945: A Design History*. Annapolis MD: Naval Institute Press, 1994.

Furman, Necah Stewart. *Sandia National Laboratories: The Postwar Decade*. Albuquerque: University of New Mexico Press, 2000.

Fursenko, Aleksandr, and Timothy Naftali. *One Hell of a Gamble: Khrushchev, Castro, and Kennedy 1958–1964*. New York: Norton, 1997.

Galantin, I. J. *Submarine Admiral: From Battlewagons to Ballistic Missiles*. Chicago: University of Illinois Press, 1995.

Garbinski, John C. *North River Depot: The Story of the United States First Operational Nuclear Weapons Storage Site*. Morrisville NC: Lulu Press, 2011.

Garthoff, Raymond. *Reflections on the Cuban Missile Crisis*. Washington DC: Brookings Institution, 1989.

George, Alexander L., and Richard Smoke. *Deterrence in American Foreign Policy: Theory and Practice*. New York: Columbia University Press, 1974.

George, Peter. *Dr. Strangelove, or: How I Learned to Stop Worrying and Love the Bomb*. New York: Bantam Books, 1963.

———. *Red Alert*. New York: Ace Books, 1958.

Ghamari-Tabrizi, Sharon. *The Worlds of Herman Kahn: The Intuitive Science of Thermonuclear War*. Cambridge MA: Harvard University Press, 2005.

Glasstone, Samuel, and Phillip J. Dolan. *The Effects of Nuclear Weapons*. 3rd ed. Washington DC: Department of Defense, 1977.

Goodman, Michael S. *Spying on the Nuclear Bear: Anglo-American Intelligence and the Soviet Bomb*. Stanford CA: Stanford University Press, 2007.

Gordin, Michael D. *Five Days in August: How World War II Became a Nuclear War*. Princeton NJ: Princeton University Press, 2015.

Gordon, Yefim, and Dmitriy Komissarov. *Soviet Air Defence Aviation 1945–1991*. Manchester, UK: Hikoki, 2012.

Gorgas, J. W. "AUTOVON: Switching Network for Global Defense." *Bell Laboratories Record*, April 1968, 106–11.

Gribkov, Anatoli I., and William Y. Smith. *Operation Anadyr: US and Soviet Generals Recount the Cuban Missile Crisis*. Chicago: Edition q, 1994.

Grove, Eric. *From Vanguard to Trident: British Naval Policy since World War Two*. Annapolis MD: Naval Institute Press, 1987.

Guier, William H., and George C. Weiffenbach. "Genesis of Satellite Navigation." *Johns Hopkins APL Technical Digest* 19, no. 1 (1998): 14–17.

Gulley, Bill. *Breaking Cover*. New York: Simon and Schuster, 1980.

Haefmeister, David. "How Much Warhead Reliability Is Enough for a Comprehensive Nuclear Test Ban Treaty?" *Forum on Physics and Society of the American Physical Society* 36, no. 2 (April 2007). https://www.aps.org/units/fps/newsletters/2007/april/articles.html.

Hall, R. Cargill. "A History of the Military Polar Orbiting Meteorological Satellite Program." Chantilly VA: Office of the Historian, National Reconnaissance Office, September 2001.

———. "The Truth about Overflights." *Quarterly Journal of Military History* 9 (Spring 1997): 24–39.

Hampton, Dan. *The Hunter Killers*. New York: William Morrow, 2015.

Hansen, Chuck. *US Nuclear Weapons: The Secret History*. New York: Orion Books, 1988.

Harder, Robert O. *Flying from the Black Hole: The B-52 Navigator-Bombardiers of Vietnam*. Annapolis MD: Naval Institute Press, 2009.

Haslam, Jonathan. *Near and Distant Neighbors: A New History of Soviet Intelligence*. New York: Farrar, Straus and Giroux, 2015.

Haynes, John Earl, and Harvey Klehr. *Venona: Decoding Soviet Espionage in America*. New Haven CT: Yale University Press, 1999.

Heefner, Gretchen. *The Missile Next Door*. Cambridge MA: Harvard University Press, 2012.

Hennessy, Peter, and James Jinks. *The Silent Deep: The Royal Navy Submarine Service since 1945*. London: Allen Lane, 2015.

Henrick, Richard P. *Crimson Tide*. New York: Avon Books, 1995.

———. *The Phoenix Odyssey*. New York: Kensington, 1986.

Henschen, Craig C. "Titan II Crew Duty." *Association of Air Force Missileers* 7, no. 3 (September 1999): 9–10.

Hersey, John. *The War Lover*. New York: Knopf, 1959.

Hill, Clint. *Five Presidents*. New York: Gallery Books, 2016.

Holland, Max. "I. F. Stone: Encounters with Soviet Intelligence." *Journal of Cold War Studies* 11, no. 3 (Summer 2009): 144–205.

Hoopaw, James. *Where the BUF Fellows Roamed*. Centralia PA: Gorham, 1999.

Horne, Alastair. *Harold Macmillan. Volume II: 1957–1986*. New York: Viking Books, 1989.

Hudlow, Rick. *Shamrock 22: An Aviator's Story*. Bloomington IN: AuthorHouse, 2011.

Hutchhausen, Peter A. *October Fury*. Hoboken NJ: John Wiley and Sons, 2002.

Immele, John D., et al. "An Exchange on Stockpile Confidence." *International Security* 13, no. 1 (Summer 1988): 196–215.

Inter-American Tropical Tuna Commission/Comision Interamericana del Atun Tropical. "Special Report." *Informe Especial*, no. 8 (1993).

Isaacson, Walter. *Kissinger: A Biography*. New York: Simon and Schuster, 1992.

Jaskoviak, Phil. *Life Aboard the Crazy Polack*. Self-published, 2010.

Jett, Charles Cranston. *Super Nuke!* Parker CO: Outskirts Press, 2016.

Johnstone, Paul H. *From Mad to Madness: Inside Pentagon Nuclear War Planning*. Atlanta GA: Clarity Press, 2017.

Justman, Ben. *Offutt Air Force Base*. Charleston SC: Arcadia, 2014.

Kahn, Herman. *On Thermonuclear War*. Princeton NJ: Princeton University Press, 1960.

Kane, Arnold. *My Meteoric Rise to Obscurity: The Life and Times of a TV Writer/Producer*. Self-published, 2008.

Kaplan, Fred. *The Wizards of Armageddon*. New York: Simon and Schuster, 1983.

Kaufman, William. *The McNamara Strategy*. New York: Harper and Row, 1964.

Kennedy, Robert F., and Theodore Sorensen. *Thirteen Days*. New York: Norton, 1969.

"Keynote Speech Summary." SAC ACCA *Flyer* 16, no. 2 (June 2010): 4–5. http://www.sac -acca.org/newsletter/flyer0610.pdf.

Kohn, Richard H., and Joseph P. Harahan. *Strategic Air Warfare: An Interview with Generals Curtis E. LeMay, Leon W. Johnson, David A. Burchinal, and Jack J. Catton*. Washington DC: Office of Air Force History, 1988.

Khrushchev, Nikita. *Khrushchev Remembers: The Glasnost Tapes*. Translated by Jerrold L. Schecter. Toronto: Little, Brown, 1990.

Khrushchev, Sergei. *Khrushchev on Khrushchev: An Inside Account of the Man and His Era*. Translated by William Taubman. Toronto: Little, Brown, 1990.

Klehr, Harvey, et al. *The Secret World of American Communism*. New Haven CT: Yale University Press, 1995.

Klie, R. H., and R. E. Masher. "The L-4 Coaxial Cable System." *Bell Laboratories Record* 45, no. 7 (July–August 1967): 210–17.

Koch, Stephen. *Double Lives: Spies and Writers in the Secret Soviet War of Ideas against the West*. New York: Free Press, 1994.

Kozak, Warren. *LeMay: The Life and Wars of General Curtis LeMay*. Washington DC: Regnery, 2009.

Krugler, David F. *This Is Only a Test: How Washington D.C. Prepared for Nuclear War*. New York: Palgrave Books, 2006.

Kuehn, Cory. "ALCS 50th Anniversary: Celebrating a Proud Heritage." AAFM *Newsletter* 25, no. 1 (March 2017): 13–16.

Kuklick, Bruce. *Blind Oracles: Intellectuals and War from Kennan to Kissinger*. Princeton NJ: Princeton University Press, 2006.

Kurdin, Igor, and Wayne Grasdock. "Loss of a Yankee SSBN." *Undersea Warfare* 7, no. 5 (Fall 2005). http://www.public.navy.mil/subfor/underseawarfaremagazine/Issues /Archives/issue_28/yankee.html.

Lapp, Ralph E. *Kill and Overkill: The Strategy of Annihilation*. New York: Basic Books, 1962.

Larzelere, Alex R. *Witness to History: White House Diary of a Military Aide to President Richard Nixon*. Bloomington IN: AuthorHouse, 2009.

Lashmar, Paul. *Spy Flights of the Cold War*. Annapolis MD: Naval Institute Press, 1994.

Leavitt, Lloyd R. *Following the Flag*. Montgomery AL: Air University Press, 2010.

LeMay, Curtis, and MacKinlay Kantor. *Mission with LeMay*. New York: Doubleday Press, 1965.

LeMay Curtis E., with Dale O. Smith. *America Is in Danger*. New York: Funk and Wagnall's, 1968.

Lheureux, Ray "Frenchy," and Lee Kelley. *Inside Marine One*. New York: St. Martin's Press, 2015.

Lister, M. D. "The Evolution and Current Status of NORAD." *The Roundel* 14, no. 5 (June 1962): 2–10.

Lloyd, Alwyn T. *A Cold War Legacy*. Missoula MT: Pictorial Histories, 1999.

MacGregor, Morris J. *Integration of the Armed Forces 1940–1965*. Washington DC: Center for Military History United States Army, 2001.

Mackenzie, Donald. *Inventing Accuracy: A Historical Sociology of Nuclear Missile Guidance*. Cambridge MA: MIT Press, 1990.

Maggelet, Michael H., and James C. Oskins. *Broken Arrow: The Declassified History of US Nuclear Weapons Accidents*. Morrisville NC: Lulu Press, 2007.

Maloney, Sean M. "The Missiles of Anadyr: Nuking Comox, 1961–1969." *Canadian Military Journal* 17, no. 1 (Winter 2016).

———. "Remembering Soviet Nuclear Risks." *Survival* 57, no. 4 (2015): 77–104.

Malucci, Louis. *Mission B-47 Stratojet: Be a Nuclear Deterrent to the Nuclear Threat of the Cold War*. Morrisville NC: Lulu Press, 2013.

Manthorpe, William H. J., Jr. *A Century of Service: The US Navy on Cape Henlopen, Lewes, Delaware*. Wilmington DE: Cedar Tree Books, 2014.

Markus, Rita, et al. *Air Force Weather: Our Heritage 1937 to 2012*. Scott AFB IL: MAC Publication, 1989.

McGill, Earl J. *Jet Age Man: SAC B-47 and B-52 Operations in the Early Cold War*. Philadelphia: Casemate, 2011.

McHale, Gannon. *Stealth Boat: Fighting the Cold War in a Fast Attack Submarine*. Annapolis MD: Naval Institute Press, 2008.

McLaren, Alfred Scott. *Silent and Unseen: On Patrol in Three Cold War Attack Submarines*. Annapolis MD: Naval Institute Press, 2015.

McLean, Jon. "The Airborne Launch Control System Part I." *AAFM Newsletter* 12, no. 2 (June 2004): 5–7.

———. "Airborne Launch Control System Part II." *AAFM Newsletter* 12, no. 3 (2004): 4.

Mercurio, Jed. *Ascent*. London: Vintage Books, 2008.

Miller, Jerry. *Stockpile: The Story behind 10,000 Strategic Nuclear Weapons*. Annapolis MD: Naval Institute Press, 2010.

Moore, John E. *The Soviet Navy Today*. London: Macdonald and Jane's, 1975.

Morgan, Patrick M. *Deterrence: A Conceptual Approach*. Beverly Hills CA: Sage, 1977.

Naftali, Timothy, and Aleksandr Fursenko. *Khrushchev's Cold War*. New York: Norton, 2007.

Natola, Mark, ed. *Boeing B47 Stratojet: True Stories of the Cold War in the Air*. Atglen PA: Schiffer Military History Books, 2002.

Neal, Roy. *Ace in the Hole: The Story of the Minuteman Missile*. Garden City NY: Doubleday, 1962.

Neufeld, Jacob. *Ballistic Missiles in the US Air Force 1945–1960*. Washington DC: U.S. GPO, 1989.

Newhouse, John. *Cold Dawn: The Story of SALT*. New York: Holt, Rinehart, and Winston, 1973.

Newman, James R. "Two Discussions of Thermonuclear War." *Scientific American* 204, no. 3 (March 1961): 197–204.

Norris, Robert Stan, et al. *Nuclear Weapons Databook V: British, French, and Chinese Nuclear Weapons*. New York: Westview Press, 1994.

Ogletree, Greg. "The 4th Airborne Command and Control Squadron." *ACCA Flyer* 6, no. 3 (November 2000): 1–4.

Palmer, Bruce. *Intervention in the Caribbean: The Dominican Crisis of 1965.* Lexington: University Press of Kentucky, 1989.

Pearson, David E. *The World Wide Military Command and Control System: Evolution and Effectiveness.* Montgomery AL: Air University Press, 2000.

Pedlow, Gregory, and Donald E. Welzenbach. *The CIA and the U-2 Program 1954–1974.* Washington DC: CIA Center for the Study of Intelligence, 1998.

Pedrozo, Pete. "The US-China Incidents at Sea Agreement: A Recipe for Disaster." *Journal of National Security Law and Policy* 6, no. 1 (2012). http://jnslp.com/2012/08/29/the-u-s-china-incidents-at-sea-agreement-a-recipe-for-disaster/.

Penley, Gary. *Deep Venture: A Sailor's Story of Cold War Submarines.* Gretna LA: Pelican, 2011.

Perlstein, Rick. *Before the Storm.* New York: Nation Books, 2001.

Petranick, M. G. *Peace Was His Profession.* Denver CO: Outskirts Press, 2011.

Pettee, George S. "A Critical Review of the Nuclear Escalation Concept." In *Four Papers on Problems of Strategy.* Washington DC: Research Analysis Corporation, 1967. http://www.dtic.mil/dtic/tr/fulltext/u2/686769.pdf.

Pfeffer, Robert, and D. Lynn Shaeffer. "A Russian Assessment of Several USSR and US HEMP Tests." *Combating Weapons of Mass Destruction,* no. 3 (January 2009): 22–38.

Podvig, Pavel. "History and the Current Status of the Russian Early-Warning System." *Science and Global Security* 10 (2002): 21–60.

———. *Russian Strategic Nuclear Forces.* Cambridge MA: MIT Press, 2001.

Polmar, Norman, and Robert S. Norris. *The US Nuclear Arsenal: A History of Weapons and Delivery Systems since 1945.* Annapolis MD: Naval Institute Press, 2009.

Poole, Walter S. *The Joint Chiefs of Staff and National Policy.* Vol. 8: *1961–1964.* Washington DC: Office of the Chairman of the Joint Chiefs of Staff, 2011.

Power, Thomas S., with Albert Arnhym. *Design for Survival.* New York: Cardinal Edition, 1965.

Prados, John. "The Navy's Biggest Betrayal." *Naval History Magazine* 24, no. 3 (June 2010). https://www.usni.org/magazines/naval-history-magazine/2010/june/navys-biggest-betrayal.

Price, Alfred. *The History of US Electronic Warfare.* Vol. 2: *The Renaissance Years 1946 to 1964.* Pikesville MD: Association of Old Crows, Port City Press, 1989.

Price, Eldon. *Senior Birdman: The Guy Who Just Had to Fly.* Bloomington IN: iUniverse, 2006.

Publication No. L58-141: Lessons Learned from Operations ALERT 1955–57, 30 April 1958. Washington DC: Industrial College of the Armed Forces, 1958.

Rapf, Johana, ed. *Sidney Lumet: Interviews.* Jackson: University Press of Mississippi, 2006.

Rascovich, Mark. *The Bedford Incident.* New York: Atheneum Press, 1963.

Raskin, Marcus. *Liberalism: The Genius of American Ideals.* New York: Rowan and Littlefield, 2004.

Redmond, Kent C., and Thomas M. Smith. *From Whirlwind to MITRE: The R&D Story of the SAGE Air Defense Computer.* Cambridge MA: MIT Press, 2000.

Reed, C. M. *KC-135 Stratotanker in Action.* Carrollton TX: Squadron-Signal Publications, 1991.

Reed, Thomas C. *At the Abyss.* New York: Ballantine Books, 2004.

Reed, Thomas C., and Danny B. Stillman. *The Nuclear Express: A Political History of the Bomb and Its Proliferation.* Minneapolis MN: Zenith Press, 2010.

Reed, W. Craig. *Red November: Inside the Secret US-Soviet Submarine War.* New York: William Morrow, 2011.

Rhodes, Richard. *Dark Sun: The Making of the Hydrogen Bomb*. New York: Simon and Schuster, 1996.

Richelson, Jeffrey. *Spying on the Bomb*. New York: Norton, 2006.

———. *Sword and Shield: Soviet Intelligence and Security Apparatus*. Cambridge MA: Ballinger 1986.

Rife, James P., and Rodney P. Carlisle. *The Sound of Freedom: Naval Weapons Technology at Dahlgren, Virginia 1918–2006*. Washington DC: GPO, 2007.

Roberts, K. G. "Air Defence Goes Underground." *The Roundel* 15, no. 7 (September 1963): 8–13.

Romerstein, Herbert, and Eric Breindel. *The Venona Secrets: Exposing Soviet Espionage and America's Traitors*. Washington DC: Regnery, 2000.

Rosenberg, David Alan. "Origins of Overkill: Nuclear Weapons and American Strategy, 1945–1960." *International Security* 7, no. 4 (Spring 1983): 3–71.

Rosenblith, Walter A., ed. *Jerry Wiesner: Scientist, Stateman, Humanist. Memories and Memoirs*. Cambridge MA: MIT Press, 2003.

Rotenstein, David S. "The Undisclosed Location Disclosed." *RPPN Bulletin* 1, no. 3 (Summer 2010): 3–8.

Sagan, Scott. *The Limits of Safety: Organizations, Accidents, and Nuclear Weapons*. Princeton NJ: Princeton University Press, 1995.

Salinger, Pierre. *John F. Kennedy, Commander in Chief: A Profile in Leadership*. New York: Penguin Studio, 1997.

Sambaluk, Nicholas Michael. *The Other Space Race: Eisenhower and the Quest for Aerospace Security*. Annapolis MD: Naval Institute Press, 2015.

Schaffel, Kenneth. *The Emerging Shield: The Air Force and Continental Defense 1945–1960*. Washington DC: Office of Air Force History, 1991.

Schelling, Thomas. *Strategies of Commitment and Other Essays*. Cambridge MA: Harvard University Press, 2006.

———. *The Strategy of Conflict*. Cambridge MA: Harvard University Press, 1980.

Schweitzer, Glenn E. *Techno-Diplomacy: US-Soviet Confrontation in Science and Technology*. New York: Springer, 1989.

Scortia, Thomas N., and Frank M. Robinson. *The Gold Crew*. New York: Warner Books, 1980.

Scrivner, John H., Jr. "Pioneer into Space: A Biography of Major General Orvil Arson Anderson." PhD dissertation, University of Oklahoma, 1971.

Serxner, Jonathan L. "An Experience in Submarine Psychiatry." *American Journal of Psychiatry* 125, no. 1 (July 1968): 25–30.

Sewell, Kenneth. *All Hands Down: The True Story of the Soviet Attack on the USS Scorpion*. New York: Simon and Schuster, 2008.

Sewell, Kenneth, and Clint Richmond. *Red Star Rogue*. New York: Simon and Schuster, 2005.

Sharfman, Peter. *The Effects of Nuclear War*. Detroit MI: Gale Research, 1984.

Siddiqi, Asif A. *Sputnik and the Soviet Space Challenge*. Gainesville: University Press of Florida, 2003.

Silver, Alain, and James Ursini. *Whatever Happened to Robert Aldrich? His Life and Films*. New York: Limelight Editions, 1995.

Silverstone, Scott A. *Preventive War and American Democracy*. London: Routledge, 2007.

"Skyking, Skyking . . . Can Anybody Hear Me?" *Klaxon* 5, no. 3 (Winter/Spring 1998): 12–15.

Smith, P. D. *Doomsday Men: The Real Dr. Strangelove and the Dream of the Superweapon*. London: Allen Lane, 2007.

Smith, Richard A. *Emergency Deep! One Man's Life in the Submarine Service*. Amazon Digital Services, 2012.

Snyder, Thomas, et al. *Air Force Communications Command 1938–1991: An Illustrated History*. 3rd ed. Scott AFB IL: AFCC Office of History, 1991.

Spinardi, Graham. *From Polaris to Trident: The Development of US Fleet Ballistic Missile Technology*. London: Cambridge University Press, 2004.

Spires, David N. *Beyond Horizons: A Half-Century of Air Force Space Leadership*. Honolulu HI: University Press of the Pacific, 2002.

Stearns, Ben W. *Arthur Collins: Radio Wizard*. Sarasota FL: First Edition, 2002.

Steiner, Barry H. *Bernard Brodie and the Foundations of American Nuclear Strategy*. Lawrence: University Press of Kansas, 1991.

Stejskal, James. *Special Forces Berlin*. Philadelphia: Casemate, 2017.

Stern, Sheldon M. *The Cuban Missile Crisis in American History: Myth versus Reality*. Stanford CA: Stanford University Press, 2012.

———. *The Week the World Stood Still*. Stanford CA: Stanford University Press, 2005.

Stine, G. Harry. *ICBM: The Making of the Weapon that Changed the World*. New York: Orion Books, 1991.

Stone, I. F. *The Best of I. F. Stone*. New York: Public Affairs, 2006.

Stumpf, David K. *Regulus: The Forgotten Weapon*. Paducah KY: Turner, 1996.

———. *Titan II: A History of Cold War Missile Program*. Fayetteville: University of Arkansas Press, 2002.

Suid, Lawrence H. *Guts and Glory: The Making of the American Military Image in Film*. Revised and expanded ed. Lexington: University Press of Kentucky, 2002.

Szasz, Ferenc Morton. *The Day the Sun Rose Twice*. Albuquerque: University of New Mexico Press, 1984.

Tansey, W. A., et al. "Analysis of Health Data from 10 Years of Polaris Submarine Patrols." *Undersea Biomedical Research Submarine Supplement* 6 (Suppl 1979): s217–s246.

Taylor, Maxwell D. *Swords and Ploughshares*. New York: Da Capo Press, 1972.

———. *The Uncertain Trumpet*. New York: Harper and Brothers, 1959.

Terrell, D. S. "What Is SAGE?" *The Roundel* 13, no. 5 (June 1961): 21–23.

Thomas, Gordon, and Max Morgan Witts. *Ruin from the Air: The Enola Gay's Atomic Mission to Hiroshima*. Chelsea MI: Scarborough House, 1977.

Tillman, Barrett. *LeMay: Lessons in Leadership*. New York: Palgrave Books, 2007.

Tomoda, Yoshibumi. "Gravity at Sea: A Memoir of a Marine Geophysicist." *Proceedings of the Japan Academy Series B Physical and Biological Sciences* 86, no. 8 (2010): 769–87.

Trew, Antony. *Two Hours to Darkness*. London: Fontana/Collins, 1963.

Troitskaya, V. A. "Effects of Earth Currents Caused by High-Altitude Atomic Explosions." *Izvestiya Akademii Nauk SSSR, Seriya Geofizicheskaya*, no. 9 (1960): 1321–29.

Turchetti, Simone, and Peder Roberts, eds. *The Surveillance Imperative: Geosciences during the Cold War and Beyond*. New York: Palgrave Books, 2014.

U.S. Department of Defense. *Dictionary of Military Terms*. New York: Arco, 1988.

"U-2 Incident Wrecks Paris Summit Meeting." In *CQ Almanac 1960*. Washington DC: Congressional Quarterly, 1960. http://cqpress.com.

Vogel, Steve. *The Pentagon: A History*. New York: Random House, 2007.

Wager, Walter. *Viper Three*. New York: Macmillan, 1971.

Walker, Chuck. *Atlas: The Ultimate Weapon*. Burlington VT: Apogee Books, 2005.

Waller, Douglas C. *Big Red: Three Months on Board a Trident Nuclear Submarine*. New York: Harper Collins, 2001.

Walsh, Kenneth T. *Air Force One: A History of the Presidents and Their Planes*. New York: Hyperion Press, 2003.

Walters, Cathy Darlene. "Perceptions Management: Soviet Deception and Its Implications for National Security." MA Thesis, Naval Postgraduate School, March 1988.

Weir, Gary E., and Walter J. Boyne. *Rising Tide: The Untold Story of the Russian Submarines That Fought the Cold War*. New York: Basic Books, 2003.

Weisgall, Jonathan M. *Operation CROSSROADS: The Atomic Tests at Bikini Atoll*. Annapolis MD: Naval Institute Press, 1994.

Weitze, Karen J. *Cold War Infrastructure for Strategic Air Command: The Bomber Mission*. Sacramento: KEA Environmental, 1999.

Wells, Selman Willard "Sundown." *The Life and Career of Lt. General Selmon "Sundown" Wells in His Own Words*. Amherst MA: Modern Memoirs, 2003.

Werrell, Kenneth P. *The Evolution of the Cruise Missile*. Montgomery AL: Air University, 1985.

Weybrew, Benjamin B., and Ernest M. Noddin. "The Mental Health of Nuclear Submariners in the United States Navy." *Military Medicine* 144, no. 3 (March 1979): 188–91.

Willeford, James D. "What Is a Military Professional?" *Marine Corps Gazette* 98, no. 9 (September 2014): 95–96.

Winkler, David F. *Cold War at Sea: High-Seas Confrontation between the United States and the Soviet Union*. Annapolis MD: Naval Institute Press, 2000.

———. "The Evolution and Significance of the 1972 Incidents at Sea Agreement." *Journal of Strategic Studies* 28, no. 2 (April 2005): 361–77.

Wittner, Lawrence S. *The Struggle against the Bomb*. Vol. 2: *Resisting the Bomb, 1954–1970*. Stanford CA: Stanford University Press, 1997.

Wohlstetter, Albert. "The Delicate Balance of Terror." In *American Strategy for the Nuclear Age*, edited by Walter F. Hahn and John C. Neff, 197–218. New York: Doubleday and Co., Inc., 1960.

Yang Kuisong. "The Sino-Soviet Border Clash of 1969: From Zhenbao Island to Sino-American Rapprochement." *Cold War History* 1, no. 1 (August 2000): 21–52.

Yengst, William. *Lightning Bolts*. Mustang OK: Tate, 2010.

Yionoulis, Steve M. "The Transit Satellite Geodesy Program." *Johns Hopkins APL Technical Digest* 19, no. 1 (1998): 36–42.

York, Herbert. *Race to Oblivion: A Participant's View of the Arms Race*. New York: Simon and Schuster, 1970.

Zubok, Vladislav, and Constantine Pleashakov. *Inside the Kremlin's Cold War*. Cambridge MA: Harvard University Press, 1997.

Zuckerman, Edward. *The Day after World War III*. New York: Viking Press, 1984.

Zumwalt, Elmo R. *On Watch*. New York: New York Times Book Company, 1976.

INDEX

ARC-27 radio, 210

ARC-98 radio, 289

Arms Control and Disarmament Agency, 165

Arnhym, A. A., 96–97, 377n71

ASROC (Anti-Submarine Rocket) system, 35, 37, 38, 302, 308–9, 312–18

AT&T phone system, 135, 144, 149, 154; breakdown of, 159–60; Direct Communications Link and, 166–67; ICBM force and, 261, 280; WWMCCS and, 293

AT&T Project Office, 172

Atlantic Command, 344, 345

Atlas ICBM, 231, 249, 250, 259, 260, 263, 266, 272, 398n1

Atmospheric Test Ban, 82

The Atomic Café (film), 70

atomic demolition munitions, 266–68

Atomic Energy Commission, 95, 101, 149, 150, 161, 162, 177, 197, 198, 204

Autery, Clarence R., 275

authentication procedures, 180, 187, 220–21, 262, 282–83, 289–90, 347; fictional, 43, 175, 275–77, 330–31

Aviation Depot Group (nuclear storage), 123

B-3 bomber, 87

B-17 bomber, 76

B-24 bomber, 88

B-29 bomber, 89, 95, 107, 200

B-36 bomber, 82, 106, 108, 110, 114, 194–203, 221–23

B-47 bomber, 68, 76, 90, 107, 108, 110, 136, 143, 203–15

B-50 bomber, 111

B-52 bomber, 47, 52, 57, 81, 82, 90, 111, 113, 114, 127, 145, 173, 175, 176, 185, 223; and Berlin Crisis (1962), 129; crash of, at Palomares, 192; crash of, at Thule, 186; crews of, on uppers, 190–91; and ECM, 224–25; and fictional release procedures, 217–18; and Head Start tests, 182; and low-level training, 118–19; Meal 88 disappearance of, 192; and Selective Employment of Air/Ground Alert, 193; Steel Trap and, 183–84; and U-2 Crisis, 124. *See also* airborne alert

B-58 bomber, 29, 91, 112, 143, 173, 175, 230–48

B-66 bomber, 113

Bailey, Charles W., II, 60, 62, 151

ballistic missiles, Soviet: R-5 MRBM (SS-3 Shy-

ster), 227; R-9A ICBM (SS-8 Sasin), 233; R-12 MRBM (SS-4 Sandal), 132, 140, 228, 233; R-14 IRBM (SS-5 Skean), 132, 228; R-16 ICBM (SS-7 Saddler), 132, 139

Barber's Point Naval Air Station, 342

Barksdale Air Force Base, 154

Bar Lock radar system, 239

Bartholomew, Frank, 18, 26, 119, 181

Bartlett, Cy, 105, 115

Basic War Plan, 186, 204

Battlestar Galactica (TV series), 171

Bay of Pigs, 62, 64

Beach, Edward N., 161, 350, 361n23

Beale Air Force Base, 262, 263

The Beast of Yucca Flats (film), 51

The Bedford Incident (book), 32–38, 189

The Bedford Incident (film), 32, 47, 148, 189, 301, 307, 308–19

Bell Canada, 156

Bell Telephone Laboratory, 154, 159

Beneath the Planet of the Apes (film), 292

Bergan, Gerald T., 92

Berlin Crisis (1948), 37, 80–81

Berlin Crisis (1959–60), 183

Berlin Crisis (1961), 122, 127–30, 134

Big Board, 28, 152–60, 187, 231, 274

The Big Lift (film), 105

Bikini Atoll nuclear tests, 81, 197

Biryuzov, Sergei, 132

"biscuit" authenticators, 163

Black Book, 163, 164

Black Forest incident, 159–60

Black Liberation Army, 285

BLU-2B pod, 235

Blue and Gold crew concept, SSBN, 349–50

Blue Cradle ECM system, 199

Blue Eagle (aircraft), 298, 344

Blue Eagle ACTU (USN), 343

Blue Phone, 155

Blue Scout ERCS system, 337

BMEWS (Ballistic Missile Early Warning System), 132, 135, 139, 160, 178, 185–86, 232, 298

Bomarc missile, 158, 285

Bomb Alarm System, 153, 158

Bomber (book), 194

Bond, James (character), 52

"boomer" submarine psychological thriller genre, 319–48

boost glide vehicle, 270–71

Box Brick electronic intelligence system, 238, 240

Braeden, Eric, 291

Braun, Wernher von, 51

Bravo Net. *See* Giant Talk HF communications system

Brezhnev, Leonid, 234

Brings, Lawrence M., 93

Brodie, Bernard, 22, 99, 102

Bronson, Charles, 257

Bruckheimer, Jerry, 329

Brugioni, Dino, 59, 100

Bryant, Peter. *See* George, Peter

Buchan, Alastair, 24

Bucher, Lloyd M., 32–33

Bulletin of the Atomic Scientists, 24, 61

Bundy, McGeorge, 58, 121, 127

Bunker Hill Air Force Base, 231

Burchinal, David, 127, 139

Burdick, Eugene, 22, 23, 24, 28, 29, 44, 182

Burpelson Air Force Base (fictional), 27, 92, 216, 221

By Dawn's Early Light (film), 47–49, 148, 163, 164, 166, 171, 173, 193, 217, 249, 269, 286, 294, 296, 300, 357

BZHRK train-mounted ICBM, 288

C-118 command-and-control aircraft, 343

C-121 communications aircraft, 341, 343

C-124 transport aircraft, 197

Cactus facility. *See* Camp David

Caddyshack (film), 59

The Caine Mutiny (book), 42, 43, 49

The Caine Mutiny (film), 328

Caldwell, Jim (character), 115

Camelot phenomenon, 58, 62, 133

Camp David, 150, 172

Camp Ritchie, 148

Canadian Chiefs of Staff Committee, 123

Cannonball presidential emergency facility, 172

Cape Canaveral Air Force Station, 337

Caribbean Crisis. *See* Cuban Missile Crisis

Caribou Air Force Station, 198

Carswell Air Force Base, 108, 143, 195, 231, 232

Carter, Jimmy, 163–64

Cartwheel presidential emergency facility, 172

Castle Air Force Base, 143, 182

Castle Bravo nuclear test, 12, 19, 82

Castle Nectar nuclear test, 207

Castle nuclear test series (1954), 12, 82, 207

Castro, Fidel, 142–43

Central Locator System, 171

chaff systems, 212, 224, 272

Chateauroux Air Base, 343

Cheyenne Mountain Complex (NORAD), 155–57, 159, 160, 276, 294

Chiang Kai-shek, 80

Chidlaw Building (NORAD), 158, 159, 160

Child 44 (film), 358

China, Communist, 76, 87–88, 109, 232–35

Chrome Dome airborne alert flights, 185, 187, 188, 189–90, 192, 235

Churchill, Winston S., 109

CIA, 59, 100, 109, 124, 205, 208, 238, 257

civil defense, 82, 95–96, 148

civil rights movement, 63

Clam Lake communications station, 345

Clancy, Tom, 37, 39

Clear Air Force Station, 185–86

Clifton, C. V., 129

Close-In Automatic Route Restoral System (CARRS), 159

cobalt bombs, 26

Coco practice alert, 209

Coded Switch System, 265–66

cognitive anchoring, 350

Cold War: historiography of, 3–4; nature of, 9, 34–35, 38, 301, 307; policy, U.S. critique of, 15

Collins, Arthur, 114

Collins Radio Corporation, 113–14, 341

Colossus (book) 26, 291

Colossus (fictional computer), 291–92, 293

Colossus: The Forbin Project (film), 26, 249, 291

Combat Defense Force, 260, 267

Combat Operations Center, North Bay Ontario, 156–59

Command Center Processing and Display System, 294–96

Commander-1 (book), 21

Commander Submarine Force Atlantic, 346

command signals decoder (Minuteman), 285

Communist front organizations, 67

Comprehensive Test Ban Treaty, 271

Connery, Sean, 307

Conrad, Robert, 39, 327

Considine, Robert, 74, 105, 111, 116

92, 113, 120, 153, 164, 171, 180, 216, 218, 249, 279, 284, 286, 300, 319; airborne alert and, 175, 183, 186; book origins of, 14; and Cuban Missile Crisis, 130, 137; Doomsday Machine and, 286–87; human reliability and, 192; as propaganda, 357; sexual aspects of, 52, 92; war room in, 151

Dr. Strangelove (screenplay), 26, 27

drug use by USAF personnel, 68

DSP (Defense Support Program) satellite system, 139, 254, 298

Duga Steel Yard, 403n63

Durning, Charles, 266

E-4B National Emergency Airborne Command Post, 294

Earth Abides (book), 12

Eatherly, Claude, 70

EC-121 aircraft, 294

EC-130 communications aircraft, 341–42

EC-135 command-and-control aircraft, 172, 288–89, 343. *See also* Looking Glass (aircraft)

EC Comics, 24–25

ECM (electronic countermeasures), 110, 210–12, 216–17, 224–25, 248

Edgertsen, Paul, 191

Eielson Air Force Base, 209

Eisenhower, Dwight D., 60, 83, 101, 112, 124, 126, 149, 150, 161, 165; administration of, 18, 19, 23, 170, 178; airborne alert and, 182, 183–84; temper of, 91

Electronic Warfare Termination Line, 210

ELF (extremely low frequency) communications system, 331, 345

Ellis, Richard, 85

Ellsberg, Daniel, 66

Ellsworth Air Force Base, 288

emergency action message, 265–66, 280–81, 282, 330, 346–47

Emergency Broadcast System, 163

Emergency Planning Committee, 169–70

Emergency War Order Network, 280

Emergency War Plan, 60, 100, 103, 178, 195–96, 210, 311

EMP (electromagnetic pulse), 227, 228, 233, 261, 262, 264, 280, 286, 288, 336, 345

The Enemy Below (film), 308

Engels Air Base, 229

Eniwetok nuclear test site, 313

Ent Air Force Base, 158

Epstein, Edmund N., 355

ERCS (Emergency Rocket Communications System), 287–88, 337

Ernest Harmon Air Base, 311

escalation, 10–11, 12, 37, 138

espionage operations, Soviet, 104, 110, 128, 132, 302

ETCRRM cipher machine, 167

European Command communications units, 343

Executive Committee of the National Security Council (EXCOMM), 60, 121

Exercise Down Field, 184–85

Exercise Keen Axe, 185

Exercise Play Back (Emergency War Order), 392n108

Exercise Steel Trap, 183–84

F-100 fighter, 158

F-102 fighter, 138

"Fail-Safe" (article), 23

Fail-Safe (book), 23, 24, 27, 28, 29, 32, 38, 70, 99, 175, 182, 256

Fail-Safe (film), 31, 32, 38, 47, 120, 148, 151, 153, 156, 164, 165, 175, 180, 182, 189, 192, 230–31, 249, 279, 298, 300, 319, 326; as basis for *Crimson Tide*, 329; and Cuban Missile Crisis, 130; and lawsuit, 23; USAF evaluation of, 32

fail-safe box (fictional), 29, 175, 180, 189, 231

fail-safe concept, 18, 174, 180, 181, 182. *See also* positive control

fail-safe point (fictional), 30, 175, 230

Fairchild Air Force Base, 255

Falken, Stephen (character), 292

fallout, 82, 95, 228, 230

Fan Song radar system, 215

Fast Freight (code word), 186

Fast Talk communications system, 261

Federal Civil Defense Administration, 150

Federal Relocation Arc, 149

Fedrick, Jack, 158

female ICBM crews, 250

Fenske, Fedrick, 158

ferret operations, 13, 35, 38, 109–10, 205–6, 211, 224, 303

F. E. Warren Air Force Base, 289

The Fifth Missile (film), 39, 302, 319, 326–27, 350

55 Days at Peking (film), 10

Hen House radar, 138

Hersey, John, 53

H-Hour Control Line, 188, 209, 219, 235, 236

Hickham Air Force Base, 343

High Dice UHF communications system, 187

High Point/Hi-Point. *See* Mount Weather special facility

Hiroshima, 11, 81, 89, 94, 268, 312

Hiroshima (book), 53

Hitler, Adolph, 147

HMS *Retaliate* (fictional submarine), 40–43

"hold-down" naval tactics, 304, 305, 315

Holland, Robert "Dutch" (character), 106, 194–95, 203–4

Holloway, Bruce, 193–94

Hollywood, 105, 108, 300, 307

Hollywood blacklist, 67

homosexuality, 43, 78

Hostile Waters (film), 301, 308

Hot Line, 148, 164–68, 170, 249, 255. *See also* Direct Communications Link

Hound Dog cruise missile (AGM-28), 220–21, 223, 225–27, 229

Hubler, Richard, 73, 85

Hudlow, Richard, 90

Hudson, Rock, 115, 155, 307

Hudson Institute (fictional), 327

Human Reliability Program, 48, 191–92, 358. *See also* Personnel Reliability Program

Hungarian uprising (1956), 17

The Hunt for Red October (book), 39

The Hunt for Red October (film), 39, 301, 305, 307, 319, 320, 326, 328, 337

ICBMs (intercontinental ballistic missiles), 249–52

Ice Station Zebra (book), 33, 37, 188

Ice Station Zebra (film), 33, 38, 188, 251, 307, 319

Iconorama display systems, 153, 158–59, 160

Ikle, Frederick, 191

IL-28 light nuclear bomber, 132

incidents at sea, 301, 302, 303–5, 323–25

Incidents at Sea Agreement (1975), 306

Increased Readiness Posture (alert level), 186, 232, 234

in-flight insertion safety mechanism 19, 198–99

influence operations, 100, 105–16, 373n5

Intelsat satellites, 168

Inter-American Tropical Tuna Commission, 33

International Information Department (KGB), 67

Ivy nuclear test series, 12, 82

jamming, Soviet, 29, 34, 188–89, 231

Japan, 4, 11, 21, 81, 87, 106, 108

Jaskoviak, Phil, 346

Jeremiah (TV series), 156

JFK (film), 131, 142, 259

John Birch Society, 63

Johnson, Lyndon, 59, 65, 127, 143, 164

Joint Chiefs of Staff, 42, 49, 80, 88, 100, 101, 121, 123, 126, 134, 151, 164, 181, 195; and Basic War Plan 1-58, 204; and destruction criteria, 208; espionage penetration of, 128; and human reliability, 191, 285; and Kennedy assassination, 142, 144; and NCA, 169; and Radford Affair, 161; and Sputnik, 176

Joint Chiefs of Staff Alerting Network (JCSAN), 30, 155

Joint Chiefs of Staff Telephone Authentication System, 162

Joint Committee on Atomic Energy, 95

Joint Strategic Target Planning Staff (JSTPS), 256, 258, 294, 322

Jones, David C., 83

Jones, Dennis Feltham, 26, 291, 293

Jones, James, 49

Jones, James Earl, 217

judo, 77, 92–93, 103–4

Jupiter IRBM, 130, 131, 132

K-19: The Widowmaker (film), 319

KAA-29/TSEC authenticator, 210, 219, 221, 236, 262, 394n132

KAC-1 authenticator, 180, 208–10

KAC-65 authenticator, 262

KAC-72/TSEC authenticator, 210, 219, 221, 236

Kadena Air Base, 232

Kahn, Herman, 24–27, 29, 53, 138, 155, 250, 251, 286, 292, 327

Kantor, MacKinlay, 65, 80

Kapustin Yar, 220, 225, 228

Kaufman, William, 26, 56, 58, 90, 128

Kaysen, Carl, 32, 84

Kaysen's raid, 127–30

KB-29 tanker, 111

KC-97 tanker, 108, 111

KC-135 tanker, 52, 76, 82, 113, 114, 173, 185–86, 232

436

Operation Head Start, 182–84

Operation Hideout, 349–50

Operation Judo, 109

Operation Ju-Jitsu, 109–10

Operation Power Flite, 111

Operation Quick Kick, 185

Operation Redwing. *See* Redwing nuclear test series (1956)

Operation Sandblast, 311, 350

Operations Coordinating Board, 19, 113

Operation Upshot-Knothole. *See* Upshot-Knothole nuclear test series

oss (Office of Strategic Services), 88

overflights, 122, 304. *See also* ferret operations

paccs (Post-Attack Command and Control System), 135

Pacific Command, 342–43

Pacific War, 76

Panay Incident, 87

Parade magazine, 165

Patuxant River Naval Air Station, 341

Pave Paws radar system, 297

Peacekeeper icbm, 249

Pearl Harbor attack, 17, 88, 98, 124, 126, 148, 179

Pearson, Drew, 69, 79

Pearson, Lester B., 78

Pease Air Force Base, 143

Peck, Gregory, 27

penetration aids, 272, 321

Pentagon Papers, 258

Pentagon war room (fictional depiction), 28

People's Liberation Army, 234

Peppard, George, 274

peripheral reconnaissance program, 109

Permissive Action Link systems, 358

Personal Inventory Barometer, 351

Personnel Reliability Program, 47, 191. *See also* Human Reliability Program

Peters, Bryan. *See* George, Peter

Petropavlovsk, 205–15

Phantom (film), 306

Philippines, 87

The Phoenix Odyssey (book), 329

Pickens, Slim, 38

"piecing" and emergency action messages, 348

Pinetree Line, 156

Plan Majestic, 195

Plan "R" (fictional), 20, 27, 53, 55, 175, 178–79, 216

Plato, 147

Playbook, 163–64. *See also* siop (Single Integrated Operational Plan)

Playboy magazine, 52, 190

Plaza Theatre, Calgary, 1

Plumbbob nuclear test series (1957), 220, 313

Point Mugu tracking station, 336

Poitier, Sidney, 309

Polaris a-1 submarine-launched ballistic missile, 320

Polaris a-2 submarine-launched ballistic missile, 320, 321

Polaris a-3 submarine-launched ballistic missile, 248, 271, 320, 321, 322, 334–35, 339

Polaris missiles, 39, 269, 321, 323, 338–39, 347–48

Policy Planning Committee (State Department), 165

political officers, Soviet, 319

Pollack, Sydney, 77

Polyarniki gru, 187

Poppy signals intelligence satellite, 254

Port Bow show of force operation, 390n75

Poseidon submarine-launched ballistic missile, 298, 320, 321, 347–48

positive control, 175, 181. *See also* fail-safe concept

positive control point, 20, 180–81

post-traumatic stress disorder, 42

Power, Mae, 54, 92, 115

Power, Thomas S., 18, 26, 56–58, 77–79, 85–98, 100–101, 106, 152, 206, 218, 219, 250, 255, 263, 291, 358; airborne alert and, 183, 186; Bartholomew interview and, 182; Black Forest incident and, 159–60; comparison of, to Ripper character, 54–55; critique of, 56–57, 60, 61, 65, 284; and Cuban Missile Crisis, 121–45; and *Design for Survival*, 19, 93, 377n71; and deterrence campaign, 99–120; disinformation campaign against, 68–70; influence of, on *Fail-Safe* and *Dr. Strangelove*, 26; influence of, on Ronald Reagan, 96; influence of, on *Seven Days in May*, 51; and judo, 103–4; and Kaysen's raid, 129; and Kennedy assassination, 143–44; and Minuteman numbers, 269, 401n49; and Nikita Khrushchev, 116–18, 184; predelegation and, 179; and use of sac for signaling, 134; views of, on nuclear war, 95–96; visit of, to Soviet Union, 94

Welles, H. G., 11
Wells, Selmon "Sundown," 89–90, 118, 263
Western Electric Co., 154
Westover Air Force Base, 154
Weybrew, Benjamin B., 349–51
Whalen, William, 128, 132
Wheeler, Harvey, 21–24, 26, 28, 29, 44, 120, 182
Whif radar system, 205
"Whiskey-on-the-rocks" incident (1981), 312
White, Thomas, 51, 134, 179, 181, 186, 269, 375n52
White Dot message, 263, 281
White House, 30, 161, 167, 258
White House bomb shelter (fictional depiction), 28, 151, 165
White House Communications Agency, 171–72, 342–43
White House Signal, 171
White Sands Proving Ground, 165
"Whiz Kids," 58, 77, 84, 96
Whoops Apocalypse (film), 218
Widmark, Richard, 66, 308
Wiesner, Jerome, 58, 59–60, 83

Wohlstetter, Albert, 17, 22, 24
WOPR (War Operations Plan Response) (fictional computer), 276, 292, 294–95
"World Targets in Megadeaths" (fictional document), 164
World War III (miniseries), 49
WS-117L satellite system, 256
WWMCCS (World-Wide Military Command and Control System), 256, 293–98
WWV radio station, 282, 335, 342

Yak-25M interceptor aircraft, 205, 211
Yak-28P interceptor aircraft, 241
Yankee box, 296–97, 307
Yom Kippur War (1973), 327
Yo-Yo radar system, 244, 248
Yugoslavia, 235, 237

zero code controversy, 284
Zhenbao Island battle, 233
The Zhukov Briefing (book), 40
Ziegele, Robert R., 89
Zogg, Lothar (character), 217–18